THE CAUSES OF THE CIVIL WAR

THE CAUSES OF THE CIVIL WAR

Institutional Failure or Human Blunder?

Edited by **HANS L. TREFOUSSE**
Brooklyn College, City University of New York

KRIEGER PUBLISHING COMPANY
MALABAR, FLORIDA

Cover illustration: Little Bo-Peep. *(The New York Public Library Print Division)*

Original Edition 1971
Reprint 1977
Reprint 1982 with corrections
Reprint 2002 with updated material

Printed and Published by
ROBERT E. KRIEGER PUBLISHING CO., INC.
KRIEGER DRIVE,
MALABAR, FLORIDA 32950

Library of Congress Cataloging in Publication Data
Main entry under title:

The Causes of the Civil War.

  Bibliography: p.
  Contents: Slavery and race: Slavery, the sole
cause/James Ford Rhodes. Slavery and the problem
of race adjustment/Allan Nevins—Economic
conflict: The approach of the second American
revolution/Charles A. and Mary R. Beard. Commitment to
laissez faire/William Appleman Williams—[etc.]
  1. United States—History—Civil War, 1861-1865—
Causes—Addresses, essays, lectures. I. Trefousse,
Hans Louis.
E459.C36   973.7'11   81-23696
ISBN 1-57524-210-9   AACR2

Printed in the United States of America

10   9   8   7   6   5   4   3   2

CONTENTS

The Ruins of the Northwest Depot, Charleston, South Carolina, 1865. (*The National Archives*)

INTRODUCTION

The Civil War has always held a particular fascination for Americans. Its impact on the United States was so immense and its results so far-reaching that every generation since 1861 has sought to reinterpret it. What were the causes that led to the catastrophe? Why did the American system break down in the 1850s and 1860s? Who was responsible for the war, and how could the holocaust have been prevented? These are the questions that have been posed over and over again, until a vast literature on the war has accumulated.

Since the causation of wars is one of the central questions of history, it is not surprising that this, the most destructive conflict between 1815 and 1914, has received a great deal of attention. And indeed, for the study of the origins of human conflict, the American Civil War offers a rich field for research. Fought between two antagonists equally schooled in parliamentary methods, in a society where newspapers and periodicals sought to record all major events in as much detail as possible, it has been studied so minutely that virtually every step of the major participants, every action of any consequence, has been the subject of historical inquiry. The manuscript depositories of the country have been scoured for the most minute scraps of evidence bearing on the conflict; national Civil War Round Tables have been established, and several publications have devoted themselves almost exclusively to it. But in spite of all the study which has already taken place, there is no sign of a lessening of interest. Books continue to pour from the presses, doctoral candidates write their dissertations, and college courses are structured around the Civil War and Reconstruction. The war goes on.

The basic outlines of events are clear enough. The existence of slavery in the South, the rise of abolitionism in the North, the persistence of an agrarian society at odds with a growing industrialism, differences in constitutional interpretation, and the failure of the democratic process to resolve these problems, all contributed to an explosive situation in which war between the sections might break out at any moment. The crisis came in 1860–61, when, after the split in the Democratic party on the question of the desirability of a federal slave code for the territories, the Republicans won the presidential election on a platform of nonextension of the "peculiar institution," and the cotton states seceded. President Abraham Lincoln then attempted to send food to beleaguered Fort Sumter, the isolated federal post in Charleston harbor, and the government of the newly formed Southern Confederacy decided to reduce the fort by force. Civil war was the result. Although all these occurrences have been extensively described, the emphasis given to the various factors contributing to the debacle has differed widely.

In view of the far-reaching coverage of the conflict and of the length of time that has elapsed since the appearance of the first books dealing with the war, it is astonishing how frequently the same explanations have recurred. That slavery was a major factor in bringing on the war was clear to contemporaries, many of whom tended to take an extremely simplistic view of the national tragedy. Henry Wilson, radical Republican and later Vice President of the United States, was certain that the slaveholders had caused the war, which he explained in terms of the *History of the Rise and Fall of the Slave Power in America,* as he entitled his three-volume work published during the Reconstruction period. Economic factors, likewise, have been stressed from the very beginning. As early as 1884, James G. Blaine, in his *Twenty Years of Congress,* emphasized the importance of the economic conflict between the agrarian South and the industrial North, and in 1861, before the war had even started, Robert Toombs, in his secession speech in the Senate, pointed to alleged Northern intentions of outlawing $4,000,000,000 worth of property as a cause for war. The constitutional issue of states rights versus nationalism was the theme of the postwar reflections of Alexander H. Stephens, the former Vice President of the Confederacy. *A Constitutional View of the Late War Between the States,* he called his book, and his old opponent, Jefferson Davis, adopted a very similar point of view. Any number of writers sought to find the explanation in the actions of extremists. Northerners like General John A. Logan, who entitled his book *The Great Conspiracy,* held the fire-eaters responsible, and Southern sympathizers like Rushmore G. Horton, the abolitionists.

As time went on, the arguments became more sophisticated, but their fundamental tenor did not change materially. By the turn of the century, a nationalist school had developed, largely centered in the North and represented by scholars like James F. Rhodes, Hermann E. von Holst, and John Burgess. These writers tended to view the national state as a supreme good and condemned the South's particularistic attitudes, although they often sympathized with the minority section's racist outlook. By the 1920s, when Edward Channing titled the sixth volume of his *History of the United States, The War for Southern Independence,* the concept of two rival civilizations had arisen, an explanation which in part had been offered by Edward Pollard as early as 1866, and by the 1930s, the economic interpretation had been restated most effectively by Charles A. and Mary R. Beard. Then, shortly before the outbreak of the Second World War, the so-called revisionist school, consisting of historians like James G. Randall and Avery O. Craven, reverted to the anti-extremist point of view, spoke of a "repressible conflict," a needless war that might have been prevented, and stressed the breakdown of the American political system.

In view of the importance of ideological and racial factors since 1945, slavery and the conflict to which it gave rise have once more attracted attention. Not that these aspects had ever been wholly neglected. Critics of abolitionism like Frank L. Owsley and Gilbert H. Barnes had earlier published works dealing with them. But writers like Arthur Schlesinger, Jr. succeeded in restating in forceful terms the moral issue confronting the nation, and the concomitant problem of racial adjustment has been more extensively studied than before. Although John S. Rosenberg, questioning the values of Northern society, has doubted whether the war justified its cost, and Arnold Whitridge has once again attacked the extremists, writers like Richard H. Sewall and Hans L. Trefousse have defended the Northern radicals, and David M. Potter, in a major synthesis of the pre-war decade, has once more emphasized the centrality of slavery in causing the sectional conflict.

The other theories of the causation of the war have also received renewed attention. A modern formulation of the economic thesis has been written by Barrington Moore, who has characterized the conflict as a last offensive of middle class democracy. William Appleman Williams, a firm believer in the expansionist nature of laissez-faire society, has likewise explained the war in economic terms, as has Raimondo Luraghi, who has stressed the resistance of the South to industrial "modernization." Eugene D. Genovese, delineating the total domination of society by the Southern ruling class, has restated the class conflict in a new form. In support of the "two civilizations" school, Eric Foner has stressed the devotion of Northern Republicans to a society of free enterprise. The difficulties of maintaining the cohesion of the Democratic party have been analyzed by Roy F. Nichols, those of a party system devoid of issues by Michael F. Holt, constitutional controversies by Arthur Bestor, institutional shortcomings by David Donald, Southern expansionism by William Barney, and the defense of narrowly conceived Southern honor by Don E. Fehrenbacher. But however the emphasis may have changed, the basic causes of slavery, economic conflict, constitutional strife, political breakdown, and supposed extremist intransigence have recurred again and again. It seems that no serious student of the war can conscientiously ignore these factors.

What is true of the fundamental causes of the war is equally true of the immediate origins of the conflict. So tangled is the web of evidence bearing on the firing on Fort Sumter that ever since General Pierre G. T. Beauregard gave orders for the first shot all manner of explanations have been offered. Southern apologists from the very beginning have blamed the Union government in general and President Lincoln in particular for forcing the issue, while Northerners with equal plausibility have argued that the guilt is clear: Jefferson Davis and the government at Montgomery ordered the fort to be reduced by force, authorized the first shot, and therefore must bear full responsibility for the bloodshed that ensued. Modern historians have further divided upon the issue of Lincoln's motives: Did the President, in ordering the expedition for the relief of Fort Sumter, desire to provoke war in such a way as to throw guilt upon the South; did he wish to prevent war by sending only supplies and giving due notice to the Governor of South Carolina; or did he consciously take a risk of provoking war without necessarily desiring it? Since the evidence bearing upon this question is incomplete, it is likely that the controversy will continue unabated.

The selections which follow are excerpts representative of the major schools of thought on the causes of the Civil War. The first section deals with those historians who have emphasized either slavery or the racial issue. James Ford Rhodes, the author of the monumental work, *History of the United States from the Compromise of 1850,* wrote at a time when the immediate passions of the post-war era had cooled, but when it was still possible to assert, as he did, that "slavery was the sole cause of the war." Living in a period in which racism was on the increase, his attitude toward the blacks was at best ambivalent, but the power of his prose and the meticulous care with which he examined his sources have made his work a classic. Believing that the system of chattel slavery was outmoded and a blot on civilization, he concludes that the great failure of the South had been its inability to solve the question long before the Civil War. That the defense of human bondage was joined with the idea of state sovereignty is to him a fatal step in the development of a sectional spirit which finally drove an entire population into an unrighteous war for the protection of slavery. But he does not roundly condemn the slaveholders. Considering the "peculiar institution" a curse for North and South alike, he merely sees them as victims of their social system.

Allan Nevins, writing after World War II, when the emphasis on slavery as an explanation for the outbreak of the conflict was once more becoming popular, set out to cover again the ground previously gone over by Rhodes. In a series of volumes entitled, *Ordeal of the Union, The Emergence of Lincoln,* and *The War for the Union,* Nevins did not merely reexamine Rhodes' premises but added his insights as one of the most productive scholars in America, a historian who consulted virtually every available manuscript collection bearing on the period. His conclusions were similar to Rhodes'. Like his predecessor, he finds the Southern system wanting, and severely criticizes Stephen A. Douglas for introducing the Kansas-Nebraska Act, which repealed the Missouri Compromise and set in train a series of events leading directly to the Civil War. But, mindful of the overriding issues of his own day, Nevins stresses the racial problem with greater understanding. It is one of his major contentions that slavery was not merely a system of human bondage but also one of racial exploitation, and his explanations for the conflict are no longer so simplistic as Rhodes'. While giving due emphasis to constitutional, political, and economic factors, Nevins nevertheless once again emphasizes slavery and "its concomitant of racial adjustment" as the main problem leading to war. His provocative analysis has stimulated much further research, and in a recent reconsideration in "The Irrepressible Conflict," a chapter in his *The Imperiled Union,* Kenneth M. Stampp has reached similar conclusions.

But was slavery the chief cause of the war? Scholars who believe in the economic interpretation of the origins of the conflict have offered differing interpretations, here represented by two selections. One is an excerpt from Charles A. and Mary R. Beard's *The Rise of American Civilization,* and the other, part of a chapter of William Appleman Williams' *The Contours of American History.* A longtime member of the faculty of Columbia University, Charles A. Beard first became famous in 1913 with the publication of *An Economic Interpretation of the Constitution of the United States.* A series of important studies followed, and he became the best-known representative of a school which believed economic rivalries to hold the key to great historical events. Because of this outlook, Beard and his followers tended to play down the importance of ideological factors such as the crusade against slavery. To them the conflict between the agrarians of the South and the industrialists of the North—a version of the class struggle—seemed sufficient explanation of the origins of America's greatest holocaust. That this interpretation enjoyed great popularity during the economic depression of the 1930s, and that Marxists adopted it with some modifications, is not surprising.

How valid were the Beards' assumptions? Were Northern capitalists really united in outlook and goals? Did the owners of large Southern plantations invariably occupy positions in the forefront of the secession movement? Modern writers have questioned both concepts. But the economic interpretation has not been abandoned. An example of a more recent approach is represented by William Appleman Williams, primarily a specialist in the history of American foreign policy, whose views have been strongly influenced by Marxist positions. Williams believes both North and South to have been expansionist. The South, according to this view, wanted to expand its plantation system toward the Caribbean. The North, on the other hand, was committed to a laissez-faire society. And laissez faire, in Williams' opinion, invariably involved westward and overseas expansion. Consequently, he argues that the demand for a society in which laissez-faire attitudes could have free rein led both Northern businessmen and Western agrarians to combine against Southern slaveholders. The antislavery movement, he holds, was chiefly motivated by economic considerations, and he looks upon Stephen A. Douglas, William H. Seward, and Abraham Lincoln as advance agents of the "*Weltanschauung* of laissez faire." This attitude, he concludes, made impossible the peaceful settlement of the differences between the sections. Although Williams' sweeping generalizations have not been widely accepted, they are a good example of the more recent contributions of economic determinists.

Can one single factor alone explain historical events? Much more comprehensive than the economic interpretation of the causes of the Civil War is the "two civilizations" school. The selections included consist of excerpts from Arthur C. Cole's *The Irrepressible Conflict* and Frank L. Owsley's essay by the same title in the compendium written by twelve Southerners, *I'll Take My Stand.* One of the volumes in the *History of American Life* series which emphasized social and economic developments rather than politics, Professor Cole's work clearly illustrates the increasingly thorough division between the sections in all lines of endeavor. This differentiation, accentuated by the emergence of industry in the North and the persistence of slavery in the South, made it increasingly difficult for the plantation system to survive. While Cole does not specifically make the point, it is evident that he believes war to have been the result, and, like Rhodes and Nevins, he broadly sympathizes with the North and its opposition to the outmoded and cruel institution of human bondage.

Not so Frank L. Owsley. Southern-born and Southern-educated, Owsley does not hesitate to defend his section and the type of civilization which it cherished. To him, the main difference between North and South was not the institution of slavery, but the persistence of an agrarian society with its concomitant of slavery in one section and its disappearance in the other. His essay ably puts forth a view no longer popular, and it serves as an important counterweight to Cole's analysis.

The next group of selections deals with the failure of the political system as one of the main causes of the Civil War. James G. Randall's presidential address before the Mississippi Valley Historical Association at Omaha on May 2, 1940, "A Blundering Generation," most clearly illustrates this point of view. "If one word or phrase were selected to account for the war, that word would not be slavery, or state rights," he asserted. "It would have to be such a word as fanaticism (on both sides), or misunderstanding, or perhaps politics." As he sees it, men made the war; they might just as easily have prevented it.

Like Randall, Roy F. Nichols examines the problem of the breakdown of the American political process. After many years of research in the history of the Democratic party in the 1850s, he published in 1948 *The Disruption of American Democracy,* a book in which he summed up his conclusions. In this penetrating analysis, he emphasizes the importance of the party structure in holding American society together. As long as the united Democratic party was in existence, it could cope with the sectional, emotional, and ideological conflicts threatening the Union; once it broke apart, the last bulwark against disaster had been removed. Like Randall, he stresses the shortcomings of the political process, but in many ways, he is more interested in institutional defects than in individual failure.

To what degree moral indignation contributed to the outbreak of the war has long been a subject of controversy among historians. It was part of Randall's argument that extremists on both sides, both abolitionists and fire-eaters, were responsible, and Avery O. Craven, like Randall a representative of the revisionist school of the 1930s and 1940s, was generally critical of Northern radicals and abolitionists. But did not the continued existence of slavery involve a real moral issue? Could a Western democratic country permit so anachronistic an institution to go unchallenged? The next selection, excerpts from Arthur M. Schlesinger,

Jr.'s article in the *Partisan Review* for 1949, "The Causes of the Civil War: A Note on Historical Sentimentalism," addresses itself to this question. Severely criticizing the revisionists' failure to condemn slavery, Schlesinger rejects "sentimental theories about the needlessness of the Civil War." "We cannot be relieved from the duty of moral judgment on issues so appalling and inescapable as those involving human slavery," he writes, thus restating the convictions of many of his predecessors in modern terms.

Once the fundamental causes of the Civil War have been determined, the subsidiary question of the immediate background of the conflict, especially the firing of the first shot at Fort Sumter, still remains. The last portion of the book deals with this problem. Did Lincoln desire peace or did he seek to break the impasse by challenging the Confederate authorities to make an aggressive move? Or did he engage in a deliberate gamble? The first selection, Charles W. Ramsdell's article, "Lincoln and Fort Sumter," reprinted from the *Journal of Southern History,* represents the extreme pro-Southern viewpoint. Arguing that Lincoln, because of his difficulties, had decided that there was no other way than war "for the salvation of his administration, his party, and the Union," Ramsdell holds the President responsible for the consequences. According to this view, Lincoln arranged things in such a way as to maneuver "the Confederates into firing the first shot in order that they, rather than he, should take the blame of beginning the bloodshed." But does the evidence bear out such an interpretation? Neither James G. Randall nor David M. Potter were convinced by Ramsdell's arguments. Both held that Lincoln was interested in preserving peace, and that all his actions pointed to this desire. The selection included is the Preface to the 1962 edition of Potter's book, *Lincoln and His Party in the Secession Crisis.* When in 1942 he had first published his findings, Potter had written that Lincoln's policy "offered maximum possibilities of avoiding conflict; a Confederate attack to prevent food from going to Sumter would constitute an offensive act; therefore Lincoln, wishing to save Sumter without a fight, sought to hold it by a policy so purely defensive that the South would hesitate to make an issue of it." Twenty years later, with additional evidence available because of the opening in 1947 of the Robert Todd Lincoln Papers, the author saw no reason to revise his opinions.

How valid were Potter's and Randall's conclusions? Reexamining the evidence, Richard N. Current, excerpts from whose book, *Lincoln and the First Shot,* constitute the final selection, arrives at slightly different conclusions. After carefully reviewing the evidence concerning the events leading to the attack on the fort and the historical controversies to which they have given rise, he argues that Lincoln, in ordering the relief expedition, was taking a calculated risk. In this assessment, he is in substantial agreement with Kenneth P. Stampp, whose study, *And the War Came,* also dealt with the immediate background of the war.

Thus, after over one hundred years of intense study, both the underlying and immediate causes of the Civil War are still in dispute, and it becomes ques-

tionable whether the issue will ever be fully resolved. Undoubtedly, every generation will continue to interpret it according to its own predilections. It is to be
hoped that the continuing controversy will shed additional light, not merely on
the American Civil War, but also on the fundamental causes of human conflict
in general. The time and energy expended on it will then have been worthwhile.

JAMES FORD RHODES (1848–1927) turned to the
writing of history in 1885 after a successful career in
business. His *History of the United States from the
Compromise of 1850,* a tribute to his scholarship as well
as his industry, is marked by an absence of wartime
passions, although it is broadly nationalistic in outlook.
The selection which follows is indicative of his
insistence that slavery was the sole cause of the Civil
War.*

James Ford Rhodes

Slavery, the Sole Cause

In the election of Lincoln the North had
spoken. Because slavery was wrong, the
majority of the Northern people had declared against its extension. South Carolina quickly made answer. Before the October elections, men in that State believed
the choice of Lincoln probable, and after
Pennsylvania and Indiana had gone Republican, only a lingering hope remained
that the issue could be other than that
dreaded by the South. The minds of men
were preparing for action in case the
event should actually take place. It was
argued that honor and pecuniary interest
alike demanded disunion. There seemed
little doubt that public opinion would
support the political leaders of the State in
promptly taking measures to put in force
the long-threatened remedy of secession.
Gist, South Carolina's governor, shaped
with alacrity his official action in conformity to the sentiment of his State. Before the October elections he had sent a
confidential letter to each of the governors of the cotton States, with the exception of Houston of Texas, saying that
South Carolina would unquestionably
consider her course in convention and
asking for cooperation on the part of her
sister States. October 12, three days after
Pennsylvania and Indiana had virtually
decided the presidential contest, Gist
called the usual session of the legislature
for the purpose of appointing presidential
electors; but at the same time he gave the
unusual intimation that some action

*James Ford Rhodes, *History of the United States from the Compromise of 1850,* Vol. III (New York:
The Macmillan Co., 1895), pp. 114–125, 146–149, 272–280, 324–325. (Footnotes omitted).

might be necessary "for the safety and protection of the State." November 5, the day before the election, the legislature assembled at Columbia. Governor Gist recommended that in case Lincoln was elected provision should be made immediately for the holding of a convention in the view of severing the connection of South Carolina with the Federal Union. . . .

If any one is inclined to doubt that there was other than a single cause for secession and the war that ensued; if he feel himself almost persuaded by the earnest and pathetic statements of Southern writers since the war, who naturally have sought to place the four years' devotion and heroism of the South on a higher basis than that of a mighty effort to conserve an institution condemned alike by Christianity and by ethics, let him read the speeches and the newspaper articles of the early days of the secession movement in South Carolina. It cannot be denied that the South Carolinians looked the matter squarely in the face, and that sincerity characterized their utterances. "The first issue," said Trenholm, "was made upon the question of a tariff in which the sympathies of the world were with the South. Now we are joining the issue with the prejudices and the sympathies of the world against us." "The question is," declared a preacher in a Sunday sermon, whether slavery "is an institution to be cherished," or whether it "must be dispensed with." While South Carolinians did not for a moment doubt the right of secession, they were not ignorant of the fact that their movement might be called revolution. "It is not a legislative revolution, but a popular revolution," truly said a member of the legislature at the Thursday meeting, and a similar manner of expression is common in the political literature of the time. . . .

Charleston and South Carolina people

felt that secession was no longer a choice, but a necessity; that they had submitted to as much aggression from the North as a free people could endure and preserve their liberties. It is a striking evidence of the mutual misunderstanding between the two sections that, while eleven twelfths of the Northern voters thought the South had lorded it over the North since the annexation of Texas, South Carolinians, almost to a man, and the majority of the men of the cotton States, were equally convinced that they had suffered grievous wrongs from the North. This sentiment was now strong in South Carolina. When her people acknowledged the greater prosperity of the North, they asserted that it had been obtained at the expense of the South by protective tariffs. In the event of separation, the South Carolinians had dreams of unrestricted direct trade with Europe, which would redound to the advantage of their agricultural interests, and would make Charleston rival Boston and New York in commercial importance. They considered the admission of California in 1850 as a free State an outrage, and asserted that insult was added to injury in the resistance by State legislation and by mobs to the enforcement of the Fugitive Slave law, when that law had been conceded by the North as an offset for the gain which destroyed the equilibrium between the two sections. The urging of the commercial question, the assertion that the South suffered grievously from the tariff acts, was a survival from 1832, and was one of those lesser arguments that are popularly supposed to add somewhat of strength to the main cause; but it did not touch the vital matter. The grievance regarding slavery resolved itself into a fierce resistance to the virtual reproach of the Republican party that the South Carolinians were living in the daily practice of a heinous wrong.

If the negro had never been brought to

America and enslaved, South Carolina would not have seceded. Nothing in all history is plainer than that the ferment of which I have been speaking was due solely to the existence of slavery. That the North had been encroaching upon the South, that it had offered an indignity in the election of Lincoln, was for South Carolinians a feeling perfectly natural, and it was absolutely sincere. The President-elect believed that slavery should ultimately be done away with, while they were convinced that it was either a blessing, or else the only fit and possible condition of the negro in contact with the white. That their cause was the cause of life, liberty, and property seemed, from their point of view, beyond question. No South Carolinian would have maintained that any overt act of oppression had yet been committed, but he would have asserted that a free people must strike at the first motion of tyranny, while for an example he might have pointed to the sons of Massachusetts in the years that preceded the American Revolution. It soon began to be apparent that the course on which the State was entering involved sacrifice as well as excited enthusiasm. Business grew bad, merchants found it difficult and even impossible to pay their debts, and, before the end of November, the banks of Charleston were forced to suspend specie payments. But the people showed no signs of faltering. During the month of November there were a round of meetings, pole-raisings, dedications of banners, fireworks, and illuminations; and the music of this nascent revolution was the Marseillaise.

Interest now became centred on the next formal step to be taken in the march of secession. December 6 had been fixed as the day on which delegates to the convention should be chosen. Voters did not divide on party lines. Indeed, since 1851, political divisions, such as were seen in the other Southern States, did not exist in South Carolina. Had the popular vote for President obtained there as elsewhere, the voice for Breckinridge would undoubtedly have been almost unanimous. The lines of 1851, of separate State action or cooperation, were sometimes referred to, but they were obliterated by the actual unanimity of sentiment. Had there been a union party or a party of delay, a contest would have been natural, but no such parties existed. It was a favorite notion of some Northern observers that a latent union sentiment existed in South Carolina, but that it was kept under by intimidation. Anonymous letters may be found scattered through the Northern journals of this period, which, were they representative, would go to substantiate this belief. But all other contemporary evidence points to the view that I have taken. It is almost certain that the nonslaveholding whites were as eager for secession as the slave-owners. The antipathy of race, always strong, had been powerfully excited by assertions that submission meant the freeing of the negroes and the bestowal on them of civil rights, and by the statement, often repeated and currently believed, that Vice-President-elect Hamlin was a mulatto.

The fact that the South, in its sentiment on slavery, was at war with the rest of the civilized world, undoubtedly lent arrogance to assertions of South Carolinians and intolerance to their acts. They were especially severe on Northerners suspected in any way of propagating abolition opinions. An example of this is seen in the action of the book-shops of Charleston, in closing their accounts with the publishers of *Harper's Weekly* and *Magazine,* and returning all the copies on hand, because the *Weekly* had published a biographical sketch and full-length portrait of Abraham Lincoln. Yet the experience of Petigru would seem to show that a union party headed by South Carolinians of character and position would have obtained a hearing and been permitted to advocate unmolested their views. The election of delegates to the convention did not turn on any party differences, nor were the candidates nominated by parties. In some places they were put up by public meetings; in Charleston the nominations were made through the advertising columns of the newspapers. The election turned on the personal standing and ability of the candidates, and, in the main, the most distinguished men of the State were chosen. Of the twenty-two delegates elected from the Charleston district, seventeen had declared for prompt secession and forever against reunion, three favored secession as soon as practicable, and two did not respond to the inquiries of the Charleston *Mercury;* but one of these was C. G. Memminger, afterwards Secretary of the Treasury of the Southern Confederacy, and he had declared in a speech that "secession is a necessity, not a choice."

Thus stood affairs on December 3, when Congress met. South Carolina was practically unanimous for secession; the President had failed utterly to rise to the emergency, while at the North there existed an overwhelming desire to preserve the Union. All eyes were directed towards Congress. Would it avert the threatened danger? As the persistent attitude of South Carolina and the warm sympathy with her of her sister States were fixed facts, the question was, What would the Republicans in Congress be willing to do to satisfy the South? Compromise had solved the difficulty in 1820, in 1833, and in 1850; and it was now apparent that the border State men and the Northern Democrats could unite on a plan which would prevent the secession of all the States except South Carolina. Would the

Republicans go as far as that? Properly to judge their action in this crisis, we must first inquire, what were the grievances of the South as made known to Congress?

The tangible grievances were the interference with the execution of the Fugitive Slave act by the Personal Liberty laws, and the denial by the North to the owners of negro slaves of the common rights of property in the territories. The wrong done the South by the Personal Liberty laws was dwelt upon by men who were opposed to secession, and who, taking an impregnable position, were willing to rest their case upon a remediable complaint. Their conspicuous exponent was Alexander H. Stephens. In the famous speech which he made before the Georgia legislature, November 14, he thrust this view into prominence. His words gave rise to much discussion. It may be positively affirmed that, if the sole grievance of the South had been the alleged nullification of the Fugitive Slave act by many Northern States, there would have been no secession but that of South Carolina. For this grievance would certainly have been redressed. Vermont, the pioneer in this sort of legislation, had already taken steps towards the revision of her Personal Liberty act. On December 17 the national House of Representatives, in which the Republicans and anti-Lecompton Democrats had a clear majority, earnestly recommended, by a vote of 153 to 14, the repeal of the Personal Liberty laws in conflict with the Constitution. These facts, with others that will be mentioned later, show that, if it would have appeased the South, every State, with the possible exception of Massachusetts, either would have rescinded this legislation, or so modified it that it no longer would have been an offence. Early in the session of Congress, however, the Republicans were told that this would not settle the difficulty. "You talk about repealing the Personal Liberty bills as a concession to the South," said Senator Iverson of Georgia. "Repeal them all tomorrow, sir, and it would not stop the progress of this revolution." Iverson spoke for a large party in the empire State of the South. Since the secession of South Carolina had become a foregone conclusion, the action of Georgia was awaited with breathless interest, and every indication of her sentiment was scanned with care. "What though all the Personal Liberty bills were repealed," asked Jefferson Davis, the leader of the cotton States; "would that secure our rights?"

The other tangible grievance—the refusal of the North to recognize that the slaveholder's human chattels had the common attributes of other property in the territories—was urged with emphasis by Davis and by Toombs. It was indeed replied that the Dred Scott decision gave them all that they claimed, but to this it was naturally rejoined that the President-elect did not accept as binding the general principle in regard to slave property as asserted by Chief-Justice Taney. The experience of the last seven years had made patent to each party the importance of a friendly executive, when the issue of freedom and slavery should come to be fought out in the territories.

The intangible grievance of the South was the sentiment of the North in regard to slavery. In most of the public declarations and confidential letters one is struck with the influence with the stigma cast by Republicans upon the slaveholders had on the Southern mind. This sensitiveness proved to be a heavy obstacle in the way of compromise. Between the idea that slavery was right, or, at least, the only suitable condition of the negro, and the idea that slavery was a blot upon the na-

tion, it seemed wellnigh impossible to hit upon the common ground of opinion which was a necessary antecedent to compromise. "The true cause of our danger," declared Jefferson Davis, "I believe to be that a sectional hostility has been substituted for a general fraternity. . . . Where is the remedy?" he asked. "In the hearts of the people" is the ready reply.

If, after the evidence I have already adduced, any one doubts that slavery was the sole cause of the war, and that, had it not existed, the doctrine of States-rights would never have been pushed to the extreme remedy of secession, let him consider the proceedings of these conventions, and give especial attention to the justifications of Mississippi and Georgia. The convention of Mississippi declared that "Our position is thoroughly identified with the institution of slavery. . . . A blow at slavery is a blow at commerce and civilization. . . . There was no choice left us but submission to the mandates of abolition, or a dissolution of the Union." Toombs's report, adopted by the Georgia convention, was of the same tenor. . . .

When one thinks of the many fruitless attempts of peoples to devise wise systems of government, and of the many admirable constitutions on paper which have been adopted, but which have failed to find a response in the character and political habits of the men for whom they were intended, one might be lost in admiration at the orderly manner in which the Southerners proceeded, at the excellent organic instrument they adopted, at the ready acceptance of the work of their representatives, were it not that they were running amuck against the civilized world in their attempt to bolster up human slavery, and in their theory of governmental particularism, when the spirit of the age was tending to freedom and to unity. The sincerest and frankest public man in the

Southern Confederacy, Alexander H. Stephens, told the true story. "The new constitution has put at rest forever," he declared, "all the agitating questions relating to our peculiar institution— African slavery as it exists amongst us— the proper status of the negro in our form of civilization. This was the immediate cause of the late rupture and present revolution. . . . The prevailing ideas entertained by Jefferson and most of the leading statesmen at the time of the formation of the old Constitution were, that the enslavement of the African was in violation of the laws of nature, that it was wrong in principle socially, morally, and politically. . . .

"Our new government is founded upon exactly the opposite idea; its foundations are laid, its corner-stone rests, upon the great truth that the negro is not equal to the white man; that slavery—subordination to the superior race—is his natural and normal condition. This, our new government, is the first in the history of the world based upon this great physical, philosophical, and moral truth. . . .

"The great objects of humanity are best attained when there is conformity to the Creator's laws and decrees, in the formation of governments as well as in all things else. Our confederacy is founded upon principles in strict conformity with these laws. This stone, which was rejected by the first builders, 'is become the chief of the corner'—the real 'corner-stone'—in our new edifice."

Allan Nevins

Slavery and the Problem of
Race Adjustment

Great and complex events have great
and complex causes. Burke, in his *Reflections on the Revolution in France,* wrote
that "a state without the means of some
change is without the means of its conservation," and that a constant reconciliation
of "the two principles of conservation and
correction" is indispensable to healthy
national growth. It is safe to say that every
such revolutionary era as that on which
the United States entered in 1860 finds
its genesis in an inadequate adjustment of
these two forces. It is also safe to say that
when a tragic national failure occurs, it
is largely a failure of leadership. "Brains
are of three orders," wrote Machiavelli,
"those that understand of themselves,
those that understand when another

shows them, and those that understand
neither by themselves nor by the showing
of others." Ferment and change must
steadily be controlled; the real must, as
Bryce said, be kept resting on the ideal;
and if disaster is to be avoided, wise leaders must help thoughtless men to understand, and direct the action of invincibly
ignorant men. Necessary reforms may be
obstructed in various ways; by sheer in-
ertia, by tyranny and class selfishness, or
by the application of compromise to basic
principles—this last being in Lowell's
view the main cause of the Civil War.
Ordinarily the obstruction arises from a
combination of all these elements. To
explain the failure of American leadership in 1846–1861, and the revolution that

*Reprinted with the permission of Charles Scribner's Sons from Volume II, *The Emergence of Lincoln,*
pp. 462–471, by Allan Nevins. Copyright 1950 Charles Scribner's Sons.

ensued, is a bafflingly complicated problem.

Looking backward from the verge of war in March, 1861, Americans could survey a series of ill-fated decisions by their chosen agents. One unfortunate decision was embodied in Douglas's Kansas-Nebraska Act of 1854. Had an overwhelming majority of Americans been ready to accept the squatter sovereignty principle, this law might have proved a statesmanlike stroke; but it was so certain that powerful elements North and South would resist it to the last that it accentuated the strife and confusion. Another disastrous decision was made by Taney and his associates in the Dred Scott pronouncement of 1857. Still another was made by Buchanan when he weakly accepted the Lecompton Constitution and tried to force that fraudulent document through Congress. The Northern legislatures which passed Personal Liberty Acts made an unhappy decision. Most irresponsible, wanton, and disastrous of all was the decision of those Southern leaders who in 1858–60 turned to the provocative demand for Congressional protection of slavery in all the Territories of the republic.* Still other errors might be named. Obviously, however, it is the forces behind these decisions which demand our study; the waters pouring down the gorge, not the rocks which threw their spray into the air.

At this point we meet a confused clamor of voices as various students attempt an explanation of the tragic denouncement of 1861. Some writers are as content with a simple explanation as Lord Clarendon was when he attributed the English Civil War to the desire of Parliament for an egregious domination of the government. The bloody conflict, declared James Ford Rhodes, had "a single cause, slavery." He was but echoing what Henry Wilson and other early historians had written, that the aggressions of the Slave Power offered the central explanation. That opinion had been challenged as early as 1861 by the London *Saturday Review,* which remarked that "slavery is but a surface question in American politics," and by such Southern propagandists as Yancey, who tried to popularize a commercial theory of the war, emphasizing a supposed Southern revolt against the tariff and other Yankee exactions. A later school of writers was to find the key to the tragedy in an inexorable conflict between the business-minded North and the agrarian-minded South, a thrusting industrialism colliding with a rather static agricultural society. Still another group of writers has accepted the theory that the war resulted from psychological causes. They declare that agitators, propagandists, and alarmists on both sides, exaggerating the real differences of interest, created a state of mind, a hysterical excitement, which made armed conflict inevitable.

At the very outset of the war Senator Mason of Virginia, writing to his daughter, asserted that two systems of society were in conflict; systems, he implied, as different as those of Carthage and Rome, Protestant Holland and Catholic Spain. That view, too, was later to be elaborated by a considerable school of writers. Two separate nations, they declared, had arisen within the United States in 1861, much as two separate nations emerged within the first British Empire by 1776. Contrasting ways of life, rival group consciousness,

---

*We stated in an earlier chapter that Southern leaders in 1857 had time for a few more decisions, but they had to think fast and think straight. This slave-code demand represented their most flagrant error. It has been said that Jefferson Davis adopted it because his blatherskite rival A. G. Brown took it up. But a true statesman does not let an irresponsible rival force him into courses he recognizes as unwise.

divergent hopes and fears made a movement for separation logical; and the minority people, believing its peculiar civilization in danger of suppression, began a war for independence. We are told, indeed, that two types of nationalism came into conflict: a Northern nationalism which wished to preserve the unity of the whole republic, and a Southern nationalism intent on creating an entirely new republic.

It is evident that some of these explanations deal with merely superficial phenomena, and that others, when taken separately, represent but subsidiary elements in the play of forces. Slavery was a great fact; the demands of Northern industrialism constituted a great fact; sectional hysteria was a great fact. But do they not perhaps relate themselves to some profounder underlying cause? This question has inspired one student to suggest that "the confusion of a growing state" may offer the fundamental explanation of the drift to war; an unsatisfactory hypothesis, for westward growth, railroad growth, business growth, and cultural growth, however much attended with "confusion," were unifying factors, and it was not the new-made West but old-settled South Carolina which led in the schism.   *economy. And*

One fact needs emphatic statement: of all the monistic explanations for the drift to war, that posited upon supposed economic causes is the flimsiest. This theory was sharply rejected at the time by so astute an observer as Alexander H. Stephens. South Carolina, he wrote his brother on New Year's Day, 1861, was seceding from a tariff "which is just what her own Senators and members in Congress made it." As for the charges of consolidation and despotism made by some Carolinians, he thought they arose from peevishness rather than a calm analysis of facts. "The truth is, the South, almost in mass, has voted, I think, for every measure of general legislation that has passed both houses and become law for the last ten years." The South, far from groaning under tyranny, had controlled the government almost from its beginning, and Stephens believed that its only real grievance lay in the Northern refusal to return fugitive slaves and to stop the antislavery agitation. "All other complaints are founded on threatened dangers which may never come, and which I feel very sure would be averted if the South would pursue a judicious and wise course." Stephens was right. It was true that the whole tendency of Federal legislation 1842–1860 was toward free trade; true that the tariff in force when secession began was largely Southern-made; true that it was the lowest tariff the country had known since 1816; true that it cost a nation of thirty million people but sixty million dollars in indirect revenue; true that without secession no new tariff law, obnoxious to the Democratic Party, could have passed before 1863—if then.

In the official explanations which one Southern State after another published for its secession, economic grievances are either omitted entirely or given minor position. There were few such supposed grievances which the agricultural States of Illinois, Iowa, Indiana, Wisconsin, and Minnesota did not share with the South—and they never threatened to secede. Charles A. Beard finds the tap-root of the war in the resistance of the planter interest to Northern demands enlarging the old Hamilton-Webster policy. The South was adamant in standing for "no high protective tariffs, no ship subsidies, no national banking and currency system; in short, none of the measures which business enterprise deemed essential to its progress." But the Republican platform in 1856 was silent on the tariff; in 1860 it carried a milk-and-water statement on the subject which Western Republicans took, mild as it was, with a wry face; the incoming President was little interested in the tariff; and any harsh legislation was impossible. Ship subsidies were not an issue in the campaign of 1860. Neither were a national banking system and a national currency system. They were not mentioned in the Republican platform nor discussed by party debaters. The Pacific Railroad was advocated both by the Douglas Democrats and the Republicans; and it is noteworthy that Seward and Douglas were for building both a Northern and a Southern line. In short, the divisive economic issues are easily exaggerated. At the same time, the unifying economic factors were both numerous and powerful. North and South had economies which were largely complementary. It was no misfortune to the South that Massachusetts cotton mills wanted its staple, and that New York ironmasters like Hewitt were eager to sell rails dirt-cheap to Southern railway builders; and sober businessmen on both sides, merchants, bankers, and manufacturers, were the men most anxious to keep the peace and hold the Union together.*

We must seek further for an explanation; and in so doing, we must give special weight to the observations of penetrating leaders of the time, who knew at firsthand

the spirit of the people. Henry J. Raymond, moderate editor of the New York *Times,* a sagacious man who disliked Northern abolitionists and Southern radicals, wrote in January, 1860, an analysis of the impending conflict which attributed it to a competition for power:

In every country there must be a just and equal balance of powers in the government, an equal distribution of the national forces. Each section and each interest must exercise its due share of influence and control. It is always more or less difficult to preserve their just equipoise, and the larger the country, and the more varied its great interests, the more difficult does the task become, and the greater the shock and disturbance caused by an attempt to adjust it when once disturbed. I believe I state only what is generally conceded to be a fact, when I say that the growth of the Northern States in population, in wealth, in all the elements of political influence and control, has been out of proportion to their political influence in the Federal Councils. While the Southern States have less than a third of the aggregate population of the Union, their interests have influenced the policy of the government far more than the interests of the Northern States. . . . Now the North has made rapid advances within the last five years, and it naturally claims a proportionate share of influence and power in the affairs of the Confederacy.

It is inevitable that this claim should be put forward, and it is also inevitable that it should be conceded. No party can long resist it; it overrides all parties, and makes them the mere instruments of its will. It is quite as strong today in the heart of the Democratic party of the North as in the Republican ranks; and any party which ignores it will lose its hold on the public mind.

Why does the South resist this claim? Not because it is unjust in itself, but because it has become involved with the question of slavery, and has drawn so much of its vigor and vitality from that quarter, that it is almost merged in that issue. The North bases its demand for

---

*South Carolina's Declaration of immediate causes of secession ignored economic issues, and concentrated upon slavery. Rhett's Address to the other slaveholding States did charge the North with gross injustice in tariff legislation; but the whole body of South Carolina's Representatives and Senators had voted for the existing tariff of 1857, and Rhett in defending his Address declared that to win the sympathy of Britain and France, a protest against protective tariffs would be more useful than a protest grounded on the slavery question. McPherson, *Political History,* 12–20.

increased power, in a very great degree, on the action of the government in regard to slavery—and the just and rightful ascendancy of the North in the Federal councils comes thus to be regarded as an element of danger to the institutions of the Southern States.

In brief, Raymond, who held that slavery was a moral wrong, that its economic and social tendencies were vicious, and that the time had come to halt its growth with a view to its final eradication, believed that the contest was primarily one for power, and for the application of that power to the slave system. With this opinion Alexander H. Stephens agreed. The Georgian said he believed slavery both morally and politically right. In his letter to Lincoln on December 30, 1860, he declared that the South did not fear that the new Republican Administration would interfere directly and immediately with slavery in the States. What Southerners did fear was the ultimate result of the shift of power which had just occurred—in its application to slavery:

Now this subject, which is confessedly on all sides outside of the constitutional action of the Government, so far as the States are concerned, is made the 'central idea' in the platform of principles announced by the triumphant party. The leading object seems to be simply, and wantonly, if you please, to put the institutions of nearly half the States under the ban of public opinion and national condemnation. This, upon general principles, is quite enough of itself to arouse a spirit not only of general indignation, but of revolt on the part of the proscribed. Let me illustrate. It is generally conceded by the Republicans even, that Congress cannot interfere with slavery in the States. It is equally conceded that Congress cannot establish any form of religious worship. Now suppose that any one of the present Christian churches or sects prevailed in all the Southern States, but had no existence in any one of the Northern States—under such circumstances

suppose the people of the Northern States should organize a political party, not upon a foreign or domestic policy, but with one leading idea of condemnation of the doctrines and tenets of that particular church, and with an avowed object of preventing its extension into the common Territories, even after the highest judicial tribunal of the land had decided they had no such constitutional power. And suppose that a party so organized should carry a Presidential election. Is it not apparent that a general feeling of resistance to the success, aims, and objects of such a party would necessarily and rightfully ensue?

Raymond and Stephens agreed that the two sections were competing for power; that a momentous transfer of power had just occurred; and that it held fateful consequences because it was involved with the issue of slavery, taking authority from a section which believed slavery moral and healthy, and giving it to a section which held slavery immoral and pernicious. To Stephens this transfer was ground for resuming the ultimate sovereignty of the States. Here we find a somewhat more complex statement of James Ford Rhodes's thesis that the central cause of the Civil War lay in slavery. Here, too, we revert to the assertions of Yancey and Lincoln that the vital conflict was between those who thought slavery right and those who thought it wrong. But this definition we can accept only if we probe a little deeper for a concept which both modifies and enlarges the basic source of perplexity and quarrel.

The main root of the conflict (and there were minor roots) was the problem of slavery *with its complementary problem of race-adjustment;* the main source of the tragedy was the refusal of either section to face these conjoined problems squarely and pay the heavy costs of a peaceful settlement. Had it not been for the difference in race, the slavery issue would have presented no great difficulties. But as the racial gulf existed, the South inarticulately but clearly perceived that elimination of this issue would still leave it the terrible problem of the Negro. Those historians who write that if slavery had simply been left alone it would soon have withered overlook this heavy impediment. The South as a whole in 1846–61 was not moving toward emancipation, but away from it. It was not relaxing the laws which guarded the system, but reinforcing them. It was not ameliorating slavery, but making it harsher and more implacable. The South was further from a just solution of the slavery problem in 1830 than it had been in 1789. It was further from a tenable solution in 1860 than it had been in 1830. Why was it going from bad to worse? Because Southern leaders refused to nerve their people to pay the heavy price of race-adjustment. These leaders never made up their mind to deal with the problem as the progressive temper of civilization demanded. They would not adopt the new outlook which the upward march of mankind required because they saw that the gradual abolition of slavery would bring a measure of political privilege; that political privilege would usher in a measure of economic equality; that on the heels of economic equality would come a rising social status for the Negro. Southern leadership dared not ask the people to pay this price.

A heavy responsibility for the failure of America in this period rests with this Southern leadership, which lacked imagination, ability, and courage. But the North was by no means without its full share, for the North equally refused to give a constructive examination to the central question of slavery as linked with race adjustment. This was because of two principal reasons. Most abolitionists and many other sentimental-minded Northerners simply denied that the problem existed. Regarding all Negroes as white men with dark skins, whom a few years of schooling would bring abreast of the dominant race, they thought that no difficult adjustment was required. A much more numerous body of Northerners would have granted that a great and terrible task of race adjustment existed—but they were reluctant to help shoulder any part of it. Take a million or two million Negroes into the Northern States? Indiana, Illinois, and even Kansas were unwilling to take a single additional person of color. Pay tens of millions to help educate and elevate the colored population? Take even a first step by offering to pay the Southern slaveholders some recompense for a gradual liberation of their human property? No Northern politician dared ask his constituents to make so unpopular a sacrifice. The North, like the South, found it easier to drift blindly toward disaster.

The hope of solving the slavery problem without a civil war rested upon several interrelated factors, of which one merits special emphasis. We have said that the South as a whole was laboring to bolster and stiffen slavery—which was much to its discredit. But it is nevertheless true that slavery was dying all around the edges of its domain; it was steadily decaying in Delaware, Maryland, western Virginia, parts of Kentucky, and Missouri. Much of the harshness of Southern legislation in the period sprang from a sense that slavery was in danger from *internal* weaknesses. In no great time Delaware, Maryland, and Missouri were likely to enter the column of free States; and if they did, reducing the roster to twelve, the doom of the institution would be clearly written. Allied with this factor was the rapid comparative increase of

Northern strength, and the steady knitting of economic, social, and moral ties between the North and West, leaving the South in a position of manifest inferiority. A Southern Confederacy had a fair fighting chance in 1861; by 1880 it would have had very little. If secession could have been postponed by two decades, natural forces might well have placed a solution full in sight. Then, too, the growing pressure of world sentiment must in time have produced its effect. But to point out these considerations is not to suggest that in 1861 a policy of procrastination and appeasement would have done anything but harm. All hope of bringing Southern majority sentiment to a better attitude would have been lost if Lincoln and his party had flinched on the basic issue of the restriction of slavery; for by the seventh decade of nineteenth century history, the time had come when that demand had to be maintained.

While in indicting leadership we obviously indict the public behind the leaders, we must also lay some blame upon a political environment which gave leadership a poor chance. American parties, under the pressure of sectional feeling, worked badly. The government suffered greatly, moreover, from the lack of any adequate planning agency. Congress was not a truly deliberative body, and its committees had not yet learned to do long-range planning. The President might have formulated plans, but he never did. For one reason, no President between Polk and Lincoln had either the ability or the prestige required; for another reason, Fillmore, Pierce, and Buchanan all held that their duty was merely to execute the laws, not to initiate legislation. Had the country possessed a ministerial form of government, the Cabinet in leading the legislature would have been compelled to lay down a program of real

scope concerning slavery. As it was, leadership in Washington was supplied only spasmodically by men like Clay, Douglas, and Crittenden.

And as we have noted, the rigidity of the American system was at this time a grave handicap. Twice, in the fall of 1854 and of 1858, the elections gave a stunning rebuke to the Administration. Under a ministerial system, the old government would probably have gone out and a new one have come in. In 1854, however, Pierce continued to carry on the old policies, and in 1858 Buchanan remained the drearily inept helmsman of the republic. Never in our history were bold, quick planning and a flexible administration of policy more needed; never was the failure to supply them more complete.

Still another element in the tragic chronicle of the time must be mentioned. Much that happens in human affairs is accidental. When a country is guided by true statesmen the role of accident is minimized; when it is not, unforeseen occurrences are numerous and dangerous. In the summer and fall of 1858, as we have seen, the revival of a conservative opposition party in the upper South, devoted to the Union, furnished a real gleam of hope. If this opposition had been given unity and determined leadership, if moderate Southerners had stood firm against the plot of Yancey and others to disrupt the Democratic Party, if Floyd had been vigilant enough to read the warning letter about John Brown and act on it, the situation might even then have been saved. Instead, John Brown's mad raid fell on public opinion like a thunderstroke, exasperating men everywhere and dividing North and South more tragically than ever. The last chance of persuading the South to submit to an essential step, the containment of slavery, was gone.

The war, when it came, was not primarily a conflict over State Rights, although that issue had become involved in it. It was not primarily a war born of economic grievances, although many Southerners had been led to think that they were suffering, or would soon suffer, economic wrongs. It was not a war created by politicians and publicists who fomented hysteric excitement; for while hysteria was important, we have always to ask what basic reasons made possible the propaganda which aroused it. It was not primarily a war about slavery alone, although that institution seemed to many the grand cause. It was a war over slavery *and* the future position of the Negro race in North America. Was the Negro to be allowed, as a result of the shift of power signalized by Lincoln's election, to take the first step toward an ultimate position of general economic, political, and social equality with the white man? Or was he to be held immobile in a degraded, servile position, unchanging for the next hundred years as it had remained essentially unchanged for the hundred years past? These questions were implicit in Lincoln's demand that slavery be placed in a position where the public mind could rest assured of its ultimate extinction.

Evasion by the South, evasion by the North, were no longer possible. The alternatives faced were an unpopular but curative adjustment of the situation by the opposed parties, or a war that would force an adjustment upon the loser. For Americans in 1861, as for many other peoples throughout history, war was easier than wisdom and courage.

CHARLES A. BEARD (1874–1948) was one of America's best known proponents of the economic interpretation of history. After an association with the renowned Europeanist, James Harvey Robinson, with whom he shared an interest in making the past relevant to all phases of modern civilization, he turned to American history. Stressing the underlying economic factors in the origins of the Constitution, the development of Jeffersonian democracy, and the evolution of society in general, he sought to apply the "new history" to the unfolding of institutional patterns in the United States. The following excerpts from *The Rise of American Civilization,* which he wrote in collaboration with his wife, illustrate his point of view of the Civil War as a "Second American Revolution," in which Northern industrial interests overthrew Southern agrarian domination of the Federal government.*

Charles A. Beard

The Approach of
the Second American Revolution

Had the economic systems of the North and the South remained static or changed slowly without effecting immense dislocations in the social structure, the balance of power might have been maintained indefinitely by repeating the compensatory tactics of 1787, 1820, 1833, and 1850; keeping in this manner the inherent antagonisms within the bounds of diplomacy. But nothing was stable in the economy of the United States or in the moral sentiments associated with its diversities.

Within each section of the country, the necessities of the productive system were generating portentous results. The periphery of the industrial vortex of the Northeast was daily enlarging, agriculture in the Northwest was being steadily supplemented by manufacturing, and the area of virgin soil open to exploitation by planters was diminishing with rhythmic regularity—shifting with mechanical precision the weights which statesmen had to adjust in their efforts to maintain the equilibrium of peace. Within each of the three sections also occurred an increasing intensity of social concentration as railways, the telegraph, and the press made travel and communication cheap and almost instantaneous, facilitating the centripetal process that was drawing people of similar economic status and

*Reprinted with permission of The Macmillan Company from *The Rise of American Civilization,* II, pp. 3–13, 35–54, by Charles A. and Mary R. Beard. Copyright 1933 by The Macmillan Company, renewed 1961 by William Beard and Miriam Beard Vagts.

parallel opinions into cooperative activities. Finally the intellectual energies released by accumulating wealth and growing leisure—stimulated by the expansion of the reading public and the literary market—developed with deepened accuracy the word-patterns of the current social persuasions, contributing with galvanic effect to the consolidation of identical groupings.

As the years passed, the planting leaders of Jefferson's agricultural party insisted with mounting fervor that the opposition, first of the Whigs and then of the Republicans, was at bottom an association of interests formed for the purpose of plundering productive management and labor on the land. And with steadfast insistence they declared that in the insatiable greed of their political foes lay the source of the dissensions which were tearing the country asunder.

"There is not a pursuit in which man is engaged (agriculture excepted)," exclaimed Reuben Davis of Mississippi in 1860, "which is not demanding legislative aid to enable it to enlarge its profits and all at the expense of the primary pursuit of man—agriculture. . . . Those interests, having a common purpose of plunder, have united and combined to use the government as the instrument of their operation and have thus virtually converted it into a consolidated empire. Now this combined host of interests stands arrayed against the agricultural states; and this is the reason of the conflict which like an earthquake is shaking our political fabric to its foundation." The furor over slavery is a mere subterfuge to cover other purposes. "Relentless avarice stands firm with its iron heel upon the Constitution." This creature, "incorporated avarice," has chained "the agricultural states to the northern rock" and lives like a vulture

upon their prosperity. It is the effort of Prometheus to burst his manacles that provokes the assault on slavery. "These states struggle like a giant," continued Davis, "and alarm these incorporated interests, lest they may break the chain that binds them to usurpation; and therefore they are making this fierce onslaught upon the slave property of the southern states."

The fact that free-soil advocates waged war only on slavery in the territories was to Jefferson Davis conclusive proof of an underlying conspiracy against agriculture. He professed more respect for the abolitionist than for the free-soiler. The former, he said, is dominated by an honest conviction that slavery is wrong everywhere and that all men ought to be free; the latter does not assail slavery in the states—he merely wishes to abolish it in the territories that are in due course to be admitted to the Union.

With challenging directness, Davis turned upon his opponents in the Senate and charged them with using slavery as a blind to delude the unwary: "What do you propose, gentlemen of the Free-Soil Party? Do you propose to better the condition of the slave? Not at all. What then do you propose? You say you are opposed to the expansion of slavery. . . . Is the slave to be benefited by it? Not at all. It is not humanity that influences you in the position which you now occupy before the country. . . . It is that you may have an opportunity of cheating us that you want to limit slave territory within circumscribed bounds. It is that you may have a majority in the Congress of the United States and convert the Government into an engine of northern aggrandizement. It is that your section may grow in power and prosperity upon treasures unjustly taken from the South, like the vampire bloated and gorged with the blood which it has secretly sucked from its victim . . . You desire to weaken the political power of the southern states; and why? Because you want, by an unjust system of legislation, to promote the industry of the New England states, at the expense of the people of the South and their industry."

Such in the mind of Jefferson Davis, fated to be president of the Confederacy, was the real purpose of the party which sought to prohibit slavery in the territories; that party did not declare slavery to be a moral disease calling for the severe remedy of the surgeon; it merely sought to keep bondage out of the new states as they came into the Union—with one fundamental aim in view, namely, to gain political ascendancy in the government of the United States and fasten upon the country an economic policy that meant the exploitation of the South for the benefit of northern capitalism.

But the planters were after all fighting against the census returns, as the phrase of the day ran current. The amazing growth of northern industries, the rapid extension of railways, the swift expansion of foreign trade to the ends of the earth, the attachment of the farming regions of the West to the centers of manufacture and finance through transportation and credit, the destruction of state consciousness by migration, the alien invasion, the erection of new commonwealths in the Valley of Democracy, the nationalistic drive of interstate commerce, the increase of population in the North, and the southward pressure of the capitalistic glacier all conspired to assure the ultimate triumph of what orators were fond of calling "the free labor system." This was a dynamic thrust far too powerful for planters operating in a limited territory with incompetent labor on soil of diminishing fer-

tility. Those who swept forward with it, exulting in the approaching triumph of machine industry, warned the planters of their ultimate subjection.

To statesmen of the invincible forces recorded in the census returns, the planting opposition was a huge, compact, and self-conscious economic association bent upon political objects—the possession of the government of the United States, the protection of its interests against adverse legislation, dominion over the territories, and enforcement of the national fugitive slave law throughout the length and breadth of the land. No phrase was more often on the lips of northern statesmen than "the slave power." The pages of the Congressional Globe bristled with references to "the slave system" and its influence over the government of the country. But it was left for William H. Seward of New York to describe it with a fullness of familiar knowledge that made his characterization a classic.

Seward knew from experience that a political party was no mere platonic society engaged in discussing abstractions. "A party," he said, "is in one sense a joint stock association, in which those who contribute most direct the action and management of the concern. The slaveholders contributing in an overwhelming proportion to the capital strength of the Democratic party, they necessarily dictate and prescribe its policy. The inevitable caucus system enables them to do this with a show of fairness and justice." This class of slaveholders, consisting of only three hundred and forty-seven thousand persons, Seward went on to say, was spread from the banks of the Delaware to the banks of the Rio Grande; it possessed nearly all the real estate in that section, owned more than three million other "persons" who were denied all civil and political rights, and inhibited "freedom of speech, freedom of press, freedom of the ballot box, freedom of education, freedom of literature, and freedom of popular assemblies. . . . The slaveholding class has become the governing power in each of the slaveholding states and it practically chooses thirty of the sixty-two members of the Senate, ninety of the two hundred and thirty-three members of the House of Representatives, and one hundred and five of the two hundred and ninety-five electors of the President and Vice-President of the United States."

Becoming still more concrete, Seward accused the President of being "a confessed apologist of the slave-property class." Examining the composition of the Senate, he found the slave-owning group in possession of all the important committees. Peering into the House of Representatives he discovered no impregnable bulwark of freedom there. Nor did respect for judicial ermine compel him to spare the Supreme Court. With irony he exclaimed: "How fitting does the proclamation of its opening close with the invocation: 'God save the United States and this honorable court. . . . The court consists of a chief justice and eight associate justices. Of these five were called from slave states and four from free states. The opinions and bias of each of them were carefully considered by the President and Senate when he was appointed. Not one of them was found wanting in soundness of politics, according to the slaveholder's exposition of the Constitution, and those who were called from the free states were even more distinguished in that respect than their brethren from the slaveholding states."

Seward then analyzed the civil service of the national government and could descry not a single person among the thousands employed in the post office, the treasury, and other great departments who was "false to the slaveholding interest." Under the spoils system, the dominion of the slavocracy extended into all branches of the federal administration. "The customs-houses and the public lands pour forth two golden streams—one into the elections to procure votes for the slaveholding class; and the other into the treasury to be enjoyed by those whom it shall see fit to reward with places in the public service." Even in the North, religion, learning, and the press were under the spell of this masterful class, frightened lest they incur its wrath.

Having described the gigantic operating structure of the slavocracy, Seward drew with equal power a picture of the opposing system founded on "free labor." He surveyed the course of economy in the North—the growth of industry, the spread of railways, the swelling tide of European immigration, and the westward roll of free farmers—rounding out the country, knitting it together, bringing "these antagonistic systems" continually into closer contact. Then he uttered those fateful words which startled conservative citizens from Maine to California—words of prophecy which proved to be brutally true—"the irrepressible conflict."

This inexorable clash, he said, was not "accidental, unnecessary, the work of interested or fanatical agitators and therefore ephemeral." No. "It is an irrepressible conflict between opposing and enduring forces." The hopes of those who sought peace by appealing to slave owners to reform themselves were as chaff in a storm. "How long and with what success have you waited already for that reformation? Did any property class ever so reform itself? Did the patricians in old Rome, the noblesse or clergy in France? The landholders in Ireland? The landed aristocracy in England? Does the slaveholding class even seek to beguile you with such a hope? Has it not become rapacious, arrogant, defiant?" All attempts at compromise were "vain and ephemeral." There was accordingly but one supreme task before the people of the United States—the task of confounding and overthrowing "by one decisive blow the betrayers of the Constitution and freedom forever." In uttering this indictment, this prophecy soon to be fulfilled with such appalling accuracy, Seward stepped beyond the bounds of cautious politics and read himself out of the little group of men who were eligible for the Republican nomination in 1860. Frantic efforts to soften his words by explanations and additions could not appease his critics.

Given an irrepressible conflict which could be symbolized in such unmistakable patterns by competent interpreters of opposing factions, a transfer of the issues from the forum to the field, from the conciliation of diplomacy to the decision of arms was bound to come. Each side obdurately bent upon its designs and convinced of its rectitude, by the fulfillment of its wishes precipitated events and effected distributions of power that culminated finally in the tragedy foretold by Seward. Those Democrats who operated on historic knowledge rather than on prophetic insight, recalling how many times the party of Hamilton had been crushed at elections, remembering how the Whigs had never been able to carry the country on a cleancut Webster-Clay program, and counting upon the continued support of a huge array of farmers and mechanics marshaled behind the planters, imagined apparently that politics—viewed as the science of ballot enumeration—could resolve the problems of power raised by the maintenance of the Union.

And in this opinion they were confirmed by the outcome of the presidential campaign in 1852, when the Whigs, with General Winfield Scott, a hero of the Mexican war, at their head, were thoroughly routed by the Democratic candidate, General Franklin Pierce of New Hampshire. Indeed the verdict of the people was almost savage, for Pierce carried every state but four, receiving 254 out of 296 electoral votes. The Free-Soil party that branded slavery as a crime and called for its prohibition in the territories scarcely made a ripple, polling only 156,000 out of more than three million votes, a figure below the record set in the previous campaign.

With the Whigs beaten and the Free-Soilers evidently a dwindling handful of negligible critics, exultant Democrats took possession of the Executive offices and Congress, inspired by a firm belief that their tenure was secure. Having won an overwhelming victory on a definite tariff for revenue and pro-slavery program, they acted as if the party of Hamilton was for all practical purposes as powerless as the little band of abolitionist agitators. At the succeeding election in 1856 they again swept the country—this time with James Buchanan of Pennsylvania as their candidate. Though his triumph was not as magisterial as that of Pierce it was great enough to warrant a conviction that the supremacy of the Democratic party could not be broken at the polls.

During these eight years of tenure, a series of events occurred under Democratic auspices, which clinched the grasp of the planting interest upon the country and produced a correlative consolidation of the opposition. One line of development indicated an indefinite extension of the slave area; another the positive withdrawal of all government support from industrial and commercial enterprise. The first evidence of the new course came in the year immediately following the inauguration of Pierce. In 1854, Congress defiantly repealed the Missouri Compromise and threw open to slavery the vast section of the Louisiana Purchase which had been closed to it by the covenant adopted more than three decades before. On the instant came a rush of slavery champions from Missouri into Kansas determined to bring it into the southern sphere of influence. Not content with the conquest of the forbidden West, filibustering parties under pro-slavery leaders attempted to seize Cuba and Nicaragua and three American ministers abroad flung out to the world a flaming proclamation, known as the "Ostend Manifesto," which declared that the United States would be justified in wresting Cuba from Spain by force—acts of imperial aggression which even the Democratic administration in Washington felt constrained to repudiate.

Crowning the repeal of the Missouri Compromise came two decisions of the Supreme Court giving sanction to the expansion of slavery in America and assuring high protection for that peculiar institution even in the North. In the Dred Scott case decided in March, 1857, Chief Justice Taney declared in effect that the Missouri Compromise had been void from the beginning and that Congress had no power under the Constitution to prohibit slavery in the territories of the United States anywhere at any time. This legal triumph for the planting interest was followed in 1859 by another decision in which the Supreme Court upheld the fugitive slave law and all the drastic procedure provided for its enforcement. To the frightened abolitionists it seemed that only one more step was needed to make freedom unconstitutional throughout the country.

These extraordinary measures on behalf of slavery were accompanied by others that touched far more vitally economic interests in the North. In 1859, the last of the subsidies for trans-Atlantic steamship companies was ordered discontinued by Congress. In 1857, the tariff was again reduced, betraying an unmistakable drift of the nation toward free trade. In support of this action, the representatives of the South and Southwest were almost unanimous and they gathered into their fold a large number of New England congressmen on condition that no material reductions should be made in duties on cotton goods. On the other hand, the Middle States and the West offered a large majority against tariff reduction so that the division was symptomatic.

Immediately after the revenue law went into effect an industrial panic burst upon the country, spreading distress among businessmen and free laborers. While that tempest was running high, the paper money anarchy let loose by the Democrats reached the acme of virulence as the notes of wildcat banks flooded the West and South and financial institutions crashed in every direction, fifty-one failing in Indiana alone within a period of five years. Since all hope of reviving Hamilton's system of finance had been buried, those who believed that a sound currency was essential to national prosperity were driven to the verge of desperation. On top of these economic calamities came Buchanan's veto of the Homestead bill which the impatient agrarians had succeeded in getting through Congress in a compromise form—an act of presidential independence which angered the farmers and mechanics who regarded the national domain as their own inheritance. . . .

From what has just been said it must be apparent that the forces which produced the irrepressible conflict were very complex in nature and yet the momentous struggle has been so often reduced by historians to simple terms that a reëxamination of the traditional thesis has become one of the tasks of the modern age. On the part of northern writers it was long the fashion to declare that slavery was the cause of the conflict between the states. Such for example was the position taken by James Ford Rhodes and made the starting point of his monumental work.

Assuming for the moment that this assertion is correct in a general sense, it will be easily observed even on a superficial investigation that "slavery" was no simple, isolated phenomenon. In itself it was intricate and it had filaments through the whole body economic. It was a labor system, the basis of planting, and the foundation of the southern aristocracy. That aristocracy, in turn, owing to the nature of its economic operations, resorted to public policies that were opposed to capitalism, sought to dominate the federal government, and, with the help of free farmers also engaged in agriculture, did at last dominate it. In the course of that political conquest, all the plans of commerce and industry for federal protection and subvention were overborne. It took more than a finite eye to discern where slavery as an ethical question left off and economics—the struggle over the distribution of wealth—began.

On the other hand, the early historians of the southern school, chagrined by defeat and compelled to face the adverse judgment of brutal fact, made the "rights of states"—something nobler than economics or the enslavement of Negroes—the issue for which the Confederacy fought and bled. That too like slavery seems simple until subjected to a little scrutiny. What is a state? At bottom it is a majority or perhaps a mere plurality of persons engaged in the quest of something supposed to be beneficial, or at all events

not injurious, to the pursuers. And what are rights? Abstract, intangible moral values having neither substance nor form? The party debates over the economic issues of the middle period answer with an emphatic negative. If the southern planters had been content to grant tariffs, bounties, subsidies, and preferences to northern commerce and industry, it is not probable that they would have been molested in their most imperious proclamations of sovereignty.

But their theories and their acts involved interests more ponderable than political rhetoric. They threatened the country with secession first in defying the tariff of abominations and when they did secede thirty years later it was in response to the victory of a tariff and homestead party that proposed nothing more dangerous to slavery itself than the mere exclusion of the institution from the territories. It took more than a finite eye to discern where their opposition to the economic system of Hamilton left off and their affection for the rights of states began. The modern reader tossed about in a contrariety of opinions can only take his bearings by examining a few indubitable realities.

With reference to the popular northern view of the conflict, there stands the stubborn fact that at no time during the long gathering of the storm did Garrison's abolition creed rise to the dignity of a first rate political issue in the North. Nobody but agitators, beneath the contempt of the towering statesmen of the age, ever dared to advocate it. No great political organization even gave it the most casual indorsement.

When the abolitionists launched the Liberty party in the campaign of 1844 to work for emancipation, as we have noted, the voters answered their plea for "the restoration of equality of political rights among men" in a manner that demonstrated the invincible opposition of the American people. Out of more than two and a half million ballots cast in the election, only sixty-five thousand were recorded in favor of the Liberty candidate. That was America's answer to the call for abolition; and the advocates of that policy never again ventured to appeal to the electorate by presenting candidates on such a radical platform.

No other party organized between that time and the clash of arms attempted to do more than demand the exclusion of slavery from the territories and not until the Democrats by repealing the Missouri Compromise threatened to extend slavery throughout the West did any party poll more than a handful of votes on that issue. It is true that Van Buren on a free-soil platform received nearly three hundred thousand votes in 1848 but that was evidently due to personal influence, because his successor on a similar ticket four years afterward dropped into an insignificant place.

Even the Republican party, in the campaign of 1856, coming hard on the act of defiance which swept away the Missouri compact, won little more than one-third the active voters to the cause of restricting the slavery area. When transformed after four more years into a homestead and high tariff party pledged merely to liberty in the territories, the Republicans polled a million votes fewer than the number cast for the opposing factions and rode into power on account of the divided ranks of the enemy. Such was the nation's reply to the anti-slavery agitation from the beginning of the disturbance until the cannon shot at Sumter opened a revolution.

Moreover not a single responsible statesman of the middle period committed himself to the doctrine of immediate and unconditional abolition to be achieved by independent political action. John Quincy Adams, ousted from the presidency by Jacksonian Democracy but returned to Washington as the Representative of a Massachusetts district in Congress, did declare that it was the duty of every free American to work directly for the abolition of slavery and with uncanny vision foresaw that the knot might be cut with the sword. But Adams was regarded by astute party managers as a foolish and embittered old man and his prophecy as a dangerous delusion.

Practical politicians who felt the iron hand of the planters at Washington—politicians who saw how deeply intertwined with the whole economic order the institution of slavery really was—could discover nothing tangible in immediate and unconditional abolition that appealed to reason or came within the range of common sense. Lincoln was emphatic in assuring the slaveholders that no Republican had ever been detected in any attempt to disturb them. "We must not interfere with the institution of slavery in the states where it exists," he urged, "because the Constitution forbids it and the general welfare does not require us to do so."

Since, therefore, the abolition of slavery never appeared in the platform of any great political party, since the only appeal ever made to the electorate on that issue was scornfully repulsed, since the spokesman of the Republicans emphatically declared that his party never intended to interfere with slavery in the states in any shape or form, it seems reasonable to assume that the institution of slavery was not the fundamental issue during the epoch preceding the bombardment of Fort Sumter.

Nor can it be truthfully said, as southern writers were fond of having it, that a tender and consistent regard for the rights of states and for a strict construction of the Constitution was the prime element in the dispute that long divided the country. As a matter of record, from the foundation of the republic, all factions were for high nationalism or low provincialism upon occasion according to their desires at the moment, according to turns in the balance of power. New England nullified federal law when her commerce was affected by the War of 1812 and came out stanchly for liberty and union, one and inseparable, now and forever, in 1833 when South Carolina attempted to nullify a tariff act. Not long afterward, the legislature of Massachusetts, dreading the overweening strength of the Southwest, protested warmly against the annexation of Texas and resolved that "such an act of admission would have no binding force whatever on the people of Massachusetts."

Equally willing to bend theory to practical considerations, the party of the slavocracy argued that the Constitution was to be strictly and narrowly construed whenever tariff and bank measures were up for debate; but no such piddling concept of the grand document was to be held when a bill providing for the prompt and efficient return of fugitive slaves was on the carpet. Less than twenty years after South Carolina prepared to resist by arms federal officers engaged in collecting customs duties, the champions of slavery and states' rights greeted with applause a fugitive slave law which flouted the precious limitations prescribed in the first ten Amendments to the Constitution — a law which provided for the use of all the powers of the national government to assist masters in getting possession of their elusive property — which denied to the alleged slave, who might perchance be a freeman in spite of his color, the right to have a jury trial or even to testify in his own behalf. In other words, it was "constitutional" to employ the engines of the federal authority in catching slaves wherever they might be found in any northern community and to ignore utterly the elementary safeguards of liberty plainly and specifically imposed on Congress by language that admitted of no double interpretation.

On this very issue of personal liberty, historic positions on states' rights were again reversed. Following the example of South Carolina on the tariff, Wisconsin resisted the fugitive slave law as an invasion of her reserved rights — as a violation of the Constitution. Alarmed by this action, Chief Justice Taney answered the disobedient state in a ringing judicial decision announcing a high nationalism that would have delighted the heart of John Marshall, informing the recalcitrant Wisconsin that the Constitution and laws enacted under it were supreme; that the fugitive slave law was fully authorized by the Constitution; and that the Supreme Court was the final arbiter in all controversies over the respective powers of the states and the United States. "If such an arbiter had not been provided in our complicated system of government, internal tranquility could not have been preserved and if such controversies were left to the arbitrament of physical force, our Government, State and National, would cease to be a government of laws, and revolution by force of arms would take the place of courts of justice and judicial decisions." No nullification here; no right of a state to judge for itself respecting infractions of the Constitution by the federal government; federal law is binding everywhere and the Supreme Court, a branch of the national government, is the final judge.

And in what language did Wisconsin reply? The legislature of the state, in a solemn resolution, declared that the decision of the Supreme Court of the United States in the case in question was in direct conflict with the Constitution. It vowed that the essential principles of the Kentucky doctrine of nullification were sound. Then it closed with the rebel fling: "that the several states . . . being sovereign and independent, have the unquestionable right to judge of its [the Constitution's] infraction and that a positive defiance by those sovereignties of all unauthorized acts done or attempted to be done under color of that instrument is the rightful remedy."

That was in 1859. Within two years, men who had voted for that resolution and cheered its adoption were marching off in martial array to vindicate on southern battlefields the supremacy of the Union and the sovereignty of the nation. By that fateful hour the southern politicians who had applauded Taney's declaration that the Supreme Court was the final arbiter in controversies between the states and the national government had come to the solemn conclusion that the states themselves were the arbiters. Such words and events being facts, there can be but one judgment in the court of history; namely, that major premises respecting the nature of the Constitution and deductions made logically from them with masterly eloquence were minor factors in the grand dispute as compared with the interests, desires, and passions that lay deep in the hearts and minds of the contestants.

Indeed, honorable men who held diametrically opposite views found warrant for each in the Constitution. All parties and all individuals, save the extreme abolitionists, protested in an unbroken chant their devotion to the national covenant and to the principles and memory of the inspired men who framed it.

As the Bible was sometimes taken as a guide for theologians traveling in opposite directions, so the Constitution was the beacon that lighted the way of statesmen who differed utterly on the issues of the middle period. Again and again Calhoun declared that his one supreme object was to sustain the Constitution in its pristine purity of principle: "to turn back the government," as he said, "to where it commenced its operation in 1789 . . . to take a fresh start, a new departure, on the States Rights Republican tack, as was intended by the framers of the Constitution."

This was the eternal refrain of Calhoun's school. The bank, subsidies to shipping, protection for industries, the encouragement of business enterprise by public assistance were all departures from the Constitution and the intentions of its framers, all contrary to the fundamental compact of the land. This refrain reverberated through Democratic speeches in Congress, the platform of the party, and the official utterances of its statesmen. "The liberal principles embodied by Jefferson in the Declaration of Independence and sanctioned by the Constitution . . . have ever been cardinal principles in the Democratic faith"— such was the characteristic declaration of the elect in every platform after 1840. The Constitution warrants the peaceful secession of states by legal process—such was the answer of Jefferson Davis to those who charged him with raising the flag of revolution. Everything done by the Democratic party while in power was constitutional and finally, as a crowning act of grace, the Constitution gave approval to its own destruction and the dissolution of the Union.

It followed from this line of reasoning as night the day that the measures advanced by the Whigs and later by the

Republicans were unconstitutional. In fact, Calhoun devoted the burden of a great speech in 1839 to showing how everything done by Hamilton and his school was a violation of the Constitution. Party manifestoes reiterated the pronouncements of party statesmen on this point. In their platform of 1840, the Democrats highly resolved that "the Constitution does not confer upon the general government the power . . . to carry on a general system of internal improvement . . . the Constitution does not confer authority upon the federal government, directly or indirectly, to assume the debts of the several states . . . Congress has no power to charter a United States Bank . . . Congress has no power, under the Constitution, to interfere with or control the domestic institutions of the several states." This declaration was repeated every four years substantially in the same form. After the Supreme Court announced in the Dred Scott case that Congress could not prohibit slavery in the territories, the Democratic party added that the doctrine "should be respected by all good citizens and enforced with promptness and fidelity by every branch of the general government."

In the best of all possible worlds everything substantial desired by the Democrats was authorized by the Constitution while everything substantial opposed by them was beyond the boundaries set by the venerable instrument. Hamilton, who helped to draft the Constitution, therefore, did not understand or interpret it correctly; whereas Jefferson, who was in Paris during its formation was the infallible oracle on the intentions of its framers.

On the other hand, the Whigs and then the Republicans were equally prone to find protection under the aegis of the Constitution. Webster in his later years devoted long and eloquent speeches to showing that the Constitution contemplated a perpetual union and that nullification and secession were utterly proscribed by the principles of that instrument. He did not go as far as Calhoun. He did not declare free trade unconstitutional but he did find in the records of history evidence that "the main reason for the adoption of the Constitution" was to give "the general government the power to regulate commerce and trade." A protective tariff was therefore constitutional. Furthermore "it was no more the right than the duty" of Congress "by just discrimination to protect the labor of the American people." The provision of a uniform system of currency was also among "the chief objects" of the Fathers in framing the Constitution. A national bank was not imperatively commanded by the letter of the document but its spirit required Congress to stabilize and make sound the paper currency of the land. In fact Webster thought the Democrats themselves somewhat unconstitutional. "If by democracy," he said, "they mean a conscientious and stern adherence to the Constitution and the government, then I think they have very little claim to it."

In the endless and tangled debates on slavery, the orators of the age also paid the same sincere homage to the Constitution that they had paid when dealing with other economic matters. Southern statesmen on their side never wearied in pointing out the pro-slavery character of the covenant. That instrument, they said, recognized the slave trade by providing that the traffic should not be prohibited for twenty years and by leaving the issue open after that period had elapsed. It made slavery the basis of taxation and representation, "thus preferring and fostering it above all other property, by making it alone, of all property, an element of political power in the union, as well as a source of revenue to the federal government." The Constitution laid a binding obligation upon all states to return fugitive slaves to their masters upon claims made in due course. It guaranteed the states against domestic violence, not overlooking the possibilities of a servile revolt. "Power to abolish, circumscribe, or restrain slavery is withheld but power is granted and the duty is imposed on the federal government to protect and preserve it." The English language could hardly be more explicit.

All this was no accident; it was the outcome of design. "The framers of the Constitution were slave owners or the representatives of slave owners"; the Constitution was the result of a compromise between the North and the South in which slavery was specifically and zealously guarded and secured. Such were the canons of authenticity on the southern side.

This view of the Constitution contained so much sound historical truth that the opposition was forced to strain the imagination in its search for an answer. In an attempt to find lawful warrant for their creed in 1844, the abolitionists made a platform that became one of the prime curiosities in the annals of logic. They announced that the principles of the Declaration of Independence were embraced in the Constitution, that those principles proclaimed freedom, and that the provision of the Constitution relative to the return of fugitive slaves was itself null and void because forsooth common law holds any contract contrary to natural right and morality invalid.

Although the Republicans did not go that far in their defensive romancing, they also asserted, in their platform of 1860, that the principles of the Declaration of Independence were embodied in the Constitution and they claimed that neither Congress nor a state legislature could give legal existence to slavery in any territory of the United States. But there was one slip in this reasoning: the Supreme Court of the United States, with reference to the Dred Scott case, had read in the same oracle that Congress could not deprive any slave owner of his property in the territories and that the abolition of slavery there by Congress was null and void.

Nevertheless, the Republicans neatly evaded this condemnation of their doctrine, by calling it "a dangerous political heresy, at variance with the explicit provisions of that instrument itself, with contemporaneous exposition, and with legislative and judicial precedent." In short, the Republicans entered a dissenting opinion themselves; while it was hardly authentic constitutional law it made an effective appeal to voters—especially those fond of legal proprieties.

Even in their violent disagreement as to the nature of the Union, the contestants with equal fervor invoked the authority of the Constitution to show that secession was lawful or that the perpetuation of the Union was commanded as the case might be. With respect to this problem each party to the conflict had a theory which was finely and logically drawn from pertinent data and given the appearance of soundness by a process of skillful elision and emphasis.

Those who to-day look upon that dispute without rancor must admit that the secessionists had somewhat the better of the rhetorical side of the battle. Their scheme of historicity was simple. The thirteen colonies declared their independence as separate sovereignties; they were recognized by Great Britain in the treaty of peace as thirteen individual states;

when they formed the Articles of Confederation they were careful to declare that "each state retains its sovereignty, freedom, and independence and every power, jurisdiction, and right, which is not by this Confederation expressly delegated to the United States in Congress assembled." These were undeniable facts. Then came the formation of the Constitution. The states elected delegates to the federal convention; the delegates revised the Articles of Confederation; the revision, known as the Constitution, was submitted for approval to the states and finally ratified by state conventions.

Q. E. D., ran the secessionist argument, the sovereign states that entered the compact can by lawful process withdraw from the Union just as sovereign nations may by their own act dissolve a treaty with other foreign powers.

There was, of course, some difficulty in discovering attributes of sovereignty in the new states carved out of the national domain by the surveyors' compass and chain and admitted to the Union under specific constitutional limitations— states that now outnumbered the original thirteen. But the slight hiatus in the argument, which arose from this incongruity, was bridged by the declaration that the subject territories when taken in under the roof were clothed with the sovereignty and independence of the original commonwealths.

The historical brief of those who maintained, on the other hand, that secession was illegal rested in part on an interpretation of the preamble of the Constitution, an interpretation advanced by Webster during his famous debate with Hayne. "It cannot be shown," he said, "that the Constitution is a compact between state governments. The Constitution itself, in its very front, refutes that idea; it declares that it is ordained and established by the people of the United States. . . . It even does not say that it is established by the people of the several states; but pronounces that it is established by the people of the United States in the aggregate." That is, the Constitution was not made by the states; it was made by a high collective sovereign towering above them—the people of the United States.

This fair argument, which seemed convincing on its face, was later demolished by reference to the journals of the Convention that drafted the Constitution. When the preamble was originally drawn, it ran: "We, the people of the states of New Hampshire, Massachusetts, &c., . . . do ordain and establish the following Constitution." But on second thought the framers realized that according to their own decree the new government was to be set up as soon as nine states had ratified the proposed instrument. It was obviously undesirable to enumerate the states of the Union in advance, for some of them might withhold their approval. Therefore the first draft was abandoned and the words "We the people of the United States" substituted. The facts of record accordingly exploded the whole thesis built on this sandy foundation.

This fallacy Lincoln was careful to avoid in his first inaugural address. Seeking a more secure historical basis for his faith, he pointed out that the Union was in fact older than the Constitution, older than the Declaration of Independence. It was formed, he said, by the Articles of Association framed in 1774 by the Continental Congress speaking in the name of revolutionary America. It was matured and continued in the Declaration of Independence which proclaimed "these United Colonies" to be free and independent states. It was sealed by the Articles of Confederation which pledged the thirteen commonwealths to a perpetual Union under that form of government; it was crowned by the Constitution designed to make the Union "more perfect."

Far more effective on the nationalist side was the argument derived through logical processes from the nature of the Constitution itself, by Webster, Lincoln, and the philosophers of their school. It ran in the following vein. The Constitution does not, by express provision or by implication, provide any method by which a state may withdraw from the Union; no such dissolution of the federation was contemplated by the men who drafted and ratified the covenant. The government established by it operates directly on the people, not on states; it is the government of the people, not of states. Moreover the Constitution proclaims to all the world that it and the laws and treaties made in pursuance of its terms, are the supreme law of the land and that the judges of the states are bound thereby, "anything in the constitution and laws of any state to the contrary notwithstanding." Finally, the Supreme Court of the United States is the ultimate arbiter in all controversies arising between the national government and the states. Chief Justice Marshall had proclaimed the doctrine in beating down the resistance of Virginia, Maryland, and Ohio to federal authority; Chief Justice Taney had proclaimed it in paralyzing the opposition of Wisconsin to the fugitive slave law. Such being the grand pledges and principles of the Constitution it followed, to use Lincoln's version, that no state could lawfully withdraw from the Union; secession was insurrectionary or revolutionary according to circumstances.

What now is the verdict of history on these verbal contests? Did the delegates at the Philadelphia convention of 1787 regard themselves as ambassadors of sovereign states entering into a mere treaty of alliance? Did they set down anywhere a pontifical judgment to the effect that any state might on its own motion withdraw from the Union after approving the Constitution? The answer to these questions is in the negative. Had they thought out a logical system of political theory such as Calhoun afterward announced with such precision? If so, they left no record of it to posterity.

What then was the Constitution? It was a plan of government designed to effect certain purposes, specific and general, framed by a small group of citizens, "informed by a conscious solidarity of interests," who, according to all available evidence, intended that government to be supreme over the states and enduring. They were not dominated by any logical scheme such as Calhoun evolved in defending his cause; they were engrossed in making, not breaking, a Union; they made no provision for, and if the testimony of their recorded debates be accepted as conclusive, did not contemplate the withdrawal of the states from the federation by any legal procedure. Surely it was not without significance that James Madison, the father of the Constitution, who lived to see secession threatened in South Carolina, denounced in unmistakable terms the smooth and well-articulated word-pattern of Calhoun, condemning secession as utterly without support in the understandings of the men who made, ratified, and launched the Constitution.

But it may be said that the men of Philadelphia merely drafted the Constitution and that what counts in the premises is the opinions of the voters in the states, who through their delegates ratified the instrument. Did, then, the men who chose the delegates for the state ratifying conventions or the delegates themselves have clearly in mind a concept that made the great document in effect a mere treaty of alliance which could be legally denounced at will by any member? The records in the case give no affirmative answer. What most of them thought is a matter of pure conjecture. Were any of the states sovereign in fact at any time; that is, did any of them assume before the world the attributes and functions of a sovereign nation? Certainly not. Did the whole people in their collective capacity make the Constitution? To ask the question is to answer it; they did not.

When the modern student examines all the verbal disputes over the nature of the Union—the arguments employed by the parties which operated and opposed the federal government between the adoption of the Constitution and the opening of the Civil War—he can hardly do otherwise than conclude that the linguistic devices used first on one side and then on the other were not derived from inherently necessary concepts concerning the intimate essence of the federal system. The roots of the controversy lay elsewhere—in social groupings founded on differences in climate, soil, industries, and labor systems, in divergent social forces, rather than varying degrees of righteousness and wisdom, or what romantic historians call "the magnetism of great personalities.". . .

In the spring of 1861 the full force of the irrepressible conflict burst upon the hesitant and bewildered nation and for four long years the clash of arms filled the land with its brazen clangor. For four long years the anguish, the calamities, and the shocks of the struggle absorbed the energies of the multitudes, blared in the headlines of the newspapers, and loomed impressively in the minds of the men and women who lived and suffered in that age. Naturally, therefore, all who wrote of the conflict used the terms of war. In its records, the government of the United States officially referred to the contest as the War of the Rebellion, thus by implication setting the stigma of treason on those who served under the Stars and Bars. Repudiating this brand and taking for his shield the righteousness of legitimacy, one of the leading southern statesmen, Alexander H. Stephens, in his great history of the conflict, called it the War between the States. This, too, no less than the title chosen by the federal government, is open to objections; apart from the large assumptions involved, it is not strictly accurate for, in the border states, the armed struggle was a guerrilla war and in Virginia the domestic strife ended in the separation of several counties, under the aegis of a new state constitution, as West Virginia. More recently a distinguished historian, Edward Channing, entitled a volume dealing with the period The War for Southern Independence—a characterization which, though fairly precise, suffers a little perhaps from abstraction.

As a matter of fact all these symbols are misleading in that they overemphasize the element of military force in the grand dénouement. War there was unquestionably, immense, wide-sweeping, indubitable, as Carlyle would say. For years the agony of it hung like a pall over the land. And yet with strange swiftness the cloud was lifted and blown away. Merciful grass spread its green mantle over the cruel scars and the gleaming red splotches sank into the hospitable earth.

It was then that the economist and lawyer, looking more calmly on the scene, discovered that the armed conflict had been only one phase of the cataclysm, a transitory phase; that at bottom the so-called Civil War, or the War between the States, in the light of Roman analogy, was a social war, ending in the unquestioned establishment of a new power in the government, making vast changes in the arrangement of classes, in the accumulation and distribution of wealth, in the course of industrial development, and in the Constitution inherited from the Fathers. Merely by the accidents of climate, soil, and geography was it a sectional struggle. If the planting interest had been scattered evenly throughout the industrial region, had there been a horizontal rather than a perpendicular cleavage, the irrepressible conflict would have been resolved by other methods and accompanied by other logical defense mechanisms.

In any event neither accident nor rhetoric should be allowed to obscure the intrinsic character of that struggle. If the operations by which the middle classes of England broke the power of the king and the aristocracy are to be known collectively as the Puritan Revolution, if the series of acts by which the bourgeois and peasants of France overthrew the king, nobility, and clergy is to be called the French Revolution, then accuracy compels us to characterize by the same term the social cataclysm in which the capitalists, laborers, and farmers of the North and West drove from power in the national government the planting aristocracy of the South. Viewed under the light of universal history, the fighting was a fleeting incident; the social revolution was the essential, portentous outcome.

To be sure the battles and campaigns of the epoch are significant to the military strategist; the tragedy and heroism of the contest furnish inspiration to patriots and romance to the makers of epics. But the core of the vortex lay elsewhere. It was in the flowing substance of things limned by statistical reports on finance, commerce, capital, industry, railways, and agriculture, by provisions of constitutional law, and by the pages of statute books—prosaic muniments which show that the so-called civil war was in reality a Second American Revolution and in a strict sense, the First.

The physical combat that punctuated the conflict merely hastened the inevitable. As was remarked at the time, the South was fighting against the census returns—census returns that told of accumulating industrial capital, multiplying captains of industry, expanding railway systems, widening acres tilled by free farmers. Once the planting and the commercial states, as the Fathers with faithful accuracy described them, had been evenly balanced; by 1860 the balance was gone.

WILLIAM APPLEMAN WILLIAMS (1921–   ) is one of the most prominent of modern left-wing historians. Primarily interested in the development of American diplomatic relations, which he has taught at the University of Wisconsin and Oregon State University, he turned to the question of the causation of the Civil War in his book, *The Contours of American History.* Arguing that an exclusive laissez-faire philosophy was fundamental to the antislavery crusade, he tends to downgrade the idealistic motivation of the abolitionists, while presenting a more complicated view of the basic conflict between Northern business, Western agriculture, and Southern slavery than the Beards. Excerpts from *The Contours of American History* follow.*

William Appleman Williams

Commitment to Laissez Faire

Long after it has ceased to be an effective weapon of personal recrimination or political strategy, Americans remain haunted by the Civil War. One is sometimes tempted to conclude that never have so many said so much about the same thing that is redundant or irrelevant. Underlying that persistent involvement is the realization that the war undercuts the popular mythology that America is unique. Only a nation that avoided such a conflict could make a serious claim to being fundamentally different. In accordance with the logic and psychology of myth, therefore, it has become necessary to turn the war itself into something so different, strange, and mystic that it could have happened only to the chosen people.

Whatever the appeals and sublimations of that approach, it seems more pertinent to history as a way of learning to examine the Civil War through the convergence of the three moralities of laissez faire that began in the late 1830s and reached an early climax in the Free Soil movement. As they merged in a consolidated system, the religious, political, and economic ethics were also distilled into a few key symbols. These handholds of thought, discourse, and judgment became the most potent and yet inclusive words of the age: *expansion, antislavery, freedom.* As indicated by their use as early as Jackson's time, as well as by their more formal denotations and connotations, they implied that the integrated value system of laissez faire was almost wholly negative. Freedom was defined as release from restriction. Expansion and antislavery were but the two sides of the coin that bought such liberty. But while the defining of evil is a vital function, it is no more than half the responsibility of any philosophy. Lacking a creative vision of community, laissez faire was weak in an essential respect: it provided no basis upon which to deal with evil in a nonviolent way. Its solutions were persistently aggressive and acquisitive.

For these reasons, the northern critics of the Compromise of 1850 were more influential than the southern extremists whose first fuse sputtered out at the Nashville Convention. While many of these northerners were ostensibly anti-expansionists, their position was in reality far more complex. They favored overseas economic expansion and defined the rest of foreign policy largely in terms of the trans-Mississippi west. Most westerners and eastern would-be capitalists shared the latter part of this outlook, and on the issue all of them were vigorous expansionists. Since that region was in fact America's colonial (i.e., underdeveloped) empire, their view was realistic.

But it was also extremely provocative because it defined the issue in very severe terms: would expansion into the trans-Mississippi west be undertaken within the framework of the Constitution, or would that basic law be rewritten in accordance with the abstract principles of laissez faire? The compromises under which the Constitution was adopted, the clauses of that document pertaining to representation in the Congress (which counted three-fifths of each slave) and the rights of states, and the pattern of legislation, and the decisions of the Supreme Court all pointed to a choice between two ways of handling the western territories. Either

they would be opened to slaveholders as well as nonslaveholders, or the region would be divided into slave and nonslave areas. Southerners were willing to accept either of these solutions. So were a good many northerners.

But the advocates of antislavery laissez faire insisted that no one who did not accept their version of the axioms of laissez faire should be permitted to share the territorial empire. And as far as they were concerned, slavery was a violation of those principles. For them, at any rate, the arrival of the Age of Laissez Nous Faire meant that the Constitution had to be interpreted—that is, rewritten—in the light of this outlook. Since the divergence of opinion ultimately defined *the* question, the basic cause of the Civil War was the *Weltanschauung* of laissez faire. Unwilling to compete within the framework and under the terms of the Constitution, northern antislavery advocates of laissez faire finally undertook to change the rules in the middle of the game—and in the middle of the continent—by denying the south further access to the expanding market place.

In the meantime, from 1851 to 1861, the nation and its politicians fruitlessly sought a way to reconcile laissez faire with the Constitution. But since all their proposals hinged on expansion, they never broke free of the impasse. Seward had the keenest insight into this determining factor. "I cannot exclude the conviction," he concluded as early as 1846, "that the popular passion for territorial aggrandizement is irresistible." Small wonder, therefore, that he later called the struggle between north and south an "irrepressible conflict." Nor is it surprising that most leaders of the decade offered little more than Polk's strategy of balancing the gains between competing expansionist elements. Any more positive approach was almost discredited. One congressman with a sense of history expressed the attitude with great perceptiveness: any efforts to co-ordinate and balance the country's development "should be expunged as a disgrace to the country and to the nineteenth century." President Franklin Pierce vented the same spirit in his inaugural assertion that he would "not be controlled by any timid forebodings of evil from expansion." President James Buchanan put it even more bluntly. "Expansion is in the future the policy of our country, and only cowards fear and oppose it."

Thus the issue became dangerously oversimplified: expansion for whom? Throughout the 1850s, moreover, the debate took place against a backdrop prepared by America's first female primitive artist in words and ideas. *Uncle Tom's Cabin,* Harriet Beecher Stowe's landscape of slavery, was published in March, 1852. Though the form had not really been established (Erastus Beadle launched it in 1860), it might fairly be called the first dime novel. It was a crude, jerky, inaccurate, and violent morality play based on the manipulation of a few type-cast characters in one black-and-white situation.

By populating the south exclusively with evil slaveholders and Negroes, Stowe stereotyped the south as evil. There was nothing of the anxiety and hesitance of the area, let alone its initial propensity to accept the Compromise of 1850. The moral was provided by her misleading picture of the Negro as a man who could in "one generation of education and liberty" take his place in society as a fully matured and developed individual. An application of the principles of laissez faire would enable everyone to live happily ever after. Many southerners thought Stowe no more than a typical emancipated female—"part quack and part cut-throat"

—and initially discounted the importance of the book. But the polemic became a guidebook to an enemy—the south—that had already been defined by the value system of laissez faire as it emerged in the program of the Free Soilers and the generalized antislavery spirit. Perhaps nothing defines the essence of laissez faire quite as well as the parallels between the Jacksonian campaign against the bank and the antislavery agitation. Both were negative. Both defined the enemy in secular moral terms. Both were closely tied to economic objectives. Both lacked any positive program for dealing with the problem. And both were undertaken in the name of expansion and freedom.

Even President Millard Fillmore's administration revealed itself as merely cautious (and a bit pro-northern) instead of fundamentally anti-expansionist. Fillmore allowed Commodore Matthew Perry to write his own militant instructions for opening Japan to American commerce, indicated considerable interest in Hawaii, and refused to sign a temperance pledge guaranteeing Spanish control of Cuba. Having argued in 1829 that expansion was "the *principle* of our institutions," Secretary of State Edward Everett in a more fully developed theory anticipated some features of Charles Darwin's theory of evolution. While overrated by the congressman who called it "the most 'manifest destiny' document that ever emanated from the State Department," Everett's long despatch refusing to guarantee the *status quo* in Cuba was a manifesto for empire. Once out of office, he was less verbose: "The pioneers are on the way; who can tell how far and fast they will travel?"

This vigorous spirit also infused a loose association of expansionists known as the Young Americans. Calling for commercial, territorial, and ideological expansion, they wanted to make the United States the hub of the hemisphere, the crossroads of the world, and the patriarch of global republicanism. Other expansionists followed the same general line on their own initiative. Though they ultimately failed, southerners had significant support from politicians and commercial groups in the northeast and the upper Mississippi Valley in their drive to acquire Cuba. And a similar combination of New Englanders, New Yorkers, and southerners almost turned Nicaragua into a Central American Hawaii; Buchanan even recognized their government before internal dissension and armed attack from other isthmian nations ended the colonizing venture.

Despite such involvement in southward territorial expansion, most northerners were primarily interested in overseas economic expansion, ideological empire, and control of the trans-Mississippi west. Their views won out in the Clayton-Bulwer Treaty of 1854, which facilitated trade developments in Central America while checking further territorial annexations by either Great Britain or the United States. Even so, some southerners supported the commercial push across the Pacific. Their trade interests were reinforced by the idea that such a move would help them hold their own in the territorial west, both directly and as a political *quid pro quo*. The result was a China policy designed for "maintaining order there" so that the nation's great economic opportunities would not become "the prey of European ambition."

Convinced that they were the "only powerful race" on the Pacific, some farsighted northerners like Perry McDonough Collins and Asa Whitney concentrated on plans whereby "American commercial enterprise [could] penetrate the obscure depths of Northern Asia."

Backed by President Pierce and Senator Seward, and of course the Western Union Company, Collins proposed a telegraph system reaching across to Siberia and thence south to India and west to Paris, Berlin, and London. It was a vision of a vast, global funnel with the spout (and the profits) opening into the Mississippi Valley. Whitney stressed a transcontinental railroad to consolidate the opportunity. "Here we stand forever," he exulted; "we reach out one hand to all Asia, and the other to all Europe, willing for all to enjoy the great blessing we possess . . . but *all* [of them] tributary, and at our will subject to us."

Nor was this an irrelevant flight from reality. Not only were large agricultural surpluses being exported, but by 1860, manufactured goods, including iron, amounted to nearly 20 per cent of America's direct exports. But the south received few benefits from the developing subsidizing of such railroads by cash appropriations and massive land grants (approximately 3.75 million acres in 1850, 35 additional projects between 1852 and 1857, and 174 million acres gross between 1850 and 1871). A Mobile-Chicago connection was the most significant offering to the south, and that came too late to alter the established pattern of east-west routes. Land was acquired for a southern route to the Pacific, but such a gulf-coast transcontinental line was never built, at least not for *that* south.

Whatever their serious internal and sectional differences, the north and the west came to define expansion ever more clearly in terms of an interrelated industrial system based on manufactures and food. Despite Buchanan's defense of it as the policy of the "good neighbor" offering a "helping hand," they opposed his plan to snip off a bit more of northern Mexico while that country was preoccupied with internal difficulties, preferring to encourage overseas revolutions that promised commercial advantages. Seward candidly referred to such governments as "the outworks of our system of politics." "We have a direct interest . . . ," agreed a westerner, "in the benefits of commercial intercourse. . . . All we want is that freedom should have a fair battlefield." . . .

On November 8, 1860, a southern gentlewoman summed it up succinctly. "That settles the hash." Since it did indeed, the reasons are important. In the broadest sense, and speaking as the heirs of the physiocratic forefathers of laissez faire, southerners insisted that the Constitution guaranteed minimum protection against *any* political economy. Its leaders interpreted Lincoln's election quite accurately as the victory of a movement to alter the Constitution and abrogate that compromise, literally in the sense of ending southern expansion, and philosophically in the sense of applying *all* the principles of a political economy in *all* the country. The south was correct about it. Lincoln's election did symbolize the coming to power of a revolutionary coalition.

ARTHUR C. COLE (1886–   ) is a recognized
authority on the antebellum period, whose sympathies,
despite a deep commitment to fairness, lay largely
with the free society of the North. During a fruitful
teaching career which culminated in the chairmanship
of the Department of History at Brooklyn College, he
published significant studies both in political and
cultural history. The best known of these is *The
Irrepressible Conflict,* Volume VII of *A History of
American Life,* edited by Arthur M. Schlesinger and
Dixon Ryan Fox, excerpts from which follow. By
tracing the development of two different civilizations in
the North and South, the author seeks to illustrate those
forces which made for the coming of the war.*

Arthur C. Cole

Two Separate Societies

In the summer of 1850 Americans
looked out upon their country with eyes
that glowed with pride and confidence.
"Manifest destiny" had been realized; the
flag had been borne in triumph to the Rio
Grande and to the Pacific shore. As if to
celebrate this great achievement the
mountains of the Far West had loosed a
mighty stream of gold. Within the vast
empire under the "Stars and Stripes" the
forces of political democracy had won
under Western leadership a mighty victory. The American example had been
enviously cited in the recent revolutionary movements in France, Italy and Germany and, lest others overlook it, the government was soon gratuitously preaching
it to Austria and Spain. The old align-
ment, of East and West, of the complacent
settled communities on the one hand and
the changing and obstreperous frontier
on the other representing to some extent
the antipathy of credits and debts was
still sensed, but less keenly than in Andrew Jackson's time. For thirty years
discerning minds had feared that it might
be supplanted by another cleavage, more
clear and strict, between the slave-planta-
tion culture of the South and the industrial and small-farm culture of the North.
Each had reached a high degree of self-
consciousness and it had seemed that their
interests might be mutually antagonistic,
especially in determining the future of
the new land gained from Mexico and
thus of national control. But moderate

*Reprinted with permission of the Macmillan Company from *The Irrepressible Conflict, 1850–1865,*
by Arthur Charles Cole, pp. 1–2, 33, 99–100, 198, 203–204, 241–242, 257–261, 283–284, 406–407. Copyright 1934
by The Macmillan Company, renewed 1962 by Arthur Charles Cole. (Footnotes omitted).

men, representing the varied propertied interests of the nation, were satisfied that—despite the work of agitators and fire eaters—intelligence, forbearance and sentimental nationalism had surmounted all that difficulty when the legislative items just narrowly passed on their own merits were shortly acquiesced in as a great and "final" compromise that should make for national accord. That this apparently perfect balance, this dualism, could not possibly continue with ideals so disparate and aggressive—in fact, that the house was hopelessly divided and on the verge of schism—this in that Indian summer calm could not be realized. . . .

The most highly organized industries, like the iron mills of Pennsylvania, suffered the worst blows [in the Panic of 1857]. In the agricultural South, on the other hand, prosperity and good prices for cotton continued, with only occasional bank failures and suspensions as reminders of the economic interdependence of the sections. Excellent cotton crops prevailed, exports increased and Negro slaves sold at prices that exceeded all past figures. All this was in marked contrast to the social revolution that seemed to threaten the industrial areas. The proud spokesmen of the South therefore boasted of the superior soundness of the cotton kingdom. "The wealth of the South," announced J. D. B. DeBow, "is permanent and real, that of the North fugitive and fictitious." Yet the census summary of industrial progress at the close of the decade showed no perceptible trace of the temporary breakdown of 1857. . . .

New Englanders often migrated in parties or in well-organized colonies. They first sought their kind in the old Yankee belt along the Great Lakes, thus avoiding the antipathy of critics who charged them

with being "sniveling, hypocritical, rascally, white-livered Yankees" afflicted with "cant, humbug, Pharisaism, bigotry, abolitionism, red republicanism." It was not long, however, before they spread out in all directions, even into lower Illinois, that "land of ignorance, barbarism, and poverty." There the Southern bias of the earlier settlers made them less welcome, but missionary zeal inspired many to carry the torch of freedom to light up the darkness of "Egypt." Migrating New Yorkers, Pennsylvanians, Ohioans, Hoosiers and the rest also played an important part. As in the case of Yankee settlers, the older Eastern influences which they brought with them, far from succumbing to frontier experiences and prejudices, came to make a deep impress upon the new environment. Thus the mingling of peoples aided further in breaking down Western suspicion of the Atlantic Seaboard.

The North-South line of cleavage, on the other hand, grew steadily more rigid. Only a few settlers hailed from the states south of the Ohio River; and these, primarily from Virginia, Tennessee and Kentucky, cherished growing doubts concerning the virtues of slavery. This stream remained insignificant until the oncoming war enlarged the flow, bringing many who felt bitterly resentful toward the South and its institutions. The heart of the South had shifted with the culture of cotton to the Gulf states. A common frontier experience no longer bound these states to those north of the Ohio. The barrier between freedom and slavery was fast becoming more effective than the old mountain barrier between the seaboard and the West. . . .

The "isms" that ravaged the country during the fifties evidenced the growing pains of an adolescent nation. Largely confined to the North, their local critics, like Walt Whitman, were usually willing to concede that they were "significant of a grand upheaval of ideas and reconstruction of many things on new bases." Proud Southerners, on the other hand, rejoiced that the land of chivalry had largely escaped the taint of the fads that were sweeping Yankeedom. In less complacent mood they sounded the tocsin of alarm against vagaries of Yankee fanaticism that found their most portentous expression in a militant abolitionism. . . .

Wealthy Southerners, as has been said, had long furnished a valuable patronage to the Northern resorts. Summer Newport was often referred to as a Southern community; a conservative proslavery atmosphere prevailed in the hotels they patronized and even in the churches they attended. In 1858 Senator Jefferson Davis of Mississippi joined a congenial group of prominent Southerners who regularly sojourned near Portland, Maine. As sectional feeling grew sharper, however, the Southern fire eaters insistently demanded a boycott of Northern resorts. Dixie had mountain and seaside attractions of her own, they pointed out. At the same time sensitive Southerners reported an increasingly rude reception upon Northern visits. "We are treated worse in the North than if we were foreign enemies," lamented the editor of the *Richmond Whig*. "Let us with one accord stay home and spend among our own people."

Under this impetus wealthy planters began to erect summer places at the already popular mineral springs in the Virginia mountains, Fauquier White Sulphur Springs becoming especially fashionable. In 1855 a number of Southerners formed a stock company to develop Southern resorts, particularly a spring at Montgomery, Virginia, a few miles from the

Tennessee line, where they hoped to create a "Southern Saratoga." A few years later, a number of small watering places with attractive summer residences grew up along the Gulf coast of Mississippi, a convenient location for inhabitants of New Orleans and for planters of the interior. Thus, as the decade drew to a close, the spirit of sectionalism was invading even the sphere of pleasure and recreation. Formerly, leisure-class Americans from both sections rubbed elbows and learned the lesson of tolerance as they exchanged social courtesies and ideas at Saratoga and Newport. But unobserved by the statesmen, coming events disclosed how badly frayed had become the bonds of fraternal feeling and mutual esteem. . . .

If the American nation had become by 1860, as some friendly foreign visitors admitted, "the most generally educated and intelligent people of the earth," this was due not only to the operation of the rapidly expanding public-school system but also to the less formal intellectual and cultural influences that ramified in almost every direction. Carl Schurz ascribed the high average of intelligence in large part to the fact that "the individual is constantly brought into interested contact with a greater variety of things, and is admitted to active participation in the exercise of functions which in other countries are left to the care of a superior authority."

Less reassuring was the circumstance that the cultural advance of these years was sectional in character. For the most part the South, hampered by its caste system, its undigested mass of poor whites and enslaved blacks, its growing antagonism to the free states, remained unaffected by the new currents of civilization. It did not share in the movement for popular education; it took a negligible part in the lyceum movement; it supported few magazines or publishing houses; it had little of a creative nature to contribute to science, scholarship, letters and the arts. More and more it lived to itself, closed in by tradition and by loyalty to a social institution which it alone in all the civilized world maintained and defended. The widening breach between the sections thus reached beyond political acerbities into the very substance of life itself. . . .

As early as the 1840's two major denominations had split upon the rock of slavery and driven their Southern brethren into independent organization. Only the Roman Catholic Church seemed free from the agitation, although its next of kin, the Protestant Episcopal Church, proud of its conservative spirit, also succeeded in steering a safe noncommittal course. It was an easy matter for churches organized in independent congregations without central legislative bodies to practise the gospel of "no fellowship with slave-holders." Moreover, most Baptist, Congregational and Unitarian churches were controlled by elements unequivocally committed to the gospel of freedom. The Western Unitarian Conference at Alton in 1857 did not allow the certain danger of the secession of the St. Louis delegation to prevent the adoption of a strong antislavery report. It is significant, too, that a group of Quakers of Chester County, Pennsylvania, opposed to the conservative stand of their brethren, formed a yearly meeting of Progressive Friends and undertook the freest discussion not only of slavery but also of war, marriage, prisons, property and other established institutions of the day.

Official spokesmen of the Methodist Episcopal Church North commonly pointed to the record of its earnest but conservative protest against the evil of slavery. On the other hand, probably as many as two hundred thousand slaves were owned by its members. Many zealous antislavery men from Northern conferences demanded that the general rule in regard to slavery be made more drastic so that the church might be freed entirely from its "criminal" connection with the institution. This issue was pressed against a declining opposition until the general conference at Buffalo in 1860 adopted a new rule in which, without excluding slaveholders from its communion, it admonished members "to keep themselves pure from this great evil, and to seek its extirpation by all lawful and Christian means."

While the Old School Presbyterians, true to their traditional conservatism, ignored the slavery question, the New School group continued in the early fifties the tactics of trying to appease the antislavery forces by mild condemnations of slavery. The radical element, however, proposed to refuse fellowship to the slaveholder, a program much too strenuous for the cautious leaders of the church and influential laymen like Cyrus H. McCormick, patron of the Theological Seminary at Chicago. Finally, in 1857 when the general assembly voted strong condemnation of a proslavery report of a Kentucky presbytery, six Southern synods with about two hundred churches and fifteen thousand communicants withdrew. With the opening of the Civil War the Old School Presbyterians of the South organized a separate church of their own.

An especial effort was made in the West to enlist the various missionary agencies under the banner of freedom. An important figure in the controversies that arose was President Jonathan Blanchard of Knox College. Convinced that "the heart of action in the Church" was the missions, he declared that from them "the foul spirit of Slavery must be dislodged before it will be *cast out of the Church.*" Accordingly, beginning in 1847, he led a fight at the annual meetings of the American Board of Commissioners for Foreign Missions in favor of barring slaveholders from the mission churches. These efforts proving fruitless, the Illinois Wesleyan Missionary Conference commended the uncompromising antislavery position of the American Missionary Association and urged affiliation with it instead of the formation of rival societies. President Blanchard showed, however, that even this body permitted membership of slaveholders. Meanwhile antislavery Baptists felt impelled to organize the American Baptist Free Mission Society. As a result a group of extreme opponents of slaveholding fellowship, meeting at Chicago in July, 1852, formed the Free Mission Society for the Northwest. For the same reason the Western Tract Convention was organized in 1859 out of antislavery seceders from the conservative American Tract Society.

Meanwhile the common cause of freedom was tending to break down the denominational barriers that separated the Christian antislavery forces. Deprecating the adoption of expediency as a substitute for the spirit of Christ, the crusaders could not but feel that the slavery issue was of more importance than sectarianism. As a result a Christian Anti-Slavery Convention assembled at Cincinnati in April, 1850; in July, 1851, an even more enthusiastic session of two hundred and fifty delegates met at Chicago with Blanchard in the chair. Though the Christian Anti-Slavery Convention disappeared as the conservative reaction set in, it was revived in October, 1859, as the Northwestern Christian Anti-Slavery Convention. Again Blanchard was a leading figure, calling the assemblage to order and justifying his support of the Republican party.

On less drastic tests of their devotion to human liberty the clergy of the nation spoke out with greater courage. Though ministers were oftentimes silent or apologetic, a strong note of protest sounded from many pulpits at the passage of the fugitive-slave law of 1850. Four years later the clergy burst out in wrath against the Kansas-Nebraska act as an assault on freedom. A memorial signed by five hundred clergymen of the Northwest denounced Douglas for "want of courtesy and reverence toward man and God." Promptly conservative editors and politicians deplored the tendency of churchmen to leave their sacred calling and incite partisan strife. "When ministers enter the arena of politics, and associate themselves with the corrupt and lying hypocrites who lead the black republican party, and utter seditious harangues from the pulpit, they are no longer entitled to that respect that their sacred calling commands," declared the *Signal* of Joliet, Illinois, when four of the local clergy participated prominently in a Republican meeting. Such warnings probably restrained the timid at a time when radical abolitionists were wondering whether the cause of freedom could triumph except upon the ruins of the church. Henry Ward Beecher, a brilliant barometer of popular progressive currents, answered critics by advancing the doctrine that any topic introduced into the pulpit became thereby consecrated. Mock slave auctions at his church vividly dramatized many of the horrors of chattel slavery.

Thus the outbreak of the war found most branches of the Christian faith embroiled by the slavery controversy. As the paramount moral question of the day it was regarded by churchgoers on one side of the Mason and Dixon line predominantly from one angle and by those dwelling on the other side predominantly from another; and both groups of

Christians espoused their convictions with a sense of inner righteousness and high scriptural sanction. However reluctant organized religion may earlier have been to enlist in the sectional strife, it failed to stay the tide of revolt and division when the national crisis appeared. . . .

Lincoln's election, indeed, inaugurated a revolution which played havoc with many existing institutions, political, social and economic. But the brunt of the upheaval fell upon the states that had taken their stand for a static, agrarian civilization in which the institution of chattel slavery held the place of paramount importance. Some Southrons consoled themselves with the thought that they were of the blood of a master race, a noble Norman stock not to be crushed by Northern Puritans of vulgar Saxon origin. They repudiated all thought of brotherhood with the Yankees; this was no fratricidal war but a renewal of the hereditary hostility between the "two races engaged." Let not the "Saxonized maw-worm" bring his taint to the soil of the South. Others, like Senator Wigfall of Texas, accepted as compliment and not reproach the description of their section as a primitive but civilized agricultural community. If, they claimed, it lacked not only a commercial marine, manufacturing and the mechanic arts but also any real cities, literature or even press, it was by choice. In such an atmosphere, of course, the plantation system and the institution of chattel slavery might flourish, although then only with the reins of power in the hands of its ardent exponents and champions. But amid the whirl and rush of modern industrial civilization its doom was certain. . . .

After four years of armed strife neither victor nor vanquished was in a mood to view in perspective the bloody struggle and assess the forces that had produced it. The South, its fields ravaged, its homes in smoking ruins, nursed a "lost cause," and mourned that righteousness had fallen before brute strength. Nor had war, "the avenger," satisfied the holy indignation of the North, for "treason" not only had struck at the foundations of the Union, but had loosed the assassin's knife in the final hour of its triumph. It was difficult to recall that but a decade and a half before Northerners and Southerners had proudly formed parts of the same great people, lying on opposite sides of the boundary between freedom and slavery. Both groups had found it wise to court or pacify the maturing West, but, as the frontier moved ever onward, the free North found it easier to assimilate the Western provinces and, at the same time, to make necessary concessions to their demands. The spirit of democracy and the cause of free land spread their influence over the industrial North. The railroad pushed its iron bands across the country binding together the young commonwealths and the old. The fruits of a new and glowing prosperity were tasted in the great agricultural empire as well as in the Eastern marts of trade and manufacture. The throbbing forces of enlightenment, culture and humanitarian reform spread over the North, while free labor, girding its loins, began to feel its power.

South of the Ohio's murky waters a plantation oligarchy basked contentedly in the waning sun of prosperity. For the few, life was easy and pleasant; culture—measured in terms of a passive leisure-class enjoyment and not in science and the creative arts—was within ready reach. An army of Negro vassals and a dependent white class made obeisance to planter rule, though the white yeomanry stirred restlessly as its opportunities of rising to a share in the plantation régime steadily declined and slave labor threatened to become a fatal incubus upon the back of Dixie. The revolutionary victory in 1860 of the forces that challenged the social institutions of the South severed the last bonds that held the cotton kingdom within the Union. Since the North and the administration that represented it refused to "allow the erring sisters to depart in peace," the issue was staked upon the arbitrament of arms. Workshop, farm, drawing-room, press and pulpit—all the gentle arts of peace were dedicated to the shrine of Mars. In the fiery furnace of war and the crushing defeat of the South the permanence of the Union was welded. Yet dislike, suspicion, fear, remained; the gaping wound lingered. Only when it could be bound up and healed could real peace and happiness come to the nation. Then emerged at length the glories of a modern America.

If Arthur C. Cole stressed the development of two separate civilizations on either side of the Mason-Dixon line from the point of view of the North, FRANK L. OWSLEY (1890–1956), a native of Alabama who for many years was Professor of History at Vanderbilt University and the University of Alabama, chronicled the differences from the vantage point of the South. In the following essay, which he contributed to the compendium written by twelve Southerners under the title, *I'll Take My Stand,* he not only defends his section but emphasizes its agrarian ideals. How does his approach differ from Cole's? To what degree does this selection foreshadow Owsley's later insistence on blaming the war on "egocentric sectionalism," with the North bearing a major portion of the guilt?*

Frank L. Owsley

Southern Agrarianism

What lay behind the bitter sectional quarreling between 1830 and 1860? What made the war which followed this quarreling so deadly? Why the cruel peace that followed war? Why the intellectual conquest of the South? The old answer for these questions and the answer which is yet given by the average Northerner is that the whole struggle from beginning to end was a conflict between light and darkness, between truth and falsehood, between slavery and freedom, between liberty and despotism. This is the ready answer of the Babbitts, who, unfortunately, have obtained much of their information from historians such as James Ford Rhodes and John Bach MacMaster. The Southern historians of the Dunning school, all the third generation "rebel historians," and many of the recent Northern historians reject such an explanation as naïve if nothing else. They have become convinced that slavery as a moral issue is too simple an explanation, and that as one of the many contributing causes of war it needs an explanation which the North has never grasped—in fact, never can grasp until the negro race covers the North as thickly as it does the lower South. They are more inclined to take seriously the Southern championship of state rights in the face of centralization as a cause of the struggle; they see that the protective tariff was as fundamental in the controversy at times as the slavery question, and that the constant

*From Frank Lawrence Owsley, "The Irrepressible Conflict," in Twelve Southerners, *I'll Take My Stand,* pp. 68–91. Copyright 1930 by Harper & Brothers; renewed 1958 by Donald Davidson. Reprinted by permission of Harper & Row, Publishers.

expansion of the United States by the annexation of territories and the constant admission of new states from these territories was a vital factor in producing the Civil War—in short, that the sectional controversies which finally resulted in the Civil War and its aftermath were deep rooted and complex in origin, and that slavery as a moral issue has too long been the red herring dragged across the trail.

Complex though the factors were which finally caused war, they all grew out of two fundamental differences which existed between the two sections: the North was commercial and industrial, and the South was agrarian. The fundamental and passionate ideal for which the South stood and fell was the ideal of an agrarian society. All else, good and bad, revolved around this ideal—the old and accepted manner of life for which Egypt, Greece, Rome, England, and France had stood. History and literature, profane and sacred, twined their tendrils about the cottage and the villa, not the factory.

When America was settled, the tradition of the soil found hospitable root-bed in the Southern colonies, where climate and land combined to multiply the richness of an agrarian economy. All who came to Virginia, Maryland, the Carolinas and Georgia were not gentlemen; in fact, only a few were of the gentry. Most of them were of the yeomanry, and they were from rural England with centuries of country and farm lore and folk memory. Each word, name, sound, had grown from the soil and had behind it sweet memory, stirring adventure, and ofttimes stark tragedy. Thoughts, words, ideas, concepts, life itself, grew from the soil. The environment all pointed toward an endless enjoyment of the fruits of the soil. Jefferson, not visualizing the industrial revolution which whipped up the multiplication of populations and tore their

roots from the soil, dreamed of America, free from England, as a boundless Utopia of farms taking a thousand generations to fill.

Men so loved their life upon the soil that they sought out in literature and history peoples who had lived a similar life, so that they might justify and further stimulate their own concepts of life and perhaps set a high goal for themselves among the great nations which had sprung from the land. The people whom they loved most in the ancient world were the Greeks and the Romans of the early republic. The Greeks did not appeal to them as did the Romans, for they were too inclined to neglect their farms and turn to the sea and to handicraft. But the even-poised and leisurely life of the Greeks, their oratory, their philosophy, their art—especially their architecture—appealed to the South. The Greek tradition became partly grafted upon the Anglo-Saxon and Scotch tradition of life. However, it was the Romans of the early republic, before land speculators and corn laws had driven men from the soil to the city slums, who appealed most powerfully to the South. These Romans were brave, sometimes crude, but open and without guile—unlike the Greeks. They reeked of the soil, of the plow and the spade; they had wrestled with virgin soil and forests; they could build log houses and were closer to many Southerners than even the English gentleman in his moss-covered stone house. It was Cincinnatus, whose hands were rough with guiding the plow, rather than Cato, who wrote about Roman agriculture and lived in a villa, whom Southerners admired the most, though they read and admired Cato as a fine gentleman with liberal ideas about tenants and slaves and a thorough knowledge and love of the soil. The Gracchi appealed to Southerners because the Gracchi were lovers of the soil and died in the attempt to restore the yeomanry to the land.

With the environment of the New World and the traditions of the Old, the South thus became the seat of an agrarian civilization which had strength and promise for a future greatness second to none. The life of the South was leisurely and unhurried for the planter, the yeoman, or the landless tenant. It was a way of life, not a routine of planting and reaping merely for gain. Washington, who rode daily over his farms and counted his horses, cattle, plows, and bushels of corn as carefully as a merchant takes stock of his supplies, inhaled the smell of ripe corn after a rain, nursed his bluegrass sod and shade trees with his own hands, and, when in the field as a soldier or in the city as President of the United States, was homesick at the smell of fresh-plowed earth. He kept vigil with his sick horses and dogs, not as a capitalist who guards his investments, but as one who watches over his friends.

The system of society which developed in the South, then, was close to the soil. It might be organized about the plantation with its wide fields and its slaves and self-sufficiency, or it might center around a small farm, ranging from a fifty-acre to a five-hundred-acre tract, tilled by the owner, undriven by competition, supplied with corn by his own toil and with meat from his own pen or from the fields and forests. The amusements might be the fine balls and house parties of the planter or the three-day break-down dances which David Crockett loved, or horse races, foot races, cock and dog fights, boxing, wrestling, shooting, fighting, logrolling, house raising, or corn-shucking. It might be crude or genteel, but it everywhere was fundamentally alike and natural. The houses were homes, where families lived sufficient and complete within themselves, working together and fighting together. And when death came, they were buried in their own lonely peaceful graveyards, to await doomsday together.

This agrarian society had its own interests, which in almost all respects diverged from the interests of the industrial system of the North. The two sections, North and South, had entered the revolution against the mother country with the full knowledge of the opposing interests of their societies; knowing this difference, they had combined in a loose union under the Articles of Confederation. Finally, they had joined together under the Constitution fully conscious that there were thus united two divergent economic and social systems, two civilizations, in fact. The two sections were evenly balanced in population and in the number of states, so that at the time there was no danger of either section's encroaching upon the interests of the other. This balance was clearly understood. Without it a union would not have been possible. Even with the understanding that the two sections would continue to hold this even balance, the sections were very careful to define and limit the powers of the federal government lest one section with its peculiar interests should get control of the national government and use the powers of that government to exploit the other section. Specific powers were granted the federal government, and all not specifically granted were retained by the states.

But equilibrium was impossible under expansion and growth. One section with its peculiar system of society would at one time or another become dominant and control the national government and either exploit the other section or else fail to exercise the functions of government for its positive benefit. Herein lies the irrepressible conflict, the eternal struggle between the agrarian South and the commercial and industrial North to control the government either in its own interest or, negatively, to prevent the other section from controlling it in its interests. Lincoln and Seward and the radical Republicans clothed the conflict later in robes of morality by making it appear that the "house divided against itself" and the irrepressible conflict which resulted from this division marked a division between slavery and freedom.

Slavery, as we shall see, was part of the agrarian system, but only one element and not an essential one. To say that the irrepressible conflict was between slavery and freedom is either to fail to grasp the nature and magnitude of the conflict, or else to make use of deliberate deception by employing a shibboleth to win the uninformed and unthinking to the support of a sinister undertaking. Rob Roy Mac-Gregor, one of the chief corruptionists of the present-day power lobby, said that the way the power companies crush opposition and win popular support is to pin the word "bolshevik" upon the leaders of those who oppose the power-lobby program. The leaders of the Northern industrial system could win popular support by tagging their opponents as *"enemies of liberty"* and themselves as "champions of freedom." This they did. Lincoln was a politician and knew all the tricks of a politician. Seward was a politician and knew every *in* and *out.* This is true of other leaders of the "party of high ideals" which assumed the name of Republican party. Doubtless, Lincoln, Seward, and others were half sincere in their idea of an irrepressible conflict, but their fundamental purpose was to win elections and get their party into power—the party of the industrial North—with an industrial program for business and a sop of free lands for the Western farmer.

The irrepressible conflict, then, was not between slavery and freedom, but between the industrial and commercial civilization of the North and the agrarian civilization of the South. The industrial North demanded a high tariff so as to monopolize the domestic markets, especially the Southern market, for the South, being agrarian, must purchase all manufactured goods. It was an exploitative principle, originated at the expense of the South and for the benefit of the North. After the South realized that it would have little industry of its own, it fought the protective tariff to the point of nullification in South Carolina and almost to the point of dissolving the Union. In this as in other cases Southerners saw that what was good for the North was fatal to the South.

The industrial section demanded a national subsidy for the shipping business and merchant marine, but, as the merchant marine was alien to the Southern agrarian system, the two sections clashed. It was once more an exploitation of one section for the benefit of the other.

The industrial North demanded internal improvements—roads, railroads, canals—at national expense to furnish transportation for its goods to Southern and Western markets which were already hedged around for the benefit of the North by the tariff wall. The South objected to internal improvements at national expense because it had less need of transportation than the North and because the burden would be heavier on the South and the benefits greater for the North—another exploitation of the Southern system. The North favored a government-controlled bank; but as corporate wealth and the quick turnover of money were confined to that section, such an institution would be for the sole benefit, the South believed, of the North. There were many other things of a positive nature which the system of society in the North demanded of the federal government, but those mentioned will illustrate the conflict of interest between North and South.

It is interesting to observe that all the favors thus asked by the North were of doubtful constitutional right, for nowhere in the Constitution were these matters specifically mentioned; it is further significant that all the powers and favors thus far demanded by the North were merely negatived by the South; no substitute was offered. The North was demanding positive action on the part of the federal government, and the South was demanding that no action be taken at all. In fact, it may be stated as a general principle that the agrarian South asked practically nothing of the federal government in domestic legislation. It might be imperialistic in its foreign policy, but its domestic policy was almost entirely negative. Even in the matter of public lands the South favored turning over these lands to the state within which they lay, rather than have them controlled by the federal government.

Had these differences, inherent in agrarian and industrial civilizations, been the only ones, it is obvious that conflict would have been inevitable and that two different political philosophies would have been developed to justify and rationalize the conflict which was foreshadowed in the very nature of the demands of the sections: centralization in the North and state rights in the South. But there was another and deadlier difference. There was the slavery system in the South. Before examining the Southern doctrine of state rights, which was its defense mechanism for its entire system of society rather than, as has been claimed, for slavery alone, let us turn to the slavery problem as one of the elements of conflict between the two sections.

Slavery was no simple question of politics; it cut across the categories of thought like a giant question mark. It was a moral, an economic, a religious, a social, a philosophical, and above all a political question. It was no essential part of the agrarian civilization of the South—though the Southerners under attack assumed that it was. Without slavery the economic and social life of the South would have not been radically different. Perhaps the plantation life would not have been as pronounced without it, yet the South would long have remained agricultural— as it still is after sixty-five years of "freedom"! Certainly the South would have developed its political philosophy very much as it did. Yet the slavery question furnished more fuel to sectional conflict and created more bitterness than any or all the other elements of the two groups.

Slavery had been practically forced upon the country by England—over the protest of colonial assemblies. During the eighteenth century it had ceased to be profitable, and colonial moral indignation rose correspondingly. However, when the Revolution came and the Southern colonies gained their independence, they did not free the negroes. The eternal race question had reared itself. Negroes had come into the Southern Colonies in such numbers that people feared for the integrity of the white race. For the negroes were cannibals and barbarians, and therefore dangerous. No white man who had any contact with slavery was willing to free the slaves and allow them to dwell among the whites. Slaves were a peril, at least a risk, but free blacks were considered a menace too great to be hazarded. Even if no race wars occurred, there was dread of being submerged and absorbed by the black race. Accordingly, all slaveholders and non-slaveholders who objected to slavery, objected even more to

egro. They ar-
never be freed
ported back to
ies. This convic-
it when the terri-
ns in Santo Do-
troyed the white
populatio.. itions almost completely and submerged the remainder
under barbarian control. All early abolitionists—which meant most of the Southern people up until around 1800—were
abolitionists only on condition of colonization. As a result there were organized
many colonization societies, mostly in the
South during this period.

But colonization was futile. It was soon
realized by all practical slaveholders that
the negroes could not be deported successfully. Deportation was cruel and expensive. Few of the black people wished to
leave the South. The Southern whites
shrugged their shoulders and deplored
the necessity of continuing the negroes in
bondage as the only alternative to chaos
and destruction.

Then the invention of the cotton gin
and the opening of the cotton lands in the
Southwest, 1810–36, made the negro slave
an economic instrument of great advantage. With the aid of the fresh cheap lands
and the negro slave vast fortunes were
made in a few years. Both North and
South having now conceded that emancipation was impossible, the Southern
planters made the most of their new cotton kingdom with a fairly easy conscience.
They had considered emancipation honestly and fairly and had found it out of the
question. Their skirts were clear. Let the
blood of slavery rest upon the heads of
those who had forced it upon the South.

But the opening of the "cotton kingdom" gave dynamic power to the agrarian
section, and new lands were desired by
the West and South. The now industrial

East saw its interest threatened if the
South should colonize the territories to
the West, including those gained and to
be gained. With the tremendous impetus
given to the expansion of the Southern
system by the growth of the cotton industry and culture, the North became uneasy
and began to show opposition to the continued balance of power. This first became
manifest in the struggle which resulted in
the Missouri Compromise of 1822. Up to
this point the objection to slavery was
always tempered by the acknowledgment
on the part of the North that the South
was a victim of the system of slavery and
ought to be sympathized with, rather than
the instigator of the system, who ought to
be condemned as a criminal.

But in 1831 a voice was raised which was
drowned only in the roar of battle in
1861–5. It was the cry of William Lloyd
Garrison that slavery was a crime and the
slaveholders were criminals. He established the famous *Liberator,* which
preached unremitting and ruthless war
upon slavery and the slaveholder. He
knew no moderation. He had no balance
or sense of consequence. His was the
typical "radical" mind which demands
that things be done at once, which tries to
force nature, which wants to tear up by the
roots. Although he was completely ignorant of the South and of negro slavery, he
dogmatically assumed an omniscient power of judgment over the section and the
institution. In the *Liberator* or in the antislavery tracts fostered by the anti-slavery
societies which he aided or instigated, he
set no bounds of accusation and denunciation. The slave master, said Garrison,
debauched his women slaves, had children by them, and in turn defiled his own
children and sold them into the slave
market; the slave plantation was primarily a gigantic harem for the master and his
sons. The handsome octaroon coachmen

shared the bed of the mistress when the master was away from home, and the daughters were frequently away in some secluded nook to rid themselves of undesirable negro offspring. Ministers of the gospel who owned or sanctioned slavery were included in his sweeping indictment of miscegenation and prostitution. In short, Garrison and the anti-slavery societies which he launched, followed soon by Northern churchmen, stigmatized the South as a black brothel. This was not all! The Southern slaveowners were not merely moral lepers; they were cruel and brooding tyrants, who drove their slaves till they dropped and died, who starved them to save food, let them go cold and almost naked to save clothing, let them dwell in filthy pole pens rather than build them comfortable cottages, beat them unmercifully with leather thongs filled with spikes, dragged cats over their bodies and faces, trailed them with bloodhounds which rent and chewed them,—then sprinkled their wounds with salt and red pepper. Infants were torn from their mothers' breasts and sold to Simon Legrees; families were separated and scattered to the four winds. This brutal treatment of the slaves reacted upon the masters and made them brutal and cruel in their dealings with their fellow whites. Such charges, printed in millions upon millions of pamphlets, were sent out all over the world. Sooner or later, much of it was accepted as true in the North.

In the South this abolition war begot Nat Turner's rebellion, in which negro slaves in Virginia under the leadership of Nat Turner, a freedman, massacred their masters, including women and children. The new situation, in turn, begot a revolution in Southern attitudes. Struck almost out of a clear sky by the Garrisonian blasts and the Nat Turner rebellion, Southern leaders were dazed. They dis-

cussed momentarily the expedient of freeing the slaves, then closed forever their minds upon the subject as too dangerous to undertake. Then came a counter-blast of fierce resentment, denying all accusations. The South threw up a defense mechanism. The ministers searched the Scriptures by day and night and found written, in language which could not be misunderstood, a biblical sanction of slavery. Abraham, Moses, the prophets, Jesus, and the disciples on many occasions had approved slavery. History from its dawn had seen slavery almost everywhere. A scriptural and historical justification was called in to meet the general indictment of the wrongfulness of slavery in the abstract. Partly as a result of this searching of the Scriptures there took place a religious revival in the South, which had tended heretofore to incline to Jeffersonian liberalism of the deistic type. The South became devoutly orthodox and literal in its theology. But the abolitionists were not willing to accept scriptural justification of slavery. There was an attempt to prove the wrongfulness of slavery by the same sacred book, but, finding this impossible, many abolitionists repudiated the Scriptures as of divine origin. Partly as a result, the North lost confidence in orthodoxy and tended to become deistic as the South had been. One could almost hear Puritan New England creaking upon its theological hinges as it swung away from its old position.

But there were philosophers and thinkers at work in the South who would meet the abolitionists upon their own grounds. Hammond, Fitzhugh, John C. Calhoun, Chancellor Harper, Thomas R. Dew, either because they felt that scriptural justification of slavery was inadequate or because they realized the necessity of getting away from the theological grounds in order that they might combat the abolitionists upon common ground, approached slavery from the social and economic standpoint. Their general conclusions were that two races of different culture and color cannot live together on terms of equality. One will dominate or destroy the other. There was no middle ground. It had ever been thus. They contended that the negro was of a backward, inferior race. Certainly his culture was inferior. He must either rule or be ruled. If he ruled, the white race would be destroyed or submerged and its civilization wiped out. For the Southern people there was no choice; the negro must be ruled, and the only way he could be controlled, they believed, was by some form of slavery. In other words, Calhoun, Fitzhugh, and the "philosophers of slavery" justified slavery upon the grounds of the "race question"—which U. B. Phillips has called the theme of Southern history, before and after the Civil War. Aside from the scriptural and social justification, these men defended slavery as an economic necessity. They contended that the culture of rice, tobacco, sugar cane, and especially cotton upon which the world depended could not be carried on without slaves. The South, including the up-country and the mountains, accepted the scriptural justification of slavery, to a great extent. The up-country did not accept the economics of slavery, but slavery, in its aspect as a race question, was universally approved in valleys, plains and mountains. It found, in fact, its strongest supporters among the poor whites and the non-slaveholding small landowners. Their race prejudice and fears were the stronger because they knew nothing of the better side of the negro and regarded him as a vicious and dangerous animal whose freedom meant war to the knife and knife to the death. It was the old fear which we have spoken of, common to all in the days

of the Revolution and in the days when Jefferson and Washington were advocating emancipation only on condition that the freedman be sent from the country. Outside of the common agrarianism of the multitudinous sections of the South which acted as a common tie, the race question which underlay slavery, magnified and aggravated by the abolition crusade, was the hoop of steel which held men together in the South in the great final argument of arms.

This abolition crusade on the part of the North and justification of slavery by the South were principally outside of the realm of politics in the beginning. The abolitionists, in fact, had a tendency to abjure politics and demand "direct action," as some of our recent radicals do. But the leaven soon spread, and slavery became a burning political issue. The political leaders of the North, especially the Whigs, after the dynamic growth of the South in the first quarter of the nineteenth century, became fixed in their determination that the agrarian section should have its metes and bounds definitely limited. Industrialism, which had undergone an even greater development than had cotton-growing, declared that the balance of power between agrarian and industrial sections must go. Because slaveholding was the acid test to whether a state would remain agrarian or become eventually industrial, the Northern leaders wished that no more slave states should be carved from the Western territories. Between 1836, when the annexation of slaveholding Texas was advocated by the South, and 1860, when Lincoln was elected upon a platform which declared that no more territory was open to slavery, the major issues in national politics were the struggles between North and South over the admission or exclusion of slavery from the national territories. That is, it was a question whether the territories would be equally open to both sections or whether the North should have an exclusive right in these territories to found its own states and system and thereby destroy the balance of power and control the federal government in the interest of its own economic and social system. Unfortunately for the South, the leaders of the North were able to borrow the language of the abolitionists and clothed the struggle in a moral garb. It was good politics, it was noble and convenient, to speak of it as a struggle for freedom when it was essentially a struggle for the balance of power.

So to the bitter war of the abolitionists and the bitter resentment of the South was added the fight over the balance of power in the form of the extension of slavery into the common territories.

As it has been suggested, had there not been slavery as an added difference between the agrarian South and industrial North, the two sections would have developed each its own political philosophy to explain and justify its institutions and its demands upon the federal government. The North had interests which demanded positive legislation exploitative of the agrarian South; the South had interests which demanded that the federal government refrain entirely from legislation within its bounds—it demanded only to be let alone. While this conflict of interest was recognized as existing in the days of the Revolution when the first attempt at union was made, it was not until the first government under the Constitution was in power that it received a philosophical statement. In the beginning of Washington's administration two men defined the fundamental principles of the political philosophy of the two societies, Alexander Hamilton for the North and Jefferson for

the South. The one was extreme centralization, the other was extreme decentralization; the one was nationalistic and the other provincial; the first was called Federalism, the other State Rights, but in truth the first should have been called Unitarianism and the second Federalism.

It has been often said that the doctrine of state rights was not sincere, but that it was a defense mechanism to protect slavery (implying that slavery was merely a moral question and the South entirely immoral). But Jefferson was an abolitionist, as nearly all the Southern people were at the time the doctrine was evolved and stated by Jefferson, and Calhoun's extreme doctrine of state sovereignty was fully evolved in South Carolina before the crusade had begun against slavery. However, there is no doubt that the bitter abolition crusade and the political controversies between the two sections between 1836 and 1861 over slavery in the territories gave added strength and exactness to the Southern doctrine. Another thrust has been made at the sincerity of the doctrine of state rights: the principle has been laid down that state rights is a cowardly defense used by the industrial interests to shield themselves against the unfriendly action of a more powerful government. Such examples are noted as the extreme sensitiveness of big business to state rights in the matter of federal child-labor laws, federal control of water power, and prohibition. It is not to be denied that it should be easier for the water-power companies to purchase a state than a national legislature—as the market price of a Comgressman is supposed to be somewhat higher than a mere state legislator (though there are certain well-known purchases of Congressmen which seem to contradict this impression). But observe the other side of the question. Big business has more often taken refuge behind the national government than behind the state. I have only to call attention to the way in which corporations take refuge behind the Fourteenth Amendment to avoid state legislation, to the numberless cases brought before the Supreme Court of the United States by corporations whose charters have been vitiated or nullified by state action, to the refuge sought by the railroads in national protection against the state granger legislation, and to the eternal whine of big business for paternalistic and exploitative legislation such as the tariff, the ship and railroad subsidies. Historically, then, the vested interests of industrialism have not had any great use for state rights. They are the founders of the doctrine of centralization, of the Hamiltonian and Republican principles; they have controlled the Republican party; why should they be unfriendly to their own principles and their own political instrument? They have not been! It may be suggested as a principle that for positive exploitation big business has desired large and sweeping powers for the national government, and that for negative business of defense it will hide behind any cover convenient, whether it be a state or the Fourteenth Amendment. The assertion that state rights was a defense mechanism evolved by slaveowners, for corporations later to hide behind, is inadequate if nothing else.

But state rights was a defense mechanism, and its defensive ramparts were meant by its disciples to protect things far more fundamental and larger than slave property. It was the doctrine of an agrarian society meant in the first place to protect the South as a whole against the encroachments of the industrial and commercial North. By upholding the doctrine of a rigid division of powers between state and nation and the literal interpretation of the Constitution such

legislation as protective tariffs, ship subsidies, national banks, internal improvements at federal expense, would be avoided. It would also protect one part of the South against another. While there were infinite diverging interests between the industrial North and agrarian South which made a doctrine of state rights the only safe bulwark against Northern exploitation and encroachment, there were great regional differences within the South itself which made legislation that was beneficial to one section, harmful to another. One section grew cotton and cane, another tobacco and rice, another produced naval stores and lumber; one had slaves, another had none. To throw all these interests into a hodge-podge under one government would be to sacrifice all the minority interests to the one which was represented by the largest population and body of voters. Even among themselves the agrarians felt their local interests safer in the hands of the state than in the hands of a national government. But this was not the end of the logic of local self-government and regional autonomy. The states in turn, because of diverging interests between the Tidewater and Piedmont areas, allowed a large sweep to county government, and built up a system of representation for both state and federal government which would tend to place legislative power in the hands of economic groups and regions rather than in the hands of the people according to their numbers.

The whole idea then was local self-government, decentralization, so that each region should be able to defend itself against the encroachment of the other regions. It was not a positive doctrine; it did not contemplate a program of exploitative legislation at the expense of other regions. An unmixed agrarian society such as Jefferson and Calhoun had in mind called for no positive program.

Such a society, as Jefferson visualized it, called for only enough government to prevent men from injuring one another. It was by its very nature, a *laissez faire* society, an individualistic society where land, water, and timber were practically free. It only asked to be let alone. State rights, local and regional autonomy, did not make for a uniform, standardized society and government. It took cognizance of the fundamental difference between the agrarian South and West on the one hand and the commerical and growing industrial system of the East on the other; and it still further took note, as we have said, of the regional and local differences within each of these systems. It might not make for a neat and orderly system of government, but this was the price of social and economic freedom, the price of bringing into one Union so many different groups and interests.

The interests pointed out have been largely economic and social. These were not the only interests which the state-rights doctrine was expected to protect from an overbearing and unsympathizing national government. Perhaps the greatest vested interest was "personal liberty," the old Anglo-Saxon principles expressed in the Magna Carta, bill of rights, habeas corpus act, supported in the American Revolution, and engrafted finally in every state constitution of the independent states, as "bills of rights." These bills of rights guaranteed freedom of religion, freedom of speech, of thought, of press, of assembly, right of petition, freedom from arbitrary arrest and imprisonment, right of trial by jury, and prohibited the taking of property without due process of law—guaranteed, in short, the fundamental rights which Jefferson had called the "inalienable rights of man" and Locke and Rousseau had called the "natural rights"—right of life, liberty, property, and the free pursuit of happi-

ness as long as the free pursuit of this object did not encroach upon the pursuit of another's just rights. The famous Virginia and Kentucky Resolutions of 1798–9 had been directed at the violation of these liberties. The Alien and Sedition laws which had been pushed through Congress during the Adams administration had struck at many of these. Under the Sedition Act men had been prosecuted for criticizing the President or members of Congress or judges and had been sent to prison in violation of the Constitutional guarantee of freedom of speech. Opinion had been suppressed, meetings broken up, arbitrary arrests made, men held without trial; in fact, the whole body of personal liberties had been brushed aside by the Federalist or centralizing party eight years after the founding of the present federal system under the Constitution. Jefferson and Madison, supported by the state-rights apostle of Virginia, John Taylor of Caroline, and the irascible old democrat, John Randolph, proclaimed that the federal government had thus shown itself to be an unsafe protector of liberty. So Jefferson announced in his inaugural, which was made possible by the excesses of the centralizing party of the East, that the states were the safest guardians of human liberty and called on all to support "the state governments in all their rights, as the most competent administrations for our domestic concerns and the surest bulwark against anti-republican tendencies." The founder of the party of the agrarian South and West upheld state rights as the safest guardian of the liberties and the domestic interests of the people.

Thus the two sections clashed at every point. Their economic systems and interests conflicted. Their social systems were hostile; their political philosophies growing out of their economic and social systems were as impossible to reconcile as it is to cause two particles of matter to occupy the same space at the same time; and their philosophies of life, growing out of the whole situation in each section, were as two elements in deadly combat. What was food for the one was poison for the other.

When the balance of power was destroyed by the rapid growth of the North, and the destruction of this balance was signalized in the election of Lincoln by a frankly sectional, hostile political party, the South, after a futile effort at obtaining a concession from Lincoln which would partly restore the balance of power, dissolved its partnership with the industrial North.

This struggle between an agrarian and an industrial civilization, then, was the irrepressible conflict, the house divided against itself, which must become according to the doctrine of the industrial section all the one or all the other. It was the doctrine of intolerance, crusading, standardizing alike in industry and in life. The South had to be crushed out; it was in the way; it impeded the progress of the machine. So Juggernaut drove his car across the South.

How "men stumbed into a ghastly war" was the theme of JAMES G. RANDALL (1881–1953) in his 1940 presidential address before the Mississippi Valley Historical Association. Considering war the ultimate evil to be avoided, Randall, for many years Professor of History at the University of Illinois, characterized those whom he held responsible for the failure to prevent armed conflict as "the blundering generation."*

James G. Randall

Human Failure

When one visits a moving picture, or reads Hergesheimer's *Swords and Roses,* which is much the same thing, he may gather the impression that the Civil War, fought in the days before mechanized divisions, aerial bombs, and tanks, was a kind of *chanson de geste* in real life. "The Civil War in America," writes Hergesheimer, "was the last of all wars fought in the grand manner. It was the last romantic war, when army corps fought as individuals and lines of assault . . . charged the visible enemy." "The war created a heroism . . . that clad fact in the splendor of battle flags." Hergesheimer feeds his readers chunks of sombre beauty, winterless climate, air stirred with faint cool music, fine houses, Spanish moss and cypress, trumpet vine and bay blossom, live oaks and linden, bridal wreath, japonica, moonflower, and honeysuckle. In his foreword to "Dear Blanche" he writes: "Here is a book of swords . . . of old-fashioned dark roses. . . . [of] the simpler loveliness of the past." His pages live up to the foreword. He gives dear Blanche "The Rose of Mississippi," "The Lonely Star," "Shadows on the Sea," and "Gold Spurs." Of "Jeb" Stuart he says:

Ladies in Maryland gave him the spurs and ladies wherever he chanced to be gave him the rosebuds. . . . Naturally he was in the cavalry. He was different. . . . [He] wore a brown felt hat . . . with . . . sweeping black plume; . . . his boots in action were heavy, . . . afterwards he changed them for immaculate boots of patent leather worked with gold thread; but he danced as well as fought in his spurs.

---

*J. G. Randall, "The Blundering Generation," *Mississippi Valley Historical Review,* XXVII (1940), pp. 3–28. (Footnotes omitted).

The picture is filled in with red-lined cape, French sabre, yellow sash and tassels, The Bugles Sang Truce, The Dew is on the Blossom, orders given when asleep, animal vitality dancing in brilliant eyes.

Escapists may put what they will between the covers of a book; unfortunately the historian must be a realist. Whatever may be the thrill, or the emotional spree, of treating the Civil War romantically, it may be assumed that this has not been neglected. This paper, therefore, will attempt a very different task, that of weighing some Civil War realities, examining some of the irrational ideas of war "causation," and pondering some aspects of the Civil War mind.

Without stressing that Zeebrugge or Westerplatte or the Karelian Isthmus matched any Civil War exploit, or that aviation is as smart as cavalry, it is sufficient to note a few comparisons. If the World War produced more deaths, the Civil War produced more American deaths. If weapons have become more brutal, at least medicine and sanitation have advanced. One seldom reads of the Civil War in terms of sick and wounded. Medical officers of the sixties repeated the experience of a British medical officer in the Burmese War who advised his commander how to avoid scurvy and was told: "Medical opinions are very good when called for." A Union surgeon at Bull Run reported extreme difficulty in inducing field officers to listen to complaints of disease resulting from foul tents into which fresh air was "seldom if ever" admitted. Because ambulances were on the wrong side of the road, this also at Bull Run, twelve thousand troops had to pass before some of the wounded could be taken to the emergency hospital. Wounded men arriving from the field were thrust into freight cars where they lay on the bare floor without food for a day; numbers died on the road. One of the officers refused hospital admittance to wounded soldiers not of his regiment. Medical supplies were thrown away for want of transportation, injured men were exposed to heavy rain, gangrene resulted from minor wounds.

Romance and glory suggest at least the memory of a name. This implies an identified grave, but after making calculations based upon the official medical history issued by the surgeon general, the student would have to inform dear Blanche, or perhaps Mr. Ripley, that if the surgeon general's figures are right the unknown dead for the Civil War exceeded the number killed in battle! In round numbers there were about 110,000 Union deaths from battle, but the surgeon general reported that in November, 1870, there were 315,555 soldier graves, of which only 172,109 had been identified by name, leaving over 143,000 unidentified graves. The number of soldiers known in the adjutant general's records to have died during the war is much greater than the number identified as to burial or reburial. It must be remembered that the soldier regularly carried no means of identification, that graves of men buried by comrades were marked by hasty devices, that Confederates appropriated Union arms and clothing, that teamsters, refugees, camp followers, or even fugitive slaves might have been buried with soldiers, and that the number reported as killed in action was inaccurate. Yet after making all these allowances, the vast number of the nameless leaves the inquiring mind unsatisfied. It is no more satisfactory to realize that about half the Union army became human waste in one form or another, as dead, disabled, deserted, or imprisoned.

"Jeb" Stuart may have worn gold spurs,

but the common soldier was more familiar with fleas. Sashes may have adorned generals but privates were often in rags. It was reported that one of the army surgeons boarded for an entire winter on Sanitary Commission stores. Camps were dirty, sanitation was faulty, cooking was shiftless. Reporting on one of the hospitals, an inspector referred to a leaky roof, broken glass, dirty stairs, insufficient sanitary facilities, and unclean disgusting beds. The soldier who was brutally struck by a sentry of his own company or who contracted malaria would hardly think of his experience as a thing of romance. Without exposing all the euphemisms that obscure the truth of this subject, it may be noted that the great majority of Union deaths were from causes medically regarded as preventable, leaving aside the cynical assumption that war itself is not preventable. Pneumonia, typhus, cholera, miasmic fever, and the like hardly find their way into the pages of war romance, but they wrought more havoc than bayonets and guns. Where there was danger of infection the rule-of-thumb principle of the Civil War surgeon was to amputate, and from operating tables, such as they were, at Gettysburg, arms and legs were carried away in wagon loads. Marching was hatefully wearisome, desertion was rampant, corruption was rife. Individual injustices of the war were shocking. Some generals got credit that was undeserved, others were broken by false report or slandered by an investigating committee of Congress. The men who languished in prison were several times more numerous than those stopped by bullets. That there was heroism in the war is not doubted, but to thousands the war was as romantic as prison rats and as gallant as typhoid or syphilis.

One does not often speak or read of the war in reality, of its blood and filth, of mutilated flesh, and other revolting things. This restraint is necessary, but it ought to be recognized that the war is not presented when one writes of debates in Congress, of flanking movements, of retreats and advances, of cavalry and infantry, of divisions doing this and brigades doing that. In the sense of full realism war cannot be discussed. The human mind will not stand for it. For the very word "war" the realist would have to substitute some such term as "organized murder" or "human slaughterhouse." In drama as distinguished from melodrama murder often occurs offstage. In most historical accounts, especially military narratives, the war is offstage in that its stench and hideousness do not appear.

With all the recent revisionist studies it is difficult to achieve a full realization of how Lincoln's generation stumbled into a ghastly war, how it blundered during four years of indecisive slaughter, and how the triumph of the Union was spoiled by the manner in which the victory was used. In the hateful results of the war over long decades one finds partisanship at its worst. To see the period as it was is to witness uninspired spectacles of prejudice, error, intolerance, and selfish grasping. The Union army was inefficiently raised, poorly administered, and often badly commanded. In government there was deadlock, cross purpose, and extravagance. One can say that Lincoln was honest, but not that the country was free from corruption during the Lincoln administration. There was cotton plundering, army-contract graft, and speculative greed. Where Lincoln was at his best, where he was moderate, temperate, and far-seeing, he did not carry his party with him. Even those matters dissociated from the war, such as homesteading and railroad extension, came to be marred by exploitation and crooked finance. The period of the Civil War and the era of Jim Fisk and Jay Gould were one and the same generation.

If it was a "needless war," a "repressible conflict," as scholars now believe, then indeed was the generation misled in its unctuous fury. To suppose that the Union could not have been continued or slavery outmoded without the war and without the corrupt concomitants of the war, is hardly an enlightened assumption. If one questions the term "blundering generation," let him inquire how many measures of the time he would wish copied or repeated if the period were to be approached with a clean slate and to be lived again. Most of the measures are held up as things to be avoided. Of course it is not suggested that the generation of the sixties had any copyright on blundering. It is not that democracy was at fault. After all, civil war has not become chronic on these shores, as it has in some nations where politics of force is the rule. One can at least say that the Civil War was exceptional; that may be the best thing that can be said about it. A fuller measure of democracy would probably have prevented the war or at least have mitigated its abuses. To overlook many decades of American democracy and take the Civil War period as its test, would be to give an unfair appraisal. Nor does this probing of blunders involve lack of respect for the human beings of that generation. As individuals we love and admire them, these men and women who look at us from the tin-types and Brady photographs of the sixties, though we may have "malice toward some." The distortions and errors of the time were rather a matter of mass thinking, of social solidification, and of politics.

In the present vogue of psychiatry, individual mental processes and behavior have been elaborately studied. Psychia-

try for a nation, however, is still in embryo, though it is much the fashion to have discussions of mass behaviorism, public opinion, pressure groups, thought patterns, and propaganda. Scholars in the field of history tend more and more to speak in terms of culture; this often is represented as a matter of cultural conflict, as of German against Slav, of Japanese against Chinese, and the like. Such concepts were given overemphasis at the meeting of the American Historical Association last December. Historians are doing their age a disservice if these factors of culture are carried over, as they often are, whether by historians or others, into justifications or "explanations" of war. The note of caution here should be a note of honest inquiry. It may be seriously doubted whether war rises from fundamental motives of culture or economics so much as from the lack of cultural restraint or economic inhibition upon militaristic megalomania. Modern wars do not relieve population pressure. Whether wars are needed for economic outlets or for obtaining raw materials is highly doubtful. International trade brings all that. Those who create war throttle the very flow of trade that would promote economic objectives. Where the economy of a nation hinges upon an export market, it may happen that plotters of war in that nation will stupidly kill that market by devices of economic autarchy and then claim that they have to go to war to have trade outlets. It is the same with incoming goods. Of such is the economic argument for war. War makers do not open up economic benefit so much as they stifle it. Their relation to culture is no better than their relation to economy.

There is the word astrology for bogus astronomy and alchemy for false chemistry. Ought there not to be some such word for the economic alchemists of this world? Perhaps it exists in the word autarchy. Is it not in the category of bogus economics, or *ersatz* economics, that one should put those who study war as a matter of trade, supply, resources, needs, and production? As for the Civil War the stretch and span of conscious economic motive was much smaller than the areas or classes of war involvement. Economic diversity offered as much motive for union, in order to have a well rounded nation, as for the kind of economic conflict suggested by secession. One fault of writers who associate war-making with economic advantage is false or defective economics; another is the historical fault. It is surprising how seldom the economic explanation of war has made its case historically, *i.e.* in terms of adequate historical evidence bearing upon those points and those minds where actually the plunge into war occurred. One hears war treated as a matter of culture, but cultural and racial consciousness are as strong in Scandinavia or the Netherlands or Switzerland as in militarist-ridden countries. To make conquest a matter of culture is poor history. It may be the vanquished whose culture survives. Culture is not easily transplanted if force be the method. When war comes by the violence of a few in control and by the stifling of economic and cultural processes, it ill becomes the scholar to add his piping to the cacophonous blare of militaristic propaganda.

War causation tends to be "explained" in terms of great forces. Something elemental is supposed to be at work, be it nationalism, race conflict, or quest for economic advantage. With these forces predicated, the move toward war is alleged to be understandable, to be explained, and therefore to be in some sense reasonable. Thought runs in biological channels and nations are conceived as organisms. Such thought is not confined to philosophers; it is the commonest of mental patterns. A cartoonist habitually draws a nation as a person. In this manner of thinking Germany does so and so; John Bull takes this or that course, and so on. When thought takes so homely a form it is hardly called a philosophical concept; for that purpose the very same thing would appear under a Greek derivative or Freudian label. However labeled, it may be questioned whether the concept is any better than a poor figure of speech, a defective metaphor which is misleading because it has a degree of truth.

Ruritania—to be no more specific—does so and so in the sense that it has a government, the government acts for the nation, and for political purposes there is no other way in which the country can act. The doubtful part is to infer that there is one directing mind for Ruritania which is the distillation of all the millions of minds. Where government has a bogus quality such an inference is more doubtful than if government has a well grounded or established quality. Give certain conditions of forced leadership and suppressed thought, the oneness of excutive action in a nation may in fact represent nothing at all in terms of consolidated will and intent distilled from the whole mass. What passes for mass thought these days is not so much distilled as it is translated from golden plates handed down on some ideological Hill of Cumorah and read through the magic of authoritarian Urim and Thummim. The terrifying fact is that such bogus thought can be manufactured; it can be produced wholesale and distributed at top speed; it can control a nation; it is the shabby mental *ersatz* of an abnormal period.

War-making is too much dignified if it is told in terms of broad national urges, of great German motives, or of compelling

Russian ambitions. When nations stumble into war, or when peoples rub their eyes and find they have been dragged into war, there is at some point a psychopathic case. Omit the element of abnormality, or of bogus leadership, or inordinate ambition for conquest, and diagnosis fails. In the modern scene it fails also if one omits manipulation, dummies, bogeys, false fronts, provocative agents, made-up incidents, frustration of elemental impulses, negation of culture, propaganda that is false in intent, criminal usurpation, and terrorist violence. These are reflections on the present bedeviled age, but their pertinence to the subject at hand is seen in the fact that scholarly discussions in explanation of war on the economic or cultural basis frequently include the Civil War as a supposedly convincing example. The writer doubts seriously whether a consensus of scholars who have competently studied the Civil War would accept either the cultural motive or the economic basis as the effective cause.

If one were to explain how this or that group or individual got into the Civil War, he could rely on no one formula. He would have to make up a series of elements or situations of which the following are only a few that might be mentioned: the despairing plunge, the unmotivated drift, the intruding dilemma, the blasted hope, the self-fulfilling prediction, the push-over, the twisted argument, the frustrated leader, the advocate of rule or ruin, and the reform-your-neighbor prophet. Robert Toombs said he would resist Stephen A. Douglas though he could see "nothing but . . . defeat in the future"; there is your despairing plunge. Young Henry Watterson, a Tennessee antislavery Unionist who fought for the Confederacy, is an example of the unmotivated drift. To many an individual the problem was not to fight with the side whose policies he approved of, but to be associated with the right set. Such an individual motive could not by a process of multiplication become in any reasonable sense a large-group motive. Yet it would be understandable for the individual. Usually in war time individuals have no choice of side, though in the American Civil War they sometimes did, especially on the border. Even where such choice was possible, the going to war by the individual in the sixties was due less to any broad "cause" or motive than to the fact that war existed, so that fighting was the thing to do. The obtaining of soldiers is not a matter of genuine persuasion as to issues. War participation is not a proof of war attitude.

The intruding dilemma was found in the great border and the great upper South where one of two ugly courses had to be chosen, though neither choice made sense in terms of objectives and interests in those broad regions. The self-fulfilling prediction is recognized in the case of those who, having said that war must come, worked powerfully to make it come. The blasted hope, i.e. the wish for adjustment instead of butchery, was the experience of most of the people, especially in the border and upper South. The frustrated leader is seen in the Unionist who came to support secession, or in such northerners as Thurlow Weed and William H. Seward who sought compromise and then supported war. The plea that "better terms" could be had out of the Union, which implied a short secession gesture though uttered by determined secessionists, was the crafty argument for secession to be used in addressing Unionists. This might be dubbed the twisted argument. The push-over is seen in the whole strategy of secession leaders by which anti-secession states and Union-loving men were to be dragged in by the accelerated march of events.

These are things which belong as much

to the "explanation" of the Civil War as any broad economic or cultural or elemental factor. It should be remembered how few of the active promoters of secession became leaders of the Confederacy; their place in the drama was in the first act, in the starting of trouble. Nor should sectional preference cause one to forget how large a contribution to Union disaster, and how little to success, was given by northern radicals during the war. Clear thinking would require a distinction between causing the war and getting into the war. Discussion which overlooks this becomes foggy indeed. It was small minorities that caused the war; then the regions and sections got into it. No one seems to have thought of letting the minorities fight it out. Yet writers who descant upon the causation of the war write grandly of vast sections, as if the fact of a section being dragged into the slaughter was the same as the interests of that section being consciously operative in its causation. Here lies one of the chief fallacies of them all.

In writing of human nature in politics Graham Wallas has shown the potent effect of irrational attitudes. He might have found many a Civil War example. None of the "explanations" of the war make sense, if fully analyzed. The war has been "explained" by the choice of a Republican president, by grievances, by sectional economics, by the cultural wish for southern independence, by slavery, or by events at Sumter. But these explanations crack when carefully examined. The election of Lincoln fell so far short of swinging southern sentiment against the Union that secessionists were still unwilling to trust their case to an all-southern convention or to cooperation among southern states. In every election from 1840 to 1852 Lincoln voted for the same candidate for whom many thousands of southerners voted. Lincoln deplored the demise of the Whig party and would have been only too glad to have voted in 1856 for another Harrison, another Taylor, or another Fillmore. Alexander Stephens stated that secessionists did not desire redress of grievances and would obstruct such redress. Prophets of sectional economics left many a southerner unconvinced; it is doubtful how far their arguments extended beyond the sizzling pages of *De-Bow's Review* and the agenda of southern commercial congresses. The tariff was a potential future annoyance rather than an acute grievance in 1860. What existed then was largely a southern tariff law. Practically all tariffs are one-sided. Sectional tariffs in other periods have existed without producing war. Southern independence on broad cultural lines is probably more of a modern thesis than a contemporary motive of sufficient force to have carried the South out of the Union on any cooperative, all-southern basis.

It was no part of the Republican program to smash slavery in the South, nor did the territorial aspect of slavery mean much politically beyond agitation. Southerners cared little about actually taking slaves into existing territories; Republicans cared so little in the opposite sense that they avoided the prohibition of slavery in those territorial laws that were passed with Republican votes in February and March, 1861. Things said of "the South" often failed to apply to southerners, or of "the North" to northerners. Thwarted "Southern rights" were more often a sublimation than a definite entity. "The North" in the militant pre-war sense was largely an abstraction. The Sumter affair was not a cause, but an incident resulting from pre-existing governmental deadlock; Sumter requires explanation, and that explanation carries one back into all the other alleged factors. In contemporary southern comments on Lincoln's course at Sumter one finds not harmony but a jangling of discordant voices. Virginia resented Lincoln's action at Sumter for a reason opposite to that of South Carolina; Virginia's resentment was in the anti-secessionist sense. By no means did all the North agree with Lincoln's course as to Sumter. Had Lincoln evacuated Sumter without an expedition, he would have been supported by five and a half of seven cabinet members, Chase taking a halfway stand and Blair alone taking a positive stand for an expedition. What Lincoln refused as to Sumter was what the United States government had permitted in general as to forts and arsenals in the South. Stronger action than at Sumter was taken by Lincoln at Pickens without southern fireworks. There is no North-versus-South pattern that covers the subject of the forts. Nor is the war itself to be glibly explained in rational North-versus-South terms.

Let one take all the factors—the Sumter maneuver, the election of Lincoln, abolitionism, slavery in Kansas, cultural and economic differences—and it will be seen that only by a kind of false display could any of these issues, or all of them together, be said to have caused the war if one omits the elements of emotional unreason and overbold leadership. If one word or phrase were selected to account for the war, that word would not be slavery, or state-rights, or diverse civilizations. It would have to be such a word as fanaticism (on both sides), or misunderstanding, or perhaps politics. To Graham Wallas misunderstanding and politics are the same thing.

The fundamental or the elemental is often no better than a philosophical will o' the wisp. Why do adventitious things, or glaringly abnormal things, have to be elementally or cosmically accounted for? If, without proving his point, the historian makes war a thing of "inevitable"

economic conflict, or cultural expression, or *Lebensraum,* his generalizations are caught up by others, for it would seem that those historians who do the most generalizing, if they combine effective writing with it, are the ones who are most often quoted. The historian's pronouncements are taken as the statement of laws whether he means them so or not; he is quoted by sociologists, psychologists, behaviorists, misbehaviorists, propagandists, and what not; he becomes a contributor to those "dynamic" masses of ideas, or ideologies, which are among the sorriest plagues of the present age. As to wars, the ones that have not happened are perhaps best to study. Much could be said about such wars. As much could be said in favor of them as of actual wars. Cultural and economic difficulties in wars that have not occurred are highly significant. The notion that you must have war when you have cultural variation, or economic competition, or sectional difference is an unhistorical misconception which it is stupid in historians to promote. Yet some of the misinterpretations of the Civil War have tended to promote it.

What was the mind of America in Lincoln's day? It was human, which means it was partly simian! It was occidental. It was New World. It was American, though one would have to be a Stephen Benét to state what that means. It had somewhat of a sense of humor, though not enough. It was southern, or Yankee, or midwestern, or otherwise sectional. It was the mind of the McGuffey reader, by which a world of ready-made ideas is suggested. It was Victorian; it had inhibitions which today appear as droll as its unrepressed whiskers. It was less mechanized than today, being of the horse-and-buggy age. It was soul-searching. It was Christian and it was chiefly Protestant; yet the one most numerous faith was Catholic. Religiously it was fundamentalist. It was not profoundly philosophical and took with resentment the impact of Darwinism. Though polyglot it was far from cosmopolitan. The soapbox flavor or the backwoods tang was characteristic of its humorists. It was partly conditioned by racial backgrounds, such as the Dutch, German, Irish, Anglo-Saxon, or Scandinavian. It differed in the degrees of its Americanization; there was a staggering at variant distances from immigrant ancestors. Often the recent immigrant, such as the German or Scandinavian, took American democracy with more simple faith than the seasoned American. When disillusion came to such, it came hard.

The mind of the time was many things socially, being of the four hundred if one considers the De Peysters and Van Courtlands, or Boston Brahmin, or mountaineer, or of the numerous small farmer group, or of the unvocal laboring class. If one were to have searched for class consciousness in this age, it would have been found less among underprivileged masses than among the aristocrats, the planters, the capitalists; it was they who were indeed class-conscious. Such a matter as the southern gentleman's conventionalized code of honor, including the *code duello,* was a bulwark of exclusiveness and a deliberate social barrier.

As to its war attitude, the mind of Lincoln's day was in part a mind during war, in part pro-war, in part anti-war, in part merely at war. Where it was pro-war it was not necessarily militaristic. Where it was German it was usually not Prussian, being spiritually closer to Weimar or Frankfort-on-Main. What is meant here are minds that were more or less genuine; this would rule out the politician whose mind was usually a synthetic affair made up for the vote-getting occasion. The mind of the time was often the product of intra-American migration. Thus it was Virginia or Kentucky in Illinois, Tennessee in Missouri, Vermont in Indiana, Massachusetts or upstate New York in Ohio. Rural areas had contributed more to these migrations than cities; not much relief of urban congestion had come by way of the westward movement. Perhaps predominantly the mind of America was rural. Yet hardly at all was it a peasant mind, much less proletarian. Never would its educated people have called themselves the intelligentsia. To refer to its middle class as bourgeois would be to use a non-American concept. The middle class did not function as a set social type or bloc.

It would be of interest to examine this mind in segments, but they would have to be complex segments. There would be the American-Victorian-New York élite mind, the midwest-German-farmer mind, the Irish-Tammany-Eastside mind, the immigrant-labor mind, the old American frontier mind, and so on. Quite generally it was three things: Victorian, restless, and habituated to politician-like thinking. The puritanical Victorianism of the age combined with financial imperatives when one of Jay Cooke's cashiers committed the astounding indiscretion of driving a four-in-hand in Central Park on a Sunday afternoon. Cooke warned him that if that were known "amongst financial People" it would bring "great discredit to the Bank." "Credit," he admonished, "is a tender plant." Its delicate growth would be affected by "such a stupid display as a four-in-hand." Business men who did not walk the straight and narrow were "under suspicion." Wall Street was an uplifting factor. Sabbath observance had its Bradstreet rating. Yet it may have been the appearance of evil that was detrimental, for corruption was rampant and social disapproval by no means always attached to methods of questionable financial dealing. Graft and special privilege were respectable. Many a fortune of Civil War origin belonged to the ill-gotten class. Defrauding the government did not make one a social pariah.

In spite of much nobility of sentiment, the Civil War mind seems a sorry *melange* of party bile, crisis melodrama, inflated eloquence, unreason, religious fury, self-righteousness, unctuous self-deception, and hate. Bad party feeling was evident when Seward appeared in the Senate on January 9, 1860, "& not a man from the democracy save Douglas . . . came to greet him." "D——n their impudence," was the comment of William P. Fessenden. Yet this was more than a year before the war opened. It was a time of crisis psychosis. Men felt they were living in great days. The generation had its self-consciousness of mission and destiny. Even the private soldier filled his letters with exalted talk. At the beginning of the war a Massachusetts soldier, telling of a rail journey from Boston to New York, wrote: "Refreshments were lavished upon us . . . cannon sent their boom over hill and dale and bells peeled [sic] their tocsin of warning . . . that our train was approaching bearing a Regiment of brave hearts to the defence of our country's capitol [sic]." Passing the "Constitution" he wrote: "May they [the colors] ever float over that notable ship . . . as she rides proudly upon the waters of the Union." This proudly riding epistle was but a soldier's letter to his brother. Similar attitudes were characteristic of the South; Mrs. Chesnut referred to "the high-flown style which of late seems to have gotten into the very air."

What the war did to the mind of Ralph Waldo Emerson deserves careful study, though here it can be only hinted. To the Emerson of the sixties New England was the custodian of sense and elegance, Boston superiority was axiomatic, the South was boorish as well as wicked, and John Brown, well-known in Concord, was a martyr. There are "crises which demand nations," he thought, and a generation might well perish to insure a better life for generations that follow. "What a healthy tone exists!" he wrote in May, 1861. To Emerson not merely *the war* but *war* was an elemental, purifying force. Ridiculing the sentimentalist, demanding that the North must conquer as a matter of culture, he wrote grandly of a strong wind, of "one energetic mind" where there had been "incapacity to move," of war as a searcher of character. War to Emerson was a "dynamometer," taking the fop in the street, the beau at the ball, and lifting them up by something "in the air." "A civil war," he naively wrote, "sweeps away all the false issues." "This revolution," he said, "is the work of no man, but the effervescence of Nature." Reaching almost Nietzschean ecstacy, he burbled: "War is a realist, shatters everything flimsy and shifty, sets aside all false issues . . . breaks through all that is not real." "On with the war" might have been his slogan. "Let it search," he said, "let it grind, let it overturn, and . . . when it finds no more fuel, it burns out."

To illustrate the benefit of war he looked for a simile and found it in the cholera! On this theme he wrote: "We watch its course [that of the war] as we did the cholera, which . . . took only the susceptible, set its seal on every putrid spot . . . followed the limestone, and left the granite." What to David Starr Jordan was an annihilator of the finest and of potential descendants of those best fit to reproduce, was to Emerson a beneficial cosmic force finding its origin in the motion of the planets. Norman Angell's great illusion counted its mental victims among those who passed for philosophers.

When philosophers turned war mongers it was not to be expected that pacifists would have a hearing. The broad cause of peace was one of the casualties of war. In its antebellum background the peace crusade in America was a small affair of humanitarian groups with variant attitudes. It embraced men of intelligent idealism, but its efforts never bore fruit as did other crusades such as that of Dorothea Dix for the neglected insane or of Horace Mann for public elementary education. The Peace Society, launched with the impetus of Christian evangelism by William Ladd in 1828, and promoted by Elihu Burritt and other choice spirits, was thirty-three years old when the guns spoke at Sumter. In those years the society had not been idle. It had made use of the familiar techniques of agitation: lectures, local agents, local chapters, tracts, prize essays, magazines, books, national congresses, and petitions to the seat of government. A vigorous literature was produced, world peace congresses were held, arguments against war were marshalled, arbitration among nations urged, and disarmament advocated. Diverse elements were enlisted, such as Quakers, insurance men, free-traders, and merchants.

Pacifism of the early nineteenth century differed from that of the twentieth chiefly in this, that it was economically and socially conservative. Peace agitation was a matter of Christian evangelism and of social stability. It drew more from the Gospel than from fundamental philosophy. Its swing was to the right rather than the left. It did not march with socialism. It contained sectional trouble-makers in its ranks. Christian and conservative as it was, it often met opposition or at least non-cooperation from ordained ministers. Taking a stand against war was diffi-

cult and complex. Questions arose touching the duty of fighting a defensive war or concerning the right of revolution. To favor peace in the sense of having governments avoid the outbreak of war was very different from avoiding individual participation once war had broken out. Organized peace men were chiefly northerners, rather northeasterners, and the movement was interlocked with collateral movements, especially antislavery. Peace advocacy might or might not mean nonresistance. Not all peace men could accept Garrison's formula of doing nothing to preserve the Union against armed secession.

When war came and as the struggle dragged on, demands for peace were regarded as a kind of defeatism, of surrender to forces which northern idealists considered destructive and evil. Peace became a matter of politics, of anti-Lincoln agitation, of what was called Copperhead disloyalty. Forces that stood outwardly for Christianity denounced it the loudest. Though praising Seward's peace efforts before Sumter, the Peace Society formulated its war-time position after Sumter as follows: "*Peace is always loyal. . . . We cannot . . . tolerate rebellion. . . . The cause of Peace was never meant to meet such a crisis as is now upon us.*" The society was a negligible thing; indeed one could read many tomes of American history without seeing it mentioned. It did not associate itself with opposition to the war powers, with anti-Lincoln demands for civil rights, with Vallandigham partisanship, nor with obstruction of the draft. It never made enough of a stir to become notorious. It did not arouse the horrendous and vindictive ire of any Dies committee. Many of its members preferred war to the continuance of slavery; others preferred war to disunion; still others deemed human slaughter not too high a price for ascendancy of a favorite party.

Denunciation of war easily became denunciation of rebellion; this readily passed over into a demand to put down rebellion. The cause of peace as a crusade found a new orientation when war actually existed, for non-resistance could not stop the torrent. It was the dilemma of the pacifist. When peace men face an existing war begun by what they consider an aggressor, their attachment to peace becomes outraged indignation against those who, in their opinion, have broken the peace. Such a feeling is consistent with the motive of stopping the war maker. It is only the cynic who would laugh at the discomfiture of the pacifist when once war exists and when the choice of peace is no longer open. The self-contradiction belongs to those who would put the label of war monger upon peace-time efforts to implement international cooperation and to buttress war prevention. The inconsistency is in misapplying the term "peace bloc" to those isolationist groups which have worked to frustrate international security by way of peaceful organization among nations.

For the Civil War generation the problem of the advocate of peace was only in a limited sense the problem of the conscientious objector. Objectors in the Lincoln period were chiefly associated with established anti-war creeds of religious groups. General objectors on other than religious grounds were not much in evidence. In this the Civil War presented a contrast to the World War, wherein refusal to fight was associated not only with specific Quaker-like groups but with broad liberal attitudes. In both wars the mass effect of organized religion was the opposite of pacifist. In each war administrative authorities of the United States respected the idealism of the objector and gave him

the alternative of noncombatant service. In the World War more objectors were relieved than imprisoned, though the imprisoned received the most attention. Imprisonment of objectors as such was not a Civil War practice.

If the pacifist had a dilemma, so did the government. The sincere and serene Christianity of the Quakers could not but command respect, and those who stood their ground were, as a rule, honorably excused from fighting. In the Civil War this leniency was at first an administrative adjustment in a situation where the objector might have expected severe treatment; late in the war it was a matter of statutory amendment to the conscription act. As originally passed the Conscription Act of 1863 did not even exempt ministers. For the objector to stand his ground in early Civil War days meant defiance of the government; the government was demanding a service which the objector refused; leniency was an afterthought. Non-resistance was a Quaker tenet, but here the Quakers, or rather the strictest of them, would have to resist, as did Cyrus Pringle of Vermont, unless their government would make a concession which in such cases it did make. No government can be completely unbending. Government is, after all, an art, perhaps a compromise. If the objector remained obdurate, either the government had to withdraw somewhat from the principle of compulsory military service or a man would be punished for being a Christian. The government took an attitude toward Quakers which it could not take toward all, if conscription were its principle. The Quaker came through the dilemma with less compromise than the government.

It is not of record that Lincoln's Cabinet contained a "minister of national enlightenment and propaganda"; yet propaganda itself was not lacking. In the public "enlightenment" of that time there was boasting, there was rumor, there were atrocity tales, and there was falsehood. Atrocity stories were found not only in newspapers but in congressional reports. There were circumstantial accounts of Confederates bayoneting wounded captives, kicking heads about like footballs, insulting women, and engaging in gruesome tortures. William B. Hesseltine has shown that anti-southern horror tales were not without governmental inspiration in the North and that the secretary of war, the surgeon general, and the committee on the conduct of the war took pains to spread tales of the sufferings of northern prisoners in the South. Motives were various: tales might be spread to carry forward the abolitionist's denunciation of southern cruelty, to satisfy the moral sense by besmirching the foe, or to discourage surrender into southern hands. When the backfire came and these atrocity stories led to questions as to why prisoners were not exchanged, it became necessary to invent the tale that exchange had been stopped by a vicious South intent upon destroying the lives of prisoners. Even the humanitarian motive promoted atrocity tales, and the report of the Sanitary Commission on this subject in no way fell short of governmental accounts.

Lincoln's attitude on such matters was expressed in a speech delivered at a Sanitary Fair in Baltimore in 1864. Referring to the rumored massacre of colored prisoners at Fort Pillow, Lincoln carefully avoided pointing up the reputed atrocity, declared that the event was not known to have occurred, and promised an investigation. He also promised retribution if needed, but, as in the case of similar threats by the Confederacy, the motive was humanitarian. The threat of retaliation was intended to make actual retaliation unnecessary, as well as to satisfy that type of vindictiveness at the North which was strangely bound up with humanitarianism. On this point Lincoln reached the height of caution when he said: "It will be a matter of grave consideration in what exact course to apply the retribution." What seemed to worry Lincoln was not a vicious South, but the need to satisfy his own northern public, including the humanitarianly vindictive public. For the latter he gave a threat of retribution which in fact he never carried out, and probably never intended to.

In spite of its lack of modern techniques such as radio and the movies, Civil War propaganda found many devices. There were drawings in *Harper's, Leslie's,* and *Vanity Fair,* though not daily cartoons. There were popular songs such as "Father Abraham" which gave the chief a nickname and personified the cause in a benevolent President. There was recruiting propaganda by poster and otherwise, and there was partisanly patriotic propaganda in appeals for soldier votes. Generals of the political variety made flourishing speeches. The Loyal Publication Society sent out its material by the bushel, including stereotypes to local editors, tracts, broadsides, pamphlets, and in one case a forged speech attributed to Alexander H. Stephens, whose alleged language was startlingly similar to that of Helper's *Impending Crisis.*

The word "propaganda" is an inexact expression which eludes definition. Every public appeal to support a cause could be loosely called propaganda. An advertisement might be propaganda in this broad sense, so also an editorial, a parade, a novel, a Sanitary Fair, a request for funds, a Thanksgiving proclamation, an anecdote, an envelope, a letter-head, a postage stamp, a dollar bill, a legislative preamble, a sermon, a petition, a sewing circle, or a school primer. One might use propaganda in christening a baby, naming a street, or addressing the Almighty. Motives in reaching the public were mixed. Propaganda in Lincoln's day was more often complex than simple, hybrid oftener than thoroughbred; it had one purpose grafted upon another. Publicity for the national cause was universal, but this broad appeal was often linked with an ulterior purpose which was in fact the main interest of the promoting agency. Thus a party rally would masquerade as a Union mass meeting, an appeal for peace in England might be an effort to withhold ironclads from the Confederacy, a volunteer fire brigade would be a unit of Tammany Hall, and the anniversary at Baltimore in 1862 of the anti-Union riot of April, 1861, was a boost for the newly elected mayor and council which had become Unionist. When Jay Cooke urged people to buy bonds he did not hesitate to blend self-interest with patriotism as he stressed the advantages of tax-free seven per cents. Even the name "Union" applied to the Republican party in Civil War days was an example of this tendency. Among themselves Republican leaders understood each other perfectly and continued to refer to their party as Republican, while for public consumption it was called "Union."

Much could be said of party propaganda, but this was not peculiar to war time; party agitation is always with us. That the national cause was appropriated for a party purpose was seen in the Union League. It is unnecessary to comment on the league at large, with its expensive club buildings, its social impressiveness, its exploitation of the American propensity for joining, its masses of war literature, and its showy efforts toward recruiting and soldier relief; but there is need for further study of the league's campaign activities, especially the procedures of its local chap-

ters. The minute-book of a local league in the nineteenth ward of New York City belongs to the type of sources that are seldom dug up. The minutes here recorded are generally quite sterile as they creep along with routine matters till the approach of election time. Indeed it was not until September 19, 1864, that the nineteenth-ward leaguers "heartily approved" the early June nomination of Abraham Lincoln and Andrew Johnson at Baltimore. It was in October and the first days of November, 1864, that this local league suddenly came alive, sending loyal newspapers to soldiers, passing sizzling anti-Democratic resolutions, publishing campaign documents, and appointing poll-watchers to swing into action at sunrise on the eighth of November. Just after the election the minutes report "no quorum," and from that time this patriotic organization sank back into utter inactivity. Repeatedly there was the "no quorum" record; in February, 1865, it was voted to adopt measures to increase interest in the meetings. On April 3, 1865, the minutes flicker out altogether. Similar accounts with different terms, including the names of Tammany and the Knights of the Golden Circle, would illuminate the history of the Democratic party.

Official propaganda took many forms, including governmentally inspired foreign missions of prominent Americans. Thurlow Weed promoted the Union cause in the British press, Archbishop John Hughes sought contact with Catholics in Europe, Bishop McIlwaine of the Episcopal Church made his appeal to the British clergy. In addition, the irrepressible Robert J. Walker appealed to British financial groups in opposition to southern bond sales, while John M. Forbes and William H. Aspinwall labored to halt naval building for the Confederacy in Britain. President Lincoln, who once owned a newspaper, by no means neglected publicity. Naturally he addressed the people in occasional speeches, in his two inaugurals, his proclamations, and his messages to Congress. Beyond this there was the use of patronage for newspapers, an obscure subject yet to be explored, and there was the case of J. W. Forney whose Philadelphia *Chronicle* and Washington *Chronicle* were known as Lincoln organs. In March, 1862, the President asked Henry J. Raymond for an article in the *Times*. So much of the writing on Lincoln has been of the sentimentally stereotyped variety that people have overlooked Lincoln's trenchant comments on his own times, on wartime profits, on corruption, and on the manner in which every "foul bird" and "every dirty reptile" came forth in war time. It is safe to say that Lincoln saw the war more clearly and faced it more squarely than Emerson. He faced it with an amazing lack of hatred and rancor.

The Civil War generation, not alone military and political events, but life and *mores*, social conditions and thought-patterns that accompanied the war as well as non-war aspects of the age, will receive further attention by inquisitive historians. In Arthur C. Cole's pages in the Fox-Schlesinger series one finds many a cue for further investigation and many a product of mature study. Beyond the boundaries of even the newer books lie disappearing and forgotten stories. Where the stories are recoverable the present age of historiography, as shown in Cole's book, is more capable of accomplishing the recovery than previous ages. History has its vogues and its movements. Just as Americans beginning about 1935 executed something like an about-face in their interpretation of the World War, including American participation in it and attitudes preceding it, so the retelling of the Civil War is a matter of changed and changing viewpoints. In the present troubled age it may be of more than academic interest to reexamine the human beings of that war generation with less thought of the "splendor of battle flags" and with more of the sophisticated and unsentimental searchlight of reality.

Stressing the failure of the American political system,
ROY F. NICHOLS (1896–   ), Professor Emeritus
at the University of Pennsylvania has written a series
of important works on the political history of the 1850s.
In *The Disruption of American Democracy* he argues
that the coming of the Civil War was the result of
divisive attitudes of Democratic party factions and
leaders. To what degree does the concluding chapter of
his study, which follows, agree with Randall? Does
Nichols offer a valid conclusion?*

Roy F. Nichols

Party Failure

The disruption of the American Democracy was complete in 1861. Secession had split the Republic, and the guns of civil war were thundering. The breakup of the Democratic party and the beginning of armed conflict were almost simultaneous; they were intimately related phenomena. The shattering of the party of Jackson was the bursting of a dike which unloosed an engulfing flood.

On the reasons for the Civil War there has been a vast amount of theorizing. Writers have been prone to select patterns—economic, cultural, political, racial, moral, and others—and to devise and emphasize theories in conformity with them. Long arguments as to whether the conflict was repressible or irrepressible, whether the war was inevitable or might have been avoided, have preoccupied historians. As they have unearthed more and more "causes," as they have introduced into the picture more and more elements, they have not altogether succeeded in answering the moot question: Why a civil war? Most of the principal "causes"—ideological differences, institutional differences, moral differences, cultural differences, sectional differences, physiographic differences—have existed in other times and places, without necessarily causing a war. Then why should they set the people of the United States to killing one another in 1861? . . .

People fight under the stress of hyper-emotionalism. When some compelling

*Reprinted with permission of The Macmillan Company from *The Disruption of American Democracy* by Roy F. Nichols, pp. 513–517. Copyright 1948 by The Macmillan Company.

drive, whether it be ambition, fear, anger, or hunger, becomes supercharged, violence and bloodletting, thus far in human history, seem "inevitable." Now why was emotion in the United States in 1861 supercharged?

The basic reasons for this hyperemotionalism cannot be neatly formulated and weighted. Fundamentally the process was an illustration of what Machiavelli describes as the "confusion of a growing state." The population of the United States was rapidly multiplying, partly by natural increase and partly by foreign immigration, at the same time that it was arranging itself in rapidly changing patterns. Many Americans were creating new communities, others were crowding together into older urban centers. In old and new, change was continual, with a ceaseless moving out and coming in. The rate of growth, however, could not be uniform; for it was determined in large part by physiographical considerations and the Republic extended from the temperate into the semitropical zone. In the semitropical-to-temperate agricultural South, enterprise was less active, mobility less noticeable. In the northerly states, on the other hand, the variety of realized and potential wealth was greater, the stimulus from climate was sharper, the interest in projects of all sorts was more dynamic. There the vision of wealth and of the needs of the growing society continually inspired the creation of new and more powerful interests, under zealous and ambitious leaders.

So rapid and uneven a rate of social growth was bound to inflict upon Americans this "confusion of a growing state." Characteristic of it and dominant in it were pervasive, divisive, and cohesive attitudes which, as Whitman put it, were "significant of a grand upheaval of ideas and reconstruction of many things on new bases." The social confusion in itself was the great problem confronting statesmen and politicians. Turn where they would, they could not escape it; they themselves were confused by it, and yet they must wrestle with it.

The political system which was in the process of evolving reflected their predicament. They knew that they were operating a federal system, but they oversimplified their problem by believing that it was only a political federalism. They did not grasp the fact that it was a cultural federalism as well. Not only were they dealing with a political federation of states, they must understand this cultural federation of attitudes. The inability to understand contributed much to their failure to organize partisanship and to create political machinery which would be adequate to deal with the complexities of this cultural federation.

This lack of understanding was accompanied by a deep-seated enjoyment of political activity by Americans which proved dangerous. They gave themselves so many opportunities to gratify their desire for this sport. There were so many elections and such constant agitation. Contests were scheduled automatically by the calendar, at many different times and seasons; there were thirty-three independent state systems of election. Within each state the parties, despite their national names, were really independent, each a law unto itself, and none was subjected to much if any central direction; there were nearly eighty such party organizations. A great disruptive fact was the baneful influence of elections almost continuously in progress, of campaigns never over, and of political uproar endlessly arousing emotions. The system of the fathers might possibly bear within itself the seeds of its own destruction.

This constant agitation certainly furnishes one of the primary clues to why the war came. It raised to ever higher pitch the passion-rousing oratory of rivals. They egged one another on to make more and more exaggerated statements to a people pervasively romantic and protestant, isolated and confused. The men and women exhibiting these different attitudes were not isolated and separated by boundaries—they dwelt side by side, and the same person might be moved by more than one attitude at a time, or by different attitudes at different times. The emotional complex which was created by the variety of these attitudes, and the tension which their antagonisms bred, added confusion to that already provided by the chaotic electoral customs and poorly organized parties; the total precipitated a resort to arms. The baffling problem was not how to maintain a balance among states but how to preserve a balance among a number of emotional units or attitudes. It was this that proved beyond the political capacity of the time.

The Democratic party was not unaware of some of the danger. Its most enlightened leaders had sought to quiet such divisive attitudes as antislaveryism in the North and southernism in the South by encouraging such cohesive attitudes as nationalism. Unhappily they did not understand the pervasive romanticism and protestantism sufficiently to make use of them in strengthening the cohesive attitudes. No leader in the Democracy could find the formula. Buchanan, Douglas, the justices of the Supreme Court, Davis, Hammond, and Hunter all tried and failed. The Republicans, such as Lincoln and Seward, grasped the realities: a house so divided against itself could not stand; with such divisive attitudes in the ascendant and unchecked, the conflict was irrepressible.

Under the stimulus of constant agita-
tion the leaders of the southern branch of the Democracy forbade the voters to elect a Republican President unless they wished him to preside over a shattered government. A number of voters sufficient to create a Republican majority in the Electoral College defied the prohibition. Then southerners, in a state of hyperemotion, moved by pride, self-interest, a sense of honor and fear, rushed to action; they were numerous enough and effective enough to force secession. They would flee the peril; in the spirit of 1776, they would organize a second American Revolution, this time against the tyranny not of a monarch but of "a mob." They would create a reformed confederacy free from corruption and centralization in which their social and economic institutions would be safe.

Also under the stimulus of constant agitation, the newly organized Republican administration decided to put down what it called the "Rebellion." Backed by an angered constituency including most northern Democrats, it determined to fight rather than permit the seceding states to break up a profitable partnership, a source of wealth and power, and an experiment in liberty and equality which Lincoln felt was the hope of the world. It undertook a "people's contest" to insure that "government of the people, by the people, for the people" should "not perish from the earth."

Thus war came when the American people for the first time refused to abide by a national election. The parties which had been promoting the cohesive attitudes had broken down, and their disorganization had permitted the new Republican organization to win through direct appeal to the divisive attitudes. The constant heat generated in the frequent elections brought an explosion. The social, economic, and cultural differences had been so used by the political operators as to produce secession and civil war.

War broke out because no means had been devised to curb the extravagant use of the divisive forces. Statesmanship seemed poverty-stricken. The work of the nationalists who sought to find a formula with which to overcome the divisive attitudes was vain. Too few even saw the need for the formula; they ran heedlessly down the path to disruption. The war was the product of the chaotic lack of system in ascertaining and directing the public will, a chaos exploited with little regard for the welfare of the general public by irresponsible and blind operators of local political machinery unchecked by any adequate central organization.

Finally, carrying the analysis even further, it may be postulated that the war came because of certain interests and activities characterized for convenience as the processes of human behavior, in which individual and general attitudes and emotional drives are constantly interacting—provoking and conditioning one another. At certain times and in certain circumstances, cooperative behavior predominates; but competitive behavior is seldom if ever absent, and when too vigorously aroused leads to a strife which ranges from argument to war. Indeed argument is itself a form of conflict short of war, more or less, and if pressed without checks and restraints easily passes over into war.

The American Democracy sought from 1850 to 1860 to keep in power by encouraging cooperative behavior. But, deeply affected by the shocks of the collisions occurring within the society in which it operated and of which it was a part, the party failed to overcome the divisive attitudes and was shattered. The disruption of the American Democracy eventuated in defeat, secession, and civil war.

ARTHUR SCHLESINGER, JR. (1917–   ) has written
authoritative volumes on the age of Jackson, the age of
Roosevelt, and the Kennedy era. A trusted adviser of
President John F. Kennedy and of Senator Robert
Kennedy, Schlesinger has been closely identified with
the liberal attitudes of the New Frontier. Because of his
personal involvement in public issues, his article on
"The Causes of the American Civil War: A Note on
Historical Sentimentalism," which appeared in the
Partisan Review in 1949, has special significance. How
does he refute the revisionists? In particular, how does
he differ from Randall? Is his criticism valid? His
approach also invites comparison with earlier
assessments by James F. Rhodes.*

Arthur Schlesinger, Jr.

A Moral Problem

The Civil War was our great national trauma. A savage fraternal conflict, it released deep sentiments of guilt and remorse—sentiments which have reverberated through our history and our literature ever since. Literature in the end came to terms with these sentiments by yielding to the South in fantasy the victory it had been denied in fact; this tendency culminated on the popular level in *Gone with the Wind* and on the highbrow level in the Nashville cult of agrarianism. But history, a less malleable medium, was constricted by the intractable fact that the war had taken place, and by the related assumption that it was, in William H. Seward's phrase, an "irrepressible conflict," and hence a justified one.

As short a time ago as 1937, for example, even Professor James G. Randall could describe himself as "unprepared to go to the point of denying that the great American tragedy could have been avoided." Yet in a few years the writing of history would succumb to the psychological imperatives which had produced *I'll Take my Stand* and *Gone with the Wind;* and Professor Randall would emerge as the leader of a triumphant new school of self-styled "revisionists." The publication of two vigorous books by Professor Avery Craven—*The Repressible Conflict* (1939) and *The Coming of the Civil War* (1942)—and the appearance of Professor Randall's own notable volumes on Lincoln—*Lincoln the President: Springfield to Gettysburg* (1945), *Lincoln and the South* (1946), and *Lincoln the Liberal Statesman*

*Arthur Schlesinger, Jr., "The Causes of the American Civil War: A Note on Historical Sentimentalism," *Partisan Review*, XVI, No. 10 (1949), pp. 969–981. Reprinted by permission from Professor Schlesinger.

[handwritten marginalia: fundamental rivalries don't → war]

(1947)—brought about a profound reversal of the professional historian's attitude toward the Civil War. Scholars now denied the traditional assumption of the inevitability of the war and boldly advanced the thesis that a "blundering generation" had transformed a "repressible conflict" into a "needless war."

The swift triumph of revisionism came about with very little resistance or even expressed reservations on the part of the profession. Indeed, the only adequate evaluation of the revisionist thesis that I know was made, not by an academic historian at all, but by that illustrious semi-pro, Mr. Bernard De Voto; and Mr. De Voto's two brilliant articles in *Harper's* in 1945 unfortunately had little influence within the guild. By 1947 Professor Allan Nevins, summing up the most recent scholarship in *Ordeal of the Union,* his able general history of the eighteen-fifties, could define the basic problem of the period in terms which indicated a measured but entire acceptance of revisionism. "The primary task of statesmanship in this era," Nevins wrote, "was to furnish a workable adjustment between the two sections, while offering strong inducements to the southern people to regard their labor system not as static but evolutionary, and equal persuasions to the northern people to assume a helpful rather than scolding attitude."

This new interpretation surely deserves at least as meticulous an examination as Professor Randall is prepared to give, for example, to such a question as whether or not Lincoln was playing fives when he received the news of his nomination in 1860. The following notes are presented in the interests of stimulating such an examination.

The revisionist case, as expounded by Professors Randall and Craven, has three main premises. First:

1) that the Civil War was caused by the irresponsible emotionalization of politics far out of proportion to the real problems involved. The war, as Randall put it, was certainly not caused by cultural variations nor by economic rivalries nor by sectional differences; these all existed, but it was "stupid," as he declared, to think that they required war as a solution. "One of the most colossal of misconceptions" was the "theory" that "fundamental motives produce war. The glaring and obvious fact is the artificiality of warmaking agitation." After all, Randall pointed out, agrarian and industrial interests had been in conflict under Coolidge and Hoover; yet no war resulted. "In Illinois," he added, "major controversies (not mere transient differences) between downstate and metropolis have stopped short of war."

Nor was the slavery the cause. The issues arising over slavery were in Randall's judgment "highly artificial, almost fabricated. . . . They produced quarrels out of things that would have settled themselves were it not for political agitation." Slavery, Craven observed, was in any case a much overrated problem. It is "perfectly clear," he wrote, "that slavery played a rather minor part in the life of the South and of the Negro."

What then was the cause of war? "If one word or phrase were selected to account for the war," wrote Randall, ". . . it would have to be such a word as fanaticism (on both sides), misunderstanding, misrepresentation, or perhaps politics." Phrases like "whipped-up crisis" and "psychopathic case" adorned Randall's explanation. Craven similarly described the growing sense of sectional differences as "an artificial creation of inflamed minds." The "molders of public opinion steadily created the fiction of two distinct peoples." As a result, "distortion led a people into bloody war."

If uncontrolled emotionalism and fanaticism caused the war, how did they get out of hand? Who whipped up the "whipped-up crisis"? Thus the second revisionist thesis:

2) that sectional friction was permitted to develop into needless war by the inexcusable failure of political leadership in the fifties. "It is difficult to achieve a full realization of how Lincoln's generation stumbled into a ghastly war," wrote Randall. ". . . If one questions the term 'blundering generation,' let him inquire how many measures of the time he would wish copied or repeated if the period were to be approached with a clean slate and to be lived again."

It was the politicians, charged Craven, who systematically sacrificed peace to their pursuit of power. Calhoun and Adams, "seeking political advantage," mixed up slavery and expansion; Wilmot introduced his "trouble-making Proviso as part of the political game;" the repeal clause in the Kansas-Nebraska Act was "the afterthought of a mere handful of politicians;" Chase's Appeal to the Independent Democrats was "false in its assertions and unfair in its purposes, but it was politically effective"; the "damaging" section in the Dred Scott decision was forced "by the political ambitions of dissenting judges." "These uncalled-for moves and this irresponsible leadership," concluded Craven, blew up a "crack-pot" crusade into a national conflict.

It is hard to tell which was under attack here—the performance of a particular generation or democratic politics in general. But, if the indictment "blundering generation" meant no more than a general complaint that democratic politics placed a premium on emotionalism, then the Civil War would have been no more nor less "needless" than any event in our blundering history. The phrase "blunder-

ing generation" must consequently imply that the generation in power in the fifties was *below* the human or historical or democratic average in its blundering. Hence the third revisionist thesis:

3) that the slavery problem could have been solved without war. For, even if slavery were as unimportant as the revisionists have insisted, they would presumably admit that it constituted the real sticking-point in the relations between the sections. They must show therefore that there were policies with which a non-blundering generation could have resolved the slavery crisis and averted war; and that these policies were so obvious that the failure to adopt them indicated blundering and stupidity of a peculiarly irresponsible nature. If no such policies could be produced even by hindsight, then it would seem excessive to condemn the politicians of the fifties for failing to discover them at the time.

The revisionists have shown only a most vague and sporadic awareness of this problem. "Any kind of sane policy in Washington in 1860 might have saved the day for nationalism," remarked Craven; but he did not vouchsafe the details of these sane policies; we would be satisfied to know about one.* Similarly Randall declared that there were few policies of the fifties he would wish repeated if the period were to be lived over again; but he was not communicative about the policies he would wish pursued. Nevins likewise blamed the war on the "collapse of American statesmanship," but restrained himself from suggesting how a non-collapsible statesmanship would have solved the hard problems of the fifties.

---

*It is fair to say that Professor Craven seems in recent years to have modified his earlier extreme position; see his article "The Civil War and the Democratic Process," *Abraham Lincoln Quarterly*, June 1947.

In view of this reticence on a point so crucial to the revisionist argument, it is necessary to reconstruct the possibilities that might lie in the back of revisionism. Clearly there could be only two "solutions" to the slavery problem: the preservation of slavery, or its abolition.

Presumably the revisionists would not regard the preservation of slavery as a possible solution. Craven, it is true, has argued that "most of the incentives to honest and sustained effort, to a contented, well-rounded life, might be found under slavery. . . . What owning and being owned added to the normal relationship of employer and employee is very hard to say." In describing incidents in which slaves beat up masters, he has even noted that "happenings and reactions like these were the rule [sic], not the exception." But Craven would doubtless admit that, however jolly this system might have been, its perpetuation would have been, to say the least, impracticable.

If, then, revisionism has rested on the assumption that the nonviolent abolition of slavery was possible, such abolition could conceivably have come about through internal reform in the South; through economic exhaustion of the slavery system in the South; or through some government project for gradual and compensated emancipation. Let us examine these possibilities.

1) *The internal reform argument.* The South, the revisionists have suggested, might have ended the slavery system if left to its own devices; only the abolitionists spoiled everything by letting loose a hysteria which caused the southern ranks to close in self-defense.

This revisionist argument would have been more convincing if the decades of alleged anti-slavery feeling in the South had produced any concrete results. As one judicious southern historian, Professor Charles S. Sydnor, recently put it, "Although the abolition movement was followed by a decline of antislavery sentiment in the South, it must be remembered that in all the long years before that movement began no part of the South had made substantial progress toward ending slavery. . . . Southern liberalism had not ended slavery in any state."

In any case, it is difficult for historians seriously to suppose that northerners could have denied themselves feelings of disapproval over slavery. To say that there "should" have been no abolitionists in America before the Civil War is about as sensible as to say that there "should" have been no anti-Nazis in the nineteen-thirties or that there "should" be no anti-Communists today. People who indulge in criticism of remote evils may not be so pure of heart as they imagine; but that fact does not affect their inevitability as part of the historic situation.

Any theory, in short, which expects people to repress such spontaneous aversions is profoundly unhistorical. If revisionism has based itself on the conviction that things would have been different if only there had been no abolitionists, it has forgotten that abolitionism was as definite and irrevocable a factor in the historic situation as was slavery itself. And, just as abolitionism was inevitable, so too was the southern reaction against it—a reaction which, as Professor Clement Eaton has ably shown, steadily drove the free discussion of slavery out of the South. The extinction of free discussion meant, of course, the absolute extinction of any hope of abolition through internal reform.

2) *The economic exhaustion argument.* Slavery, it has been pointed out, was on the skids economically. It was overcapitalized and inefficient; it immobilized both capital and labor; its one-crop system

was draining the soil of fertility; it stood in the way of industrialization. As the South came to realize these facts, a revisionist might argue, it would have moved to abolish slavery for its own economic good. As Craven put it, slavery "may have been almost ready to break down of its own weight."

This argument assumed, of course, that southerners would have recognized the causes of their economic predicament and taken the appropriate measures. Yet such an assumption would be plainly contrary to history and to experience. From the beginning the South has always blamed its economic shortcomings, not on its own economic ruling class and its own inefficient use of resources, but on northern exploitation. Hard times in the eighteen-fifties produced in the South, not a reconsideration of the slavery system, but blasts against the North for the high prices of manufactured goods. The overcapitalization of slavery led, not to criticisms of the system, but to increasingly insistent demands for the reopening of the slave trade. Advanced southern writers like George Fitzhugh and James D. B. DeBow were even arguing that slavery was adapted to industrialism. When Hinton R. Helper did advance before the Civil War an early version of Craven's argument, asserting that emancipation was necessary to save the southern economy, the South burned his book. Nothing in the historical record suggests that the southern ruling class was preparing to deviate from its traditional pattern of self-exculpation long enough to take such a drastic step as the abolition of slavery.

3) *Compensated emancipation.* Abraham Lincoln made repeated proposals of compensated emancipation. In his annual message to Congress of December 1, 1862, he set forth a detailed plan by which States, on an agreement to abolish slavery

by 1900, would receive government bonds in proportion to the number of slaves emancipated. Yet, even though Lincoln's proposals represented a solution of the problem conceivably gratifying to the slaveholder's purse as well as to his pride, they got nowhere. Two-thirds of the border representatives rejected the scheme, even when personally presented to them by Lincoln himself. And, of course, only the pressure of war brought compensated emancipation its limited hearing of 1862.

Still, granted these difficulties, does it not remain true that other countries abolished slavery without internal convulsion? If emotionalism had not aggravated the situation beyond hope, Craven has written, then slavery "might have been faced as a national question and dealt with as successfully as the South American countries dealt with the same problem." If Brazil could free its slaves and Russia its serfs in the middle of the nineteenth century without civil war, why could not the United States have done as well?

The analogies are appealing but not, I think, really persuasive. There are essential differences between the slavery question in the United States and the problems in Brazil or in Russia. In the first place, Brazil and Russia were able to face servitude "as a national question" because it was, in fact, a national question. Neither country had the American problem of the identification of compact sectional interests with the survival of the slavery system. In the second place, there was no race problem at all in Russia; and, though there was a race problem in Brazil, the more civilized folkways of that country relieved racial differences of the extreme tension which they breed in the South of the United States. In the third place, neither in Russia nor in Brazil did the abolition of servitude involve constitutional issues; and the existence of these issues played a great part in determining the form of the American struggle.

It is hard to draw much comfort, therefore, from the fact that other nations abolished servitude peaceably. The problem in America was peculiarly recalcitrant. The schemes for gradual emancipation got nowhere. Neither internal reform nor economic exhaustion contained much promise for a peaceful solution. The hard fact, indeed, is that the revisionists have not tried seriously to describe the policies by which the slavery problem could have been peaceably resolved. They have resorted instead to broad affirmations of faith: if only the conflict could have been staved off long enough, then somehow, somewhere, we could have worked something out. It is legitimate, I think, to ask how? where? what?—at least, if these affirmations of faith are to be used as the premise for castigating the unhappy men who had the practical responsibility for finding solutions and failed.

Where have the revisionists gone astray? In part, the popularity of revisionism obviously parallels that of *Gone with the Wind*—the victors paying for victory by pretending literary defeat. But the essential problem is why history should be so vulnerable to this literary fashion; and this problem, I believe, raises basic questions about the whole modern view of history. It is perhaps stating the issue in too portentous terms. Yet I cannot escape the feeling that the vogue of revisionism is connected with the modern tendency to seek in optimistic sentimentalism an escape from the severe demands of moral decision; that it is the offspring of our modern sentimentality which at once evades the essential moral problems in the name of a superficial objectivity and asserts their unimportance in the name of an invincible progress.

The revisionists first glided over the implications of the fact that the slavery system was producing a closed society in the South. Yet that society increasingly had justified itself by a political and philosophical repudiation of free society; southern thinkers swiftly developed the anti-liberation potentialities in a social system whose cornerstone, in Alexander H. Stephen's proud phrase, was human bondage. In theory and in practice, the South organized itself with mounting rigor against ideas of human dignity and freedom, because such ideas inevitably threatened the basis of their own system. Professor Frank L. Owsley, the southern agrarian, has described inadvertently but accurately the direction in which the slave South was moving. "The abolitionists and their political allies were threatening the existence of the South as seriously as the Nazis threaten the existence of England," wrote Owsley in 1940; ". . . Under such circumstances the surprising thing is that so little was done by the South to defend its existence."

There can be no question that many southerners in the fifties had similar sentiments; that they regarded their system of control as ridiculously inadequate; and that, with the book-burning, the censorship of the mails, the gradual illegalization of dissent, the South was in process of creating a real machinery of repression in order more effectively "to defend its existence." No society, I suppose, encourages criticism of its basic institutions. Yet, when a democratic society acts in self-defense, it does so at least in the name of human dignity and freedom. When a society based on bond slavery acts to eliminate criticism of its peculiar institution, it outlaws what a believer in democracy can only regard as the abiding values of man. When the basic institutions are evil, in other words, the effect of attempts to defend their existence can only be the moral and intellectual stultification of the society.

A society closed in the defense of evil institutions thus creates moral differences far too profound to be solved by compromise. Such a society forces upon every one, both those living at the time and those writing about it later, the necessity for a moral judgment; and the moral judgment in such cases becomes an indispensable factor in the historical understanding.

The revisionists were commendably anxious to avoid the vulgar errors of the post-Civil War historians who pronounced smug individual judgments on the persons involuntarily involved in the tragedy of the slave system. Consequently they tried hard to pronounce no moral judgments at all on slavery. Slavery became important, in Craven's phrase, "only as a very ancient labor system, probably at this time rather near the end of its existence"; the attempt to charge this labor system with moral meanings was "a creation of inflamed imaginations." Randall, talking of the Kansas-Nebraska Act, could describe it as "a law intended to subordinate the slavery question and hold it in *proper* proportion" (my italics). I have quoted Randall's even more astonishing argument that, because major controversies between downstate and metropolis in Illinois stopped short of war, there was reason to believe that the Civil War could have been avoided. Are we to take it that the revisionists seriously believe that the downstate-metropolis fight in Illinois—or the agrarian-industrial fight in the Coolidge and Hoover administrations—were in any useful sense comparable to the difference between the North and South in 1861?

Because the revisionists felt no moral urgency themselves, they deplored as fanatics those who did feel it, or brushed aside their feelings as the artificial product of emotion and propaganda. The revisionist hero was Stephen A. Douglas, who always thought that the great moral problems could be solved by sleight-of-hand. The phrase "northern man of southern sentiments," Randall remarked, was "said opprobriously . . . as if it were a base thing for a northern man to work with his southern fellows."

By denying themselves insight into the moral dimension of the slavery crisis, in other words, the revisionists denied themselves a historical understanding of the intensities that caused the crisis. It was the moral issue of slavery, for example, that gave the struggles over slavery in the territories or over the enforcement of the fugitive slave laws their significance. These issues, as the revisionists have shown with cogency, were not in themselves basic. But they were the available issues; they were almost the only points within the existing constitutional framework where the moral conflict could be faced; as a consequence, they became charged with the moral and political dynamism of the central issue. To say that the Civil War was fought over the "unreal" issue of slavery in the territories is like saying that the Second World War was fought over the "unreal" issue of the invasion of Poland. The democracies could not challenge fascism inside Germany any more than opponents of slavery could challenge slavery inside the South; but the extension of slavery, like the extension of fascism, was an act of aggression which made a moral choice inescapable.

Let us be clear what the relationship of moral judgment to history is. Every historian, as we all know in an argument that surely does not have to be repeated in 1949, imports his own set of moral judgments into the writing of history by the very process of interpretation; and the phrase "every historian" includes the category "revisionist." Mr. De Voto in his paraphrases of the revisionist position has put admirably the contradictions on this point: as for "moral questions, God forbid. History will not put itself in the position of saying that any thesis may have been wrong, any cause evil. . . . History will not deal with moral values, though of course the Republican radicals were, well, culpable." The whole revisionist attitude toward abolitionists and radicals, repeatedly characterized by Randall as "unctuous" and "intolerant," overflows with the moral feeling which is so virtuously excluded from discussions of slavery.

An acceptance of the fact of moral responsibility does not license the historian to roam through the past ladling out individual praise and blame: such an attitude would ignore the fact that all individuals, including historians, are trapped in a web of circumstance which curtails their moral possibilities. But it does mean that there are certain essential issues on which it is necessary for the historian to have a position if he is to understand the great conflicts of history. These great conflicts are relatively few because there are few enough historical phenomena which we can confidently identify as evil. The essential issues appear, moreover, not in pure and absolute form, but incomplete and imperfect, compromised by the deep complexity of history. Their proponents may often be neurotics and fanatics, like the abolitionists. They may attain a social importance only when a configuration of non-moral factors—economic, political, social, military—permit them to do so.

Yet neither the nature of the context nor the pretensions of the proponents

alter the character of the issue. And human slavery is certainly one of the few issues of whose evil we can be sure. It is not just "a very ancient labor system"; it is also a betrayal of the basic values of our Christian and democratic tradition. No historian can understand the circumstances which led to its abolition until he writes about it in its fundamental moral context. "History is supposed to understand the difference between a decaying economy and an expanding one," as Mr. De Voto well said, "between solvency and bankruptcy, between a dying social idea and one coming to world acceptance. . . . It is even supposed to understand implications of the difference between a man who is legally a slave and one who is legally free."

"Revisionism in general has no position," De Voto continues, "but only a vague sentiment." Professor Randall well suggested the uncritical optimism of that sentiment when he remarked, "To suppose that the Union could not have been continued or slavery outmoded without the war and without the corrupt concomitants of war is hardly an enlightened assumption." We have here a touching afterglow of the admirable nineteenth-century faith in the full rationality and perfectibility of man; the faith that the errors of the world would all in time be "outmoded" (Professor Randall's use of this word is suggestive) by progress. Yet the experience of the twentieth century has made it clear that we gravely overrated man's capacity to solve the problems of existence within the terms of history.

This conclusion about man may disturb our complacencies about human nature. Yet it is certainly more in accord with history than Professor Randall's "enlightened" assumption that man can solve peaceably all the problems which overwhelm him. The unhappy fact is that man occasionally works himself into a log-jam; and that the log-jam must be burst by violence. We know that well enough from the experience of the last decade. Are we to suppose that some future historian will echo Professor Nevins' version of the "failure" of the eighteen-fifties and write: "The primary task of statesmanship in the nineteen-thirties was to furnish a workable adjustment between the United States and Germany, while offering strong inducements to the German people to abandon the police state and equal persuasions to the Americans to help the Nazis rather than scold them?" Will some future historian adapt Professor Randall's formula and write that the word "appeaser" was used "opprobriously" as if it were a "base" thing for an American to work with his Nazi fellow? Obviously this revisionism of the future (already foreshadowed in the work of Charles A. Beard) would represent, as we now see it, a fantastic evasion of the hard and unpleasant problems of the thirties. I doubt whether our present revisionism would make much more sense to the men of the eighteen-fifties.

The problem of the inevitability of the Civil War, of course, is in its essence a problem devoid of meaning. The revisionist attempt to argue that the war could have been avoided by "any kind of sane policy" is of interest less in its own right than as an expression of a characteristically sentimental conception of man and of history. And the great vogue of revisionism in the historical profession suggests, in my judgment, ominous weaknesses in the contemporary attitude toward history.

We delude ourselves when we think that history teaches us that evil will be "outmoded" by progress and that politics consequently does not impose on us the necessity for decision and for struggle. If historians are to understand the fullness of the social dilemma they seek to reconstruct, they must understand that sometimes there is no escape from the implacabilities of moral decision. When social conflicts embody great moral issues, these conflicts cannot be assigned for solution to the invincible march of progress; nor can they be bypassed with "objective" neutrality. Not many problems perhaps force this decision upon the historian. But, if any problem does in our history, it is the Civil War.

To reject the moral actuality of the Civil War is to foreclose the possibility of an adequate account of its causes. More than that, it is to misconceive and grotesquely to sentimentalize the nature of history. For history is not a redeemer, promising to solve all human problems in time; nor is man capable of transcending the limitations of his being. Man generally is entangled in insoluble problems; history is consequently a tragedy in which we are all involved, whose keynote is anxiety and frustration, not progress and fulfillment. Nothing exists in history to assure us that the great moral dilemmas can be resolved without pain; we cannot therefore be relieved from the duty of moral judgment on issues so appalling and inescapable as those involved in human slavery; nor can we be consoled by sentimental theories about the needlessness of the Civil War into regarding our own struggles against evil as equally needless.

One must emphasize, however, that this duty of judgment applies to issues. Because we are all implicated in the same tragedy, we must judge the men of the past with the same forbearance and charity which we hope the future will apply toward us.

CHARLES W. RAMSDELL (1877–1942) was perhaps the most eloquent spokesman for the Southern interpretation of the immediate causes of the Civil War. A loyal son of his section, Ramsdell, who taught for many years at the University of Texas, attempted to prove that Lincoln deliberately provoked the Confederacy into firing the first shot at Fort Sumter. The article which follows represents the summary of his findings.*

Charles W. Ramsdell

Fort Sumter a Deliberate Plot

When the Confederate batteries around Charleston Harbor opened fire on Fort Sumter in the early morning hours of April 12, 1861, they signaled the beginning of the most calamitous tragedy in the history of the American people. Because the Confederate authorities ordered the attack it is generally held that they were directly responsible for the horrors of the ensuing four years. Certainly that was the feeling in the North, then and afterwards, and it became the verdict of austere historians.

Whether the war was inevitable, in any case, is a question that need not be raised here. It has been the subject of endless disputation and is one to which no conclusive answer can be given. But even though it be conceded that if the conflict had not arisen from the Fort Sumter crisis it would have sprung from some other incident growing out of the secession of the "cotton states," the actual firing of the "first shot" placed the Southerners under a great moral and material disadvantage. The general Northern conviction that the "rebels" had made an unprovoked attack upon the little Federal garrison added thousands of volunteers to the Union armies and strengthened the determination of the Northern people to carry the struggle through to the complete subjugation of the South.

The Confederate leaders who ordered the bombardment were not vicious, feeble-minded, irresponsible, or inexperi-

*Charles W. Ramsdell, "Lincoln and Fort Sumter," *Journal of Southern History,* III (1937), 259–288. (Footnotes omitted). Copyright 1937 by the Southern Historical Association. Reprinted by permission of the Managing Editor.

enced men. As even a casual investigation will show, they had been fully aware of the danger of taking the initiative in hostilities and had hoped for peace. How then could they be so blind as to place themselves at this manifest disadvantage?

The story of the development of the Fort Sumter crisis has been told many times, but it is so full of complexities that there is little wonder that many of its most significant features have been obscured with a resultant loss of perspective. On the one hand, most accounts have begun with certain assumptions which have affected the interpretation of the whole mass of evidence; on the other, too little credit has been given to Abraham Lincoln's genius for political strategy, which is truly surprising in view of all the claims that have been made for the abilities of that very remarkable man. The purpose of this paper is to place the facts already known in their logical and chronological order and to re-evalutate them in that setting in the belief that when thus arranged they will throw new light upon this momentous affair.

The early stages of the Sumter problem can be dealt with in summary form. It is well known that six days after the secession of South Carolina Major Robert Anderson, who had been stationed at Fort Moultrie in command of all the United States forces in Charleston Harbor, abandoned Moultrie and moved his command into the new and still unfinished Fort Sumter where he thought his force would be better able to resist attack. The South Carolina authorities evidently had had no intention of attacking him for they thought they had an understanding with President Buchanan for maintaining the military status quo; but they immediately occupied Fort Moultrie and Castle Pinckney and made protest to Buchanan, demanding that Anderson be sent back to Moultrie. Buchanan refused to admit their ground of protest or to order Anderson back; then early in January he ordered relief to be sent secretly to the garrison on a merchant steamer. This vessel, *The Star of the West,* was forced back from the entrance of the harbor by the military authorities of the state, and the South Carolinians were with some difficulty restrained by the leaders in other Southern states from assaulting Fort Sumter. Thereafter Buchanan refrained from the use of force, partly because Anderson insisted that he was in no danger, partly because he still hoped for some peaceful adjustment, if not by Congress itself, then by the Peace Conference which was soon to assemble in Washington, and partly because he was averse during the last weeks of his term to beginning hostilities for which he was unprepared.

By February 1 six other cotton states had passed ordinances of secession and each of them, as a matter of precaution and largely because of the happenings at Charleston, seized the forts, arsenals, customs houses, and navy yards within its own borders. There were two exceptions, both in Florida. Fort Taylor, at Key West, was left undisturbed; and Fort Pickens, at the entrance of Pensacola Bay and on the extreme western tip of Santa Rosa Island, was occupied by a small Federal force much as Fort Sumter had been.

Since Fort Pickens plays a part in the development of the Sumter crisis, some explanation of the situation at that point becomes necessary. In the beginning this fort was not occupied by troops, but a company of artillery, under Lieutenant Adam J. Slemmer, was stationed at Barrancas Barracks, across the neck of the bay about a mile and a half to the north of Pickens, and close by the Navy Yard. The town of Pensacola was some six miles farther up the bay. On January 10 Lieutenant Slemmer, hearing that the governors of Florida and Alabama were about to send troops to seize the forts and the Navy Yard and in accordance with instructions from General Winfield Scott, removed his small command to Fort Pickens. On the twelfth the Navy Yard capitulated to the combined state forces under Colonel W. H. Chase. Chase then demanded the surrender of Fort Pickens, which Slemmer refused. After some further correspondence between the two opposing officers, a group of nine Southern senators in Washington, on January 18, urged that no attack should be made on Fort Pickens because it was "not worth a drop of blood." These senators believed that the Republicans in Congress were hoping to involve the Buchanan administration in hostilities in order that war might open before Lincoln's inauguration. On January 29 an agreement was effected at Washington by Senator Stephen R. Mallory of Florida, and others, with President Buchanan and his secretaries of War and the Navy to the effect that no reinforcement would be sent to Fort Pickens and no attack would be made upon it by the secessionists. The situation at Fort Pickens then became somewhat like that at Fort Sumter; but there were certain differences. Fort Pickens did not threaten the town of Pensacola as Fort Sumter did Charleston; it was easily accessible from the sea if reinforcements should be decided upon; and there was no such excitement over its continued occupation by United States troops as there was about Sumter.

As soon as the new Confederate government was organized the Confederate Congress, on February 12, by resolution took charge of "questions existing between the several States of this Confederacy and the United States respecting the occupation of forts, arsenals, navy yards and other pub-

lic establishments." This hurried action was taken in order to get the management of the Sumter question out of the hands of the impatient and rather headlong Governor Francis W. Pickens of South Carolina, who, it was feared, might precipitate war at any time. In fact, the public mind, North and South, sensed accurately that the greatest danger to peace lay in Charleston Harbor.

This danger, of course, was in the irreconcilable views of the two governments concerning their respective claims to the fort. To the Washington officials Sumter was not merely the legal property of the Federal government; its possession was a symbol of the continuity and integrity of that government. To withdraw the garrison at the demand of the secessionists would be equivalent to acknowledging the legality of secession and the dissolution of the Union. There was also, especially with the military officials, a point of honor involved; they could not yield to threats of force. The attitude of the Southerners was based upon equally imperative considerations. In their view the Confederate States no longer had any connection with the government on the Potomac; they were as independent as that other seceded nation, Belgium. No independent government could maintain its own self-respect or the respect of foreign governments if it permitted another to hold an armed fortress within the harbor of one of its principal cities. When South Carolina had ceded the site for the fortification it had done so for its own protection. That protection was now converted into a threat, for the guns of Sumter dominated not only every point in the harbor but the city of Charleston itself. We may conceive an analogous situation by supposing that Great Britain at the close of the American Revolution had insisted upon retaining a fortress within the harbor of Boston or of New York. The Confederate government could not, without yielding the principle of independence, abate its claims to the fort.

During the last six weeks of Buchanan's term the situation at Charleston remained relatively quiet. Anderson and his engineers did what they could to strengthen the defenses of Sumter; while the state and Confederate officers established batteries around the harbor both to repel any future relief expedition and, in case of open hostilities, to reduce the fort. Although Governor Pickens had wished to press demands for surrender and to attack the fort if refused, he had first sought the advice of such men as Governor Joseph E. Brown of Georgia and Jefferson Davis of Mississippi. Both advised against any such action, partly because they still had some hope of peace and partly because they saw the danger of taking the initiative. Although Anderson was under constant surveillance, he was allowed free use of the mails and was permitted to purchase for his men fresh meats and vegetables in the Charleston market. Other necessities, which under army regulations he must procure from the regular supply departments of the army, he was not allowed to receive because that would be permitting the Federal government to send relief to the garrison and involve an admission of its right to retain the fort. Anderson consistently informed the authorities at Washington during this time that he was safe and that he could hold out indefinitely. The Confederate government, having taken over from the state all negotiations concerning the fort, was moving cautiously with the evident hope of avoiding hostilities. On February 15 the Confederate Congress by resolution requested President Davis to appoint three commissioners to negotiate with the United States "all questions of disagreement between the two governments" and Davis appointed them on February 25. They reached Washington on March 5, the day after Lincoln's inauguration.

Southern as well as Northern men waited anxiously to learn what policy would be indicated by the new President of the United States in his inaugural address. It is not necessary to dwell long on what Abraham Lincoln said in that famous paper. He stated plainly that he regarded the Union as unbroken, the secession of the seven cotton states as a nullity. In this he merely took the position that Buchanan had taken. He also said that he would enforce the laws of the Union in all the states; but he immediately softened this declaration by saying that he would not use violence unless it should be forced upon the national authority. Then he added, "The power confided to me will be used to hold, occupy and possess the property and places belonging to the government, and to collect the duties and imposts; but beyond what may be necessary for these objects, there will be no invasion, no using of force against or among the people anywhere." And later on: "In your hands, my dissatisfied fellow countrymen, and not in mine, is the momentous issue of civil war. The government will not assail you. You can have no conflict without being yourselves the aggressors." How is it possible to reconcile the declaration that he would occupy "the property and places belonging to the government" with the promise that the government would not assail his dissatisfied fellow countrymen who either held or claimed the right to those places? While ostensibly addressing the Southerners, was he really directing these last soothing words to the anxious antiwar elements in the North? Although it is improbable that he had this early any definite plan in mind, his warning that the secessionists would be the aggressors, if civil war should come, may be significant in view of what he was to be engaged in exactly a month from that day.

But the inaugural should not be regarded as the declaration of a definite program; for while the new President was careful to lay down the general principle that the Union was legally unbroken, he refrained with equal care from committing himself to any course of action. If he hedged at every point where a statement of active policy was expected, it was because he could not know what he would be able to do. Caution was necessary; it was not merely political expediency, it was at that juncture political wisdom. Cautious reticence, until he knew his way was clear, was a very marked trait of Abraham Lincoln. There is another characteristic quality in this address. Lincoln had developed an extraordinary skill in so phrasing his public utterances as to arouse in each special group he singled out for attention just the reaction he desired. To the extreme and agressive Republicans the inaugural indicated a firm determination to enforce obedience upon the secessionists; to the Northern moderates and peace advocates, as well as to the anxious Unionists of the border slave states, not yet seceded, it promised a conciliatory attitude; in the seceded states it was interpreted as threatening coercion and had the effect of hastening preparations for defense.

In the latter part of the address Lincoln had counseled the people generally to avoid precipitate action and to take time to think calmly about the situation. He doubtless hoped to be able to take time himself; but he discovered within a few hours that there was one problem whose solution could not be long postponed. On the very day of his inauguration Buchanan's secretary of war, Joseph Holt, received a letter from Major Anderson in which for the first time the commander at

Fort Sumter expressed doubt of his ability to maintain himself. More than this, Anderson estimated that, in the face of the Confederate batteries erected about the harbor, it would require a powerful fleet and a force of twenty thousand men to give permanent relief to the garrison. Since it was his last day in office, Buchanan had the letter referred to Lincoln; and when on March 5 Holt submitted it to the new President he accompanied it with a report sharply reviewing Anderson's previous assurances of his safety. Lincoln called General Scott into conference and the General concurred with Anderson. After a few days of further consideration Scott was of the same opinion and was sustained by General Joseph G. Totten, chief of the Army Engineers. These men considered the question primarily as a military problem, although Scott could not refrain from injecting political considerations into his written statement. In doing this the aged General was suspected of following the lead of Secretary William H. Seward who was already urging the evacuation of Sumter, in order to avoid precipitating hostilities at that point, and the reinforcement of Fort Pickens in order to assert the authority of the government. Lincoln accepted at least a part of Seward's plan, for on March 12, General Scott, by the President's direction, sent an order to Captain Israel Vogdes, whose artillery company was on board the U.S. Steamer *Brooklyn,* lying off Fort Pickens, directing him to land his company, reinforce Pickens, and hold it. Instead of sending the order overland, Scott sent it around by sea with the result that it did not reach its destination until April 1, and then the navy captain in command of the ship on which the artillery company was quartered refused to land the troops because the orders from the former Secretary of the Navy directing him to respect the truce with the Confederates had never been countermanded. The fort was not reinforced at that time, a fact of which Lincoln remained ignorant until April 6. We shall return to the Fort Pickens situation later.

Meanwhile Lincoln was considering the Fort Sumter problem. He had learned that Anderson's supplies were running short and that the garrison could not hold out much longer without relief. Although both General Scott and General Totten had advised that the relief of the fort was impracticable with the forces available, Gustavus V. Fox, a former officer of the navy and a brother-in-law of Postmaster-General Montgomery Blair, believed that it would be possible to reach the fort by running small steamers past the Confederate batteries at the entrance to the harbor. Fox had first proposed this to Scott early in February; he now came forward again with the backing of Montgomery Blair and presented his plan and arguments to Lincoln on March 13. The President seems to have been impressed, for on March 15 he asked for the written opinions of his cabinet on the question whether, assuming that it was now possible to provision Sumter, it was wise to attempt it. All, save Montgomery Blair, advised against an expedition. Apparently this overwhelming majority of his cabinet at first decided him against the plans, for there is considerable evidence, although it is not conclusive, that he was about to order Anderson to evacuate. Certainly rumors of impending orders for evacuation were coming from various high official circles in Washington aside from those for which Seward seems to have been responsible. There is the familiar story of how old Frank Blair, brought to the White House by his son Montgomery, found the President about to sign the evacuation order and protested so vigorously that Lincoln did not sign it.

Lincoln now found himself facing a most difficult and dangerous situation and the more he considered it the more troublesome it appeared. It seems reasonably certain that he never wanted to give up Sumter. As early as December 24, 1860, having heard a wild rumor that the forts in South Carolina were to be surrendered by the order or consent of President Buchanan, he had written from Springfield to Senator Lyman Trumbull that he would, "if our friends at Washington concur, announce publicly at once that they are to be retaken after the inauguration." After he had arrived at Washington and had taken up the burden of office he saw that the problem was not so simple as it had looked from the frontier town of Springfield. His Secretary of State, a man of far greater political experience than himself, was urging him to make his stand for the authority of the government at Fort Pickens and not at Sumter, for Seward could not see how it would be possible to reinforce Sumter without putting the administration in the position of the aggressor. That would be a fatal mistake. Fort Pickens, on the other hand, could be relieved from the Gulf side without coming into direct conflict with the Confederates.

It would be extremely interesting to know what was passing through Lincoln's mind during those difficult days when, bedeviled by importunate office seekers, he could find little time for considering what he should do about the re-establishment of Federal authority in the seceded states and especially about the imperiled fort at Charleston. As was his habit, he left few clues to his reflections and it is impossible to say with assurance what ideas he picked up, examined, and discarded. One plan which he seems to have entertained for a short while, just after the adverse cabinet vote on relieving Sumter, contemplated the collection of customs duties on revenue vessels, supported by ships of war, just outside the Confederate ports; and there were hints in the press that Anderson's force was to be withdrawn to a ship off Charleston. If it were seriously considered, the plan was soon abandoned, possibly because of legal impediments or more probably because it did not fully meet the needs of the situation. But although Lincoln kept his thoughts to himself he must have studied public opinion closely, and we may be able to follow his thinking if we examine for ourselves the attitudes of the several groups in the North as they revealed themselves in those uncertain days of March.

It must not be forgotten that, notwithstanding Lincoln's smashing victory in the free states in November, his party was still new and relatively undisciplined. His support had come from a heterogeneous mass of voters and for a variety of reasons. The slavery issue, the drive for a protective tariff and internal improvements, the promise of free homesteads in the West, and disgust at the split among the Democrats had each played its part. Many voters had been persuaded that there was no real danger of a disruption of the Union in the event of his election. The secession of the border states had now thrown the former issues into the background and thrust to the front the question whether the discontented Southerners should be allowed to depart in peace or whether the government should, as Lincoln phrased it, "enforce the laws" and in so doing bring on war with the newly formed Confederacy. As always, when a new and perilous situation arises, the crosscurrents of public opinion were confusing. As Lincoln, pressed on all sides, waited while he studied the drift, he could not fail to note that there was a strong peace party in the North which was urging the settlement of difficulties without resort to force. On the other hand the more aggressive party men among the Republicans, to whom he was under special obligations, were insisting that he exert the full authority of the government even to the extent of war. This group included some of the most active and powerful members of his party whom he could not afford to antagonize. One disturbing factor in the situation was the marked tendency of many voters who had supported him in November to turn against the Republicans, as was shown in a number of local elections in Ohio and New England. While the peace men attributed this reversal to fear of war, the more aggressive Republicans insisted that it was caused by disgust at the rumors that Fort Sumter would be given up to the secessionists. Reinforcing the Northern conservatives were the majorities in the eight border slave states who had thus far refused to secede but who were openly opposed to any "coercive" action against their brethren in the Lower South. The Virginia State Convention, which had convened on February 13 and was in complete control of the conditional Unionists, was still in session, evidently awaiting his decision. Therefore, if he should adopt a strongly aggressive policy he might find himself opposed by the large group of peace men in the North while he precipitated most if not all of the border slave states into secession and union with the Confederacy. If, on the other hand, he failed to act decisively, he was very likely to alienate the radical Republicans who were already manifesting impatience. In either case he would divide his party at the very beginning of his administration and increase the risk of utter failure. There was, however, some cheering evidence among the business elements of a growing irritation against the secessionists because of the depression which had set in with the withdrawal of South Carolina; and if the Confederates should add further offense to their low tarriff policy or adopt more aggressive tactics with respect to the forts, this feeling might grow strong enough to overcome the peace men.

He had promised to maintain the Union, but how was he to attempt it without wrecking his chances at the very outset? It was now too late to restore the Union by compromise because, having himself rejected all overtures in December, he could not now afford to offer what he had recently refused. Moreover, there was no indication that the Confederates would accept at this late date any compromise he might proffer. He must do something, for the gradual exhaustion of the supplies of the garrison in Fort Sumter would soon force his hand. He could not order Anderson to evacuate without arousing the wrath of the militant Unionists in the North. If he continued to let matters drift, Anderson himself would have to evacuate when his supplies were gone. While that would relieve the administration of any charge of coercion, it would expose the government to the accusation of disgraceful weakness and improve the chances of the Confederacy for foreign recognition. If he left Anderson to his fate and made ostentatious display of reinforcing Fort Pickens, as Seward was urging him to do, would he gain as much as he lost? Was it not best, even necessary, to make his stand at Sumter? But if he should try to relieve Anderson by force of arms, what was the chance of success? Anderson, supported by the high authority of General Scott, thought there was none. If, as Captain Fox believed, swift steamers could run the gauntlet of the Confederate batteries and reach the fort with men and supplies, would they then be able to hold it against attack? Failure in this military movement might seriously damage the already uncertain prestige of the administration. Would it not be looked upon as aggressive war by the border state men and perhaps by the peace men in the North? Could he risk the handicap of appearing to force civil war upon the country? In every direction the way out of his dilemma seemed closed.

There was one remote possibility: the Confederates themselves might precipitate matters by attacking Sumter before Anderson should be compelled to evacuate by lack of supplies. But the Confederates, though watchful, were showing great caution. General P. G. T. Beauregard, in command at Charleston since March 6, was treating Major Anderson with elaborate courtesy. The government at Montgomery was in no hurry to force the issue, partly because it was quite well aware of the danger of assuming the aggressive and partly because it was waiting to see what its commissioners would be able to effect at Washington, where Seward was holding out hopes to them of the eventual evacuation of Sumter. At some time, while turning these things over in his mind, this daring thought must have occurred to Lincoln: Could the Southerners be *induced* to attack Sumter, to assume the aggressive and thus put themselves in the wrong in the eyes of the North and of the world? If they could, the latent irritation perceptible among the Northern moderates might flame out against the secessionists and in support of the government. The two wings of his party would unite, some at least of the Democrats would come to his support, even the border-state people might be held, if they could be convinced that the war was being forced by the secessionists. Unless he could unite them in defense of the authority of the government, the peaceable and the "stiff-backed" Republicans would split apart, the party would collapse, his administration would be a failure, and he would go down in history as a weak man who had allowed the Union to crumble in his hands. As things now stood, the only way by which the Union could be restored, his party and his administration saved, was by an unequivocal assertion of the authority of the government, that is, through war. But he must not openly assume the aggressive; that must be done by the secessionists. The best opportunity was at Fort Sumter, but the time left was short for Anderson was running short of essential supplies.

Let us examine closely what Lincoln did after the middle of March, taking care to place each movement as nearly as possible in its exact sequence. We have seen that Captain Fox made his argument to Lincoln for a combined naval and military expedition on March 13 and that the cabinet, with the exception of Montgomery Blair and the equivocal Chase, had voted against it on the fifteenth. Fox then offered to go in person to Fort Sumter to investigate the situation and Lincoln gave him permission. He arrived in Charleston on March 21 and was allowed to see Anderson that night. He and Anderson agreed that the garrison could not hold out longer than noon of April 15. Although Anderson seems to have remained unconvinced of its feasibility, Fox returned to Washington full of enthusiasm for his plan.

On the very day that Fox arrived in Charleston, Lincoln had dispatched to that city a close friend and loyal supporter, Ward H. Lamon, a native of Virginia and his former law partner in Illinois. This sending of Lamon on the heels of Fox is an interesting incident. The precise nature of his instructions has never been fully revealed. Lamon himself, in his *Recollections,* merely says he was sent "on a confidential mission" and intimates that he was to report on the extent of Unionist feeling in South Carolina. He arrived in Charleston on the night of Saturday, March 23; visited James L. Petigru, the famous Unionist, on Sunday and learned from him that there was no Unionist strength in the state, that "peaceable secession or war was inevitable"; and on Monday morning obtained an interview with Governor Pickens. In reply to questions the Governor stated very positively that any attempt on the part of President Lincoln to reinforce Sumter would bring on war, that only his "unalterable resolve *not* to attempt any reinforcement" could prevent war. Lamon, whether through innocence or guile, left the impression with the Governor, and also with Anderson whom he was permitted to visit, that the garrison would soon be withdrawn and that his trip was merely to prepare the way for that event. He left Charleston on the night of the twenty-fifth, arrived in Washington on the twenty-seventh, and reported to Lincoln what he had learned. What had he been sent to Charleston to do? There must have been some purpose and it could hardly have been to prepare the way for Anderson's evacuation. Does it strain the evidence to suggest that it was chiefly to find out at first hand how strong was the Southern feeling about relief for Fort Sumter and that this purpose was camouflaged by the vague intimations of evacuation? But it is quite probable that Lamon himself did not understand the real purpose, for it is altogether unlikely that the cautious Lincoln would have divulged so important a secret to his bibulous and impulsive young friend. But if there was such an ulterior purpose, Lincoln now had the information directly from Charleston that any sort of relief would result in an attack upon the fort.

According to Gideon Welles, whose account of these events was written several years later, Lincoln sometime in the latter half of March had informed the members of his cabinet that he would send relief to Sumter. During a cabinet meeting on March 29 (two days after Lamon's return), when the matter was again discussed, Lincoln, at the suggestion of Attorney General Edward Bates, again requested each member to give his opinion in writing on the question of relieving Sumter. Whether Lincoln's known determination, political pressure, or some other influence had effected it, there was a marked change from the advance given just two weeks earlier. Now only Seward and Caleb Smith were for evacuating Sumter, but they both wished to reinforce Fort Pickens. Bates proposed to strengthen Pickens and Key West and said that the time had come either to evacuate Sumter or relieve it. The rest were unequivocally for a relief expedition. Later that day Lincoln directed the secretaries of War and the Navy to co-operate in preparing an expedition to move by sea as early as April 6. The destination was not indicated in the order, but it was Charleston.

On the same day Seward, intent upon the reinforcement of Fort Pickens, brought Captain M. C. Meigs of the Engineers to Lincoln to discuss an expedition to that place. On March 31 Meigs and Colonel Erasmus D. Keyes, of General Scott's staff, were directed to draw up a plan for the relief of Fort Pickens. They took it to Lincoln who had them take it to Scott to be put into final form and executed. On the next day, April 1, Seward, Meigs, and Lieutenant D. D. Porter of the navy went to the Executive Mansion and after consultation with Lincoln finished the plans for the Pickens expedition. It was to be conducted with such absolute secrecy, lest information leak out to the Confederates, that even the secretaries of War and the Navy were to know

nothing of it. The orders were signed by the President himself. It was only because the same ship, the *Powhatan,* was selected for both expeditions that the Secretary of the Navy learned of the expedition to the Gulf of Mexico. Energetic preparations began in New York and Brooklyn to collect vessels, men, arms, and provisions for the two expeditions.

In the first days of April came the disquieting returns from the elections in Ohio, Connecticut, and Rhode Island. April 4 proved to be an important day. Early that morning Lincoln seems to have had a mysterious conference with a group of Republican governors, said to be seven or nine in number. Among them were Andrew G. Curtin of Pennsylvania, William Dennison of Ohio, Richard Yates of Illinois, Oliver P. Morton of Indiana, Israel Washburn of Maine, and Austin Blair of Michigan. How did all these governors happen to be in Washington at the same time? The newspapers, in so far as they noticed the presence of these gentlemen, assumed that they were looking after patronage; but rumors were soon current that they had gone to demand of the President that he send relief to the garrison at Fort Sumter. This is not improbable since all these men belonged to the aggressive group of Republicans who had been alarmed at the rumors of evacuation and they could hardly have known what Lincoln had already planned. Several questions arise here. If Lincoln was still hesitating, did they bring pressure upon him and force him to a decision? Or did Lincoln allow them to think they were helping him to decide? Or, if the President had not actually summoned them to a conference, did he seize the opportunity to make sure of their powerful support in case the Confederates should show fight? Were mutual pledges of action and support exchanged that morning?

Later that same morning occurred the much-discussed Lincoln-Baldwin interview. On April 2, apparently at the suggestion of Seward, Lincoln had sent Allan B. Magruder, a Virginia Unionist living in Washington, to Richmond to ask G. W. Summers, the leader of the Unionists in the State Convention, to come to see him at once or to send some other representative from that group. Magruder reached Richmond the next day. As Summers could not leave, John B. Baldwin, another leader of the group, was selected; and Baldwin and Magruder were in Washington early on the morning of April 4. They went to Seward who conducted Baldwin to Lincoln at eleven o'clock. Lincoln took Baldwin alone into a bedroom, locked the door and exclaimed "You have come too late!" In the conversation which followed, according to Baldwin's statement, the President asked why the Unionists in the Virginia Convention did not adjourn sine die, as the continuance of the session was a standing menace to him. Baldwin replied that if they should so adjourn without having accomplished anything for the security of the state, another convention would certainly be called and it would be more strongly secessionist. He then urged the President to assure peace to the country and strengthen the border-state Unionists by evacuating both Sumter and Pickens and calling upon the whole people to settle their differences in a national convention. Lincoln replied that his supporters would not permit him to withdraw the garrisons. Baldwin then warned him that if a fight started at Fort Sumter, no matter who started it, war would follow and Virginia would go out of the Union in forty-eight hours. Lincoln became greatly excited and exclaimed, "Why was I not told this a week ago? You have come too late!" This is Baldwin's account, but it is substantiated by several other Virginia Unionists, at least to the extent that it was what Baldwin told them when he returned to Richmond the next day.

But John Minor Botts, a violent Virginia Unionist who by invitation talked with Lincoln on the night of April 7, insisted that Lincoln then told him that he had offered to Baldwin to withdraw Anderson's force from Sumter if the Virginia Convention would adjourn sine die, that he would gladly swap a fort for a state; but that Baldwin refused the offer. When Botts offered to take the proposition to Richmond at once Lincoln replied, "Oh, it is too late; the fleet has sailed and I have no means of communicating with it."

Baldwin always denied that Lincoln had made any such proposal as Botts reported. Did Baldwin lie? He seems to have had a much better reputation for accuracy than Botts and his account of his journey to Washington is accurate as far as it can be checked, whereas Botts' story is full of minor inaccuracies. Besides, Baldwin was a sincere Unionist and voted against secession to the last. Why should he have refused Lincoln's offer and failed to report it to his fellow Unionists in Richmond? Did Botts lie about what Lincoln told him? His extreme prejudices and frequently unwarranted statements on other matters would easily bring this conclusion into the range of possibility, were it not for the fact that Lincoln seems to have told much the same story to others. If Lincoln did, then the question whether the President offered to evacuate Sumter at this stage of his plan becomes an issue of veracity between Lincoln and Baldwin, which obviously places the Virginian at a great disadvantage. But let us consider other factors in the situation. Lincoln had just been holding conferences with the militant Republican governors and evidently had come to some agreement with them, else why should he greet his visitor with the exclamation, repeated later in the conversation, "You have come too late"? Certainly he could not have referred to the final orders to Fox, for those orders were given later that day. And why did he refuse on the night of April 7, if the Botts story is correct, to permit Botts to take his proposition to Richmond, alleging that the fleet had sailed, when in fact none of the vessels left New York until the next night? Is there not some basis for suspecting that Lincoln had not actually made the offer to Baldwin to evacuate Sumter because he was already bound by some sort of agreement with the Republican governors to send the expedition forward; and that later, desiring above all things to leave the impression that he had done everything in his power to avoid a collision, he dropped hints about an offer which had been flatly refused?

During the afternoon of April 4 Lincoln saw Captain Fox, who was to have charge of the Sumter expedition, and told him of his final determination to send relief to Anderson and that notification of the relief expedition would be sent to the Governor of South Carolina before Fox could possibly arrive off Charleston Harbor. Fox hurried back to New York to push his preparations. At some time that same day Lincoln drafted a letter to Major Anderson, which was copied and signed by the Secretary of War, informing him that relief would be sent him.

On the afternoon of April 6 Secretary Welles received a letter from Captain Henry A. Adams of the navy, stationed off Fort Pickens, explaining that he had not landed the artillery company at the fort in accordance with General Scott's order of March 12 because of controlling orders from the former Secretary of the

Navy to respect the truce of February 29, but stating that he was now ready to obey if ordered to land the men. Welles consulted the President and then hurried off Lieutenant John L. Worden with verbal orders to Captain Adams to land the men at once. This incident gave occasion for a strange statement of Lincoln which deserves notice. In his special message to Congress of July 4, he stated that the expedition for the relief of Sumter was first prepared "to be ultimately used or not according to circumstances," and intimated that, if Pickens had been relieved in March, Sumter would have been evacuated, and that it had not been decided to use the expedition until word came that Fort Pickens had not been reinforced in accordance with the order of March 12. The strange thing about this statement is that word was not received from Adams until April 6, while positive orders had been given two days before to Captain Fox to go ahead with his expedition and at the same time Anderson had been notified to expect it. Had Lincoln become confused about the order of these events? It does not seem probable. Or was he, for effect upon public opinion, trying to strengthen the belief that his hand had been forced, that his pacific intentions had been defeated by circumstances?

On April 1 Lincoln had passed the promise through Seward and Justice John A. Campbell to the Confederate Commissioners in Washington that he would notify Governor Pickens if any relief expedition should be sent to Fort Sumter. When they learned of it, several members of his cabinet objected to such notification, but Lincoln insisted; he had his own reasons for so doing. The formal notice which he drafted with his own hand, dated April 6, is interesting not only for its careful phrasing but for the evident importance which he attached to it. It was embodied in a letter of instruction to R. S. Chew, an official of the state department who was to be accompanied by Captain Theodore Talbot, directing him to proceed to Charleston where, if he found that Fort Sumter had not been evacuated or attacked and that the flag was still over it, he was to seek an interview with Governor Pickens, read to him the statement and give him a copy of it. If he found the fort evacuated or attacked he was to seek no interview but was to return forthwith. The message to Governor Pickens was in these words:

I am directed by the President of the United States to notify you to expect an attempt will be made to supply Fort Sumter with provisions only; and that, if such an attempt be not resisted, no effort to throw in men, arms, or ammunition will be made without further notice, or in case of an attack upon the fort.

Was the purpose of this message merely to fulfill a promise? Is there not special significance in the fact that Lincoln entrusted the form of it to no one else, but carefully drafted it himself? It is unnecessary to call attention again to the fact that Lincoln was a rare master of the written word, that he had the skill of an artist in so phrasing a sentence that it conveyed precisely the meaning he wished it to convey. He could do more than that: he could make the same sentence say one thing to one person and something entirely different to another and in each case carry the meaning he intended. It is obvious that the message to be read to Governor Pickens was intended less for that official than for General Beauregard and the Confederate government at Montgomery. But it was intended also for the people of the North and of the border states. To the suspicious and apprehensive Confederates it did not merely give information

that provisions would be sent to Anderson's garrison—which should be enough to bring about an attempt to take the fort—but it carried a threat that force would be used if the provisions were not allowed to be brought in. It was a direct challenge! How were the Southerners expected to react to this challenge? To Northern readers the same words meant only that the government was taking food to hungry men to whom it was under special obligation. Northern men would see no threat; they would understand only that their government did not propose to use force if it could be avoided. Is it possible that a man of Lincoln's known perspicacity could be blind to the different interpretations which would be placed upon his subtle words in the North and in the South?

The message was not only skillfully phrased, it was most carefully timed. It was read to Governor Pickens in the presence of General Beauregard on the evening of April 8. News of the preparation of some large expedition had been in the newspapers for a week; but as the destination had not been officially divulged, newspaper reporters and correspondents had guessed at many places, chiefly the coast of Texas and revolutionary Santo Domingo. It was not until April 8 that the guessing veered toward Charleston, and not until the next day was any positive information given in the press of the notice to Governor Pickens. The Confederate officials had regarded these preparations at New York with suspicion while conflicting reports came to them from Washington concerning Lincoln's designs about Sumter. The first of Captain Fox's vessels were leaving New York Harbor at the very hour that Chew read the notification to Governor Pickens. The Confederates were given ample time, therefore, to act before the fleet could arrive off Charleston. They did not know that a portion of the vessels which had left New York were really destined not for Charleston but for Fort Pickens at Pensacola. The utmost secrecy was maintained about the Pensacola expedition, thus permitting the Confederates to believe that the whole force was to be concentrated at Charleston.

The tables were now completely turned on the Southerners. Lincoln was well out of his dilemma while they, who had heretofore had the tactical advantage of being able to wait until Anderson must evacuate, were suddenly faced with a choice of two evils. They must either take the fort before relief could arrive, thus taking the apparent offensive which they had hoped to avoid, or they must stand by quietly and see the fort provisioned. But to allow the provisioning meant not only an indefinite postponement to their possession of the fort which had become as much a symbol to them as it was to Lincoln; to permit it in the face of the threat of force, after all their preparations, would be to make a ridiculous and disgraceful retreat. Nor could they be sure that, if they yielded now in the matter of "provisions only," they would not soon be served with the "further notice" as a prelude to throwing in "men, arms, and ammunition." This, then, was the dilemma which they faced as the result of Lincoln's astute strategy.

Events now hurried to the inevitable climax. As soon as President Lincoln's communication was received General Beauregard telegraphed the news to the Confederate secretary of war, L. P. Walker. Walker at once ordered that the Sumter garrison be isolated by stopping its mails and the purchase of provisions in Charleston. On this same day the Confederate commissioners at Washington had received a copy of a memorandum filed in the state department by Seward, dated March 15, in which the Secretary declined to hold any official intercourse with them. They telegraphed the news to their government and at once, feeling that they had been deceived and knowing that their mission had failed, prepared to leave Washington. Jefferson Davis was thus, on April 8, apprised of two movements by the Federal government which, taken together or singly, looked ominous. On the following day Beauregard seized the mails as they came from Fort Sumter and discovered a letter from Anderson to the war department which disclosed that he had been informed of the coming of Fox's expedition and indicated that the fleet would attempt to force its way into the harbor. This information also was at once communicated to the Montogomery government. On the tenth came the news that the fleet had sailed from New York. Walker then directed Beauregard, if he thought there was no doubt of the authorized character of the notification from Washington (meaning Lincoln's), to demand the evacuation of Fort Sumter and, if it should be refused, "to reduce" the fort. The Davis administration had waited two full days after receiving word of Lincoln's notification before deciding what to do. It is said that Robert Toombs, secretary of state, objected vigorously to attacking the fort. "It is unnecessary; it puts us in the wrong; it is fatal!" If Toombs protested, he was overruled because Davis and the rest believed that Lincoln had already taken the aggressive and they regarded their problem now as a military one. To them it was the simple question whether they should permit the hostile fleet to arrive before they attacked the fort or whether they should take Sumter before they had to fight both fort and fleet.

At two o'clock on the eleventh Beauregard made the demand upon Anderson, who rejected it but added verbally to the officer sent to him that if not battered to pieces, he would be starved out in a few days. When Beauregard reported this remark to Walker, that official informed him that the government did "not desire needlessly to bombard Fort Sumter" and that if Major Anderson would state when he would evacuate, Beauregard should "avoid the effusion of blood." Evidently the Montgomery officials thought there was still a chance to get the fort peaceably before the fleet could arrive. Had not Lincoln so carefully timed his message with the movement of Fox there might have been no attack. But late in the afternoon of the same day Beauregard received information from a scout boat that the *Harriet Lane,* one of Fox's ships, had been sighted a few miles out of the harbor. It was expected that all the fleet would be at hand by next day. Nevertheless, Beauregard about midnight sent a second message to Anderson, in accordance with Walker's instructions, saying that if he would state the time at which he would evacuate and would agree not to use "your guns against us unless ours should be employed against Fort Sumter, we will abstain from opening fire upon you." To this Anderson replied that he would evacuate by noon on the fifteenth and would in the meantime not open fire upon Beauregard's forces unless compelled to do so by some hostile act "against this fort or the flag it bears, should I not receive prior to that time controlling instructions from my government or additional supplies." This answer was conditional and unsatisfactory for it was clear that, with Fox's fleet arriving, Anderson would not evacuate. Thereupon the two aides who had carried Beauregard's message, in accordance with their instructions from that

officer, formally notified Anderson—it was now 3:20 in the morning of the twelfth—that fire would be opened upon him in one hour's time.

What followed we all know. The bombardment which began at 4:30 on the morning of April 12 ended in the surrender of Anderson and his garrison during the afternoon of the following day. The three vessels of the fleet which lay outside were unable to get into the harbor because of the high seas and the failure of the rest of the fleet—the tugboats and the *Powhatan*—to arrive. Although there were no casualties during the bombardment, the mere news that the attack on the fort had begun swept the entire North into a roaring flame of anger. The "rebels" had fired the first shot; they had chosen to begin war. If there had been any doubt earlier whether the mass of the Northern people would support the administration in suppressing the secessionists, there was none now. Lincoln's strategy had been completely successful. He seized at once the psychological moment for calling out the militia and committing the North to support of the war. This action cost him four of the border slave states, but he had probably already discounted that loss.

Perhaps the facts thus far enumerated, standing alone, could hardly be conclusive evidence that Lincoln, having decided that there was not other way than war for the salvation of his administration, his party, and the Union, maneuvered the Confederates into firing the first shot in order that they, rather than he, should take the blame of beginning bloodshed. Though subject to that interpretation, they are also subject to the one which he built up so carefully. Is there other evidence? No one, surely, would expect to find in any written word of his a confession of the stratagem; for to acknowledge it openly would have been to destroy the very effect he had been at so much pains to produce. There are, it is true, two statements by him to Captain Fox which are at least suggestive. Fox relates that in their conference of April 4 the President told him that he had decided to let the expedition go and that a messenger would be sent to the authorities at Charleston before Fox could possibly get there; and when the Captain reminded the President of the short time in which he must organize the expedition and reach the destined point, Lincoln replied, "You will best fulfill your duty to your country by making the attempt." Then, again, in the letter which Lincoln wrote the chagrined Captain on May 1 to console him for the failure of the fleet to enter Charleston Harbor, he said: "You and I both anticipated that the cause of the country would be advanced by making the attempt to provision Fort Sumter, even if it should fail; and it is no small consolation now to feel that our anticipation is justified by the result." Was this statement merely intended to soothe a disappointed commander, or did it contain a hint that the real objective of the expedition was not at all the relief of Sumter?

Lincoln's two secretaries, John G. Nicolay and John Hay, in their long but not impartial account of the Sumter affair come so close to divulging the essence of the stratagem that one cannot but suspect that they knew of it. In one place they say, with reference to Lincoln's solution of this problem of Sumter, "Abstractly it was enough that the Government was in the right. But to make the issue sure, he determined that in addition the rebellion should be put in the wrong." And again, "President Lincoln in deciding the Sumter question had adopted a simple but effective policy. To use his own words, he

determined to 'send bread to Anderson'; if the rebels fired on that, they would not be able to convince the world that he had begun the civil war." And still later, "When he finally gave the order that the fleet should sail he was master of the situation . . . master if the rebels hesitated or repented, because they would thereby forfeit their prestige with the South; master if they persisted, for he would then command a united North."

Perhaps not much weight should be given to the fact that before the expedition reached Charleston his political opponents in the North expressed suspicion of a design to force civil war upon the country in order to save the Republican party from the disasters threatened in the recent elections and that after the fighting began they roundly accused him of having deliberately provoked it by his demonstration against Charleston. And perhaps there is no significance in the further fact that the more aggressive members of his own party had demanded action to save the party and that the administration newspapers began to assert as soon as the fleet sailed that, if war came, the rebels would be the aggressors.

There is evidence much more to the point than any of these things. Stephen A. Douglas, senator from Illinois, died on June 3, 1861. On June 12 the Republican governor of that state, Richard Yates, appointed to the vacancy Orville H. Browning, a prominent lawyer, a former Whig, then an ardent Republican, and for more than twenty years a personal friend of Abraham Lincoln. Browning was one of the group who from the first had favored vigorous measures and had opposed compromise. He was to become the spokesman of the administration in the Senate. On July 2, 1861, Browning arrived in Washington to take his seat in the Senate for the special session which had been called to meet on July 4. On the evening of the third he called at the White House to see his old acquaintance. Now Browning for many years had kept a diary, a fact that very probably was unknown to Lincoln since diarists usually conceal this pleasant and useful vice. In the entry for July 3 Browning relates the conversation he had with the President that evening, for after reading the new Senator his special message to Congress, Lincoln laid aside the document and talked. The rest of the entry had best be given in Browning's own words:

He told me that the very first thing placed in his hands after his inauguration was a letter from Majr Anderson announcing the impossibility of defending or relieving Sumter. That he called the cabinet together and consulted Genl Scott—that Scott concurred with Anderson, and the cabinet, with the exception of P M Genl Blair were for evacuating the Fort, and all the troubles and anxieties of his life had not equalled those which intervened between this time and the fall of Sumter. He himself conceived the idea, and proposed sending supplies, without an attempt to reinforce giving notice of the fact to Gov Pickens of S.C. The plan succeeded. They attacked Sumter—it fell, and thus, did more service than it otherwise could.

This statement, condensed from the words of Lincoln himself by a close friend who wrote them down when he returned that night to his room at "Mrs. Carter's on Capitol Hill," needs no elaboration. It completes the evidence.

It is not difficult to understand how the usually secretive Lincoln, so long surrounded by strangers and criticized by many whom he had expected to be helpful, talking that night for the first time in many months to an old, loyal, and discreet friend, though a friend who had often been somewhat patronizing, for once forgot to be reticent. It must have been an emotional relief to him, with his pride over his consummate strategy bottled up within him for so long, to be able to impress his friends Browning with his success in meeting a perplexing and dangerous situation. He did not suspect that Browning would set it down in a diary.

There is little more to be said. Some of us will be content to find new reason for admiration of Abraham Lincoln in reflecting on this bit of masterful strategy at the very beginning of his long struggle for the preservation of the Union. Some, perhaps, will be reminded of the famous incident of the Ems telegram of which the cynical Bismarck boasted in his memoirs. And some will wonder whether the sense of responsibility for the actual beginning of a frightful war, far more terrible than he could possibly have foreseen in that early April of 1861, may have deepened the melancholy and the charity toward his Southern foemen which that strange man in the White House was to reveal so often before that final tragic April of 1865.

Unlike Ramsdell, the distinguished Lincoln scholar DAVID M. POTTER (1910–   ), who was born in Georgia and has taught in the South, at Yale, and at Stanford University, absolves the President from the charge of having provoked the Confederacy. In the following excerpts from the preface to the 1962 edition of his book, originally published in 1942, he reaffirms his conviction that Lincoln sought to preserve peace rather than to provoke war when he ordered the expedition for the relief of the beleaguered fort. How does Potter refute Ramsdell? Does his argument exculpate the President?*

David M. Potter

Lincoln's Peaceful Intentions

Along with the debate as to what policy ought to have been adopted in 1861, there is also a disagreement as to what policy actually was adopted, for there has been a spirited dispute concerning the real intent of the Lincoln administration. This brings me to the second controversial aspect of my study. My narrative emphasized the idea that Lincoln wanted peace and believed until the last moment that he might be able to preserve it. Many very able historians, like Bruce Catton, David Donald, and Allan Nevins, hold a similar view, but there are other scholars whose work must be taken very seriously who deny that Lincoln wanted peace or, if not that he wanted it, that he either expected it or thought it practicable to seek.

When I wrote in 1942, the chief exponent of this view was the late Professor Charles W. Ramsdell. Ramsdell, a Texan and a man of Southern sympathies, took a fairly clear-cut position. Lincoln, he said, was in a dilemma from which he perceived that he could escape if the Southerners "could . . . be *induced* [his italics] to attack Sumter." Therefore Lincoln deliberately "maneuvered the Confederates into firing the first shot." He adopted a "stratagem," and when Sumter was fired upon he knew that his "strategy had been completely successful." Ramsdell compared Lincoln's handling of the Sumter situation to Bismarck's handling of the Ems telegram. . . .

A few years after Ramsdell's paper,

*David M. Potter, *Lincoln and His Party in the Secession Crisis* 2d ed., (New Haven: Yale University Press, 1962), pp. xxiii–xxxii. (Footnotes omitted). Reprinted by permission of Yale University Press.

Kenneth M. Stampp published another interpretation of Lincoln's policy, which was formulated in his paper entitled "Lincoln and the Strategy of Defense in 1861" and in his book *And the War Came. . . .* Stampp's argument was a subtle and balanced one, less easy to summarize than Ramsdell's, but he seemed to say first that, without really wanting war, Lincoln *expected war*—he saw it was on the way, and he prepared not to be caught at a disadvantage by its coming; and second, that without actually *inducing* (Ramsdell's word) the Confederates to start a war, Lincoln took a position to which he foresaw the Confederates would react by starting a war. In Stampp's opinion, Lincoln was quite satisfied with the outcome. Both writers spoke of Lincoln's action as a "maneuver," and Stampp spoke distinctly of Lincoln's "coercionist views," and of his policy as one of "casting coercion in the mold of defense." According to Stampp, Lincoln saw the possibilities in the situation where "the Union government could easily pretend to forego aggressive action and simulate a defensive pose."

It would be a neat question to determine wherein Ramsdell and Stampp agreed, and wherein they disagreed. Certainly Ramsdell laid emphasis upon the thought that Lincoln actually desired war, while Stampp stressed the thought that he accepted it as something that could not be averted and must be handled in an advantageous way. Also, Ramsdell pictured him as scheming to provoke the Confederates to attack, while Stampp portrays him rather as taking a position which he shrewdly foresaw that they would attack. But these differences sometimes blur at the edges, and to some extent both writers are saying the same things: Lincoln concluded that he could only save the Union by means of war; he perceived that it would be greatly to his advantage if the

adversary did the first shooting; he therefore worked out a policy at Fort Sumter which he clearly foresaw would result in an initiation of hostilities by the Confederates; his claims of a peaceful intent merely to provision the fort were disingenuous; and when war came, he was well satisfied with the result.

The most substantial difference between Ramsdell and Stampp clearly turns not upon what they think Lincoln was doing but upon how they feel about what they think he was doing. Ramsdell, with his Southern sympathies, was shocked and disapproving. Stampp, on the contrary, with solidly Northern sympathies, says in effect that the War was worth what it cost, that it had to be, and that Lincoln is to be admired for putting his adversaries in the wrong and for facing up to the situation without shirking it.

Professor Stampp is a most resourceful scholar, and so is Richard N. Current, who has to some extent associated himself with Stampp's position. They make an impressive presentation. For instance, Stampp adduces a very strong argument that Lincoln must have known that war was likely to result from sending provisions to Sumter. He knew that the Confederates had fired on the *Star of the West* when it brought provisions; members of the cabinet told him plainly that the sending of provisions would result in war; and, as Current emphasizes, his special emissary to Charleston, Stephen A. Hurlbut, reported to him on March 17 that any attempt to send provisions would result in war.

It is certainly true, as Stampp and Current contend, that Lincoln must have seen the likelihood of war, and that his thought must have reckoned with that contingency. I now believe that I should have recognized this fact more clearly and explicitly than I did, and if I were rewriting my account now, I would do so. But for reasons which I will indicate further on, it seems to me that, whatever other effects his recognition of the increasing likelihood of war may have had upon Lincoln, it did not cause him to deviate a single step from a course of action which can be precisely defined. This course was to avoid any menacing action or any action which might precipitate a clash, just as far as was possible consistently with maintaining the principle of Union. As I have argued at some length, ... Lincoln pointedly refrained from the exercise of all the customary forms of federal authority in the seceded states, any of which he would have been perfectly justified in asserting.

Not all of Stampp's and Current's arguments seem to me as convincing as their demonstration that Lincoln must have realized the increasing likelihood of war. For instance, they have made very detailed computations to discredit Lincoln's statement in his message to Congress in July 1861 that he had decided upon sending the final expedition to Fort Sumter only after his attempt to reinforce Fort Pickens had failed. He stated that he had wanted to demonstrate, by the reinforcement of Pickens, "a clear indication of policy," and that if he had been able to do this it would have "better enable[d] the country to accept the evacuation of Fort Sumter as a military necessity." Stampp's analysis emphasizes, quite correctly, that Lincoln had certainly ordered the Sumter expedition prepared before he learned that the reinforcement of Pickens had miscarried. It also emphasizes the even more important points that Lincoln had actually gone to the length of ordering the expedition to move, and of sending word to Major Anderson that it would move. But it is crucial that the evidence still indicates that Lincoln did not inform the

Governor of South Carolina that the Sumter expedition would be sent until exactly the time when news reached Washington that the orders of March 11 for the reinforcing of Pickens had not been carried out. This news left Pensacola on April 1 and arrived at Washington on April 6, the same day on which Lincoln's message to the Governor of South Carolina was sent. The labored nature of Stampp's and Current's arguments on this point makes it all the more striking that they have found the essential point unassailable: the one irrevocable step, the message to the Governor, was taken on the very day when news arrived of the failure to reinforce Pickens. The first ships of the Sumter expedition did not leave port until two days later.

The assertions, therefore, that Lincoln's later statement about this matter is "scarcely consistent with the known facts" and that "the President had dealt with Sumter and Pickens as separate problems" seem to me arbitrary and insufficiently proved. Also it seems unsatisfactory to say that Lincoln did not need to wait for news of the reinforcement of Pickens, since he "had no reason to doubt that his order would be executed." In fact, his order instructed Union troops to occupy a position which he knew that Confederate forces might try to prevent them from occupying, and he had very real reason to await the result with anxiety. And, of course, his order was not executed, though the Fort was later reinforced.

Another case in point is the question of Lincoln's offer to the Virginians to evacuate Fort Sumter if they would adjourn the Virginia Convention. Historians have fallen into an endless dispute over the insoluble question whether Lincoln made such an offer to John B. Baldwin. But this focus upon Baldwin is unfortunate, for the testimony of Governor Morehead of Kentucky and of John Hay, reporting the statement of Lincoln himself, has long given evidence that Lincoln did propose to the Border State men terms on which he would abandon the Fort. . . . Since the opening of the Lincoln Papers, new evidence in the form of a letter from George Plumer Smith to John Hay on January 9, 1863, asking Hay to secure Lincoln's confirmation of the fact that Lincoln had told him (Smith) of the offer to Baldwin, and a reply from Hay to Smith on January 10 giving this confirmation, tend to corroborate this further. Professor Stampp deals with this evidence by doubting that Lincoln "seriously expected the Virginians to accept the offer," and Professor Current by saying that "these letters, it seems to me, by no means settle the controversy as to whether Lincoln actually made an offer to give up the fort."

There is certainly a substantial amount of evidence, whether it is conclusive or not, both in general terms and in specific terms, that Lincoln thought, until very late in the crisis, if not until the end, that he could achieve both peace and Union and would not have to choose between them. In this connection it is important to remember how consistently the Republicans had ridiculed all threats of secession, and how much they were the captives of their own mental set when secession came. In the light of this mental set, it is not really necessary to attribute such adroit hidden purposes as Stampp attributes to Lincoln in explaining his statement that "there is no crisis but an artificial one."

It is also important to remember that in some respects the secession movement, as of March 1861, had failed and that Seward, at least, regarded it as a failure. Eight slave states were still in the Union; only seven had seceded. The secessionists had been beaten in Virginia, North Caro-

lina, Tennessee, Arkansas, and Missouri, and the efforts to create a united South had divided the South as never before.

Another point which it is essential to keep in view if Lincoln's thinking is to be understood is that the President-elect made all his calculations, until March 5, on the assumption that Major Anderson's position at Fort Sumter was secure and that the existing status could continue for some time without any positive action on the part of the new administration. Not until March 5 did Secretary Holt and General Scott confront him with the news that a decision would have to be made at once either to abandon Fort Sumter or to take positive action for the support of the Fort.

Without being repetitious about evidence which is discussed more fully in the main body of this work, I would argue also that there are several items of evidence which indicate that Lincoln did quite seriously consider the evacuation of Fort Sumter. For instance: the fact that he made overtures to the Virginians about this possibility; the fact that Seward expected evacuation with enough confidence to make promises to the Confederates, based upon the expectation; the fact that Trumbull feared evacuation enough to introduce monitory resolutions in the Senate reminding the new head of the Republican party of his duty "to hold and protect the public property." Could these things have happened if the idea of evacuation had not seemed very much a reality?

The dispute concerning evidence, however, could go on endlessly for two reasons. First, because there were large factors working toward war and large factors working for peace, and both left a substantial residue of evidence. Thus one can marshal extensive material to show the magnitude of the demands upon Lincoln to hold Sumter or the extent of the pressure upon him to evacuate the Fort. Applying this ambivalence to Lincoln's own situation, one can legitimately stress his seeming expectation in March that he would abandon Sumter, or one can with equal validity emphasize the deep reluctance with which he arrived at this expectation. The historian can show that many of Lincoln's contemporaries regarded the first inaugural address as a threat of coercion, or he can show that many others thought it was too mild and was a promise of peace. That this disagreement continues is evident from the fact that, in our own time, Stampp sees it primarily as a statement "in which he [Lincoln] took such enormous pains to absolve himself from the charge of aggression," while Allan Nevins sees it as "one long plea for patience, forebearance, and the avoidance of rash action," and Roy F. Nichols calls it "a stirring plea to avoid hostilities."

A second reason that the review of evidence can never be conclusive is that the dispute turns not only upon what Lincoln did but upon what he thought. In other words, it is a question of motive as well as of action. Motive lies to a considerable extent beyond historical proof, partly because historical judgments must depend upon acts, and the same act may be performed with diverse motives by different persons. Thus a man may perform an act which is honest in its effect because he is an honest man on principle, or because he wants whatever policy will prove most advantageous to him and he believes that honesty is the best policy. This example is not far from the point at issue here, for essentially I am arguing that Lincoln followed a peaceable-seeming course because he was a peaceable man who wanted peace and thought he could attain it. Stampp and Current are essentially arguing that he wanted an effective policy, knew that a peaceable-seeming policy

would be most effective, and therefore took care to make his policy appear peaceable, though there was a covert element of coercion and of aggressiveness in it. They contend that he did not really mind fighting a war to protect the national interest.

If motive cannot be accurately determined, there will always be room both for the beliefs that Lincoln's purposes were peaceable or, alternatively, that the peaceable appearance of his position cloaked a purpose far from pacific. But if the question of motive must, by its very nature, be forever open to doubt, it becomes doubly important to turn back to the question of actions. At this level, the historian faces a different problem: given Lincoln's determination to save the Union, and given his belief that the loss of Fort Sumter, without being sure of Fort Pickens, would make it impossible to save the Union, could he have followed any more peaceable course than he did? Was there any possible means of holding Sumter that would have been less provocative than informing the Confederates that "an attempt will be made to supply Fort Sumter with provisions only and that if such attempt be not resisted, no effort to throw in men, arms, or ammunition will be made, without further notice or [except] in case of an attack upon the Fort." The existence of such an alternative and the demonstration that Lincoln rejected it is essential to any argument that Lincoln was not following the most peaceable course available to him.

Unless the historians who charge Lincoln with coercive or covertly aggressive policies can name a less provocative course that he might have followed, they are in the curious position of arguing that a man may pursue a course which offers the maximum possibility of peace and may at the same time be open to the accusation of scheming to bring about war.

If the very nature of human motivation

is such that no one can ever say categorically whether Lincoln's purposes were peaceable, perhaps it is more nearly possible to say categorically whether his course of action was peaceable. Here the crucial fact is that no one who attributes to him a purpose to see that the war got started in a way that would be advantageous to him has yet said what else he could have done that would have been more peaceable than what he did, given his purpose not to abandon the principle of Union.

No doubt he must have recognized that war might ensue; no doubt he must have seen that if it did ensue, it would come in a way disadvantageous to the Confederacy; no doubt he was glad this was true. But when we say this, we are back in the realm of motive again. If we confine ourselves to scrutinizing his overt course, the question persists: what could he have done that would have been more peaceable? Two outstanding scholars have defined this point well. J. G. Randall stated it with superb precision when he wrote: "To say that Lincoln meant that the first shot would be fired by the other side, *if a first shot was fired* [Randall's italics], is by no means the equivalent of saying that he deliberately maneuvered to have the shot fired. This distinction is fundamental." Allan Nevins stated it with wonderful force when he said: "'In your hands, not mine,' he [Lincoln] had told Southerners, 'lies the issue of peace or war.' The shells that burst over a Federal fort awaiting a victualizing expedition which had orders not to fire unless it was fired upon, gave the answer to that statement."

RICHARD N. CURRENT (1912–   ), Distinguished
Professor at the University of North Carolina at
Greensboro, offers still another interpretation of
Lincoln's motives. Faced with the dilemma of the
rapidly worsening situation at Fort Sumter, the
President, deciding to send only supplies to Major
Anderson and to warn the South Carolina authorities
of his intentions, according to Current's account, took
a deliberate risk. How does the following selection from
his book, *Lincoln and the First Shot*, refute Potter's
thesis?*

Richard N. Current

Lincoln's Risky Gamble

To most Northerners of the Civil War
generation, it seemed obvious that the
Southerners had started the war. The
Southerners had fired the first shot and,
what was worse, had done so without real
provocation. They had begun the bloodshed on being informed that the Federal
government would attempt to carry food
to a few dozen hungry and beleaguered
men.

To certain Northerners, however, and
to practically all Southerners, it seemed
just as obvious that Lincoln was to blame.
While the war was still going on, one
New York Democrat confided to another
his suspicion that Lincoln had brought
off an "adroit manoeuver" to "precipitate
the attack" for its "expected effect upon

the public feeling of the North." A one-
time Kentucky governor, speaking in
Liverpool, England, stated that the Republicans had schemed to "provoke a collision in order that they might say that the
Confederates had made the first attack."
The Richmond journalist E. A. Pollard
wrote in his wartime history of the war
that Lincoln had "procured" the assault
and thus, by an "ingenious artifice," had
himself commenced the fighting. "He
chose to draw the sword," the *Petersburg
Express* asserted, "but by a dirty trick succeeded in throwing upon the South the
seeming blame of firing the first gun."

When, soon after the war's end, Alexander H. Stephens wrote his memoirs,
he had no doubt as to who the real aggres-

*From the book *Lincoln and the First Shot* by Richard N. Current, pp. 182–208. Copyright, ©, 1963 by
Richard N. Current. Reprinted by permission of J. B. Lippincott Company. (Footnotes omitted).

sor had been in 1861. In the book he conducted an imaginary colloquium. "Do you mean to say, Mr. Stephens, that the war was inaugurated by Mr. Lincoln?" he had one of his listeners ask. "Most assuredly I do," Stephens replied. "Why, how in the world . . . ?" the incredulous one persisted. "It is a fact that the *first gun* was fired by the Confederates," Stephens conceded. Then he patiently explained that the aggressor in a war is not the first to use force but the first to make force necessary.

Jefferson Davis, in his account of *The Rise and Fall of the Confederate Government* (1881), agreed with Stephens on this point, though he had agreed with him on little else while the two were president and vice president of the Confederacy. "He who makes the assault is not necessarily he who strikes the first blow or fires the first gun," Davis wrote. Referring to the Republicans and the Sumter expedition, he elaborated: "To have awaited further strengthening of their position by land and naval forces, with hostile purpose now declared, would have been as unwise as it would be to hesitate to strike down the arm of the assailant, who levels a deadly weapon at one's breast, until he has actually fired."

Some Northerners, defenders of Lincoln, took a view rather similar to that of his Southern critics but presented it in a very different light. They praised Lincoln for essentially the same reasons that Davis, Stephens, and others blamed him. In a book (1882) purporting to give the "true stories" of Sumter and Pickens, and dedicated to the "old friends" of Robert Anderson, a lieutenant colonel of the United States Army maintained that the advice of Scott and Seward to withdraw from Sumter was quite sound from a merely military standpoint. "But Mr. Lincoln and Mr. Blair judged more wisely that it would be better to sacrifice the garrison of Sumter for political effect." They sent the expedition "with the knowledge that it would compel the rebels to strike the first blow. If the last man in the garrison of Sumter had perished, it would have been a cheap price to pay for the magnificent outburst of patriotism that followed."

In their ten-volume history (1890) Lincoln's former private secretaries, John G. Nicolay and John Hay, wrote that Lincoln cared little whether the Sumter expedition would succeed in its provisioning attempt. "He was not playing a game of military strategy with Beauregard." He was playing a game for much higher stakes than Sumter itself. "When he finally gave the order that the fleet should sail he was master of the situation . . . master if the rebels hesitated or repented, because they would thereby forfeit their prestige with the South; master if they persisted, for he would then command a united North." He was "looking through and beyond the Sumter expedition to the now inevitable rebel attack and the response of an awakened and united North." The government, of course, was in the right. "But to make the issue sure, he determined in addition that the rebellion should be put in the wrong." His success entitled him to the high honors of "universal statesmanship."

In later generations a number of writers repeated the view that Lincoln himself had compelled the Confederates to fire first. Most of these writers inclined to the opinion that, in doing so, he exhibited less of universal statesmanship than of low cunning. Not till 1935, however, did a professional historian present a forthright statement of the thesis with all the accouterments of scholarship. In that year Professor Charles W. Ramsdell, of the University of Texas, reading a paper at the

annual meeting of the American Historical Association, thus summed up the
case:

"Lincoln, having decided that there was
no other way than war for the salvation of
his administration, his party, and the
Union, maneuvered the Confederates
into firing the first shot in order that they,
rather than he, should take the blame of
beginning bloodshed."

According to the Ramsdell argument,
Davis and the rest of the Confederate
leaders desired peace. They were eager to
negotiate a settlement and avoid a resort
to arms. But Lincoln, not so peaceably
inclined, refused to deal with them.

During the weeks that followed his inauguration he was beset on two sides.
Coercionists demanded that he take forceful action to rescue Fort Sumter. Moderate men advised him to yield the fort. If
he should use force, he might impel the
states of the Upper South to secede, and
perhaps the border states as well. If he
should abandon the fort, the majority of
his party would probably abandon him.
While he hesitated, his fellow Republicans bickered among themselves, his administration declined in prestige, and the
country drifted toward ruin. He had to
make up his mind soon, before the Sumter
garrison was starved out.

At last he hit upon a way out of his dilemma. The thought occurred to him—
must have occurred to him—that he could
induce the Confederates to attack the
fort. Then, the flag having been fired
upon, he would gain all the benefits of an
aroused patriotism. Republicans and
Democrats would forget their quarrels of
party and faction, the border states would
respond with an upsurge of loyalty, and
wavering millions throughout the North
would rally to the Union cause. The
party, the administration, and the Union
would be saved.

The stratagem was a shrewd one,
worthy of the shrewd man that Lincoln
was. He decided to send the expedition
and—most cleverly—to give advance
notice. A genius with words, he could
make them mean different things to different people. This is what he did with the
words he addressed to the governor of
South Carolina. To Northerners these
words would seem quite innocent. The
government was taking groceries to starv-
ing men and would not use force unless
it had to. That was all. To Southerners
the same words carried a threat, indeed
a double threat. First, Sumter was going
to be provisioned so that it could hold
out. Second, if resistance should be offered, arms and men as well as food were
going to be run in!

The notice was timed as carefully as it
was phrased. It was delivered while the
ships of the expedition were departing
from New York. These could not reach
their destination for three days at least,
and so the Confederates would have
plenty of time to take counteraction before the ships arrived. Already the Confederates had news that a sizable expedition was being prepared, and they were
left to suppose that the entire force (including the part of it actually being dispatched to Pensacola) was heading for
Charleston. With such a large force
presumed to be on the way, they had all
the more reason to move quickly.

The ruse worked perfectly. True, the
expedition neither provisioned nor reinforced Sumter; it gave the garrison no
help at all. But that was not the object.
The object was to provoke a shot that
would rouse the Northern people to fight.

This Ramsdell thesis was elaborated,
with variations, in a book written by a
Southern lawyer, John S. Tilley, and published during that fateful year 1941 (when
another President was to be accused of a

first-shot "maneuver"). Writing in a spirit more appropriate to a criminal court than a scholarly forum, Tilley contended that, at the time of Lincoln's inauguration, there existed no real need for provisioning Sumter. Indeed, Tilley left the impression that Lincoln had invented the story of short supplies at the fort so as to have an excuse for forcing the issue with the Confederacy. One of Tilley's chapter titles announced: "Lincoln Got What He Wanted." The implication was that Lincoln wanted war and went out of his way to get it.

While the Ramsdell thesis has attracted other and more responsible adherents, it has also been challenged by formidable critics. Professor James G. Randall, of the University of Illinois, maintained in the *Abraham Lincoln Quarterly* (1940) and in two books on Lincoln (1945, 1947) that Lincoln intended and expected a peaceful provisioning of the fort. After an independent study of *Lincoln and His Party in the Secession Crisis* (1942), Professor David M. Potter, then of Yale University (now of Stanford University), presented essentially similar conclusions. Lincoln counted upon a resurgence of Unionism in the South to overcome secession eventually, without war. To facilitate reunion, he planned to refrain from forcible assertion of Federal authority so long as he could do so without an obvious and outright surrender of it. He would have evacuated Fort Sumter if he had been able promptly enough to reinforce and secure Fort Pickens, so that it could serve as a substitute symbol of Federal authority. Events, however, compelled him to act. Finally he accepted the necessity of the Sumter expedition, but he took care to make it as unprovocative as possible. By means of it he hoped merely to preserve the existing status in Charleston Harbor. His policy was a failure, since it culmi-

nated in war. Such is the contention of Professors Randall and Potter.

In between the Randall-Potter thesis of the peace policy and the Ramsdell-Tilley thesis of the war maneuver, there is yet a third interpretation which sees Lincoln's policy as aiming at neither war nor peace, as such, but as risking the chance of war. Professor Kenneth M. Stampp, of the University of California, stated this thesis of the calculated risk in the *Journal of Southern History* (1945) and restated it in his book *And the War Came* (1950). According to Stampp, Lincoln's primary purpose was to preserve the Union and to do so by a "strategy of defense" which would avoid even the appearance of initiating hostilities.

One version of the Sumter story— Tilley's insinuation that Lincoln faked the hunger crisis at the fort—may be immediately ruled out. This insinuation was based mainly upon the absence of evidence. Tilley could not find the letter, or even a copy of the letter, that Lincoln was supposed to have seen on the day after his inauguration, the letter in which Major Anderson revealed shortages of certain essential supplies and the necessity of either replenishing these or abandoning the fort. Now, it may be good legal practice to argue from the absence of evidence. It is not sound historical scholarship. Even at the time Tilley wrote, there were documents available referring to the Anderson letter and indicating clearly enough that it actually had been written and sent. Later, after the opening of the Robert Todd Lincoln Collection of Lincoln papers in the Library of Congress, in 1947, lo! there was the missing letter which Tilley had been at such pains to prove nonexistent.

The Ramsdell thesis itself does not necessarily fall with the collapse of Tilley's case, though much of Ramsdell's evidence is either inconclusive or irrelevant. He devoted a considerable part of his essay merely to showing that various pressures or supposed pressures had induced Lincoln to decide in favor of sending the Sumter expedition, but this line of argument has little bearing upon the main issue to which Ramsdell had addressed himself. As his critic Randall aptly commented: "The inducing-to-attack argument does not proceed very far before it involves a subtle change of approach, so that the very decision to send the expedition is treated as the aggressive or provocative thing, whereas the point at issue . . . is whether the sending of supplies to feed the garrison was not in Lincoln's mind compatible with continued peace efforts."

This is indeed a crucial question. It may be restated thus: Did Lincoln think, or did he have good reason to think, that he could send his expedition to Sumter and his advance notice to the South Carolina governor without encountering resistance on the part of the Confederate forces at Charleston? Unfortunately, there is no direct, contemporary evidence to show what Lincoln *actually thought* about the probable Confederate reaction. There is, however, plenty of evidence to indicate what he *had good reason to think*.

Lincoln was familiar with the news of recent events at Charleston—events illustrating the readiness of the Confederate batteries to open up. He knew that in January his predecessor, President Buchanan, had sent an unescorted and unarmed merchant steamer with provisions and (below deck) troops for Sumter, and that the Charleston batteries had fired upon this vessel and compelled her to turn back. Now, Lincoln was sending not one ship but several, including warships. He had reason to expect that his expedi-

tion would meet with at least the same degree of hostility as Buchanan's had met with, if not more. Before Lincoln's expedition had actually sailed, he received confirmation of this probability in the report that, on April 3, the Confederate batteries fired upon the Boston schooner *R. H. Shannon*, which innocently had put in at Charleston Harbor to get out of the ocean fog.

When Lincoln called upon his cabinet for written advice, on March 15 and again on March 29, he got little assurance the first time and still less the second time that a peaceful provisioning would be likely. The first time only two of the seven members favored making the attempt, and only one of the two, Secretary Chase, was confident that it could be made without armed conflict. The second time only one definitely opposed the attempt, but even Chase, who still favored it, had lost his confidence that it could be carried out peaceably. Secretary Welles, who had changed from opposition to approval, now expressed an opinion similar to Chase's. "There is little possibility that this will be permitted," Welles stated, "if the opposing forces can prevent it."

The objection may be raised that, nevertheless, Lincoln had reason to think *his* Sumter expedition, unlike Buchanan's, might be tolerated by the authorities in Charleston because he intended to give, and did give, advance notice of its coming, whereas Buchanan had not done so. Though Ramsdell has characterized this notice as a threat, and a double-barreled one at that, his critics have replied that it was no such thing. They say it was given "to show that hostile surprise was not intended" and to make clear Lincoln's "non-aggressive purpose." Whether the notification, with its reference to "men, arms, or ammunition," constituted a threat, we need not stop to debate. We need only to recall what Lincoln had learned recently from Hurlbut, his secret emissary to Charleston. Hurlbut reported his conclusion "that a ship known to contain *only provisions* for Sumpter would be stopped & refused admittance." In the light of this information, Lincoln would have had little ground for expecting that his notice would mollify the Confederates even if he had confined it to a simple announcement that he would attempt to supply "provisions only."

If Lincoln had intended and expected nothing but a peaceful provisioning, he no doubt would have been surprised and disappointed at the actual outcome. In fact, however, he repeatedly expressed a feeling of at least qualified satisfaction and success. When he replied to the Virginia delegates at the White House, on April 13, he said in an almost triumphant tone that the "unprovoked assault" would set him "at liberty" to go beyond the self-imposed limitations of his inaugural and to "repossess" as well as "hold, occupy, and possess" Federal positions in the seceded states. When he consoled the frustrated Fox, on May 1, he wrote: "You and I both anticipated that the cause of the country would be advanced by making the attempt to provision Fort Sumpter, even if it should fail; and it is no small consolation now to feel that our anticipation is justified by the result." When he drafted his first message to Congress, for the July 4 session, he emphasized the point that, by the "affair at Fort Sumpter," he had succeeded in making good his earlier declaration that, if war should come, the seceders would have to be the aggressors. And when he read the message to Browning, on July 3, he went on to remark, as Browning paraphrased him: "The plan succeeded. They attacked Sumter—it fell, and thus, did more service than it otherwise could."

In short, it appears that Lincoln, when he decided to send the Sumter expedition, considered hostilities to be *probable*. It also appears, however, that he believed an unopposed and peaceable provisioning to be at least barely *possible*. It is reasonable to suppose that he shared the expectation of his Attorney General, who wrote in his diary at the time Fox was leaving New York for Charleston: "One of two things will happen—either the fort will be well provisioned, the Southrons forebearing to assail the boats, or a fierce contest will ensue." If the first rather than the second of the two possibilities had materialized, then Lincoln doubtless could have said afterwards, just as he said when the second of the two occurred, that his plan had succeeded. Doubtless he would have been equally well satisfied, perhaps even better satisfied. Either way, whether the Confederates resisted or not, he would have been (in the words of Nicolay and Hay) "master of the situation."

It follows, then, that neither the Randall-Potter nor the Ramsdell view of Lincoln's intentions and expectations seems quite accurate. On the one hand, Lincoln did not count confidently upon peace, though he thought there was a bare chance of its being preserved for the time being. On the other hand, he did not deliberately provoke war. He thought hostilities would be the likely result, and he was determined that, if they should be, they must clearly be initiated by the Confederates. "To say that Lincoln meant that the first shot would be fired by the other side *if a first shot was fired*," as Randall has most admirably put the matter, "is not to say that he maneuvered to have the first shot fired."

The Ramsdell thesis, with its war-maneuver charge, is essentially an effort to document the rationalizations of Davis, Stephens, and other Confederates or Confederate sympathizers. Similarly, the Randall-Potter thesis, in one of its important aspects, is essentially an effort to substantiate the explanation that Lincoln gave after the events, in his July 4 message to Congress.

Interestingly, Potter observes that, to understand Lincoln's plans at the time of his inauguration, "it is necessary to exclude the misleading perspective of hindsight, and to view the problem as he viewed it at the time, rather than as he later viewed it." Yet, in dealing with Lincoln's policy after the inauguration, Potter neglects this very principle. Like Randall, he bases his argument largely on the misleading perspective of hindsight, on the way Lincoln viewed the problem in July rather than the way he viewed it in March and April.

According to Potter, who paraphrases Lincoln's July 4 message, the Sumter expedition was only tentative, the Pickens expedition definite. The Sumter expedition "was withheld until the fort was almost starved out, and it was withheld because Lincoln still hoped that he could transfer the issue of Union to Fort Pickens before the Sumter question reached a crisis." To both Potter and Randall the critical date is April 6. This was the date when, as Lincoln said in the message, he received a report that his order to land the troops already on shipboard in Pensacola Harbor, to reinforce Fort Pickens, had not been carried out. And this was the date when Lincoln sent to Major Anderson, by special messenger, the letter informing him that the expedition was going ahead (though the letter was dated April 4). "Up to April 6, then," Randall says, "the expedition, though prepared, could have been held back." And the plain implication of Randall and Potter,

as well as of Lincoln himself, is that if the troops had been landed at Fort Pickens, and if Lincoln had known of it by April 6, he would have called off the Sumter expedition.

There is undoubtedly an element of truth in this story of a Sumter-for-Pickens sacrifice. During March and early April the idea was discussed in the newspapers, was recommended by a number of Lincoln's Republican correspondents, and was urged again and again by Seward. At one time or another, Lincoln must have given some consideration to it. He could hardly have avoided doing so. Possibly, if he had been assured before March 29 that the troops had been landed and Fort Pickens was safe, he might not have decided at that time to prepare the Sumter expedition. But it appears (in the light of contemporary evidence) that, having ordered the Sumter preparations on March 29, he did not thereafter make his policy for Charleston contingent upon events at Pensacola.

Actually, the key dates regarding the Sumter decision are March 29 and April 4, not April 6. After the order for preparations had been given on March 29, there followed a period of vacillation and delay which was exasperating to Fox. The causes were twofold: the fears that visible preparations would hurt the prospects on the New York money market for the government loan to be subscribed on April 2, and the hopes (on the part of Seward) that a last-minute Sumter-for-Virginia deal could be arranged. After the successful sale of the bonds, and after the fiasco of Lincoln's conversation with the Virginia representative, Lincoln decided definitely to go ahead with the Sumter plans. On April 4 he arranged the details with Fox and wrote the letter informing Anderson that supplies would be on the way. That same day a copy of the letter was mailed to Anderson, and Anderson received it three days later. Not sure that the mail had got through, Lincoln sent the second copy by special messenger on April 6. His sending it on that day is no indication whatever that he waited until then to make his final decision regarding Sumter.

True, on April 6, Lincoln learned that his nearly-a-month-old order to land the troops at Pensacola had not been executed. But, to him, this was hardly unexpected news: it was merely a confirmation of what he already had guessed. As early as March 29 he had suspected that the order somehow had gone astray. On April 1 he was informed, by a communication from Pensacola, that the forces there had (as of March 21) been out of touch with the government. When the report of April 6 arrived, it had only one visible effect upon the administration: it caused the prompt dispatch of a messenger overland to Pensacola with new orders from Secretary Welles to land the troops already there.

Meanwhile, Seward had never given up his obsession with the idea of yielding Sumter and holding Pickens as a kind of substitute. The idea was Seward's, not Lincoln's. Seward stressed it in his brash April 1 memorandum, "Some Thoughts for the President's Consideration," and Lincoln in his written reply on the same day said his own domestic policy was the same as Seward's "with the single exception, that it does not propose to abandon Fort Sumter."

Why, then, did Lincoln tell Congress, in the July 4 message, that he *had* proposed to abandon Fort Sumter if Fort Pickens could be made secure in time? One conceivable reason is that, after the months of preoccupation with the widening war, he had forgotten some of the chronological details of his earlier policy formation. He may well have remembered that on some occasion or other, possibly in mid-March, he had actually given at least fleeting consideration to the proposal. He may not have remembered exactly when, or how seriously. Another conceivable reason is that he was still concerned, in July, about the opinions of those peace-minded Northerners, including many Republicans, who in March and early April had been willing or even eager for Sumter to be evacuated on the condition that Pickens be firmly held. Lincoln may have felt it advisable now to reassure those timid and hesitant ones that he had, indeed, exhausted all the possibilities for peace and, in particular, had carefully considered the Sumter-for-Pickens alternative.

In stressing this alternative as an essential element of Lincoln's April policy, Randall and Potter confuse Lincoln's March and April thinking with Seward's. They make the same error in characterizing Lincoln's overall approach to the secession problem. Potter, for instance, asserts that "Republican policy was consistent" and that party leaders "insisted that delay and avoidance of friction would create a condition under which the Unionists in the South could regain the ascendancy." Certain party leaders, yes, and above all Seward, but Lincoln never fully shared Seward's faith in the do-nothing panacea.

In truth, Republican policy was far from being consistent. The policy of Seward was, at many points, inconsistent with that of Lincoln. The assumption that time would heal all wounds, the hints and promises of an early withdrawal from Sumter, the notion of bargaining Sumter for Virginia, the proposal to abandon Sumter and concentrate on Pickens—all these were hobbies of Seward's. Lincoln had great respect for Seward's abilities and for his political value to the administration. He listened to Seward's suggestions and urgings. To some extent he was influenced by them, but he was by no means converted. Nor did he authorize all of Seward's undertakings. Some of them he knew nothing about until after they had been well advanced.

The worst fault in the Ramsdell thesis is a lack of balance and perspective. Ramsdell makes Lincoln appear too much the warmonger, Davis too much the peace lover; Lincoln too much the controlling force, Davis too much the passive agent. Ramsdell argues that the Confederate government "could not, without yielding the principle of independence, abate its claims to the fort." He fails to see that, likewise, the Federal government could not abate its claims without yielding the principle of Union.

Davis made the decision that led directly to war. True, early on the morning of April 12, Beauregard sent Roger A. Pryor, James Chestnut, and two others from Charleston to the fort to present Davis's final terms, and these men on their own rejected Anderson's reply—which was that he would hold his fire and evacuate in three days, unless he should meanwhile receive "controlling instructions" or "additional supplies." Instead of taking responsibility upon themselves, Pryor and the other hot-headed underlings might have referred Anderson's reply to Beauregard, and he in turn to Walker and Davis. Since Pryor and his colleagues went ahead without thus referring to higher authority, the story arose that they and not Davis had made the real decision. The story seemed to be confirmed by the testimony that Pryor gave to an historian many years later, in 1909. Accepting Pryor's account, the historian wrote: "Pryor and his associates did not report to the General, but, thinking that

Davis was trying to reconstruct the Union and negotiate with Seward to that end and that the chance of war was about to slip away forever, they conferred together and decided to give the signal to the gunners to fire—and war began, and such a war!" War began, all right, but the main point of Pryor's testimony has no foundation in fact. When Pryor and his associates rejected Anderson's reply, they were faithfully following the line of Davis's policy, and Davis afterwards fully approved what they had done. The real decision was his, not theirs.

Davis justified his decision on the ground that "the reduction of Fort Sumter was a measure of defense rendered absolutely and immediately necessary." In fact, however, Sumter in April, 1861, offered no immediate threat to the physical safety of Charleston or of South Carolina or of the other six Confederate states. Nor did the approach of Fox's small fleet suddenly create such a threat. The landing of supplies—or even of men, arms, and ammunition—would have made little difference in the existing power balance.

Writers of the Ramsdell school insist that there was no *military* reason for Lincoln's effort to provision the fort. They cannot have it both ways. If there was no military reason for Lincoln's attempt, there could have been none for Davis' effort to forestall it.

Indeed, the Ramsdell thesis, turned inside out, could be applied to Davis with as much justice as it has been applied to Lincoln. One could argue that political and not military necessity led Davis to order the firing of the first shot. The very life of the Confederacy, the growth upon which that life depended, was at stake. So were the pride, the prestige, and the position of Davis. Ramsdell himself, a distinguished authority on Confederate history, might appropriately have devoted his talents to an essay on

"Davis and Fort Sumter" instead of "Lincoln and Fort Sumter."

Biographers of Davis and historians of the Confederacy have evaded or obscured their hero's role in the Sumter affair. They have digressed to levy accusations or innuendoes at Lincoln. If they have any concern for historical objectivity, however, they should face frankly the question of Davis's responsibility for the coming of the war. Upon them, upon *his* partisans, should rest the burden of proof. It should not have to be borne forever, as it has for far too many years, by Lincoln's champions. After all, Lincoln did not order the guns to fire. Davis did.

Authorities agree pretty well as to what actually happened in March and April, 1861. They disagree about the meaning of the events and, in particular, about the aims of Lincoln. To judge historical significance involves a certain amount of guessing, and to ascertain a man's intentions (especially when the man is so close-mouthed as Lincoln or, for that matter, Davis) requires a bit of mind reading. For these reasons, the true inwardness of the Sumter story will, in some of its aspects, always be more or less moot. The probable truth may be summarized as follows:

At the time of his inauguration Lincoln was determined to retake the Federal positions already lost to the seceding states as well as to hold the positions not yet lost. When he revised his inaugural, so as to announce only the "hold, occupy, and possess" objective, he did not really change or limit his original purpose. He meant to achieve this purpose, however, without appearing to initiate the use of force. He did not yet know precisely how he was going to manage so delicate a task, but he assumed that he would have plenty of time in which to deal with the problem.

Then, for about three weeks, he hesitated with regard to Fort Sumter, though not with regard to Fort Pickens, which he promptly ordered to be reinforced by means of the troops already available there. In the case of Sumter, the bad news from Anderson and the deterring counsel from Scott and the cabinet gave him pause. During the period of hesitation he considered alternative lines of action as at least temporary expedients—the collection of customs on ships off Southern ports, the evacuation of Sumter if and when Pickens had been made absolutely secure, the provisioning (with advance notice) but not the reinforcing of Sumter.

On March 29 he gave orders for the preparation of an expedition to provision Sumter—and also, conditionally, to reinforce it. He had decided to act because, from various sources of advice and information, he had concluded that a retreat at any point (except in the face of superior force) would lead eventually to a retreat at all points. If he were to yield to the demand for Sumter, he would still face the demand for Pickens and the other Florida forts, to say nothing of the demand for recognition of the Confederacy. True, if he took a stand, he would run the risk of antagonizing and losing Virginia and other still-loyal slave states. But if he declined to take a stand, he would still risk losing those states, through conferring new prestige and attractiveness upon the Confederacy. And, besides, he would surely alienate many of his adherents in the North.

Soon afterward, at Seward's urging, Lincoln ordered also the preparation of another expedition, this one to be secret, unannounced, and intended for the immediate reinforcement of Fort Pickens. Even its sponsor, Seward, did not expect the enterprise to be peaceably received: he merely thought Pensacola a better place than Charleston for war to begin. The Pickens expedition got off first, the Sumter preparations running into various snags, including Seward's efforts at sabotage.

On April 4, in consultation with Fox, Lincoln made the final arrangements for the Sumter effort. According to these carefully laid plans, Fox's men would try to run in supplies by boats or tugs. If challenged, the pilot would hand over a note explaining that the aim was only to take food to the garrison, and that if the Confederates fired upon the boats, they would be firing upon unarmed and defenseless men. Already the South Carolina governor would have received his notice. Thus the arrival of the boats would put the Confederates in a dilemma. If they fired, they would convict themselves of an atrocity. If not, they could hardly prevent the fort from being supplied. Either way, they would lose.

And if they fired, the guns of the warships offshore and of the fort itself would fire back and, hopefully, clear the way for the supplies to be taken in, along with reinforcements. This would, no doubt, entail a certain amount of bloodshed, but surely the Federal government would appear to be justified, in the eyes of most Northerners and of many Southerners as well. Even the majority of Virginians, under these circumstances, would possibly think twice before countenancing the secession of their state.

In certain respects the outcome was not to be quite what Lincoln anticipated.

The policy of the Montgomery government was less passive, less cautious, than he supposed. That policy aimed to get control of Sumter and the other forts as soon as it could be done, by negotiations if feasible, by siege or assault if not. The mission to Washington had a twofold function: on the one hand, to seek recognition of the Confederacy and a peaceful transfer of the forts and, on the other, to gain time for military preparations to be

used in case diplomacy should fail. Once the preparations had proceeded far enough, the termination of diplomacy was to be the signal for the beginning of military measures. By early April, in Charleston, Beauregard was ready. Soon he would have begun actual operations for taking Sumter—even if Lincoln had never planned or sent an expedition of any kind (unless Anderson should promptly have given up, which was a possibility, or Lincoln should have invited the commissioners to talk with him, which was not).

When Davis heard of Lincoln's notice to the South Carolina governor, on April 8, his immediate response was to order Beauregard to prevent the landing of the supplies. It is interesting to speculate about what might have happened if Davis had stuck to this decision. Most likely, Beauregard then would have waited for the actual approach of the provisioning boats. But Fox, considering the storm-caused delays and the nonappearance of the flagship, *Powhatan,* probably would have decided not to send the boats in. In that event, the Sumter expedition would have proved an utter fiasco. Lincoln would have lost prestige and Davis gained it. Or, after hesitation, Fox might have made a token effort. Then things would have happened pretty much as Lincoln had calculated, except that the expedition would not have had the power to open the way for the supplies.

But Davis and his advisers did not remain content with their decision of April 8. Two days later they made a new one, and orders went to Beauregard to demand a surrender and, failing to get that, to reduce the fort.

This reaction, though more than Lincoln had counted on, was somewhat better, from his point of view, than the previous one. If the Confederates were going to fire at all, it was well that they should do so without even waiting until the food-laden boats were in sight. The eagerness of the Confederates would the more surely convict them of aggression, and this was all to the good, even though it would mean that Sumter would have less chance of being actually reinforced and held.

The first shot having been fired, the response of the North more than reconciled Lincoln to the loss of the fort, if not also to the loss of Virginia, Arkansas, Tennessee, and North Carolina. The response of the North certainly went far toward making possible the ultimate redemption of the Union.

In those early April days both Lincoln and Davis took chances which, in retrospect, seem awesome. The chances they took eventuated in the most terrible of all wars for the American people. Lincoln and Davis, as each made his irrevocable decision, could see clearly enough the cost of holding back. Neither could see so clearly the cost of going ahead. Both expected, or at least hoped, that the hostilities would be limited in space and time. Lincoln thought of blockade and boycott and a few seaborne operations against coastal forts. Davis thought of accessions and allies—in the slave states, in foreign countries, and in the North itself—which would make the Confederacy too strong for its independence to be long contested.

The Sumter incident itself did not lead at once to general war. Neither side was yet prepared for that. By a kind of escalation, however, war rapidly developed, and the lines were soon drawn. Through his proclamation of April 15, calling for 75,000 volunteers, Lincoln unintentionally contributed to the growth of the martial spirit on both sides. Perhaps if in that proclamation he had stressed his defensive purposes, especially the need for troops to protect the capital, he might at least have strengthened the Unionists in Virginia and the other non-seceded slave states.

The charge of "aggression," which has been bandied for so long, should not concern historians except as it figured in the propaganda of 1861 and after. From the Confederate point of view the United States had made itself the aggressor long before Lincoln acted to strengthen any fort. It was aggression when, on December 26, 1860, Major Anderson moved his small force from their exposed position at Fort Moultrie to the somewhat more secure one at Fort Sumter. Indeed, it was a continuing act of aggression every day that United States forces remained in Sumter or any other place within the boundaries of the Confederacy. And from the Union point of view the Confederacy had committed and was committing aggression by its very claim to existence, to say nothing of its seizures of Federal property and its preparations to seize Sumter and Pickens. Viewed impartially, both sides were guilty of aggression, and neither was.

When Lincoln expressed his desire for peace he was sincere, and so was Davis when he did the same. But Lincoln thought of peace for one, undivided country; Davis, of peace for two separate countries. "Both parties deprecated war," as Lincoln later put it, "but one of them would *make* war rather than let the nation survive; and the other would *accept* war rather than let it perish. And the war came."

Suggestions for Further Reading

The literature on the causes of the Civil War is so extensive that it has given rise to a number of convenient historiographical works, which may serve as a handy introduction to the subject. A full size well researched study of this type is Thomas J. Pressly, *Americans Interpret Their Civil War* (Princeton, 1954), which superseded the perceptive article by Howard K. Beale, "What Historians Have Thought About the Civil War," in *Theory and Practice in Historical Study,* Social Science Research Bulletin No. 54 (New York, 1946). Eric Foner's "The Causes of the Civil War: Recent Interpretations and New Directions," *Civil War History,* XX (1974), 197-214 brings the subject up to the date of publication. Edwin C. Rozwenc, ed., *The Causes of the Civil War* (Boston, 1972) is a useful collection of primary and secondary sources, as is Kenneth M. Stampp, ed., *The Causes of the Civil War* (Englewood Cliffs, N.J., 1974). Don E. Fehrenbacher, *Manifest Destiny and the Coming of the Civil War* (New York, 1970) and David Donald, *The Nation in Crisis* (New York, 1969) are two helpful bibliographies, as are the two volumes by Allan Nevins, James L. Robinson, Jr., and Bell I. Wiley, *Civil War Books: A Critical Bibliography* (2 vols., New York,1967).

A series of one volume books covering the period may be helpful for the study of the causes of Civil War. The most comprehensive of these are J. G. Randall and David Donald, *The Civil War and Reconstruction* (2d ed., Boston, 1969), Peter Parish, *The American Civil War* (New York, 1975), and James M. McPherson, *Ordeal by Fire: The Civil War and Reconstruction* (New York, 1981). These may be supplemented with such more recent studies as Curt Anders, *Hearts in Conflict* (New York, 1994), Allen C. Guelzo, *The Crisis of the American Republic: A History of the Civil War and Reconstruction*

Era (New York, 1995), Brooks D. Simpson, *America's Civil War* (Wheeling, IL 1996), Stephen B. Oates, *The Approaching Storm: Voices of the Storm 1820-1861* (New York, 1997), and Russell F. Weigley, *A Great Civil War: A Military and Political History, 1861-1865* (Bloomington, IN, 2000). Other works include William H. Brock, *Conflict and Transformation: The United States, 1844-1877* (Baltimore, 1973), Robert Cruden, *The War That Never Ended: The American Civil War* (New York, 1977), David Herbert Donald, *Liberty and Union: The Crisis of Popular Government, 1830-1860* (Boston, 1978), Donald M. Jacobs and Raymond H. Robinson, *America's Testing Time, 1844-1877* (Boston, 1973), Ludwell H. Johnson, *Division and Reunion: America 1848-1877* (Boston, 1973), Robert H. Jones, *Disrupted Decades: The Civil War and Reconstruction Years* (New York, 1973), David Lindsay, *Americans in Conflict: The Civil War and Reconstruction* (Boston, 1974), Thomas H. O'Connor, *The Disunited States: The Era of the Civil War and Reconstruction* (New York, 1978), David M. Potter, *Division and the Stresses of Reunion, 1846-1876* (New York, 1973), and Emory Thomas, *The American War and Peace, 1860-1877* (Englewood Cliffs, N.J., 1973).

Among the earlier works of participants and contemporaries, Horace Greeley, *The American Conflict* (2 vols., Hartford, 1864-1866), Henry Wilson, *History of the Rise and Fall of the Slave Power in America* (3 vols., Boston, 1872-1877), James G. Blaine, *Twenty Years of Congress* (2 vols., Norwich, Conn., 1884-1886), and John A. Logan, *The Great Conspiracy: Its Origin and History* (New York, 1886, are representative of the Northern point of view, generally emphasizing slavery (although Blaine well understood economic problems), and Edward A. Pollard, *The Lost Cause* (New York, 1866), Rushmore G. Horton, *A Youth's History* of the Great Civil War in the United States, from 1861 to 1865 . . . (New York, 1866), Jefferson Davis, *The Rise and Fall of the Confederate Government* (2 vols., New York, 1881), and Alexander H. Stephens, *A Constitutional View of the Late War Between the States* (2 vols., Chicago, 1868-1870), of the Southern, which either stressed abolitionism or constitutional issues.

In the half century following the Civil War, the most important works written by historians generally nationalist in outlook are Hermann E. von Holst, *The Constitutional and Political History of the United States* (8 vols., Chicago, 1877-1892), James Schouler, *History of the United States under the Constitution* (7 vols., New York, 1880-1913), John W. Burgess, *The Middle Period 1817-1858* (New York, 1897) and *The Civil War and the Constitution* (2 vols., New York, 1901), and James Ford Rhodes, *History of the United States from the Compromise of 1850* (7 vols., New York, 1893-1906), and *Lectures on the Civil War* (New York, 1913). By and large, these writers deplored slavery and praised the superiority of a free society held together by a strong Union.

The best known example of the economic interpretation of the coming of the Civil War is Charles A. and Mary R. Beard, *The Rise of American Civilization* (2 vols., New York, 1927). Marxist variations of this theme include the earlier study by Algie Simons, *Social Forces in American History* (New York, 1911), Louis Hacker, *The Triumph of American Capitalism* (New York, 1940), and Philip S. Foner, *Business and Slavery* (Chapel Hill, N.C., 1941). A Marxist interpretation emphasizing the role of the blacks is Herbert Aptheker, *Essays in the History of the American Negro* (New York, 1945). More recent treatments include the appropriate chapters in William Appleman Williams, *The Contours of American History* (Cleveland, 1961), Barrington Moore, Jr., *Social Origins of Dictatorship and Democracy* (Boston, 1966), Eugene D. Genovese, *The World the Slaveholders Made* (New York, 1969), and Raimondo Luraghi, *La Storia della Guerra Civile Americana* (Turin, 1966).

The point of view stressing the existence of two different civilizations may be studied in Arthur C. Cole's *The Irrepressible Conflict,*

1850-1865 (New York, 1934), Volume VII of Arthur M. Schlesinger and Dixon Ryan Fox, eds., *A History of American Life* (13 vols., New York, 1927-1948). Other books taking either this approach or focusing on the separate cultural developments of the sections include Edward Channing, *A History of the United States*, Vol. VI, *The War for Southern Independence* (New York, 1925), Jesse T. Carpenter, *The South as a Conscious Minority, 1789-1861* (New York, 1930), Ten Southerners, *I'll Take My Stand* (New York, 1930), especially the essay by Frank L. Owsley, *The Irrepressible Conflict,* stressing Southern loyalty to the agrarian ideal, Ulrich B. Phillips, "The Central Theme of Southern History," *The American Historical Review*. XXXIV (1928), 30-43, and his *The Course of the South to Secession* (New York, 1939), E.M. Coulter, ed., Rollin G. Osterweis, *Romanticism and Nationalism in the Old South* (New Haven, 1949), Clement Eaton, *The Growth of Southern Civilization, 1790-1860* (New York, 1961), and Eric Foner, *Free Soil, Free Labor, Free Men: The Ideology of the Republican Party before the Civil War* (New York, 1970). A variety of this approach is represented by Don E. Fehrenbacher, *The South and Three Sectional Crises* (Baton Rouge, 1980), which emphasizes the South's defense of its honor in the face of world-wide attacks on slavery as one of the causes of the war, and by William Barney, *The Road to Secession* (New York, 1972), which focuses on the expansive nature of Southern society as a disturbing factor. James Oakes, *Slavery and Freedom: An Interpretation of the Old South* (New York, 1990), focuses on the section's relationship to liberal capitalism.

The older revisionist school which stressed the failure of the political system was foreshadowed by the study of Mary Scrugham, *The Peaceable Americans of 1860-1861* (New York, 1921). It is best represented in the writings of James G. Randall. These include *The Civil War and Reconstruction* (Boston, 1937), since revised by David Donald from a different point of view (Boston, 1961, Lexington, 1969), and the best one volume study available, *Lincoln the Liberal Statesman* (New York, 1947), "The Blundering Generation," *The Mississippi Valley Historical Review,* XXVII (1940), 3-28, and his multivolume biography of Lincoln the President (see below). Avery O. Craven's *The Repressible Conflict, 1830-1861* (Baton Rouge, 1939), *The Coming of the Civil War* (New York, 1942), *The Growth of Southern Nationalism, 1848-1861* (Baton Rouge, 1953), and *Civil War in the Making, 1815-1860,* though later differing somewhat in approach, are examples of this school, which is also characterized by an anti-extremist position. George Fort Milton, *The Eve of the Conflict: Stephen A. Douglas and the Needless War* (New York, 1934), and Albert J. Beveridge, *Abraham Lincoln, 1809-1858* (2 vols., Boston, 1928), present the Senator from Illinois in a favorable light, while Philip G. Auchampaugh, *James Buchanan and His Cabinet on the Eve of Secession* (Lancaster, Pa., 1926) and Philip S. Klein, *President James Buchanan* (University Park, Pa., 1962) constitute attempts to rehabilitate the fifteenth President of the United States. Roy F. Nichols, *The Disruption of American Democracy* (New York, 1948) emphasizes the failure of the political system, especially the collapse of the Democratic party; David Donald, *An Excess of Democracy* (Oxford, 1960), stresses the institutional inability of the American people to meet the crisis, Michael F. Holt, *The Political Crisis of the 1850's* (New York, 1978), the breakdown of the second party system, and Arthur Bestor, "State Sovereignty and Slavery: A Reinterpretation of Pro-Slavery Constitutional Doctrine, 1846-1860," *Journal of the Illinois State Historical Society,* LIV (1961), 117-180, and "The American Civil War as a Constitutional Crisis," *The American Historical Review,* LXIX (1964), 327-352, focus once more on the constitutional issues which gave rise to the conflict.

The related problem of extremism is represented by such Southern oriented works as many of Craven's volumes, mentioned above, which put a great deal of blame on the abolitionists, Frank L. Owsley's "The Fundamental Cause of the Civil War: Egocentric Sectionalism," *Journal of Southern History,* VII (1941), 3-18, and Charles W. Ramsdell's "The Natural Limits of Slavery Expansion," *Mississippi Valley Historical Review,* XVI (1929), 151-171. Arnold Whitridge, *No Compromise: The Story of the Fanatics Who Paved*

the Way to the Civil War (New York, 1960), takes a similar point of view, although the author is as critical of the fire-eaters as of the abolitionists. The other side is presented by Hans L. Trefousse, *The Radical Republicans: Lincoln's Vanguard for Racial Justice* (New York, 1969), and a more favorable treatment of abolitionist and radicals in general may be found in Dwight L. Dumond, *Anti-Slavery Origins of the Civil War in the United States* (Ann Arbor, 1939), Russell B. Nye, *Fettered Freedom* (Lansing, 1949), Louis Filler, *The Crusade Against Slavery* (New York, 1960), James M. McPherson, *The Struggle for Equality: Abolitionists and Negroes in the Civil War and Reconstruction* (Princeton, 1964), James Brewer Stewart, *Holy Warriors: The Abolitionists and American Slavery* (New York, 1976), Richard H. Sewall, *Ballots for Freedom: Antislavery Politics in the United States, 1837-1860,* (New York, 1976) and Jane H. and William H. Pease, *Bound With Them in Chains: A Biographical History of the Antislavery Movement* (Westport, Conn., 1972). Gilbert Barnes, *The Antislavery Impulse* (New York, 1933), emphasizes the contributions of Western abolitionists, and Aileen S. Kraditor, *Means and Ends in American Abolitionism: Garrison and His Critics on Strategy and Tactics, 1834-1850* (New York, 1969), the importance of radicalism. Michael A. Morrison, *Slavery and the American West: The Eclipse of Manifest Destiny and the Coming of the Civil War* (Chapel Hill, N.C., 1997) details the controversy about the territories, and Michael H. Holt, *The Rise and Fall of the Whig Party and the Onset of the Civil War* (New York, 1999), returns to the question of political causation.

The most comprehensive post-World War II work, which stresses racial factors as well as slavery in spite of great fairness to the South, is Allan Nevins, *Ordeal of the Union* (2 vols., New York, 1947), *The Emergence of Lincoln* (2 vols., New York, 1950), and *The War for the Union* (4 vols., New York, 1959-1971). A similar explanation may be found in Kenneth P. Stampp, *The Imperiled Union* (New York, 1980). Bernard De Voto, in his remarks in "The Easy Chair," *Harper's Magazine,* CXCII (1946), 123-126, 234-237, severely criticizes the revisionists, as does Arthur Schlesinger, Jr, in "The Causes of the American Civil War: A Note on Historical Sentimentalism," *Partisan Review,* XIV (1949), 968-981, which seeks to reestablish the relevance of abolitionism and the earnestness of the antislavery crusade. This approach has been criticized by John S. Rosenberg in "Toward a New Civil War Revisionism," *American Scholar,* XXXVIII (Spring, 1969), 250-272, but the most important modern synthesis, David Potter's *The Impending Crisis, 1848-1861* (New York. 1976) once more attaches importance to the primacy of the slavery issue. Gerald Gunderson, "The Origins of the American Civil War," *Journal of Economic History,* XXXIV (1974), 915-950, in an economic treatment of the problem, comes to the same conclusion.

The entire institution of slavery has been subjected to a new and critical analysis, reversing, in many ways, the assessment in U. B. Phillips, *American Negro Slavery* (New York, 1918), and *Life and Labor in the Old South* (Boston, 1929). Among these works are Kenneth M. Stampp, *The Peculiar Institution: Slavery in the Ante-Bellum South* (New York, 1956), Stanley M. Elkins, *Slavery: A Problem in American Institutional and Intellectual Life* (Chicago, 1949), John W. Blassingame, *The Slave Community* (New York, 1972), William Brion Davis, *The Problem of Slavery in Western Culture* (Ithaca, 1966), and *The Problem of Slavery in the Age of Revolution, 1770-1823* (Ithaca, 1975), Leslie Howard Owens, *This Species of Property: Slave Life and Culture in the Old South* (New York, 1976), Nathan Huggins, *Black Odyssey* (New York, 1977), and the Marxist interpretation by Eugene D. Genovese, *The Political Economy of Slavery* (New York, 1965), and *Roll, Jordan, Roll* (New York, 1974). Robert William Fogel and Stanley L. Engerman, *Time on the Cross: The Economics of American Negro Slavery* (Boston, 1974) is a highly controversial work ably refuted by Herbert G. Gutman, the author of *The Black Family in Slavery and Freedom, 1750-1925* (New York, 1976), in *Slavery and the Numbers Game* (Urbana, Ill., 1975). Ira Berlin, *Many Thousands Gone: The First Two Centuries of Slavery in North America* (Cambridge, MA, 1998) is a more recent work on the subject.

The Southern view of the immediate causes of the Civil War is represented by Charles W.

Ramsdell, "Lincoln and Fort Sumter," *Journal of Southern History,* III (1937), 259-288, and J. S. Tilley, *Lincoln Takes Command* (Chapel Hill, 1941). Sympathetic to Lincoln and the North are David M. Potter, *Lincoln and His Party in the Secession Crisis* (2d ed., New Haven, 1962); J. G. Randall, *Lincoln the President* (4 vols., New York. 1945-1955, final volume co-authored by Richard N. Current); W. A. Swanberg, *First Blood: The Story of Fort Sumter* (New York, 1958); Dwight I. Dumond, *The Secession Movement, 1860-1861* (New York, 1931); and, with modifications, Kenneth M. Stampp, *And the War Came: The North and the Secession Crisis* (Baton Rouge, 1950), and Richard N. Current, *Lincoln and the First Shot* (Philadelphia, 1963). Current's *The Lincoln Nobody Knows: Portrait in Contrasts of the Greatest American* (New York, 1958), contains an excellent chapter on the outbreak of the war. Whether or not the South was justified in seceding is the problem discussed by Arthur C. Cole, "Lincoln's Election an Immediate Menace to Slavery in the States?" *The American Historical Review,* XXXVI (1931), 740-767, who answers the question in the negative, and by J. G. de Roulhac Hamilton, "Lincoln's Election an Immediate Menace to Slavery in the States?" *The American Historical Review,* XXXVII (1932), 700-711, who comes to the opposite conclusion.

The problem of the irrepressible conflict has been reexamined by Pieter Geyl, "The American Civil War and the Problem of Inevitability," *New England Quarterly,* XXIV (1951), 147-168, and by Thomas A. Bonner, "Civil War Historians and the 'Needless War' Doctrine," *Journal of the History of Ideas,* XVII (1956), 193-216. Convenient collections of source material include Robert W. Johannsen, ed., *The Union in Crisis, 1850-1877* (New York, 1965), and Frank Moore, ed., *The Rebellion Record . . .* (12 vols., New York, 1862-1868).

SUBSTANCE ABUSE COUNSELING

FOURTH EDITION

Judith A. Lewis
Governors State University

Robert Q. Dana
University of Maine

Gregory A. Blevins
Governors State University

BROOKS/COLE
CENGAGE Learning™

Australia • Brazil • Japan • Korea • Mexico • Singapore • Spain • United Kingdom • United States

BROOKS/COLE
CENGAGE Learning

Substance Abuse Counseling, Fourth Edition
Judith A. Lewis, Robert Q. Dana, Gregory A. Blevins

Editor, Counseling, Social Work, and Human Services: Seth Dobrin

Assistant Editor: Arwen Petty

Editorial Assistant: Conor Allen

Media Editor: Dennis Fitzgerald

Marketing Manager: Trent Whatcott

Executive Advertising Project Manager: Brian Chaffee

Marketing Communications Manager: Tami Strang

Content Project Management: Pre-Press PMG

Creative Director: Rob Hugel

Art Director: Caryl Gorska

Production Technology Analyst: Lori Johnson

Print Buyer: Paula Vang

Rights Acquisitions Account Manager, Text: Bob Kauser

Rights Acquisitions Account Manager, Image: Leitha Etheridge-Sims

Production Service: Pre-Press PMG

Copy Editor: Mark Mayell

Cover Designer: Irene Morris

Cover Image: Veer Photography

Compositor: Pre-Press PMG

For product information and technology assistance, contact us at **Cengage Learning Customer & Sales Support, 1-800-354-9706.**
For permission to use material from this text or product, submit all requests online at **www.cengage.com/permissions**.
Further permissions questions can be e-mailed to **permissionrequest@cengage.com.**

Library of Congress Control Number: 2009934825

Student Edition:
ISBN-13: 978-0-534-62845-1

ISBN-10: 0-534-62845-1

Brooks/Cole, Cengage Learning
20 Davis Drive
Belmont, CA 94002-3098
USA

Cengage Learning is a leading provider of customized learning solutions with office locations around the globe, including Singapore, the United Kingdom, Australia, Mexico, Brazil, and Japan. Locate your local office at **www.cengage.com/global.**

Cengage Learning products are represented in Canada by Nelson Education, Ltd.

To learn more about Brooks/Cole, a part of Cengage Learning, visit **www.cengage.com/brookscole**

Purchase any of our products at your local college store or at our preferred online store **www.ichapters.com**

Printed in the United States of America
1 2 3 4 5 6 7 13 12 11 10 09

To the many clients and students who have kept us centered on the reality of lives touched by substance abuse

To my wife Cookie, our daughters Jennifer, Katherine, and Elizabeth

To Vicki and Stacy

To Keith, Christine, and Langston

CONTENTS

NEW IN THIS EDITION

TWENTY-FIRST-CENTURY substance abuse counseling differs in truly fundamental ways from the predominant models of the past. The field is in the midst of a paradigm shift that is changing the central assumptions guiding the counselor's work. This practice revolution has begun to move programs and practitioners from a penchant for coercion to a predilection for collaboration, from scare tactics to empowerment, from reliance on mythology to confidence in science.

We believe that this edition of *Substance Abuse Counseling* not only responds to these positive changes but also helps to move them forward. In the three previous editions of this book, we emphasized the need to close the gap between research and practice, to treat clients with respect and dignity, to recognize the social context of substance use behavior, and to employ a multicultural perspective. In the past, some of these ideas were viewed as if they were outside the mainstream of addiction-related treatment models. Now, the substance abuse field has found its way toward a hard-won consensus that change is needed, and our fourth edition maintains its place at the cutting edge.

The new substance abuse paradigm accepts the centrality of evidence-based practices and recognizes the key role of respectful collaboration. The confluence of these two factors has brought Motivational Interviewing (MI) to the center of accepted practice and made competence in MI a requirement for excellence. This edition of *Substance Abuse Counseling* includes a new chapter devoted solely to this important topic, explaining MI concepts and practices and including examples from such divergent fields as criminal justice, health care, and family therapy. We have also increased our attention to the connection between research and implementation, reviewing up-to-date applications of evidence-based practices in individual, group, and family counseling. Our long-time recognition of the importance of the social context of substance use has brought us to introduce a new principle that has not been seen before in the substance abuse counseling literature: the notion that client advocacy is central to the counselor's role. We review the competencies involved in effective advocacy and apply them to the substance abuse counselor's work. Of course, client and advocacy and respect for diversity go hand-in-hand, and we have infused a multicultural perspective throughout the book.

ACKNOWLEDGMENTS

This book could not have been completed without the support of a number of people. Our students and colleagues at Governors State University and the University of Maine helped by providing fresh perspectives and by allowing us to share our earliest conceptualizations. We would like to mention in particular Dr. Jacque Elder, a member of the Governors State University faculty, who shared her expertise on MI.

We would also like to acknowledge the reviewers of previous editions whose wise counsel led us toward significant improvements. Finally, we want to recognize our publisher, especially the very talented staff who brought this project to fruition. We are especially indebted to Seth Dobrin. We often see statements from authors that their books would not have been completed without the help and support of their editors. In regard to Seth Dobrin, this statement is truer than usual. We would also like to thank Mary T. Stone for all her capable guidance and support.

Judith A. Lewis
Robert Q. Dana
Gregory A. Blevins

ABOUT THE AUTHORS

Dr. Judith A. Lewis retired in 2008 from Governors State University, where she served as Professor and Chair of Addictions Studies and Behavioral Health. She is a past president of the American Counseling Association (ACA) and the International Association of Marriage and Family Counselors. She is the coauthor of three texts for Brooks/Cole including *Substance Abuse Counseling, Management of Human Service Programs*, and *Community Counseling: Empowerment Strategies for a Diverse Society*. Dr. Lewis received her PhD from the University of Michigan and is a licensed psychologist in Illinois.

Dr. Robert Q. Dana is the vice president for Student Affairs at the University of Maine. He has direct responsibility for all campus life programs including Greek Life, Alcohol and Drug Education Programs, Residence Life, Counseling Services, and campus-wide crisis management services.

He received his doctorate in Human Development Counseling (Addictive Behaviors) from Vanderbilt University in Nashville, Tennessee. Dr. Dana spent a substantial part of his career as an addictive behaviors researcher and practitioner. He writes frequently on substance abuse and has conducted numerous studies on epidemiology and etiology of alcohol and other drug abuse. Dana has served as an extramural reviewer for state and federal agencies and as a journal reviewer for *Addictive Behaviors*. He teaches courses on addictions and is a member of the graduate faculty at University of Maine.

Dr. Gregory A. Blevins is interim assistant dean of the College of Health and Human Services, chair of the Addictions Studies and Behavioral Health Department, and professor of Addictions Studies. He completed the Specialty Certificate in Alcohol and Drug Abuse in 1974 and a doctorate in Sociology in 1979 at Western Michigan University. Dr. Blevins is a founder and life member of the International Coalition for Substance Abuse Educators and has served as a trainer for the Bemidji Area Office of Indian Health Services since 1988. Dr. Blevins has been married to Vicki Lyn for 30 years and has a daughter named Stacy.

INTRODUCTION

CHAPTER

I

Substance Abuse Counseling for the 21st Century

THE PRACTICE OF 21st century substance abuse counseling is well on its way toward fundamental change. In fact, the field is moving rapidly toward a paradigm shift that will leave 20th century models far behind. Looking back now, it is difficult to believe that only a few years ago the American "conventional wisdom" about substance abuse was built more on mythology than on science.

> This mythology is built on the premise that people who are grappling with issues related to addictions or substance abuse somehow belong in a different category of species from other human beings. The implication of the myths is that the collaborative partnerships that counselors like to build with their clients must suddenly be put aside when alcohol or other drugs find their way into the conversation. The stereotype about how substance abuse counselors must operate has become a self-propelling "conventional wisdom" that inspires avid belief with no basis in fact. (Lewis & Elder, in press)

Many members of the community of helping professionals actually joined with the general public in believing that successful interventions required "aggressive confrontation, a tearing down of defenses, coercion, and a wariness to avoid being deceived or conned" (Miller, 1996, p. 840).

In contrast, 21st century substance abuse counselors know that a collaborative and respectful approach is not just humane but also effective. They are aware that the most successful interventions are the ones that best fit the client's current life situation and concerns. They view their clients within a context that includes family, community, and even national policy. They are committed to the process of closing the gap between research and practice. As Miller and Carroll (2006,

p. 310) point out, "It is long overdue for science, rather than opinion and ideology, to shape interventions for drug problems."

The quest for advancement in substance abuse counseling practice is not just an intellectual exercise. It is a path to real improvement in real people's lives. Look at the following examples and then consider what kind of help might best meet the needs of human beings who are in pain.

- Marvin was caught selling a small amount of cocaine and served some time in prison. After his release, he was determined to put that bitter part of his life behind him. Now, however, he is back at home, and he has begun to lose hope. His family, his friends, and the people he knows in the neighborhood all seem to be involved in drug use. He says he can't find a way out.
- Last week, Kathy's drug and alcohol abuse created a medical crisis that brought her to the hospital emergency room. She had tried to withdraw from drug use a number of times over the last few years, but every time she sought help, her life partner, Roy, threatened to leave her. She knows she should choose recovery, but this relationship still comes first.
- Carlos, a high school honor student, was accepted into his first-choice university as he planned to be the first one in his family to participate in higher education. His celebration got out of hand as he went to school intoxicated and with alcohol in his possession. On the basis of the school's zero-tolerance policy, he risked being suspended and prevented from graduating with his class. He feels as though his entire future has been destroyed by this one incident.
- Nine-year-old Melissa has always seemed to be a bright, outgoing, and well-adjusted child. Lately, she has come to school more exhausted every day, falling asleep at times when she would normally have been actively engaged. Melissa insists that nothing is wrong, but the reality is that her father has returned to binge drinking after years in recovery. Though her mother's attention has been focused on this crisis, Melissa has been shouldering much of the responsibility for taking care of her two preschool siblings.
- Marian is very serious about her career in sales. She is aware of the glass ceiling that has kept women from progressing very far in her company, so she does everything she can to fit in. She goes to the bar with her colleagues when they invite her, and she dines with clients when she can. Recently, she has had some warnings at the office that her drinking is getting out of hand. She is worried that she is suddenly careening off her desired career path.

The situations just described illustrate just a few of the ways substance abuse can destroy the hopes and plans that people hold dear. Marvin, Kathy, Carlos, Melissa, and Marian also help to demonstrate just how heterogeneous the faces of substance abuse really are. The fact is that counselors in all settings find themselves confronting substance abuse issues every day. Marvin might seek help from a substance abuse specialist, but he would be just as likely to enter the helping system through contact with a counselor in the community mental health or criminal justice system. Carlos or Melissa might come to the attention of a school or family counselor. Kathy might be reached through the health system, but could also be helped effectively by a counselor specializing in work with couples. Marian might be referred to an employee assistance or career counselor. Wherever an individual enters the network of helpers, however, he or she deserves competent attention.

A national initiative designed to improve substance abuse treatment pointed out that there should be no wrong door to treatment. "Effective systems must ensure that an individual needing treatment will be identified and assessed and will receive treatment, either directly or through appropriate referral, no matter where he or she enters the realm of services" (Center for Substance Abuse Treatment, 2000, p. 14). The implication of this statement is that all helpers, whether or not they consider themselves "addiction specialists," have a responsibility to respond to problems associated with substance use. The school counselor who hopes to prevent the negative consequences of adolescent drug use, the family therapist who wonders why a particular family system seems unusually rigid and secretive, the mental health counselor facing a client's steady deterioration—all these people confront substance abuse issues every day. They can appropriately deal with these issues if they learn to recognize the abuse of alcohol and other drugs and adapt their counseling or referral skills to meet the needs of affected clients.

The purpose of this book is to help counselors develop the basic knowledge and skills they will need to deal with their clients' substance abuse problems. Some counselors will choose to specialize, devoting a major portion of their professional careers to substance abuse issues. For them, this text will provide a general framework on which to base further study. Other practitioners will see themselves as generalists, working with heterogeneous client populations and addressing substance abuse problems as they arise. These counselors will find guidelines in the book for adapting their current skills and techniques to the special needs of substance-dependent clients. Our intention is not to promote any one theory at the expense of others but, rather, to describe the methods that are best supported by current research and, above all, to encourage an individualized approach based on the unique needs of each client.

SUBSTANCE ABUSE: A WORKING DEFINITION

A counselor who wants to carry out appropriate assessments and collaborate on action plans for clients needs to begin with at least a working definition of substance abuse. For general counseling purposes, a problem is related to substance abuse if a client's use of alcohol or other mood-altering drugs has undesired effects on his or her life or on the lives of others. The negative effects of the substance may involve impairment of physiological, psychological, social, or occupational functioning. In terms of our working definition, use of a drug that modifies the mood or behavior of the user is not necessarily considered substance abuse unless the user's functioning is negatively affected. We also differentiate between substance abuse and addiction, defining a client's problem as addiction only when physical symptoms of withdrawal or tolerance to the substance are present. Among the psychoactive substances associated with abuse or addiction are alcohol, sedative hypnotics, opioids, amphetamines, cannabis, cocaine, and tobacco. (Chapter 2 provides an overview of these drugs and their physiological effects.)

Of all of the substances likely to cause problems among clients, alcohol is the most common. Alcohol abuse has major effects on the physical health of drinkers.

In addition, it plays a major role in many of society's most pressing concerns, including accidents, violence, criminal behavior, family problems, and productivity loss. Clearly, a problem of this magnitude affects so many clients in so many ways that no counselor can overlook it.

Counselors in virtually any setting can also expect to see a large number of clients affected by drugs other than alcohol. Many people routinely use marijuana, cocaine, stimulants, sedatives, and tranquilizers, and millions are addicted to nicotine. As we have said, the mere use of a drug is not automatically problematic. The substance users who need the assistance of counselors are those who have developed life problems or health risks from their drug use. Thus, the counselor should recognize individual differences among substance-using clients and try to address drug use in the context of the client's total life functioning.

PRINCIPLES FOR 21ST CENTURY SUBSTANCE ABUSE COUNSELING

The emergent paradigm for substance abuse counseling represents a fresh approach and a new mindset. Although this perspective is broad, it does lend itself to practical guidelines for implementation. Counselors at the cutting edge of practice tend to adhere to the following general principles:

1. Focus on evidence-based practices.
2. Use a respectful and positive approach with all clients.
3. View substance abuse problems on a continuum from nonproblematic to problematic use rather than as an either/or situation.
4. Collaborate with clients on the creation of individualized plans for change.
5. Build interventions based on the recognition that substance abuse occurs in a social context.
6. Use a multicultural perspective to meet the needs of diverse client populations.
7. Acknowledge the idea that client advocacy is central to the counselor's role.

The rest of this section details how these principles can be put into everyday use.

EVIDENCE-BASED PRACTICES

One of the major shortcomings of substance abuse treatment in the past has been a certain rigidity in the choice of methods, a tendency of treatment centers to rely too heavily on their familiar practices at the expense of fresh possibilities. Although a number of options are available in some areas of the United States, treatment alternatives in many regions are severely limited, and clients who find themselves unable to fit into mainstream approaches have few choices. Especially in alcoholism facilities, certain practices have become so common that caregivers, managers, community members, and even clients tend to accept these practices without question. Yet these methods are grounded neither in theory nor in behavioral research. Many counselors assume, for instance, that "educating clients about alcoholism" is a necessary and possibly even sufficient mechanism for engendering sobriety; yet one would be hard pressed to find real support for the generalization that the provision of information can be counted on to bring about desired changes in attitude or behavior. Similarly, confrontational counselor behaviors, long thought to be the key components of addiction treatment, have not shown evidence of effectiveness. If anything, methods designed to convince clients of their impairment have been associated not only with resistance but also with a lack of behavior change.

> Creating a close connection between research and practice is a high priority in the field of substance abuse. The time lag between empirical findings and application to services is still longer than it should be, but the body of research on the effectiveness of various modalities has shown vast improvement in recent years and the existence of evidence-based practices is widely recognized. (Center for Substance Abuse Treatment, 2000)

In general terms, *evidence-based practices* are "approaches to prevention or treatment that are validated by some form of documented scientific evidence…(and) stand in contrast to approaches that are based on tradition, convention, belief, or anecdotal evidence" (Substance Abuse and Mental Health Services Administration [SAMHSA], 2009a). When a substance abuse professional is in the process of making a decision about whether to use a particular method, he or she normally takes into account whether the procedures "have been subjected to randomized clinical trials or other experimental research designs and have been found to be more effective than 'treatment as usual'" (Eliason, 2007, p. 22). Additionally, an evidence-based practice should carry with it a specific set of procedures that are disseminated in a manual that allows for accurate replication.

A focus on evidence-based practices does not imply the existence of a concrete list of treatments that would be applied to every client and therefore become the new treatment as usual. In fact, focusing on evidence is more likely to be a mindset that allows practitioners to think through their treatment decisions by weighing available scientific information and considering client needs. The very notion of a scientific approach brings with it the assumption that any list of "what works" is bound to be in constant flux as new data become available. The key to success for a substance abuse counselor is simply to be aware of the advances in the field and to integrate these advances into one's practice.

Full-time helping professionals, including counselors, have always found it difficult to keep up with research by regularly perusing scientific journals. It is reasonable, however, to expect that awareness of current research studies will continue to grow because of Internet access. Consider, for example, the enormous benefit of SAMHSA's National Registry of Evidence-Based Programs and Practices (SAMHSA, 2009b). This online, searchable registry lists interventions that have gone through extensive review processes. Each listing includes not only descriptive information about the program but also ratings of outcome research, dissemination materials, and populations studied. Some of the programs listed are designed for specific populations, for example, adolescent-focused programs such as Adolescent Community Reinforcement (Dennis et al., 2004) and Multidimensional Family Therapy (Liddle, Rowe, Dakov, Henderson, & Greenbaum, 2009). Among the general interventions with strong ratings are Motivational Enhancement Therapy (Ball et al., 2007), Motivational Interviewing (Carroll et al., 2006), Relapse Prevention Therapy (Marlatt, Parks, & Witkiewitz, 2002), Twelve-Step Facilitation (Nowinski, 2006), Behavioral Couples Therapy (Fals-Stewart, Birchler, & Kelley, 2006), and

Skill Training (Rohsenow et al., 2004). Each of these approaches tends to appear in "what-works" lists, but this registry includes the backup data and literature reviews that a scientifically oriented counselor would always want to have.

A RESPECTFUL AND POSITIVE APPROACH

In contrast to the now-discredited notion that substance abuse clients are unable to participate in their own treatment planning, current thinking emphasizes the idea that "treatment must be respectful and empowering to the individual" (Center for Substance Abuse Treatment, 2000, p. 20). Counselors have learned that a respectful and supportive approach can bring better results than an aggressive one. In fact, use of a respectful and positive approach is an evidence-based practice. As Miller and Carroll (2006) point out,

> When randomly assigned, counselors' clients often differ widely in outcomes even if they are ostensibly delivering the same manual-guided treatment. Counselors who are higher in warmth and accurate empathy have clients who show greater improvement in drug use and problems. As early as the second session, clients' ratings of their working relationship with the counselor are predictive of treatment outcome. (p. 301)

The body of research in support of motivational interviewing provides even more potent evidence of the power of the collaborative relationship. *Motivational Interviewing* is "a directive, client-centered counseling style for eliciting behavior change by helping clients explore and resolve ambivalence" (Rollnick & Miller, 1995). The *spirit* of motivational interviewing arises from the basic idea that the motivation for change comes from within the client and is elicited by a skilled and supportive interviewer who recognizes that the client holds the decision-making responsibility for his or her own life. The motivational interviewer knows that the decision to change comes not from the client's basic traits but from the counselor–client interaction. A large and growing body of literature indicates that this seemingly simple intervention brings about significant change (Hettema, Steele, & Miller, 2005; Rubak, Sandboek, Lauritzen, & Christensen, 2005).

Clients tend to enter the counseling process feeling ambivalent about change; the last thing a counselor would want to do is to create a situation that engenders defensiveness. Moreover, people dealing with substance abuse concerns frequently begin treatment at a time when their hope for a better life is at a low point. They can benefit from a dose of optimism, a sense of possibility, and a feeling that their lives are worth saving. Think about the examples discussed at the beginning of this chapter. Marvin, for instance, is very much aware of the problems that have dogged him for as long as he can remember. Given his sense of hopelessness, the best possibility of change for him depends on his developing a new ability to visualize success.

A counselor who has a respectful attitude toward people grappling with addiction recognizes that clients hold the ultimate responsibility for their own recovery. Encouraging clients to accept this challenge is not just humane; it is also empirically supported. People who believe in the possibility of controlling their own lives seem better able to engage in health-enhancing behaviors, including those relating to substance abuse. In fact, "people's belief that they can motivate themselves and regulate their own behavior plays a crucial role in whether they even consider changing detrimental health habits or pursuing rehabilitative activities" (Bandura, 1997, p. 119).

An individual's belief that he or she can solve a problem, accomplish a task, or function successfully has been labeled by Bandura (1997) as self-efficacy. Efficacy involves an ability to deal with one's environment, mobilizing whatever cognitive and behavioral skills are needed to manage challenging situations. Perceived self-efficacy entails people's judgment about their own coping abilities. This judgment affects all aspects of performance; those who lack self-efficacy tend to avoid challenges and give up quickly when they face obstacles. In contrast, people who believe in their own efficacy concerning a particular task are more likely to persevere.

> Such beliefs influence the courses of action people choose to pursue, how much effort they put forth in given endeavors, how long they will persevere in the face of obstacles and failures, their resilience to adversity, whether their thought patterns are self-hindering or self-aiding, how much stress and depression they experience in coping with taxing environmental demands, and the level of accomplishments they realize. (Bandura, 1997, p. 3)

Thus, clients dealing with any pressing life problem are most likely to succeed in making and maintaining behavior changes if they have positive perceptions of their self-efficacy. When they are dealing with substance abuse issues, self-efficacy becomes even more important as a means of preventing relapse. Given the importance of self-efficacy for the maintenance of positive behaviors and the prevention of relapse, the counselor should reinforce each client's sense that control is possible. Treatment should focus on enhancing the client's feelings of personal mastery, especially through the provision of opportunities to plan for and practice appropriate coping behaviors.

SUBSTANCE ABUSE DIAGNOSIS: CONTINUUM, NOT DICHOTOMY

Treatment providers sometimes oversimplify the assessment of substance abuse problems, creating a dichotomy that fails to confront the complexity of the diagnostic process. Such oversimplification is particularly common in dealing with alcohol problems. Many people assume that they can identify alcoholism as a unitary disease and that once this identification has been made, a particular course of treatment can be described. In fact, what is usually called *alcoholism* is a multivariate syndrome. Drinkers vary in terms of consumption, physical symptoms, patterns of drinking behavior, life consequences of drinking, personality, social environment, gender, culture, and a variety of other factors. Given the differences among individuals, no one treatment plan—and no one label—could possibly be appropriate for all clients.

The difficulty with the dichotomous classification of *yes* or *no* for addiction-related concerns lies in its implicit assumption that because we know that a client is an "alcoholic" or an "addict" we know how to treat him or her. If we are to make appropriate treatment decisions, we need to do a great deal more than labeling a client's dysfunction. Use of a dichotomous diagnosis, whether of alcoholism or drug addiction, actually interferes with treatment planning by masking individual differences. This simplistic approach to assessment also lessens the potential effectiveness of treatment by discouraging early intervention in cases of problematic drinking or drug use. An either/or diagnosis leads inexorably to a generalized, diffuse treatment package that at worst may be ineffective and at best may meet the needs only of individuals with serious, chronic, long-standing substance abuse disorders. Insistence on a clear diagnosis of "alcoholism," for instance, drives away from treatment many people who are not necessarily dependent on alcohol but who could benefit from assistance in dealing with life problems associated with incipient alcohol abuse. If we wait until people are ready to accept a diagnosis of "alcoholism" or "addiction," we may be missing an opportunity to help them when they are best able to benefit from counseling. Miller and Carroll (2006) point out that "there is ... no clear moment when a person 'becomes' dependent or addicted" and that "interventions appropriate to one region of the continuum may be unhelpful or even counterproductive at another level of development" (p. 296).

Suppose that instead of conceptualizing substance abuse disorders merely as present or absent, we view drug or alcohol use along a continuum from nonproblematic to highly problematic, as shown in Figure 1.1. The figure shows, from left to right, six categories of substance use.

Such a continuum does not imply progression. An individual who begins to develop problems does not necessarily move along the continuum from left to right. On the contrary, the various points on the continuum may represent different individuals, some of whom move from less serious to more serious involvement, some of whom stay at one point for an indefinite length of time, and some of whom may move back and forth between problematic and nonproblematic substance use.

Because of the difficulty in predicting the course of substance use for any one individual, counselors need to be as helpful as possible in responding to the client's needs as they are presented at the time of first contact. The notion that substance abuse problems will increase in seriousness over time is understandably difficult for clients with as yet minor difficulties to accept. Many treatment providers label the client's hesitancy as "denial" and wait for the individual to develop a sufficient number of problems to warrant acceptance of the label of "alcoholic" or "addict." More appropriately, counselors should attempt to devise treatment plans that fit the nature and seriousness of the client's current difficulties. Consider, for example, the case of Carlos, who was introduced at the beginning of this chapter. It is apparent that Carlos could benefit from assistance in addressing the life problems that are associated with his drinking. It is much less apparent that Carlos's drinking could be termed *alcoholic*. The counselor's focus should be on helping this student make decisions and plans for getting his life back on track. Insisting on the acceptance of a specific diagnosis might well be damaging to the process.

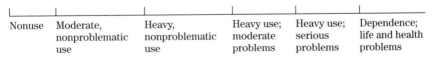

| Nonuse | Moderate, nonproblematic use | Heavy, nonproblematic use | Heavy use; moderate problems | Heavy use; serious problems | Dependence; life and health problems |

FIGURE 1.1 | CONTINUUM OF SUBSTANCE ABUSE.

A counselor can explore a client's life situation and get a sense of where the individual stands on the continuum from nonproblematic to severely problematic drug use. It is not possible, however, to determine through the use of any objective measure whether an individual client should be helped. The fact that traditional treatment approaches have tended to be appropriate only for those clients clustered at the far right of the continuum means that services have in effect been withheld from people exhibiting minor or moderate problems. Where is the cutoff point below which a client should be denied services? Someone with many serious life problems related to drug use clearly needs help, but an individual whose problems are only at the beginning stage may also benefit from assistance, albeit of a less intensive nature. Thus, an individual who has been arrested for driving under the influence of alcohol deserves a chance to learn how to discriminate his or her blood alcohol level. A young person developing problems associated with careless use of substances deserves an opportunity to learn responsible decision making. A person who has learned to abuse drugs as a way of dealing with grief or stress deserves the services of a counselor who can help in the formation of more appropriate coping methods. These clients need help that is not sullied by the process of labeling or by the assumption that progression of their problems is easily predictable. They need to be seen as individuals who can be assisted without being forced to accept diagnoses that they see as inapplicable.

Individualized Plans for Change

Counselors who move away from dichotomous diagnoses find themselves increasingly able to provide help tailored to the individual needs of their clients. When we think of the people we serve as complex, multifaceted human beings, we can work in collaboration with our clients to develop change plans that are as unique as the clients themselves. This process depends on the counselor's recognition that no one goal or treatment outcome is likely to be appropriate for every client.

The client's substance abuse must be considered in the context of other life problems, although not necessarily in terms of causality. Substance abuse tends to be associated with a variety of social, psychological, familial, and financial problems. The counselor does not need to determine whether these problems are a cause or a result of substance abuse. Each of a client's major concerns should be addressed as part of the counseling process under the assumption that a favorable outcome involves rehabilitation across several life domains. Only a collaborative assessment process that sets individualized goals and takes note of individual strengths as well as deficits can lead to comprehensive treatment. Thus, each client's plan for change should include long- and short-term goals that reflect the individual's commitments and deal with both substance use and other issues. Among the general life areas that might be addressed, depending on the individual's concerns, are the following:

- resolving or avoiding legal problems
- attaining financial stability
- attaining stability in family relationships
- setting and meeting career goals
- improving social skills

- improving assertion skills
- enhancing physical health and fitness
- learning more effective methods for coping with stress
- developing more effective problem-solving and decision-making skills
- learning relaxation skills
- learning to recognize and express feelings
- adapting more effectively to work or school
- developing social-support systems
- increasing involvement in recreation and social pursuits
- dealing with mental health issues
- increasing self-esteem and self-efficacy

Obviously, not every client needs to set goals in each of these areas. The assessment process should identify issues that can be addressed through treatment, with interventions then tailored to the specific outcomes desired.

The assessment process should also guide the counselor and client toward individualized goal setting with regard to future substance use. One of the goals of substance abuse counseling, by its very definition, is a change from a problematic level of substance use to a nonproblematic level (abstinence or responsible use). Yet even this one generalization is subject to adaptation from client to client. In each individual case, the client and counselor must work together to decide on the most desirable outcome in terms of substance use. This decision is especially complex when the drug of choice is alcohol. A debate has raged for many years over the possibility that people who have had concerns about alcohol use might be able to achieve moderation. Yet much of the controversy surrounding the concept of "controlled drinking" arises from the way the issue is framed. Writers and clinicians concerned about the dangers of controlled drinking tend to ask whether that goal is "possible for alcoholics." Instead, the question should be "What outcomes seem to be most appropriate for what types of clients in what situations?" Clearly, there are individuals for whom controlled drinking is an inappropriate objective, just as there are individuals more likely to relapse when they attempt abstinence. People who have long-standing problems with alcohol, who now have many life problems associated with drinking, who show signs of being physically addicted to alcohol, who have health problems that might be exacerbated by alcohol use, or who have been unsuccessful at drinking moderately are not good candidates for moderation and should be encouraged to opt for a goal of abstinence.

It is not surprising that those who treat alcoholism tend to be put off by any mention of controlled drinking as an option. Until recently, almost all of the clients who sought help for alcohol problems fit the profile of the person for whom abstinence was the only safe goal! Now, however, the client population has become more heterogeneous. As we see younger, less seriously impaired people in treatment, we need to consider involving clients more actively in deciding on their own treatment aspirations. Clinicians who are frightened by the concept of controlled drinking tend to believe that although many people would be harmed by a goal of moderation, none would be put at any particular risk by striving for abstinence. In fact, however, "for nondependent persons the risk of relapse from controlled drinking is, if anything, lower than that from abstinence" (Miller, 1985, p. 590).

If drinkers are young and healthy, if they have not shown signs of physical dependence on alcohol, if their problem drinking is of recent duration, if they have few life problems associated with alcohol use, and if they object to abstinence, they may do best working toward moderating their drinking.

In every case, a client's commitment to a goal is a major factor in his or her ability to reach it. The key to setting goals in this important area is a recognition that differential outcomes are not only possible but may also be preferable to a rigid insistence that each client must fit the counselor's preconceived ideal. Marlatt's (1998) discussion of harm reduction provides a helpful conceptualization. Stating that "harm reduction recognizes abstinence as an ideal outcome but accepts alternatives that reduce harm" (p. 50), Marlatt points out that requiring abstinence as a precondition for receiving help may place an unnecessary barrier in the way of entry into treatment. Instead, he suggests, we should meet people on their own terms and thereby encourage small steps toward positive change.

The counselor who has worked out a reasonable set of goals with the client can use a number of techniques for reaching those goals. Among the counseling methods most frequently used in the substance abuse field are behavioral self-control training (teaching clients the techniques they need to monitor to change their own behaviors); contingency management (identifying and manipulating environmental contingencies that reward or punish the substance use behaviors); relaxation, assertion, and social skills training; couple and family therapy; career counseling; cognitive restructuring (helping clients alter their appraisals of self and environment); assistance with problem solving and decision making; aversive conditioning (coupling substance use with a real or imagined unpleasant experience); stress management training; group counseling; lifestyle and recreational planning; provision of information about the effects of psychoactive drugs; and referral to such self-help organizations as Alcoholics Anonymous and Narcotics Anonymous. Of course, the counseling process often takes place in the context of an agency which also uses pharmacological components.

Any combination of the methods mentioned earlier may be appropriate for a specific client. It would not be effective, however, to use this entire group of interventions as a package for all substance-abusing clients. Addressing problems beyond the narrow band of substance use behaviors is an important strategy, but it can be workable only to the degree that it is adapted to match each client's actual needs.

Social Context

The *fundamental attribution error* (FAE) is a common error that skews the ways in which people explain human behaviors. In reviewing the FAE, Gladwell (2000) explained that we all tend to use a "dispositional" explanation of events as opposed to an explanation based on context. "When it comes to interpreting other people's behaviors, human beings invariably make the mistake of overestimating the importance of fundamental character traits and underestimating the importance of the situation and context" (Gladwell, 2000, p. 160).

Unfortunately, people in the helping professions are as prone to misattribution as anyone else and the tendency to overlook the role of environmental factors permeates many approaches to counseling and therapy. To the detriment of their clients, helpers still focus more attention on negative internal characteristics than on the social, cultural, political, and economic factors that affect their clients' lives. All too often, the counseling spotlight stays on the clients' diagnoses, rather than on their strengths, and on their personal vulnerabilities, rather than their environments. The result is that clients feel increasingly powerless.

The tendency to view problems as internal to the client is especially prevalent in substance abuse treatment, where addictive behaviors are often viewed as resulting from personal traits that are resistant to change. In fact, however, substance use behaviors are powerfully affected by social context. Moos (2006) examined four theoretical perspectives that provide explanations of the role of social context in substance use. *Social control theory* emphasizes the degree to which "strong bonds with family, school, work, religion, and other aspects of traditional society motivate individuals to engage in responsible behavior and refrain from substance use" (Moos, 2006, p. 182). In contrast, the absence of these bonds makes substance abuse more likely. Similarly, *behavioral choice theory* sees substance abuse as less likely to occur when the individual's environment provides reinforcements that serve as alternatives to the reinforcing effects of substance use. *Social learning theory* emphasizes that the modeling effects of drug-related attitudes and behaviors are prevalent in the individual's environment. *Stress and coping theory* explains that stressors in the social environment can lead to substance abuse in the absence of healthier coping skills. What all of these perspectives indicate is that the individual's social context—from family, to community, to the public arena—can increase the risk of substance abuse or protect against it. A counseling process that is built on the awareness of social context emphasizes both client empowerment and multidimensional treatment.

EMPOWERMENT STRATEGIES   As important as it is for counselors to recognize the impact of the social environment, it is even more important that their clients come to understand it. People who fail to see the broader context of their problems often feel bogged down, mired in self-blame, and become helpless. Understanding one's life in a broader context is actually empowering. As Lewis et al. (2002) pointed out, counselors who use an empowerment-based approach with their clients should be able to

- Identify strengths and resources of clients and students.
- Identify the social, political, economic, and cultural factors that affect the clients/students.
- Recognize the signs indicating that an individual's behaviors and concerns reflect responses to systemic or internalized oppression.
- At an appropriate developmental level, help the individual identify the external barriers that affect his or her development.
- Train students and clients in self-advocacy skills.
- Help students and clients create self-advocacy action plans.
- Assist students and clients in carrying out action plans.

MULTIDIMENSIONAL TREATMENT   When clients eliminate problematic substance abuse from their lives, they are sometimes surprised when other concerns fail to fade away. Some problems remain in effect, either because their etiology was independent of substance abuse or because years of heavy drinking or drug use have created multiple life problems too serious to be ignored. It is for this reason that counseling must be multidimensional, focusing on specific drug-use behaviors but seeing them in the context of the client's psychological, social, and vocational functioning.

Counselors who believe in individualized, efficacy-enhancing treatment tend to appreciate the importance of a number of factors beyond the individual's specific substance-abusing behaviors. They realize that in the long run clients' recovery depends not just on their intrapersonal qualities but also on the nature of their social environments and on their repertoire of skills for coping with the "real world" in which sobriety must be maintained.

Social, cultural, biological, and psychological factors interact reciprocally in both the etiology and the resolution of substance-related problems. A major implication of this view is that efforts toward prevention and rehabilitation aimed at changing alcohol and drug use may not be maximally effective if they are limited in focus to the substance use behavior itself or to an isolated domain of the individual's life. Instead, interventions should focus simultaneously on multiple domains.

At the beginning of this chapter, for instance, we met Marian, whose work setting was characterized by widespread alcohol use. At one time, counselors would have perceived Marian's drinking behaviors to be provoked entirely by internal mechanisms. They might have assumed that it was her alcoholism alone that motivated her drinking and that her statements about the work setting were mere excuses. This notion of recovery would have required that she abstain regardless of environmental factors. Now, experienced counselors tend to be more cognizant of the idea that behaviors are affected by both internal and external factors. Of course, Marian must examine her vulnerability to addiction, as well as such personal dimensions as spirituality, physical health, cognitions, behaviors, and attitudes. At the same time, however, she and her counselor would address environmental factors, asking what skills she would need to cope with the risks to sobriety that are prevalent in her workplace. She might even have to decide whether this job was worth the risk or whether she should consider other career options.

The multidimensional nature of recovery has major implications for the counseling process. First, treatment goals need to take into account not just substance use behavior but also rehabilitation in such areas as occupational functioning, psychological well-being, and social involvement. Second, levels of functioning in these aspects of life may have strong influences on the individual's ability to maintain healthy new behaviors. The social and physical environments that surround all people hold the potential to support health or to place it at risk. Like Marian, any person trying to make a difficult life change must find ways to avoid some of the stressful situations that are most dangerous to sobriety and to cope with others.

It is a rare counseling setting that successfully addresses these issues and prepares clients to face the social and economic realities of their environment after treatment. Such treatment programs do exist, however, with one of the best documented examples provided by the Community Reinforcement Program

(Meyers & Smith, 1995). This program is unusual in its comprehensiveness, providing treatment that includes the following components:

- job counseling
- couples counseling
- resocialization and recreation
- problem prevention rehearsal
- early warning system (a daily "happiness scale")
- supportive group sessions
- "buddy" procedures utilizing recovering peer advisers
- written contracts focused on counselor and client responsibilities

A multidimensional approach like the Community Reinforcement Program is built on a recognition of the very real pressures faced by clients when they return to their familiar social and work environments. Expanding positive social-support systems and building personal resources for health are major challenges and important opportunities for any client.

MULTICULTURAL PERSPECTIVE

A multicultural perspective is central to competent practice in substance abuse counseling. The rationale for emphasizing this point of view is based on some of the current realities of the field, including the increasing diversity of client populations, the importance of context for all clients, the need for fresh perspectives, and the need for flexibility.

- Diverse Client Populations. Addiction counselors work with a client population that is becoming more diverse every day. Because their clients are so different, counselors must have many strategies in their repertoires. What works for one client—or even one group of clients—will not necessarily work for another.
- The Importance of Context. All clients are affected not just by their own addictions but also by the world around them. A multicultural perspective helps counselors understand how great an impact our cultural context has on all of us. Counseling strategies should take into account the realities of the world that the recovering client will reenter. One of those realities is the pervasiveness of oppression.
- Fresh Perspectives. The models that are most frequently used in addiction treatment were first developed to meet the needs of a homogeneous group of clients. Now we need new models, innovative techniques, and fresh perspectives.
- The Need for Flexibility. Counselors need to be aware that their own cultural backgrounds affect their worldviews. The assumptions that we make about the world are not always in tune with the views of others. All people have multiple cultural identities that affect their risk factors for addiction, their responsiveness to specific forms of treatment, and their prospects for recovery. If we listen closely to our clients we can tailor our work to their specific goals and needs.

Until recently the bulk of information about substance abuse treatment was based on research carried out with White male subjects. Many of the generalizations accepted by substance abuse counselors were therefore severely limited. Most counselors have now come to accept the fact that their clients may be members of highly diverse groups with widely varying goals, needs, and social pressures. In this milieu, successful practice requires multicultural competence. As Sue, Arredondo, and McDavis (1992) suggest that multicultural competencies fall into three general areas: the counselor's awareness of his or her own assumptions, values, and biases; the counselor's understanding of the worldview of the culturally different client; and the counselor's ability to develop appropriate intervention strategies and techniques. Gaining a multicultural perspective is, in many ways, a life-changing process for counselors, leading them to make changes in deeply held assumptions and to examine both their own worldviews and the cultural biases that are implicit in mainstream counseling practices.

A multicultural perspective has much in common with the awareness of social context that was emphasized in Principle 5, earlier.

> When we view our counseling relationships through the lens of multiculturalism, we see ourselves and our clients in an environmental context. This awareness of context enables us to make an important transition in our own thinking from assuming that our clients' problems are caused solely by intrapsychic or intrafamilial factors to recognizing that political, social, and economic explanations are often more accurate. ... We notice oppression. (Lewis & Arnold, 1998, p. 52)

An environment characterized by *oppression* is one in which membership in a particular group places limits on one's access to the rights, resources, and benefits that are normally available to members of more privileged groups. Oppression of this kind remains ubiquitous in today's world, making it unlikely that any counselor could avoid dealing with its effects on his or her clients. "It is a short step from becoming aware of the impact of the cultural milieu to noticing the role of oppression in our clients' lives" (Lewis & Arnold, 1998, p. 51).

In working with gay male, lesbian, bisexual, and transgendered clients, for instance, the counselor should be alert to heterosexism as a stressor, particularly when this oppression appears in the guise of religious condemnation (Pecoraro, 2000). In working with women, counselors should take note of the high correlation between addiction and experiences of sexual victimization. They should also note that access to treatment is affected by gender, because many treatment facilities overlook women's special health problems, ignore the need for child care, or fail to deal with the fact that so many women are poor and underinsured.

Racial discrimination and social inequality are, of course, "rooted in the social organization of our society" (Holcomb-McCoy & Mitchell, 2007, p. 137) and must never be overlooked in a counseling situation.

> Oppression in a counseling context designates the disadvantage and injustice some people suffer not because tyrannical power coerces them, but because of the everyday practices of a society. Oppression in this sense is embedded in unquestioned norms, habits, and symbols; in the assumptions underlying institutional rules; and in the collective consequences of following those rules. (Holcomb-McCoy & Michell, 2007, p. 137)

Clearly, an effective one-to-one, family, or group counseling process would depend on the counselor's willingness to address head-on any issues of racism and other oppressions that have an impact on the client's well-being. The days of forcing the client to focus solely on his or her internal traits are long gone.

In addition to integrating oppression-related issues into direct client services, counselors should be knowledgeable about the impact of societal inequality on their clients' development. Two notable examples of this inequality have direct effects that are specific to substance abuse and health: health care disparities and unequal treatment in the criminal justice system.

HEALTH CARE DISPARITIES   Although disparities in health outcomes, including life expectancy, are widely known to exist, there remains some disagreement about causal factors, with some writers still focusing on the possibility that cross-population differences in individual health behaviors and help seeking might account for the gaps. The weight of current research, however, seems to indicate that the quality and amount of service provided to patients do differ across racial and ethnic lines. A study carried out by the Institute of Medicine (IOM) solidly confirmed what health professionals have known for some time: Clear disparities exist between health care services received by racial and ethnic minorities and those received by White patients.

> An IOM study committee reviewed well over 100 studies that assessed the quality of healthcare for various racial and ethnic minority groups, while holding constant variations in insurance status, patient income, and other access-related factors. Many of these studies also controlled for other potential confounding factors, such as racial differences in the severity or stage of disease progression, the presence of co-morbid illnesses, where care is received (e.g., public or private hospitals and health systems) and other patient demographic variables, such as age and gender. Some studies that employed more rigorous research designs followed patients prospectively, using clinical data abstracted from patients' charts, rather than administrative data used for insurance claims. The study committee was struck by the consistency of research findings: even among the better-controlled studies, the vast majority indicated that minorities are less likely than whites to receive needed services, including clinically necessary procedures. These disparities exist in a number of disease areas, including cancer, cardiovascular disease, HIV/AIDS, diabetes, and mental illness, and are found across a range of procedures, including routine treatments for common health problems. (Institute of Medicine, 2002, p. 2)

The issue of health disparity cuts across all types of conditions and treatments, and substance abuse is no exception. In fact, the National Institute on Drug Abuse (NIDA) has embarked on an effort to address disparities in treatment and outcome for minority populations. The NIDA report emphasizes the fact that the stigma that is generally applied to drug users is actually magnified for African Americans and Latinos.

> Racial/ethnic minority populations are perhaps most adversely affected by this stigma and its effects, leading to misperceptions about drug abuse and addiction in minority communities. ... For example, the common perception is that minority groups, particularly Blacks and Hispanics, use drugs more than Whites even though epidemiological data show little difference in overall use by race/ethnicity. In fact, in some instances

minority groups are less likely to use licit or illicit drugs. There are, however, great differences in the consequences of drug use for racial/ethnic minorities, creating a great need to better understand the unique prevention, treatment, and health services needs of these communities. (National Institute on Drug Abuse, 2004)

If substance-abusing patients are subjected to greater stigma by society as a whole and possibly are subjected to lower standards of health care as well, then oppression is at work and should be recognized as such by counselors.

CRIMINAL JUSTICE INEQUITIES   A decades-long "War on Drugs" greatly increased the numbers of people incarcerated in federal or state prisons in the United States. According to the Sentencing Project,

> Sentencing policies brought about by the "war on drugs" resulted in a dramatic growth in inmates convicted of a drug offense. At the Federal level, prisoners incarcerated on a drug charge make up more than half of all inmates while the number of drug offenders in state prisons has increased thirteen-fold since 1980. Most of these persons are not high-level actors in the drug trade, and most have no prior criminal record for a violent offense. (Sentencing Project, 2009)

Some changes in public policy are moving into the forefront, with one federal official, Drug Czar Gil Kerlikowske, stating that the concept of a "War on Drugs" should be changed. "Regardless of how you try to explain to people it's a 'war on drugs' or a 'war on a product,' people see a war as a war on them," he said, "We're not at war with people in this country" (Fields, 2009, p. A3). A renewed emphasis on addressing drug problems through the health system rather than the criminal justice system is sorely needed in light of the impact the "War on Drugs" has had on communities of color. According to the Drug Policy Alliance (2002),

- Though African Americans constitute 13% of the United States' monthly drug users, they represent 35% of those persons arrested for drug possession, 55% of drug possession convictions, and 74% of those sentenced to prison for drug possession.
- Under federal legislation enacted in 1986, it takes 1/100 as much crack cocaine as powder cocaine to trigger equal mandatory minimum sentences. In 1995, although American crack users were 52% Whites and 38% African Americans, Blacks accounted for 88% of those sentenced for crack offenses and Whites just 4.1%.
- Almost 1.4 million African American males or 14% of the adult Black male population are currently disenfranchised as a result of felony convictions.

Statistics like this make clear that a "multicultural perspective" goes beyond the knowledge of varying cultures, as important as that may be, to a recognition of the role of oppression in clients' lives. "Once we begin to notice systemic oppression, it is just one more short step to accepting our responsibility for social action" (Lewis & Arnold, 1998, p. 51). The new paradigm for substance abuse counseling adds the advocacy role to the direct-service component of the counselor's professional life.

ADVOCACY

Every human being is powerfully influenced by his or her social context, but clients grappling with substance abuse concerns often have environmental stressors that go beyond the norm. First, their drug use behaviors came into being in settings that facilitated experimentation or, at the very least, failed to provide protection against the development of this health problem. Second, once the problem arose, they became subject to the stigma that societies frequently impose on drug users. Third, their attempts to obtain help in overcoming the difficulty came up against barriers because, at this point, the help they needed was complex and multifaceted. These difficulties in their immediate environments—their own families, schools, and communities—exist in a still larger social, cultural, economic, and political climate. In this broader arena, they might be subject to oppression and they surely will be affected by public policies that are based on negative views of substance abusers' lives rather than on positive views of their potential for change.

Because their clients cannot always be successful in navigating an imperfect environment, counselors often find it important to advocate on their clients' behalf. The practice of advocacy can run the gamut from helping one client find the help he or she needs to promoting changes in public policies that affect everyone. The American Counseling Association's (ACA) Advocacy Competencies (Lewis et al., 2002) identify three domains in which advocacy might take place: the individual, the school or community, and the larger public arena. At the level of the individual, advocacy can involve working *with* the client through empowerment efforts or working *on behalf of* the client by carrying out such efforts as negotiating service systems; helping clients gain access to resources; identifying barriers to clients' well-being; and developing and carrying out action plans for change. At the school or community level, the counselor might develop alliances with groups that are working for change or lead the way toward needed community change. In the larger public arena, the counselor might focus on using his or her expertise to disseminate information for public consumption. Sometimes, however, the counselor might become aware that his or her own advocacy efforts are needed. The ACA Competencies for this domain include the following:

In influencing public policy in a broad public arena, advocacy-oriented counselors are able to

- Distinguish those problems that can best be resolved through social/political action.
- Identify the appropriate mechanisms and avenues for addressing those problems.
- Seek out and join with potential allies.
- Support existing alliances for change.
- With allies, prepare convincing data and rationales for change.
- With allies, lobby legislators and other policy makers.
- Maintain open dialogue with communities and clients to ensure that the social/political advocacy is consistent with the initial goals.

In the larger public arena, challenges for advocacy exist in abundance. A number of political issues call for advocacy efforts by professionals who are knowledgeable about substance abuse. Many substance abuse counselors are active in such efforts as promoting policies that encourage harm reduction efforts such as needle exchange programs; supporting efforts to allow first-time drug offenders to have the option of treatment rather than incarceration; and fighting for the elimination of laws that unfairly target minority group members, including differential punishments for the possession of crack or powder cocaine. The future will bring additional environmental challenges that will call on the advocacy competencies of substance abuse counselors.

COUNSELOR ROLES AND SETTINGS

The principles just discussed have in common an emphasis on individualized, multidimensional, and culturally competent practices. Substance abuse counseling that follows these principles will tend to be oriented toward empowering the individual and addressing the impact of the environment.

It is readily apparent that the approach we are suggesting cannot be limited to any one setting or counseling specialization. In fact, providing for each client's special needs requires a number of alternative settings and forms of treatment. Thinking of drug or alcohol use as one aspect of a client's unique constellation of behaviors and characteristics also has two major implications for counselors' roles. First, generalist counselors must be expected to assess substance abuse issues routinely, just as they would be expected to identify any other behaviors or health concerns affecting their clients' well-being. Second, addiction specialists should recognize their responsibility for dealing with psychological, social, and vocational issues that might interact with drug use, rather than assuming that they can limit the scope of their assessments and interventions to drinking or drug-taking behaviors alone.

Counselors' work settings have substantial effects on the issues they face and the day-to-day roles they must perform. In this section we will examine generalized settings in the community and a variety of specialized settings dealing with substance abuse problems.

GENERAL COMMUNITY SETTINGS

Counselors in health care venues, community agencies, and educational settings play a major role in recognizing and confronting substance abuse among members of their general client population. Appropriate identification and referral of clients with alcohol or drug problems can make the difference between timely treatment for the real problem and hours wasted on therapy that fails to address a primary concern.

An expert panel convened by the National Quality Forum (2005) reviewed evidence-based treatments for people with substance use disorders and recommended that treatment takes place in a continuum including (a) screening, diagnosis, and assessment; (b) active treatment; and (c) long-term chronic care. The Forum placed emphasis on screening and brief interventions in health care settings, suggesting that "all patients in general and mental healthcare settings...should be screened for alcohol misuse whenever a care encounter provides the opportunity" and that "all patients with a positive screen should receive a brief intervention by a healthcare practitioner trained in this technique" (p. viii). A number of studies have demonstrated the efficacy of screening and brief interventions, particularly for alcohol-abusing patients (Maisto et al., 2001; Miller, 2000). Brief interventions are also becoming common in other general settings, including, for instance, education (Burke, Da Silva, Vaughan, & Knight, 2005; Monti, Colby, & O'Leary, 2004; Mun, White, & Morgan, 2009) and criminal justice (Ginsburg, Mann, Rotgers, & Weekes, 2002).

Thus, counselors working in such diverse arenas as health care, social services, education, and criminal justice have a major role to play, not only in referring clients for specialized treatment but also in providing brief services themselves. Because vast numbers of seriously impaired clients still need specialized treatment, "it is reasonable, as well as practical at present, for nonspecialists to offer a generalized brief intervention" (Institute of Medicine, 1990, p. 37).

In the case of both alcohol problems and abuse of other drugs, the primary decisions about clients' treatment needs are made not in specialized substance abuse facilities but in community agencies dealing with a general client population. Counselors who see themselves as generalists, rather than as substance abuse specialists, bear the bulk of responsibility both for making initial diagnoses and for helping their clients choose the most appropriate treatment strategies.

Specialized Substance Abuse Settings

Substance abuse counselors are employed in a variety of settings, each of which meets distinct client needs and tends to raise different concerns regarding the quality of care being offered. Among the most prevalent organizations focusing on substance abuse issues are detoxification centers, inpatient rehabilitation programs, therapeutic communities, methadone maintenance programs, outpatient counseling agencies, and employee assistance programs.

DETOXIFICATION CENTERS   Detoxification is short-term treatment designed to oversee the client's safe withdrawal from the substance to which he or she is addicted. Whether the abused substance is alcohol or another drug, the initial period of abstinence may bring a high degree of discomfort and may, in fact, constitute a medical emergency for some.

Although detoxification is a physiological phenomenon through which the individual's body becomes free of the abused substance, it also has psychological and social implications that call for a counselor's best efforts. In the context of a detoxification center, the counselor's important role involves:

• Working with the client to develop an appropriate plan for treatment
• Linking the client to appropriate community and agency resources
• Monitoring the client's progress and referring for medical assistance as needed
• Providing personal/emotional support to the client
• Encouraging the client and his or her family to use the crisis of detoxification as an opportunity for change
• Assessing the client's needs and potential for further treatment

Perhaps the most important question for counselors working in detoxification centers is which clients should be detoxified under the close supervision that these facilities offer. Detoxification centers may be medical, with supervision provided by medically trained personnel, frequently within a hospital. In these centers, physicians may routinely offer medications to enhance the client's safety and comfort. In contrast, nonmedical, or social, detoxification centers provide counseling, support, and supervision outside of a hospital. Medical personnel will be on call in such facilities, but many social detoxification centers eschew the use of medications and depend instead on nonpharmacological withdrawal.

Clearly, then, clients have at least three choices for detoxification: remaining at home, entering a nonmedical detoxification center, or seeking treatment in a medical setting. They need to take a number of factors into account in their decision-making process, including the stability of their home situation and the personal and social support available to them. Especially important is the question of the seriousness of their physical condition and the likelihood that withdrawal will involve major health risks. Many substance-abusing clients are routinely placed in inpatient detoxification facilities before being provided with additional treatment. In fact, only those clients who demonstrate physical dependence on a drug should need supervised detoxification. Even these clients, if medically stable, can be treated effectively in a nonmedical setting. Thus, the principle that treatment should be as unintrusive as possible becomes especially important when we consider the role of the detoxification facility in the general continuum of care.

Individual care is another important issue for counselors working in this milieu. Detoxification can never be more than a first step in treatment and recovery. The counselor working with clients at this stage needs to conduct complete assessments and develop individual treatment plans that include both long- and short-term goals.

RESIDENTIAL REHABILITATION PROGRAMS   Like detoxification facilities, rehabilitation programs may be housed either in hospitals or in nonmedical settings. In fact, the number of treatment alternatives is increasing as providers experiment with partial hospitalization (providing a full rehabilitation program in the daytime but allowing patients to go home at night) and variable lengths of stay. In general, however, rehabilitation programs tend to have a great deal in common. Whether the facility is run by a general hospital, a freestanding medical treatment unit, or a social agency, the primary emphasis tends to be on psychological rather than physiological factors and on education rather than medicine.

The general purpose of a rehabilitation program is to help individuals gain understanding of their problems and to prepare them for long-term recovery. Ideally, the time spent in the rehabilitation setting should allow clients the opportunity to develop personal recovery goals, to learn the skills needed to prevent a relapse, to prepare for their resocialization into the community, and to plan and rehearse an abstinent lifestyle. The goals of such programs include providing clients with a social learning frame for understanding their drinking behaviors, helping clients assess their drinking problems, helping them identify the antecedents of their drinking, teaching them skills for maintaining abstinence, helping them learn how to reinforce their abstinence, and teaching them about relapse management.

Unfortunately, some rehabilitation programs lack this kind of attention to individual assessment, skill development, and relapse prevention. All too often, inpatients are forced to fit into predetermined and nondifferentiated activities that may not have any relationship to their unique personal needs. Such programs are especially problematic when they focus almost exclusively on didactic methods, assuming that if clients are "educated" about their disease, rehabilitation will follow. In fact, clients need more than to be sold on the idea of abstinence. They also need help in developing the skills and resources that can increase their control over their lives. They need to know not just why abstinence is desirable but how it can be attained.

Another vital issue in any inpatient setting involves the question of its appropriateness for individual clients. In general, outpatient or partial hospital treatment is preferable to hospitalization because of the opportunities clients have to try out their learning in a real-life environment. Clients who have been isolated for weeks from work, family, and social ties may not be accurate in their assessments of their own progress and in their expectations regarding their coping skills. If clients are socially stable, physically healthy, and reasonably motivated, a hospital stay should be avoided. If individuals do need inpatient treatment, every effort should be made to ease their transition back to the community at large.

THERAPEUTIC COMMUNITIES   Unlike the shorter inpatient rehabilitation program, which has its roots in alcoholism treatment, the therapeutic community has become most prevalent as an intervention for drug abusers, particularly those addicted to opiates. Although the earliest therapeutic communities were staffed by recovering addicts, professional counselors have become increasingly involved with them over the years. Mutual help, however, remains a core value.

As therapeutic communities have evolved, members have been expected to remain in these isolated residential environments for extremely long stays of a year or more. This model depends for its efficacy on a high degree of commitment on the part of each individual to the community as a whole.

Cohen (1985) summarizes the 12 characteristics that therapeutic communities tend to have in common: (a) an arduous admission policy, (b) charismatic leadership, (c) emphasis on personal responsibility, (d) mutual assistance, (e) self-examination and confession, (f) structure and discipline, (g) a system of rewards and punishments, (h) status as an extended family, (i) separation from society, (j) staff members who are not seen as authority figures, (k) fostering of such characteristics as nonviolence and honesty, and (l) emphasis on work.

Some of the greatest concerns about therapeutic communities are based on these characteristics. The shortcomings of the model lie in the core values of separation from society, long-term isolation, and insistence on conformity to the collective unit. As in other treatment settings, the key factor in effectiveness remains the appropriateness of the approach for the individual client.

METHADONE MAINTENANCE PROGRAMS   The use of methadone as a treatment for heroin addiction was pioneered by Dole and Nyswander (1965) in New York in the 1960s. Their goal in using this synthetic opiate was to focus on rehabilitation rather than on abstinence and to help addicts live productive, if not drug-free, lives.

Methadone maintenance has grown in importance as a treatment approach in recent decades, at least in part because it is seen as a way to separate the client from the dangers and instability of a lifestyle devoted to obtaining and using an illegal drug. Ideally, methadone "frees the client from the pressures of obtaining illegal heroin, from the dangers of injection, and from the emotional roller coaster that most opiates produce" (Polich, et al., 1984, p. 95). The treatment requires that the client come to a clinic regularly to receive methadone and allow a urine check to ensure that other drugs are not being used. Methadone is seen as a positive alternative to heroin because it is legal; it is administered orally, rather than by injection; it does not produce the level of euphoria of heroin; and it blocks both the effects and the withdrawal symptoms of the abused opiates. Thus, its use allows for a level of physical, social, and emotional stability that might not be possible if heroin use were continued. This stability is enhanced by the fact that methadone is longer acting than heroin, allowing all doses to be given under clinical observation.

Over the years questions have arisen, not so much about the use of methadone but about the context within which it is used. Originally, many agencies provided methadone maintenance in a vacuum, with no other treatment deemed necessary. Now, they recognize the need to place this method in the context of a treatment plan including counseling and other efforts at rehabilitation. They also recognize that more attention must be paid to the question of whether methadone maintenance is a short-term solution or a long-term panacea.

OUTPATIENT COUNSELING AGENCIES   Substance abuse counseling is offered to outpatients in a number of settings, running the gamut from comprehensive community mental health centers to the offices of private practitioners, from highly intensive nightly group meetings to biweekly individual sessions, and from brief interventions to long-term therapy. Although outpatient counseling varies among counselors and agencies, its positive aspects seem fairly consistent.

First, outpatient counseling allows for a high degree of individualization. Of course, inpatient counselors always attempt to individualize treatment plans to the degree possible. In reality, however, the constraints of group-oriented treatment and the need for daily structure often make true differentiation impractical. Outpatient counseling, in contrast, is based entirely on the notion that each intervention can be planned with the unique needs of the specific client in mind.

Second, outpatient counseling encourages the development of treatment plans based on both long- and short-term goals. Again, it is difficult for counselors and inpatients to think far into the future. Distal goals are seen as ideals, but because the typical rehabilitation program can meet only immediate objectives, both counselors and clients tend to focus on concrete, readily achievable ends. The outpatient counselor, in contrast, can work with the clients, one issue at a time, until all their needs have been addressed. Short-term objectives may still be given priority, but the counselor and client can evaluate each achievement as one step in the direction of the ultimate goal.

Third, outpatient counseling gives the client an opportunity to try out new behaviors in ordinary environments. Much of the potency of substance abuse treatment comes from the client's opportunity to reexamine habitual behaviors, to study the environmental cues that tend to affect drinking or drug use, and to develop a broader repertoire of coping behaviors. Outpatient counseling enhances this process by giving the individual a chance to try new behaviors and attitudes, knowing that the results of each experiment can be discussed at the next counseling session. Furthermore, outpatient counseling allows for easy alteration of the treatment plan in response to any unforeseen difficulties the client may encounter.

Although outpatient counseling should be seen as a preferred modality, it is not appropriate for all clients. The most suitable candidate for an outpatient intervention is one who is able to function independently on a day-to-day basis, who has sources of social support for a sober or straight lifestyle, who is medically stable, and who has the ability and motivation to abstain from substance use until a new lifestyle has been established. As earlier recognition of substance abuse problems becomes the norm, an ever-larger proportion of clients can be expected to exhibit this profile.

EMPLOYEE ASSISTANCE PROGRAMS   One of the reasons that substance abuse problems are being identified earlier than previously is the growth of drug and alcohol programs in business and industry. Counseling programs designed for employees in their work settings are now known as "employee assistance programs" and they deal not just with substance abuse but with a variety of issues of mental and physical health that might affect job performance. But the employee assistance concept has its roots in the industrial alcoholism programs of the 1940s, and alcohol and drug issues remain central among the concerns of employee assistance counselors, if for no other reason than that the connection between substance abuse and deteriorating work standards is clear. Counselors who work in an employee assistance program (EAP) are expected to be knowledgeable and skilled in assessing and dealing with substance abuse problems. Their primary role involves assessment and referral, not the formation of long-term counseling relationships.

In the context of an employee assistance program, clients with major health problems, whether physical or psychological, are linked with treatment resources outside of the employing organization. Thus, EAP counselors are not expected to provide treatment or long-term therapy. When they counsel employees, their goal is to give temporary support and assistance so that clients can gain or regain self-responsibility. Employee assistance professionals engage in counseling in the true sense of the word: helping individuals gain skills and mobilize resources so that they can manage problem situations and achieve the highest possible degree of mastery over their environments. The help provided by the employee assistance counselor is short-term, pragmatic, and oriented toward problem solving.

An employee assistance program is not a treatment modality in itself. Rather, it is a method for helping work organizations to resolve, efficiently and humanely, problems relating to productivity. Thus, an EAP counselor is both a human resource consultant to the organization and a service provider to the employee.

Perhaps the most difficult challenge faced by substance abuse counselors in business and industry involves their ability to wear these two hats to utilize their clinical skills while working to ensure that the organization as a whole accepts the employee assistance concept as a viable way of solving difficulties. Potential value conflicts are avoided if the program is seen as an organizationally based system that includes the following components:

* written policy statements that demonstrate the organization's commitment to referral and treatment for troubled employees
* training for supervisors that encourages referrals to the employee assistance program on the basis of job performance criteria

- information for employees that clarifies the nature, purpose, and confidentiality of the services provided
- provision of confidential counseling, assessment, and referral that is easily accessible to all employees
- educational and preventive efforts focused on the organization as a whole

Employee assistance practitioners, like all effective substance abuse counselors, recognize the importance of adapting their methods to the needs of the individuals they serve.

Counseling Competencies

As we have seen, counseling that addresses issues of substance abuse and addiction takes place in a variety of settings. In general, however, the competencies associated with effective practice tend to be similar across specialties. The Addiction Technology Transfer Centers National Curriculum Committee (2006) spelled out the competencies underlying successful work in this field, identifying eight practice dimensions that were seen as necessary for effective performance of the substance abuse counseling role. The practice dimensions include the following: (a) clinical evaluation, which encompasses screening and assessment; (b) treatment planning; (c) referral; (d) service coordination; (e) counseling, which encompasses individual, group, and family counseling; (f) client, family, and community education; (g) documentation; and (h) professional and ethical responsibilities.

Although the competencies needed for carrying out each of the dimensions were identified, those that relate specifically to the counseling dimension are especially relevant to the purposes of this book. Following are the individual counseling competencies that were identified by the Addiction Technology Transfer Centers National Curriculum Committee (2002, pp. 101–111):

Counseling
Definition: *A collaborative process that facilitates the client's progress toward mutually determined treatment goals and objectives.*

Counseling includes methods that are sensitive to individual client characteristics and to the influence of significant others, as well as the client's cultural and social context. Competence in counseling is built upon an understanding of, appreciation of, and ability to appropriately use the contributions of various addiction counseling models as they apply to modalities of care for individuals, groups, families, couples, and significant others.

Element: Individual Counseling

- Establish a helping relationship with the client characterized by warmth, respect, genuineness, concreteness, and empathy.
- Facilitate the client's engagement in the treatment and recovery process.
- Work with the client to establish realistic, achievable goals consistent with achieving and maintaining recovery.
- Promote client knowledge, skills, and attitudes that contribute to a positive change in substance use behaviors.

- Encourage and reinforce client actions determined to be beneficial in progressing toward treatment goals.
- Work appropriately with the client to recognize and discourage all behaviors inconsistent with progress toward treatment goals.
- Recognize how, when, and why to involve the client's significant others in enhancing or supporting the treatment plan.
- Promote client knowledge, skills, and attitudes consistent with the maintenance of heath and prevention of HIV/AIDS, tuberculosis, sexually transmitted diseases, and other infectious diseases.
- Facilitate the development of basic life skills associated with recovery.
- Adapt counseling strategies to the individual characteristics of the client, including but not limited to disability, gender, sexual orientation, developmental level, culture, ethnicity, age, and health status.
- Make constructive therapeutic responses when client's behavior is inconsistent with stated recovery goals.
- Apply crisis management skills.
- Facilitate the client's identification, selection, and practice of strategies that help sustain the knowledge, skills, and attitudes needed for maintaining treatment progress and preventing relapse.

These counseling competencies are consistent with the focus of the chapters that follow.

SUMMARY

Counselors can consider a client's problem as relating to "substance abuse" if continuous use of alcohol or another drug affects his or her social or occupational functioning. In dealing with substance abuse issues, counselors should take into account the individual differences among their clients. Among the general principles that can help substance abuse counselors to be effective are the following: (a) Focus on evidence-based practices; (b) use a respectful and positive approach with all clients; (c) view substance abuse problems on a continuum from nonproblematic to problematic use rather than as an either/or situation; (d) collaborate with clients on the creation of individualized plans for change; (e) build interventions based on the recognition that substance abuse occurs in a social context; (f) use a multicultural perspective to meet the needs of diverse client populations; and (g) acknowledge the idea that client advocacy is central to the counselor's role.

These guidelines lead in the direction of treatment that is individualized rather than diffuse and that focuses on other areas of life functioning beyond the specific drinking or drug-use behaviors. Among the contexts in which such counseling might take place are general community settings, detoxification centers, inpatient rehabilitation programs, therapeutic communities, methadone maintenance programs, outpatient counseling agencies, and employee assistance programs. Whether practitioners view themselves as counseling generalists or as substance abuse specialists, they can adapt the methods described in this text to the special needs of their clients. Our general purpose in this book is to describe the approaches best supported by current research and to encourage an individualized, multidimensional approach to the complex problems of substance abuse.

QUESTIONS FOR THOUGHT AND DISCUSSION

1. Chapter 1 suggests that we should view substance abuse problems as occurring along a continuum rather than thinking of addiction or alcoholism as a dichotomy. The chapter also presents the idea that the treatment selected for each client should be individualized to meet his or her individual needs and goals. What implications might these ideas have for the following client?

    Bob, who is in his early 20s, is arrested for driving under the influence of alcohol. Because this is his second arrest, he is ordered to participate in alcoholism treatment. The counselor who assesses his situation refers him to a 28-day, inpatient treatment program and recommends that he attend meetings of Alcoholics Anonymous.

    Bob does begin this program, because he knows there is no other hope of getting his driver's license back. He needs the license in his work as an electrician. After a few days in the program, however, he drops out, saying that he does not feel he belongs there. He has never experienced physical signs of addiction to alcohol and does not believe that his life is out of control. The treatment providers and the other patients press him to recognize and verbalize that he is an alcoholic, but he refuses to do so. He says he will drive without his license if necessary and will try to avoid drinking and driving in the future.

2. This chapter suggests that treatment should be multidimensional, self-efficacy–enhancing, and sensitive to the needs of diverse client populations. How might these ideas affect treatment for the following client?

    Jeanine used cocaine throughout her first pregnancy and feels fortunate that her 2.5-year-old child is healthy. When she becomes pregnant for the second time, her mother convinces her to seek drug treatment. It takes some time to find a program that will accept a pregnant patient, but she finally does check into a hospital program. Her second child is now 3 months old, and Jeanine is trying hard to stay straight.

    Her counselor feels somewhat pessimistic about Jeanine's future, for several reasons. Jeanine, who was a good student, dropped out of high school when she became pregnant. She has not been able to get a job due to her drug history, her lack of education, and her child care responsibilities. She does not get any emotional or financial support from either of her children's fathers. Her mother is very helpful, but she also has limited resources. Jeanine loves her children but says she is not as good a mother as she would like to be. She is afraid of losing her children.

REFERENCES

Addiction Technology Transfer Centers National Curriculum Committee. (2006). *Addiction counseling competencies: The knowledge, skills, and attitudes of professional practice* (2nd ed.). Rockville, MD: U.S. Department of Health and Human Services.

Ball, S. A., Martino, S., Nich, C., Frankforter, T. L., Van Horn, D., Crits-Christoph, P., et al. (2007). Site matters: Multisite randomized trial of motivational enhancement therapy in community drug abuse clinics. *Journal of Consulting and Clinical Psychology, 75*(4), 556–567.

Bandura, A. (1997). *Self-efficacy: The exercise of control.* New York: Freeman.

Burke, P. J., Da Silva, J. D., Vaughan, B. L., & Knight, J. R. (2005, December 26). Training high school counselors on the use of motivational interviewing to screen for substance abuse. *Substance Abuse, 26*(3–4), 31–34.

Carroll, K. M., Ball, S. A., Nich, C., Martino, S., Frankforter, T. L., Farentinos, C., et al. (2006). Motivational interviewing to improve treatment engagement and outcome in individuals seeking treatment for substance abuse: A multisite effectiveness study. *Drug and Alcohol Dependence, 81*(3), 301–312.

Center for Substance Abuse Treatment. (2000). *Changing the conversation: Improving substance abuse treatment: The national treatment plan initiative.* Vol. 1. Rockville, MD: U.S. Department of Health and Human Services.

Cohen, S. (1988). *The Chemical Brain – The Neurochemistry of addictive Disorders.* Irvine, CA: CareInstitute.

Drug Policy Alliance. (2002). *Effectiveness of the War on Drugs.* Retrieved February 24, 2009, from http://www.drugpolicy.org/library/factsheets/effectivenes/

Dennis, H., Godley, S. H., Diamond, G., Tims, F. M., Babor, T., Donaldson, J., et al. (2004). The cannabis youth treatment study: Main findings from two randomized trials. *Journal of Substance Abuse Treatment, 27*(3), 197–213.

Dole, V. P., & Nyswander, M. E. (1965). A medical treatment for diacetyl morphine (heroin) addiction: A clinical trial with methadonehydrochloride. *Journal of the American Medical Association, 193,* 64ff.

Eliason, M. J. (2007). *Improving substance abuse treatment: An introduction to the evidence-based practice movement.* Thousand Oaks, CA: Sage.

Fals-Stewart, W., Birchler, G. R., & Kelley, M. L. (2006). Learning sobriety together: A randomized clinical trial examining behavioral couples therapy with alcoholic female patients. *Journal of Consulting and Clinical Psychology, 74,* 579–591.

Fields, G. (2009, May 14). White House Czar calls for end to War on Drugs. *Wall Street Journal,* A3.

Ginsburg, J. I. D., Mann, R., Rotgers, F., & Weekes, J. R. (2002). Motivational interviewing with criminal justice populations. In W. R. Miller & S. Rollnick (Eds.), *Motivational interviewing: Preparing people for change* (pp. 333–346). New York: Guilford.

Gladwell, M. (2000). *The tipping point: How little things can make a difference.* Boston: Little, Brown & Company.

Hettema, J., Steele, J., & Miller, W. R. (2005, April). Motivational interviewing. *Annual Review of Clinical Psychology, I,* 91–111.

Holcomb-McCoy, C., & Mitchell, N. A. (2007). Promoting ethnic/racial equality through empowerment-based counseling. In C. C. Lee (Ed.), *Counseling for social justice* (pp. 137–157). Alexandria, VA: American Counseling Association.

Institute of Medicine (1990). *Broadening the base of treatment for alcohol problems.* Washington, DC: National Academy Press.

Institute of Medicine. (2002). *Unequal treatment: Confronting racial and ethnic disparities in health care.* Washington, DC: National Academy Press.

Lewis, J. A., & Arnold, M. S. (1998). From multiculturalism to social action. In C. C. Lee & G. Walz (Eds.), *Social action: A mandate for counselors* (pp. 51–66). Alexandria, VA: American Counseling Association.

Lewis, J. A., Arnold, M. S., House, R., & Toporek, R. L. (2002). *American Counseling Association Advocacy Competencies.* Retrieved January 15, 2005, from http://www.counseling.org/Publications

Lewis, J. A., & Elder, J. (In press). Substance abuse counseling and social justice advocacy. In M. Ratts, R. Toporek, & J. A. Lewis (Eds.). *ACA Advocacy Competencies: A social justice framework for counselors*. Alexandria, VA: American Counseling Association.

Liddle, H. A., Rowe, C. L., Dakof, G. A., Henderson, C. E., & Greenbaum, P. E. (2009). Multidimensional family therapy for young adolescent substance abuse: Twelve-month outcomes of a randomized controlled trial. *Journal of Consulting and Clinical Psychology, 77*(1), 12–25.

Maisto, S. A., Conigliaro, J., McNeil, M., Kraemer, K., Conigliaro, R. L., & Kelley, M. E. (2001). Effects of two types of brief intervention and readiness to change on alcohol use in hazardous drinkers. *Journal of Studies on Alcohol, 62*(5), 605–614.

Marlatt, G. A. (1998). Basic principles and strategies of harm reduction. In G. A. Marlatt (Ed.), *Harm reduction: Pragmatic strategies for managing high-risk behaviors* (pp. 49–66). New York: Guilford Press.

Marlatt, G. A., Parks, G. A., & Witkiewitz, K. (2002). *Clinical guidelines for implementing Relapse Prevention Therapy: A guideline developed for the Behavioral Health Recovery Management Project*. Seattle: University of Washington, Addictive Behaviors Research Center.

Meyers, R. J., & Smith, J. E. (1995). *Clinical guide to alcohol treatment: The community reinforcement approach*. New York: Guilford Press.

Miller, W. R. (1985). Controlled drinking: A history and critical review. In W. R. Miller (Eds.). *Alcoholism: Theory, research, and treatment* (pp. 5838–595). Lexington, MA: Ginn Press.

Miller, W. R. (1996). Motivational interviewing: Research, practice, and puzzles. *Addictive Behaviors, 21*, 835–842.

Miller, W. R. (2000). Rediscovering fire: Small interventions, large effects. *Psychology of Addictive Behaviors, 14*(1), 6–18.

Miller, W. R., & Carroll, K. M. (2006). Drawing the scene together: Ten principles, ten recommendations. In W. R. Miller & K. M. Carroll (Eds.), *Rethinking substance abuse: What the science shows, and what we should do about it* (pp. 293–311). New York: The Guilford Press.

Moos, R. H. (2006). Social contexts and substance use. In W. R. Miller & K. M. Carroll (Eds.), *Rethinking substance abuse: What the science shows, and what we should do about it* (pp. 182–200). New York: The Guilford Press.

Monti, P. M., Colby, S., & O'Leary, T. (2004). *Reaching teens through brief interventions*. New York: The Guilford Press.

Mun, E. Y., White, H. R., & Morgan, T. J. (2009). Individual and situational factors that influence the efficacy of personalized feedback substance use interventions for mandated college students. *Journal of Consulting and Clinical Psychology, 77*(1), 88–102.

National Institute on Drug Abuse (2004). *National Institute on Drug Abuse: Strategic plan on reducing health disparities*. Retrieved February 25, 2009, from http://www.drugabuse.gov/StrategicPlan/HealthStratPlan.html

National Quality Forum (2005). *Evidence-based treatment practices for substance use disorders: Executive summary*. Retrieved April 30, 2009, from http://www.qualityforum.org/publications/reports/sud.asp

Nowinski, J. (2006). *The twelve step facilitation outpatient program: The Project MATCH twelve step treatment protocol. Facilitator guide*. Center City, MN: Hazelden Foundation.

Pecoraro, C. (2000, December). Understanding gay, lesbian and bisexual issues in treatment. *Counselor: The Magazine for Addiction Professionals, 1*, 23–32.

Polich, J. M., Ellickson, P. L., Reuter, P., & Kahan, J. P. (1984). *Strategies for controlling adolescent drug use.* Santa Monica, CA: Rand Corp.

Rohsenow, D. J., Monti, P. M., Martin, R. A., Colby, S. M., Myers, M. G., Gulliver, S. B., et al. (2004). Motivational enhancement and coping skills training for cocaine abusers: Effects on substance use outcomes. *Addiction, 99*(7), 862–874.

Rollnick, S., & Miller, W. R. (1995). What is motivational interviewing? *Behavioural and Cognitive Psychotherapy, 23*, 325–334.

Rubak, S., Sandboek, A., Lauritzen, T., & Christensen, B. (2005). Motivational interviewing: A systematic review and meta-analysis. *British Journal of General Practice, 55*(513), 305–312.

Sentencing Project. (2009). *Drug policy.* Retrieved April 30, 2009, from http://sentencingproject.org/IssueAreaHome.aspx?IssueID=5

Substance Abuse and Mental Health Services Administration. (2009a). *What is evidence-based?* Retrieved April 1, 2009, from http://www.nrepp.samhsa.gov/about-evidence.asp

Substance Abuse and Mental Health Services Administration. (2009b). *SAMHSA's National Registry of Evidence-based Programs and Practices.* Retrieved April 1, 2009 from http://www.nrepp.samhsa.gov/listofprograms.asp?textsearch=&ShowHide=1&Sort=1&T5=5

Sue, D. W., Arredondo, P., & McDavis, R. J. (1992). Multicultural counseling competencies and standards: A call to the profession. *Journal of Counseling & Development, 70*, 477–486.

2 | DRUGS AND THEIR EFFECTS

INTRODUCTION

Throughout recorded history, chemical substances have been both exalted for their benefits and vilified for the problems they can cause. This can be seen in the common contemporary distinction between medicines and drugs. However, it must be noted that some of the alleged problems related to drug use are based more on societal values and perceptions about drug use and drug users than on the pharmacological properties of the drugs themselves. Only by understanding how drugs work and what they are capable of can we begin to distinguish drug effects from other possible causes of behavior (e.g., mental illness, racial, cultural, gender, age, or developmental factors).

There are a number of reasons why substance abuse professionals should be well versed in pharmacology. These include facilitating communication, rapport, and empathy with clients; making consultations and referrals with other professionals; and maintaining professional competence (staying current). In addition, substance abuse professionals can influence social policy by dispelling myths, misconceptions, and misinformation related to drug use and abuse.

FACTORS THAT AFFECT A DRUG'S EFFECTS

Drug effects can best be understood as the results of complex interactions among four groups of variables: (a) characteristics of the substance itself, (b) the physiological functioning of the user, (c) the psychological state of the user, and (d) the sociocultural environment in which the drug is used. For simplicity we will discuss each of these groups independently while remembering that they are interacting (Meyer & Quenzer, 2005).

CHARACTERISTICS OF DRUGS

Let us begin by defining a drug as any substance that alters the structure or function of some aspect of the user. Such a definition is wide-ranging (Klein & Thorne, 2007); conceivably, it would include not only the abusable drugs, which will be the focus of this chapter, but also antibiotics, antitoxins, vitamins, minerals, and even water and air.

Water, air, and food are considered to be essential to the survival of organisms and are therefore not conceived as drugs. However, consider the use of oxygen to revitalize a fatigued athlete or the effects of spices and food additives on blood pressure, cardiac function, water retention, and allergic reactions. Similarly, though vitamins and minerals are generally thought of as nutritional supplements, they can produce toxic reactions and other alterations in physiological structure and function. On a different level, numerous drugs used to restore and maintain health are generally not considered to be abusable substances despite risks in the use or overuse of such drugs by susceptible individuals.

Thus, drugs, even abusable drugs, are not good or bad per se. Rather, the benefits and risks of substance use depend on how much, how often, in what manner, and with what other drugs a particular substance is used.

DRUG DOSAGE

Generally, drugs can produce multiple effects. Which effects are produced and how strong those effects are depend partly on the amount of drug ingested. At lower doses, for example, alcohol can relax and disinhibit as well as stimulate hunger; at higher doses it can cause one to become fatigued and nauseous. The connection between a drug's dose and its effects is called a dose/response relationship. As Figure 2.1 illustrates, below a certain dosage, called the threshold, there is no

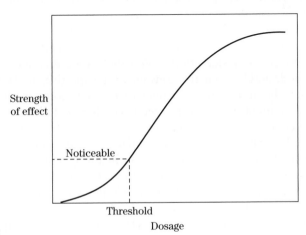

FIGURE 2.1   DOSE/RESPONSE CURVE.

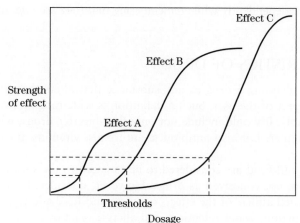

FIGURE 2.2 | MULTIPLE DOSE/RESPONSE CURVE.

noticeable effect. As the dosage increases, the effect becomes increasingly strong until it reaches some maximum value. The maximum effect attainable is determined by physiological capabilities (you can only become so relaxed or sedated without falling asleep).

As Figure 2.2 illustrates, the threshold dose may vary with the drug being studied. We see that effect A has a low threshold dosage and it maximizes at a relatively low dose. Effects B and C require higher dosages to initiate. Notice also that effect B terminates well before effect C. Thus, the drug dosage affects both what responses will be produced and how strong the responses are. In practical terms this means that users experience quantitatively and qualitatively different effects when they use different dosages of the same drugs.

CATEGORIES OF DRUG EFFECTS   The multiple effects of drugs can be usefully categorized as follows. The desired effect of a drug, or the reason it is used, is the therapeutic effect. All other effects of the drug are collectively referred to as *adverse drug reactions* (ADRs). Reliable, anticipated, and frequently encountered ADRs are generally referred to as side effects. We should note that side effects may not be adverse or undesirable from the consumer's perspective. In fact, many drugs are used precisely because they contribute to two or more simultaneous effects; for example, acetaminophen and aspirin reduce both pain and fever. Allergic effects differ from side effects in the frequency of occurrence and the ability to anticipate their occurrence. Idiosyncratic reactions are highly unusual effects that are unanticipated and unreliable. Toxic effects result from ingesting lethal or near-lethal doses of a drug (commonly referred to as *overdoses*). For example, the therapeutic effect of morphine is pain relief; the side effects include pinpoint pupils (miosis) and nausea; an allergic effect might be a mild skin rash; idiosyncratic reactions might include excitation and stimulation; and the toxic effects could include respiratory depression, coma, and death.

POTENCY   Potency is the amount of drug necessary to produce a certain effect. The more potent a drug is the smaller the dosage required to produce the desired effect. Alcohol is a relatively impotent drug, because ounces or grams of the drug are required to produce noticeable effects. LSD, on the other hand, is very potent, with dosages measured in micrograms, or millionths of a gram.

The potency of a drug is determined by two factors, affinity and efficacy. *Affinity* refers to the drug's ability to attach itself to, or bind with, a receptor, or site of action. Receptors are "slots" on the neural membrane that accept and respond to particular chemical structures, much as a lock will accept and respond to particular keys. Drugs with higher affinity bind well with receptors. *Efficacy* refers to the stimulatory power of the drug on the receptor. Drugs with high efficacy strongly stimulate receptors. To have an effect, a drug must have both affinity and efficacy, and the higher the affinity and efficacy, the more potent the drug is (that is, the smaller the dosage required to produce an effect).

THERAPEUTIC RATIO OR SAFETY MARGIN   The *therapeutic ratio* (or safety margin) refers to the relationship between the lethal dose and the effective dose of a drug. The *effective dose* (ED) refers to the dose required to produce a particular effect in a certain proportion of the population. For example, ED_{50} refers to the effective dose for 50% of the population. The *lethal dose* (LD) refers to the dose required to kill a particular proportion of the recipients. Again, this is generally specified as LD_{50}, referring to the lethal dose for 50% of the population. The ratio of the LD to the ED allows us to compare the relative safety of various drugs as well as giving us some sense of the safety of a particular dose of a drug. This relationship is known as the therapeutic ratio, or safety margin, of a drug. Because the lethal dose for some psychoactive drugs is not well established, we cannot reliabily compute a therapeutic ratio.

COMPOSITION

Pharmaceutical preparations are composed of several ingredients. In addition to an active ingredient, a capsule or tablet may also contain binders, fillers, dissolving agents, coloring compounds, coatings, and perhaps even a taste ingredient. Although these "inactive" ingredients generally do not affect users, some people can react adversely to one or more of them (perhaps because of an allergy or a genetic predisposition). Thus, two apparently identical compounds can have different effects on a user because of sensitivity to the "inactive" ingredients.

Street drugs are not generally subjected to the same quality controls as are prescription and over-the-counter drugs. Street drugs vary in quality, quantity, and purity. *Quality* simply means that the actual composition of a drug may be different from what it is alleged to be; common mushrooms dusted with phencyclidine can be sold as psilocybin. *Quantity* and *purity* refer to the fact that street drugs often vary in the proportions of active ingredients and adulterants. Street cocaine, for example, may vary from 10% to 90% (averaging about 50%) cocaine, with the remainder consisting of almost anything that is white, flaky, or sparkly (talc, strychnine, phencyclidine, boric acid, and various sugars).

DRUG EQUIVALENCE *Drug equivalence* refers to the ways in which two or more drugs can be compared with one another. There are three separate ways of assessing the equivalence of drug compounds: (a) chemical equivalence, (b) – biological equivalence, and (c) clinical equivalence. Chemical equivalence simply means that the active ingredients of the compounds are identical. More broadly, chemical equivalence can be used to compare both the active and inactive ingredients of compounds.

The second measure of equivalence is biological equivalence, or bioavailability. Drug compounds that are biologically equivalent provide the same amount of the active ingredient to the user.

The third measure is clinical equivalence, which is based on the observable effects of compounds. Thus, two preparations are said to be clinically equivalent if they produce identical effects.

It is important to realize that these are separate measures of equivalence. When we compare two chemically equivalent drugs, one of them may dissolve incompletely; hence, the bioavailability and clinical effects will be different. Likewise, two or more related but chemically different drugs with differing bioavailabilities can produce the same clinical effects.

FREQUENCY OF USE

How frequently an individual uses a drug has important implications for the effects the drug produces. First, as we will discuss in more detail later, frequent use of a drug increases the likelihood of both physiological and psychological changes in the user. Thus, the user is different from one drug-using episode to the next, and a different user experiences different effects. Second, if a drug is used frequently enough, it or its metabolic by-products can accumulate in the body. Such drug accumulation, in effect, changes the dosage available at any given time and is referred to as a cumulative effect. Figure 2.3 depicts a cumulative-effect curve for four successive doses of a drug.

As Figure 2.3 indicates, the first dose of the drug is administered at t_0 when there is none of the drug in the user. The second dose, at t_1, is administered before the entire first dose has left the user. Thus, the second dose greatly increases the

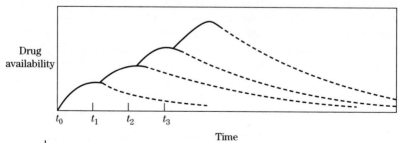

FIGURE 2.3 | ENHANCED CUMULATIVE-EFFECT CURVE.

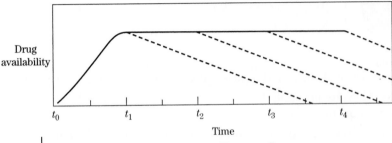

Drug availability

t_0 t_1 t_2 t_3 t_4

Time

FIGURE 2.4 | MAINTENANCE CUMULATIVE-EFFECT CURVE.

amount of drug in the body. Likewise, the third and fourth doses are administered before previous doses can be excreted. The overall effect of this series of doses is to produce a much greater effect (and probably more different kinds of effects) than any one dose.

Figure 2.4 depicts a different type of cumulative-effect curve. The doses are spaced in such a way as to establish and maintain a particular drug effect. Figure 2.3 typifies a drinking episode in which the user consumes alcohol faster than the body can excrete it and therefore becomes increasingly intoxicated. Figure 2.4, on the other hand, is typical of a prescription-use pattern designed to achieve and maintain a particular level of the drug in the bloodstream. Figure 2.4 may also be typical of a "speed run," in which the user spaces dosages in such a way as to achieve and maintain a desired "high."

ROUTE OF ADMINISTRATION

There are a number of ways of administering a drug. The three most common methods are swallowing, injection, and inhalation. However, buccal, sublingual, otic, optic, nasal, rectal, vaginal, and topical routes can also be used to administer drugs. We will focus primarily on the oral, injection, and inhalation routes.

How a drug is administered affects the onset of effects, the peak effects, and the duration of effects. Drugs administered orally typically take at least 15 min to produce an effect and can take much longer, depending on the contents of the stomach and the composition of the drug. Swallowed drugs produce a lower peak, or maximum, effect but typically have a longer duration of effect than either injected or inhaled drugs. Injected drugs typically have quick onsets (a few seconds to a few minutes), very high peak effects, and relatively short durations of action. Inhalation of a drug is, in most respects, very similar to injecting the drug. That is, inhalation produces a quick onset, high peak effect, and relatively short duration of action.

In addition to onset, peak, and duration, several other factors should be taken into consideration in the administration of drugs. Some of these factors are identified in the accompanying box.

Benefits and Risks of Drug-Administration Methods

Swallowing

Convenience: Tablets and liquids are very convenient for most people.

Cost: They are generally less expensive to purchase than drugs designed for injection or inhalation.

Safety: In the event of an overdose, they can sometimes be removed by gastric lavage or diluted.

Gastric irritation: They can cause stomach or intestinal distress.

Dose precision: Part or all of the drug may not be well absorbed or may be chemically altered by stomach, intestine, or liver action before it can affect the individual.

Injection

Efficiency: The entire drug dose enters the bloodstream directly.

Pain: Many people avoid injections because of the pain involved.

Overdose: It is difficult, if not impossible, to remove, dilute, or neutralize an injected drug.

Disease: Unclean needles and improper techniques can result in infections, abscesses, collapsed veins, or scarring.

Inhalation

Dosage regulation: Rapid onset allows for relatively accurate dose titration.

Efficiency: Unless carefully controlled, part of the drug is lost or is diluted by air.

Damage: Injury to nose, mouth, trachea, and lungs may occur.

Drug Interactions

When examining the frequency of use, we noted that doses of a drug could be administered in proximity to one another so as to increase the intensity of the effects and to prolong their duration. Similarly, two or more drugs can be administered in proximity to one another such that they alter the type or strength of the effects.

Such drug interactions are categorized into three basic types: additive, synergistic, and antagonistic. Additive interactions occur when the various drugs combine to increase the intensity, number, or duration of the separate drug effects. These additive interactions can be predicted if we know the separate drug effects. For example, Tuinal is a combination of secobarbital and amobarbital designed to achieve the more rapid sedative/hypnotic onset of the secobarbital in combination with the longer effects found with amobarbital. On the street, alcohol or marijuana is sometimes used in conjunction with another drug to enhance the effects of the second substance.

Synergistic interactions are unexpected drug interactions. That is, knowledge of the separate drug effects does not accurately predict the resultant combined effects. It is not always easy to distinguish additive from synergistic effects. For example, combining alcohol (a depressant) with Seconal (a depressant) may result in severe central nervous system depression, including coma and death, rather than relaxation or sleep, but this effect is largely predictable from knowledge of both drugs. On the other hand, taking "T's" with "blues" or Talwin with Valium results in a clearer example of synergistic effects. Combining T's (Talwin, a synthetic opiate) with blues (pyribenzamine, an antihistamine) greatly enhances the narcotic effects of the Talwin, or pentazocine. Likewise, combining Tagamet with Valium greatly enhances the sedative/hypnotic properties of the Valium.

In antagonistic interactions, the drugs counter each other's effects. Antagonistic interactions can occur when separate drugs compete for the same receptor (pharmacological antagonism), stimulate opposing physiological reactions (physiological antagonism), or chemically combine to neutralize each other (chemical antagonism). The classic example of pharmacological antagonism occurs with the combination of morphine and naltrexone. Naltrexone has greater binding power (affinity) than morphine but has no apparent efficacy (stimulatory power). Thus, naltrexone occupies the receptor sites, blocks the morphine, and produces no effects of its own. Dexamyl, "speedballs," and "goofballs" are examples of physiological antagonism. Dexamyl is a combination of dextroamphetamine (a stimulant) and amobarbital (a depressant). Speedballs and goofballs are combinations of a stimulant and an opiate or depressant. The purpose of these combinations is to "take the edge off" the drugs—that is, to avoid too much stimulation or depression. An example of chemical antagonism is the combining of dairy products rich in calcium with tetracycline (an antibiotic), which neutralizes the antibiotic.

Clearly, the effects of a drug depend on several factors, including the dose, composition, frequency of use, route of administration, and its interaction with other drugs (sometimes food products have druglike effects). Once the drug is administered, the physiological characteristics of the user become important in determining what effects the drug will produce.

PHYSIOLOGICAL FUNCTIONING OF THE USER

The dynamic physiology of the user often influences a drug's effects. Thus, it is important to understand how a human body responds to and processes a drug. No two users will experience exactly the same effects from a drug, and one user may have different experiences with the same drug at different times.

Drugs, in turn, often produce direct and indirect changes in the physiological functioning of users. Direct changes occur as a result of chemical actions on the cells, tissues, organs, and systems of the user. Such direct changes occur through irritation, alteration, or destruction of biological constituents. Similarly, drugs may indirectly influence physiological processes through the induction of disease, damage, or malnutrition in the user. However, these direct and indirect changes in physiological processes can often be desirable, as when a drug enhances immune-system activity, reduces irritation or pain, or improves the utilization of nutrients. Thus, physiological processes both affect and are affected by the characteristics of the substances being used.

This section is organized into two parts (Meyer & Quenzer, 2005). The first part focuses on the pharmacokinetics of drugs, which is concerned with the physiological processes involved in the body's absorption, distribution, metabolism, and excretion of a drug. The second part focuses on pharmacodynamics, which is concerned with the study of where and how a drug produces its effects. Thus pharmacodynamics involves, for our purposes, the neurological functioning of the user.

PHARMACOKINETICS

ABSORPTION   Before a substance can have an effect, the user must absorb it. The three principal methods of administering drugs have already been discussed. It is also important to understand that conditions at the site of administration affect the user's absorption of the substance.

The main consideration with injections is the volume of blood flow in the area of the injection. Intravenous (IV) and intra-arterial (IA) injections are generally most rapidly absorbed, because the substance, or bolus, is deposited directly in the blood. The speed of absorption for intramuscular (IM) and subcutaneous (SQ) injections depends on the blood flow in the area of the injection. Similarly, the absorption of inhaled substances varies with disease or damage to the nasal and oral cavities, trachea, and lungs.

Absorption of oral drugs is somewhat more complicated. First, the drug must be placed in solution. Liquids are more readily absorbed than tablets or capsules, and absorption of the latter can be enhanced by the use of disintegrating agents or retarded through special coatings to delay disintegration. Second, swallowed drugs are generally absorbed more readily in the intestines than in the stomach. Thus, the presence of food may delay absorption. Third, the acidity/alkalinity of the stomach and intestines affects solubility. The acidity of the stomach and the alkalinity of the intestines can be altered by a number of factors, including foods, other drugs, and disease or damage. Fourth, higher doses produce higher concentrations of the drug, and high concentrations are absorbed more readily than low concentrations. Finally, fat-soluble drugs can pass through the membrane walls of the digestive system and enter the bloodstream faster than water-soluble drugs.

DISTRIBUTION   Unless it is directly injected into the site of action, a substance must travel there from the site of administration. This transportation depends on the cardiovascular functioning of the user. Several variables affect a substance's distribution in the body.

First, the distribution of a substance is systemic. That is, the drug is distributed throughout the body as it travels with the blood. Second, in order to travel in the bloodstream, the drug must have an affinity for (must attach itself to) some element of the blood chemistry or move by hydraulic pressure. Third, the speed at which a drug is distributed depends on the efficiency of the heart. Cardiac efficiency, in turn, depends on the health and stimulation of the heart muscle. Finally, whether enough drug reaches the site of action depends on both the dose (because it will be diluted throughout the entire body) and the affinity of the drug for various biological components of the organism (the drug may be stored in inactive or nonresponsive areas of the body).

METABOLISM   As a drug is distributed throughout the body, it eventually arrives at the liver, the primary chemical detoxification system of the body. The liver is capable of chemically altering the original substance to form a new and often inactive drug. The liver may perform any of four chemical alterations on the initial drug: oxidation, hydrolysis, reduction, or conjugation (combining the drug molecule with a biological compound). These chemical alterations produce metabolic by-products, which are generally deactivated forms of the original substance that can be excreted from the body.

One of the disadvantages of swallowed drugs is that significant proportions of them are transported from the digestive system to the liver and metabolized before having any effect on the user's behavior (first-pass metabolism). In addition, although metabolic by-products are generally less active than the original substance, occasionally (as with chloral hydrate) the liver produces an active drug from an inactive one. Finally, we need to be aware that small amounts of the drug may be metabolized outside the liver and that small amounts of most drugs are often excreted unmetabolized.

The metabolization rate of a drug depends on several factors. Disease or damage to the liver can retard metabolization. Malnutrition can alter metabolism, because vitamins, minerals, and other compounds essential for the production of enzymes and catalysts are unavailable. Cardiovascular functioning is important, because the slower the distribution of the drug to the liver, the slower the rate of metabolism will be. Sequestration, or storage, of the drug in body tissues also inhibits metabolism. One factor that can enhance metabolism is the user's previous use of a substance or related drug. Use of a drug often stimulates the production of the enzymes and catalysts essential to its metabolism. Thus, the liver becomes more efficient at metabolizing the substance because of the increased availability of these chemicals. This increased efficiency, or metabolic tolerance, is one factor in the development of tolerance to a drug.

Metabolism of a substance is the primary method by which a drug's actions are terminated. After absorption and during the initial stages of distribution, the relative concentration of the drug is higher in blood plasma than in other tissues. As distribution progresses, a relative balance of the drug in blood plasma and in other tissues is established through homeostatic equilibration. As the liver metabolizes the drug, it is redistributed from other tissue sites back into the bloodstream in order to maintain a relative equilibrium. This redistribution means that the substance leaves the site of action, and the effects terminate.

EXCRETION   The final stage in the pharmacokinetics of a drug is the excretion of the drug and its metabolic by-products. For drugs, the primary method of excretion is through urination. However, some of the drug or its derivatives can also be excreted in defecation, respiration, or perspiration.

Because urination is the principal method of drug excretion, kidney and bladder functioning becomes an important consideration. First, the ability of the kidneys to remove drugs and their metabolic by-products is dependent on cardiovascular and hepatic (liver) functions. Second, disease or damage to the kidneys or bladder can impair the rate of excretion. Finally, pure drugs and their by-products can be reabsorbed into the bloodstream from the urinary system. Thus, impairment of excretory functions can prolong the duration of a drug's effects or produce different effects. For example, significant amounts of pure phenobarbital and mescaline are found in the urine of users. Delay in the excretion of these drugs, once removed from the bloodstream, can result in significant reabsorption of the active drug.

The half-life of a drug is the amount of time required to metabolize and excrete one-half of the original dose (Coombs & Howatt, 2005). The half-life is therefore a measure of the drug's duration of action. Half-life measures assume "normal" cardiovascular, metabolic, and excretory functioning. If these functions are enhanced or (more likely) impaired, the duration of action for a particular user is decreased or increased.

PHARMACODYNAMICS

Pharmacodynamics is the study of where and how a drug produces its effects. Generally speaking, psychoactive substances produce their major effects through acting on the nervous system (Cooper, Bloom, & Roth, 2003). Thus, to better understand the site of action and the mechanism of action for various drugs, we begin with a general review of human neurobiology.

REVIEW OF NEUROBIOLOGICAL PRINCIPLES   The neurological system has three parts. The peripheral nervous system (PNS) fans out in all directions over the surface of the body. It carries messages (such as touch, warmth, cold, and pain) from throughout the body to the central nervous system (CNS) and carries reflexive and voluntary action messages back to muscles. The autonomic nervous system (ANS) is responsible for the more or less automatic functions of the body. It governs heart rate, respiration, digestion, and similar functions. The ANS is divided into two parts, the parasympathetic nervous system (PSNS) and the sympathetic nervous system (SNS). These two systems complement each other, so that when the PSNS is active, the SNS is inactive, and vice versa. The PSNS is the "normal" operating state of the autonomic system and is energy efficient. The SNS is the aroused state of the ANS and prepares for high-energy use as in a fright/fight/flight condition. The effects of PSNS and SNS activation on various physiological functions are summarized in the accompanying box.

 | ## EFFECTS OF PARASYMPATHETIC AND SYMPATHETIC CONTROL

Organ system	Parasympathetic	Sympathetic
Heart	Normal rate and volume	Increased rate and volume
Vascular	Dilated	Constricted
Gastrointestinal	Increased tone and motility; facilitated excretion	Decreased tone and motility; inhibited excretion
Liver	Glycogenesis	Glycogenolysis
Skin	None	Stimulated sweat secretion and Piloerection (gooseflesh)
Respiratory	Normal rate and efficiency	Increased rate and efficiency
Eye	Constricted iris and lens (near vision, or myopia)	Dilated iris and lens (far vision, or hyperopia)

The third and probably most significant part of the nervous system for understanding psychoactive substances is the CNS, which consists of the brain and spinal cord. Although many PNS and ANS actions take place below the level of awareness, they are all reflected in the CNS and can be modified by CNS activation.

The neuron, or nerve cell, is the basic building block of the nervous system. The neural system contains billions of neurons with the majority found within the brain. These neurons vary in length from a few millimeters to about one meter. The basic components of a neuron are represented in Figure 2.5.

Messages are conducted throughout the nervous system by electrochemical processes (see Figure 2.5). A message travels along the neuron from the dendrites to the cell body, axon, and terminals by an electrochemical process involving the exchange

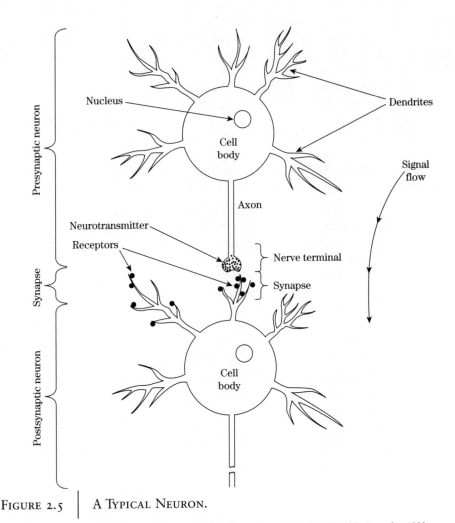

FIGURE 2.5 | A TYPICAL NEURON.

Source: Reproduced from Fifth Special Report to the U.S. Congress on Alcohol and Health, December 1983.

of chemical ions through the membrane of the neuron. However, this electrical current is insufficient to "jump" the synaptic cleft, or gap, between the terminals of one neuron and the dendrites or axons of successive neurons.

In order for a message to traverse the synapse, the electrochemical force is converted into a chemical. This conversion occurs when the chemicals, known as neurotransmitters, are released from storage areas or vesicles. The neurotransmitters flood the synapse and stimulate a receptor site on the next neuron. This receptor stimulation alters the electrochemical characteristics of the successor neuron. The change in electrochemical characteristics may be either excitatory or inhibitory. That is, by stimulating a receptor, the neurotransmitter may initiate a corresponding electrochemical flow in the successor neuron, or the neurotransmitter may act to impede the transmission of a signal that would otherwise occur in the neuron (Cooper et al., 2003). These electrochemical processes occur so fast that impulses travel in the neurological system at about 240 miles per hour, or 350 feet per second. In general, psychoactive substances act by disrupting these electrochemical processes.

There are approximately 40 known neurotransmitters, with some estimates ranging as high as 200. Each neuroterminal releases only one neurotransmitter, and dendritic receptors are responsive to only one neurotransmitter. Thus, neurological impulses follow relatively predetermined pathways in the neurological system. Interconnections within the neural systems, particularly the brain, are accomplished when a neuron responds to one neurotransmitter but releases a different neurotransmitter, thus stimulating a collateral pathway.

NEUROTRANSMITTERS   Of the many postulated neurotransmitters, we will review only a few that are of special concern in the study of psychoactive drugs:

Acetylcholine Probably the most widely distributed neurotransmitter. It is found in the peripheral, autonomic, and central nervous systems. Acetylcholine sometimes excites and sometimes inhibits neurotransmission. It is involved in diverse processes such as voluntary behavior, sleep and arousal, food and water intake, learning and memory, and mood.

Catecholamines A group of neurotransmitters with similar chemical composition. Dopamine is involved in motor activity, reward and reinforcement, and learning. Adrenaline (epinephrine) and noradrenaline (norepinephrine) are involved in autonomic neural activity, where they play a major role in the fright/fight/flight arousal reaction, body temperature, and intake of food and water.

Serotonin Also referred to as 5-hydroxytriptamine, serotonin is involved in mood, aggressive behavior, appetite, and sleep/arousal.

Gamma-aminobutyric acid GABA is the major inhibitory neurotransmitter of the brain and modulates sedation, sleep, and convulsions/seizures.

Endorphins These are naturally occurring morphinelike compounds with considerable analgesic (pain-relief) action.

As the scientific inquiry into neurophysiology and neuropharmacology continues to expand, we expect to acquire greater knowledge of how the brain operates and what effects various chemicals have on those processes.

DRUG EFFECTS ON NEUROTRANSMISSION   A drug or externally administered chemical can alter neurotransmission pathways in several ways:

Destruction of neurons The chemical may be toxic, destroying neurons and thereby interrupting the neurotransmission pathways. Chemical-warfare agents are sometimes designed to have this effect.

Alteration of neuron membranes By altering the permeability of the neuron membrane, a drug can inhibit or stimulate the ion exchange that carries impulses along the neuron.

Effects of enzymes Neurotransmitters are synthesized by enzymes. If a substance affects those enzymes, the synthesis of neurotransmitters will also be affected.

Release of neurotransmitters Once synthesized, neurotransmitters are stored in tiny vesicles. A drug may cause the release of a neurotransmitter from these sacs, thus simulating neural stimulation.

Destruction of neurotransmitters One way in which neurotransmitter action is terminated is by enzymatic, or chemical, destruction of the neurotransmitter. A drug may facilitate or retard this breakdown, thereby reducing or enhancing stimulation of the postsynaptic neuron.

Uptake inhibition A second method of terminating a neurotransmitter's activity is through reabsorption (uptake) of the transmitter substance. A drug can facilitate or inhibit this reabsorption, thereby reducing or enhancing the action of the transmitter.

Mimicking of neurotransmitters A drug can have both receptor affinity and efficacy, thereby creating a false neurotransmission.

Production of a false neurotransmitter A drug can be absorbed by the neuron and used to produce a neurotransmitter that lacks either affinity or efficacy.

Blocking of the receptor A drug can have receptor affinity without efficacy, which would allow the drug to occupy the receptor and block neurotransmission.

Change in receptor sensitivity By attaching to the postsynaptic receptor, a drug can alter the sensitivity of the receptor, thereby enhancing or retarding the neurotransmitter's action on the receptor.

Drugs disrupt neural transmission by acting in one or a combination of the foregoing methods. For some drugs this mechanism of action is well understood; for others, it is a matter of speculation (Sherman, 2007). Table 2.1 identifies some of the drug–neurotransmitter relationships that have been proposed to exist.

HOMEOSTASIS   One of the fundamental principles of physiological functioning is that the organism and its various systems strive to maintain a homeostatic balance. This means there is a dynamic, or changing, equilibrium, such that every change in some element of the organism is compensated for by a change in some other part. For example, increases in cardiovascular volume, peripheral vascular dilation, and perspiration in an effort to return the body temperature to normal limits compensate for increases in internal body temperature. Similarly, the neurological system

TABLE 2.1 | DRUG–NEUROTRANSMITTER RELATIONSHIPS

Drug	Neurotransmitter	Effect
Alcohol	Neural membranes	Hyperpolarization and Neurotoxicity
	Gaba	Enhances
Amanita muscaria	Gaba	Enhances
Amphetamine	Dopamine	Increases
	Norepinephrine	Increases
Anticholinergics	Acetylcholine	Inhibits
Antidepressants	Norepinephrine	Blocks reuptake
	Serotonin	Blocks reuptake
Antipsychotics	Dopamine	Blocks receptors
	Acetylcholine	Blocks receptors
	Norepinephrine	Blocks receptors
	Serotonin	Blocks receptors
	Histamine	Blocks receptors
Aspirin	Prostaglandin	Inhibits
Barbiturates	Gaba	Increases
Benzodiazepines	Gaba	Increases
Caffeine	Adenosine	Blocks receptors
Cocaine	Dopamine	Increases
	Serotonin	Increases
Inhalants	Neural membranes	Hypopolarization and neurotoxicity
Lithium	Serotonin	Increases
LSD	Serotonin	Enhances
	Norepinephrine	Increases
Marijuana	Anandamide	Increases
	Dopamine	Enhances
	Norepinephrine	Enhances
	Serotonin	Enhances
Mescaline	Serotonin	Enhances
Nicotine	Acetylcholine	Increases then decreases
	Dopamine	Increases
	Norepinephrine	Increases
Opioids	Endorphins	Enhances
Phencyclidine (PCP)	Glutamate	Inhibits
Psilocybin	Serotonin	Enhances

operates through such compensatory processes. Drug-induced changes in neural transmission can stimulate homeostatic changes in other neurological processes. Such compensatory changes can result in tolerance to the effects of a drug, referred to as *neurological*, or *psychodynamic, tolerance*.

Rebound and Withdrawal   The compensatory physiological changes in response to the ingestion of a substance account at least partly for the phenomena of rebound and withdrawal. In response to the ingestion of a drug, the body compensates through homeostatic processes for that drug's effects. The individual is now functioning on a new homeostatic plane, which requires the presence of the drug in order to be maintained. As the drug is metabolized and excreted, disequilibrium is created, and physiological adjustments must occur once again. In occasional or periodic usage, this compensation results in rebound, as the individual goes from normal to intoxicated to a state opposite from intoxication. For example, stimulant use is often followed by a period of depression, lethargy, and fatigue. In long-term, repeated usage of a drug, the compensatory processes in response to the absence of the drug can require more time and be more difficult to achieve physiologically. Thus, withdrawal can be viewed as a protracted rebound effect. For example, tolerance to depressants and narcotics generally requires frequent use of the drugs. The withdrawal from these drugs equally requires a fairly lengthy period to achieve (or reachieve) a normal state.

Age   For several reasons, the age of the user is an important variable in determining drug dosages and effects. First, body weight varies with age, with infants and senior citizens typically weighing less than adolescents, young adults, and middle-agers. Second, physiological functions vary by age, with a gradual slowing of cardiovascular, metabolic, and excretory functions over time. Third, neurological development and functions vary with age. Fourth, the proportions of body fat, protein, and water vary with age. Finally, a number of psychosocial factors vary with age. Thus, there are recommended pediatric doses for many drugs, and geriatric standard doses have been established for some drugs.

Gender   The gender, like the age, of the user is a summary factor representing several variables. First, body weight is generally greater for men than for women. Second, there are male/female differences in the proportions of body fat and muscle. Third, hormonal differences between men and women can affect drug effects. Fourth, there are differences between women and men in physiological functioning, particularly as those differences relate to hormone variations. Finally, the psychosocial matrix for men and women is often different. Thus, a drug may affect a male differently than it does a female (Meyer & Quenzer, 2005).

Weight   The weight, or body mass, of a user is perhaps the most frequently used variable in adjusting drug dosages in medical practice. Like age and sex, weight is actually an indicator of several variables, including fat and protein proportions, volume of blood, and cardiovascular function. Thus, the more a user weighs, the more drug he or she can typically consume without experiencing undesirable drug effects.

Race   The user's race may directly and indirectly influence the effects of a drug. Directly, racial variations in blood chemistry and other physiological characteristics can determine the results a drug produces. Indirectly, the psychosocial matrix of an individual is often partly determined by racial characteristics. Thus, how one is expected to act both when drug-free and when under the influence of a drug often varies along racial lines.

NUTRITION   The body requires a variety of proteins, carbohydrates, vitamins, and minerals for normal physiological functioning. Likewise, the enzymes necessary for the metabolism of drugs are built from nutritional sources. Hence, a mildly or severely imbalanced diet can alter the course of a drug's effects.

FOOD AND DRUG INTERACTIONS   Just as two drugs may interact with each other to potentiate or counter the effects of either or both, various foods and nutrients may interact with drugs to alter the effects of the drugs. Most commonly, the presence of food in the stomach delays the onset of swallowed drugs by interfering with absorption. However, food products also contain natural and added chemicals that can inactivate a drug (e.g., calcium-rich foods with tetracycline or acidic foods with penicillin) or stimulate a dangerous reaction (e.g., monoamine oxidase inhibitors with tyramine-rich foods).

DISEASE AND DAMAGE   Clearly, disease or damage to various organs can alter the absorption, distribution, metabolism, or excretion of a drug. Similarly, disease or damage to the neural system can alter both the extent and types of effects a drug produces. Because disease and injury are often corollaries of drug use, chronic users may react very differently to a drug than naive users. This same principle applies to individuals who experience disease or injury that is not drug related. For example, both the type and amount of analgesic required to alleviate pain depend on the source and the intensity of the pain (e.g., headaches versus postoperative pain).

GENETICS   Both professionals and the public have shown considerable interest in recent years in the role genetics plays in the effects of drugs (Hasin, Hatzenbuehler, & Waxman, 2006). Allergic reactions by some individuals to certain substances have long been noted. Recent research has begun to explore more systematically the role of heredity in individual susceptibility and immunity to various drugs. Of particular note is the research on sensitivity to alcohol among Asians and the proclivity to alcohol abuse or alcoholism among children of alcoholic parents.

BIORHYTHMS   Many physiological processes are cyclic. These cycles may be monthly (as in menstrual cycles); may be daily, or circadian (as in periods of alertness or sleep); or may occur several times within a 24-hour period (as in hunger). Research suggests that a drug's effects may depend on the time of day or month it is administered. For example, stimulants should have less impact on a well-rested and alert individual than on one who is fatigued.

We have reviewed a number of physiological principles and individual characteristics that can affect the way a user responds to a drug. Clearly, there is considerable variation among users. We should not be surprised to learn that different users, or the same user on different occasions, can experience somewhat different effects from the same drug administered in the same way at identical doses. Even in medical situations it is difficult to predict exactly what effects a drug will have, and "street-use" conditions are hardly ideal environments for predicting drug effects. However, it is easier in many respects to understand how physiological factors influence a drug's effects than it is to predict the influence of psychological and sociocultural factors on drug reactions (Erickson, 2007).

PSYCHOLOGICAL CHARACTERISTICS OF THE USER

The effects of a drug that have been demonstrated by double-blind placebo studies to be related to the chemistry of the drug are referred to as *specific effects*. Those effects that depend on psychological and sociocultural variables are referred to as *nonspecific effects*. Often, a drug's nonspecific effects are more powerful than its specific effects. In this section we discuss some of the psychological variables that alter a drug's effects; in the next section, we will look at some of the sociocultural variations that contribute to a drug's effects. There are four major psychological variables: previous drug experience, expectations or set, mood, and task.

Previous Drug Experience

Experience with a substance similar to the one about to be ingested is clearly an important determinant of the drug's effects. Of primary importance is the fact that previous usage has a major impact on our expectations about the drug's effects (discussed in more detail in the next subsection).

For some drugs (e.g., marijuana) the effects can be so subtle that one has to learn what to look for and to define those effects as pleasurable. In addition, with exposure to a substance we learn how to adjust our behavior to compensate for drug-induced changes in sensations, voluntary behavior control, cognitions, and moods. We also learn that the effects are transient—they will wear off—and thus an experienced user is less likely to panic and less likely to experience "bad trips." This learning process is extremely important in maintaining some semblance of control over one's state of intoxication, and it accounts for a significant proportion of the tolerance that experienced users show for a substance. That is, tolerance is in part a learned response to a drug.

Cross-tolerance, reverse tolerance, and rapid tolerance (tachyphlaxis) can be explained at least partially through learning mechanisms. Cross-tolerance occurs when previous experience with one drug or class of drugs increases the user's tolerance to a second substance or class of drugs. For example, the various sedative/hypnotic drugs show considerable cross-tolerance, as do some hallucinogens. Reverse tolerance is said to occur when smaller successive doses are required to produce the same effects. The classic example of reverse tolerance occurs with marijuana, as experienced users find that it requires less to get high than when they began using the drug. Acute, or rapid, tolerance occurs with several drugs, the most notable being alcohol. For the same blood-alcohol level (BAL), intoxication is often more noticeable when the BAL is rising than when it is falling, thereby illustrating a rapid tolerance to the effects of alcohol.

EXPECTATIONS OR SET

A user's expectations about a drug's effects are derived from several sources, including his or her previous experience with the substance, friends' accounts, the mass media, education and training, and professional descriptions. These expectations have a considerable impact on the effects one obtains from a drug.

Placebo studies using inactive materials provide clear information on the effects of expectations on drug reactions. Depending on the manner in which the placebo is administered, the information provided, and even the physical characteristics of the placebo itself (size, color, and taste), significant proportions of users have reported cognitive, sensory, and emotional changes related to the use of the placebo. Similarly, the user's behaviors are generally consistent with the reported subjective changes. Thus, the effects a user experiences are often determined by the user's beliefs about a substance rather than the drug's chemistry.

MOOD

The effects that a substance can have depend on the user's initial mood relative to his or her maximum capabilities. This principle is known as Wilder's law of initial value. Basically, Wilder's law states that a drug cannot make a user exceed his or her capabilities behaviorally, emotionally, or cognitively. Further, it notes that a drug's effect depends on the user's predrug state: The further one is from one's maximum, the greater the potential effect. Thus, if you are already highly stimulated, a stimulant will have relatively little effect, but when you are fatigued, that same drug at the same dose can have considerable impact. Wilder's law also suggests that paradoxical effects (effects opposite to those expected) occur when users are already at or near their maximum and ingest a drug to further enhance their state; for example, methylphenidate, a stimulant, is effective in controlling hyperkinetic children.

TASK

The final psychological characteristic is the nature of the tasks a user attempts while under the influence of a drug. Tasks can vary along at least four dimensions: complexity, abstractness, recency of acquisition, and performance motivation. Substances impair complex, abstract, recently acquired, or low-motivation tasks more than they impair simple, concrete, well-learned, or highly motivated behaviors. Thus, it requires a very high dose to keep you from tying your shoes or performing a similar task, but it requires a very small dose to interfere with studying for an examination.

Clearly, users' drug-using experiences, their expectations regarding the effects of a drug, their mood before taking the drug, and the tasks they attempt after ingesting it influence the effect the drug has on them. To some degree the sociocultural environment of the user, to which we now turn, determines the tasks, predrug state, and expectations.

SOCIOCULTURAL ENVIRONMENT

The sociocultural environment of drug use can be separated into physical and social aspects. We must not forget, however, that each influences the other. That is, the physical environment prescribes and proscribes both the types of individuals found there and the types of interactions. Likewise, people and their interactions help define the physical environment and may be the most important characteristic of the environment.

PHYSICAL ENVIRONMENT

It is difficult, if not impossible, to engage in certain behaviors when appropriate props are absent. Thus, one cannot play pool without a pool table. Similarly, the physical environment both constrains and facilitates various behaviors for a drug user. A drug will result in very different behavior when used in a hospital or other medical setting than when used at a party. Thus, the physical environment becomes an important determinant of a drug's effects and a user's behaviors.

SOCIAL ENVIRONMENT

Other people and their behavior influence the relationship between an individual and a drug in several ways. First, others provide a milieu that defines the environment as happy or sad and thereby establishes a general mood, or emotional tone. Second, it is from others that we learn the rules and rituals regarding the use of a substance. Third, the behavior of others becomes a reference point or standard of comparison according to which we judge our own behavior and against which our behavior is judged. Fourth, others act as guides and interpreters to help us identify, define, and assess the effects of a substance. Finally, throughout all of the foregoing, others provide social support and sanctions for appropriate and inappropriate behavior regarding substance use and abuse.

Our actions, whether we are drug-free or high, are likely to be very different in the presence of friends at a party than in the presence of strangers at a formal dinner. Likewise, preparing a fix, rolling a joint, and freebasing require skills and techniques acquired from others. We quickly learn that it is acceptable to say and do under the influence of a drug some things that are not permissible when we are drug-free. Often, especially with novices, one person stays "straight" to help the users understand and interpret a drug's effects and thereby help alleviate panic, tension, and other factors that can contribute to a bad trip. Finally, through their encouragement, acceptance, and support, our peers, friends, family, and associates provide important rewards and punishments for the use or nonuse of substances.

The sociocultural environment, consisting of physical objects and social beings, can either facilitate or hinder the effects of a drug. The resulting drug-related experiences play an important role in shaping our attitudes, values, and beliefs regarding the general use of drugs in society and our own personal use of substances. Thus, the physical and social environments have a considerable impact on both the present and future effects of drugs on behavior.

We have reviewed four groups of variables that contribute to the effects that substance users experience. Clearly, different users or even the same user on different occasions can experience considerable variation in response. Thus, drug effects are generally discussed in terms of the proportion of users who experience a particular effect at a given dosage. For example, a 10-mg dose of morphine will induce analgesia among most nontolerant users.

Nevertheless, both in medical practice and on the street, relatively consistent effects can be achieved. These effects, including analgesia, hallucinations, hypnosis, sedation, and stimulation, are possible even among drug-tolerant individuals if the dosage is increased to obtain the desired or expected effect. We now turn to a discussion of these commonly experienced drug effects.

DRUG-CLASSIFICATION SYSTEMS

There are several ways of classifying drugs, according to the needs of the classifier. Drugs can be classified by chemical structure, a system useful to biochemists because common chemical structures often, but not always, imply similar effects. Substances are also classified according to their origin, or source (e.g., cannabinoids derived from marijuana). Drug-classification systems have also been developed that rely on the site of action or mechanism of action because of the rather obvious utility in understanding where or how a drug produces physiological changes. Finally, and most useful for our present purposes, drugs can be classified on the basis of their effects, such as prototype (amphetaminelike), therapeutic use (sedative/hypnotic), or street use (as "uppers"). The end result of each classification is the same: to facilitate the search for commonalities and differences among drugs and their interactions with physiological systems.

COMMON DRUG-RELATED EFFECTS

Table 2.2 summarizes some of the more frequently encountered drug-related effects. These effects are classified by drug categories as follows:

Opioids natural, semisynthetic, and synthetic narcotic analgesics

Depressants barbiturates, minor tranquilizers, and other sedative/hypnotic drugs, including alcohol

Stimulants amphetamines, cocaine, amphetaminelike drugs, and caffeine

Hallucinogens LSD, psilocybin, mescaline, and stimulant-related substances

Phencyclidine categorized by itself because it possesses analgesic, depressant, and hallucinogenic properties

Cannabinoids marijuana derivatives categorized separately because of their combined depressant and hallucinogenic properties

Inhalants a diverse group of volatile chemicals whose effects are largely related to anoxia or hypoxia

For each group of drugs, the effects of acute intoxication, overdose, and withdrawal are presented.

TABLE 2.2 | COMMON EFFECTS OF DRUGS

	Intoxication							Overdose							Withdrawal		
Autonomic	Opioids	Depressants	Stimulants	Hallucinogens	Phencyclidine	Cannabinoids	Inhalants	Opioids	Depressants	Stimulants	Hallucinogens	Phencyclidine	Cannabinoids	Inhalants	Opioids	Depressants	Stimulants
Abdominal cramps											X				X	X	
Angina			X							X							
Arrhythmia										X							
Chest pain										X							
Chills								X							X	X	
Circulatory collapse										X	X						X
Coryza											X	X			X	X	
Diarrhea				X	X						X				X		
Flushing	X			X						X							
Hypertension			X	X						X					X	X	
Hyperthermia			X							X							
Hypotension (orthostatic)	X	X						X	X								
Hypotonia	X	X						X	X								X
Lacrimation							X								X		
Mouth, dry			X							X	X						

TABLE 2.2 | COMMON EFFECTS OF DRUGS (*Continued*)

	Intoxication							Overdose							Withdrawal		
	Opioids	Depressants	Stimulants	Hallucinogens	Phencyclidine	Cannabinoids	Inhalants	Opioids	Depressants	Stimulants	Hallucinogens	Phencyclidine	Cannabinoids	Inhalants	Opioids	Depressants	Stimulants
Nystagmus		X			X				X			X					
Piloerection (gooseflesh)															X		
Pupils, dilated			X	X	X	X				X	X				X		
Pupils, pinpointed	X							X									
Reflexes, hyperactive			X	X						X	X					X	
Respiration, slow and shallow								X	X					X			
Rhinorrhea							X								X		
Sweating										X					X		
Tachycardia			X	X	X				X	X	X	X			X	X	
Vomiting					X					X	X				X		
Yawning															X		
Sensorimotor Aches, muscle															X		
Analgesia					X			X		X		X					
Ataxia		X			X			X	X			X					
Coma								X	X			X					
Convulsions		X								X		X					X

	Intoxication							Overdose							Withdrawal		
	Opioids	Depressants	Stimulants	Hallucinogens	Phencyclidine	Cannabinoids	Inhalants	Opioids	Depressants	Stimulants	Hallucinogens	Phencyclidine	Cannabinoids	Inhalants	Opioids	Depressants	Stimulants
Diplopia		x															
Dysmetria		x			x												
Facial grimacing					x					x							
Headaches							x									x	
Motor seizures (grand mal)										x	x	x				x	
Muscle spasm (rigidity)					x							x			x		
Nausea			x							x	x	x			x	x	
Paresthesia			x	x						x					x		
Skin pricking	x		x							x							
Sleep disturbance			x	x						x							
Sleepiness	x	x				x	x										
Speech, slurred		x			x		x										
Stare, blank					x							x					
Tremor			x	x						x	x					x	x
Violent behavior		x			x							x					
Psychological Affect, labile			x		x							x					x
Anorexia			x	x	x					x	x						
Anxiety	x		x	x						x	x	x			x	x	

TABLE 2.2 | COMMON EFFECTS OF DRUGS (Continued)

	Intoxication							Overdose							Withdrawal		
	Opioids	Depressants	Stimulants	Hallucinogens	Phencyclidine	Cannabinoids	Inhalants	Opioids	Depressants	Stimulants	Hallucinogens	Phencyclidine	Cannabinoids	Inhalants	Opioids	Depressants	Stimulants
Body image changes	x			x	x					x	x	x					
Comprehension, slow	x	x			x			x	x	x		x					x
Delirium		x	x		x			x	x	x	x	x		x		x	x
Depressed mood		x			x												x
Dizziness	x	x	x	x	x		x				x						
Euphoria	x	x	x	x	x												
Fatigue		x								x							
Floating feeling	x	x		x	x												
Hallucinations			x	x	x	x					x	x				x	
Hyperphagia																	x
Irritability		x	x		x				x	x	x				x	x	
Memory, poor		x			x												
Psychosis (toxic)		x		x	x					x	x	x					
Restlessness			x	x						x	x				x	x	
Suspiciousness			x	x	x					x	x	x					
Talkativeness			x			x				x							

Table 2.2 identifies various signs and symptoms that can occur with substance use. These effects are sorted into three broad categories: autonomic, sensorimotor, and psychological. Autonomic effects are those related to the autonomic nervous system and include involuntary muscle control, cardiovascular, respiratory, digestive, and related effects. Sensorimotor effects refer to voluntary muscle control and sensory changes. The psychological category includes perceptual, emotional, and cognitive effects. It should be clear from a review of Table 2.2 that, in general, no single effect is sufficient to determine either the class of drug or the level of dosage that has been used. Unless one has access to body fluid (blood, urine) or tissue (brain, liver) samples and biochemical testing processes, identifying the type of drug used and the approximate dosage administered requires one to look for and determine a pattern of signs and symptoms.

ALCOHOL AND OTHER DRUGS: A CAVEAT

We can see in Table 2.2 that there are a number of similarities as well as significant differences among diverse classes of drugs. Alcohol, as a drug, is generally classed as a depressant on the basis of its pharmacological actions and behavioral effects. However, alcohol abuse and alcoholism have been considered throughout much of the 20th century to constitute a separate entity from other forms of drug abuse.

The basis for the distinction between alcohol abuse and other types of drug abuse is primarily sociocultural. With repeal of Prohibition in the United States in 1933, alcohol use was legalized subject to various state and local restrictions (e.g., drinking age, hours of sale, outlets). Because the use of alcohol has been socially acceptable and beverage alcohol has been widely available, definitions of what constitutes abuse of alcohol have been developed that focus on the pattern of use (e.g., more than 3 oz of absolute alcohol per day or a BAL in excess of 0.08) or on the consequences of use (poor work or school performance and marital or family problems). Definitions of drug abuse, on the other hand, have relied on legal considerations regarding the manufacture, distribution, sale, possession, or use of controlled substances. Any use of a controlled drug other than under the direction of a doctor is considered to be drug misuse or abuse by the general public and by many professionals.

We have taken the position in this text that the pharmacological and behavioral similarities between alcohol and other drugs are more important than the differences. Thus, unless otherwise noted, we prefer the term substance abuse to the distinction between alcohol abuse (or alcoholism) and drug abuse.

PHARMACOTHERAPY OF DRUG ABUSE

Administering a drug can modify the effects of a second drug, and both the National Institute on Drug Abuse and the National Institute on Alcohol Abuse and Alcoholism have supported research to develop pharmacotherapies for drug abuse. This research has focused on three types of pharmacological interventions: symptom amelioration, agonist substitution, and antagonistic therapies.

Symptom amelioration therapy explores the use of various drugs to control the symptoms of substance withdrawal. This approach uses antinauseant, antidepressant, analgesic, and similar prescription or over-the-counter medications to help clients cope with physiological withdrawal problems. Although symptom amelioration therapy is the least controversial of the pharmacotherapies, it remains unclear whether it improves treatment outcomes.

The second form of pharmacotherapy, agonist substitution, has been the focus of much controversy within both professional and popular arenas. Agonist substitution therapy replaces the abused substance (e.g., heroin) with a legal drug having a similar pharmacological profile (methadone). The rationale behind such an approach is that the replacement drug will control or avoid withdrawal symptoms and craving for the abused drug. By removing the withdrawal and craving, the agonist substitute facilitates client participation in psychosocial treatment activities and reintegration into family/community life (e.g., parenting, occupational/educational careers). The controversy over agonist substitution therapy has focused primarily on the goals of treatment (i.e., should clients be drug-free?).

The final area of pharmacotherapy involves the use of antagonists to block the effects of a preferred drug (e.g., naltrexone and heroin) or make the use of the abused drug aversive (e.g., disulfiram and alcohol). The expectation is that the user will learn that his or her drug of choice no longer produces the desired effects (or produces very undesirable effects) and will stop using that drug. Of course, the clients may switch preferred drugs (e.g., methadone clients using cocaine) or avoid taking the antagonist so that they can resume using their drug of choice.

Although there is considerable interest in developing pharmacotherapies for substance abuse, there are at least two barriers to their integration into treatment practices. The first issue concerns questions of efficacy in the use of such therapies, which are researchable questions. The second barrier has been the apparent resistance among many substance abuse counselors to using drugs to treat drug abuse, which is a question of education and training.

SUMMARY

Substance abuse professionals are often expected to explain the effects of drugs, both to their clients and to the community. A wide variety of pharmacological, physiological, psychological, and sociocultural factors contribute in complex ways to the effects experienced by substance users.

The pharmacological variables that influence the effects of a drug include its dosage and composition, the frequency or pattern of use, the method of administration, and its interaction with other drugs. Physiological factors include those processes that are involved in the absorption, distribution, metabolism, and excretion of the drug. In addition, a drug user's sensations, emotions, cognitions, and behaviors change in response to alterations in neurotransmission processes. Psychological influences include the user's previous drug experience, expectations, mood, and the task the user is attempting. Finally, we must consider the influence of physical and social environments on drug effects.

Given the large number of variables and the complexity of the interactions among them, it should be clear that there could be considerable heterogeneity in the effects of drugs. However, there is also considerable consistency in users' experiences. Recognition of the diversity as well as the commonality of drug effects is important in the assessment, treatment, and aftercare of clients. Moreover, developments in the pharmacotherapy of substance abuse suggest some intriguing possibilities for improving treatment outcomes.

SOME IMPLICATIONS OF PHARMACOLOGY FOR COUNSELING

In the initial assessment process, counselors should focus on the user's perceptions and perceived effects of their drug use rather than the pharmacology of the putative drug because analysis of drug samples are not always what they are claimed and user reactions to the same drug can be different (same drug, different effect).

Though it should be obvious that it can be very difficult to work with a client who is "under the effects" of a drug, it may not be so obvious that the indirect effects of using drugs can result in a postacute withdrawal syndrome that may persist for days, weeks, or longer. These postacute effects can be the result of malnutrition, sleep disturbances, physical or mental trauma from long duration or high dosages of drug use.

Because most psychoactive drugs affect cognitive or emotional experiences (that is why they are desired), counselors must avoid making assumptions related to client perceptions, memories, and feelings. Clients may be having a memory lapse, there could be a failure to process events as a memory, or even distrust of the counselor rather than resistance/denial.

It is unlikely that any two clients have experienced the same or even similar drug-using histories.

An advantage that recovering helpers have over nonrecovering helpers is their personal experiences with the drug(s). These experiences enhance the development of rapport and trust with the client. However, the differences in experiences between client and counselor can also become an obstacle to later counseling sessions. One or more courses in pharmacology can be of great help to both the recovering and nonrecovering counselor in developing an understanding of the client's experiences.

The treatment plan and activities need to be regularly reassessed as the client begins to function with less drug ingestion. In particular, if the drug-using behavior was functional for the client, then alternative behaviors serving similar functions need to be found or developed.

QUESTIONS FOR THOUGHT AND DISCUSSION

1. People tend to think of some drugs as inherently and absolutely bad and other drugs as acceptable. In fact, as you have noted in this chapter, the effect of a drug comes from a combination of the drug itself, the psychology of the user, the physiology of the user, and the sociocultural environment. How does this phenomenon affect your views about specific drugs? How would you objectively compare cigarettes, coffee, marijuana, and heroin?

2. George says that after having successfully recovered from a long-term problem with an overuse of caffeine, he has recently had a relapse and is drinking more coffee than ever. The occasion of his relapse had to do with a change in his workplace. Smoking is no longer allowed in the building. George says that

because he can no longer enjoy a cigarette during his break, he has begun drinking coffee instead. Think first about why the substitution of caffeine for nicotine might be considered unusual. Given this background, how might you explain George's behavior?

REFERENCES

Coombs, R., & Howlatt, W. (2005). *The adiction counselor's desk reference.* Hoboken, NJ: Wiley.

Cooper, J. R., Bloom, F. E., & Roth, R. H. (2003). *Biochemical basis of neuropharmacology* (8th ed.). New York, NY: Oxford University Press.

Erickson, C. K. (2007). *The science of addiction—From neurobiology to treatment.* New York, NY: W. W. Norton and Company.

Hasin, D., Hatzenbuehler, M., & Waxman, R. (2006). Genetics of substance abuse disorders. In W. R. Miller, & K. M. Carroll (Eds.), *Rethinking substance abuse—What the science shows and what we should do about it.* New York, NY: Guilford Press.

Klein, S. B., & Thorne, B. M. (2007). *Biological psychology.* New York, NY: Worth Publishers.

Meyer, J. S. & Quenzer, L. F. (2005). *Psychopharmacology: Drugs, the brain, and behavior.* Sunderland, MA: Sinauer Associates.

Sherman, C. (2007). *Impacts of drugs on neurotransmission.* NIDA, Washington, DC: NIDANotes.

MOTIVATIONAL INTERVIEWING

CHAPTER 1 BEGAN with our portrayal of substance abuse counseling as a field in the midst of a paradigm shift from coercion to collaboration, from scare tactics to empowerment and respect, from assumptions based on mythology to models based on science. These strides toward a 21st century perspective could not have been made without the key contribution of Motivational Interviewing (MI). If one myth dominated the 20th century view of addiction treatment, it was "the myth of the unmotivated patient" (Rollnick, Miller, & Butler, 2008, p. 5). There was a time when people believed that motivation was a character trait seldom found in people with substance abuse problems. Derived from this assumption was the notion that substance-abusing clients would be likely to change only when (a) their lives became too painful to endure or (b) they received strong external pressures to push them toward action. Motivational interviewing suggests an entirely different view of motivation.

> Many of the clients we see have had no dearth of suffering. Humiliation, shame, guilt, and angst are not the primary engines of change. Ironically, such experiences can even immobilize the person, rendering change more remote. Instead, constructive behavior change seems to arise when the person connects it with something of intrinsic value, something important, something cherished. Intrinsic motivation for change arises in an accepting, empowering atmosphere that makes it safe for the person to explore the possibly painful present in relation to what is wanted and valued. (Miller & Rollnick, 2002, p. 12)

In order to be successful in MI, a counselor would have to believe in and commit to this way of understanding the process of change. Only when counselors have internalized this respectful view of their clients can they begin to create the safe, accepting, and empowering atmosphere that is at the heart of competent practice.

THE MEANING OF MOTIVATIONAL INTERVIEWING

Motivational Interviewing is defined as *"a goal-directed, client-centered counseling style for eliciting behavior change by helping clients to explore and resolve ambivalence"* (SAMHSA's National Registry of Evidence-based Programs and Practices, 2007b). Each aspect of the definition of MI bears exploration, beginning with the unusual combination of *goal-directedness* and *client-centeredness*.

BOTH CLIENT-CENTERED AND DIRECTIVE

MI is rooted in the time-tested therapy of Carl Rogers (1957). Rogers's theory, even as it evolved from "client-centered" to "person-centered," maintained a central focus on the counselor–client relationship. The facilitative dimensions underlying effectiveness included the counselor's ability to exhibit genuineness, unconditional acceptance of the client, and empathic understanding. The strength of the relationship set the stage for client growth, even to the degree of being seen as not only necessary but also sufficient for positive growth.

If one were to observe an authentic motivational interview, one would again see these same facilitative dimensions in action. Although the competent motivational interviewer is empathic and accepting of the client, the positive relationship would be seen as necessary but not, in itself, sufficient.

> MI can be thought of as client-centered therapy with a twist. Unlike client-centered therapy, MI has specific goals: to reduce ambivalence about change and to increase intrinsic motivation to change. In this sense, MI is both client-centered and directive. The MI therapist creates an atmosphere in which the client rather than the therapist becomes the main advocate for change as well as the primary agent of change. (Arkowitz & Miller, 2008, p. 4)

Motivational interviewers use the finely honed listening skills of the person-centered therapist, but they are intentional in listening for and reinforcing the client's *change talk*. When clients talk about the positive aspects of change, when they express optimism about the possibilities of a different kind of life, when they speak of intentions for something new: Those utterances represent the change talk that underlies positive movement. When interviews move in this direction, motivational interviewers use reinforcement to keep the momentum going. At the same time, they maintain a strong hold on their client-centered approach, knowing that giving unsought expert advice is the one way guaranteed to stop change talk in its tracks.

ELICITING BEHAVIOR CHANGE

Miller and Moyers (2006) point out that if counselors can recognize change talk they can learn how to elicit more of it, explaining that:

> This intentional effort to elicit client change talk, rather than simply waiting for it to occur, is a strategic skill that differentiates MI from other therapeutic approaches. ... For example, the MI counselor asks open questions the answer to which is change talk (e.g., "In what ways might this change be a good thing?"), and is cautious with questions the answer to which is resistance (e.g., "Why haven't you changed?"). When

change talk occurs, the counselor may reflect it, affirm it, or ask for elaboration or examples—all of which are likely to elicit more change talk. (p. 8)

Eliciting talk of change and keeping focus on change itself are at the heart of MI. The assumptions about motivation that lie beneath MI are that (a) people possess within themselves all that they need for change to happen and (b) the will toward change is awakened within an interpersonal context.

Resolving Ambivalence

Although people have the seeds of motivation within themselves they also have the seeds of doubt. No one should be surprised that clients feel ambivalent about changing their substance use behaviors. Ambivalence accompanies most major life changes—and altering one's substance use is, for many, a major adjustment. Counselors who adhered to the old conventional wisdom about substance abuse used to interpret ambivalence as a sign of resistance, denial, or lack of motivation. In fact, ambivalence is a natural state and it is easy for people to get "stuck." They are uncertain about what the future holds for them if they move away from what is familiar to them, but they have doubts about whether their familiar life fits their life goals. The motivational interview process is designed to help individuals move past the barriers that have kept them in place. The safe environment that is created through a collaborative and supportive relationship helps to make that movement possible.

> Resolving ambivalence can be a key to change, and, indeed, once ambivalence has been resolved, little else may be required for change to occur. However, attempts to force resolution in a particular direction (as by direct persuasion or by increasing punishment for inaction) can lead to a paradoxical response, even strengthening the very behavior they were intended to diminish. (Miller & Rollnick, 2002)

Counselors may find it frustrating to hold back their advice when they "know" what the person should do. It is clear, however, that the spirit and principles of MI, in sharp contrast with pressure and advice-giving, do lead toward a resolution of ambivalence and, finally, toward positive change.

MI SPIRIT

Recently, it has become common for addiction professionals to be sent for mandatory training in MI. On the surface, it would appear that MI, like other evidence-based practices, should be learned by everyone. The fact is, however, that MI should not be considered a "technique" to be added to any treatment provider's repertoire. MI is built on a set of assumptions about how people change and how helpers can best facilitate that process. Some treatment providers continue to believe that the helper's "expertise" should overrule the client's self-knowledge. They believe that the client cannot be "allowed" to make his or her own decisions about drug use. MI is too inconsistent with such beliefs to make it possible for MI "procedures" to be added to the methods implemented by the believer. The MI spirit, which forms the basis for practice, is "*collaborative, evocative,* and honoring of patient *autonomy*" (Rollnick et al., 2008, p. 6). Real effort is required to learn MI, and effective practice requires that the MI spirit be authentic.

COLLABORATION

A true collaboration depends on mutual respect. In the context of MI, counselors can be seen as adhering to the MI spirit when their interactions demonstrate respect for their clients' ability to plan and manage their own lives. Collaboration, of course, is a behavior that can be exhibited only through the participation of two or more people. The give-and-take of a true collaboration is recognizable by a comfortable sharing of thoughts and a willingness to support the ideas put forth by the other. In MI, it is the responsibility of the counselor to be clear in demonstrating his or her respect for the client and to minimize the differentials in status and power that so often characterize the helper–client relationship. Collaborative counselors know that their clients are authorities on their own lives and therefore they are uniquely qualified to make choices about the direction their lives should take.

In contrast, counselors who are less collaborative have difficulty trusting in the possibility that their clients might be able to make life decisions that are right for them. This orientation comes into plain view when the counselor takes a strong lead, deciding what is best for the client and then trying to convince him or her of the rightness of the counselor's perception. The differences between the highly collaborative counselor and the less collaborative helper provide a clue to the presence or absence of a trained motivational interviewer.

EVOCATION

The belief that the individual holds within himself or herself the potential for motivation and action provides clear direction concerning the role of the counselor: evoking the client's ideas about change. Through exploring and expressing their thoughts about the potential for altering their behaviors, people can come to terms with their ambivalence and move toward resolution. Counselors who are skilled in drawing out their clients' thoughts can help bring to light the clients' hopes for positive change. One side of any individual's ambivalence is the side that desires change. Through evocation, the counselor can help the client find and express that side.

The other side of the individual's ambivalence, of course, involves a reluctance to change. Sometimes counselors choose to disregard their clients' ideas and focus instead on selling their own notions of what the plan of action should be. When this happens, the opportunity to elicit positive thoughts is lost. Clients are left with the thankless task of arguing against the change that the counselors desire.

AUTONOMY

A key factor in MI is the notion that the client—not the counselor—must bear the decision-making power. It seems obvious that the person who will actually live with any decisions that are made must obviously be the one in control. In real life, away from the counseling office or the treatment setting, the counselor has no power to determine what steps the client will take. Despite this reality, some counselors prefer to hold onto the illusion that they are in charge. In doing so, they undercut their clients' autonomy and thereby lessen the likelihood of change.

Change is most likely to occur when people believe that it is within their own power to make it happen. When counselors reinforce and support even their clients' smallest movements toward autonomy, they vastly increase the chances for success. It is for this reason that the counselor's ability to support client autonomy forms such an important component of MI spirit. Sometimes clients make decisions that appear, at least in the short term, to be terribly wrong. In those situations, it may be difficult for counselors to let go of the reins until they remind themselves that the reins were never theirs to hold.

MOTIVATIONAL INTERVIEWING PRINCIPLES

Counselors whose work is infused with MI spirit appreciate the centrality of collaboration, evocation, and client autonomy. This understanding forms the foundation upon which the principles of MI are based. The principles that guide the counselor's behaviors include the following (Miller & Rollnick, 2002):

1. Express empathy.
2. Develop discrepancy.
3. Roll with resistance.
4. Support self-efficacy.

EXPRESS EMPATHY

Empathic counselors use their listening and communication skills to understand what their clients are conveying and then demonstrate this understanding in their own responses. Empathy, which is at the heart of MI practice, allows counselors to comprehend the thoughts and feelings behind their clients' actual utterances. They reflect these thoughts and feelings back to the client in a way that not only shows understanding but also helps clients see their own thoughts in a new light.

Counselors who express accurate empathy do not allow the prism of judgmentalism to distort their own understanding. They do not have to agree with their clients' statements; they only have to respect them. Treatment providers who are accustomed to dispensing detailed advice sometimes view empathic behaviors as overly passive.

> Some treatment providers may be so passionate about the problem of substance abuse that they will not be comfortable using any but the most extreme responses when they believe that such a problem is present. Motivational interviewing is probably not for them. (Moyers & Yahne, 1998, p. 31)

The evidence is clear, however, that the respectful and empathic responses of a trained motivational interviewer can increase the likelihood that clients will make life changes (Carroll, Ball, Nich, Martino, Frankforter, & Farentinos, 2006; Rubak, Sandbaek, Lauritzen, & Christensen, 2005; Vasilaki, Hosier, & Cox, 2006) even though the process may look deceptively easy.

Consider the situation of Maria, a young woman who is on parole after serving time in prison for a drug-related offense. She had been doing very well in the months after her release. Now, however, she has tested positive for marijuana. She and the interviewer, a parole agent who was trained in MI, talk about the situation in this brief segment. She has just explained that she is living with her fiancé and her cousin, both of whom are regular users of marijuana.

INTERVIEWER: I can understand how difficult it must have been for you to keep on track all this time when your fiancé and your cousin have been smoking in front of you.

CLIENT: Yeah, it has been hard sometimes. But I think it's been worth it because it's such a good living situation—being with people who love me, who are supportive. Usually I can say no when they offer me some but I just came from a job interview that went bust and I was feeling awful.

INTERVIEWER: This time because you were feeling down anyway you didn't have your usual strength that it takes to say no.

CLIENT: That's exactly what happened. If other things are going okay then I don't feel like using it at all. It's just when there's no job, no really great future that I can see … it's kind of like, why bother?

INTERVIEWER: I know what you mean. Things that you can stand up against when you're feeling good about yourself just get to be too much when you're under some kind of stress or feeling hopeless.

CLIENT: That's it! I was under stress. I just felt like I was so glad to be home after the day I had. But I was still feeling so awful. Otherwise I could walk right by without a thought. I've done it a million times. But there was the stress and then they were saying to me, "Come on. You'll feel better." They shouldn't have done that. But I should have just walked out. I absolutely should have.

INTERVIEWER: It sounds like your living situation feels really good when other things are going along okay. But when things are difficult, when you're stressed out, you don't feel like you can count on yourself as well to stay clean and sober. Having that invitation to use just hit you at the wrong time.

CLIENT: I couldn't seem to see my way clear to say no at the time. I know it sounds hard to believe but I absolutely did not want to smoke.

INTERVIEWER: Even though you lose hope sometimes, it sounds like you're still very committed to staying clean. Do I have that right?

CLIENT: Yes. I just can't go back to prison.

INTERVIEWER: I know you've been thinking about this a lot. What ideas have you come up with so far?

CLIENT: I'm going to have to decide what to do. I thought I was strong enough for anything but this scared me. I might even have to think about moving somewhere temporarily where there aren't drugs. Maybe I could go to my mother's house or something for a while. Or maybe I could get another copy of that list of halfway houses that I threw out.

If the interviewer had wanted to give unsolicited advice, he could have told Maria that she was not in "a good living situation" with people who loved and supported her. He could have told her that her living situation was lethal and that she needed to move out at once. Even assuming the truth of that assessment, however, we need to ask what the result of that intervention would have been. The greatest likelihood is that Maria would have responded by defending her choice of home, defending her choice of fiancé, and, ultimately, deciding that no change was warranted. But the interviewer avoided advice-giving and confrontation, working instead to understand what Maria was thinking and feeling. His use of empathic responses made it possible for the client to think through her options and move toward change.

DEVELOP DISCREPANCY

Motivational Interviewing helps clients notice discrepancies between their current behaviors on the one hand and their goals and values on the other. Their awareness of the gaps between what is and what could be can lead toward motivation, especially if the goals in question are especially important to them. Counselors can help move this process along by listening for and reinforcing clients' statements of values or goals that are meaningful to them. When clients speak intensely about their aspirations, they are in a good position to begin talking about the steps they would have to take in order to break down the barriers between themselves and their desired outcomes. This process can work only if the aspirations are authentically the clients', not the goals that others find appropriate.

In the course of MI, clients might see discrepancies not just between their current behaviors and their external goals but also between their current behaviors and their sense of the people they believe themselves to be. This factor highlights the importance of the respectfulness that is inherent in MI spirit. If a person believes himself or herself to be a good person who is responsible and cares about others, he or she might see a discrepancy in such behaviors as taking an extra-long lunch devoted to drinking and then getting behind the wheel to rush back to work. If a counselor was to take the approach that many addiction professionals did in the past, he or she might focus on encouraging the client to take on the "alcoholic" label. Unfortunately, the label might make the behaviors logical and thereby lessen the individual's sense of the existence of a discrepancy. Respectfulness awakens the client to discrepancies in a way that confrontation could not.

Maria, in the interview cited earlier, began to see discrepancies between her goal of staying clean and sober and her current living situation. The interviewer helped the process along first by double-checking to make sure that his perception of her goal was accurate and then by asking her an open-ended question about what options she had been considering. In this case, the client saw the discrepancies at the center of her life and began to explore possibilities that she had discarded (literally) in the past. If she had not moved in this direction on her own, the counselor could have said something like the following: "I know you're committed to staying clean and it sounds like your current situation might be making that hard. If you're seeing that too, would it be okay with you to maybe talk about it a little bit?"

ROLL WITH RESISTANCE

In the past, many substance abuse treatment providers assumed that *resistance* and *denial* were both internal traits shared by most addicts. They assumed that the only way to address these characteristic attributes was to confront them directly. If clients refused to accept labels or diagnoses, they were bombarded with evidence proving that the labels or diagnoses were beyond question. If clients refused to believe that they belonged in treatment, they heard again about the "proof" that they were just like all the other patients. In essence, some of the characterizations of resistance were simply reflections of the fact that the client disagreed with the helper's view of the problem. The more the treatment provider pressed the issue, the more the client resisted. The ensuring quarrel often involved the treatment provider arguing that a problem existed and the client insisting that it did not. Needless to say, the client often found his or her own arguments the most compelling.

The advent of MI brought an entirely different focus. The "resistance" born of disagreement with the counselor's "truth" could never gain a foothold because counselors no longer wanted to replace the client's truth with their own. Of course, the motivational interviewer does want to facilitate the client's movement from the status quo to a healthier state. In that context, the concept of resistance focuses primarily on those clients who stand firm against engagement in the process. In those situations, the counselor does not oppose the client, knowing how easy it is to fall into the trap of arguing in favor of change whereas the client continues to oppose it. Instead, the counselor rolls with the resistance (Miller & Rollnick, 2002), recognizing that ambivalence about whether to participate in an interview is as natural as ambivalence about changing one's substance use behaviors. Because the notion of resistance, like the notion of denial, takes place in a relational context, counselors might respond by changing their own approach. More often, counselors are able to tamp down the heat of resistance by avoiding participation in the conflict.

The following brief segment is drawn from an interchange between a nurse and a patient named Ralph who has been referred by a worried spouse.

PATIENT: There's absolutely nothing wrong with me. I haven't been sick at all. My wife thinks I've been too tired and sleeping too much. Of all things! She's a teacher. She just has to worry about little kids and she gets home by 3:00 in the afternoon. I'm a manufacturing foreman. I work the evening shift and I have to work hard every minute of it. Why shouldn't I be tired?

NURSE: So even though your wife worries, when you feel tired it doesn't feel to you like anything out of the ordinary.

PATIENT: I've been doing this for a long time. See, she comes home in the afternoon and if I'm sleeping instead of already gone to work she gets all upset. Says she can't get me up. Couple of times she came home later and I was gone but there were messages from work about where was I. And she says that there are too many bottles in the garbage. She got all in a huff about it. See, we've been doing this schedule since the kids were small so we'd take turns at home. Now this isn't working right. Maybe it's time for her to change jobs.

NURSE: Normally you're already gone when she gets home or you're up and ready to leave. Lately you've been having a harder time getting up when it's time to go to work.

PATIENT: That's what she says.

NURSE: So if I understand right, you don't feel you have a health problem right now—at least not enough of one that you would have come in on your own. But you're hearing a lot from your wife about her worries.

PATIENT: Maybe she's just in the mood to get after me. But yeah, maybe she's worried. So ... my wife is worried about me. I'm not worried about me. Except that I'm worried I'll never hear the end of this ... so here I am.

NURSE: I can see that you and your wife are in different places about this whole thing. Even though you're not worried, I think you were really wise to come in. I'd like to just ask you some questions about the sleeping patterns and tiredness. Is that okay with you?

PATIENT: Yeah. We might as well look into it.

This interchange seems mild, but the potential for Ralph to become belligerent was there. The fact that there were "too many bottles in the garbage" will probably come up again sometime in the future, but responding to it at this point would have brought the interview to a halt or taken the participants on a detour down a dead-end street. Another likely scenario for a treatment provider bent on fighting against resistance might have involved the patient's accusation that the nurse was siding with his wife against him. The nurse, who had been trained in MI, avoided being drawn into conflict. Moreover, she treated Ralph with respect. His willingness to participate in the health visit was most likely sealed by one key utterance: "Is that okay with you?"

SUPPORT SELF-EFFICACY

Bandura (1997, p. 3) defines perceived self-efficacy in terms of "beliefs in one's capabilities to organize and execute the courses of action required to produce given attainments." When individuals believe that they are capable of solving a problem or completing a task, they are more likely to attempt it and, in fact, more likely to succeed. If, in contrast, they lack that sense of possibility, the likelihood of success is diminished.

> People's beliefs in their efficacy have diverse effects. Such beliefs influence the courses of action people choose to pursue, how much effort they put forth in given endeavors,
> how long they will persevere in the face of obstacles and failures, their resilience to adversity, whether their thought patterns are self-hindering or self-aiding, how much stress and depression they experience in coping with taxing environmental demands, and the level of accomplishments they realize. (Bandura, 1997, p. 3)

The relevance of self-efficacy for people who are considering changes in their substance use behaviors is palpable. The act of modifying longstanding habits is daunting at best and terrifying at worst, and the individual's judgment of his or her self-efficacy around this issue has major implications for the decisional balance. To the person contemplating change, the perceived potential for success or failure weighs heavily.

Motivational Interviewing emphasizes the importance of supporting self-efficacy because a person's belief about the likelihood of success is a key factor that affects both initial motivation and longer-term perseverance. MI contrasts sharply with earlier approaches that accentuated the bad outcomes related to substance use instead of exploring the good outcomes related to change. Treatment providers and clients thereby missed out on opportunities for enhancing self-efficacy.

The MI spirit clearly buttresses self-efficacy. When counselors enter into collaborative relationships with their clients, they communicate their belief in their clients' ability to change. When they draw out their clients' ideas through evocation, they help their clients notice—many for the first time—that their own ideas make sense. When they support and reinforce their clients' autonomy, they send a strong message of optimism.

MOTIVATIONAL INTERVIEWING ACROSS SETTINGS

Over the years since MI was first introduced, its reach has broadened across health, human services, criminal justice, therapeutic, and educational settings. Motivational interviewers with a variety of professional titles carry out interventions that may be as brief as one short session but generate life changes even so. Sometimes an interview is all that is needed for clients to resolve their ambivalence and make changes on their own. Sometimes the interview helps a client make the decision to seek treatment. And sometimes the interview opens up new possibilities for a client who might decide on change now, a little later, or much later. All of these situations have in common an interviewer who moves the discussion purposefully in the direction of change but who never tries to wrest the decision-making power from the client.

MOTIVATIONAL INTERVIEWING IN THE CONTEXT OF FAMILY THERAPY: AN EXAMPLE

In the following example, a family therapist carries out a motivational interview with a couple. The therapist is both client-centered and directive, listening carefully but keeping the interview focused on the possibility of change. As the interview moves to a close, she gives one clear message to the clients: The decision about whether to change is yours to make.

MOTIVATIONAL INTERVIEW WITH JIM AND MARCIA[1]

COUNSELOR: Marcia and Jim, it is good to meet you. Jim, I appreciate you agreeing to come in. I know you were feeling like you didn't want to. And yet you did. Thanks.

JIM: You're welcome. But like I said on the phone, I don't think we need counseling.

COUNSELOR: You did tell me that, so I was wondering if it would be OK for Marcia to tell us what she thinks the problem is. Then I would really like to hear from you. Would that be all right with both of you to begin that way?

MARCIA: Sure.

JIM: I guess, but I don't like this counseling stuff. We didn't do this counseling stuff in my family.

COUNSELOR: Your family found other ways of dealing with problems.

JIM: You bet! But I told you I would be here, so let's get this over with.

MARCIA: That's the kind of attitude that makes me mad, Jim. When we first started dating in school, you never treated me like that, and with the problems of your drinking and not having a job, you must be out of your mind to think that I would even consider getting married.

COUNSELOR: Marcia, tell me more about how you see the problem, what concerns you about Jim's drinking.

MARCIA: Well, he is just so different from the Jim I know. We met in graduate school, and we hit it off right away. We were both partying more then; but we were younger and we knew that when we got out of school we would have to start behaving ourselves and be more responsible. I don't drink much at all any more. I am working about 60 hours of week...

COUNSELOR: It must be hard to work that long.

MARCIA: It is hard, but it's a really good corporate job. I should continue to do well in it, even though the economy is so iffy right now. I worked hard in school and got this job on the first try around. Jim here was the "golden boy" of the university. He barely had to study and he got straight A's. All the professors loved him and gave him tons

---

[1]Adapted from an interview by Dr. Jacquelyn Elder. Used with permission.

of recommendation letters. Even though he has had a couple of interviews, he doesn't get the jobs, and I don't get that. Then to top it off, he is out drinking almost every night with guys. He doesn't call, and I stay up all night worrying about him. He came home one night last week and when he woke up, he didn't know where his car was!

COUNSELOR: Jim, what ended up happening that night?

JIM: She is making a big deal out of it out of that car thing. So I couldn't remember where it was, so what? I called around and asked my buddies what had happened the night before. One of them knew I was loaded, and he took me home. He told me exactly where my car was. We found it right away.

COUNSELOR: That's a good friend who got you home safely. Marcia seems to think you drink too much, and I am wondering what you make of that.

JIM: She is blowing it way out of proportion. Everyone our age drinks like we do, especially when we were in school. I told her I would cut down once I get a job, but no one wants to hire anyone right now. She's acting like she doesn't know that.

MARCIA: What do you mean? You had that interview as a manager for Walgreen's a few weeks ago, and that should have been a shoo-in for you. I mean, I talked on the phone to the guy that got your application; and he was ready to hire you over the phone. You came home in a terrible mood after that, and drank yourself into oblivion that night. You couldn't remember anything about that night either. That makes for about four blackouts you've had. And some of them have been while you were driving.

JIM: Hey I made it home OK, and Walgreen's just ended up being a terrible job. They wanted to start me at a ridiculously low salary, and I did not go to graduate school just to make $10 an hour.

COUNSELOR: Jim, you were such a good student and worked hard. That must have been like walking off a cliff to have that interview not go well. Sounds like drinking seemed like the obvious thing to do that night. It's hard to get your hopes up for a job and not get it.

JIM: It is hard, and she just doesn't want to acknowledge that. She lucked out getting her job right away, and I am getting screwed in this job market.

COUNSELOR: You're the golden boy, and Marcia got the job that maybe you should have gotten.

JIM: No, no, no. I don't feel that way at all. Marcia got good grades, too; and she works hard. Really hard. Harder than me.

COUNSELOR: In what way?

MARCIA: Jim, what are you talking about? You never told me you thought I worked harder than you, and you have three other interviews coming up. I know you did your best on those interviews. They just don't know what they are missing out on by not hiring you. I cannot for the life of me figure out what could have gone wrong. We should follow up and try to find out. I'm gonna call that guy from Walgreen's myself.

JIM: Okay, okay. Marcia, stop. I have to tell you something. I have wanted to tell you for a while, but I was embarrassed. I just don't know what to do about it.

MARCIA: Jim, now you are starting to worry me. Are you OK?

JIM: No, no. I mean yes, I am OK. Marcia, I didn't make it to the Walgreen's interview, though I got to the place. When I walked in, I was told that I would have to do a urine drug test, and I knew I wouldn't have passed. I've been smoking some weed when you're at work, and I didn't know that they would ask for a test. I would have to stop smoking for at least a month, and I have been trying. I get to about 3 days of no weed; and then I think, "I need a little smoke."

COUNSELOR: You wanted that job, but now you are frightened that each one will do a drop on you.

MARCIA: Jim, I can't believe you are still smoking weed! What are you, in high school or what? This is our future we are talking about here. You can't stop smoking pot, and then you take it out on me by going out drinking all night?

JIM: Marcia, I feel bad enough about this as it is. I wish I hadn't had to tell you. I know money is tight, and I can't believe that I am in this mess. I can't believe that after all my hard work and dreams about having a good job that I can't stop smoking! The drinking wouldn't even count in a drop.

COUNSELOR: Jim, it sounds like you would be willing to work on quitting the weed so you can get a job. You might have to stay off weed if they do random testing. Sounds like the alcohol was causing some problems between the two of you as well, like the weed and alcohol are kind of wrapped up with each other.

JIM: I wanted that job so bad, and yet I would tell myself, "Screw them. They can't tell me not to smoke weed…"

COUNSELOR: You don't like people telling you that you can't smoke weed, and now it is getting in the way of this other chapter of your life, like the "grown up and got a job" chapter. Jim, a lot of people go through that, and they come out of it OK. You get to decide which road you are going to take; you are smart enough to know where each road takes you.

JIM: I don't know. I just know I want to stop, because I want that job. I want us to be together like we planned. I have always been a hard worker. Marcia, you know that. I will do anything you ask me to. I have wanted to tell you, but there was a part of me that was so embarrassed.

COUNSELOR: Because that's not who you really are. You're really that hard worker who earned that degree. You love Marcia and want it to work out. You are asking for help from her, and that's new territory for you. Kinda scary.

JIM: You have no idea. Marcia, you know me well enough that I wouldn't be telling you this if I wasn't willing to do something about it. I could have just kept lying, but I have been feeling worse and worse about what this has been doing to us. I mean, a few months ago we were planning a wedding and thinking our future was set. Then I messed it up by acting like a stupid kid. I am willing to stop, Marcia. I want us to work it out.

MARCIA: Jim, I don't know how I feel. I love you; but I will not put up with this kind of lying, not working, and being a partying kid. It just won't happen, not if you're not going to do something about it and I mean now, and I mean serious.

COUNSELOR: Marcia, what exactly do you want and need Jim to do? Then maybe Jim has some ideas, too.

MARCIA: Jim, I need you to stop smoking and drinking now. If you need help to do that, go and get the help, and I will be there for you. I need to know that you are clean and that you are getting a job. At this point, I wouldn't care if you worked at McDonald's. I would at least know that you really are that guy I once knew who did work hard.

JIM: I can't tell you how bad it makes me feel to see you doing so well, and I am a loser. I didn't think I would end up in a spot like this. I don't know that I want to go into one of those treatment programs with all those groups and stuff, but I would be willing to get counseling and get tested. I really don't want to go to any group stuff. That is not for me. And if you want to keep on with the two of us seeing Dr. Smith, I would do that. I think I could do that.

COUNSELOR: Marcia, how does that sound to you?

MARCIA: Dr. Smith, what do you think? Don't most people need those treatment programs?

COUNSELOR: I think Jim's ideas are actually good ones, and he knows himself best. He went 3 days without smoking, which is a long time and I bet there were certain things he did during those 3 days that helped him. That's pretty resourceful and when he put everything together, it sounded like a good Plan A. I think that Jim is a capable and smart guy and if it doesn't work out, you two could decide on a Plan B. You two could decide on what Plan B is and we could talk about that next week, since Jim is willing to add me into the mix. I appreciate that, considering how you felt coming in, Jim. What would that be like for the two of you?

JIM: Dr. Smith, I do need a counselor's name and drug testing. Can you give me someone's number?

COUNSELOR: I have a couple of people that you could check out. If you wanted to, you could call both of them; and whichever one sounds like they would be a better fit, you could pick one.

MARCIA: I am a little worried about this because I thought everyone had to go through some rehab but I feel better knowing that we will have a Plan B to fall back on. I think I would feel more comfortable if you would help us with that right away, rather than waiting.

COUNSELOR: That is a good idea, Marcia. That way you have both Plan A and B. I can share with you what has worked for some other folks in the past if they need more structure.

If Jim isn't successful with what he has planned so far, my guess would be outpatient treatment for him, but first the other counselor who sees him would have to find how much alcohol and weed use is going on. They have work to do together, and outpatient counseling really varies on how often and how long they meet. It also depends on things like insurance and what programs are around you.

JIM: I don't have insurance right now.

COUNSELOR: Honestly, that changes things right there but there are some good programs that see folks on a sliding scale, and that's a road you can cross if you ever have to.

MARCIA: I feel better knowing that he is going to get some help because I could not figure out what was going on with him! He just wasn't the guy I knew before.

COUNSELOR: Your radar was picking up on something.

MARCIA: I think you're right, and at least I have a better sense of it. I thought I was going a little crazy.

COUNSELOR: Maybe Jim felt that way, too.

JIM: I did, and I felt bad, maybe depressed.

COUNSELOR: And you might be right about being depressed, and we can sort that out once you get off everything. That might give you a better idea of what you are feeling, and we can also work on that feeling of depression, if it remains a problem.

I wanted to wrap things up as we are out of time today. I am going to give Jim a couple of numbers of individual therapists who work with substance abuse, and he is going to shop around and check them out, picking out the one that he thinks best fits him. Either that therapist or myself will set up the testing. Jim, it says a great deal that you came up with that idea to put that safety net underneath you to make sure you stay straight. Most folks don't even think of that.

JIM: Thanks. I want Marcia to know I am serious.

COUNSELOR: Jim, you'll be seeing the therapist and the two of you will work out the details of you staying clean. Marcia, I can see you and Jim weekly, if that works for you two. At any time, if something doesn't seem to be working, we can get back together. Jim could get that Plan B in place, so there's another safety net.

And I'll tell you, Jim. You have been a golden boy before and I wouldn't be surprised if you shine again. You know what to do and you'll be the one to choose the road you go down.

JIM: Yeah, that sounds right. I can either make this work or not by what I do or don't do.

MOTIVATIONAL ENHANCEMENT THERAPY

Although MI is used in a variety of settings, its offshoot, Motivational Enhancement Therapy (MET), was designed primarily for use in settings where substance abuse clients were seen. MET is sometimes confused with MI, but differs primarily because it includes the steps of assessment and feedback.

> Motivational Enhancement Therapy (MET) is an adaptation of motivational interviewing (MI) that includes one or more client feedback sessions in which normative feedback is presented and discussed in an explicitly non-confrontational manner. Motivational interviewing is a directive, client-centered counseling style for eliciting behavior change by helping clients to explore and resolve their ambivalence and achieve lasting changes for a range of problematic behaviors. This intervention has been extensively tested in treatment evaluations of alcohol and other drug use/misuse. MET uses an empathic but directive approach in which the therapist provides feedback that is intended to strengthen and consolidate the client's commitment to change and promote a sense of self-efficacy. MET aims to elicit intrinsic motivation to change substance abuse by resolving client ambivalence, evoking self-motivational statements and commitment to change, and "rolling with resistance." (SAMHSA's National Registry of Evidence-based Programs, 2007a)

The connection between MI and MET is readily apparent because of the shared spirit and principles. MET, however, is a structured therapy adapted from the MI model for the purposes of treatment. The use of an extensive assessment makes the MET distinctive, but the feedback session is characterized by an affirmative climate that recognizes the client's power to use the assessment results as he or she sees fit.

SUMMARY

Across settings and specialties, trained motivational interviewers share a commitment to the MI spirit, which is collaborative, evocative, and supportive of client autonomy. MI can be defined as a goal-directed, client-centered counseling style for eliciting behavior change by helping clients to explore and resolve ambivalence. The principles underlying MI include expressing empathy, developing discrepancy, rolling with resistance, and supporting self-efficacy. The spirit and principles of MI mark a sharp departure from the harsh confrontation and advice-giving that once characterized substance abuse treatment in the United States. Many counselors now accept the notion that their clients rightly own the power to decide whether or not to change. Once counselors make the commitment to respect and heed their clients' wishes, they are ready to learn how to help people get past the ambivalence that often accompanies change.

QUESTIONS FOR THOUGHT AND DISCUSSION

1. In this chapter you read brief excerpts of motivational interviews with Maria, a young woman on parole, and Ralph, a patient being interviewed by a nurse. You also read a longer interview involving a couple, Marcia and Jim. Look at these interviews and see whether you can identify spots where the interviewer

could have confronted the client but chose not to. What do you think about the choices that the interviewers made in those situations? Should they have pushed the clients harder? Or should they stay with the MI spirit and support the clients' autonomy?

2. If you are familiar with substance abuse treatment, you know that it often focuses on breaking down the client's denial. MI presents a completely different view, seeing denial not as a characteristic of the client but as a result of the client–counselor relationship. How comfortable do you feel with the MI approach to helping?

REFERENCES

Arkowitz, H., & Miller, W. R. (2008). Learning, applying, and extending motivational interviewing. In H. Arkowitz, H. A. Westra, W. R. Miller, & S. Rollnick (Eds.), *Motivational interviewing in the treatment of psychological problems* (pp. 1–25). New York: Guilford Press.

Bandura, A. (1997). *Self-efficacy: The exercise of control.* New York: W. H. Freeman.

Carroll, K. M., Ball, S. A., Nich, C., Martino, S., Frankforter, T. L., & Farentinos, C. (2006). Motivational interviewing to improve treatment engagement and outcome in individuals seeking treatment for substance abuse: A multisite effectiveness study. *Drug and Alcohol Dependence, 81*(3), 301–312.

Miller, W. R., & Moyers, T. B. (2006). Eight stages in learning motivational interviewing. *Journal of Teaching in the Addictions, 5*(1), 3–17.

Miller, W. R., & Rollnick, S. (2002). *Motivational interviewing: Preparing people for change* (2nd ed.). New York: Guilford Press.

Moyers, T. B., & Yahne, C. E. (1998). Motivational interviewing in substance abuse treatment: Negotiating roadblocks. *Journal of Substance Misuse, 3*, 30–33.

Rogers, C. (1957). The necessary and sufficient conditions of therapeutic personality change. *Journal of Consulting Psychology, 21*, 95–103.

Rollnick, S., Miller, W. R., & Butler, C. C. (2008). *Motivational interviewing in health care: Helping patients change behavior.* New York: Guilford Press.

Rubak, S., Sandbaek, A., Lauritzen, T., & Christensen, B. (2005). Motivational interviewing: A systematic review and meta-analysis. *British Journal of General Practice, 55*(513), 305–312.

SAMHSA's National Registry of Evidence-based Programs and Practices. (2007a). *Motivational enhancement therapy.* Retrieved June 1, 2009, from http://www.nrepp. samhsa.gov/programfulldetails.asp?PROGRAM_ID=182#outcomes

SAMHSA's National Registry of Evidence-based Programs and Practices. (2007b). *Motivational interviewing.* Retrieved April 30, 2009, from http://www.nrepp.samhsa. gov/programfulldetails.asp?PROGRAM_ID=183

THE PROCESS OF
BEHAVIOR CHANGE

II

4 | Assessment and Treatment Planning

THE PROCESSES OF assessment and treatment planning work most effectively when clients are actively involved in setting goals and deciding on strategies for change. In substance abuse, as with any other problem, the following basic questions need to be addressed:

- What are the differences between a client's life as it is now and what he or she would like it to be?
- What strategies are most likely to help clients achieve their goals?
- What barriers might stand in the way of clients' progress?
- How can these barriers be lessened?
- What internal and external resources can help clients reach their goals?
- How can these resources be used effectively?

Although clients urgently need the technical help of the counselor, they are the ones who can best answer these questions.

When given the opportunity, substance abuse clients can participate actively and honestly in assessment and treatment planning. All too often, however, assessment procedures focus on labeling the problem as "alcoholism" or "addiction" and convincing clients that the label is accurate. Unfortunately, this narrow and confrontive operation jeopardizes the counseling process by increasing clients' defensiveness and decreasing their self-efficacy.

William Miller and his associates developed the concept of motivational interviewing (MI) (discussed at length in chapter 3) as an alternative to the directive, confrontational style that many people use with substance abuse clients (Miller, 2006). According to Miller, "denial," far from being an innate characteristic of addicts, may be a function of the way we tend to interact with these clients. When counselors actively press clients to accept the view that substance use underlies all of their problems, they encounter resistance that becomes more entrenched as the debate continues. In contrast, MI tries to encourage change by avoiding labels and accepting the notion that the decision-making responsibility belongs in the hands of the client. The counselor completes a careful assessment and shares the resulting data with the client. Ultimately, however, the client decides how to use the data:

> What motivational interviewing does is to overcome the myth that substance abuse clients are so different from others that the usual principles of human behavior fail to apply to them. As long as we assume that people with alcohol or drug problems are unable to make responsible choices and must therefore be told what to do, we will be forced to deal with defensiveness and denial. If we recognize the unassailable truth that behaviors are based on individuals' choices—not therapists' wishes—we are more likely to see motivated clients.

Motivational interviewing is essential in the assessment phase of counseling and proceeds through a step-by-step process, beginning with a nonjudgmental exploration of the client's view of the problem. The following dialogue provides an example of the kind of initial interview that might take place using this approach. Jade, a high school junior, is being seen for the first time by a substance abuse counselor in a community agency:

COUNSELOR: I'm glad you could come in, Jade. I did talk to your mother on the phone, and she said she was concerned about your drinking, but right now I'd like to hear what you think about this. Could we begin by having you tell me what you've become aware of about your drinking?

JADE: Oh, I don't really have a problem at all. My mother thinks so, and she's been trying to tell me to come in for a long time, but to tell you the truth, I think that's just her way of blaming anything that goes wrong on just this one thing.

COUNSELOR: So this has been going on for a while, but something made you decide to come in now.

JADE: Well, actually, my mother said I couldn't use the car unless I came in. But she's said that before, and I got out of it. This time I thought I'd see about it.

COUNSELOR: Something's convinced you to take a look at your drinking now?

JADE: Well, something did happen last weekend. There was this party that all the kids were going to, and my boyfriend was out of town with his parents. So I told my friend Jackie I'd pick her up and we could go together. I figured she'd want to come with me because she just broke up and I knew she didn't have a date and this wasn't that kind of party anyway. All kinds of kids were going by themselves or in groups. Just one of those things. Anyway, Jackie said she wouldn't ride with me because I always end up drinking too much at these things and she'd rather not get in a car with me. She said she'd ask her parents for the car and pick me up, but I said, "no, forget it, I'll go myself." Well, I did, and on the way home I saw this cop car in my rearview mirror, and I thought he was following me. He turned off, but I was scared to death. I knew if I got a DUI I'd be in nothing but trouble.

COUNSELOR: So other people have started to notice things, and it took you by surprise that Jackie kind of predicted what actually happened. Are there other things you've noticed that make you think there might be a problem?

JADE: Not really. I've been drinking more than usual these last few months, but I don't think I drink more than my friends do. And a lot of the kids are still into cocaine and marijuana. Everybody knows they're the ones who are really headed for trouble.

COUNSELOR: One thing you've noticed is that you're drinking more than you used to.

JADE: Yes, but it doesn't really affect me all that much. Back when I was a freshman, I used to really get drunk on a little bit of alcohol.

COUNSELOR: Your tolerance for alcohol is higher than it used to be.

JADE: Is that what it is? Tolerance?

COUNSELOR: Yes, that means that you can drink more without feeling the effects as much. Have you noticed anything else?

JADE: Well, a couple of times I didn't remember everything that happened at a party or something. I went to my boyfriend's brother's graduation party, and the next day John—that's my boyfriend—said I'd acted like a fool and people had talked about it. I didn't remember anything happening. It made me feel kind of nervous.

COUNSELOR: What other kinds of things have happened after an evening of heavy drinking. Ever have hangovers or feel like having a drink in the morning?

JADE: Yeah, I've had some bad hangovers, but I never drink in the morning. I know that's a sign of alcoholism. One time I put some vodka in my orange juice when I had a hangover. But that was the late morning, not the early morning.

COUNSELOR: What other things have happened? Do you get along OK with everybody when you're drinking?

JADE: I wouldn't normally say rude things to people. In psych class we learned about assertiveness, and I think I'm not even as assertive as I ought to be. But I have gotten into a couple of arguments that got people mad at me.

COUNSELOR: It sounds as if some things have been worrying you about the drinking.

JADE: I guess so, but I know I'm not an alcoholic. I know some kids at school who had alcoholism treatment, and they're nothing like me. They were completely flunking before they got treatment, and everybody knew about them. I'm nothing like them. I'm still doing perfectly well at school. You can't be an alcoholic and get the kind of grades I get and participate in activities the way I do. For God's sake, I'm the secretary of the National Honor Society. Does that sound like somebody with an alcohol problem?

COUNSELOR: So you're worried about your drinking, but you have a picture in your own mind of a teenage alcoholic, and you don't see yourself as looking like that picture.

JADE: Right. I may have some problems, but I'm no druggie.

COUNSELOR: So you haven't been thinking about it that much, but now you've decided to accept your mother's suggestion.

JADE: Well, to tell you the truth, my relationship with my boyfriend is a little shaky, and I'm starting to wonder what'll happen about college and everything.

COUNSELOR: You're not so worried about how things have been up till now, but you're worried things could get worse, and you want to keep that from happening.

JADE: Yes, that's right.

COUNSELOR: Would you be willing to spend a couple of hours on an assessment? There are some questionnaires we use here that help us get a pretty objective look at the situation. It could help you make some decisions about what you'd like to do. Is that OK with you?

JADE: That would be fine.

In the interview with Jade, the counselor actively avoided confronting her or labeling her behavior. He focused on her own views and away from the opinions of other people, thus encouraging her to see herself as responsible for making decisions. He did stimulate and reinforce comments indicating her possible willingness to recognize and act on her problem.

This approach minimizes clients' defensiveness and makes it more likely that they will participate actively in an objective assessment and, finally, in a negotiation of alternatives for action. The fact that the client is seen as the primary decision maker does not mean that the objective assessment is eliminated. On the contrary, it makes the process even more comprehensive.

THE COMPREHENSIVE ASSESSMENT PROCESS

Frequently, substance abuse practitioners oversimplify the problems presented by their clients. This reductionism ignores critical scientific and clinical distinctions and fails to recognize substance abuse problems as complex and multiply determined. When this complexity is not acknowledged, treatment proceeds on a simplistic level, with abstinence being equated with health and nonabstinence with illness. Unfortunately, this either/or view does not allow for changes in other areas of life function and maintains the myth that substance abuse and dependence are unitary, well-defined, and predictable disorders that can be treated simply by stopping the client from ingesting his or her drug of choice. It is increasingly clear, however, that abstinence is not the only goal of successful treatment (MacCoun, 2009). Rather, it is important to view substance abuse problems as multivariate syndromes that should be treated individually and differentially because they are associated with different problems for different people. In recent years, a broadened concept of substance abuse has emerged (Moos, 2009). This emergent view recognizes that chemical dependency can involve multiple patterns of use, misuse, and abuse; that multiple causal variables combine to produce problems; that treatment must be multimodal to correspond to a client's particular pattern of abuse; and that treatment outcomes vary from individual to individual. Based on this broader view, it is now possible for us to better understand substance abuse problems and to diagnose and treat them less dogmatically.

Assessment is the act of determining the nature and causes of a client's problem. During the early sessions of treatment, counselors gather data and increase their understanding of their clients. At the same time, clients can ask questions and clarify their role in counseling. At this point the counselor should fully address confidentiality and other expectations.

To understand our clients' substance abuse problems, we must try to understand our clients. This involves interviewing them, taking a history, and administering psychological tests. It is vital that clinicians avoid preconceived notions about the client and that they make treatment determinations based only on data collected during the initial evaluation. In this respect, a client's merely walking into a substance abuse treatment facility does not, in and of itself, warrant a diagnosis of "chemical dependency" or "alcoholism." Rather, clinicians must carefully evaluate clients and only then work with them to make decisions concerning treatment. These decisions must take into account each client's culture and background. Insensitivity to these critical issues and the consequent homogenization of treatment seriously limits counselors' effectiveness. Clinicians must guard against these preventable sources of treatment contamination.

SUBSTANCE USE HISTORY

Collection of data about the client begins with a lengthy interview. It is designed to elicit information about the client's background, problems, current functioning, and motivation for treatment. Its primary purpose is to lay the groundwork for planning treatment. Counselors must make their clients feel welcome and as comfortable as possible (some anxiety is expected and quite appropriate). They must create a situation in which they can elicit all the information they need, which is best done by keeping a clear focus on the agenda. In essence, then, counselors ask a series of questions and attempt to get the clearest possible answers. To do this effectively, counselors must maintain structure and keep the client calm and on track. To elicit a clear and broad understanding of the client, the interview should include the following:

1. referral source
2. chief complaint
3. history of present problem (illness)
4. history of substance use and abuse
5. life situation
   a. living arrangements
   b. marriage or cohabitation
   c. children
   d. social life
   e. current functioning
6. family history
   a. siblings
   b. parents or other family
   c. discipline
   d. how and where the client was raised
7. religious history
8. work history of client, siblings, parents, and spouse
9. legal history
10. sexual history
11. mental status
    a. appearance, behavior, and attitude
       (1) general appearance
       (2) motor status
       (3) activity
       (4) facial expression
       (5) behavior
    b. characteristics of talk
       (1) blocking
       (2) preservation
       (3) flight of ideas
       (4) autism
    c. emotional state: affective reactions
       (1) mood
       (2) affect
       (3) depression
       (4) mania
    d. content of thought: special preoccupations and experiences
       (1) hallucinations
       (2) delusions
       (3) compulsions

        (4) obsessions
        (5) ritualistic behaviors
        (6) depersonalization
        (7) fantasies or daydreams
    e. anxiety
        (1) phobia(s)
        (2) generalized (diffuse) anxiety
        (3) specific anxiety
    f. orientation
        (1) person
        (2) place
        (3) time
        (4) confusion
12. memory
    a. memory power
        (1) remote past experiences
        (2) recent past experiences
        (3) immediate impressions
        (4) general grasp and recall
    b. general intellectual evaluation
        (1) general information
        (2) calculation
        (3) reasoning and judgment
    c. insight

Although the above outline is helpful in forming the evaluation agenda and in clarifying the client's condition, it is wise to add substance to each category. In this vein a standardized format is helpful in guiding the interview and providing structure so that all essential information is gained. An example of such a history form is provided in Appendix A.

BEHAVIORAL ASSESSMENT

Once the substance use history has been completed, the counselor is ready to do a behavioral assessment and functional analysis. A behavioral assessment allows the counselor to discover the triggers to and consequences of the client's substance abuse behaviors and to examine the acquisition of these behaviors. (Donovan & Marlatt, 2005). The behavioral assessment and functional analysis (Cooney, Kadden, & Steinberg, 2005) also let the counselor determine what is reinforcing and punishing for the client and specify the factors correlated with a high probability of substance abuse. The functional analysis, a component of behavioral assessment, clearly shows when and why a client abuses substances, and the counselor can then use this information to tailor a treatment plan to the unique needs of each client. The behavioral assessment and functional analysis interview (Appendix B) is designed to be administered orally by the counselor. An attempt should be made to gather as much information as possible in each content area. The counselor should be both sensitive and directive in conducting this interview.

ASSESSMENT DEVICES

The assessment instruments described or listed in this section were chosen because they are readily available, reliable, valid, easily administered, easily scored, and practical. Their results can be applied easily to the clinical setting.

COMPREHENSIVE DRINKER PROFILE

The Comprehensive Drinker Profile (CDP) is a structured intake interview to assess alcohol problems. It is in the public domain and can be freely used by all practitioners. It is included in its entirety in appendix C. It has been used and validated with both clinical and research populations, is appropriate for use with men and women in any type of treatment modality, and is culture-sensitive.

The CDP provides an intensive and comprehensive history and status of clients' use and abuse of alcohol with a clear focus on determining treatment type indicators (Tarter, Kirisci, & Mezzich, 1999). The interview focuses on information that is relevant to the selection, planning, and implementation of treatment.

The CDP covers a wide array of important information about the client, including basic demographics, family and employment status, history of drinking, pattern of alcohol use, alcohol-related problems, severity of dependence, social aspects of use, associated behaviors, relevant medical history, and motivations for drinking and treatment. The CDP has incorporated the widely used Michigan Alcoholism Screening Test (MAST). It yields quantitative indexes of other dimensions, including duration of the problem, family history of alcoholism, alcohol consumption, alcohol dependence, range of drinking situations, quantity and frequency of other drug use, range of beverages used, emotional factors related to drinking, and life problems other than drinking.

The interview can be administered, with proper training and practice, by most mental health or substance abuse workers. It is complex, and counselors should carefully read the manual in the CDP kit before they undertake any interviews. In addition, it is suggested that counselors engage in role-played practice interviews before trying client interviews. The CDP kit also contains individual interview forms and eight reusable card sets needed to administer the interview.

The CDP is the most comprehensive empirically derived instrument of this kind. It is carefully constructed and proceeds in a logical order:

1. demographic information
   a. age and residence
   b. family status
   c. employment and income information
   d. educational history
2. drinking history
   a. development of the drinking problem
   b. present drinking pattern
   c. pattern history
   d. alcohol-related life history
   e. drinking settings
   f. associated behaviors
   g. beverage preferences
   h. relevant medical history

3.   motivational information
     a.   reasons for drinking
     b.   effects of drinking
     c.   other life problems
     d.   motivation for treatment
     e.   rating of type of drinker

ADDITIONAL ASSESSMENT TOOLS

The CDP is unusually complete and well researched, but the counselor may also wish to choose from among a variety of additional instruments that can assist in the assessment process. At this point we will review a number of these tools, a few of which will be presented for examination. The counselor should gather as much information as possible before working with the client to design a treatment plan. The following measurement devices will prove to be of help in this respect. For a comprehensive library of research-tested assessment instruments, counselors are encouraged to visit http://casaa.unm.edu/inst.html or http://pubs.niaaa.nih.gov/publications/arh28-2/78-79.htm where one can access and view different instruments.

SUBSTANCE ABUSE PROBLEM CHECKLIST   A useful clinical aid for practitioners is the Substance Abuse Problem Checklist (SAPC). The checklist is a self-administered inventory containing 377 specific problems grouped into eight categories: (1) problems associated with motivation for treatment, (2) health problems, (3) personality problems, (4) problems in social relationships, (5) job-related problems, (6) problems associated with the misuse of leisure time, (7) religious or spiritual problems, and (8) legal problems. The client benefits by assuming the role of an active collaborator in the treatment process. Furthermore, the SAPC aids the clinician in diagnosing and treating drug abusers and has a potential use in research. The results of a study of 114 SAPCs completed in a Pennsylvania hospital reflect the contribution of suppressed and depressed feelings to the evolution of chemical dependency and provide a clear indication of the importance of the ecological perspective. One problem with the SAPC is its unsuitability for clients with limited ability in English. In addition, clients may consciously or unconsciously deny or conceal problems when responding.

MICHIGAN ALCOHOLISM SCREENING TEST   The MAST contains 24 items that ask about drinking habits, and its usefulness has been consistently supported by empirical evaluations. MAST scores range from 0 to 53. A score of 0 to 4 indicates no problem; a score greater than 20 indicates severe alcoholism. The MAST is reproduced in its entirety in Appendix D.

The Short Michigan Alcoholism Screening Test (SMAST), is a useful and manageable measurement device for the clinician. It is composed of 17 yes-or-no questions chosen as the most discriminating of alcoholism from the original MAST. Many counselors find the shorter form easier to administer. The SMAST does not tend toward false positives, as does the MAST, and it is more accurate in correctly diagnosing alcohol problems. The SMAST, then, is a simple, quick test with a high degree of reliability and validity. It is useful in targeting all types of alcohol-abusing populations, and it correlates highly (0.83) with the full MAST. On the SMAST, weighted scores range from 0 to 53. Scores of 20 or more indicate severe alcoholism.

ALCOHOL DEPENDENCE SCALE   The Alcohol Dependence Scale (ADS) is a brief, self-administered instrument. Its 25 multiple choice items focus on such aspects of alcohol dependence as withdrawal symptoms, obsessive/compulsive drinking style, tolerance, and drink-seeking behavior.

ADDICTION SEVERITY INDEX   The Addiction Severity Index assesses seven areas: medical status, employment status, drug use, alcohol use, legal status, family/social relationships, and psychological status. It is one of the few well-tested instruments that addresses drugs other than alcohol. Using a structured interview format, the instrument yields severity ratings for each area, from 0 (no treatment necessary) to 9 (treatment needed to intervene in a life-threatening situation).

ALCOHOL DEPENDENCE SCALE   The Alcohol Dependence Scale is a short, self-administered screening device which measures the severity of alcohol dependence. There are 25 multiple choice questions focusing on alcohol withdrawal symptoms, obsessional drinking, tolerance, and alcohol-seeking behavior.

ALCOHOL TIMELINE FOLLOW BACK   The Alcohol Timeline Follow Back (TLFB), a daily drinking estimation method, provides a detailed picture of a person's drinking over a designated time period. The TLFB method was originally developed as a research tool for use with alcohol abusers, but it has since been adapted for use in clinical settings and has been extended to measure drug and cigarette use. The TLFB is a calendar-based form in which people provide retrospective estimates of their daily drinking, including abstinent days over a specified period of time ranging up to 12 months prior to the interview. Memory aids are used to enhance recall. The amount of time needed to administer the TLFB varies as a function of the assessment interval (e.g., 90 days = 10–15 min; 12 months = 30 min). The TLFB can generate a number of variables that provide more precise and varied information about a person's drinking than is produced by a simple assessment of quantity and frequency of use. The TLFB can generate variables to portray the pattern, variability, and level of drinking. Administration of the TLFB is flexible: It can be self-administered or administered in person by trained interviewers, and it is available in pencil-and-paper and computerized formats.

ADOLESCENT DRINKING INDEX   The Adolescent Drinking Index measures the severity of drinking behaviors for adolescents in four domains: loss of control of drinking, social indicators of drinking problems, psychological problems, and physical indicators of a drinking problem. This device measures rebellious drinking and self-medicating behavior.

ALCOHOL USE INVENTORY   The Alcohol Use Inventory is a self-report inventory which identifies patterns of behavior, attitudes, and symptoms associated with the use and abuse of alcohol. Used for people 16 plus years old, it assesses drinking-related problems and differentiates drinking styles.

CAGE   The CAGE is a simple four-item self-report assessment device. Clients are asked the following questions: C—Have you ever tried to *cut* back on your use of chemicals?, A—Have you ever been *annoyed* by people criticizing your substance use?, G—Have you ever felt *guilty* about your substance use behavior?, and E—Have you ever used alcohol or other drugs as an *eye-opener* to get going after a heavy night of use?

ADDICTION SEVERITY INDEX   The Addiction Severity Index assesses seven areas of concern for substance abusers. These are: medical, employment, family and social relationships, drug and alcohol use, legal status, and psychological status.

ADOLESCENT DRUG INVOLVEMENT SCALE   The Adolescent Drug Involvement Scale is a 12-item scale that addresses levels of adolescent drug use, excluding alcohol. Drug use frequency, reasons for use, social context, effects of use, and self-appraisal of use are measured.

DRUGS, ALCOHOL, AND GAMBLING SCREEN   The Drugs, Alcohol, and Gambling Screen is a 45-question assessment looking at risk for developing problems in any of the target areas. Potential risk is ranked on a scale from mild to serious.

DRUG USE SCREENING INVENTORY   The Drug Use Screening Inventory is a 159-item assessment designed to determine drug use related problems in both adults and adolescents. Substance abuse, psychiatric disorders, behavior problems, school adjustment, peer relations, social competency, family adjustment, and leisure and recreation aspects of the client's life are examined. The ultimate outcome of the assessment is a description of current status and the identification of problem areas.

SUBSTANCE ABUSE SUBTLE SCREENING INVENTORY   The Substance Abuse Subtle Screening Inventory assesses individuals for substance abuse and substance dependence disorders. It provides separate scoring for men and women.

INSTRUMENTS TO ASSESS COGNITIVE-BEHAVIORAL FACTORS

Several instruments can be used to complement the behavioral analysis process and help clients identify situations that place them at risk for drug or alcohol use. Toward this end three useful assessment instruments: the Inventory of Drinking Situations (IDS), the Situational Confidence Questionnaire (SCQ), and the Cognitive Appraisal Questionnaire (CAQ) have been developed for practitioner use.

INVENTORY OF DRINKING SITUATIONS   The IDS helps the client identify situations associated with drinking. These situations are placed in eight categories: negative emotional states, negative physical states, positive emotional states, testing of personal control, urges and temptations, interpersonal conflict, social pressure to drink, and pleasant times with others. The resulting profile shows the client's high- and low-risk situations. This profile helps the client understand the antecedents of drinking so that coping strategies can be identified for dealing with them.

SITUATIONAL CONFIDENCE QUESTIONNAIRE   The SCQ asks clients to react to a number of drinking situations. They are asked to imagine themselves in these situations and to indicate their degree of confidence in their ability to handle the situation without drinking. This instrument helps clients design a hierarchy of drinking situations so that they can begin by handling tasks about which they feel confident and then progress gradually to situations about which they feel less confident.

COGNITIVE APPRAISAL QUESTIONNAIRE   The CAQ helps clients identify cognitive factors that might interfere with their self-efficacy. Unlike the previous two questionnaires, which clients complete in writing, the CAQ is based on a structured interview. The questionnaire explores the cognitions that influence the individual's appraisal of success.

These instruments are used in conjunction with the clinical interview and other assessment procedures. It is unwise to depend solely on one assessment device. Doing so increases the likelihood of a false-negative or false-positive diagnosis that could lead to inappropriate and unsuccessful treatment.

DIAGNOSIS

Once the assessment has been completed, the counselor is in a position to form a diagnostic impression. Diagnosis allows counselors to communicate with other professionals and helps provide a framework for treatment. Counselors should treat their diagnoses as tentative. If they see that the client is not doing well with a certain treatment or if new information is uncovered during counseling, they should feel free to make a new and more accurate diagnosis and, consequently, a new treatment plan. It is perfectly appropriate to admit that an initial impression was incorrect.

A useful diagnostic approach for clinicians comes from the *Diagnostic and Statistical Manual of Mental Disorders, Fourth Edition, Text Revision (DSM-IV-TR)* (American Psychiatric Association, 2002). The *DSM-IV-TR* makes a distinction between substance abuse and substance dependence. Psychoactive substance use is considered a disorder only (1) when the individual demonstrates an inability to control his or her use despite cognitive, behavioral, or physiological symptoms, and (2) when the symptoms have clustered for at least 1 month over the course of 12 months.

A client is diagnosed as being dependent on the substance only if at least three of the following seven symptoms are present (American Psychiatric Association, 2002, pp. 197–198):

1. Marked tolerance: need for markedly increased amounts of the substance (i.e., at least a 50% increase) in order to achieve intoxication or desired effect, or markedly diminished effect with continued use of the same amount.
2. Characteristic withdrawal symptoms and substance often taken to relieve or avoid withdrawal symptoms.
3. Substance often taken in large amounts or over a longer period of time than the person intended.
4. Persistent desire or one or more unsuccessful efforts to cut down or control substance use.
5. A great deal of time spent in activities necessary to obtain the substance (e.g., theft), to use the substance (e.g., chain smoking), or to recover from its effects.
6. Important social, occupational, or recreational activities given up or reduced because of substance use.
7. Continued substance use despite knowledge of having a persistent or recurrent social, psychological, or physical problem that is caused or exacerbated by the use of the substance (e.g., using heroin despite family arguments about it, experiencing cocaine-induced depression, or having an ulcer made worse by drinking).

Source: Reprinted by permission from the Diagnostic and Statistical Manual of Mental Disorders, Text Revision, Fourth Edition, (Copyright 2000). American Psychiatric Association.

Substance dependence diagnoses included the following specifiers (American Psychiatric Association, 2002, p. 168):

With Physiological Dependence: This specifier should be used when substance dependence is accompanied by evidence of tolerance or withdrawal.

Without Physiological Dependence: This specifier should be used when there is no evidence of tolerance or withdrawal. In these individuals, substance dependence is characterized by a pattern of compulsive use (at least three items from criteria 3–7).

Early Full Remission: This specifier should be used if for at least 1 month but less than 12 months, no diagnostic criteria have been met.

Early Partial Remission: This specifier should be used if for at least 1 month but less than 12 months, some, but not all, diagnostic criteria have been met.

Sustained Full Remission: This specifier should be used if no diagnostic criteria have been met for 1 year or more.

Sustained Partial Remission: This specifier should be used if full criteria for dependence have not been met for 1 plus years, but one or more criteria are met.

On Agonist Therapy: This specifier should be used if the individual is using a prescribed medication, like Naltrexone, to avoid substance use.

In a Controlled Environment: This specifier should be used if the individual is closely supervised in a controlled environment where access to alcohol and controlled substances is restricted, for instance, a jail or hospital.

Source: Reprinted by permission from the Diagnostic and Statistical Manual of Mental Disorders, Text Revision, Fourth Edition, (Copyright 2000). American Psychiatric Association.

In the *DSM-IV-TR*, the diagnostic category of substance abuse is used for an individual whose patterns of use are maladaptive but whose use has never met the criteria for dependence. Nine classes of psychoactive substances are associated with both abuse and dependence: alcohol; amphetamines, or similarly acting sympathomimetics; cannabis; cocaine; hallucinogens; inhalants; opioids; phencyclidine, or similarly acting arylcyclohexylamines; and sedatives, hypnotics, or anxiolytics. Nicotine has a dependence diagnosis but not an abuse diagnosis. Each class of substance has its own code number (for example, alcohol dependence is coded as 303.90 and amphetamine abuse is coded as 305.70), but the general criteria for abuse and dependence are consistent across categories.

The *DSM-IV-TR* uses a multiaxial system, with each person evaluated on each of the five axes. Axis I describes clinical syndromes; substance abuse and dependence are Axis I diagnoses. Axis II identifies developmental and personality disorders, and Axis III specifies physical disorders and conditions. Axis IV is used to assess psychosocial and environmental problems affecting the individual with the clinical listing issues that might affect the diagnosis, treatment, or prognosis of the presenting problem. Axis V ratings assess the client's global functioning.

The *Diagnostic and Statistical Manual of Mental Disorders, Fifth Edition (DSM-V)* is tentatively scheduled for publication in 2012. Counselors should be cautious when using diagnostic tools such as the *DSM-IV-TR* to avoid inappropriate diagnosing or labeling of clients. Because of the complexities associated with diagnostic schema counselors should seek advanced training in both the use and the application of diagnostic schema.

TREATMENT PLANNING

The treatment plan is the foundation for success, giving both counselor and client a structure within which to function. Expectations become clear, and any misunderstandings are relatively easy to resolve. Treatment plans allow counselors and clients to specify goals and monitor and evaluate progress. With such a plan, counseling can proceed in a straightforward, outcome-oriented fashion. Without it, the client–counselor relationship will be poorly defined and less likely to succeed.

A treatment plan can be either simple or elaborate, as long as it addresses all the problems that must be dealt with in treatment. In this respect, the counselor needs to articulate short-term goals (for those problems that can be solved in 3 to 6 months) and long-term goals (for those problems that may take up to 1 year to solve and are likely to involve continuous monitoring for the duration of the client's life).

Coombs and Howatt (2005) suggest that setting long- and short-term goals is affected by such factors as the extent and seriousness of the client's problem, the client's motivation, the setting, the projected treatment time, the preferences of the client and the therapist, and the cooperation of significant others.

In substance abuse counseling, the seriousness of the client's condition sometimes dictates the priorities. For example, clients who are physically dependent on drugs or alcohol must be medically detoxified before other treatment can begin. Suicidal clients must have their depression treated before the chemical dependency issue is addressed, and psychotic individuals must be stabilized before chemical dependency treatment can begin.

The client's motivation also strongly affects goal setting. Clients who appear to have little hope and no faith in treatment should be given small tasks that they can quickly and successfully accomplish. These successes will improve their self-esteem and bolster their confidence in the treatment process. This technique, called shaping, is extremely effective in increasing motivation and, consequently, in improving treatment outcomes.

Certain treatments can be used only in an inpatient setting (for example, detoxification). Others (such as in vivo desensitization and maintenance of a job) are best completed on an outpatient basis.

The projected treatment time is always of concern to the client. Based on the initial evaluation and diagnosis, counselors will be able to give their clients a fairly accurate timetable to go by. Certain treatments for certain problems take certain lengths of time, and with experience and practice, counselors become adept at predicting these times.

Client and counselor preferences are important variables in choosing goals. For example, a client may choose to deal with issues 1, 2, and 3 during a course of treatment but not with issues 4, 5, and 6. Similarly, counselors may advise against addressing certain issues in treatment because they perceive them to be too resistant to therapy or believe that their introduction into therapy is contraindicated. The counselor and client must jointly articulate their respective preferences and then, through negotiation, determine the treatment goals.

The involvement of significant others is quite important. The family or other people close to the client can be either natural therapists (helping the client, administering contingencies and rewards, and providing support and encouragement) or saboteurs (undermining therapy, disrupting the client, or punishing the client). Counselors must set the stage for cooperation and, if they see it is not forthcoming, advise the client on appropriate ways to proceed. Significant others are critical allies, and therapists should struggle to gain their support.

An effective treatment plan need not be complex and can take the form illustrated in Exhibit 4.1. Examples of completed treatment plans are found in Exhibits 4.2 and 4.3. Once the treatment has been recorded, formal counseling can begin.

SUMMARY

A comprehensive assessment is an important first step in substance abuse counseling. Ideally, this process should be a joint effort, with the client and counselor collaborating in identifying problem areas and specifying goals. It should include a general substance use history and assessment instruments chosen with the client's specific needs in mind.

In terms of diagnosis, the most helpful criteria are those provided by the *Diagnostic and Statistical Manual of Mental Disorders, Fourth Edition, Text Revision (DSM-IV-TR)* of the American Psychiatric Association. The *DSM-IV-TR* differentiates among substance use, substance abuse, and substance dependence, offering clear guidelines for identifying the presence of a disorder.

The initial assessment and diagnosis provide the framework for the development of a treatment plan. The treatment plan should be based on clearly defined short- and long-term goals and should specify interventions designed to meet each goal. The quality and clarity of the treatment plan does a great deal to determine the success of the entire counseling process.

EXHIBIT 4.1	TREATMENT PLAN FORM

Name _____ Date _____

Date entered treatment _____ Gender _____ Birth date _____

Review date (every 3 months) _____

DSM-IV-TR diagnosis(es):

Axis I _____

Axis II _____

Axis III _____

Axis IV _____

Axis V _____

A. Brief history: _____

_____

_____

_____

_____

continued

B. Case formulation: _____
_____
_____
_____
_____

C.

Short-Term Goals	Intervention	Time Frame	Measurement Device	Goal Met? (Yes or No)
1.				
2.				
3.				
4.				

D.

Long-Term Goals	Intervention	Time Frame	Measurement Device	Goal Met? (Yes or No)
1.				
2.				
3.				
4.				

E. Comments: _____
_____
_____

F. Review updates (every 3 months). Plan redone at 1 year.
Review 1 _____
Review 2 _____
Review 3 _____
Review 4 _____

EXHIBIT 4.2	TREATMENT PLAN FOR AN ALCOHOL USER

Name John Doe   Date 1-15-2009

Date entered treatment 1-10-2009   Gender M   Birth date 5-20-1982

Review date (every 3 months) 3-15-2009, 6-15-2009, 9-15-2009

DSM-IV-TR diagnosis(es):

Axis I   Alcohol dependence, severe

          Generalized anxiety disorder

Axis II   Dependent personality disorder

Axis III Fatty infiltration of the liver

Axis IV   Psychosocial and environmental problems: loss of girlfriend,

          financial difficulty due to recent loss of job.

Axis V   GAF 45 (current)

A. Brief history: This 28-year-old White male began daily drinking (9 to 18 12-oz beer per day) about 1 year ago when his girlfriend of 3 years left him for another man. She complained of his "always being nervous and weak." Client has, in the past year, been arrested three times for alcohol-related offenses (one drunken driving, two public intoxications). He claims to drink for anxiety reduction and for a sense of protection afforded by the alcohol. Client recently lost job due to absenteeism and intoxication, and in the last month he was diagnosed as having fatty infiltration of the liver. The client has increased tolerance but no withdrawal symptoms.

B.   Case formulation: Client with an old dependent personality disorder began drinking excessively and detrimentally when his girlfriend (on whom he was very dependent) left him. Before this heavy drinking period the client typically consumed three to four alcoholic drinks per day to calm himself, to facilitate social interaction, and to hasten the onset of sleep.

C.

Short-Term Goals	Intervention	Time Frame	Measurement Device	Goal Met? (Yes or No)
1. Enforced abstinence	250 mg Antabuse every day	6 months	Biweekly blood screening for Antabuse	
2. Functional analysis of behavior/ anxiety	Functional analysis protocol	3 months	Standard forms	
3. Decreased anxiety	Progressive muscle-relaxation training	3 months	Client's self-report/self-monitoring of anxiety	
4. Education of client about his current dysfunction	Individualized education	1 month	Posttest on specific dysfunctions	
5. Improved problem-solving and decision-making skills	Training in decision making and problem solving	2 months	Problem-solving inventory and therapist discretion	
6. Engaging client in therapy; increased treatment alliance	Generic techniques; small-success experiences	3 months	Client compliance	

D.

Long-Term Goals	Intervention	Time Frame	Measurement Device	Goal Met? (Yes or No)
1. Continued abstinence	Self-monitoring support-group participation	1 year and then ongoing	Client and collateral report	
2. Decreased dependency	Contingency contracting; individual counseling	1 year	Client, collateral, and therapist report	

continued

Long-Term Goals	Intervention	Time Frame	Measurement Device	Goal Met? (Yes or No)
3. Decreased anxiety	Perfection of relaxation skills; alternatives training, stimulus control and cognitive restructuring	6 months	Client and therapist report; anxiety scale	
4. Engaging in productive and fulfilling relationships	Relationship training; communication training; skills training	1 year	Therapist and client perception	
5. Termination of relationship; successful goal accomplishment	Phasing out of schedule	1 year +		

E.   Comments: Client seems highly motivated and interested in treatment. His parents are willing to be involved. Client is bright and will do well with a combination of behavioral and insight-oriented psychotherapy. Termination should be designed to ease client out of this relationship. Counseling should proceed from weekly sessions to biweekly to one per month to a standard booster schedule.

F.   Review updates (every 3 months). Plan redone at 1 year.

Review 1 Reviews will be used to add any newly found pertinent information and to comment on new stressors, problems, or successes.

Review 2 _____

Review 3 _____

Review 4 _____

EXHIBIT 4.3 | TREATMENT PLAN FOR AN OXYCONTIN USER

Name Jane Doe _____   Date 1-15-2009 _____

Date entered treatment 1-4-2009 _____   Gender F ____ Birth date 1-8-1982 _____

Review date (every 3 months) 4-8-2009, 7-8-2009, 10-8-2009 _____

DSM-IV-TR diagnosis(es):

Axis I   Opiod dependency, severe (Oxycontin) _____

Axis II Antisocial personality disorder _____

Axis III Client has elevated serum triglycerides, history of venereal disease. _____

Axis IV Psychosocial and environmental problem stressors: drug addiction, prostitution, unstable living environment, multiple arrests

Axis V GAF 35
Highest level of adaptive functioning past year

A. Brief history: 28-year-old White female with 7-year history of opioid dependence. Client currently uses 100 to 160 mg of Oxycontin per day and prostitutes to support this habit. Client was repeatedly raped by her father between the ages of 12 and 16. Client's mother died when she was 3. No prior treatment. No current court involvement. Self-referred. No stable living environment.

B. Case formulation: Client began experiencing difficulty early in life. She was repeatedly lying, fighting, and stealing, beginning at age 8. Client began abusing a number of drugs at age 14 in an effort to escape her home reality. Given her mother's death and her father's aberrant behavior, it is evident that this woman has had no stable positive role models and has been unable to form stable relationships. She used drugs initially for symptom relief and escape and now for maintenance of dependence.

C.

Short-Term Goals	Intervention	Time Frame	Measurement Device	Goal Met? (Yes or No)
1. End of illicit drug use	Methadone maintenance 100 mg, by mouth, every day	6 months	Random urine tests	
2. Therapeutic treatment alliance	Individual counseling twice a week	6 months	————	
3. Improved social skills	Skill-training	6 months	Weekly attendance	
4. Legitimate employment	Placement in job club	6 months	Weekly attendance with contingency for failure to have gainful employment within 6 months	

D.

Long-Term Goals	Intervention	Time Frame	Measurement Device	Goal Met? (Yes or No)
1. Continued abstinence	Methadone, Narcotics Anonymous; detoxification and contingency management	1 year	Urine screens	
2. Stable employment	Job Club	1 year	Work reports	
3. Increased behavioral coping skills	Assertion training; relaxation training,	8 months	Assertion scale; biofeedback data	

continued

Long-Term Goals	Intervention	Time Frame	Measurement Device	Goal Met? (Yes or No)
4. Improved physical condition	Nutrition counseling; exercise regime; doctor visits	Ongoing	Physical correlates	
5. End of therapy	Phaseout from weekly to biweekly to monthly to booster schedule	2 years		

E. Comments: <u>Client is ambivalent about seeking treatment. She is fully ensconced in a</u> <u>drug-using culture and has no insight into the relationship between drug use and her</u> <u>current problem. Client has antisocial personality disorder, and this makes the treat-</u> <u>ment prognosis grim.</u>

F. Review updates (every 3 months). Plan redone at 1 year.
Review 1 <u>Reviews will be used to add any newly found pertinent information and to</u> <u>comment on new stressors, problems, or successes.</u>

Review 2 _____

Review 3 _____

Review 4 _____

Questions for Thought and Discussion

1. Early in this chapter, we met Jade, a high school junior being seen for an initial interview by a substance abuse counselor. Jade said she did not believe she really had a problem. Now, after learning the results of an assessment, she feels that she should do something about her drinking. The counselor did not confront her about her drinking and did not press her to enter treatment, believing that the choice had to be hers. Some counselors would have taken a different approach, insisting that Jade recognize and address her problem with alcohol.

    Clearly, there are pros and cons on this issue. What do you think is the most likely outcome for Jade? If the counselor had used a more confrontive approach, how might the outcome have been different? To what degree does Jade's age affect your beliefs about how she should be treated?

2. If Jade had been your client, what additional information would you want to have about her? What assessment methods would help you obtain this information? How might the data affect her treatment plan?

REFERENCES

American Psychiatric Association. (2002). *Diagnostic and statistical manual of mental disorders Text Revision* (4th ed.). Washington, DC: Author.

Coombs, R., & Howatt, W. (2005). *The addictions counselor desk reference.* Hoboken, NJ: Wiley.

Cooney, N., Kadden, R., & Steinberg, H. (2005). Assessment of alcohol problems. In D. Donovan & G. Marlatt (Eds.), *Assessment of addictive behaviors* (2nd ed.). NY: Guilford Press.

Donovan, D., & Marlatt, G. (2005). *Assessment of addictive behaviors* (2nd ed.). NY: Guilford Press.

Lewis, J. A. (1992). Applying the motivational interviewing process. *The Family Psychologist, 8*(1), 31–32.

MacCoun, R. J. (2009). Toward a psychology of harm reduction. In G. A. Marlatt & K. Witkiewitz (Eds.), *Addictive behaviors: New readings on etiology, prevention, and treatment.* Washington, DC: APA.

Miller, W. R. (2006). Motivational factors in addictive behaviors. In W. R. Miller & K. M. Carroll (Eds.), *Rethinking substance abuse: What the science shows, and what we should do about it.* NY: Guilford Press.

Moos, R. (2009). Addictive disorders in context: principles and puzzles of effective treatment and recovery. In G. A. Marlatt & K. Witkiewitz (Eds.), *Addictive behaviors: New readings on etiology, prevention, and treatment.* Washington, DC: APA.

Tarter, R., & Kirisci, L., & Mezzich, A. (1999). Psychometric assessment of substance abuse. In P. Ott, R. Tarter, & R. Ammerman (Eds.), *Sourcebook on substance abuse: Etiology, epidemiology, assessment, and treatment.* Boston: Allyn & Bacon.

5 | HELPING CLIENTS CHANGE

SOMEHOW, A MYTHOLOGY has developed about substance abuse counseling, with the conventional wisdom holding that clients must be treated with mistrust and even disrespect. In fact, counselors, who normally believe that the therapeutic relationship should be based on collaboration, mutual trust, and empathy, should strive to keep this principle intact when the issue at hand is drug abuse. The skills, attitudes, and characteristics that make a counselor facilitative in a general counseling practice are just as important when the client has a drug-related concern. The establishment of the counseling relationship is a first step toward healing.

THE COUNSELING RELATIONSHIP

The strength of the counseling relationship depends on two separate but closely related factors: (a) the facilitative qualities that the counselor brings to the process and (b) the strategies that he or she uses to create a positive environment for exploration and change.

FACILITATIVE QUALITIES

The personal dimensions that characterize facilitative relationships include such qualities as empathy, genuineness, immediacy, warmth, and respect. Although these characteristics are often associated with a client-centered or person-centered approach, they actually underlie most successful interactions. Successful relationship-building also depends on the counselor's ability to demonstrate cultural sensitivity.

EMPATHY   *Empathy* refers to the ability to take the feelings, sensations, or attitudes of another person into oneself. In other words, we have the capacity for vicariously experiencing other's feelings, thoughts, or posture. For example, a counselor may listen to a client explain how hopeless and useless, how unable to go on, he or she feels. An empathic response would be direct and comforting. The response does not indicate that the counselor is experiencing what the client is experiencing but, rather, that the counselor is beginning to develop a clear picture of what the client is describing. An empathic response to this situation might be: "I hear you saying that you're useless and that you don't feel hopeful about the future. It's as if you're very sad, very depressed—just feeling overwhelmed. Am I reading the situation correctly?" Thus, empathy is caring, but it is not sympathy. Obviously, counselors cannot know their client's experience, but they can share with the client their feelings as they perceive that experience. Empathy is a here-and-now quality, and it will occur only if counselors pay very close attention to their clients. They must be "present" with the client. Appropriate empathy will help the client feel understood, and this feeling is extremely curative for substance-abusing individuals.

An important aspect of being present with the substance abuse client involves the counselor's acceptance of the client's ambivalence about behavior change. The transformation from a drug-focused lifestyle to recovery is a daunting one. The counselor's empathy can help clients take the important step of openly examining their feelings about both the positive and the negative aspects of drug use.

GENUINENESS   Another important counselor quality is *genuineness*, which refers to the ability to be oneself in a situation. Genuine counselors avoid playing false roles and abstain from defensiveness. Their external behavior matches their internal feelings. This type of behavior improves the alliance between counselor and client and increases adherence to treatment (that is, how well the client follows through in therapy). Genuineness is a natural state, but counselors may need to be purposeful about practicing it. The counselor's willingness to be genuine both affects and is affected by the degree of trust in the relationship. Counselors often find it difficult to behave genuinely and trustingly when they perceive their clients as dishonest and manipulative. With substance abuse clients, who are accustomed to being perceived in these negative terms, an honest relationship is especially important.

It is within this context of genuineness that counselor's self-disclosure might sometimes be appropriate. Self-disclosure is the sharing of the counselor's personal experiences, feelings, and attitudes with a client—but only for the sake of the client. It is a powerful tool, and it can sometimes be used in a counter therapeutic fashion. Self-disclosure is never to be used to facilitate the counselor's own development. In order for this technique to be of any help, it must be relevant to the situation at hand. Self-disclosure should be utilized only when the client can tolerate the information imparted by the counselor and make use of it.

Appropriate self-disclosure may improve clients' self-esteem by making them feel less alone, less pathological, and more at ease with the ups and downs of life. In addition, it may equalize the client–counselor relationship and consequently strengthen the therapeutic alliance and improve treatment outcomes. Citing the importance of self-disclosure does not imply that a counselor should have experienced problems that are comparable to those facing clients. Rather, it implies that the counselor can sometimes help clients by sharing feelings and attitudes that relate to his or her immediate concerns.

IMMEDIACY   *Immediacy*, like genuineness, involves real feelings between the counselor and the client in the here and now. Ideally, counselor and client are constantly sharing what is going on between them in an open, honest way. This technique focuses the client on reality and is very effective at keeping the counseling process moving. When working with substance abuse clients, the counselor needs to strive to keep the process focused and on track. The quality of immediacy helps make this happen.

WARMTH   *Warmth* is also related to genuineness. This quality typically shows up in nonverbal ways, through such behaviors as smiling and nodding one's head. These responses show that the counselor, too, is a human being, and they reinforce the client's humanness. Warmth demonstrates openness and responsiveness, and it teaches clients that the counselor, at a bare minimum, will respond positively to them when they need it. A warm counselor improves the quality of treatment by helping the client feel a sense of being accepted. Substance abuse clients deserve to be treated with warmth and respect, despite the fact that their previous behaviors might have been unacceptable in terms of the counselor's values.

RESPECT   *Respect* refers to the counselor's ability to communicate to clients that they are capable of surviving in a difficult environment and that they are bright enough and free enough to choose their own alternatives and participate in the therapeutic decision-making process. This orientation empowers clients and begins the process of returning focus of control and responsibility to an internal orientation. When counselors treat their clients with respect, they send a clear message that they expect them to take responsibility for their behaviors.

One way to show respect for clients is to treat them as people who have the power to make changes in their lives. In the past, substance abuse clients were frequently pressured to accept treatment providers' definitions of their problems and to accept treatment plans devised by others. One way to help clients move in the direction of responsible behavior is to treat them as we would treat any responsible, competent adult. Honest respect is empowering to people because it encourages them to believe in their own potential for positive change.

CULTURAL SENSITIVITY   In the development of the counseling relationship, respect and *cultural sensitivity* are closely aligned. In order to set the stage for helpful interactions, the counselor must demonstrate the ability to reach out across differences.

Clients in any setting come to counseling with wide variations in terms of their expectations and in terms of the degree of trust they are likely to exhibit. The counselor should not be surprised or defensive when clients who are members of oppressed groups exhibit distrust toward the counselor and the counseling process.

The only counseling many of these people have received has been a forced, rather than a voluntary, experience with a culturally insensitive agent of some social welfare agency. In addition, counseling has often followed some crime. Generally, in both situations the goal of counseling is not developmental, but either remediation or punishment. Many people from diverse cultural backgrounds, therefore, perceive counseling as a process that the dominant society employs to forcibly control their lives and well-being (Coombs and Howatt, 2005).

The suspicions that people have about the health and human service systems are, if anything, exacerbated when the issue at hand is drug-related. Although it is true that counselors need to change their clients' perceptions before they can be therapeutic, it is also true that the best way to change these perceptions is to change the reality upon which they are based. Although it takes patience, the counselor needs to work through these issues in a way that shows respect and concern.

Culturally sensitive counselors also realize that the act of receiving help from a professional is alien to many cultural traditions.

Even though it is difficult to generalize about group similarities and differences as they relate to psychotherapeutic relationships, it is useful to recognize that some clients in all cultural groups respond to counseling differently because of their cultural experiences. For many clients, the idea of self-analysis and self-disclosing is the cause for high anxiety (Coombs and Howatt, 2005).

The entire counseling process is enhanced when counselors are willing to increase their clients' comfort by making adaptations in their own methods and styles.

Strategies to Create an Environment for Change

As the counseling relationship begins to develop, the counselor should focus on creating a safe situation in which the client feels encouraged to move toward openness. The skills of inviting communication and listening carefully are primary at this point in the process.

LEAD-INS *Lead-ins* and open-ended invitations to respond are designed to encourage clients to begin active exploration. The counselor might use a lead-in in an effort to get more information from clients about their problems or to get them to feel more comfortable while talking about their specific situation. A lead-in used in this way is simply a "nudge" given to clients that encourages them to further explore or expand an issue. Simple statements such as "Could you tell me more about that?" or "I'm not sure I understand. Can you talk more about that issue?" are particularly useful in getting clients to draw a clearer picture for themselves and for the counselor.

RESTATEMENTS In restatement, a counselor takes what a client has said and rephrases it in a clearer and more articulate way. This technique decreases the negative effects of confused or defensive self-statements and strengthens the therapeutic relationship while facilitating the counseling. *Restatement* is frequently referred to as paraphrasing, and this process lets the client know that the counselor is paying attention, cares, and thinks that the client is an important person. In addition, this procedure clarifies issues for the client and facilitates growth. Suppose, for instance, that a client says: "Everyone says my drinking is a problem. Well, I don't think it is, and it's probably a better idea to talk with my family. They're the ones with a problem—not me!" The therapist can facilitate communication and movement by responding: "It seems that you're unhappy with all the pressure that's being put on you and that you're not sure you have a problem. If I were to speak with your family, how would that help you?" This type of response is unthreatening and powerfully reinforcing. It is an essential component of the counseling relationship that provides needed organization and, consequently, increased insight and improved treatment outcomes.

REFLECTION The technique of *reflection*, a parroting of a cognitive or emotional statement, facilitates communication, gives the client a feeling of being understood, and allows the counseling relationship to grow. In this regard counselors may find that they have to reflect what the client is feeling or what he or she has said or is thinking. If they choose not to use reflection, they run the risk of prematurely ending the counseling relationship, stalling the therapeutic process, frustrating or confusing the client, or generally wasting the client's time. Use of this tool, conversely, hastens the process, improves the client's self-esteem, deepens the counseling relationship, and generally improves the therapeutic outcome. Here is an example of a counselor's response to a woman with a drinking problem:

CLIENT: Every time I think of my drinking, I want to crawl into a hole and cry. Sometimes it seems easier to keep drinking—maybe I'll die soon.
COUNSELOR: It sounds as if you're awfully embarrassed by your drinking. You seem to feel hopeless and very depressed.

Here the therapist has reflected the client's feelings and uncovered her thinking process. This exchange allows the client to be heard and gives her a strong sense of being heard. Therapy is advanced, and the relationship with the client is strengthened. Counselors can reflect either feelings or thoughts. Both forms of reflection serve to move treatment along and provide an impetus for continued progress.

QUESTIONING *Questioning* allows the counselor to clarify the client's needs, feelings, and beliefs. It facilitates the expansion of ideas, therapeutic growth, and self-understanding. Questioning should not be used arbitrarily or solely to fill time. Continual questioning is regressive. Facilitative questioning can effectively enlighten the client; short-circuit maladaptive defense mechanisms; and move the therapeutic process along to deeper, more meaningful, levels. Questions are typically most useful when they ask "what" or "how." A "why" question implies a right/wrong dichotomy; fosters the use of defense mechanisms such as intellectualization, rationalization, and denial; and generally impedes useful counseling. Compare these three types of questions:

COUNSELOR: What is it about your drinking that is important to you?
COUNSELOR: How does your drinking make you feel?
COUNSELOR: Why do you drink?

It is evident that the "what" and "how" questions are nonjudgmental and likely to facilitate open communication. The "why" question, however, sounds judgmental and almost punitive. It immediately puts the client on guard and is very likely to bear little fruit other than a litany of denial and rationalization.

Questions can also be either direct or, more effectively, open-ended. Open-ended questions expand the therapeutic process and aid the client in establishing a free-flowing pattern of communication. In this respect counselors will do well to avoid questions like "Do you want to die?" in favor of questions like "What sorts of burdens will be lifted if you kill yourself?" Questioning done in a sensitive and therapeutic way will facilitate growth and begin the process of separating behavior from self. It will encourage discussion while improving self-acceptance, self-disclosure, and honesty.

SILENCE   All of the skills we have mentioned so far encourage the client—not the counselor—to do most of the talking. In order to be adept at practicing these skills, counselors have to learn to feel comfortable with some degree of silence. It may seem odd to think of *silence* as a competency, but counselors do need to develop the skill of using silence effectively. Silence at the appropriate time facilitates introspection and the creation of therapeutic dissonance (anxiety). This dissonance often serves as a spur in getting a client to take difficult and painful steps in therapy. Counselors sometimes feel that silence is taboo and contraindicated in "talking therapies." This is not true, and the adage that silence is golden could easily be revised to say that silence is potent.

COGNITIVE RESTRUCTURING   As clients share more about themselves, the counselor can begin to deepen the level of communication. Another basic counseling technique, *cognitive restructuring*, is helpful in this regard. It allows clients to restate their beliefs and ideas in a fashion that more closely represents reality as opposed to fantasy. For example, a client who says "I can't change my behavior" would be encouraged to say "I won't change my behavior." This type of self-statement more accurately reflects reality and gives clients a spur to initiative, because they will begin to "own" their behavior. In addition, the statements that clients make will begin to be less overwhelming ("Some people dislike me" as opposed to "Everyone hates me") and consequently easier to deal with in the therapeutic relationship. In essence, this technique will help ensure that clients' cognitions, emotions, and actions are more rational. To promote cognitive restructuring, counselors should teach their clients to ask the following questions as they evaluate their thoughts and feelings:

- Is my thinking in this situation based on an obvious fact or on fantasy?
- Is my thinking in this situation likely to help me protect my life or health?
- Is my thinking likely to help me or hinder me in achieving my short- and long-term goals?
- Is my thinking going to help me avoid conflict with others?
- Is my thinking going to help me feel the emotions I want to feel?

Cognitive restructuring of this sort will serve to decrease negative self-statements, negative self-fulfilling prophecies, hopelessness, anxiety, and fear and to increase realistic cognitions, positive self-image, and self-esteem. It requires consistent attention to what the client is saying and a continuous orientation back to reality.

CONFRONTATION   In the past, some treatment providers believed that confrontation was the only skill they needed. Confrontation is an important tool that can be helpful in propelling clients forward, but it can be effective only in the context of a solid helping relationship and only when the client is ready to receive it. In this context, confrontation takes place when the counselor perceives a discrepancy between what clients say and what they are experiencing, between what they say now and what they said earlier, or between what they say and their actual behavior. There are five types of confrontation:

1. experiential confrontation
2. strength confrontation
3. weakness confrontation

4. action confrontation
5. factual confrontation

An experiential confrontation occurs when clients say one thing but the counselor perceives that they feel it in a different way. A strength confrontation takes place when clients claim weakness or helplessness and the counselor empowers them by pointing out the disparity between this claim and evidence of their ability. A weakness confrontation, on the other hand, is appropriate when clients refuse to admit to painful feelings and put up a façade of invulnerability. The counselor encourages clients to drop this defensive posture so that they can experience true feelings. An action confrontation occurs when clients engage in helpless behavior and the counselor actively encourages them to complete tasks that are important to their success. Finally, a factual confrontation occurs when the counselor disabuses clients of myths or errors in fact. This opportunity will present itself frequently in typical clinical practices, and it is advisable to let substance-abusing clients know the facts concerning the substances they are using and the problems they are encountering.

In all of these situations, the confrontation must be presented tentatively. The clients are the ones who are the experts on their own lives. Whether to accept or reject the counselor's suggestion must always be their free choice.

The use of these very basic skills will improve counseling relationships and improve treatment outcomes. These techniques require practice and cannot be taken for granted. Counselors should not rely exclusively on any one skill. Rather, techniques should be used in concert and only when they will serve the client.

INTERRUPTING SUBSTANCE USE BEHAVIORS

Clients should have treatment plans that address both substance use and other related issues. We believe, however, that they are most likely to make good progress if the counselor can help them address their drug use behaviors in a very direct way. The specific techniques we discuss in this section for use with substance-abusing clients are designed to interrupt substance abuse behaviors. To use these techniques effectively, counselors must refer back to the initial assessment and evaluation. In this way, they will be able to choose specific techniques (for example, relaxation training) to treat specific concerns that have been identified during the initial evaluation (for example, anxiety).

All clients are unique and have unique problems that must be individually addressed and treated. The label "alcohol-dependent" or "opioid-dependent" cannot dictate treatment. For example, not all clients with barbiturate problems should receive assertion training, relaxation training, and a referral to Narcotics Anonymous, rather, each should be treated for the specific problems he or she has exhibited. Included in this section are several techniques that are helpful in changing substance use behavior.

IDENTIFYING AND COPING WITH HIGH-RISK SITUATIONS

A comprehensive assessment provides the base on which effective counseling can be built. A functional analysis of the individual's substance use supplies some of the information that both counselor and client will need in order to interrupt the behaviors in question. When clients are aware of the situations that tend to trigger their substance use, they can make plans for coping with those situations in different and more effective ways. Carroll (1998), in describing the use of functional analysis with cocaine-using clients, suggests that determinants of cocaine use be identified across five domains: social, environmental, emotional, cognitive, and physical. In the social domain, clients should consider such factors as with whom they spend their time, with whom they use drugs, and how their relationships and social networks interact with their drug use. Determinants in the environmental domain relate to the cues associated with their drug use, including particular times and places. Emotional determinants include negative and positive feeling states that link with substance use. The cognitive domain includes thoughts that frequently precede cocaine use. Finally, the physical domain includes particular physical states or sensations that are precursors to substance use.

Clients can identify these situations either through day-to-day monitoring or through recollecting past challenges. Another alternative is to use instruments such as the Inventory of Drinking Situations, which helps individuals categorize the experiences that place them at highest risk for substance use. When clients identify these situations, they can move in the direction of choosing and practicing coping strategies for dealing with them. Clients may decide to avoid certain situations that seem too formidable at the moment; they can work their way up a hierarchy of situations, from those that they see as moderately difficult to those that are more challenging. A client can prepare for anticipated situations, planning strategies to avoid or cope with them.

In general, the active coping strategies selected by clients can be categorized as either cognitive or behavioral (Miller & Brown, 2009). Cognitive coping strategies include, for example, self-statements that clients use as reminders about their commitment or as ways to reappraise the situation. Behavioral methods include learning alternative behaviors or the use of such skills as assertion, which is discussed in more detail later in this chapter. Each client needs to have enough alternative coping skills available so that he or she has choices in dealing with challenges. The counselor can help enlarge the client's repertoire of coping mechanisms through instruction, modeling, behavioral rehearsal, and homework assignments. Another way to enhance coping behaviors is through contingency contracting, which is also discussed later in this chapter.

RELAXATION TRAINING

Anxiety is very frequently a precipitant to substance use and abuse. This is not to say that anxiety is the root cause of excessive alcohol or drug use. Clearly, however, people who have long histories of substance use frequently report having no way to deal with anxiety except through the drug of choice. In light of this reality it is wise to have a tool to help clients reduce their anxiety. This tool is relaxation training. It is vital that counselors understand that anxiety does not occur in a vacuum. There are always a number of social, emotional, and cognitive components from which anxiety (fear) is created. Therefore, one should never solely use relaxation training to "cure" anxiety. Rather, this technique should be used to treat the specific symptom of anxiety, and other techniques should be used to enable clients to deal with the situations that have led to anxiety (that is, assertion deficit, fear of rejection, and poor self-esteem).

Relaxation training, widely called progressive muscle relaxation is a procedure that involves successively tensing and then relaxing muscle groups in the body. The technique is used because relaxation is incompatible with anxiety. It is easy to administer and easy to learn. Substance abusers with anxiety respond well to this technique because it allows them to (1) reduce generalized anxiety and normal tension, (2) reduce anxiety and tension that are generated in highly charged emotional or social situations, (3) relax before sleep, and (4) diminish the intensity of urges and cravings that often precede a relapse to drug or alcohol use. These uses are quite positive for substance abusers, who are used to treating many, if not all, of their symptoms with alcohol or any other drug. This relaxation response, once learned, is easy to use, positively reinforcing, and effective in reducing negative outcomes (such as unremitting anxiety or a relapse) in clients' lives.

Learning to use progressive muscle relaxation is relatively simple. It requires that the counselor carefully and fully explain to the client what progressive muscle relaxation is, why it is being used, how it works, and how to make it work. In general, a statement such as the following is an acceptable introduction to this technique:

Counselor: *Today I'm going to begin teaching you a new technique to handle your anxiety. It's called relaxation training, or progressive muscle relaxation. It's a simple technique that you can use to reduce and eliminate unpleasant anxiety that you carry around with you or that presents itself in specific situations or at specific times. This tool will become an effective deterrent to anxiety, and you can use it to eliminate your urges and cravings for alcohol [or other drugs].*

Relaxation works on a simple system. Basically, if you're relaxed, you can't be uptight or anxious. We're going to spend plenty of time seeing to it that you learn this skill and that it becomes a part of you. People will often use relaxation constantly, and by doing this they greatly improve the quality of their life. You'll see when you're first learning this skill that it requires a lot of activity on your part. You'll be required to tense and then relax a lot of muscles throughout your body. You're probably asking yourself, "How can I possibly use this all day or anywhere but in private?" Well, quite simply, once you learn to do relaxation, it becomes another habit, and relaxation will occur spontaneously in response to signs and signals that your body gives you. No one will ever know you're practicing relaxation.

Now then, in order to learn relaxation and have it become a part of who you are, it's very important that you practice. I can get you to relax here in the office, but with practice you'll begin to "own" the behavior, and you'll find that it becomes easier and easier to relax. With practice, relaxation will become a part of you. Now, do you have any questions?

In order to do relaxation training, the counselor will need a comfortable, moderately firm recliner or couch. The client should be instructed to remove all jewelry and to loosen restrictive clothing and to assume as comfortable a position as possible. The lights should be dimmed, and the noise level should be kept low. During relaxation one wants to minimize external stimulus intrusions so clients can relax and concentrate on the counselor's voice and on their increasing relaxation. Before relaxation begins, the counselor should instruct clients that their level of relaxation will be monitored as the procedure progresses and that they are to signify persistent tension in a muscle group, when asked, by raising an index finger.

Relaxation should be sequential and should proceed in the following fashion:

1. Relax the muscles in the dominant and nondominant hand.
2. Relax muscles in the dominant and nondominant arm.
3. Relax muscles in the head.
4. Relax muscles in the neck.
5. Relax muscles in the face.
6. Relax muscles in the jaw.
7. Relax muscles in the shoulders.
8. Relax muscles in the back.
9. Relax muscles in the chest.
10. Relax muscles in the stomach.
11. Relax muscles in the upper legs.
12. Relax muscles in the lower legs.
13. Relax muscles in the feet.

With practice the counselor will probably be able to complete two or three muscle groups per session of 30 to 60 min. The client is simply instructed to contract the muscle group being worked on and, during this contraction, to experience as vividly as possible the tense, tight, and uncomfortable feelings that are produced. When the muscle group has been appropriately tensed, the client is instructed to release the tension and to focus on the positive and soothing feelings associated with relaxation. For each muscle group this contraction/relaxation pattern should be executed two or three times so that the client learns the difference between the two feeling states.

When the client is fully able to relax the different muscle groups, full body relaxation training can begin. In this procedure the counselor still follows the musclegroup sequence but goes through all groups during the training session. It is advisable to tape relaxation training sessions so that the client can use them to practice with at home.

In an effort to get relaxation in all muscle groups, the following instructions to clients will be useful:

1. *Hands and arms*—Make a very tight fist, and fully extend your arms.
2. *Head*—Roll your eyes to the back while straining to look up.
3. *Neck*—(a) Rotate your head fully to the left and hold; (b) rotate your head fully to the right and hold; (c) bring your head all the way back, and try to touch your back with the back of your head; and (d) move your head forward as far as possible so that your chin makes contact with your chest.
4. *Face and jaw*—Grit your teeth, furrow your forehead, purse your lips, squeeze your eyes shut, and smile and frown in an exaggerated fashion. After gritting your teeth to tense your jaw, you must allow your mouth to open slightly in order to achieve relaxation.
5. *Shoulders*—Raise your shoulders in an effort to touch your ears. Rotate your shoulders toward the middle of your chest.
6. *Back*—Arch your back while moving your shoulders in reverse as if you were trying to get them to connect. Hold your head still, and roll your shoulders forward toward the middle of your chest.

7. *Chest*—Puff out your chest, and then inhale deeply. Hold your breath for 3 to 5 seconds, and then slowly exhale.

8. *Stomach*—Suck in your belly, and then push it out. Finally, take a deep breath, hold it for 3 to 5 s, and then slowly exhale.

9. *Legs*—Elevate your legs slightly off the relaxation chair, and extend them fully.

10. *Feet*—Fully extend or arch your foot and toes in a downward position, and then do this in an upward position.

Each muscle group must be fully relaxed before the client moves to the next group. Remember to have the client indicate continued tension in a muscle group or area by raising an index finger. Muscle groups should be tensed and held for approximately 15 s, and relaxation in the muscle group should be slowly phased in over 15 to 20 s.

The following case example demonstrates a full body relaxation procedure.

Counselor: OK, John, please make yourself comfortable. Get completely relaxed now, and when you're ready to begin, signal me by raising the index finger on your right hand. OK. Now let's begin with your left hand and arm. I'd like you to make a very powerful fist with your left hand. Good. Make it tighter now, hold it, hold it, good. Feel the tension, notice how uncomfortable it is, hold it, good. Now slowly begin to open your fist, slowly now, feel the good feelings, and notice the difference between tension and relaxation. Good. Now feel the feelings, notice how nice it feels.

OK, John, let's move to your arm now. Begin to extend your arm, John, feel the tension building, feel it building. Notice the discomfort, the pain. Feel your arm shaking, and recognize that you can control this feeling, hold it, hold it. OK, now let's slowly begin relaxing your arm. Feel the bad feelings draining away, feel the tension leaving your body and notice how good your arm is beginning to feel. Notice the difference between tension and relaxation, keep relaxing, and keep feeling the good feelings. If any tension is left in your hand or arm, please tell me by raising your right index finger. OK, good, continue to relax. [Now move to the right arm and hand, using the same procedure, and then move to the head.]

OK, John, now we're going to relax your head. Feel the tension there, and know that you can control these feelings. OK, now let's arch your eyebrows, and without moving your head look straight up. OK, good, now hold it, hold it, good. Feel the tension, notice the feelings, hold it, good. Now let the tension slip away, and feel it being replaced by good feelings, a sense of relaxation. Good, feel it, good. [Have the client do appropriate neck exercises, always pointing out the positive differences between relaxation and tension. Once the client has fully relaxed the neck, move on to the face and jaw.]

OK, John, let's begin to relax your jaw. I want you to notice the tension and fatigue in your jaw and to understand that through relaxation you can remove these bad feelings. OK, now, John, let's grit your teeth, tighter, tighter. OK, hold it, feel the discomfort, notice how it feels, hold it, OK. Now slowly begin to relax your jaw, OK, separate your teeth and open your mouth slightly. Good, now feel the relaxation, relax, relax now. OK, let's relax your face now. [Have the client do facial exercises, and when relaxed, move to the shoulders and then to the back and on to the chest.]

OK, John, feel the tension in your chest, feel the anxiety and all the bad feelings that build up there and know, John, that you can control these feelings. OK, John, let's take a deep, deep breath, good, good, now hold it, hold it, feel that tension, hold it, good, feel the tension, feel the discomfort. OK, now slowly begin to let it come out, and as the air leaves your body, notice how good you feel, notice how the pressure is *leaving you. Good, feel those good feelings. Now breathe normally. [Move now to the stomach and then to the legs.]*

Finally, John, let's see about relaxing your feet and toes. OK, John, feel the tension there, and understand that your body is fully free of tension now and all that remains is to let the tension go from your feet, so let's tense your foot. [Do only one appendage at a time.] Now, make it tense, feel the tension, more tense, more, hold it, hold it, feel the discomfort. OK, now, let's start shaking that tension loose, let it go, let it go, feel the relaxation, feel the difference and know that you can control these feelings.

OK, good, good, are you completely relaxed? If not, raise the index finger on your right hand. Good, feel the relaxation and now relax even more deeply, good, good, rest now, relax, let it all go, good, and now just keep relaxing and enjoy these feelings for a moment. [Silence for 1 min.]

And now we're slowly going to begin to move about, stay relaxed now, and I'd like you to keep your eyes closed and wiggle your toes, arch your feet, and stretch your legs. OK, now take a deep breath, good, let it out and move your stomach and chest, and now begin to flex your hand and fingers and stretch your arms. Stay relaxed now, good, and let's move your shoulders and rotate your neck and scrunch up your face, lift your eyebrows, and close your eyes tightly. Good. Now, I'd like you to continue to be relaxed, and as I count backward from 5, slowly open your eyes, 5-4-3-2-1-0. Good, very good, you did a great job today.

These sessions should last from 30 to 60 min. The therapist's voice should be low, smooth, and comforting. Be relaxed, and encourage the client to maintain the relaxation response throughout the day and to ask any questions that he or she may have.

After five to eight 1-hr sessions and two 15-min practice periods per day throughout the treatment period, the relaxation response should be well learned. The client will be better equipped to handle both underlying anxiety and the tension evoked when he or she is placed in highly charged social or emotional situations.

Modeling

Modeling refers to learning through the observation and imitation of others. In general, this social learning technique allows us to foster desired behaviors in our clients simply by demonstrating these behaviors. For example, we can model appropriate communication skills, eye gaze, posture, sympathy, and refusal of drugs (Miller and Brown, 2009).

When a client observes the counselor or an actor performing appropriate behaviors, it is thought, the model acts as a stimulus for similar thoughts, attitudes, or behaviors on the part of the client. There are a number of ways to present modeled behavior. These include live modeling, in which the counselor performs the desired behavior in the presence of the client; modeling by video or audio recordings (relaxation tapes, assertion tapes); the use of multiple models (simulating real-life situations); and covert modeling with projected consequences (the counselor uses relaxation procedures and then has the client imagine situations in which he or she is engaging in the desired behavior). Live modeling tends to permit more flexible feedback, because there is always an opportunity for the model to adjust and improvise as the situation dictates. This type of modeling is frequently ad-libbed, however, and it does require a significant time commitment on the counselor's part. Recording of the desired model behavior allows editing of the work and a focus on specific problems. Another advantage of recorded modeling is that tapes of modeled behavior can be used repeatedly, reducing the long-term costs while freeing the counselor to do other work.

Multiple models can demonstrate flexibility and variability. The client sees a number of different behavioral styles in situations requiring the behavior in question. This variant requires several "helpers" to act as models, and it can be costly and difficult to arrange on a day-to-day basis. Another variant of the modeling technique is to have the client simply think of projected consequences of a model's behavior. This method is easily done in the office, is cost-effective, and is nonintrusive. Unfortunately, it is not as powerful as live or recorded models, and therefore its utility is limited.

Modeling is a powerful tool in therapy. Counselors tend to constantly model a number of behaviors, such as warmth, genuineness, and appropriate listening skills, but they must turn to well-designed modeling interventions for clients' specific deficits or problems.

Contingency Contracting and Management

Another tool that can significantly improve substance abuse counseling is contingency contracting and management. This technique might be used to limit the amount of alcohol consumed per occasion, encourage the ingestion of an Antabuse tablet each day, or facilitate open communication in a relationship dyad. It is readily applicable to a broad range of other situations and can be used in the treatment of all types of drug dependence to foster either abstinence or moderation.

Contingency contracting is an operant-conditioning procedure that links a reward (reinforcer) or a punisher to the occurrence or absence of a specified response. A reinforcer that follows a specific behavior (and only that behavior) is called a contingent reward. For instance, if one doesn't smoke during a 4-day period, one gets a gourmet dinner; as is evident, getting the reward is contingent on not smoking. Maxine Stitzer and her colleagues (2009) have reviewed a large body of literature showing that there is little doubt that the contingent dispensation of reinforcement is an effective method for controlling behavior. In fact, it has been convincingly demonstrated that noncontingent reinforcement fails to control behavior, whereas the contingent application of the same reinforcer does exert effective control. As an example, consider a drug abuser who receives an achievement pin and a testimonial dinner every 2 months, regardless of his ability to maintain abstinence, as opposed to a drug abuser who receives an achievement pin and testimonial dinner every 2 months only if she has successfully maintained abstinence. The first client is unlikely to strive for abstinence, because he is noncontingently reinforced, whereas the second client is likely to be highly invested in abstinence, because her reinforcement is contingent on such behavior. In a similar vein, it is ineffective to use a contingent reinforcer that has no value to the client. For instance, a night on the town will not be a potent reinforcer for the individual who dislikes crowds and spending money, nor will the opportunity to take an out-of-town vacation be an effective reinforcer for a homebody.

Contingency management, then, consists of the contingent presentation and withdrawal of rewards and punishments. Counselors can use these procedures themselves, and it is equally effective to train others (spouses, friends, children) to function as natural contingency managers. In addition, clients must be trained in contingency management so that they can exercise increased self-control over their own problem behaviors.

Many more skills are involved in this procedure than the simple dispensation of reinforcements. For example, counselors must discover a number of reinforcers that can be manipulated and that are effective for the client whose behavior is being changed. In addition, they must determine what behaviors will be changed, their frequency of occurrence (baseline), the situations in which they occur, and the reinforcers that appear to be responsible for the maintenance of these maladaptive behaviors. This knowledge will be gained through functional analysis. Failure to establish a baseline rate of behavior frequency, institute procedures for measuring behavioral change, and assess such things as the behaviors to be treated results in limited treatment effectiveness and a consequent waste of therapist and client time. Contingency management techniques are flexible and can be applied in the community, individually, in a group, and in both inpatient and outpatient settings. They require creative treatment planning and individualizing and are both cost- and time-effective.

SYSTEMATIC DESENSITIZATION

Systematic desensitization (SD) is frequently talked about in terms of its relationship to relaxation training. In fact, all clients must be trained in relaxation before SD can be utilized. SD is used in combination with relaxation training to deal with specific environmental factors (such as highly feared situations) that typically provoke anxiety or resultant substance abuse. This procedure involves the gradual association between relaxation and images of anxiety-producing situations, presented in a hierarchical order. Initially, SD was used solely as a treatment for phobic clients, but it is now widely applied to a number of dysfunctions in which anxiety is thought to provoke an undesirable response. The rationale behind this procedure is that fears will diminish if they are repeatedly experienced and associated with a feeling of relaxation, both in imagination and, eventually, in real life. In terms of chemical-dependency counseling, this technique is particularly helpful with clients who are experiencing difficulty in using the standard relaxation training as a self-control technique in their day-to-day living because of intrusive and extreme anxiety. It is also helpful for clients having difficulty implementing new social skills in interpersonal situations because of persistent anxiety and apprehension.

Before SD training begins, counselors must help clients develop a hierarchical list of situations within one general category that causes anxiety. The client who reports anxiety secondary to socializing in large groups, conducting romantic interactions, and dealing with authority figures will need assistance in developing a separate list for each of these categories. Situations (or images) should be rank-ordered, from those producing the least anxiety near the bottom of the list to those producing the most anxiety near the top. For example, a systematic desensitization hierarchy could take the following form:

Most Anxiety-Provoking
7. At a large social gathering where you know no one
6. At an office party where you are familiar with everyone but a few spouses
5. In a restaurant, with a friend, when you are introduced to someone you don't know

4. In a shopping center where you know no one, and no one knows you
3. At a small party with five or six of your closest friends
2. In your home with an old friend

Least Anxiety-Provoking
1. Alone in your bedroom

In constructing hierarchical lists, one must take special care to ensure that they are long enough so that they are gradual in terms of anxiety; large jumps in anxiety-producing situations could present difficulty in successful progression up the hierarchy.

Once the counselor and client have completed the hierarchy(ies), progressive muscle relaxation training, as previously outlined in this chapter, is begun. Once the client is relaxed, he or she is instructed to imagine the least anxiety-provoking situation on the list. The client is further instructed to maintain the relaxation response while continuing to imagine the anxiety-provoking situation. If the client begins to feel any anxiety, he or she is asked to indicate this to the counselor simply by raising the right index finger. At this signal, the counselor immediately advises the client to terminate the anxiety-provoking image and to engage in simple relaxation. This procedure is repeated until the client is able to imagine the scene for 2 min without experiencing any anxiety. Once the anxiety is reduced, the client should repeat the scene three to five times to consolidate gains and to create a learning history. Every item on the hierarchy list will be presented in just this fashion until the client is able to imagine all the scenes while maintaining a complete sense of relaxation.

SD will typically be accomplished over a number of sessions, but there are no set rules for time span. In general, progress is determined through the client's self-report. Following desensitization to the hierarchy list, the counselor should attempt to generalize these results to the client's real world. This is easily accomplished by establishing another hierarchical list that revolves around real-life situations that the client is likely to encounter in the days and weeks ahead.

Systematic desensitization is highly effective and easily utilized in all settings. It should be used as an adjunct to a comprehensive therapy program, and it will be particularly useful when anxiety or fear inhibits clients' ability to abstain or to moderate their substance abuse. This is a broadly used technique that enhances multifaceted treatment programs, but as with other techniques, it is not useful for all substance abusers, and it should be used only when indicated.

SKILLS TRAINING

Life skills are vital to the change process for substance-abusing clients. First, clients need coping skills in order to deal with situations that would otherwise be associated with drug use. Second, as clients develop life skills, they can begin to find success in achieving the related goals of their treatment plans. Third, intrapersonal and interpersonal skills are important for long-term maintenance of new, positive lifestyles. Seven skills that are particularly helpful in recovery are: (1) assertiveness, (2) social skills, (3) behavioral self-control, (4) identifying alternatives to drug and alcohol use, (5) problem solving, (6) dealing with emotions, and (7) stress management.

SUBSTANCE REFUSAL AND ASSERTIVENESS

Behavioral training techniques are especially important in helping clients develop the specific core skills needed to refuse drugs or alcohol. Similar skills and training processes can be used for both prevention and treatment. Coombs and Howatt (2005) list a number of core refusal skills that they find important for adolescent substance abusers. In fact, the same skills are urgently needed by all clients in the process of recovery. It appears that people with generally good interpersonal skills will be likely to be successful in carrying out the specific task of drink or drug refusal. These skills include the following:

- asking for help
- giving instructions
- convincing others
- knowing your feelings
- expressing your feelings
- dealing with someone else's anger
- dealing with fear
- using self-control
- standing up for your rights
- responding to teasing
- avoiding trouble with others
- keeping out of fights
- dealing with embarrassment
- dealing with being left out
- responding to persuasion
- responding to failure
- dealing with an accusation
- getting ready for a difficult conversation
- dealing with group pressure
- making a decision

The refusal skills training program is conducted through modeling, role playing, and performance feedback, with major attention being focused on the transfer of learning to adapt to real-life environments.

Closely related to substance refusal is a common concern of substance-abusing clients: the difficulty they have in asserting themselves. Assertion is the behavior or trait that allows people to appropriately express their personal rights and feelings. In this respect, assertion may be an expression of positive feelings ("I love you") or negative feelings ("I'm angry because you're insensitive"). Assertion, too, can be as simple as saying "yes" or "no" or even expressing an opinion that runs counter to the group opinion. The appropriateness of the assertive response, or the indicator that a response is assertive, is judged by three criteria:

1. Does the assertion result in a desired outcome; that is, does something change in the direction you want it to change as a result of your being assertive?
2. Is the assertive response acceptable to you; that is, do you feel good about your style and good about the way you handled and resolved the situation?

3. Is your assertion acceptable to and good for the person you are asserting
    yourself to? Aggression, which might bring about a behavior change and make
    you feel more powerful, is inappropriate, because it is unacceptable for the
    other person.

Assertion is best understood when compared with three other behavioral responses: (1) aggression, (2) passivity/aggression, and (3) passivity. A short vignette
will clarify the differences.

> Joe was a polydrug abuser who had recently discontinued all substance use. He was
> feeling pretty good about this accomplishment and had not had any urges to use sub-
> stances. To celebrate his victory, Joe asked his wife to join him for a special dinner at a
> local restaurant. The sky was the limit, and he ordered his favorite meal, very rare
> prime rib of beef. When his meal came, he quickly realized that his beef was over-
> cooked. He had been given assertion training in his therapy, and he chose to make the
> following response to the waiter who had brought his dinner.

WAITER: Is everything OK here?
JOE: No. I ordered very rare prime rib, and this meat is overcooked. Would you
please take it back to the kitchen and get me a rare one.
WAITER: I'm very sorry, sir. Certainly.
JOE: Thank you.

> After this conversation Joe felt very good. He had a slight amount of anxiety but
> recognized that it was his right to ask for and receive exactly what he had ordered. He
> discussed the situation with his wife and recounted to her three other ways he might
> have responded in the past.
> When he was intoxicated, for example, the situation might have gone as follows:

WAITER: Is everything OK here?
JOE: This damn steak is a piece of crap, and I'm not going to put up with this. Get
the manager, you idiot.

> Here Joe would have been aggressive. He would have upset his wife, angered the
> waiter, and been forced to leave without eating. This response would not have been
> appropriate, because it would not have been acceptable to him, his wife, the waiter,
> or the manager.
> When he was angry with himself and everybody else but not intoxicated, this
> might have been the result:

WAITER: Is everything OK here?
JOE: Yes, thank you.
JOE (TO HIS WIFE): Can you believe this crap? Look at this lousy prime rib. I'm never
coming back here.

Throughout the course of the meal Joe makes a mess with bread crumbs and spills
water, but he never voices his discontent to the waiter. He leaves a very small tip.

> This response would have been passive/aggressive. Joe would have felt slighted and
> angry but would have been fearful of expressing his feelings or of demanding his rights.
> The response would have upset his wife, made him feel weak and powerless, and
> confused the waiter, who would have wondered why such a small tip was left and why
> Joe had made such a mess. Clearly this response would not have been appropriate.

When everything seemed to be going all right and Joe was not intoxicated, this might have happened:

WAITER: Is everything OK here?

JOE: Yes, thank you—everything is lovely.

> Joe feels a slow burn in his stomach and becomes very anxious. He does not like the prime rib but is afraid to say anything for fear that the waiter will retaliate and his wife will be upset.

Joe would have convinced himself that it was no big deal and would have tried to enjoy himself. He would have left a big tip. He would have felt weak, powerless, and overwhelmed. He would have become angry later that evening and would have drunk to overcome his negative emotional state. This passive response would have diminished his self-esteem. Despite being perfectly acceptable to the waiter and his wife, this response would also have been inappropriate.

Clearly, the assertive response is the most acceptable for all involved. It improves one's self-image, self-esteem, and self-confidence, and it does not injure anyone in the process. Joe had a long history of nonassertion followed by decreased self-esteem, feelings of self-pity, and consequent intoxication. With assertion training he felt that he had much more personal power, his self-esteem improved, and he had far fewer episodes of self-pity and drinking. Thus, the use of assertion training with Joe, as with other substance abusers, is justified by the fact that by teaching new ways of coping with difficult social and emotional situations, we effectively eliminate many cues to excessive drinking (such as anxiety due to nonassertion). In essence, assertion training provides substance abusers with a healthy alternative to substance use.

Assertion consists of both verbal and behavioral components. These components should be melded to form an appropriate response that, after practice, is comfortable for the client, appears rational, and is not too anxiety-provoking:

1. *The assertive statement*—The appropriate assertive response should include the following components: "I feel _____ [emotion] because you _____ [action]. Would you please _____ [change statement]."
2. *Duration*—Assertive responses should be slightly longer than nonassertive responses.
3. *Voice tone*—Assertive responses should be made in a firm, slightly loud (not yelling, whining, or shrieking) voice.
4. *Request for a behavior change*—Requests to change behavior can be framed in the present ("Please leave now") or in the future ("Next time please call before you visit").
5. *Eye contact*—During assertive responses clients should maintain a steady (not glaring) eye contact.
6. *Gesticulation*—During assertive responses clients should use their hands to effectively accentuate what they are saying.
7. *Posture*—During assertive responses the client should sit or stand up straight, with shoulders squared and trunk slightly forward.
8. *Affect*—During assertive responses the client's affect must be appropriate to the situation. If the situation is serious, look serious; if it is humorous, look amused.

These components are taught to clients in assertion training. Some clients need to work in all areas, others in only a few. The initial evaluation will enable the counselor to clearly understand what type of training is needed. Before assertion training can be done, the client must be prepared for the treatment. The counselor should spend time discussing assertion as a behavior, its utility in people's lives, and the client's lack of assertiveness. This should not be a punitive exercise but rather an exploratory process in which clients are enlightened about behavioral patterns. Once they have explored their fears and myths concerning assertion and are fully prepared, training can begin. The most frequently used treatment components in assertion training programs are behavioral rehearsal, modeling, coaching, and feedback.

In behavioral rehearsal, clients are given the opportunity to practice and role-play appropriate assertive responses in problem situations. Brief scenes are enacted to closely approximate natural situations. As clients practice appropriate assertion, their ability to be assertive increases, as does the likelihood that the assertive response tendency will be strengthened. Sometimes, especially for homework assignments, it is effective to have clients do covert behavioral rehearsal in which they simply imagine themselves responding to problem situations in an effective, assertive fashion.

Another important form of behavioral rehearsal is known as role reversal. Clients are required to play the recipient of the assertive response, and the counselor plays the role of the client in an assertive way. This type of rehearsal provides clients with a deeper understanding of their assertion deficit.

In modeling, clients observe the counselor acting in an appropriately assertive way. The model acts as a stimulus for similar behavior in the client. The counselor can adjust and improvise for the client's benefit. In addition, the client is able to ask questions, and the counselor can demonstrate a broad array of responses. This live modeling in the office is a relatively efficient and inexpensive method to teach appropriate assertive behavior. Coaching is similar to modeling, but in this procedure the counselor describes appropriate assertive behavior to the client.

Finally, feedback lets clients know how well their assertion training is progressing. Positive feedback ("You're doing a great job") is more effective than negative feedback ("No, that was a passive response"). It more rapidly changes the client's style of behavioral response and ultimately increases self-confidence, self-esteem, and assertive ability.

The major treatment components for assertion training are most effective when used in combination. Assertion is a complex behavior that substance abusers often lack, but acceptable assertion training can nevertheless usually be given in eight to ten 1-hr sessions. Again, practice and positive reinforcement from the therapist are essential if one expects the behavior to be ingrained and well learned. Assertion training results in the expression of some anxiety. Therefore, it should always be preceded by a competent protocol of relaxation training.

Social Skills

Fields (2010, in press) suggests that interpersonal skills training is an important aspect of treatment for people with substance use problems. Such skills are important because they can provide a means for coping with high-risk situations and can be used to obtain social support. Many clients may have failed to learn social skills or have lost the use of their skills through years of heavy drinking or other drug use. Among the key interpersonal skills they address in their client training program are the following:

- starting conversations
- giving and receiving compliments
- nonverbal communication
- feeling talking (the ability to describe emotional states) and listening skills
- learning to be assertive
- giving criticism
- receiving criticism about drinking
- refusing a drink
- refusing requests
- forming close and intimate relationships
- enhancing social support networks

Counselors help their clients build these skills by providing guidelines, using modeling, guiding clients in behavioral rehearsal role playing, and equipping them with practice exercises and work sheets.

BEHAVIORAL SELF-CONTROL

Behavioral self-control training teaches clients how to make desired changes in their own behaviors. People learn how to analyze their own substance use, monitor their consumption, and use self-reinforcement and stimulus control methods to reach their abstinence or moderation goals. In the long run, people tend to find that they can use these same self-control skills to meet goals in other aspects of their lives.

In order for people to implement the skill of self-control, they have to identify very clear and measurable behavioral goals. In most instances, clients need assistance from the counselor in making the transition from diffuse, general goals ("I want to use crack a lot less next year" or "I want to be more physically fit") to specifics ("I am going to limit my drinking to a maximum of three drinks per day next week" or "I will spend one-half hour on the treadmill before going to work each day next week").

Having measurable short-term goals enables clients to monitor their activities and observe their own progress toward long-term success. Self-monitoring also makes it possible for people to set up rewards that can help them stay motivated. Clients can be encouraged to identify motivators that are meaningful to them and to create plans for giving themselves periodic rewards for good efforts. There is great variation in the kinds of rewards that people find motivating. The important factor here is for clients to set challenging but doable goals and to identify rewards that fit their own interests.

Clients who are trying to lessen or change current behaviors should also be asked to identify aspects of the behavior that they like. The question they ask themselves is, "What is the desired effect that I get from drinking? Smoking? Overeating?" Clients also identify the situations in which their urge to participate in the negative behavior is strongest. Finally, as clients recognize that the behaviors being addressed fill certain functions in their lives, they are asked to identify new ways for achieving the same desired effects.

Providing training in the skills of behavioral self-control places in clients' own hands a technology they can use for addressing a variety of different goals as they arise. When a client's self-control goal involves drinking, say, in moderation, the counselor will need to provide advice about safe drinking levels and information about the complex strategies involved. A goal of moderation may be realistic for an individual who is young and healthy, who has not shown symptoms of physical addiction to alcohol, whose problem is of short duration, who has not yet developed a large number of life problems associated with alcohol, and who objects to abstinence. Even so, controlled drinkers are not normal social drinkers. They should be willing to be on guard and to carefully choose the time, the place, the amount, and the circumstances of any drinking that takes place. They also need to learn how to approximate the behaviors of social drinkers by using such techniques as spacing, measuring, and mixing their drinks.

Those clients who choose to work toward moderation must make clear decisions about their level-of-consumption goals. Based on the results of much research with early-stage problem drinkers, it is suggested that clients should be discouraged from setting goals involving more than four drinks a day, from drinking even a small amount on a daily basis, and from drinking in situations that have been problematic in the past. The setting of "drinking limits" is essential and should involve a careful analysis of the clients' coping skills, their environment, and their commitment. Some research has suggested that safe consumption never exceeds two drinks per day, but the drinking should be spaced out and not conglomerated so that instead of a two drink per day limit the client chooses to have it all in one 14-drink event! Clients trying to moderate drinking are well advised to accept the recommendation of a 3-week period of total abstinence, whether they were working toward long-term outcomes of abstinence or moderation. This initial period of abstinence gives people the chance to improve their cognitive functioning, to identify situations associated with urges to drink, to identify the coping methods that worked for them, and to have an early experience of success.

ALTERNATIVES TO SUBSTANCE USE

As people remove alcohol and other drugs from the center stage of their lives, they often find it difficult to fill the gap that has been left. After years of substance abuse, they are left with few other activities that bring them pleasure. Activities that they have enjoyed are usually associated with alcohol use.

When counselors work with clients on developing alternative activities, they should begin by asking people to brainstorm as long a list as they can to devise activities that they might enjoy. From this list, clients choose one or two that they could picture themselves getting involved in immediately. The aspect of this process that most calls on new skills is moving an activity from imagination to reality. Asking clients what obstacles might stand in the way of beginning to participate in a selected activity within a week will assure open discussion and problem solving around the assumption of nonproblematic alternative behaviors.

Once potential obstacles have been identified, people can consider and select strategies for overcoming the obstacles either on their own or with the help of others.

PROBLEM SOLVING

Niaura and Abrams (2009) address problem-solving skills suggesting that substance-abusing clients need practical strategies for daily hassles without returning to alcohol or drug use. The authors also suggest that clients should learn to conceptualize their difficulties as problems that can be solved. The steps their clients learn include defining the problem, generating alternatives, deciding on a solution, and evaluating the outcome.

Some counselors use a problem-solving conceptualization that is based on the Alcoholics Anonymous (AA) serenity prayer:

> Grant me the serenity to accept what I cannot change, the courage to change the things I can, and the wisdom to know the difference.

As the therapist teaches clients the steps of identifying and solving problems, he or she adds an additional component: a decision point for considering whether it is more appropriate to take action in response to a particular issue or to move into acceptance instead.

DEALING WITH EMOTIONS

Substance use tends to mask emotions and fend off strong feelings, so people in early recovery sometimes have difficulty identifying and dealing with affect. Gaining skills in this area involves learning first to recognize emotions and then to deal with them. Once clients have begun to focus on recognizing their emotions they can learn to accept them. Part of the skill training around emotions is cognitive, in the sense that people learn to replace thoughts like "I shouldn't be feeling this way" with ideas like "I accept that it's okay to have this feeling as long as my behavior is appropriate." The skill set around dealing with emotions can then move in the direction of deciding what behaviors are acceptable and helpful in response to the feelings that have been identified. Clients can decide among such options as expressing their feelings to others, changing their own self-talk around emotions, taking action to change situations that invoke negative feelings, or getting help from others. Learning this skill can both lead to a fuller emotional life and, at the same time, address the issue that negative or positive feeling states can be risk situations for relapse.

STRESS MANAGEMENT

Stress management skills are especially important as people embark on the journey to recovery. People who have routinely used drugs to cope with stress in the past are unlikely to have learned other methods for dealing with environmental demands. When stressful situations arise, the individual's sobriety and health are placed at risk.

Training in this area should focus on helping clients to have a repertoire of skills available for coping with new demands. People can deal with stress by changing their thinking, by changing their responses, or by changing the environment itself. A person who has learned effective stress management is one who can choose freely from among these options.

People can often deal with stress by purposely changing their thought processes. Physiological stress responses arise because people interpret a particular situation as stressful. A change in thinking patterns helps clients recognize that their assumptions are not the only ones possible. Clients can develop cognitive skills that help them identify and rehearse different thoughts about the situations they encounter. They can change their "self-talk" to the degree that a physical stress response is actually avoided.

Of course, stressors can be very real despite our attempts to interpret them differently. Relaxation methods like the ones introduced earlier in this chapter can be used on a regular basis to limit the physical effects of stress.

Sometimes, though, people can reduce their levels of stress by making changes in their environments and thereby preventing stressful situations from occurring. Clients can adapt their problem-solving skills to deal more effectively with situations that relate either directly or indirectly to substance use.

In fact, all of the skills we have discussed in this section have a dual purpose: helping to interrupt substance use behaviors as well as improving healthy functioning. Training across all the skills normally includes a combination of modeling, practice, and feedback and can take place in either individual or group settings.

MEDICATIONS

A substantial amount of work has occurred to make medications available for the treatment of substance use disorders. The most widely used medicines are for opiate dependence and alcohol dependence. They have been tested in numerous research trials and are now routinely prescribed by physicians in their offices and in substance abuse treatment agencies. Methadone is a very common "agonist" drug used as a maintainence medication because it has a slow onset of action and a long half-life. The use of Methadone is called replacement therapy, and it is given to dependent opiate users as a replacement for their opiate of choice. Methadone programs also require that clients receive counseling services. A partial agonist called Buprenorphine (Suboxone) has recently been made available for the treatment of opiate addiction. This drug reduces opiate cravings and it has fewer negative effects than Methadone such as few or no withdrawal symptoms upon withdrawal and less chance of overdose even if combined with other opiates. Buprenorphine also has little street value and it can be dispensed in a doctor's office thus avoiding the need to attend Methadone treatment clinics. Counseling is also required for appropriate case management when clients are using Buprenorphine.

Antabuse has been used in the treatment of alcohol dependence for years. This drug produces vomiting, nausea, facial flushing, and severe headaches if taken following the consumption of alcohol. The severe alcohol–antabuse reaction means that only motivated and well–supervised clients receive this medication.

Naltrexone is another medication used to help in the treatment of alcohol dependence. This drug blunts some of the "high" associated with alcohol use. Similarly, a drug called Acamprosate is an alcohol effects blocking agent. Clients who use Naltrexone or Acamprosate have lower relapse rates than those not using the medications. Physicial prescribing and supervision are required for both of these drugs.

Substantial controversy exists over whether any drug should be employed in the treatment of alcohol or drug-dependent clients. However, the research is clear that these preparations can be significant contributors to successful treatment outcome for some clients. A careful analysis of motivation, commitment, physical health, and client desire must be completed before the decision to use medication to support counseling outcomes is made.

LINKING CLIENTS TO 12-STEP AND OTHER SELF-HELP GROUPS

Many people are helped by "12-step" programs, including AA and related groups such as Narcotics Anonymous (NA) and Cocaine Anonymous (CA). These self-help groups operate around the world and provide a social support system for recovery and a process for personal development that encourages looking inward and addressing issues obscured by alcohol and drug use (Coombs and Howatt, 2005). In general, this program should not be conceptualized as a form of treatment. Rather, the groups exist to support recovering alcoholics or drug abusers in their rehabilitation process. The description that is read at the beginning of most 12-step meetings is as follows:

> Alcoholics Anonymous [Narcotics Anonymous] is a fellowship of men and women who share their experience, strength, and hope with each other that they may solve their common problem. The only requirement for membership is a desire to stop drinking [drug abuse]. There are no dues or fees for AA membership; we are self-supporting through our own contributions. AA is not allied with any sect, denomination, political group, organization, or institution; does not wish to engage in any controversy, neither endorses nor opposes any causes. Our primary purpose is to stay sober and help other alcoholics to achieve sobriety.

These organizations have minimal formal structure, and they have no method of punishment or exclusion. They shun professionalism and report that their only authority is shared experience. The AA and NA programs are expressed in two sets of principles that have been developed since the inception of AA in 1935. The Twelve Steps came first as a program for personal recovery from drug or alcohol problems, and the Twelve Traditions, which are principles for relationships between groups, came second. NA, which was developed after AA, is a separate organization that uses most of the ideas and principles of AA.

The Twelve Steps of AA and NA are introduced with this sentence: "Here are the steps we took, which are suggested as a program for recovery":

Step 1: Admitted we were powerless over alcohol [drugs] that our lives had become unmanageable.

Step 2: Came to believe that a Power greater than ourselves could restore us to sanity.

Step 3: Made a decision to turn our will and our lives over to the care of God as we understood Him.

Step 4: Made a searching and fearless moral inventory of ourselves.

Step 5: Admitted to God, to ourselves, and to another human being the exact nature of our wrongs.

Step 6: Were entirely ready to have God remove all these defects of character.

Step 7: Humbly asked Him to remove our shortcomings.

Step 8: Made a list of all persons we had harmed and became willing to make amends to them all.

Step 9: Made direct amends to such people wherever possible, except when to do so would injure them or others.

Step 10: Continued to take personal inventory and when we were wrong, promptly admitted it.

Step 11: Sought through prayer and meditation to improve our conscious contact with God as we understood Him, praying only for knowledge of His will for us and the power to carry that out.

Step 12: Having had a spiritual awakening as the result of these Steps, we tried to carry this message to alcoholics [drug abusers] and practice these principles in all our affairs.

Source: From Alcoholics Anonymous World Services, Inc., New York, NY. Used with permission.

As the Twelve Steps became more broadly known, AA grew. This growth necessitated guidelines for the interrelationships among groups, and hence the Twelve Traditions of AA were developed. These were consequently melded into the experiences of other Twelve Steps groups:

1. Our common welfare should come first; personal recovery depends upon AA unity. Each member of AA is but a small part of a great whole. AA must continue to live or most of us will surely die. Hence our common welfare comes first. But individual welfare follows close afterward.
2. For our group purpose there is but one ultimate authority—a loving God as He may express Himself in our group conscience. Our leaders are but trusted servants; they do not govern.
3. The only requirement for AA membership is a desire to stop drinking. Our membership ought to include all who suffer from alcoholism. Hence we may refuse none who wish to recover. Nor ought AA membership ever depend on money or conformity. Any two or three alcoholics gathered together for sobriety may call themselves an AA group.
4. Each group should become autonomous except in matters affecting other groups or AA as a whole.
5. Each group has but one primary purpose—to carry its message to the alcoholic who still suffers.
6. An AA group ought never endorse, finance, or lend the AA name to any related facility or outside enterprise, lest problems of money, property, and prestige divert us from our primary purpose.
7. Every AA group ought to be fully self-supporting, declining outside contributions. No contributions or legacies from nonmembers are accepted at the General Service Office in New York City, and no more than $500,000 per year from any one member, and for only one year after death.
8. AA should remain forever nonprofessional, but our service centers may employ special workers.
9. AA, as such, ought never be organized; but we may create service boards or committees directly responsible to those they serve. The small group may elect its

secretary, the large group its rotating committee, and the groups of large metropolitan areas their central committee, which often employs a full-time secretary. The AA General Service Board serves as the custodian of AA tradition and is the receiver of voluntary AA contributions. It is authorized by the groups to handle our overall relations, and it guarantees the integrity of all our publications.

10. AA has no opinion on outside issues; hence the AA name ought never be drawn into public controversy.

11. Our public relations policy is based on attraction rather than promotion; we need to always maintain personal anonymity at the level of press, radio, and film.

12. Anonymity is the spiritual foundation of all our traditions, ever reminding us to place principles before personalities.

Source: From Alcoholics Anonymous World Services, Inc., New York, NY. Used with permission.

AA and NA meetings are available almost everywhere. The recovering substance abuser can, if he or she looks hard enough, usually find at least one meeting each day. There are two types of meetings, open and closed. Anyone is welcome at the open meetings, where one or two members typically tell their own stories of "how I used to be" and "how I am now." Only members are allowed to attend closed meetings, because these tend to be much more personal and intimate. During these meetings, personal problems or interpretations of the Twelve Steps or Twelve Traditions are usually discussed.

AA and NA, then, are widely available, cost-effective support programs for those alcoholics or drug-dependent individuals who choose to use them. We reiterate that AA is not a treatment modality. While a client is in the process of receiving professional services, participation in self-help can be seen as a supportive adjunct. Subsequently, 12-step groups can serve as a source of support and inspiration throughout the recovery process for those people who are attracted to them. AA is not for everybody, as no approach is, and it is unwise to force this modality on clients. AA members clearly have a great belief in the Twelve Steps and Twelve Traditions, and if these are not compatible with a client's thinking or belief system, it is probably unwise to coerce him or her to conform to this mode of thought. It is a good idea, however, to encourage clients to try out 12-step participation and to seek groups that are comfortable for them. "Twelve-step programs are fundamentally 'programs of attraction' and the therapist must achieve a fine balance between getting someone over the initial obstacles to attendance and engagement and exerting a level of coercion that inspires rebellion" (Zweben, 1995, p. 125).

It is ultimately the counselor's responsibility to design individualized plans with clients, as opposed to forcing them to adapt themselves to what is easily available. Counselors should be aware not only of 12-step groups but also of other self-help groups that might be of interest to some of their clients.

For instance, Self Management and Recovery Training (SMART) (SMART Recovery, 2009) is not "professional treatment", rather, it offers freely available peer support groups based on a different philosophy of recovery. The differences between SMART Recovery and 12-step programs are outlined here www.smartrecovery.org, as a broader introduction to this alternative to traditional self-help groups.

SMART offers free face-to-face and online mutual help groups. SMART helps people recover from all types of addictive behaviors, including: alcoholism, drug abuse, substance abuse, drug addiction, alcohol abuse, gambling addiction, cocaine addiction, and addiction to other substances and activities. SMART is an alternative to AA and NA. Smaller than AA, SMART sponsors more than 500 face-to-face meetings around the world, and 16 plus online meetings per week. In addition, they host an online message board which is used as a forum in which to learn about SMART and seek support.

SMART's stated purpose is to support individuals who have chosen to abstain, or are considering abstinence from any type of addictive behaviors (substances or activities), by teaching how to change self-defeating thinking, emotions, and actions; and to work towards long-term satisfactions and quality of life.

They state in their materials:

1. We help individuals gain independence from addictive behavior.
2. We teach how to
   a. enhance and maintain motivation to abstain
   b. cope with urges
   c. manage thoughts, feelings and behavior
   d. balance momentary and enduring satisfaction
3. Our efforts are based on scientific knowledge, and evolve as scientific knowledge evolves.
4. Individuals who have gained independence from addictive behavior are invited to stay involved with us, to enhance their gains and help others.

Source: From SMART Recovery®, Mentor, OH. Used with permission.

SMART assumes that addictive behavior can arise from both substance use (e.g., psychoactive substances of all kinds, including alcohol, nicotine, caffeine, food, illicit drugs, and prescribed medications), and involvement in activities (e.g., gambling, sexual behavior, eating, spending, relationships, exercise, etc.), and that there are degrees of addictive behavior, and that all individuals to some degree experience it. For some individuals the negative consequences of addictive behavior (which can involve several substances or activities) become so great that change becomes highly desirable.

Much of the SMART rationale is based on the field of cognitive-behavioral therapy (CBT), and particularly from Rational Emotive Behavior Therapy, as developed by Albert Ellis, Ph.D. In general, CBT views addictive behavior more as a complex maladaptive behavior than as a disease.

In sum, then,

1. SMART Recovery has a scientific foundation, not a spiritual one.
2. SMART Recovery teaches increasing self-reliance, rather than powerlessness.
3. SMART Recovery views addictive behavior as a maladaptive, bad habit, rather than as a disease.
4. SMART Recovery meetings are discussion meetings in which individuals talk with, encourage, and share ideas with one another.
5. SMART Recovery encourages attendance for months to years, but probably not a lifetime.
6. There are no sponsors in SMART Recovery.
7. SMART Recovery discourages use of labels such as "alcoholic" or "addict."

Source: From SMART Recovery®, Mentor, OH. Used with permission.

Clearly, this program has been designed to provide an alternative for people whose approach to substance abuse is incompatible with that of AA.

Outlined below are common ideas behind SMART and Rationale Recovery (another rational–emotive approach which is an alternative to traditional AA or NA groups):

1. People are largely responsible for their drug and alcohol use behaviors.
2. People do "get over", that is, completely recover from their addictions.
3. Lifetime membership is not a requirement. It is thought that some people recover quickly, others in one or two years.
4. Labeling oneself as an addict or alcoholic is discouraged to avoid the negative outcomes associated with labeling.
5. Alcohol dependence or other drug dependencies are not "diseases" in the common sense. They are, instead, life consuming, massive behavioral problems with broad ramifications and people with these problems need to learn to cope with them and take direct responsibility for their life course.
6. People with alcohol and other drug use problems are good people. Removing the alcohol or drug problem makes people happier and healthier, but it does not in and of itself make them "better people."
7. Denial is a self-preservation method and counselors should work to help their clients get to a process of change that is internally motivated, safe, and productive. Confrontation of denial often mobilizes defenses even more so counselors can be most effective using motivational techniques to help ease the transition from problem use to nonuse.
8. Self-recovery, spontaneous remission, and user directed change happens all the time. A person's own resources and decision making capacity coupled with other variables such as familial support is often the key to a life free of substances. Many times counselors can be part of this process but it requires a belief that clients can do it on their own and that the capacity for change is respected. In cases like this the counselor might be seen as a consultant and only seen once or twice. This speaks to the need to view every interaction we have with a person suffering from substance use problems as a discreet opportunity to instill hope, provide encouragement, and bolster self confidence and self efficacy.

Source: From SMART Recovery®, Mentor, OH. Used with permission.

Women for Sobriety (2009) (Web site: www.womenforsobriety.org) also provides an alternative to AA. Some women express the need for a philosophical approach that is positive in nature and that emphasizes empowerment, rather than powerlessness. The New Life Acceptance Program of Women for Sobriety has its own set of affirmations:

1. I have a life-threatening problem that once had me.
2. Negative thoughts destroy only myself.
3. Happiness is a habit I will develop.
4. Problems bother me only to the degree I permit them to.
5. I am what I think.
6. Life can be ordinary or it can be great.
7. Love can change the course of my world.
8. The fundamental object of life is emotional and spiritual growth.
9. The past is gone forever.

10. All love given returns.
11. Enthusiasm is my daily exercise.
12. I am a competent woman and have much to give life.
13. I am responsible for myself and for my actions.

Source: From Women For Sobriety, Inc. Quakertown, PA. Used with permission.

Judicious use of these systems involves collaborative planning between counselor and client. As always, the final choice about strategies for recovery remains in the hands of the client.

CO-OCCURRING SUBSTANCE ABUSE AND MENTAL HEALTH PROBLEMS

Counselors working with substance abuse issues will find that many of their clients are also dealing with mental health concerns. Fields (2010, in press) reports that about one-third of patients with psychiatric disorders experience substance abuse and that more than one-half of substance-abusing clients have met the diagnostic criteria for a psychiatric disorder. The most common mental health issues for substance-abusing clients are anxiety and mood disorders, especially major depression.

Approaching this issue is complex because of the difficulty in identifying causal relationships. According to Fields, substance abuse or drug withdrawal can cause psychiatric symptoms, mimic psychiatric disorders, worsen the severity of psychiatric disorders, or mask psychiatric symptoms. The reverse is also true: Psychiatric behaviors can mimic behaviors associated with substance abuse or interfere with recovery from addiction. Of course, psychiatric and substance problems can coexist.

> One disorder may prompt the emergence of the other, or the two disorders may exist independently. Determining whether the disorders are related may be difficult, and may not be of great significance, when a patient has long-standing, combined disorders. Consider a 32-year-old patient with bipolar disorder whose first symptoms of alcohol abuse and mania started at age 18, who continues to experience alcohol dependence in addition to manic and depressive episodes. At this point, the patient has two well-developed independent disorders that both require treatment.

In the past, many addiction treatment providers insisted that mental health issues should be addressed only after a period of sobriety could serve to rule out alcohol or other drugs as the primary cause of behavioral symptoms. On the other hand, mental health treatment providers often focused on psychiatric issues and failed to recognize the role of substances in the symptoms being observed. Now, there is broad recognition that the only possible way to meet the needs of clients with co-occurring substance abuse and mental health concerns is through interdisciplinary teamwork and integrated treatment plans.

Effective work with individuals who are dually diagnosed requires monitoring the client's psychiatric symptoms on an ongoing basis. If the client is placed on medication for the treatment of psychiatric symptoms, provide support and try to help him or her gain understanding of the medication being used. Wallen and Weiner (1989) have also cautioned that one must be cautious with intense confrontation early in the treatment process to avoid increasing anxiety, which might worsen the client's psychiatric symptoms. As with all clients, present and discuss issues in a concrete and straightforward manner and help develop the coping skills necessary to deal with environmental and interpersonal stressors without having to resort to substance use.

Structure, guidance, and support as well as a focus on identifying cues for substance use and developing plans to deal with them effectively are key components to an effective therapy regime.

Another important issue with dually diagnosed individuals is to be on the alert for any changes in the individual's mental status that might indicate a worsening of his or her psychiatric problem.

Wallen and Weiner (1989) also suggest that competent care providers promote and support involvement in constructive leisure-time activities while supporting involvement in educational and vocational programs.

Where appropriate and in consultation with the client, involvement in 12-step programs should be considered. In this regard the counselor should consider specialized 12-step program meetings where the issues of dual diagnosis can be attended to and where there is an understanding of, and appreciation for, the complexities associated with taking medications associated with psychiatric illness.

In every other way treating an individual with co-occurring psychiatric problems is exactly like treating someone without one. The client must be respected and treated with dignity and compassion.

Like Wallen, Zweben (1995) also emphasizes the importance of encouraging people who are dealing with coexisting problems to attend 12-step meetings that are hospitable for people on medication.

The integrated and supportive approach suggested earlier is also strongly endorsed by Sciacca (1997), who points out

> Support, encouragement, and the belief in the possibility of change are essential. For clients who have severe mental health symptoms that may impair a vision for the future, the therapist must envision the outcome of change and present such possibilities to the client. The client participates in the course of action for change. (p. 45)

It is interesting to note that a strengths-based approach to treatment is also encouraged in a Treatment Improvement Protocol paper addressing substance abuse clients who have physical or cognitive disabilities.

> For treatment to succeed, all clients must understand the particular strengths that they can bring to the recovery process. A strengths-based approach to treatment is especially important for people with disabilities who may, because they have so frequently been viewed in terms of what they cannot or should not attempt, have learned to define themselves in terms of their limitations and inabilities. (Moore, 1998, chap. 3, p. 2)

In the context of this philosophy, treatment should be adapted to accommodate the needs of people with disabilities and individualized treatment plans should be the norm.

SUMMARY

The first step in the counseling process involves the establishment of a collaborative relationship. The counselor's success in establishing such relationships depends on such facilitative characteristics as empathy, genuineness, immediacy, warmth, respect, and cultural sensitivity. Skill in carrying out strategies that create a positive environment for change are also important for relationship-building.

Once a strong counseling relationship has been developed, the counselor can use various possibilities to interrupt substance use behaviors. Among the possibilities are helping the client identify and cope with high-risk situations, and using strategies such as relaxation training, modeling, contingency contracting, systematic desensitization, and covert aversion therapy. Life skills training addresses substance related behavior change and helps the client move toward accomplishment of other goals in his or her treatment plan. The skills training described in this chapter focuses on assertiveness, social skills, behavioral self-control, alternatives to drug and alcohol use, problem solving, dealing with emotions, and stress management. We also suggest that, although clients should not be coerced to join 12-step or other self-help groups, they should have the opportunity to try these popular and supportive programs. The application of these strategies for clients with co-occurring mental health problems and disabilities was also discussed.

QUESTIONS FOR THOUGHT AND DISCUSSION

1. Matt comes to the attention of the counselor through the employee assistance program at the factory where he works. He was referred because of absenteeism and what his supervisor considered "mood swings." Matt says that he is having a lot of stress at the plant. He has worked there for 12 years and believes himself to be good at his job. He says that his boss, who was transferred there from another location 2 years ago, is giving him a great deal of trouble. The two have had so many conflicts that Matt thinks his job is in jeopardy.

    Matt says that every morning the boss gets on his back about something. Matt wants to fight back, but he knows that he has to avoid trouble. Recently, he has been spending each morning seething. By the time the lunch break comes, he wants to explode. What he does instead is go to a neighborhood bar with a group of coworkers who have been going to the same place for years. Lately, Matt has found that he is drinking more beer than usual at lunchtime. Twice the supervisor said he smelled beer on his breath in the afternoon. The second time, Matt was declared unfit for duty and sent to the medical office. Most of the time, he feels as stressed in the afternoon as he does in the morning. As he puts it, "I can't wait to get home, put my feet up, smoke a couple of joints, and drink enough beer so I can go to sleep and start the whole thing again the next morning."

    Matt is interested in making some changes, because both his job and his marriage are close to being over. He feels limited in what he can do, however, because of his belief that the supervisor is the problem.

    Given Matt's situation, how might each of the following behavioral interventions be useful?

    a. identifying high-risk situations and discovering better coping strategies for dealing with them
    b. relaxation training
    c. contingency contracting
    d. assertiveness training

In general, how would you help Matt make changes in his substance use behavior?

2. Behavioral self-control training has been used to help people achieve moderation in their alcohol use. The idea of controlled drinking has become controversial, at least in part because people try to generalize about whether it is possible as an outcome. In fact, the question can be addressed most rationally if we think about individuals and the goals that might be right for them. In your own experience, have you worked with or known a person for whom moderation, rather than abstinence, might have been an appropriate goal? What characteristics did this person have? In contrast, what characteristics would make a person a poor candidate for moderation and a good candidate for abstinence?

REFERENCES

Carroll, K. M. (1998). A cognitive-behavioral approach: Treating cocaine addicts. In *Manual I: Therapy manual for drug addicts*. Rockville, MD: NIDA, DHHS.

Coombs, R., and Howatt, W., (2005). *The addictions counselor's desk reference*. Hoboken, NJ: Wiley.

Fields, R. (2010, in press). *Drugs in Perspective*. San Francisco: McGraw Hill.

Miller, W., & Brown, S. (2009). Why psychologists should treat alcohol and drug problems. In A. Marlatt and K. Witkiewitz (Eds.), *Addictive behaviors*. Washinton, DC: American Psychological Association.

Moore, D. (1998). Substance-use disorder treatment for people with physical and cognitive disabilities. In *Treatment improvement protocol 29*. Rockville, MD: Center for Substance Abuse Treatment.

Niaura, R., & Abrams, D. (2009). Smoking cessation: Progress, priorities, and prospectus. In A. Marlatt & K. Witkiewitz (Eds.), *Addictive behaviors*. Washington, DC: American Psychological Association.

Sciacca, K. (1997, February). Removing barriers: Dual diagnosis and motivational interviewing. *Professional Counselor, 12*(1), 41–46.

SMART Recovery. (2009, March). Retrieved March 26, 2009, from http://www.smartrecovery.org

Stitzer, M., Pierce, J., Petry, N., Kirby, K., Roll, J., Krasnansky, J., Cohen, A., Blaine, J., Vandrey, R., Kolodner, K., and Rui, L. (2009). Abstinence-based incentives in methadone maintainence: Interaction with intake stimulant test results. In A. Marlatt and K. Witkiewitz (Eds.), *Addictive behaviors*. Washington, DC: American Psychological Association.

Wallen, J. (1994). *Addiction in human development perspectives on addiction and recovery*. Binghamton, NY: Haworth Press.

Wallen, M., & Weiner, H. (1989). The dually diagnosed patient in an inpatient chemical dependency treatment program. *Alcoholism Treatment Quarterly 5*(1/2), 197–218.

Women for Sobriety. (2009). *New life program*. Retrieved February 26, 2009, from http://www.womenforsobriety.org

Zweben, J. A. (1995). Integrating psychotherapy and 12-step approaches. In A. M. Washton (Ed.), *Psychotherapy and substance abuse: A practitioner's handbook* (pp. 124–140). New York: Guilford Press.

6 | Empowering Clients Through Group Work

FOR SUBSTANCE-ABUSING clients, recovery is powerfully affected by the success of interpersonal relationships and the quality of social skills. Because group counseling focuses directly on these issues, it has great potential as a component of treatment.

> One of the main reasons the group approach has become so popular is that it is frequently more effective than the individual approach. This effectiveness stems from the fact that group members not only gain insight but practice new skills both within the group and in their everyday interaction outside the group. In addition, members of the group benefit from the feedback and insights of other group members as well as those of the practitioner. Groups offer many opportunities for modeling, and members can learn how to cope with their problems by observing others with similar concerns. (Corey, 2008, pp. 4–5)

The combination of collaborative group interaction and the practice of new skills has an excellent fit with the needs of clients who are dealing with substance abuse issues.

Clients with drug problems frequently come into treatment with distorted views of themselves and the world, primarily because years of drug use have clouded their perceptions. Years of drug use also tend to be associated with deficits in the social skills that are needed in a drug-free milieu. People seeking treatment often feel isolated and distrustful, especially when they have lost or destroyed any healthy relationships they might have had, because of involvement with drugs. Virtually all clients seeking help with substance-related issues have a need to develop and practice behaviors that are new or long-forgotten. Thus, for substance abuse clients, the opportunity to test distorted perceptions, to try out new behaviors, to receive feed-back about self-defeating actions, and to reach out to others in a safe environment is of clear value.

Although group counseling holds great promise as a strategy for substance abuse treatment, that promise has not always been realized. Unfortunately, the "conventional wisdom" of the past led to group work that either emphasized verbal confrontation or depended on didactic presentations of information. These methods were inconsistent with what is known about human behavior change and lacked many of the very characteristics that make group work effective.

In the past, group sessions for substance abusers focused on confrontation, with leaders and members putting a great deal of effort into "breaking through denial," or convincing clients to accept the reality of their addiction. In these sessions, the group process was considered successful only when the client verbalized his or her acceptance of the label "alcoholic" or "addict." This approach became prevalent, especially in inpatient settings, perhaps because group leaders failed to recognize how tenuous the connections are between "correct" verbalizations and actual be-havior change. It is possible that many clients bow to coercion and accept, at a su-perficial level, conceptualizations that they have not internalized. Using the group interaction for the purpose of encouraging this kind of compliance fails to take into account the realities of group interaction and influence. It has long been under-stood that there are clear differences between compliance and internalization. Compliance takes place because the individual accepts the influence of the group and wishes—consciously or unconsciously—to gain acceptance. Internalization takes place when the individual actually believes in the efficacy of the newly ac-quired cognitions or behavior. If substance abusers accept their new labels only at the compliance level, the effects on their behaviors may be limited to the context of the group or treatment setting. What has been seen as the success of "breaking through denial" may not, in fact, have any influence on the real-life behaviors we seek to influence.

Similarly, group modalities that focus on providing cognitive information may also lack relevance to behavior change. "Educational" approaches in the form of lectures about the dangers of drugs and alcohol were at one time used very widely, both as preventive tools and as treatment methods. Inpatient alcoholism treatment programs, for instance, were likely to spend a great deal of time on lectures con-cerning the disease concept and the negative effects of alcohol. Although this ap-proach might have affected cognitive knowledge, it does not appear to have had any measurable effect on behavior. As is the case with confrontation groups, clients may appear to have changed, but these changes do not make the transition to an-other environment.

The group modality will be more likely to live up to its promise as a component of substance abuse treatment if counselors help to create group environments that are empowering for clients. True empowerment is unlikely to occur in isolation, be-cause it includes components of both individual development and mutuality. Thus, groups with an empowerment focus have several commonalities:

1. The group structure is based on a collaborative style.
2. Interventions support clients' movement toward change.

3. Clients develop personal skills and strategies that are transferable to other settings.
4. The group leader models supportiveness and multicultural competence.

We will explore these positive aspects of group counseling in the remainder of this chapter.

THE COLLABORATIVE STYLE

A collaborative style of interaction respects the fact that clients can act as valuable resources for one another. This mode of interacting also recognizes that a group is most likely to be successful if members have a sense that the group belongs to them. Leadership of a group focused on substance abuse does require that the counselor work actively to keep the group focused and structured. It is possible, however, to accomplish this task in an environment of shared leadership, with the counselor acting as a facilitator. Groups that are collaborative and empowering share several characteristics, including the following:

- All group members are recognized as having something to offer in an atmosphere of shared leadership.
- Group members participate equally in decisions about the nature of the group process.
- The counselor, as group leader, models a respectful and supportive demeanor.
- The counselor appreciates the strengths and experience that each member brings to the process and encourages participants to acknowledge one another's strengths as well.

This approach may be especially important for substance abuse clients. These individuals may have little recent experience with mutually respectful interactions, so the counselor may need to model respect in order to help clients achieve that attitude in their behaviors toward one another. Many substance abuse clients also lack recent experience in having their contributions valued. This, too, is a perspective that the counselor can model as long as it is authentic.

GROUND RULES

In the substance abuse field, when a new group is being formed or when new members join an existing group, leaders usually provide clear guidelines on regular attendance, punctuality, confidentiality, and the like. In addition, such a group generally has a firm rule against attending in an intoxicated state.

The group process can be more empowering if the group as a whole has the opportunity to develop some of its own ground rules in addition to those set by the agency or program. Many substance abuse groups are time-limited, with most members joining at the same time. For these groups, ground rules can be set at the first session. Other groups in the substance abuse field are ongoing, with clients joining as they reach particular points in their recovery. In these groups, the ground rules should be reexamined regularly so that all group members have a chance to give input.

The rule-setting task is important because it provides an opportunity for early, meaningful interaction and invokes a sense of responsibility among group members.

It is also important because the ground rules themselves can be more responsive to client needs than leader-imposed regulations would be. Consider, for example, some of the ground rules devised by one group.

"Group members can swear, but not at one another."

This statement, which reflects a hard-won group consensus, provides a good example of a ground rule that differs from one that a leader might have devised. Group members believed that a general rule against use of "cuss words," which was suggested by one member, would be both unrealistic and overly moralistic. Their agreement to avoid swearing at one another came not from a discomfort with swearing per se but from an effort to encourage mutual respect. The members had first considered a rule stating that they would treat one another respectfully. The ensuing discussion of the meaning of the term *respect* led them to decide that the concept needed to be made more concrete if the rule were to be enforceable. The group reached consensus that a rule against swearing at one another, along with a rule proscribing physical violence of any kind, would help ensure at least minimally courteous interactions.

"Group members have the right to be quiet if they do not wish to take part in a particular discussion. Other members do not have the right to force them to participate but do have the right to ask them questions and encourage them to participate."

Group members realized that participation would be expected and that their success—individually and as a group—depended on their active commitment. Many clients, however, had previously experienced highly confrontive groups that placed pressure on individuals to respond to questions. They wanted to have the right to "pass" in a discussion, but they also wished to avoid situations in which members would remain passive and isolated. The solution on which they reached consensus involved an acceptance of group members' responsibility to encourage full participation but a refusal to use coercion as a means toward this end.

"Group members should not accuse one another of stupidity when they describe self-defeating behaviors."

Substance abuse clients know that many of their thoughts and behaviors have been self-defeating. In fact, one of the primary purposes of group counseling is to provide feedback regarding such distortions. The group members' concern had to do with the nature and style of the feedback being offered. The relevance of this ground rule became clear when it was actually used. Maria, a client who was attempting to abstain from cocaine use, was discussing her plans for the following Friday night:

MARIA: I've really been pleased with how well I've been doing avoiding tough situations. I've been spending a lot of time home with my ma and the kids, and I've been going to the church group. This Friday I'm going to see Paul, so things are going great.

JOE: Isn't that the guy you said was dealing? The guy that was your source?

MARIA: Yeah, but we've worked it all out. He's not gonna offer me any. He doesn't use that much, but when he does, he just goes in another room 'cause he knows I'm not using.

JANET: Maria, I can't believe you're talking about doing this when you've been working so hard staying straight. How could you do something so stupid?

MARIA: It is not stupid! I know I can handle it. He loves me, and I'm not going to spend the rest of my life locked up in the house. I don't want to hear any more about it.

JOE: Wait a minute. Let's back up. Janet, we sort of agreed we'd try to work with this kind of stuff without calling people stupid.

JANET: You're right. I know. Maria, I'm sorry. I'm just scared for you because I remember you saying when we were talking about triggers that going out with this guy was one of yours. Could we help you think of some other things you could do on the weekend for fun, or other people you might be able to spend time with?

MARIA: It's just that I feel so closed in being home all the time. I know it sounds like I don't want to stay straight, but I do. I wouldn't mind some help.

It was important to raise this issue with Maria and to help her recognize that she was walking into a perilous situation. Her reaction to Janet's first confrontation, however, was one of defensiveness. Substance abuse clients usually report having had many opportunities to hear their decisions labeled self-defeating or stupid. This group found it more useful to focus on practical strategies for working toward positive goals. Their ground rule reflected this preference.

SETTING GROUP GOALS

Group members often find the process of group goal setting to be an empowering experience. Khantzian, Halliday, and McAuliffe (1990) suggest that members be asked in an orientation session to discuss their hopes and expectations for the group, as well as their individual recovery goals. As individual clients share their thoughts, common themes emerge.

> While the members talk about their goals, the leader listens for shared themes, such as regaining control of one's life, rebuilding a sense of self, restoring and renewing damaged relationships, and returning to reality. He or she then reflects this common ground back to the group. This is the beginning of a basic technique and thrust of the work throughout the life of the group, whereby the leader identifies that common ground where the concerns of the members intersect, where cohesiveness grows, and where insight occurs. (pp. 57–58)

In fact, as this search for commonality is modeled by the leader, members learn how to approach one another in much the same way. When consensus about goals is reached at an early stage of the group's development, a climate of mutual support is engendered.

SUPPORT FOR CHANGE

As group leaders have moved away from the use of harsh confrontation and fact-filled lectures to inspire their clients, they must seek new ways to help their clients commit to change. The group counseling milieu provides a healthy environment for the use of evidence-based practices that have the potential to help participants embark on the journey toward transformation. Motivational interviewing (MI) and stages-of-change provide two examples of well-accepted practices being applied in the context of structured counseling groups.

MOTIVATION GROUP   Fields (2004) has built a group curriculum around MI. As clients are introduced to the purpose of their new group in the first session, they learn that the decisions they will make as part of the group process are under their own control. A handout about the purpose of the group reads as follows:

> This group is to help you gain back some control over your own choices and decisions about this time in your life, by giving you a chance to reevaluate your life, and what you may want to do about the concerns related to your behavior.... What you do with this information is up to you. The final choice and decisions about any changes you make in your lives is always your own. (Fields, 2004, p. 23)

Subsequent sessions are structured so that group exercises move clients through the step-by-step process involved in resolving their ambivalence about change. The second session asks group members to express their feelings related to change and to complete a self-assessment. Subsequent sessions focus in turn on ambivalence, allowing clients to weigh the costs and benefits of their behavior, and on the values that guide their life decisions. The fifth and final session emphasizes vision-building as a way to "evoke the client's intentions to change and strengthen optimism that change is possible" (p. 72) and ends with a reassessment of the clients' motivation for change.

STAGES-OF-CHANGE GROUP   Velasquez, Maurer, Crouch, and DiClemente (2001) have designed a structured group treatment based on the transtheoretical model of behavior change (DiClemente & Prochaska, 1998; Prochaska, DiClemente, & Norcross, 1992). This model views change as a progression through five stages: (1) *precontemplation*, when the person has not yet begun to consider the possibility or desirability of change; (2) *contemplation*, when the person does acknowledge a problem but is not yet ready to commit to change; (3) *preparation*, when plans for change begin to take shape; (4) *action*, when behavior modifications actually occur; and (5) *maintenance*, when the challenging, long-term effort involved in safeguarding one's new life takes place.

Velasquez and her colleagues use 14 group sessions to bring participants to a point of readiness for action. This 14-session sequence, *Thinking About Changing Substance Abuse*, is "designed to increase motivation and facilitate change in clients who (1) do not recognize they have a problem or are not motivated to change, (2) are thinking about changing, and (3) are preparing to change" (Velasquez et al., 2001, p. 3). The clients move through a number of interventions from learning about the stages of change in the first session; to increasing awareness of their current substance use; to weighing the positive and negative aspects of their substance use; to exploring the problems and challenges that might make change difficult; and, finally, to choosing goals and creating change plans. A second sequence, *Making Changes in Substance Use*, helps clients who are in the action or maintenance stages manage the myriad of issues related to the process of change.

Both the MI curriculum and the stages-of-change therapy demonstrate the importance of fitting interventions to clients' readiness for change. Once clients have made at least a tentative commitment to change, they are ready to embark on the development of recovery skills that are transferable to real-life situations.

TRANSFERABLE SKILLS

The group modality is most useful when clients have the opportunity to transfer newly learned attitudes and behaviors to other settings. Most promising are those group activities that focus on the development of concrete, usable skills and that provide the opportunity to rehearse new behaviors. Many of the approaches used in the group parallel the methods used in individual counseling. The group context, however, provides increased opportunities for modeling, for rehearsing interpersonal behaviors, for sharing feelings and ideas, and for gaining reinforcement as attempts at behavior change begin to succeed. Among the activities that lend themselves well to the group modality are analysis of drinking or drug-taking behaviors, development of alternative methods of coping, and training in problem solving and assertiveness.

Behavior Analysis

Substance-abusing clients, whether seen in individual or group situations, need to begin by assessing their current behaviors. This can be accomplished either through homework assignments completed individually and then shared with other group members or through group activities designed to elicit ideas concerning the antecedents and reinforcements associated with target behaviors.

If clients are being seen as outpatients, an initial homework assignment can involve keeping an alcohol consumption record. An example of such a record-keeping device is shown as Exhibit 6.1. This form has been used for members of a group of clients being seen as outpatients because of multiple arrests for driving under the influence (DUI) of alcohol. The careful record keeping involved helps them become more conscious of the amount they have been drinking; the people, places, and feelings associated with their drinking; and the risks and potential problems that their drinking behaviors might bring.

Clients are asked to complete the consumption record during the week between group meetings. When they return, they are asked to share the results with a partner and then to discuss their general impressions with the group as a whole. This set of activities helps individuals increase their knowledge of their own drinking behaviors, recognize similarities and differences with other group members, and perceive their own difficulties more clearly through identification with the behaviors of others. The fact that the forms are discussed in a group helps reinforce careful and accurate reporting.

In an inpatient setting or in a group whose participants have already achieved abstinence, similar results can be achieved through exercises carried out in the group. For example, McCrady, Dean, Dubreuil, and Swanson (1985) describe a group situation in which alcoholic clients are asked to brainstorm as many responses as they can think of to the question "Why do you think some people develop drinking problems?"

Usually, the brainstormed answers fit into the following categories: (1) life stresses (retirement, death of a loved one); (2) emotional or physiological problems (recurring anxiety, depression, chronic pain); (3) other people's behavior (unfaithful spouse, recalcitrant business partner, alcoholic parent); (4) drinking environments ("All my friends drink"); (5) heredity and early socialization ("My father is an alcoholic"); and (6) positive consequences ("I could socialize better") (McCrady et al.,

EXHIBIT 6.1	ALCOHOL-CONSUMPTION RECORD

Name _____

Date record begun _____ Date record ended _____

Date								
Place where drinking occurred								
Whom were you drinking with (relationship and number of people)?								
Feeling before drinking (see #3)								
Time drinking began								
Why did you begin drinking at this time?								
Number of standard drinks consumed (see #1)								
Feelings during drinking (see #3)								
Time drinking stopped								
Feelings after drinking (see #3)								
Amount of money spent on alcohol								
Did you drive after drinking?								
How risky do you think this drinking was for you on a scale of 1–4 (see #2)								

#1 *Standard drink*
10 oz beer
4 oz wine
1 oz hard liquor

#2 *Risk scale*
4—very risky
3—moderately risky

2—slightly risky
1—no risk

#3 *Feelings codes*
1. happy
2. bored
3. tense, nervous

4. relaxed
5. angry
6. tired, sleepy

7. calm, at ease
8. sick
9. depressed

1985, p. 432). Once the brainstormed items have been placed in these categories, responses can be labeled as antecedents or as reinforcements, thus laying the groundwork for a discussion of behavioral models of problem drinking while helping clients recognize similarities in their responses.

In another exercise used by McCrady and her colleagues (1985), clients focus on antecedents to drinking. Group brainstorming allows clients to become aware of the many possible antecedents to drinking by asking them to list as many triggers as they can. Group sessions can also focus on individuals, asking one client at a time to list the antecedents that seem to trigger drinking behaviors. Other group members provide support and help individuals identify connections or problems that might not otherwise be readily apparent. Although similar activities can be carried out on an individual basis, the group context for this effort helps generate fresh ideas and encourages the recognition that people can learn to take active responsibility for meeting their own special needs.

COPING MECHANISMS

Group exercises also lend themselves well to the process of helping clients develop methods for coping with stressors or high-risk situations. A workshop strategy can be used both to help group members recognize situations that serve as substance use triggers and to assist them in developing more effective mechanisms for dealing with these pressures. Clients can learn to deal with environmental demands and their responses to them by (1) altering their environment through problem solving, lifestyle changes, and the development of assertiveness and other interpersonal skills; (2) altering their own mental processes; or (3) altering nervous system activation through relaxation training, meditation, or biofeedback. A number of group exercises can be used to bring about this kind of learning.

IDENTIFYING STRESSORS AND HIGH-RISK SITUATIONS   Group members can work together to brainstorm a list of environmental factors that they tend to find stressful or that trigger their own drinking or other drug-taking behaviors. When the list has been generated, clients can identify both the scope and the commonality of their concerns. Even more important is the fact that this list-building brings stressors to the conscious level so that they can be addressed in a realistic fashion.

COGNITIVE RESTRUCTURING   The group context can also be helpful for working on clients' reactions to situations that may be evaluated as demanding. Restructuring involves helping clients recognize the role of their own cognitions in mediating arousal. This recognition allows them to change unrealistic cognitions into more rational interpretations that will, in turn, lead to more appropriate responses. Group members can assist one another in recognizing examples of their own irrational responses and identifying and rehearsing alternate self-messages that can, in time, become automatic.

RELAXATION TRAINING   Not all stressors can be prevented or reinterpreted. Clients also need to be able to intervene at the point of the physiological stress response. Probably most appropriate for use in a group situation is the muscle relaxation procedure which we discussed in Chapter 5, with clients being trained to tense and relax muscles and to note the difference between tension and relaxation. Clients can also practice relaxation exercises on their own between sessions and learn to monitor their tension levels.

IDENTIFYING SUCCESSFUL APPROACHES   As group members become more familiar with models of stress reduction and coping, they can also begin to identify methods they have used in the past to cope with situations that might otherwise have been connected with drinking or drug use. As they discuss these coping mechanisms, they might tend to notice that their strategies include a combination of environmental problem solving, cognitive changes, and relaxation methods. This recognition can, in turn, lead to the development of individual plans for dealing with issues that have tended to be troublesome. Group members can help one another identify alternatives to substance-abusing behaviors—ideally, choices that can come close to being as reinforcing as drinking or other drug use had been in the past.

PROBLEM SOLVING

Exercises can be designed both to help group members understand problem-solving concepts and methods and to provide practice in applying these methods to general and substance-abuse-related examples. The concept of problem solving should be introduced with a discussion of its relevance for substance abuse. The discussion can focus on the fact that some people tend to ignore their problems and expect drinking or other drug use to solve them. Approaching problems in an orderly fashion is a better choice for all types of issues. In addition, problem-solving skills can be useful for dealing with specific substance use problems (e.g., avoiding driving under the influence of alcohol or planning alternatives to celebrations involving alcohol or other drug use).

For example, a series of sessions that has been used by one of the authors with groups of multiple DUI offenders begins with an overview of the following problem-solving steps:

1. recognizing and defining the problem
2. generating alternatives
3. judging the alternatives
4. implementing and evaluating solutions

The four steps are explained one by one, with the group leader then applying the model to several general examples. As members become more familiar with problem-solving steps and substeps, they contribute additional problem situations and assist one another by refining problem definitions, brainstorming alternatives, listing positive and negative aspects of proposed solutions, and preparing implementation plans.

Learning is enhanced by written homework assignments that give participants a chance to apply their problem-solving skills to hypothetical problem situations such as the following:

- There is a big party next Saturday that you want to attend, but you usually get very drunk at this person's parties.
- Your bowling team always meets at a bar after bowling. You plan to go but want to keep your drinking under control.
- Your friends like to stop for a drink after work, and you think they'll be upset if you don't join them.
- Your car has broken down and you need to find some way to get to work.
- You never seem to have enough money.

This exercise allows clients to choose between applying the problem-solving exercise to a drinking-related issue or to a more general problem. Once participants have completed the activity on their own, they bring their solutions to the next group meeting to compare notes. Such practice allows group members to become adept at using the model when real-life problems present themselves.

ASSERTIVENESS TRAINING

Assertive behaviors, like problem-solving skills, depend for their development on both conceptual understanding and extensive practice. In the group setting, assertiveness needs to be defined first, with participants learning to differentiate among assertiveness, aggressiveness, and passivity and to recognize the suitability of assertion in human interaction. Group discussion can also point up the relationships between assertiveness deficits and drinking problems; people may drink to overcome dissatisfaction with their nonassertive behavior or to attempt assertions that they find difficult in a sober state. Most important for alcohol-abusing clients attempting sobriety is the fact that assertiveness skills will be needed when refusing a drink.

Conceptual understanding of the assertiveness model needs to be followed by observing models of assertive behavior and by rehearsing assertive behaviors in the group. A group exercise designed for clients with alcohol-related problems can focus on assertive drink refusal, with the leader explaining that the same skills can be applicable to a variety of interpersonal situations. After the leader models assertive refusal of a drink offered by a role-playing group member, participants can role-play similar situations, alternating between the roles of drink "pusher" and assertive refuser. The leader's coaching and feedback can help improve each client's skills. Repetitions of the behavior rehearsal can focus on issues that clients currently face. As with all group interventions, the ultimate purpose must be to develop healthy, adaptive behaviors that can be transferred from the group setting to the client's real-life situation.

PREPARING FOR "REAL-WORLD" CHALLENGES: AN EXAMPLE   Sharon, a substance abuse inpatient, was preparing to leave the hospital in mid-November. When her group began to discuss coping skills that they would need when they returned to their homes, she shared a problem that was troubling her. Sharon, who was married and the mother of two children, was planning to prepare Thanksgiving dinner for an extended family that included her parents, her brothers and sisters, and her nieces and nephews. She was worried because her father and her two brothers were heavy drinkers and because alcohol had always played a major role in family get-togethers. The family tradition was to bring a keg of beer to her home each Thanksgiving. She recognized that her newfound sobriety would be in jeopardy if she allowed alcohol in her home, but she felt very uncomfortable with the idea of a complete break with tradition. She did not want to sacrifice having her family over on Thanksgiving even though her sister had offered to play host to the dinner this year.

The group members encouraged Sharon to assert her right to have an alcohol-free home. After a discussion about her family situation, she decided that the one person she most needed to talk to was her father. With another client playing the part of the father, Sharon attempted several verbalizations, with varying results. The assertive statement that seemed most promising to her was: "Dad, I need your help. I'm just beginning my recovery, and it's important to me to keep alcohol out of the house, at least for now. Could you talk to the others and let them know that I won't have any alcohol in the house and that they shouldn't bring any?"

After extensive rehearsal, Sharon felt that she would feel comfortable approaching her father in this way. Even though her assertiveness skills were adequate, however, the leader suggested that she should have an alternate backup plan. Clients should have good interpersonal skills in their repertoires so that they have behavioral choices available, but even the most practiced assertive responses do not guarantee acquiescence from others. Sharon's family had a long history of abusive drinking, and these habits might not be eradicated by good intentions. A brainstorming session gave group members an opportunity to talk about options that they had tried in their own lives when facing the stress of holidays. One client said that she always went out of town or to a restaurant with her husband and children rather than spending holidays with her family of origin. Another suggested that the alcohol-free dinner take place early in the day and that family members could then go to another home to drink beer and watch football games. A suggestion that family members drink in another location and then go on to Sharon's house for dinner was rejected because of the danger of drunken driving.

The discussion helped Sharon weigh her options. She decided that she did place a high value on spending the holiday with her extended family and that she did have the skill and motivation to confront her father about the issue of alcohol. At the same time, she realized that the traditional Thanksgiving dinner in her own home would be problematic both because she associated this occasion with drinking and because she would have no escape, short of severe conflict, if the keg made an appearance. She decided to request that alcohol be eliminated from the occasion, to ask her father to use his influence in that direction, but to accept her sister's offer to have the dinner at her house. As a result of the exercise, Sharon judged herself prepared for a difficult situation. At the same time, the rest of the group had a valuable opportunity both to consider their own reactions to comparable problems and to take part in a highly supportive interaction.

SUPPORTIVENESS AND MULTICULTURAL COMPETENCE

People often assume that substance abuse clients are so defensive and resistant that they must be subjected to intense confrontations. In fact, however, a climate of positive support is often helpful in lessening defensiveness and may actually increase the likelihood of openness. The counselor's empathic responses can lead the group in this direction.

Vannicelli (1992) discusses appropriate leader responses to clients who violate group norms by engaging in drug use. This behavior cannot be ignored, but empathic responses by the leader can bring about a resolution without sacrificing the supportive relationship. Consider, for example, the client who has been using but who refuses to acknowledge it. Vannicelli suggests that the leader express concern about the client but emphasize his or her understanding about why the client might be hesitant to acknowledge the problem:

> This is an empathic response that says to the patient, I can understand your not leveling with us—it's not that you are a bad person or that you want to put one over on the group, but rather that you are worried about what people will think of you. In my own experience, I have found that patients are sometimes willing to assent to an empathic comment such as this even when direct questions about whether they have been drinking continue to be refuted. (1992, pp. 65–66)

Group members are discouraged from forcing the individual to confess to the behavior and encouraged to focus on helping the person move on.

When clients come to a session intoxicated, Vannicelli suggests, the leader can encourage them to get a cup of coffee or some fresh air and return when they are ready to participate. "This is somewhat less rejecting than simply asking a patient to leave, and less likely to evoke a struggle" (1992, p. 63). Thus, even in those situations that are most likely to lend themselves to conflict, the leader can use interventions that protect the client's self-respect. As this demeanor is modeled by the counselor, it is more likely to become part of the repertoire of each group member.

Just as counselors must model a supportive demeanor, they must also learn to adapt their own behaviors to the needs of a culturally diverse clientele. Although multicultural competence is necessary for all counselors, the group milieu may require distinct skills in this area. For instance,

1. Counselors must always be prepared to work with clients who are different from themselves, but in group counseling, client-to-client differences also come to the fore.
2. The counselor must be prepared to help group members adapt to diversity and might, in fact, need to deal directly and smoothly with member-to-member prejudices.
3. The counselor must be sensitive to the cultural impact of group interventions.
4. The counselor as group leader must be able to model multicultural and diversity competencies that will also stand their clients in good stead.

As the Association for Specialists in Group Work (ASGW) (1992) explains in the association's *Principles for Diversity-Competent Group Workers*,

> Diversity-competent group workers are able to engage in a variety of verbal and nonverbal group-facilitating function, dependent upon the type of group ... and the multiple, self-identified status of various group members (such as Indigenous Peoples, African Americans, Asian Americans, Hispanics, Latinos/Latinas, gays, lesbians, bisexuals, or transgendered persons, and persons with physical, mental/emotional, and/or learning disabilities). They demonstrate the ability to send and receive both verbal and nonverbal messages accurately, appropriately, and across/between the differences represented in the group. They are not tied down to one method or approach to group facilitation and recognize that helping styles and approaches may be culture-bound. When they sense that their group facilitation style is limited and potentially inappropriate, they can anticipate and ameliorate its negative impact by drawing upon other culturally relevant skill sets (ASGW, 1992, p. 5).

SUMMARY

The group modality is appropriate for substance abuse clients because it offers opportunities to test perceptions, to practice new behaviors, to receive feedback, and to reduce isolation. In the past, many substance abuse groups focused on confrontive efforts to "break through denial" or on the provision of didactic information. In fact, group experiences can be more effective if they are based on empowerment strategies. Such groups share four commonalities: (1) The group structure is based on a collaborative style, (2) interventions support clients' movement toward change, (3) clients develop personal skills that are transferable to other settings, and (4) the group leader models supportiveness and multicultural competence.

The collaborative style involves shared leadership, with clients participating in setting the goals and ground rules of the group. Development of transferable skills can be accomplished through training in behavior analysis, coping skills, problem solving, and assertiveness. All of these goals can be accomplished most effectively within a framework of empathy and positive support.

QUESTIONS FOR THOUGHT AND DISCUSSION

1. What do you see as the main strengths of a group approach for working with substance-abusing clients? What can a group do for a client that could not be accomplished as effectively through individual sessions?

2. Given the goals of group work you provided in your answer to question 1, what would you say are the best group strategies for achieving these ends?

REFERENCES

Association for Specialists in Group Work. (1998). *Principles for diversity-competent group workers.* Retrieved May 1, 2009, from http://www.asgw.org/diversity.htm

Corey, G. (2008). *Theory and practice of group counseling.* Belmont, CA: Thomson Brooks/Cole.

DiClemente, C. C., & Prochaska, J. O. (1998). Toward a comprehensive, transtheoretical model of change. In W. Miller & N. Heather (Eds.), *Treating addictive behaviors* (pp. 3–24). New York: Plenum Press.

Fields, A. (2004). *Curriculum-based motivation group: A five-session motivational interviewing group intervention.* Vancouver, WA: Hollifield Associates.

Khantzian, E. J., Halliday, K. S., & McAuliffe, W. E. (1990). *Addiction and the vulnerable self: Modified dynamic group therapy for substance abuse.* New York: Guilford Press.

McCrady, B. S., Dean, L., Dubreuil, E., & Swanson, S. (1985). The problem drinkers' project: A programmatic application of social-learning based treatment. In G. A. Marlatt & J. R. Gordon (Eds.), *Relapse prevention: Maintenance strategies in the treatment of addictive behaviors* (pp. 417–471). New York: Guilford Press.

Prochaska, J. O., DiClemente, C. C., & Norcross, J. C. (1992). In search of how people change: Applications to addictive behavior. *American Psychologist, 47,* 1102–1114.

Vannicelli, M. (1992). *Removing the roadblocks: Group psychotherapy with substance abusers and family members.* New York: Guilford Press.

Velasquez, M., Maurer, G. G., Crouch, C., & DiClemente, C. (2001). *Group treatment for substance abuse: A stages-of-change therapy manual.* New York: Guilford Press.

Maintaining Change in Substance Use Behaviors

CHANGING LONG-TERM SUBSTANCE use behaviors is an imposing challenge for anyone. Unfortunately, however, the modification of substance use behavior is only one step in a longer and more difficult process. The client's success in maintaining change over time requires vigilance, hard work, and access to a variety of coping strategies.

The process of change in addictive behaviors has been clarified most effectively by Prochaska, DiClemente, and Norcross (1992) (Marlatt & Donovan, 2005; Kern, 2009; Fields, 2010, in press). According to their model, people move through several stages of change: *precontemplation*, when they have no intention of altering their behaviors; *contemplation*, when they are aware of a problem and are considering the possibility of acting; *preparation*, when they have begun making some small alterations in their behaviors and are serious about making changes; *action*, when they make successful behavior modifications; and *maintenance*, when they work to preserve their gains and prevent a return to their previous, unacceptable behaviors. Originally, Prochaska and his colleagues (1992) saw this process as linear, with people moving through the stages in an orderly fashion. They learned, however, that "relapse is the rule rather than the exception with addictions" (Prochaska et al., 1992; Kern, 2009) (see Figure 7.1).

Most people who make behavior changes do relapse, and it is common for people to recycle through the earlier stages several times before they achieve long-term success. This finding has clear implications for substance abuse counseling. Helping the client maintain change and prevent relapse is an important part of the counseling process (see Table 7.1).

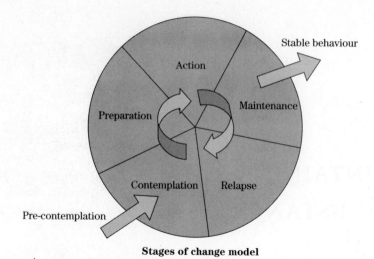

Stages of change model

FIGURE 7.1 | STAGES OF CHANGE

Source: From *Stages of Change Model*, by Marc Kern, 2009. Retreived on April 23, 2009 from http://www.addictioninfo.org/articles/11/1/Stages-of-Change-Model/Page1.html

TABLE 7.1 | STAGES OF CHANGE AND COUNSELOR TASKS

Client Stage	Counselor's Motivational Tasks
Precontemplation	Raise doubt – increase the client's perception of risks and problems with current use patterns. Establish relationship. Validate client's feelings and open door to further discovery and change.
Contemplation	Tip the balance – evoke reasons to change. Outline risks associated with continued use. Strengthen self – efficacy. Deepen personal resolve to forward momentum.
Determination/Action	Help determine best approach to change. Develop a plan and help client focus on plan. Remove barriers to change.
Maintenance/Relapse Prevention	Help identify relapse triggers and high risk situations while developing and refining strategies to prevent relapse.

Source: Adapted from R. Fields (2010, in press). *Drugs in Perspective* McGraw Hill, NY.

A relapse, or an uncontrolled return to alcohol or other drug use following competent treatment, is one of the greatest problems substance abusers and their counselors face. In fact it has been reported that close to 90% of all clients treated for substance abuse relapse within 1 year after their discharge from treatment (Marlatt & Donovan, 2005). This astounding figure means that we must place high priority on relapse prevention if we expect to consolidate treatment gains, decrease the frequency of the "revolving-door" syndrome, and increase the willingness of drug and alcohol users to enter treatment programs. It is important, however, to differentiate among three different states: (1) a return to nonproblematic drinking; (2) a slip, which is a temporary lapse; and (3) a relapse, which is a return to uncontrolled substance use.

Many alcohol abusers spontaneously discontinue their pattern of abusive substance use. These people sometimes return to moderate use following a period of abstinence. This new way of using alcohol should not be considered a relapse, because use in this group is not necessarily problematic. There is great variability in patterns of substance use and abuse, and these clients show that people can move in and out of problematic use without adhering to a stereotypical pattern.

A slip should be considered a temporary lapse that is neither catastrophic nor regressive. It should provide an impetus for learning, and the client and the counselor should spend time examining what precipitated the slip and what the client can learn by analyzing it. A slip does not have to be damaging in itself, but it can be devastating if it is defined as a disaster or a personal failure. The counselor should help the client understand slips—for example, as testing behavior or as responses to environmental cues—and redefine them as learning experiences. This redefinition should reduce guilt, anxiety, and embarrassment and enable the client to get back on track without turning the slip into a full-blown relapse.

A true relapse, in contrast, is a serious situation. It occurs when the client resumes an abusive pattern of use after a period of treatment-induced abstinence or controlled use. Thus a relapse occurs, in our conception, following a slip. A slip, if not managed correctly and redefined as a learning experience, may result in what has been called the abstinence violation effect (AVE). Clients who believe that absolute abstinence and utter loss of control are their only options often have strong reactions to what could have been minor lapses. They experience great confusion, profound guilt, decreased self-esteem, extreme embarrassment, and a pervasive sense of shame. These powerful negative emotions lead to pessimism about the possibility of recovery and a resumption of substance abuse to manage the resultant negative emotional states.

This painful experience can be avoided if we train clients to redefine lapses as learning experiences that, when analyzed, will tell them and their counselors a great deal about environmental stressors and gaps in treatment. This view reduces shame, doubt, and guilt; allows clients to maintain their integrity; and encourages them not to elope from treatment but rather to embrace it. There is no going back to square one, and all treatment gains are consolidated. If a client relapses for 3 weeks after 4 months of sobriety, he or she simply has 120 days of sobriety and 21 days of substance use. There are no moral injunctions against the client and no hints of failure. Ideally, the experience of relapse is seen as therapeutic, understandable, and acceptable.

RELAPSE PREVENTION MODELS

Prevailing models of addiction heavily influence which treatments we use with our clients and, consequently, how we address the issues of relapse and relapse prevention (RP).

DISEASE MODEL

The disease model was first conceptualized by Jellinek (1960) as a way to understand alcoholism and has since been applied to the general field of addictions. This view accepts the basic assumptions that alcohol- and drug-dependent individuals have virtually irresistible physical cravings for the substance and that they experience loss of control over drinking or other drug use. The disease of alcoholism or drug dependence is seen as progressive and irreversible.

The disease concept is widely accepted by the public and is an implicit component of the Alcoholics Anonymous (AA) and Narcotics Anonymous approaches. The shortcoming of this model for RP lies in its potential for a dichotomous view of both the disorder and the problem of relapse. This view, which characterizes the thinking of some adherents of the disease concept, defines the client as either abstinent or relapsed. Because it is so difficult to fight against the powerful and uncontrollable forces of the disease, relapse is seen as a probable event. Relapse is, in fact, considered part of the disease.

Many adherents of the disease concept view all slips as relapses, and a client's slip is thought to obviate prior success. Thus, substance abusers must, if they are willing, reinitiate the process of recovery and begin at the beginning. In traditional circles, the significance of a slip is great. It is thought and taught that one drink, one joint of marijuana, one pill, or one shot of a narcotic will lead, inevitably, to intoxication and pretreatment levels of abuse. This belief stems from the disease conception of drug and alcohol dependence, which holds that these conditions are progressive. In this view substance abusers, whether using drugs or not, are involved with a progression of their disease, and any substance use will immediately reactivate the disease process. Within this framework, clients are taught that their only chance of recovery is abstinence; it is commonly thought that *abstinence* means health and *substance use* means illness. In addition, traditionalists tell their clients that alcoholism and other drug dependence are chronically relapsing diseases. These two injunctions ("You must be abstinent to be well" and "You have a chronically relapsing disease") may create a double bind for substance-abusing clients. This double bind, combined with the belief that a relapse leads inevitably to complete deterioration, can be confusing and anxiety-provoking for clients.

Gorski (2009) has dealt with this issue by integrating components of the disease concept into an RP model. Gorski believes that physiological dysfunctions place the addict at risk for relapse, but he posits a developmental model of recovery. Once clients have sought treatment, they move toward *stabilization* and acute withdrawal; *early recovery*, when they begin to learn how to live without the drug; *middle recovery*, when they attempt balanced lifestyles; *late recovery*, when they address long-term psychological and family issues; and *maintenance*, which involves a permanent state of attention to the possibility of relapse. Gorski suggests that most substance abuse treatment programs excel at the stage of early recovery but fail to address the varying needs of clients at other stages. In order to reach the goals of total abstinence and lifestyle change, clients need to build skills at each stage. The role of the RP counselor is to help clients develop daily structure, conduct self-assessments, learn about the nature of addictive disease, identify and manage warning signs of relapse, and monitor their own recovery. The counselor also works with family members or others who can play a role in preventing relapses. Gorski's approach is educational, with clients receiving training in the developmental model of recovery, the general warning signs of relapse, and the skills they will need for long-term maintenance.

This approach integrates the fundamental principles of AA with professional counseling and therapy to meet the needs of relapse-prone clients by integrating knowledge of chemical addiction into a biopsychosocial model and 12-step principles with advanced cognitive, affective, behavioral, and social therapy principles to produce a model for both primary recovery and RP.

The biopsychosocial model Gorski espouses states that chemical addiction is a primary disease or disorder resulting in abuse of and addiction to mood-altering chemicals. Long-term use of mood-altering chemicals causes brain dysfunction that disorganizes personality and causes social and occupational problems. In this respect this approach is based on the belief that total abstinence plus personality and lifestyle change are essential for full recovery. People raised in dysfunctional families often develop self-defeating personality styles (AA calls them character defects) that interfere with their ability to recover. Addiction is thought of as a chronic disease that has a tendency toward relapse. Relapse is the process of becoming dysfunctional in recovery, which ends in physical or emotional collapse, suicide, or self-medication with alcohol or other drugs. This model, then, incorporates the roles of brain dysfunction, personality disorganization, social dysfunction, and family-of-origin problems to the problems of recovery and relapse.

Brain dysfunction, Gorski argues, occurs during periods of intoxication, short-term withdrawal, and long-term withdrawal. Clients with a genetic history of addiction are thought to be more susceptible to this brain dysfunction. As the addiction progresses, the symptoms of this brain dysfunction cause difficulty in thinking clearly, managing feelings and emotions, remembering things, sleeping restfully, recognizing and managing stress, and psychomotor coordination. The symptoms are conceptualized as being most severe during the first 6 to 18 months of sobriety, but there is thought to be a lifelong tendency of these symptoms to return during times of physical or psychosocial stress.

Personality disorganization occurs, according to Gorski, because the brain dysfunction interferes with normal thinking, feeling, and acting. Some of the personality disorganization is temporary and will spontaneously subside with abstinence as the brain recovers from the dysfunction. Other personality traits will become deeply habituated during the addiction and will require treatment to subside.

Social dysfunction, which includes family, work, legal, and financial problems, emerges as a consequence of brain dysfunction and resultant personality disorganization.

Addiction can be influenced, not caused, by self-defeating personality traits that result from being raised in a dysfunctional family. Personality is the habitual way of thinking, feeling, acting, and relating to others that develops in childhood and is unconsciously perpetuated in adult living. Personality develops as a result of an interaction between genetically inherited traits and family environment.

Being raised in a dysfunctional family can result in self-defeating personality traits or disorders. These traits and disorders do not cause the addiction to occur. They can cause a more rapid progression of the addiction, make it difficult to recognize and seek treatment during the early stages of the addiction, or make it difficult to benefit from treatment. Self-defeating personality traits and disorders also increase the risk of relapse. As a result, family-of-origin problems need to be appropriately addressed in treatment.

The relapse syndrome is an integral part of the addictive disease process. The disease is a double-edged sword with two cutting edges—drug-based symptoms that manifest themselves during active episodes of chemical use and sobriety-based symptoms that emerge during periods of abstinence. The sobriety-based symptoms create a tendency toward relapse that is part of the disease itself. Relapse is the process of becoming dysfunctional in sobriety because of sobriety-based symptoms that lead to renewed alcohol or other drug use, physical or emotional collapse, or suicide. The relapse process is marked by predictable and identifiable warning signs that begin long before alcohol and other drug use or collapse occurs. RP therapy teaches clients to recognize and manage these warning signs and to interrupt the relapse progression early and return to positive progress in recovery.

Gorski conceptualizes recovery as a developmental process that goes through six stages. The first stage is *transition*, where clients recognize that they are experiencing alcohol- and other drug-related problems and they need to pursue abstinence as a lifestyle goal so they can resolve these problems. The second stage is *stabilization*, where clients recover from acute and postacute withdrawal and stabilize their psychosocial life crisis. The third stage is *early recovery*, where clients identify and learn how to replace addictive thoughts, feelings, and behaviors with sobriety-centered thoughts, feelings, and behaviors. The fourth stage is *middle recovery*, where clients repair the lifestyle damage caused by the addiction and develop a balanced and healthy lifestyle. The fifth stage is *late recovery*, where clients resolve family-of-origin issues that impair the quality of recovery and act as long-term relapse triggers. The sixth stage is *maintenance*, where clients continue a program of growth and development and maintain an active recovery program to ensure that they do not slip back into old addictive patterns.

The Gorski Relapse Model suggests three primary psychological domains of functioning and three primary social domains of functioning. Each of these domains is considered equally important.

The primary psychological domains are

1. thinking
2. feeling
3. acting

The primary social domains are

1. work
2. friendship
3. intimate relationships

The clinical goal is to help clients achieve competent functioning within each of these domains.

Clients usually have a preference for one psychological domain and one social domain. These preferred domains become overdeveloped whereas the others remain underdeveloped. The goal is to reinforce the skills in the overdeveloped domains while focusing the client on building skills in the underdeveloped domains. The goal is to achieve healthy, balanced functioning.

Learning theories of substance abuse have emerged from a larger body of knowledge relating to reinforcement theory. Social learning theorists think that substance use and abuse are a result of a certain history of learning in which the behavior of drinking alcohol or using drugs has been increased in frequency, duration, and intensity for the psychological benefits it affords (Marlatt & Witkiewitz, 2009). There are many divergent learning theories.

One variant of learning theory is a drive reduction theory, which defines the stimulus as internal tension that, regardless of its cause, creates a drive state. Drinking or drug use becomes a prepotent response (habit) in an effort to reduce the drive. The psychological effects of alcohol or other drugs are thought to be initially tension-reducing and, therefore, reinforcing. The reinforcement, in turn, strengthens the drinking response, which will therefore occur more frequently in response to tension. This cycle, then, eventually leads to habitual drinking or other drug use (Coombs and Howatt, 2005).

Learning theory also deals with the seeming incongruity that people engage in excessive drug use even though it brings on social punishment in the forms of job loss, social ostracism, emotional upset, and psychological and physical deterioration. This incongruity is explained by the principle of delayed reinforcement. Thus, the morning after hangover or social punishment will not be effective in stopping a drinking response because of the delayed negative reinforcing effects. Furthermore, if the drive is intense, the immediate drive reduction effects afforded by substance use will be heeded more than competing social punishment, which may actually cause new stress and lead to more substance use (Fields, 2010, in press).

A second social learning perspective suggests that excessive substance use is initiated by environmental stressors and is maintained by the hypothesized depressant and anesthetic effects of alcohol and other drugs on the central nervous system. In this view the potential substance abuser has acquired substance use, through differential reinforcement and modeling, as a widely generalized dominant response to stress because of the substance's reinforcing qualities. This powerful reinforcement cements the substance-taking response, and continued drug or alcohol use leads, eventually, to a physiological state of dependence that manifests itself by producing withdrawal symptoms when the substance is removed.

Consequently, the drug use or drinking response is continued in order to forestall withdrawal. Avoiding the withdrawal symptoms is itself a reinforcement of drug and alcohol use and thus becomes a secondary maintaining mechanism for excessive consumption. One major advantage of learning theory is that it can be integrated with many other theories that suggest a drive (anxiety, depression, need to fit in, need to feel better, etc.) which can be reduced or affected by substance ingestion.

Social scientists have given careful consideration to the conceptualization of substance abuse. The resulting model respects psychosocial factors and implies the need for change in the individual and his or her relations with the environment. The model goes beyond an exclusively medical approach and encompasses a broad range of human experiences.

The social learning model has stimulated new investigations and interpretations of addictive behaviors, and it has been concluded that excessive substance use is the result of a combination of factors, including cognitive, emotional, situational, social, and physiological variables. This approach is proactive, because it allows us to pinpoint the cues and high-risk situations that may lead to a slip or relapse in our clients. In this regard RP is possible, and relapse as an ultimate outcome is not inevitable. Substance-abusing clients are given skills training and other interventions that allow them to function normally in an environment that is ordinarily very hostile to the recovering substance abuser. Treatments based on social learning theory are manageable and flexible. They respond to the needs of clients and allow for a lifestyle of moderation, which, in all respects, improves the quality of life.

The medical model considers relapse to be an all-or-nothing endeavor in which any use of a substance following abstinence is a relapse. In addition, relapse is viewed as a major symptom of the "disease of chemical dependency," and clients are typically urged to exert their will to prevent a relapse. The social learning perspective, however, looks at a return to substance use as a learning experience that can be successfully used to bolster gains previously made in treatment. Furthermore, social learning theorists think that relapse is a response to environmental cues that constantly impinge on clients. In this regard determinants of relapse and high-risk situations can be detected early on, and clients can be treated and given RP strategies that effectively decrease the probability of an initial reuse of a substance (slip) and a consequent full-blown relapse.

BIOPSYCHOSOCIAL MODEL

The biopsychosocial model (different from Gorski's conceptualization of a biopsychosocial model) sees addiction as a complex, progressive behavior pattern with biological, psychological, sociological, and behavioral components (Miller & Brown, 2009). According to this approach, multiple systems interact both in the development of addictive behaviors and in their treatment. Marlatt and Donovan (2005) have applied this model to RP, pointing out that biological, psychological, and social systems hold the potential for relapse risks. The biological risks that can place individuals in jeopardy for relapse include such factors as neurological impairments, cravings resulting from cue reactivity, and biochemical deficiencies. Psychological risk factors include beliefs and expectancies about substance use, as well as deficiencies in coping skills.

Among the social factors affecting relapse are negative life events, socioeconomic status, employment, stability of residence, and family issues. The biopsychosocial approach suggests that individual risk should be assessed through measurement and analysis of historical, biological, psychological, and social factors.

Similarly, RP strategies include attention to each system. The way clients deal with physical and cognitive problems related to withdrawal affects their risks for relapse. The biopsychosocial model calls for information to be provided in a way that recognizes the reality of short-term memory problems. Behavioral training focuses on recognizing cues associated with cravings and developing options for coping with them. Skill training and careful time management help lessen the need for overstimulation. The client's physical health and well-being are also addressed. Because expectancy concerning the effects of the substance is seen as a risk factor, the model calls for cognitive interventions that address clients' beliefs about the positive and negative outcomes of drug use. It also pays attention to building psychosocial skills, including problem solving, cognitive coping, social skills, and stress management. It focuses on social systems, especially the family, with marital and family interventions playing an important role in the RP process.

DETERMINANTS OF RELAPSE

Each RP model recognizes the importance of identifying the factors associated with relapse. Understanding the determinants of relapse—those telltale signs—will enable the client to prevent the disastrous return to substance abuse that many individuals experience.

High-Risk Situations

It is important to consider first the precipitants to a slip; that is, what are the conditions or situations that initially lead an abstinent or controlled substance user back to substance abuse and all the associated problems? We must start by considering the notion of perceived self-control, or self-efficacy, that clients possess while they are successfully adhering to a prescribed treatment regime. During these times, clients feel strongly that they can control themselves and their environment, and they develop a strong sense of self-efficacy. This powerful feeling of mastery tends to maintain itself nicely while the client is in the hospital and for some period after discharge. Unfortunately, these feelings of self-control quickly give way to feelings of insecurity, anxiety, and doubt when the client is confronted by a high-risk situation (Marlatt & Donovan, 2005).

High-risk situations are, very generally, incidents, occurrences, or situations that threaten clients' sense of self-control (for example, walking into a room where all their old drinking buddies are drinking) and increase the probability of their return to substance use. In an analysis of the precipitants to relapse in a large number of substance abusers it has been found that negative emotional states accounted for about one-third of relapses, interpersonal conflicts accounted for nearly 15%, and social pressure accounted for 20% (Marlatt & Donovan, 2005). Negative emotional states are feelings like anger, anxiety, frustration, depression, and boredom. Interpersonal conflicts are arguments or confrontations that occur between clients and their family members, friends, lovers, or coworkers. Social pressure involves situations in which clients respond to environmental or peer pressure to drink or use drugs. These categories, then, represent high-risk situations that can result in a return to uncontrolled substance use. No two clients are ever identical in their responses to situations. What is challenging for one may be quite manageable for another. Each individual needs to formulate his or her own plan for identifying problem areas and coping with the world.

Consider the client who says that he has been feeling depressed and hopeless. His wife accuses him of self-pity, and they wind up having a fight. After the fight, the client goes for a walk in his old neighborhood, and he happens to run into some of his old friends, who offer him cocaine. Given his depression, his fight with his spouse, and the fact that he has met some drug-using friends, he abandons abstinence in favor of consumption. He has no coping skills to lessen his negative feelings or to resist the advances of his friends. According to Marlatt and Gordon's (1985) cognitive behavioral model, this client would begin to feel less self-control and more anxiety as soon as he realized that he had no effective coping response available. These feelings would yield positive thoughts about what the drug could do for him, and he would find himself snorting cocaine. Following this ingestion the client would experience the abstinence-violation effect, and the guilt, shame, embarrassment, and dissonance that he felt would lead to further use (to relieve his psychological discomfort) and, inevitably, to a full-blown relapse.

RP training could have helped the client avoid this predicament in a number of ways. First, he might have recognized the risk involved in the situation and taken steps to avoid it. Alternatively, he might have been able to handle his emotional upset and the presence of his drug-using friends if he had had a repertoire of effective coping strategies.

Had this client been given coping skills training in treatment, he could have used these skills in the high-risk situation and effectively short-circuited his initial use of the substance. Utilization of a coping response would have resulted in increased self-efficacy, positive reinforcement, and a strong sense of self-control. These positive feelings, of course, greatly reduce the likelihood of an initial reuse of the substance and a consequent relapse. This scenario is illustrated in Figure 7.2.

As the figure indicates, entry into a high-risk situation (left) can lead in either of two directions. When clients enter such situations and have no effective coping responses available, they tend to experience a decrease in self-efficacy, along with a positive expectation concerning the effects of the substance. Once initial use has taken place, feelings of guilt, conflict, and shame play a role, in turn, in increasing the probability of relapse.

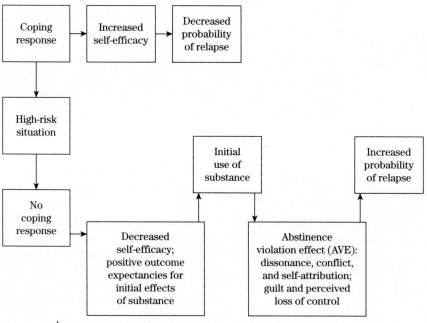

FIGURE 7.2 | A COGNITIVE-BEHAVIORAL MODEL OF THE RELAPSE PROCESS.

Source: From *Relapse Prevention: Maintenance Strategies in the Treatment of Addictive Behaviors,* edited by G. A. Marlatt and J. R. Gordon, 1985, New York: Guilford Press. Reprinted by permission.

On the other hand, entry into a high-risk situation can actually increase the sense of self-efficacy if adequate coping responses are available and are used successfully. Even if it were possible for clients to avoid all risky situations, they should not attempt this degree of self-protectiveness. Success in handling risk enhances self-efficacy and makes it increasingly likely that success will be experienced again. Maintenance of positive change seems to require that clients move carefully, attempting to handle situations usually associated with drug use only when they have selected and rehearsed appropriate coping strategies.

COGNITIVE RISK FACTORS

Subtle changes in clients' ways of thinking about themselves and about a drug may initiate a relapse process in much the same way that a high-risk situation can. A cognitive behavioral approach suggests that certain attitudes and thought patterns can serve as warning signs. For example, people in the early stages of recovery from cocaine abuse sometimes feel euphoric about their abstinence and refuse to believe that any problems will arise. When normal life problems do occur, these clients may be unprepared to respond effectively. They may also allow overconfidence to place them in high-risk situations that they are not ready to handle. Some clients, in contrast, stay mired in negative thinking or unhealthy attitudes. They may avoid the reality of the hard work involved in RP, wallow in self-pity, express impatience with the slow speed of treatment, refuse responsibility, or remain chronically dissatisfied.

Many clients have difficulty overcoming negative moods, and find that feelings of boredom, depression, loneliness, unhappiness, anger, anxiety, shame, and guilt, as well as painful memories, are often precursors to relapse. Frequently, the pain of these emotions has been anesthetized by the drug, and the drug's absence prompts an urge to self-medicate. The negative feelings being experienced contrast with the client's selective memory of the pleasures of drug use. On the other hand, positive moods and feelings of success can also trigger initial reuse, with the client feeling that recovery is secure or that a reward is deserved.

LIFESTYLE RISKS

Cognitive processes can play a role in the client's failure to make necessary lifestyle changes. A lifestyle imbalance can act as a covert antecedent, initiating a chain of events that propels the client toward high-risk situations. According to this view, lifestyle imbalances occur when people's balance between external demands (their "shoulds") and pleasure and self-fulfillment (their "wants") is inordinately weighted to the side of the "shoulds." When this happens, clients begin to feel imposed on and deprived, and are very likely to begin believing that they deserve indulgence and gratification. People who feel "put upon" all day may very well believe that they deserve to fully indulge themselves at night by getting intoxicated. According to the Marlatt and Gordon model, these people would, following the desire for indulgence and gratification, begin to have increasingly strong urges and cravings for their preferred substance. These cravings and urges tend to grow stronger over time because the client begins to think very positively about the immediate effects of the substance ("I'll feel so relaxed; it'll taste so good"). As the urges and cravings grow and the desire for indulgence increases, clients will begin to rationalize ("I owe myself") and begin to deny any possible negative outcomes that could be associated with reinitiation of substance use.

As their cognitive processes change, clients move ever closer to the high-risk situation, and as this movement occurs, they begin to make apparently irrelevant decisions based on rationalizations ("What I'm doing is OK") and denial ("This behavior is acceptable and has no relationship to relapse"). These thought processes are best conceptualized as "mini-decisions" that are made over time and that, when combined, lead the client closer to the brink of substance use. An example of such a decision is provided by a recovering alcohol abuser's refusal to empty her liquor cabinet because her problem should not adversely affect other people's ability to drink in her house. Another example is the smoker who refuses to tell his office mates that he has quit smoking because "it's nobody's business but my own." This person may neglect advertising the situation so that he can more easily approach a coworker for a cigarette ("Oh, I've run out").

Clients also need to make lifestyle changes that help them feel healthy and positive. If an individual quits a substance use behavior but doesn't replace it with equivalently easy and satisfying behaviors he or she will quickly confront the reality that life indeed is "boring and meaningless without drugs". The client who is involved in a wellness program, is active in his or her community, and is enthusiastic about work and leisure pursuits, has a high probability for success.

THE RELAPSE CHAIN

Washton (2008) suggests that although the sequence of events leading to a relapse can take many forms, the following "relapse chain" provides an example of the process in action:

1. A buildup or onset of stress is caused by either negative or positive (but usually negative) changes and life events.
2. Overly negative or positive thoughts, moods, and feelings, including confusion, bewilderment, irritability, depression, elation, or instead, complete numbness are activated.
3. The patient overreacts or fails totally to take action in response to the situation or stress, which leads to a perpetuation and escalation of problems.
4. The patient denies that the problem is serious or even exists and fails to utilize his or her existing support system and other tools of recovery.
5. The original problems "snowball"—and new ones are created as the patient continues to categorically ignore them.
6. The patient perceives the situation as being beyond the point of no return and feels totally incapable of doing anything about it. Positive thoughts about the "good times" on cocaine cross the patient's mind with increasing frequency.
7. The patient increasingly finds himself or herself in high-risk situations or engaging in other subtle and not-so-subtle acts of self-sabotage.
8. Stress further increases as the patient's life continues to skid out of control while he/she becomes increasingly isolated and alienated from his/her support

system. Frustration, despair, embarrassment, hopelessness, and self-pity set in and trigger obsessive thoughts about using cocaine.

9. Irresistible cravings and urges lead the patient to obtain and use cocaine and/or other drugs. The relapse chain is complete.

The chain of events described above is as applicable to other drugs as it is to cocaine. The function of RP is to interrupt this process so that the presence of life problems does not lead inexorably to relapse.

RELAPSE PREVENTION STRATEGIES

Relapse prevention is a broad-spectrum approach involving specific intervention procedures to avoid or limit slips and relapses as well as global procedures aimed at lifestyle balance. Counselors often express concern about addressing RP. Conventional wisdom suggests that discussing relapse might act as a self-fulfilling prophecy and cause this unfortunate situation to occur. In fact, however, clients who well understand and thoroughly practice RP skills are the ones most likely to succeed in maintaining the behavior changes they have worked so hard to bring about. Maintenance strategies can help clients prevent relapses and, just as important, limit the length and destructiveness of lapses that do occur.

Although treatments will vary, all clients should receive comprehensive RP training. This type of training will typically weave through the entire treatment period, but the specific concept of relapse and the training central to this issue should be introduced just beyond the midpoint of treatment and continue until termination. Further, RP strategies should be bolstered after termination at brief (half-hour) booster sessions 1, 3, 6, 9, 12, 15, 18, and 24 months after formal treatment ends. In addition to the booster sessions, clients should be advised that they can come in or call at any time. This open-door policy plus booster sessions will consolidate treatment gains, provide a sense of continuity, and greatly decrease the probability of a relapse.

Relapse prevention strategies do not work if clients are told that they have no control over their lives. They are not, in this perspective, seen as "victims of disease," but, rather, as objective participants in a process designed to understand why they do what they do. This participant–observer model is critical if we are to restore a sense of control and ability in our clients, and it is this self-efficacy that will enable substance abusers to operate on their environment as opposed to having the environment operate on them. The counselor does need to move slowly enough so that clients are not overwhelmed. They need to be able to pick and choose acceptable techniques and strategies in a fashion that enhances their self-efficacy and allows them to feel good about the process.

Strategies for Alleviating Risk

Marlatt and Donovan (2005) have discussed specific intervention strategies to be used after a client is exposed to a high-risk situation. Specific interventions can be used to deal with each step in the relapse process as it was shown in Figure 7.1. Thus, clients are taught to monitor their own behaviors so that they can plan for avoidance of or mastery over high-risk situations. When such situations arise, skills training and stress-management work have ensured the presence of workable coping responses. Decreases in self-efficacy are countered through cognitive strategies. Even initial use of the substance is converted into a positive learning experience through reminder cards and cognitive restructuring. Booster sessions and treatment for RP focus on mastery of these techniques as well as mastery of the global intervention techniques to be discussed in the next section.

SELF-MONITORING   The first tool in training clients to recognize high-risk situations is called self-monitoring. Clients keep track of when, where, and why they want to use drugs or alcohol. Self-monitoring is a simple tool that requires clients to keep a complete record of their substance abuse or their urges to use substances. Self-monitoring sheets can be used to show what feelings the clients were having and what coping skills they used to avoid substance use or limit the amount consumed.

Self-monitoring in this fashion serves as both an assessment procedure and an intervention strategy. The counselor gathers a great deal of information about cues to substance use and existing coping skills, and clients develop a much more acute awareness of their urge, and use patterns as they continue to self-monitor. Clients and counselors also become alert to the critical points where choices are made and to the alternative responses that have worked for them.

Addictive behaviors such as drug and alcohol abuse tend to take on a life of their own after many years and to look like automatic responses. Self-monitoring forces clients to be consciously aware of their actions, and this awareness is very effective in dehabitualizing the substance use response. As clients become more aware, they tend to use less and to report fewer pleasurable feelings from the drugs.

DIRECT OBSERVATION METHOD   Another set of techniques that helps identify high-risk situations is known as the direct observation method. Clients are presented with a comprehensive list of situations and asked to rate them for degree of temptation and the level of confidence they would have in their capacity to avoid a relapse. Similarly, the Situational Confidence Questionnaire (Annis, 1982) can be used to elucidate exactly what clients would do in high-risk situations. In this test, clients imagine themselves in each of a number of situations and report on a scale how confident they are that they would be able to resist drinking ("What would you do if you found yourself at a wedding reception where everyone was drinking?"). This technique allows counselors to determine their clients' coping skills level and to increase their awareness of high-risk situations. Other exercises involve the client's recounting of past relapse episodes and analysis of relapse fantasies. Past episodes provide a way for both client and counselor to see more clearly what led up to these relapses, what high-risk situations were involved, and how these unfortunate experiences could have been avoided. Relapse fantasies, too, will tell a great deal about the expectancies involved in a relapse and will give clear indications of what situations are seen as high-risk.

COPING SKILLS   Once the counselor and the client have identified the high-risk situations, the client can be taught to respond to these situations in an adaptive and forthright manner. Some situations should simply be avoided. Others will require the use of coping skills to negotiate the difficult situation without relapsing.

Relapse prevention is a strategy of preparedness that is based on the client's ability to cope with high-risk situations. Relaxation training, assertion, and proper communication are coping skills. The therapist needs to help clients assess which skills they possess, which skills need to be bolstered, and which skills they need to learn. Frequently, clients are able to identify coping skills that work for them when they deal with nonsubstance-related challenges and that they can adapt to this special necessity.

Stress management techniques, too, are coping skills. These include such cognitive and behavioral components as the following: (1) taking one thing at a time; (2) working tension off physically; (3) learning not to be a perfectionist; (4) using humor; (5) seeking outside help when needed; (6) allowing time alone; (7) adopting hobbies and activities that do not involve substance use; (8) striving for moderation, as opposed to rigidity, in thought and action; (9) sleeping and eating correctly; and (10) balancing the costs and benefits of life.

EFFICACY ENHANCEMENT   Another tool is an efficacy-enhancing imagery technique. Here, counselors help clients to fully relax and then present them with images of possible relapse situations. Clients imagine that, instead of relapsing, they have a great degree of control and can manage the difficult situation effectively. This tool is very similar to relapse rehearsal, in which clients imagine a situation in which they successfully apply a coping skill and therefore avoid using drugs or alcohol.

Coping skills tend to be quite effective, when learned correctly, in avoiding further progression of the process. If, however, clients do not at first succeed with coping skills and proceed to the next step in the process, experiencing decreased self-efficacy and positive expectancies of drug use, they can use their coping skills or use decision making skills or even a decision matrix which is a form on which clients list immediate and delayed positive and negative consequences for both continuation and discontinuation of abstinence. Clients should be trained in the use of this matrix before treatment ends and should be advised to create (on paper) a new matrix every time they are considering a resumption of substance use. For example, Arthur, a client considering a return to heroin use, listed the following positive consequences of continued abstinence: keeping his family together, keeping his job, maintaining physical health, and feeling better about himself. The negative consequences he thought would occur if he remained abstinent included loss of his close friends, boredom, and depriving himself of intense pleasure and excitement. He also considered the favorable and unfavorable consequences of a return to heroin use. Positive consequences included gratification, excitement, anxiety reduction, and the ability to avoid dealing with the straight world. Perceived negative consequences included shame, self-hatred, loss of job and family, and poor health. The fact that Arthur could share these thoughts with his counselor made it possible for him to explore his feelings honestly and weigh his choices carefully.

BEHAVIORAL CONTRACTING   The matrix in combination with factual education about the immediate and delayed effects of substances should provide clients with a great deal of staying power to avoid initial use of the substance. If, however, clients are simply swept away by the idea of using and do indeed try the substance, they can step back from a full-fledged relapse if they have received training in dealing with slips.

The client and the counselor should have a behavioral contract (signed, sealed, and delivered) to limit the extent of substance use following a slip. The contract should be simple, nonjudgmental, and nonpunitive. It should include a statement recognizing that a slip is not a failure and emphasizing the client's awareness that he or she does have the skills needed to regain control. The contract, which is signed by both the client and the counselor, should include a statement concerning the action the client plans to take if a slip has occurred. For example, a client might agree to telephone his AA sponsor, to contact the counselor, and to list the circumstances of the slip in an effort to use it as a learning experience. Of course, such contracts are not legal documents, but they can have a powerful effect on client behavior. Clients tend to take them seriously and become invested in their ability to keep the contract.

In addition, each client should be given a small wallet card that has tips on what to do should a slip occur. This card should outline coping skills, thoughts to be engaged in, and numbers to call. It should be simple and straightforward. Its importance lies in the fact that it operationalizes the concept of the slip as a learning experience. At a time when they might not otherwise be thinking clearly, clients have a series of steps to follow. If they carry out the suggested actions, they will have an opportunity to examine and learn from their experience. Curry and Marlatt (1987) suggest that the points clients need to keep in mind include the following: (1) stop, look, and listen (to what is happening); (2) keep calm; (3) renew the commitment to behavior change; (4) review the situation leading up to the lapse; (5) make an immediate plan for recovery; and (6) ask for help.

COGNITIVE RESTRUCTURING Finally, if clients advance through the relapse process and are experiencing the abstinence violation effect, they will have one final technique left to them. The cognitive restructuring that will have been done while they were still in treatment enables them to "rethink" what is happening to them. They are trained to use different thought processes, so that a slip becomes a mistake that they can learn from. In addition, they are imbued with the notion that the slip is a product of the situation and not a reflection of the self ("I am not a bad person!"). This procedure requires some effort and is often referred to as *positive mental attitude training*. Clients are taught to be objective, rational, and fair. They are taught to reframe the situation while recognizing that not all is lost. If this technique does not halt the process, clients may go on to relapse. Even then, however, a positive outcome is possible. Clients will still be able to utilize all that they have learned and may, at some point in the future, end the relapse.

GLOBAL INTERVENTION STRATEGIES

Global self-control strategies can be used to bolster the RP effort. These skills and techniques will, in some cases, allow clients to completely avoid high-risk situations precipitated by imbalanced lifestyles.

SEEKING LIFESTYLE BALANCE   The relapse process begins with a lifestyle imbalance. This imbalance manifests itself as too much stress or as negatives in a client's life. Global self-control strategies are intended to increase the client's overall capacity to deal with stress and to cope with high-risk situations with an increased sense of self-efficacy; to train the client to identify and respond to situational and covert early warning signals; and to help the client exercise self-control strategies to reduce the risk level of any situation that might otherwise trigger a slip (Marlatt & Donovan, 2005).

The initial goal is to avoid the onset of an imbalanced lifestyle. In this regard it is critical that clients effectively balance their "shoulds" and "wants." This effort involves balancing work and recreation, good and bad times, happiness and sadness, and pain and pleasure. Such a balance can best be effected by alerting clients to the fact that they may become obsessive and overwhelmed, now that they are sober, with a million details that can present themselves in day-to-day life. These details can be managed, but not to the exclusion of the "good things" in life. Clients should be encouraged to have leisure activities, nonstressful hobbies, and plenty of time for themselves. In addition, positive addictions such as jogging, meditation, and knitting are therapeutic and effective stress reduction techniques. These activities, when combined with a healthy style of living (sleeping and eating correctly), greatly promote a balanced lifestyle. Such activities are easy to do, inexpensive, and always available. Booster sessions and follow-up should always assess these activities, and, if necessary, corrective action should be taken to maintain a balanced lifestyle.

PROVIDING ADAPTIVE INDULGENCES   The frustrating experience of a lifestyle imbalance frequently leads the client toward a desire to feel better or to live it up. If a desire to indulge manifests itself, clients must have substitute indulgences that they can engage in. These should be adaptive (good for the person) as opposed to maladaptive (bad for the person—e.g., a return to substance use), and they should be developed creatively and broadly with the client's best interests in mind. Adaptive substitute indulgences could include buying a long-wanted item or helping someone else (L. P. Dana, personal communication, April, 2009). In addition, substitute indulgences could include such things as buying or cooking a gourmet meal, going boating, vacationing, seeing a movie, taking a walk, reading, or taking a bath. Other simple ideas would include getting a massage, writing in a journal, going to bed early, or walking on a beach. The list is endless, and substitute indulgences can be developed easily for each individual client. These activities should be determined individually, and they should be very reinforcing. Remember, substance use is, in itself, exceptionally rewarding, so the substitute indulgence ideally has a reinforcement potential equal to or greater than use of the preferred substance.

AVOIDING URGES AND CRAVINGS   The desire for indulgence may manifest itself as a craving for the drug. Urges and cravings are compensatory conditioned responses that develop from an anticipation of the effects of substance use. They result from external cues (seeing a syringe, passing a favorite bar, smelling cigarette smoke) and are therefore very common experiences following discontinuance of drug or alcohol use. Given this reality, it is critical that clients be taught about cueing responses and that they learn that exposure to cues can lead to a sense of deprivation and a desire to use. To cope with this situation, the client should be taught to use coping imagery ("Imagine yourself in situation X; now, when you feel the desire to use, make the decision to flee, relax ..."). Basically, the counselor must give clients a number of scenes in which they successfully cope with an intense desire to use a substance. In addition, stimulus control techniques (removal of as many tempting stimuli as possible from clients' everyday living environment) will effectively limit the amount of cueing that goes on and will greatly diminish the frequency of urges and cravings. Stimulus control techniques are particularly useful during the early stages of recovery, because nonexposure simply results in less temptation.

LABELING AND DETACHMENT   One of the most effective tools clients can use to survive urges and cravings is labeling and detachment. In this method, clients are taught to be critical observers of their bodily responses, and they become exceptionally sensitive to environmental influences on their behavior. Use of this technique would allow a client to say: "I'm experiencing a conditioned response that manifests itself as craving. This response stems directly from my walking by Fifth Street, where I used to do all my drinking. This feeling is temporary, and it will pass. If I respond to it, I will strengthen it and consequently be forced to experience this feeling more and more frequently. If I experience the feeling and do not give in to it, it will pass, and eventually the frequency of these feelings will decrease greatly." In this example, the client assumes a sense of control and objectivity. She has a heightened awareness of what is happening and is consequently less anxious and less likely to succumb to the urge.

DEALING WITH RATIONALIZATION AND DENIAL   If the techniques used to this point fail and clients begin to engage in rationalization, denial, and apparently irrelevant decisions, they will be able to call on the training previously received that shows rationalization and denial to be precursors of a high-risk situation. In this regard a decision matrix can be formulated that shows the positive aspects of a behavior change that will lead away from a return to substance use. Clients can also be sensitized to the dangers of apparently irrelevant decisions. They can recognize these decisions as warning signs and effectively abort the relapse process.

If the process continues on to introduction of a high-risk situation, the client should be able to fall back on relapse rehearsals (see the previous section) or engage in an avoidance strategy such as calling the counselor, fleeing from the situation, or calling a friend.

CASE EXAMPLE

Shontay, a 35-year-old account executive, seeks counseling to help her maintain her abstinence from alcohol. Shontay had become concerned about her drinking, and she achieved abstinence almost a year ago. Her initial behavior change had come about because of comments from her friends about her drinking, pressure from her husband, and her concern that her career might be jeopardized if she became known as an out-of-control drinker.

Shontay prides herself on her discipline and control and feels that these characteristics helped her quit drinking. Now, however, she is beginning to feel that her discipline may be crumbling. She feels anxious and worried about the possibility that the cravings she is beginning to feel may lead to a relapse. Her career is very important to her, and she tends to work 60-hr weeks. There is no sharp dividing line between work and leisure for her and her husband. Their social life is largely based on corporate "networking," and most of their friends are business associates.

One of Shontay's concerns has to do with the expectation of alcohol consumption among her coworkers. As she points out, "A certain amount of drinking is expected, especially with clients, and it's hard enough for a woman to be accepted where I work as it is."

She feels that people at her corporate level have to walk a narrow line: Drink enough to be accepted but not enough to be noteworthy. She also feels uncertain about how to handle the cocktail parties that she is expected to attend, not only by her company but also by her husband.

During the first months of her abstinence from alcohol, Shontay went through a honeymoon period when she was excited about her recovery and actively avoided situations where alcohol would be present. She has put most of her boundless energy into the challenge of becoming sober. Now, however, she is feeling more pressure. She perceives that she has put her career on hold and that it is important for her to renew her contacts, but she is frightened about what that might mean.

Shontay identifies several situations as risky for her because they have always been associated with drinking. These situations include (1) lunches with clients, (2) after-work socializing with coworkers, and (3) business-related cocktail parties. She identifies some alternatives that can help her avoid risk—for example, asking clients to meet her for breakfast rather than lunch. She also selects and practices a number of coping strategies that work for her. She decides in advance what nonalcoholic beverages she will order and rehearses placing her order with the waiter. She identifies a nondrinking colleague and arranges to sit next to her at restaurants. She practices drink refusal skills intensively until she feels prepared to cope with social pressures to consume alcohol. She avoids cocktail parties in favor of other networking events when possible, but she carefully prepares for occasions she feels should not be missed.

In addition to coping with specific situations, Shontay makes adjustments in her general lifestyle. She joins a health club and jogs or swims laps during lunchtime, when she normally would have been fighting off pressures to drink at restaurants. When she does have lunch appointments—rarely since she discovered the "power breakfast"—she exercises after work and arrives home feeling much more relaxed than usual. She and her husband arrange to have one social night out each week that involves neither drinking nor business.

Some substance abuse counselors might view Shontay's intense involvement with work as problematic. Some might even question the validity of her assumptions that both alcohol consumption and 60-hr workweeks are expected by her employers. In fact, however, these expectations may be very real. At this point, Shontay feels that she needs to take some risks, such as going to business-related social events, in order to advance her career. Her counselor helps her clarify her options and recognizes the need to help her live in accordance with her own values.

SUMMARY

As difficult as it is to change behaviors, it is even more challenging to maintain changes once they have been made. Relapse prevention (RP) is therefore an important part of the process of substance abuse counseling.

Counselors and clients, working in collaboration, can develop effective plans for preventing returns to uncontrolled drug use. Cognitive and lifestyle risks, as well as entry into specific high-risk situations, can serve as determinants of relapse. Individuals need to identify the situations that place them at risk and make decisions about avoiding or coping with these situations. If coping strategies are learned and used effectively, clients' self-efficacy is enhanced. If coping strategies are not available, clients may lose confidence and experience an urge for substance use. Even if substance use is reinitiated, a client can avoid disaster if he or she has received intense training in coping with slips. With RP, as with other counseling interventions, the counselor needs to be sensitive to individual differences and use strategies that closely match the needs and experiences of individual clients.

It is clear that the determinants of both lapses (brief return or one-time use) and relapses (resuming a problem behavior) are *self-efficacy* (Do I have control to avoid this behavior or do another more adaptive behavior?), *outcome expectancies* (Will this behavior make me feel better?), *motivation* (Is the client well motivated to seek positive and adaptive resolutions to the problems at hand?), *coping* (Does the person have the skill base to deal with stress and temptation?), *emotional states* (Are moods modulated and can negative emotional states including boredom be understood and managed?), and *craving* (the jet-fueled feeling that "I must use" is critically important in provoking a return to use and it must be well discussed and clients must be well prepared to manage these states) (Marlatt & Gordon, 2005) and these provoking conditions need to be fully and bravely addressed in any counseling relationship which hopes to positively reduce the likelihood of relapse and the resultant intensity of any resumption of substance use. Without careful consideration of the relapse phenomena clients will be at an unacceptably high risk of falling back, of feeling that they have failed, and of feeling that treatment is an ineffective path to change.

QUESTIONS FOR THOUGHT AND DISCUSSION

1. People sometimes question the use of RP training as part of treatment, saying that if clients expect to relapse, they will. What do you see as the pros and cons of addressing the issue of relapse as part of treatment? At what point would you introduce the subject?

2. The abstinence violation effect is also subject to controversy. Some people suggest that if clients are told that they must be absolutely abstinent at all costs, they will be unable to cope with a slip. Other people suggest that an all-or-none approach is necessary because clients must be discouraged from thoughtlessly experimenting with drugs. What are the strengths of each of these arguments? How do you think this issue can be resolved most effectively?

3. Suppose you had a client who had been recovering for some time but who had begun to make subtle changes in her life. If you became aware that she had

stopped going to meetings of her support group, that she had stopped her regular regimen of exercise, and that she had started to associate with alcohol-using friends, what would you do?

REFERENCES

Annis, H. M. (1982). *Situational confidence questionnaire*. Toronto: Addiction Foundation of Ontario.

Coombs, R., & Howatt, W. (2005). *The addictions counselor handbook*. Hoboken, NJ: Wiley Press.

Curry, S. G., & Marlatt, G. A. (1987). Building self-confidence, self-efficacy, and self-control. In W. M. Cox (Ed.), *Treatment and prevention of alcohol problems: A resource manual* (pp. 117–136). New York: Academic Press.

Fields, R. (2010, in press) *Drugs in perspective*. New York: McGraw Hill.

Gorski, T. (2009). *The CENAPS model of relapse prevention*. Retreived on April 23, 2009, from http://www.tgorski.com/

Jellinek, E. M. (1960). *The disease concept of alcoholism*. New Brunswick, NJ: Millhouse Press.

Kern, M. (2009). *Stages of Change Model*. Retreived on April 23, 2009, from http://www.addictioninfo.org/articles/11/1/Stages-of-Change-Model/Page1.html

Marlatt, G., & Donovan, D. (2005). *Relapse prevention: Maintainence strategies in the treatment of addictive behaviors*. New York: Guilford Press.

Marlatt, G. A. (1985). Relapse prevention: Theoretical rationale and overview of the model. In G. A. Marlatt & J. R. Gordon (Eds.), *Relapse prevention*. New York: Guilford Press.

Marlatt, G. A., & Gordon, J. R. (Eds.). (1985). *Relapse prevention*. New York: Guilford Press.

Marlatt, G., & Witkiewitz, K. (Eds.). (2009). *Addictive behaviors*. Washington, DC: American Psychological Association.

Miller, W., & Brown, S. (2009). Why psychologists should treat alcohol and drug problems. In A. Marlatt & K. Witkiewitz (Eds.), *Addictive behaviors*. Washington, DC: American Psychological Association.

Prochaska, J. O., DiClemente, C. C., & Norcross, J. C. (1992). In search of how people change: Applications to addictive behaviors. *American Psychologist, 47,* 1102–1114.

Velicer, W. F, Prochaska, J. O., Fava, J. L., Norman, G. J., & Redding, C. A. (1998). Smoking cessation and stress management: Applications of the transtheoretical model of behavior change. *Homeostasis, 38,* 216–233.

Washton, A. M. (2008). *Quitting cocaine*. St. Paul, MN: Hazelden.

THE CONTEXT OF
CHANGE

8 | Working with Families

NO SUBSTANCE ABUSER—in fact, no client—can be treated effectively unless his or her social interactions are taken into account. People influence their social environments and are influenced by them in return. When they develop substance abuse problems, the issues are not limited to them alone but affect all of their social systems. At the same time, these systems have a reciprocal effect on the maintenance or resolution of the problem.

The system that tends to be most widely recognized as closely associated with addictive behaviors is the family. Substance abuse counselors clearly need to pay close attention to the family dynamics affecting each client. Family systems obviously have the potential to influence the outcome of treatment for the individual. Just as important, however, is the fact that the family system itself can be seen as an appropriate target for change. As family therapists have learned, one cannot legitimately separate the individual from the family.

In her review of what is known, through research, about the interaction between families and substance abuse, McCrady (2006, pp. 168–174) explains that

- Persons with alcohol and other drug use disorders live in and have relationships with a network of family and friends...
- Family relationships may protect against the development of alcohol or drug problems...
- Families and others close to the drinker or drug user may contribute to the development and maintenance of substance use disorders...
- Families and others close to drinkers and drug users play a role in helping a user recognize a problem and seek help...
- Families and others close to drinkers and drug users have a significant impact on the change process and treatment success...

• Families and others close to drinkers or drug users play an important role in the maintenance of change.

A number of evidence-based programs have been built on the understanding that an individual's behaviors cannot appropriately be viewed in isolation from the family system. For example, *Brief Strategic Family Therapy (BSFT)* (Szapocznik & Hervis, 2004; Szapocznik, Hervis, & Schwartz, 2003), a program designed for adolescents and their families, appears on the Web site of National Registry of Evidence-based Programs and Practices (Substance Abuse and Mental Health Services Administration, 2009a). The clear focus of this program is on the context within which adolescents' behavior takes place.

> The social influences an individual encounters have an important impact on his or her behavior. Such influences are particularly powerful during the critical years of childhood and adolescence. The BSFT approach asserts that the counselor will not be able to understand the adolescent's drug-abusing behavior without understanding what is going on in the various contexts in which he or she lives. Drug-abusing behavior does not happen in a vacuum; it exists within an environment that includes family, peers, neighborhood, and the cultures that define the rules, values, and behaviors of the adolescent (Szapocznik et al., 2003).

In recognition that "the family is the primary context in which the child learns and develops" (Szapocznik et al., 2003), the program focuses on family therapy as the primary mechanism for change in the adolescent's substance use and related behaviors.

MULTIDIMENSIONAL FAMILY THERAPY (MFT)   (Liddle, Rowe, Dakof, Henderson, & Greenbaum, 2009) also centers on family therapy as a pathway to adolescent well-being. This program, like BSFT, has been assessed as an evidence-based program (Substance Abuse and Mental Health Services Administration, 2009b) and attends to multiple contexts. In a discussion of the application of MFT to a population of adolescent cannabis users, Liddle (2002) describes the theory of change as follows:

> Adolescent developmental psychology and psychopathology research has determined that (1) the family is the primary context of healthy identity formation and ego development, (2) peer influence operates in relation to the family's buffering effect against the deviant peer subculture, and (3) adolescents need to develop an interdependent rather than an emotionally separated relationship with their parents. Therefore, a multidimensional change perspective holds that symptom reduction and enhancement of prosocial and normative developmental functions in problem adolescents occur by (1) targeting the family as the foundation for intervention and (2) simultaneously facilitating curative processes in several domains of functioning and across several systemic levels. Particular behaviors, emotions, and thinking patterns known to be related to problem formation and continuation are replaced by new behaviors, emotions, and thinking patterns associated with appropriate intrapersonal and familial development (p. 19).

BEHAVIORAL COUPLES COUNSELING   (Fals-Stewart, Birchler, & Kelley, 2006; O'Farrell & Fals-Stewart, 2006), like the adolescent interventions described earlier, also emphasizes the family context as a focus for change. When using this evidence-based approach, counselors help couples to build support for substance use change, improve communication, and increase positive family activities—all behaviors that are associated with recovery.

All of these evidence-based family interventions depend on changing family systems. As systems theory makes clear, helping a family transform from a system that supports substance abuse to one that supports healthy alternatives is always challenging.

SYSTEMS THEORY

General systems theory is most often associated with the work of von Bertalanffy (1968), who developed it as an alternative to Newtonian science. Traditional Newtonian physics was reductionistic in its attempt to break complex phenomena down into the smallest possible parts and was linear in its attempt to understand these parts as a series of less complex, cause-and-effect relationships. Systems theory represents an entirely different mode of thought, viewing all living things as open systems best understood by an examination of their interrelationships and organizing principles. It pays attention not to linear, causal relationships but to consistent, if circular, patterns of interaction. A system can be thought of as a set of units that have a consistent, organized, and predictable relationship with one another. Living organisms are open systems in that they interact with their environment, taking in and discharging information or energy through boundaries that are sufficiently permeable to allow these transactions to take place. The system itself also encompasses subsystems, which interact in a predictable manner within the context of the larger system.

In order to apply the systems paradigm to family interactions, the counselor needs to understand several basic features of the approach (Umbarger, 1983, p. 17). It devotes attention not to the part but to the whole, not to the isolated unit but to the transactional process among the units that make up the system. The ongoing process is based on information and feedback loops. When a unit gets a signal that its behavior is deviating from the system's customary organization, this behavior may need to be corrected. Only then can homeostasis, the system's steady state of being, be maintained. Causes and effects are circular, rather than linear, and interventions into any part of the system affect the whole.

Although family counselors may differ in their personal approaches and theories, they tend to share a general perception that the family is a system, clearly conforming to systemic principles:

> The human family is a social system that operates through transactional patterns. These are repeated interactions which establish patterns of how, when, and to whom to relate.... Repeated operations build patterns, and these patterns underpin the family system. The patterns which evolve become familiar and preferred. The system maintains itself within a preferred range, and deviations which pass the system's threshold of tolerance usually elicit counterdeviation mechanisms which reestablish the accustomed range. (Minuchin, 1979, p. 7)

Thus, each family has its own homeostasis, or preferred steady state, that may or may not be "healthy" but that is monitored through feedback and control mechanisms and protected by the system as a whole. Each family has a set of rules that governs its interactions and makes them predictable. Each includes subsystems (e.g., spousal, parental, or sibling) that carry out specialized functions and attempt to preserve the integrity of the overall system. Each is an organized whole, making it impossible to consider intervening in one part without taking the others into account.

SUBSTANCE ABUSE AND THE FAMILY SYSTEM

Family counseling calls for a reframing of the presenting problem from a focus on individual symptoms to a focus on family structure and interactions. Even when the identified client is dependent on alcohol or another drug, the family counselor sees the goal of intervention not just as abstinence for the affected family member but also as improved functioning for the family unit as a whole.

Substance abuse or dependence, like any other presenting problem, is usually deeply embedded in a family's life. Over the years, substance abuse can become central to a family's functioning, becoming a primary organizing factor in the family system's structure. A family with an alcohol-abusing member, for instance, learns to maintain its homeostasis around that person's drinking. Alcohol may even be a stabilizing factor, allowing the family to solve problems in familiar ways.

These concepts do not imply that unstable family dynamics "cause" alcohol problems or that the homeostasis found by alcohol-affected families should be considered a healthy or positive state. What they do imply is that families develop consistent, predictable methods for adapting to substance abuse, just as they create rules and interactional styles for dealing with other problems. At the same time, abuse of alcohol or another drug may also be one method—if a spectacularly ineffective one—for coping with the stresses of a family system. Family members adapt to the substance abuse as though it were part of the family. The family develops ways of existing in the world that allow—even encourage—the drug or alcohol use to continue. This process cannot be understood from a viewpoint of linear causality. The process is circular, which makes it all the more difficult to alter.

If a counselor recognizes this conceptualization as being based in reality and wants to work from a family perspective, he or she is forced to reconsider most of the commonly held assumptions related to substance abuse, its etiology, and its treatment. A family systems therapist tends to view the substance-abusing individual simply as the identified symptom-bearer in the family, rather than as the primary focus of attention, and wants to know what function the substance use behaviors perform in the family unit. With this perception comes a major alteration in desired outcome goals. When the entire family is viewed as "the client," the goal of treatment broadens from a focus strictly on the individual's substance use to a focus on the health and functioning of the entire system. Working toward this goal requires an understanding of the family's situation at the time of the intervention. Methods for working with families vary widely, especially when we take into account the stage in the development and resolution of the substance abuse problem.

STAGES IN FAMILY RECOVERY

Families have distinctive needs at various stages of the recovery process. The goals of counseling differ according to whether substance abuse is active, whether the drug use behavior is in the process of alteration, or whether behavior change has been established.

As is the case with an individual client, recovery is a process, rather than an event. Just as individuals move through the stages of precontemplation, contemplation, preparation, action, and maintenance (Prochaska, DiClemente, & Norcross, 1992), families may also move through the process of change in predictable stages. Systems interventions are most effective if they fit the family's stage of readiness. Of course, stages of family change differ in one important way from those of individual change: Not all family members reach points of readiness at the same time. The counselor needs to be ready to help any family member who chooses to alter his or her part in the ongoing pattern of interaction. Growth and change can take place, whether or not the substance-abusing member takes part, as long as other family members make changes in their customary roles. One way to conceptualize the process of family change is to think in terms of stages of systemic change. The first two stages can be thought of as (a) making initial systemic changes and (b) adjusting to early recovery (Carlson, Sperry, & Lewis, 2005). Once a reasonable level of stability has been reached, the family may be ready to deepen and maintain change through family therapy.

MAKING INITIAL SYSTEMIC CHANGES

As treatment begins, the counselor helps family members interrupt the patterns that have been characteristic of the family system in the past. Part of the counselor's role at this point involves helping the members decide between the alternatives of (1) confronting the substance use behaviors and pressing the substance-abusing member into accepting treatment, (2) trying to disengage and change behaviors that have perpetuated an unhealthy system, or (3) helping family members learn skills for changing the social environment in positive ways that will make the substance-abusing individual more likely to choose treatment.

CONFRONTATION   An approach to confrontation that has remained popular for several decades is the "intervention," which was pioneered by Johnson (1973) for people with alcohol problems. When an intervention takes place, family members, friends, and associates gather to confront the individual as a group. All of the participants present concrete evidence of the impact that the person's drinking has had on them. In a supportive manner, they press the individual to admit that he or she does have an alcohol-related problem. The purpose of the intervention is to change the person's perceptions so that he or she comes to understand that drinking or other drug use is the source of the problems being described. The desired outcome is that the client accepts the need to enter treatment.

Many clients report that their entrance into treatment was the result of an intervention, but this procedure is not a panacea:

> For families in pain, the appeal of this approach, with its promise of treatment as a potential "happy ending," is obvious. Unfortunately, however, it is in the very simplicity of the intervention that its shortcomings lie. The overriding purpose of the intervention is to make a convincing case that alcohol is the root cause of the problems affecting the individual and the family and to present treatment as an immediately available solution. Thus, the approach oversimplifies problem attribution, conceptualizing issues in linear, cause-and-effect terms. (Lewis, 1991, p. 43)

When family members see treament as a happy ending, they may fail to recognize the need to make the systemic changes that are central to long-term health.

Family members must also explore in great depth the implications of the procedure. Usually, an intervention is built on the notion that there will be consequences if the client refuses treatment: The spouse will leave, the colleague will stop covering up problems at work, or the friend will cut off ties. Before taking any action, intervenors need to consider carefully the impact that these consequences might have on their own lives:

> One of the reasons the intervention should be approached with great caution is that this type of ultimatum can have life-shattering implications if the alcoholic refuses treatment, has unsuccessful treatment, or reacts violently to the confrontation. Great care must be taken in preparing a family for the intervention so that each member has a clear understanding of the risks involved and a concrete plan for dealing with each contingency. (Lewis, 1991, p. 44)

DISENGAGEMENT   Sometimes it is neither necessary nor appropriate to press the individual into treatment. Family members may need to begin the change process without the participation of the substance abuser. Sometimes family members who are ready to make a commitment to change should be encouraged to take steps to improve their own lives, with their goals focusing on their own growth and health, not on the drinking or drug use behavior. Through a process of disengagement, family members can interrupt rigid patterns of interaction and move away from accepting responsibility for others' behavior. For many families, a referral to AlAnon or another self-help organization at this point provides much needed support as sober family members attempt to withdraw from the performance of roles that have enabled the substance abuser to avoid the negative consequences of drinking or drug use. As family members begin to take care of themselves, the family structure is no longer built solely on a foundation of substance abuse. As they begin to refocus away from the substance abuse—and from the energy it takes to maintain secrecy—they can seek the support that they, themselves, may require. The initial purpose of these changes might have been to help family members cope with the current situation, but they also improve the family's ability to adjust effectively if the substance-abusing member does change his or her behavior.

COMMUNITY REINFORCEMENT AND FAMILY TRAINING   A viable alternative to either the confrontational intervention or the act of disengagement is provided by Community Reinforcement and Family Training (CRAFT) (Meyers & Smith, 1995; Smith & Meyers, 2009; Smith, Meyers, & Austin, 2008). The approach taken by the CRAFT program is to work directly with concerned significant others (CSOs), helping them gain the skills needed to engage their substance-abusing family members into treatment. CRAFT teaches CSOs how to make changes in their own behaviors so that they reinforce positive changes in the substance abusers' drug or alcohol use rather than focusing their attention on the most problematic situations.

> Without the drinker present, the CRAFT therapist works with the family member to change the drinker's social environment in a way that removes inadvertent reinforcement for drinking and instead reinforces abstinence. The therapist also helps the family

member prepare for the next opportunity when the drinker may respond favorably to an offer of help and support and may be willing to enter treatment. (Miller, Meyers, & Hiller-Sturmhofel, 1999, p. 119)

Research studies (Meyers, Miller, Hill, & Tonigan, 1999; Miller, Meyers, & Tonigan, 1999) have indicated that, after just four or five sessions, almost two-third of clients succeeded in their efforts to engage their family members into treatment.

ADJUSTING TO EARLY RECOVERY

When the substance-abusing family member does achieve sobriety, the counselor is in a position to help the family cope with what is, in fact, a crisis. If we think of a crisis as a situation requiring coping skills outside of one's usual repertoire, we know that families faced with a newly abstinent member clearly fit the definition. Families that have built their lives on transactional patterns involving alcoholism or addiction often find it difficult to adapt to the sudden need for change. Frequently, they realize that after years of using alcohol or other drugs to cope with any problem, they have not learned problem-solving or conflict resolution skills. The dearth of effective coping skills may be exacerbated by pent-up anger and distrust. Problems that the family has always attributed to alcohol or other drugs continue to exist, leading to feelings of intense disappointment. The family's repertoire of behaviors is adaptive to the presence of a substance-abusing member but not to the entrance of a newly sober person no longer able to act as the identified patient. Finding a new homeostatic state can be difficult.

> Families with a long history of transactional patterns based around a family member's addiction frequently face crises when the individual's substance use subsides. Behaviors that have been reasonably adaptive to the presence of the addiction are no longer appropriate when the identified patient moves out of his or her role. Families with newly abstinent members now need coping skills outside of their usual repertoires. The sudden need for change often comes as a shock, especially because substance use has previously replaced problem-solving and conflict resolution skills. In addition, families are often disappointed to find that the problems they have always attributed to substance use alone continue to exist. (Carlson et al., 2005, p. 148)

Sometimes families navigate successfully through this drastic alteration in the life of each member. Many families, however, respond to the crisis by splitting up. Family members may maintain their old behaviors and stick to their customary roles, making relapse more likely to occur. This phenomenon should not be interpreted in terms of one family member "sabotaging" another's success but should always be recognized as the system's attempt to reestablish equilibrium.

Counselors can be especially useful at this point by helping family members understand the concept of the family in crisis. The family needs to be helped to weather the immediate crisis situation by focusing on short-term, concrete goals; by making small changes in the family structure, and by learning or relearning how to give one another mutual support. A useful strategy is to ask each family member to identify a specific need or goal that he or she would like to meet. Through a process of negotiation, the family members can work out compromises so that each person gets something that he or she wants. When this happens, family members feel that some of their own needs are being addressed. At the same time, each member can experience being helpful to the others. Such simple, immediate solutions can help the family gain enough stability to withstand the pressures of this difficult time. After a few months, the members may be ready to consider more basic, long-lasting alterations in family structure. They can begin to work toward making more in-depth systemic changes and developing the roles and relationships that characterize healthy, effectively functioning social units.

Several well-researched efforts have demonstrated success in the use of couples counseling during the period of early recovery (O'Farrell, 1992; O'Farrell & Fals-Stewart, 2006). These approaches build on long-standing evidence of the success of behavioral couples therapy. McCrady, Noel, Abrams, Stout, & Nelson (1986) compared three treatments. Minimal spouse involvement (MSI) allowed the spouse to observe the alcoholic's individual therapy. Alcohol-focused spouse involvement (AFSI) taught the spouse some specific skills for dealing with alcohol-related situations. Alcohol behavioral marital therapy (ABMT) added behavioral marital therapy to the skills taught in the other conditions. All of the treatments were associated with decreased drinking. The ABMT approach led to more stable marriages and increased marital satisfaction as well as a lessening of drinking behaviors. The Counseling for Alcoholics' Marriages (CALM) project studied couples in which the husband was receiving alcoholism counseling (O'Farrell, 1992). The treatment conditions included (1) no marital treatment, (2) a group combining an Antabuse contract with a behavioral skill-building approach, and (3) an interactional couples group focusing on feelings. Participation in couples counseling enhanced the marital adjustment and drinking behaviors of the alcoholics who received the counseling.

All of these approaches hold great promise for helping families deal with the issues of early recovery and prepare for long-term maintenance of change.

Deepening and Maintaining Change

Family therapy, like all other approaches to counseling, reflects divergent viewpoints. Each of the familiar models can be useful to families affected by substance abuse, once they are ready for long-term changes.

Among the general approaches to family therapy that are frequently used for substance abuse treatment are the following: (1) psychodynamic, (2) experiential/humanistic, (3) Bowenian/multigenerational, (4) structural, (5) communication, and (6) behavioral. Each of these perspectives has unique characteristics. Yet each is built—although to varying degrees—on the notion that individual clients affect and are affected by their family units. Each examines the development of the individual in a social context. Each recognizes the potential inherent in interventions that go beyond individual, intrapsychic phenomena.

PSYCHODYNAMIC FAMILY THERAPY   In 1970, the Group for the Advancement of Psychiatry (GAP) attempted to put varying theories of family therapy into perspective by placing them on a continuum, with the two extreme positions indicating the degree to which a theoretical orientation tended to emphasize the individual or the family system:

> At one extreme, position A, were those therapists who saw the family as a means of gathering information about specific family members. These therapists retained a primary focus on the individual and were contrasted with their hypothetical opposite, the positions therapists, who focused entirely on the family as the unit of both change and pathology. Consequently, positions therapists were more likely to view traditional psychiatric problems as social and interpersonal symptoms of maladaptive family functioning. (Kolevzon & Green, 1985, pp. 26–27)

PSYCHODYNAMIC APPROACH   Among the theoretical frameworks in common use, the psychodynamic approach may come closest to the position A pole of GAP's hypothetical continuum. This approach, which is based to a large degree on psychoanalytic thought, emphasizes the effects of individual pathologies on the family system, tends to view the family as a group of interlocking personalities, and stresses the importance of insight for personal change.

The psychoanalytic bases of this model are apparent in its emphases on bringing unresolved conflicts to the surface, on dealing with past experiences, and on addressing both intrapsychic and interpersonal change. Yet the psychodynamic viewpoint as it is applied to family practice has been strongly affected by systems thought and is therefore very different from analytic therapy as it is applied to individuals. Nathan Ackerman, one of the earliest pioneers in family therapy, has probably done more than any other single theorist to bridge the gap between these two epistemologies. In his summary of the family therapist's role and function (Ackerman, 1981), he suggests that therapists should establish empathy and communication between themselves and the family members, as well as among the members themselves, and that this rapport should be used as a catalyst for the expression of major conflicts. The therapist tries to give clients an accurate understanding of their problems by counteracting defenses and converting dormant conflicts into open interpersonal exchange. To Ackerman, the therapist plays the role of "a great parent figure" (p. 172), an instrument of reality testing, an educator, and a model. Thus, Ackerman succeeds in focusing concurrently on individual pathology and family patterns "intrapersonal conflict" and "interpersonal exchange." Although he and other psychodynamic family therapists stop short of labeling all individual symptoms as indications of system dysfunction, they do recognize the high degree of reciprocity between individual and family problems and conflicts.

EXPERIENTIAL/HUMANISTIC THERAPY   The work of Virginia Satir (1967, 1972) has been closely associated with that of the communication theorists, but it can be placed in an experiential/humanistic category because of her concern for feelings and because of the strongly humanistic underpinnings of her approach:

> To Satir ... the rules that govern a family system are related to how the parents go about achieving and maintaining their own self-esteem; these rules, in turn, shape the context within which the children grow and develop their own sense of self-esteem. Building self-esteem, promoting self-worth, exposing and correcting discrepancies in how the family communicates—these are the issues Satir tackles as she attempts to help

each member of the family develop "wellness" and become as "whole" as possible. The humanistic influence of the human-potential movement on these goals is unmistakable. (Goldenberg & Goldenberg, 1985, p. 160)

The process of family counseling, as practiced by Satir, focuses on the communication patterns that typify the functioning of the specific family. Among the dysfunctional communication styles that Satir has identified are those of the placater who always agrees with others at the expense of the self; the blamer, who dominates and accuses others; the super-reasonable person, who avoids emotional involvement and tends to intellectualize; and the irrelevant person, who distracts others and communicates material that is out of context. In contrast to these dysfunctional communicators, the congruent communicator is able to express his or her messages clearly and genuinely; there is true congruence between what is meant and what is said, what is felt and what is expressed. One of the primary goals of the family therapy of Satir and other humanistic theorists is to make congruent communication the norm for the family as a whole.

Closely associated with the family's communication patterns are the self-esteem of the members and the rules that govern family interactions. Functional families reflect and enhance the self-esteem of individual members and are free to develop reasonably flexible rules that encourage open communication. Dysfunctional families, in contrast, fail to maintain the members' self-esteem and tend toward rules that limit authentic communications. Therapy attempts to move family systems away from dysfunctional patterns and toward congruent, flexible, open transactions.

BOWENIAN FAMILY THERAPY   The approach developed by Murray Bowen places a unique emphasis on the differentiation of the self:

> This concept is a cornerstone of the theory.... [It] defines people according to the degree of fusion or differentiation between emotional and intellectual functioning. This characteristic is so universal that it can be used as a way of categorizing all people on a single continuum. At the low extreme are those whose emotions and intellect are so fused that their lives are dominated by the automatic emotional system.... These are the people who are less flexible, less adaptable, and more emotionally dependent on those about them.... At the other extreme are those who are more differentiated.... Those whose intellectual functioning can retain relative autonomy in periods of stress are more flexible, more adaptable, and more independent of the emotionality of those about them. They cope better with life stresses, their life courses are more orderly and successful, and they are remarkably free of human problems. (Bowen, 1982, p. 362)

Bowen's formulation sees those who are less differentiated as being most likely to develop any type of emotional problem. Moreover, those who show low degrees of differentiation between emotion and intellect—the ones at the end of the continuum characterized by fusion—also show intense fusion in their marriages. People tend to choose partners with equal degrees of differentiation. Thus, two poorly differentiated individuals, each with a weak sense of self, will join together into a "common self" with a high potential for dysfunction.

According to Bowen, the poorly differentiated family will tend to be subject to one of several common symptoms: marital conflict, dysfunction in one spouse, or the projection of problems onto children. Whether these symptoms become serious—whether, for instance, the projection of problems onto children brings about impairment in one or more—depends on the degree of stress with which the family must contend. If anxiety remains low, the family may remain reasonably functional. High anxiety levels bring more intense symptoms. Whether or not the family actually becomes dysfunctional, the potential for problems is transmitted through multiple generations, both because undifferentiated individuals have difficulty in detaching from their parents and because impaired children tend to marry other poorly differentiated individuals and pass their problems on to the next generation.

Just as anxiety affects the degree of fusion within the family, it also affects the working of triangles, which Bowen sees as the smallest stable relationship systems and therefore as the building blocks on which all human systems are based. The intensity of these triangles within the family is affected both by the degree of differentiation of self among the members and by the level of anxiety that is present.

Bowenian therapy, then, is based on the concepts of differentiation, of triangulation, and of multigenerational transmission processes. Therapists focus on modifying the central triangle in a family, on encouraging the process of differentiation, and on "slowly increasing intellectual control over automatic emotional processes" (Bowen, 1982, p. 307). Gradually, the therapeutic process leads to the increased differentiation of each family member and therefore to the increased health of the family system as a whole.

STRUCTURAL FAMILY THERAPY   Salvador Minuchin (1974, 1979) has had a major impact on family practice through his development of structural family therapy, a strongly systems oriented approach. In Minuchin's terms, a family system can be understood only to the degree that its structure is observed and recognized. This structure involves "enduring interactional patterns that serve to arrange or organize a family's component subunits into somewhat constant relationships" (Umbarger, 1983, p. 13). These patterned relationships regulate the family's transactions, allowing the system to remain consistent over time.

Family subsystems form an important aspect of this structure. An enmeshed family system is characterized by an absence of clear boundaries between its subsystems and by a complete lack of distance among family members. In contrast, some family systems can be characterized as disengaged, the boundaries between subsystems are rigid, and personal distance among family members is great. The pathologically enmeshed family has overly rigid boundaries separating the family system from its environment, whereas the disengaged family may complement rigid internal boundaries with a lack of clear boundaries separating it from the outside world.

Family systems may be enmeshed or disengaged to varying degrees. What makes a structure dysfunctional is the family's inability to change any of its behaviors in response to the necessity for a new adaptation:

> Family members are chronically trapped in stereotyped patterns of interaction which are severely limiting their range of choices, but no alternatives seem possible.... Conflict overshadows large areas of normal functioning. Often one family member is the identified patient, and the other family members see themselves as accommodating his illness.... A family with an identified patient has gone through a reification process which overfocuses on one member. The therapist reverses this process. (Minuchin, 1979, pp. 10–11)

Minuchin's therapeutic method begins with the counselor joining the family system, sharing and imitating its communication style, and taking a position of leadership. Once the counselor has elicited enough information to understand the family's structure, the process of change begins. Gradually, the counselor confronts the family's view of the problem by moving attention from the individual symptom-bearer to the family system, manipulating the subsystem boundaries, presenting alternate concepts of reality, and encouraging the family's attempts to grow. Ultimately, the aim of the therapy is to change the structure of the family system, making it more functional in its own environmental context.

THE COMMUNICATION MODEL   If psychodynamic therapy falls at position A of the theoretical continuum developed by the GAP, the communication model holds position Z. Rather than adapting existing therapeutic models to family practice, the communication model was developed from a systems framework.

Much of the pioneering work in applying systems theory to the study of family relationships was begun in the 1950s by a group organized in Palo Alto, California, by Gregory Bateson:

> Bateson's work was instrumental in shifting the focus of family therapy from the single individual to the exchange of information and the process of evolving relationships between and among family members. It was also Bateson who stressed the limitations of linear thinking in regard to living systems.... He called instead for an epistemological shift—to new units of analysis, to a focus on the ongoing process, and to the use of a new descriptive language that emphasizes relationships, feedback information, and circularity. (Goldenberg & Goldenberg, 1985, p. 6)

Bateson was joined in Palo Alto, in what was to become the Mental Research Institute, by Jay Haley, John Weakland, and Donald Jackson. This interdisciplinary team developed the double-bind theory of schizophrenic family relationships, hypothesizing that families with schizophrenic members tended to communicate through contradictory messages (Bateson, Jackson, Haley, & Weakland, 1956). As family therapy has evolved, the double-bind theory of schizophrenia has faded from view; more important has been the attention it focused on communication models for understanding families and other human systems. It is now readily understood that communications have both content and "command" aspects, and that the command aspects, or metacommunications, define relationships.

The communication approach is probably best exemplified by the strategic therapy of Haley (1976) and Madanes (1981), with its focus on active methods for changing repetitive communication patterns between family members. Haley suggests that "if therapy is to end properly, it must begin properly—by negotiating a solvable problem and discovering the social situation that makes the problem necessary" (1976, p. 9). If problems or symptoms serve some purpose in the social context, they can be resolved only through a strategy that focuses on interpersonal relationships.

Once the problem has been redefined in terms that make it solvable, the therapist develops a strategy unique to the needs of the specific family system. He or she then uses a variety of mechanisms, emphasizing the use of directives for families to follow between therapeutic sessions. One type of directive, the "paradoxical directive," actually prescribes that a family member continue in a behavior that would be expected to be targeted for change. The therapist redefines the symptom in terms of the function it serves and suggests that the behavior be continued or emphasized. If used very carefully, prescribing paradoxical tasks can help the therapist bring about change while avoiding resistance. To Haley, Madanes, and other communication theorists, the best way to eradicate the problem or symptom being addressed is to make it unnecessary for the stability of the family system.

BEHAVIORAL FAMILY THERAPY   Liberman (1981) sees the family as a "system of interlocking, reciprocal behaviors" (p. 152) and points out that problem behaviors are learned in a social context and maintained as long as the social system is organized to reinforce them:

> Changing the contingencies by which the patient gets acknowledgment and concern from other members of his family is the basic principle of learning that underlies the potency of family or couple therapy. Social reinforcement is made contingent on desired, adaptive behavior instead of maladaptive and symptomatic behavior. (p. 153)

The counselor helps the family members identify the behavior that they review as maladaptive; target alternative goals; and find ways to reinforce the new, positive behaviors at the expense of the undesirable actions. Family members are also more likely to exhibit positive behaviors if they have observed them in practice. Therefore, modeling positive behavior is also an important aspect of the counselor's role.

Liberman, like other family counselors using behavioral or social learning approaches, focuses attention on specific, measurable behaviors and on the environmental contingencies that tend to develop and maintain these behaviors. When behavioral therapists work with families, they set concrete goals to increase positive behaviors, at least in part by altering the patterns of reinforcement and the models offered by the social unit. Just as important is the counselor's effort to provide skills training for family members, focusing on ways to communicate effectively, techniques for managing stress, and self-controlled methods to change behavior.

In the final analysis, all of these approaches to family therapy seek verifiable changes both in the behaviors of family members and in family relationships. Although the alternate perspectives vary in their emphases, they all recognize the importance of the family as a social system that both influences and is influenced by individual behaviors. Each of the approaches holds promise as a way to help family systems deepen and maintain changes that treatment can only set in motion.

EFFECTS ON CHILDREN

The problems inherent in a family system affected by substance abuse have important implications for the development of children who must spend their preadolescent and adolescent years attempting to cope with a unique set of difficulties. Although families affected by substance abuse obviously vary, they do tend to have some common patterns, at least as far as child rearing is concerned.

In a family affected by parental alcohol problems, for instance, at least one parent is likely to be somewhat impaired in the ability to provide consistent child-rearing practices. The alcohol-abusing parent may show extreme variations, being effective or ineffective, warm or cold, affectionate or distant, depending on alcohol consumption.

The other parent may also show variations in parenting as a result of his or her focus on the partner's drinking. Thus, in some families affected by alcohol or drug abuse, neither parent is truly available to the child on a consistent basis.

The structure and boundaries of the family system may also be problematic. Within the family unit, boundaries between subsystems may be weak, with the unity of the parental subsystem broken and children taking on what should be adult responsibilities. At the same time, boundaries between the family and its environment may be overly rigid, as the family tries to maintain secrecy about the existence of the alcohol problem. Thus, children who are unable to count on consistent support from their parents may also be prevented from reaching out beyond the family for fear of breaking the family's rule of silence. The delicate homeostasis of the alcoholic family system is maintained, but at high cost to the development and self-esteem of individual family members.

Children raised in these circumstances may need to work to provide consistency and order that are otherwise lacking in their home lives. Individual children differ in the mechanisms they use to adjust to their family situations. Some writers and counselors believe that children from dysfunctional families play a limited number of identifiable roles that give their family systems a semblance of order. Each of these roles is used by the individual as a coping mechanism and by the family system as a set of transactions to maintain homeostasis.

It may be an oversimplification to identify and label a limited number of roles played by children of alcoholics and to assume that these roles differ substantially from those played by the children of non-substance-abusing parents. It is important, however, to understand that the family affected by substance abuse might have difficulty functioning at an ideal level and to recognize that children might be required to develop extraordinary mechanisms for coping.

Black (1986) points out that children of alcoholics need to cope with a great deal of stress but may have fewer physical, social, emotional, and mental resources than children living in more functional family systems. Their physical resources may be sapped because they are tired due to a lack of sleep, because they have internalized stress, or because they have been abused. (Of course, they may also be the victims of fetal alcohol syndrome, which causes developmental problems in the infants of alcoholic mothers.) Social resources may also be limited; hesitancy to bring other children into the home or to share information about the family may interfere with the development of intimate relationships. Emotional resources are affected by the pain, fear, and embarrassment that come with unstable living arrangements, financial difficulties, broken promises, accidents, and public intoxication. Even mental resources may be affected by a lack of parental help and by difficulties in maintaining regular school attendance. Children in this situation can benefit by receiving the help and support provided by counseling.

Counseling for children still living in a drug-affected home environment should concentrate on providing empathy and support and helping clients develop coping skills that can serve them effectively both in the current situation and in the future. Ideally, this process should help children deal with their uncertainties and, concurrently, prevent the development of chronic emotional problems.

One way to look at the appropriate direction for counseling is to consider again the importance of family members beginning to take care of their needs. This notion is helpful for children as well as for adults. In the isolation that might characterize the family's situation, parents try to protect children by covering up problems and by avoiding discussion of unpleasant realities. The children learn to deny their negative feelings, and coping roles may become rigidified. The most useful approach with children may be to help them move to a state of actively seeking the support that they need. If they are isolated in their home environment, counseling should help them reach out to others. If they are afraid of their feelings, counseling should help them recognize and express their previously forbidden emotions. If they feel alone in their situation, counseling should convince them that others share their problems. Children of troubled parents need to know that they are not to blame for family difficulties and that their attempts to meet their own needs are in no way detrimental to other family members. These counseling goals can often be accomplished most successfully in group settings, where children can learn that their own "family secrets" are not as unusual as they had assumed. Group counseling should follow a structured process that helps members understand more about substance dependence but that goes beyond the cognitive dimension to deal with affect and with the acquisition of skills.

FAMILY COUNSELING COMPETENCIES

Working with clients in the family context requires that counselors acquire a complex set of competencies. The Addiction Technology Transfer Centers National Curriculum Committee (2006, pp. 117–119) identified the knowledge, skills, and attitudes that underlie successful work with families affected by addiction.

Understand the characteristics and dynamics of families, couples, and significant others affected by substance use.

Knowledge:

- dynamics associated with substance use, abuse, dependence, and recovery in families, couples, and significant others
- the effect of interaction patterns on substance use behaviors
- cultural factors related to the effect of substance use disorders on families, couples, and significant others
- systems theory and dynamics
- signs and patterns of domestic violence
- effects of substance use behaviors on interaction patterns

Skills:

- identifying systemic interactions that are likely to affect recovery
- recognizing the roles of significant others in the client's social system
- recognizing potential for and signs and symptoms of domestic violence

Attitudes:

- recognition of nonconstructive family behaviors as systemic issues
- appreciation of the role systemic interactions play in substance use behavior
- appreciation for diverse cultural factors that influence characteristics and dynamics of families, couples, and significant others

Be familiar with and appropriately use models of diagnosis and intervention for families, couples, and significant others, including extended kinship, or tribal family structures.

Knowledge:

- intervention strategies appropriate for family systems at varying stages of problem development and resolution
- intervention strategies appropriate for violence against persons
- laws and resources regarding violence against persons
- culturally appropriate family intervention strategies
- appropriate and available assessment tools for use with families, couples, and significant others

Skills:

- applying assessment tools for use with families, couples, and significant others
- applying culturally appropriate intervention strategies

Attitudes:

- recognition of the validity of viewing the system...as the client views it, whereas respecting the rights and needs of individuals
- appreciation for the diversity found in families, couples, and significant others

Facilitate the engagement of selected members of the family or significant others in the treatment and recovery process.

Knowledge:

- learning how to apply appropriate confidentiality rules and regulations
- methods for engaging members of the family or significant others to focus on their concerns

Skills:

- working within the grounds of confidentiality rules and regulations
- identifying goals based on both individual and systemic concerns
- using appropriate therapeutic interventions with system members that address established treatment goals

Attitudes:

- recognition of the usefulness of working with those individual system members who are ready to participate in the counseling process
- respect for confidentiality rules and regulations

Assist families, couples, and significant others in understanding the interaction between the family system and substance use behaviors.

Knowledge:

- the effect of family interaction patterns on substance use
- the effect of substance use on family interaction patterns

- theory and research literature outlining systemic interventions in psycho-active substance abuse situations, including violence against persons

Skills:

- describing systemic issues constructively to families, couples, and significant others
- assisting system members in identifying and interrupting harmful interaction patterns
- helping system members practice and evaluate alternative interaction patterns

Attitudes:

- Appreciation for the complexities of counseling families, couples, and significant others.

Assist families, couples, and significant others in adopting strategies and behaviors that sustain recovery and maintain healthy relationships.

Knowledge:

- healthy behavioral patterns for families, couples, and significant others
- empirically based systemic counseling strategies associated with recovery
- stages of recovery for families, couples, and significant others

Skills:

- assisting system members in identifying and practicing behaviors to resolve the crises brought about by changes in substance use behaviors
- assisting clients and family members with referral to appropriate support resources
- assisting family members in identifying and practicing behaviors associated with long-term maintenance of healthy interactions

Attitudes:

- appreciation for a variety of approaches to working with families, couples, and significant others

MULTICULTURAL COMPETENCE IN FAMILY COUNSELING

Multicultural competence is always a key factor in the success of the counseling process. Effective counselors realize that their own attitudes and biases can sometimes limit their understanding of their clients. They also place a high priority on learning as much as they can about their clients' worldviews. This process is especially challenging in the context of family counseling. Differences in worldview are never more dramatic than they are in considerations of family life.

> As they proceed on the journey toward multiculturalism, many family therapists find that they must stop and reexamine their own assumptions about what the concept of family really means. Suppositions that they believe to be universal sometimes turn out, on closer examination, to be culture-bound. (Carlson et al., 2005)

Most other people, tend to assume that they know what is meant by the term *family*. In fact, however, counselors need to attend to culture and other areas of diversity even in considering the basic question of how *family* is defined. There was a time when D. W. Sue and D. Sue (1990, p. 12) could point out that "middle-class White Americans consider the family unit to be nuclear (husband/wife and children related by blood)." At this point in history, that view seems outlandishly dated. Family units have taken on many forms and we know now that even the basic assumption that a marriage must involve a man and a woman was wrong. In the past, however, these very limited views about the nature of family were so deeply ingrained that the people who held those views assumed that they were unquestionably true. In fact, the concept of the nuclear family has never been widely held, with most cultures defining the *family* as a much broader entity, often encompassing extended kinship systems.

Just as the notion of the nuclear family is culture-bound, so are the ideas that individual needs and desires should outweigh family values and that maturity requires individuation and separation. In comparison with the dominant culture in the United States, "almost all minority groups place greater value on families, historical lineage (reverence of ancestors), interdependence among family members, and submergence of self for the good of the family" (Sue & Sue, 1990, p. 123).

If counselors are to avoid imposing their own assumptions on clients with differing values, they must focus their assessment processes on some key questions about family life, including

- How are boundaries defined by the members of this family?
- How do gender, ethnicity, religion, and economic class interact to affect the family's values?
- How does the family view the balance between individual and family priorities?
- In what ways does oppression play a role in the life of the family?

When these questions are asked—and when the counselor does a real self-examination around his or her own biases—it becomes possible to replace a judgmental point of view with a family empowerment perspective.

SUMMARY

Effective treatment for individual clients depends on the counselor's recognition that substance abuse has a major impact on the individual's social network and that the social environment, in turn, affects the maintenance or resolution of each presenting problem. Human beings, like all other living organisms, need to be thought of as open systems in constant, organized interaction with their environment. Systems thinking has helped counselors focus on predictable transactions, on communication and feedback loops, on circular rather than cause-and-effect relationships, and on each system's quest for equilibrium.

Systems thinking has been useful in enhancing our understanding of the family context of substance abuse. Family counseling focuses broadly on family structure and interactions, rather than narrowly on the problems presented by one member. This focus helps substance abuse counselors see the family system as a whole as the appropriate target for change. The abuse of alcohol or another substance may become central to a family's organizational structure, with the members learning to maintain homeostasis around the continued drinking or other drug use of the affected individual. Counselors therefore need to help the family interrupt rigid patterns of interaction and find a new equilibrium after sobriety has been achieved.

The needs of each family vary according to its stage in this process. In the first stage, making initial system changes, the counselor helps family members confront, detach from, or address the substance abuse. The second stage involves the family's efforts to adapt to the cessation of substance use. This sudden change, although desired, throws many families into crisis, necessitating the development of new coping mechanisms. Finally, family therapy can help families deepen and maintain change on a long-term basis. Among the currently important theories of family counseling are (1) psychodynamic therapy, (2) experiential/humanistic therapy, (3) Bowenian family therapy, (4) structural family therapy, (5) communication models, and (6) behavioral family therapy.

Attention to family systems has also brought an emphasis on the problems faced by children of substance-abusing parents. Children utilize a variety of roles to attain stability in what may be a chaotic situation. Counseling for children still in the home generally focuses on reducing anxiety, eliminating feelings of isolation, and building coping skills. Counseling for adult sons and daughters of substance-abusing parents emphasizes such issues as control, guilt, and lingering anger.

QUESTIONS FOR THOUGHT AND DISCUSSION

1. Marcia's husband, Darrell, became a heavy polydrug user, causing him to lose a series of jobs. As his drug abuse grew more severe, he became more abusive in his treatment of her. What had been verbal abuse evolved into physical abuse. Marcia was frightened for herself and for her two children, both under the age of 5. She was also frightened about the family's financial situation. Her secretarial job could barely support the family; it could never support an expensive drug habit.

   For some time, Marcia tried everything she could to placate Darrell, believing that somehow she could solve the family's problems. Finally, she left, but only because she was worried that he might do something he had never done before: hurt the children.

   Marcia moved in with her parents temporarily until she could get on her feet economically and find good day care. Her mother helped her with the children until Marcia was able to afford an apartment of her own. Meanwhile, Darrell's drug use continued, until finally he was arrested for stealing. This was his first offense, and he was able to choose drug treatment instead of prison time. When he finished treatment, he approached Marcia, sought to make amends to her and the children, and asked for a reconciliation. She agreed.

   In this case, Marcia interrupted the family's ongoing patterns. Perhaps this change paved the way for Darrell's entry into drug treatment. Now that he is abstaining from drugs and they are reunited, the family must deal with major life changes.

   What might make this period difficult for the family? What suggestions would you have about ways in which Marcia and Darrell could deal successfully with the "crisis of abstinence"?

2. What would proponents of each of the following theories suggest about how Marcia and Darrell could achieve deeper, long-lasting change in their family system?

   a) Satir's experiential/humanistic therapy
   b) Minuchin's structural family therapy
   c) Behavioral family therapy

3. How might the children of Marcia and Darrell be affected by the family's situation? If you had an opportunity to work with them when they reached elementary school, what approach would you use?

REFERENCES

Ackerman, N. W. (1981). Family psychotherapy—Theory and practice. In G. D. Erickson & T. P. Hogan (Eds.), *Family therapy: An introduction to theory and technique* (2nd ed., pp. 165–172). Pacific Grove, CA: Brooks/Cole.

Addiction Technology Transfer Centers National Curriculum Committee. (2006). *Addiction counseling competencies: The knowledge, skills, and attitudes of professional practice* (2nd ed.). Rockville, MD: U.S. Department of Health and Human Services.

Bateson, G., Jackson, D. D., Haley, J., & Weakland, J. H. (1956). Towards a theory of schizophrenia. *Behavioral Science, 1*, 251–264.

Black, C. (1986, March). *Children of alcoholics.* Paper presented at the Conference on Children of Alcoholics, Gestalt Institute for Training, Chicago.

Bowen, M. (1982). *Family therapy in clinical practice.* New York: Aronson.

Carlson, J., Sperry, L., & Lewis, J. A. (2005). *Family therapy techniques.* New York: Routledge.

Fals-Stewart, W., Birchler, G. R., & Kelley, M. L. (2006). Learning sobriety together: A randomized clinical trial examining behavioral couples therapy with alcoholic female patients. *Journal of Consulting & Clinical Psychology, 74*(3), 579–591.

Goldenberg, I., & Goldenberg, H. (1985). *Family therapy: An overview.* Pacific Grove, CA: Brooks/Cole.

Haley, J. (1976). *Problem-solving therapy.* New York: Harper & Row.

Johnson, V. (1973). *I'll quit tomorrow.* New York: Harper & Row.

Kolevzon, M. S., & Green, R. G. (1985). *Family therapy models: Convergence and divergence.* New York: Springer.

Lewis, J. A. (1991). Change and the alcohol-affected family: Limitations of the "intervention." *The Family Psychologist, 7*(2), 43–44.

Liberman, R. (1981). Behavioral approaches to family and couple therapy. In G. D. Erickson & T. P. Hogan (Eds.), *Family therapy: An introduction to theory and technique* (2nd ed., pp. 152–164). Pacific Grove, CA: Brooks/Cole.

Liddle, H. A. (2002). *Cannabis Youth Treatment Series: Vol. 5. Multidimensional Family Therapy for Adolescent Cannabis Users.* DHHS Pub. No. 02–3660. Rockville, MD: Center for Substance Abuse Treatment, Substance Abuse and Mental Health Services Administration.

Liddle, H. A., Rowe, C. L., Dakof, G. A., Henderson, C. E., & Greenbaum, P. E. (2009). Multidimensional family therapy for young adolescent substance abuse: Twelve-month outcomes of a randomized controlled trial. *Journal of Consulting and Clinical Psychology, 77*(1), 12–25.

Madanes, C. (1981). *Strategic family therapy.* San Francisco: Jossey-Bass.

McCrady, B. S. (2006). Family and other close relationships. In W. R. Miller & K. M. Carroll (Eds.), *Rethinking substance abuse: What the science shows, and what we should do about it* (pp. 166–181). New York: The Guilford Press.

McCrady, B. S., Noel, N. E., Abrams, D. B., Stout, R. L., & Nelson, H. F. (1986). Comparative effectiveness of three types of spouse involvement in outpatient behavioral alcoholism treatment. *Journal of Studies on Alcohol, 47,* 459–467.

Meyers, R. J., Miller, W. R., Hill, D. E., & Tonigan, J. S. (1999). Community reinforcement and family training (CRAFT): Engaging unmotivated drug users in treatment. *Journal of Substance Abuse, 10*(3), 1–18.

Miller, W. R., Meyers, R. J., & Tonigan, J. S. (1999). Engaging the unmotivated in treatment for alcohol problems: A comparison of three strategies for intervention through family members. *Journal of Consulting and Clinical Psychology, 67*(5), 688–697.

Miller, W. R., Meyers, R. J., & Hiller-Sturmhofel, S. (1999). The community reinforcement approach. *Health & Research World, 3*(2), 116–120.

Meyers, R. J., & Smith, J. E. (1995). *Clinical guide to alcohol treatment: The community reinforcement approach.* New York: Guilford Press.

Minuchin, S. (1974). *Families and family therapy.* Cambridge, MA: Harvard University Press.

Minuchin, S. (1979). Constructing a therapeutic reality. In E. Kaufman & P. Kaufmann (Eds.), *Family therapy of drug and alcohol abuse* (pp. 5–18). New York: Gardner Press.

O'Farrell, T. J. (1992). Families and alcohol problems: An overview of treatment research. *Journal of Family Psychology, 5,* 339–359.

O'Farrell, T. J., & Fals-Stewart, W. (2006). *Behavioral couples therapy for alcoholism and drug abuse.* New York: The Guilford Press.

Prochaska, J. O., DiClemente, C. C., & Norcross, J. C. (1992). In search of how people change: Applications to addictive behaviors. *American Psychologist, 47,* 1102–1114.

Satir, V. M. (1967). *Conjoint family therapy* (2nd ed.). Palo Alto, CA: Science and Behavior Books.

Satir, V. M. (1972). *Peoplemaking.* Palo Alto, CA: Science and Behavior Books.

Smith, J. E., & Meyers, R. J. (2009). Community reinforcement and family training. In G. L. Fisher & N. A. Roget (Eds.), *Encylopedia of substance abuse prevention, treatment, and recovery.* Thousand Oaks, CA: Sage.

Smith, J. E., Meyers, R. J., & Austin, J. L. (2008). Working with family members to engage treatment-refusing drinkers: The CRAFT program. *Alcoholism Treatment Quarterly, 26*(1/2).

Substance Abuse and Mental Health Services Administration. (2009a). *Brief strategic family therapy.* National Registry of Evidence-based Programs and Practices. Retrieved May 10, 2009 from http://nrepp.samhsa.gov/programfulldetails.asp?PROGRAM_ID=157

Substance Abuse and Mental Health Services Administration. (2009b). *Multidimensional family therapy.* National Registry of Evidence-based Programs and Practices. Retrieved May 1, 2009 from http://nrepp.samhsa.gov/programfulldetails.asp?PROGRAM_ID=184

Sue, D. W., & Sue, D. (1990). *Counseling the culturally different: Theory and practice.* New York: John Wiley & Sons.

Szapocznik, J., & Hervis, O. E. (2004). *Brief strategic family therapy training manual.* Miami, FL: University of Miami Center for Family Studies.

Szapocznik, J., Hervis, O. E., & Schwartz, S. (2003). *Brief strategic family therapy for adolescent drug abuse.* NIDA Therapy Manuals for Drug Addiction, Manual 5. NIH Publication No. 03-4751. Rockville, MD: National Institute on Drug Abuse.

Umbarger, C. C. (1983). *Structural family therapy.* New York: Grune & Stratton.

von Bertalanffy, L. (1968). *General systems theory.* New York: Braziller.

PROGRAM PLANNING AND EVALUATION

WHETHER SUBSTANCE ABUSE programs are oriented toward treatment or toward prevention, their success depends as much on excellence in planning and management as it does on quality in service delivery. Programs flourish when they can demonstrate their attainment of clear and carefully developed goals. They fail when their objectives are diffuse, their activities poorly organized, or their accomplishments unmeasured. Counselors should involve themselves in program planning and evaluation if for no other reason than to safeguard the existence and growth of their clinically excellent programs. Effective programs depend on practitioners who are sensitive to environmental contingencies and adept at carrying out planning and evaluation processes.

ENVIRONMENTAL CONTINGENCIES

All human service organizations are affected by the constantly changing political and economic factors that form the context of their endeavors. An agency or program must continually try to adapt to trends that might have been difficult to foresee. In recent years, the context within which human service organizations exist has been so radically altered that it often feels completely unfamiliar to experienced practitioners. Current trends include the following:

- An emphasis on accountability for achievement of outcomes is replacing the traditional focus on provider-controlled methods and services.
- Privatization, contracting, and other forms of cost savings are replacing customary funding mechanisms.
- An insistence on interagency collaboration, including coalitions between public- and private-sector organizations, is replacing autonomous practice.

189

- The expectation that programs will tailor services to individuals' assessed needs is replacing the long-established routine of screening clients to determine whether they "fit" the program's methods.
- Marketing, public relations, and entrepreneurship are replacing the time-honored bureaucratic skills that formerly kept programs afloat.
- Empiricism is replacing philosophy, flexibility is replacing uniformity, and business-like orientations may well be replacing humanistic values.

In the case of substance abuse programming, these trends make themselves felt most directly through three current movements: (a) the emphasis on accountability for achievement of outcomes, (b) the continued dominance of managed care, and (c) the use of placement criteria.

ACCOUNTABILITY FOR OUTCOMES

In a study of the quality of health care delivered to adults in the United States, McGlynn et al. (2003) found that quality varied according to medical condition, ranging from a high of 78.7% of recommended care being provided to patients with senile cataracts to a low of 10.5% of recommended care for patients with alcohol dependence. McGlynn and her colleagues (2003) highlight the importance of developing strategies to reduce deficits in health care. The substance abuse field clearly has work to do!

Fortunately for the consumers of substance abuse treatment, some of the necessary changes might take place more quickly than is usually the case because of the pressures of the current political environment. The idea of emphasizing "best practices" might actually be moving from discussion to action and from optional to mandatory.

> As the conversation intensifies, there is even talk about linking payment to performance so that those who provide the most optimal results with the least amount of resources will be the most favorably reimbursed. This concept will be or can be applied to heart disease, kidney stones, the management of diabetes and a plethora of other diagnoses. Yes, it can even be applied to the treatment of addictive disease disorders. And that is where the challenge will begin. How do we begin to arrive at some consensus as to what the optimal results of treatment ought to be and how do we then compare what we individually do to that standard? (National Association of Addiction Treatment Providers [NAATP], 2009b)

The NAATP is awakening to a new reality: Treatment providers' funding might be contingent on their success! It is heartening to believe that this state of affairs might actually come to pass. At the time, however, it is seriously disheartening to know that consensus about the criteria for excellence is not yet in place.

In addition to focusing on standards related to quality and cost, provider organizations will also have to attend to the fact that the accountability movement cannot be separated from the movement toward health information technology (HIT). Redhead (2009) explains that the American Recovery and Reinvestment Act of 2009 incorporated the Health Information Technology for Economic and Clinical Health (HITECH) Act, which is intended to "promote widespread adoption of health information technology for the electronic sharing of clinical data among hospitals, physicians, and other health care stakeholders" (p. 1).

> The promise of HIT comes not from automating existing practices, but rather as a tool to help overhaul the delivery of care. HIT enables providers to render care more efficiently, for example, by eliminating the use of paper-based records and reducing the duplication of diagnostic tests. It can also improve the quality of care by identifying harmful drug interactions and helping physicians manage patients with multiple conditions. Moreover, the widespread use of HIT would provide large amounts of clinical data for comparative effectiveness research, performance measurement, and other activities aimed at improving health care quality. (Redhead, 2009, p. 1)

A mandate for electronic health records has been in place since 2004, and most treatment settings have moved to electronic health records.

> It was not all that long ago when all health records, including the records kept on addiction patients were hand written. Diagnosis, treatment plans, progress notes, staffing notes, etc., were all hand written in a sometimes large folder that stayed with the organization that provided the treatment. Sometimes the History and Physical, the "aftercare" plan and a few other pages were faxed to another provider when the patient showed up for treatment and the appropriate release forms were completed. (NAATP, 2009a)

Treatment providers do have computers now, but the current trends toward interoperable health information systems reflect a whole new order of change and it is unlikely that the addiction treatment network is at the forefront of electronic data sharing. The NAATP (2009a) understands that providers will have to get on this fast-moving train.

MANAGED CARE

Managed care is a system designed to control the quality and cost of health care through such methods as placing limits on access to services, selecting service providers, and enforcing cost containment. When managed care enters the picture, "tension naturally exists between the fiscal objective of conserving funds and the clinical goal of providing appropriate, quality services in a timely manner to all those who need them" (Center for Substance Abuse Treatment [CSAT], 1995a, p. 1).

The general definition of managed care can encompass a variety of models. The CSAT (1995b) suggests that managed care models have changed over time.

1. The first generation of managed care focused on reducing costs by restricting access to services through such means as overly rigid utilization review, limited benefits, and large co-payments.
2. The second-generation managed care organizations (MCOs) manage benefits. They focus on the development of provider networks, selective contracting, increased treatment planning, and a less rigid utilization review process.
3. Third-generation MCOs focus on managing the care of enrollees by emphasizing treatment planning and carrying out more active management of clients through the course of their treatment(s). This involves enhancing the

breadth and seamlessness of the continuum of care and actively using the least restrictive treatment settings that are clinically appropriate.

4. A fourth generation—now being aspired to—is for MCOs to manage by outcomes. This model seeks to focus primarily on the outcomes of treatment and allows great provider autonomy regarding how these outcomes are achieved. (p. 1)

Managed care may be provided through health maintenance organizations (HMOs), which charge a set amount per person and provide a variety of health services to members of the group being covered. When this model is used, substance abuse services, if they are provided at all, are integrated with other medical treatments. Managed behavioral health care organizations (MBHOs), in contrast, specialize in the provision of addiction and mental health care. Although greater focus and expertise are provided, services are not integrated with other medical services. Increasingly, managed care models are in effect in public-sector programs, such as Medicare and Medicaid, as well as in the private sector.

Potentially, managed care could have some positive effects on substance abuse treatment, moving the field in the direction of comprehensive assessments, tailored treatment, empirically based modalities, selection of appropriate cost-effective treatments, and provider accountability (Lewis, 1997, p. 298). At the same time, managed care holds some dangers for substance abuse services.

Problems include an onerous system required for authorizing treatment, confusing policies regarding benefit coverage, frequent delays and cumbersome paperwork, all of which might deter all but the most motivated (and perhaps less severely compromised) patients from receiving treatment; and increased requirements for disclosure of the specifics of treatment, thereby eroding confidentiality, a concern that may be particularly salient in addiction treatment. (American Society of Addiction Medicine, 1999, p. 12)

Clearly, the degree to which the positive or negative potential for managed care is met depends in part on the goals and quality of the specific HMO or MBHO. It also depends on the service provider's ability to adapt successfully to the managed care environment, which will probably be in effect for years to come. The CSAT (1995a) provides a checklist that can help service providers assess their agencies' readiness for managed health care (see Exhibit 9.1).

As the Readiness Checklist makes clear, adapting to the managed care environment absolutely requires that an agency have enough options available to provide assurance that the needs of the individual client are addressed.

Placement Criteria

One positive aspect of managed care systems is that they increase the likelihood that an individual will be offered the least intrusive treatment available. Clients can be helped most effectively if their treatment is based on the least intrusive possible alternative, given any special health, safety, and support needs they may have. Thus, if clients' physical, personal, and social resources are adequate, they should be referred for self-help in preference to professional treatment. If treatment is needed, outpatient counseling is preferable to inpatient, nonmedical to medical, and short-term to long-term. Outpatient clients have the greatest likelihood of maintaining effective social ties; of having individualized, multidimensional treatment; and of retaining a sense

EXHIBIT 9.1	MANAGED HEALTHCARE ORGANIZATIONAL READINESS CHECKLIST

Service Comprehensiveness

No, None, Never	Very Limited, Not Often	Partially, Frequently	Mostly, Regularly	Yes, Fully, Always
1	2	3	4	5

Please circle the answer.

For adults, do you deliver:

1. Centralized screening, assessment, intake, and crisis intervention services?   1 2 3 4 5
2. Comprehensive outpatient services?   1 2 3 4 5
3. Intensive outpatient services, or do you have strong network relationships with providers of such services?   1 2 3 4 5
4. Partial hospitalization/day treatment services, or do you have strong network relationships with providers of such services?   1 2 3 4 5
5. Short-term residential treatment, or do you have strong network relationships with providers of such services?   1 2 3 4 5
6. Inpatient treatment, or do you have strong network relationships with providers of such services?   1 2 3 4 5

For children and adolescents, do you deliver:

7. Centralized screening, assessment, intake, and crisis intervention services?   1 2 3 4 5
8. Outpatient services?   1 2 3 4 5
9. Intensive outpatient services, or do you have strong network relationships with providers of such services?   1 2 3 4 5
10. Partial hospitalization/day treatment services, or do you have strong network relationships with providers of such services?   1 2 3 4 5
11. Short-term residential treatment, or do you have strong network relationships with providers of such services?   1 2 3 4 5
12. Inpatient treatment, or do you have strong network relationships with providers of such services?   1 2 3 4 5

Service Characteristics

13. Do you have skilled clinical staff assigned to all aspects of the screening and assessment process, including initial telephone contacts?   1 2 3 4 5
14. Do your services ensure rapid access (1–2 days) to assessment services and initial placement?   1 2 3 4 5
15. Do your services have a brief intervention focus, for example, six to eight sessions for outpatient care, for most patients?   1 2 3 4 5
16. Do you have internal case management services for focusing on repeating patients and others who have high utilization patterns?   1 2 3 4 5
17. Do you have ensured linkages with primary healthcare providers for needed healthcare?   1 2 3 4 5

continued

Please circle the answer.

18. Do you adapt standard services to meet the needs of special populations, such as mentally ill substance abusers, injecting drug users, and pregnant addicts?   1 2 3 4 5

19. Are service needs constantly reevaluated, and service plans modified, based on patient progress?   1 2 3 4 5

20. Are admission, treatment, and discharge criteria in place and used consistently by staff?   1 2 3 4 5

21. Do your admission, treatment, and discharge criteria take into consideration the practice standards of managed care firms with which you have (or hope to have) contracts?   1 2 3 4 5

22. Do your services ensure rapid linkage to succeeding levels of care?   1 2 3 4 5

23. Do your services emphasize family involvement and use of natural support systems, including self-help groups?   1 2 3 4 5

24. Do your services focus on patient outcomes and satisfaction?   1 2 3 4 5

Quality Assurance (QA) and Utilization Management (UM)

25. Do you have QA and UM procedures that have been shared with clinical staff?   1 2 3 4 5

26. Does the staff you have designated to perform the QA/UM function review clinical activities for consistent use of established admission, treatment, and discharge criteria?   1 2 3 4 5

27. Is the information from the QA/UM function received rapidly enough to assist clinicians during an episode of care?   1 2 3 4 5

28. Does the QA/UM function include maintaining records of managed care appeals, and suggest strategies for improving relationships and/or modifying service delivery to reduce denials?   1 2 3 4 5

29. Do you have sufficient staff assigned to the QA/UM function?   1 2 3 4 5

30. To what extent is the QA/UM function designed to "stay ahead" of staff from managed care firms by anticipating their concerns?   1 2 3 4 5

31. Do clinicians, clinical supervisors, and management all receive and act on regular QA and UM reports?   1 2 3 4 5

32. Is the QA/UM function tied closely to your management information system?   1 2 3 4 5

33. To what extent is the QA/UM function focused on patient outcomes?   1 2 3 4 5

34. Are patient satisfaction surveys a regular function of QA/UM?   1 2 3 4 5

Managed Care and Employee Assistance Program (EAP) Experience

35. Do you have contract(s) with managed care firms or EAPs as a preferred provider?   1 2 3 4 5

36. If yes to #35, are any of your contracts paid on a fee-per-case or a capitation basis?   1 2 3 4 5

37. Do you offer an employee assistance program which includes crisis intervention, assessment and linkage to service, follow-up to assure receipt of appropriate services, and coordination of benefits?   1 2 3 4 5

Please circle the answer.

38. Does your EAP provide consultation to management on policies and procedures, training to managers and supervisors, assistance with specific cases, employee education and orientation programs, critical incident debriefing, and reporting on utilization and effectiveness?   1 2 3 4 5

39. Has your EAP business increased over the last 2 years?   1 2 3 4 5

Management Information Systems (MIS)

40. Do you have an MIS which can retrieve patient information either online or in less than 1 hour?   1 2 3 4 5

41. Does your MIS have integrated functions for client information; service utilization; financial information, including payer type by client; and client records?   1 2 3 4 5

42. To what extent does your MIS permit single-source response inquiries from managed care organizations?   1 2 3 4 5

43. To what extent does your MIS produce information that is used by clinicians, supervisors, and management?   1 2 3 4 5

44. To what extent does your MIS integrate information from various programs and sites?   1 2 3 4 5

45. Is your MIS designed so that client and service information can be reported to all major payers?   1 2 3 4 5

46. Does your MIS generate patient invoices?   1 2 3 4 5

Staff and Staff Training

47. Do clinical staff accept shared responsibility with case managers from managed care organizations for clinical decisions?   1 2 3 4 5

48. Are staff informed concerning the funding and managed care environment, including managed care criteria for admission and discharge?   1 2 3 4 5

49. Have clinical and supervisory staff resolved concerns about cost, service quality, access, and managed care?   1 2 3 4 5

50. Do you have an ongoing staff training program that includes brief service intervention skills, patient assessment and reassessment, and instructions on how to respond to managed care organizations?   1 2 3 4 5

Organizational Relationships

51. To what extent have you implemented referral and business arrangements with other behavioral healthcare organizations, e.g., mental health and substance abuse programs?   1 2 3 4 5

52. To what extent have you implemented referral and business arrangements with primary or specialty healthcare organizations, e.g., hospital emergency rooms and physician group practices?   1 2 3 4 5

53. To what extent have you been involved in economic arrangements with other healthcare?   1 2 3 4 5

continued

Board and Management

54. Do you have significant experience at contract negotiation and management? 1 2 3 4 5

55. To what extent is the board oriented to service effectiveness and business success? 1 2 3 4 5

56. Are you experienced at strategic planning, modifying plans, and developing contingency plans to meet emerging opportunities and challenges? 1 2 3 4 5

57. How well informed are board members and top management concerning healthcare reform, managed care, financing options, and interorganizational arrangements? 1 2 3 4 5

58. Are mechanisms in place which would allow for prompt shifts in response to business opportunities? 1 2 3 4 5

59. To what extent will the board and management be proactive and entrepreneurial in pursuit of managed care initiatives? 1 2 3 4 5

Marketing

60. Do you have marketing plans that target payers, referral sources, and the general public? 1 2 3 4 5

61. Do you have sufficient staff resources assigned to the marketing function? 1 2 3 4 5

62. To what extent does your service line emphasize acute and primary services (rather than long-term, rehabilitative, and wraparound care)? 1 2 3 4 5

63. Have you prepared a managed care capability statement? 1 2 3 4 5

64. To what extent have you made marketing presentations to the large employers in your service area? 1 2 3 4 5

65. Do your costs per episode and lengths of stay compare favorably with the competition? 1 2 3 4 5

Fiscal Analysis

66. To what extent is your revenue diversified? 1 2 3 4 5

67. Do you have adequate liquid reserves for at least 2–3 months operating expenses? 1 2 3 4 5

68. Have you accumulated (or can you access) venture capital sufficient to respond to a major business opportunity? 1 2 3 4 5

69. Have you maximized Medicaid revenue? 1 2 3 4 5

70. Does your fiscal system, in combination with the MIS, allow analysis of cost-per-unit of service, cost-per-episode of care, and cost by disability type and level of functioning? 1 2 3 4 5

71. Can the fiscal staff assist with pricing issues during contract negotiations, especially when capitated contracts are considered? 1 2 3 4 5

72. Can the fiscal staff readily compare actual to anticipated revenue and expense by contract? 1 2 3 4 5

Business Office

Please circle the answer.

73. Is the business office experienced at fee-for-service invoicing for Medicaid, preferred provider organization (PPO) contracts, insurance, patient fees, etc.?   1 2 3 4 5

74. Does the business office conduct internal service audits to ensure that documentation of services in patient records can withstand an external audit?   1 2 3 4 5

75. To what extent is the business office's invoicing function integrated into your MIS?   1 2 3 4 5

Summary of Answers

This section allows you to generate a score for each area. Add together the individual response scores for the questions in each of the 12 sections. Then divide the total by the number of questions in that section to generate a composite score for the section. Enter the composite score on the 1 to 5 scale at right.

	Divide Total by Composite	Weakest Position			Strongest Position	
Adult Services Comprehensiveness	6	1	2	3	4	5
Adolescent Services Comprehensiveness	6	1	2	3	4	5
Service Characteristics	12	1	2	3	4	5
QA and UM area	10	1	2	3	4	5
Managed Care and EAP area	5	1	2	3	4	5
MIS area	7	1	2	3	4	5
Staff and Training	4	1	2	3	4	5
Organizational Relations	3	1	2	3	4	5
Board and Management	6	1	2	3	4	5
Marketing	6	1	2	3	4	5
Fiscal Analysis	7	1	2	3	4	5
Business Office	3	1	2	3	4	5
All scores	75	1	2	3	4	5

of responsibility for themselves and their own recovery. Clients' self-efficacy is enhanced when they learn to recognize situations that pose risks for problematic behaviors and to acquire skills for coping with these situations. Each time clients achieve success in coping with a difficult situation in the natural environment, their sense of self-efficacy is further improved. This process is difficult to duplicate when clients are separated from their usual environments. In fact, the life-disrupting effects of hospitalization have little to offer most clients in compensation for their loss of independence. People who have had long stays in the hospital may achieve abstinence but lose some personal power in the process.

Certainly, some clients will always need more intensive treatment, especially if they have medical problems or if they lack stable support systems in their own communities. It is the responsibility of those who provide professional care to make careful decisions about the efficacy of the various treatment options that are available for clients, rather than to assume that more acute care is necessarily the safest alternative or, in contrast, to make choices based solely on cost. A number of factors need to be considered in the choice of treatment.

Any decision regarding the intensity of care should take into account both the client's personal support and resources and the likelihood that detoxification might become a medical emergency. Ideally, an assessment process should take into account all aspects of the client's functioning, should pave the way for a treatment alternative involving the least possible disruption for the individual, and should safeguard the client's physical well-being.

The ASAM Patient Placement Criteria—the Patient Placement Criteria developed by the American Society of Addiction Medicine (ASAM) (2001a) have attained very widespread use in addiction treatment. The ASAM criteria identify several levels of service, including the following:

Level 0.5:   Early Intervention
Level I: Outpatient Services
Level II: Intensive Outpatient/Partial Hospitalization
Level III: Residential/Inpatient Services
Level IV: Medically Managed Intensive Inpatient Service

The level of care that is deemed appropriate for an individual client depends on the results of a thorough assessment. Among the problem areas that are considered are such issues as acute intoxication or withdrawal potential, biomedical conditions, emotional/behavioral conditions and complications, treatment acceptance or resistance, relapse potential, and living environment. These dimensions form the basis of an assessment that should lead toward reasonably accurate projections concerning the most appropriate level of service for the individual.

> Treatment should be tailored to the needs of the individual and guided by an individualized treatment plan based on a comprehensive biopsychosocial assessment of the patient and, when possible, a comprehensive evaluation of the family as well. This evaluation and related treatment plan should list problems, objectives, methods, and a timetable for achieving the goals and objectives of treatment. As with other disease processes, length of service is linked directly to the patient's response to treatment. (ASAM, 1996, p. 6)

It is very clear that the age of lockstep treatment is coming to an end. Individualized treatment planning and tailored services are in the mainstream of substance abuse treatment. Now, more than ever, treatment providers must pay careful attention to planning and evaluating their services.

PROGRAM PLANNING

The first step in effective management is to specify the outcome that is being sought. No task should be performed until program goals have been identified and methods for achieving these goals have been selected. In fact, however, many counselors tend to focus more on the means they use than on the ends they reach, measuring their achievements by the number and type of activities performed instead of examining the ultimate effects of these activities. A program planner should not begin by asking how many clients will be seen for how many hours. In the current climate, the key question is what kind of impact he or she hopes to have on clients' lives. When one begins with this question, one's choices about appropriate interventions open up, and true creativity becomes possible. Substance abuse counselors, like other helping professionals, need to assess their work according to their success in meeting real client and community needs and in attaining objectives that can be measured in terms of client and community change. Effective programming depends on a step-by-step planning process that includes the following basic components:

- assessing needs
- identifying desired outcomes
- generating alternative methods for reaching goals and selecting among these alternatives
- devising implementation and evaluation plans
- budgeting

These steps make up a generic planning process that is appropriate for activities of such varied scope as developing an agency-wide strategy, planning for changes in an existing program, or devising a treatment plan for an individual client.

Assessing Needs

A program's planning process should always begin with a needs assessment, which for our purposes can be defined as a planning activity designed to discover the gaps between what is desirable for a community or potential client population and what currently exists. Planners need to gather data concerning existing problems and resources before they can even begin to generate agency or program goals, let alone plan for the provision of specific services.

Problem Identification   Needs assessment starts with an attempt to define the problems that services will be designed to solve. Planners must gather the kinds of data that can help them identify whatever gap exists between the current state of affairs and a more desirable situation. In the substance abuse field, planners typically focus on gathering information concerning the incidence and prevalence of drug use in the community, the incidence and prevalence of related problem behaviors, and the ability of current services to address these problems.

With particular regard to drug abuse treatment, needs assessment strategies examine how well or how poorly the current service delivery system is providing for the treatment needs of the community. Typically, the questions asked are concerned with understanding whether the existing drug treatment programs meet community needs in terms of the numbers and types of clients being served.

The specific questions for needs assessment regarding treatment may include the following: Are drug abuse treatment programs seeing a significant proportion of drug users in the community? Are drug abuse treatment programs seeing clients that reflect the drug-using characteristics of the community? Are programs seeing the particular kinds of drug users (e.g., opiate users) of concern to the community?

Because needs assessment is designed to fulfill a community concern (e.g., whether resources committed to drug treatment are adequate), the community should be involved in setting the parameters of study. The involvement of community members in formulating the questions to be explored can forestall any risk that community interests and concerns are poorly addressed. (Brown, 1997, p. 1)

Information about current drug use and current treatment options is obviously important in the process of identifying problems, but practitioners often overlook the complexity of this aspect of the needs assessment. Knowing the number of drug arrests, persons in treatment, or drug emergencies in a community may help provide a convincing case that something should be done, but it does not necessarily provide enlightenment about what should be done. Counselors and prevention specialists frequently work under the assumption that a given problem can be solved through a given intervention (for example, drug use among adolescents will be prevented by providing accurate information). In fact, however, drug use data do not provide guidance for program planners unless they are accompanied by documentation concerning the correlations between variables (for example, between knowledge and initial drug use) and the results of previous studies. For instance, providing accurate information about drugs to adolescents has not been proved to prevent substance abuse among them, yet many practitioners persist in assuming that data showing the existence of a drug problem automatically point the way toward a particular educational approach.

Thus, what might appear at first glance to be the simplest aspect of a needs assessment—measuring the amount of drug use in the community—may in fact be complex, requiring careful thought on the part of the program planner before connections between drug use and potential interventions can be made. Even greater care is required when data concerning problem behaviors, psychological characteristics, or socioeconomic conditions are gathered.

Planners tend to select certain behaviors or characteristics to measure because they assume that the targeted variables are, in fact, correlated with substance abuse. Programs may then be designed to bring about change in these areas without clear indications that such correlations actually exist. Again, such shortcomings will be lessened if planners present substantiation for their assumptions, use their own program evaluations as a basis for further examination of the connections between drug use and other characteristics or behaviors, and insist on clarity in all program objectives.

ASSESSMENT METHODS   A number of methods and tools are available for assessing needs. The approach chosen for a specific study depends both on data needs and on the existence of adequate financial resources. Among the most common approaches used in measuring substance-abuse-related needs are community surveys, studies of social indicators, canvassing of local agencies, open forums, and interviews of key informants.

Surveys provide the best opportunity to gather direct information about problems and community attitudes. Surveys can be administered either to a sample of community members or to all members of a particular target group (for example, using a questionnaire to determine drug-related attitudes of all members of a high school sophomore class) and can involve written questionnaires, telephone interviews, or personal contacts. The design of the instrument determines the kind of information it will elicit, making it important to put as much effort into planning the survey as into carrying it out. Effective use of the survey technique requires a major commitment in time and money, as well as a high degree of expertise. For this reason alone, the use of the survey approach is somewhat limited. Most agencies would find it difficult to assess needs through use of a survey for every new program being considered. Even small agencies, however, should attempt to use some form of survey at fairly regular intervals in order to keep data on needs as current as possible.

Social indicators are also helpful in maintaining information about relevant aspects of community life. Social indicators are quantitative measures of characteristics that might correlate with service needs. This approach is frequently used in combination with other methods to form a comprehensive needs assessment, because planners can use secondary data, rather than personally gathering all of the necessary information on the spot. Once planners have decided what kinds of information might be useful, they can use a combination of local data with more general information gleaned through sources such as census reports, governmental publications, statistics gathered by national or local organizations, and needs assessments carried out by planning or health departments. Data concerning demographic characteristics, socioeconomic variables, health, education, housing, employment patterns, family patterns, safety, and law enforcement all play a part in determining what services are likely to be needed in a particular geographic area or among members of a target population. These data, unlike information obtained directly from clients, act as indirect indicators of community needs. Thus, appropriate use of social indicators requires careful analysis of existing data to ensure that the variables studied do have a good chance of being related in some way to substance use or abuse.

Soliciting information from local agencies also helps in the development of realistic plans. Interviews or questionnaires can be used to elicit information from the answers of two types of questions. First, what help and resources are currently available in the community? Second, what gaps in community services have been recognized by service providers? Having accurate information about the types of programs already available can do a great deal to eliminate needless duplication. At the same time, these data can also point the way toward services that are needed by community members but not yet provided through existing agencies. Program managers are often willing to identify special problems or client groups that their agencies are unable to address but that they recognize as being important. Of course, this type of information is largely subjective and must be used in connection with other types of assessment data.

Open forums and meetings give community members a chance to speak out about their needs and priorities. A condition is only a problem if people perceive it to be a problem. The fact that substance abuse professionals perceive a situation as problematic does not necessarily mean that the community sees that situation in the same light. Only the community as a whole can decide what degree of drug or alcohol use is acceptable and how many drug-related problems it is willing to bear. If community support and resources are needed for a given program, practitioners must learn how people outside of the service-providing network feel about the issue. One way to address this issue effectively is through the use of open forums and meetings that give community members an opportunity to express their opinions about needs and priorities. Whether the approach involves informal get-togethers or formal hearings, many elements of the community can be encouraged to present views that might not otherwise have been considered. New ideas can be developed, and, concurrently, the community's commitment to the new program can be enhanced through a sense of participation in the decision-making process.

Key informants can also play an important role in the assessment of community needs. In any geographical area, it is possible to find people who are known to be well informed about a given issue or about local opinions on a variety of topics. These key informants may be neighborhood leaders, political figures, or individuals whose positions make them sensitive to community needs. Planners can use meetings, individual interviews, or even questionnaires to tap into this valuable information resource, asking respondents to share their admittedly subjective perceptions about current problems and community members' ideas about them. In the substance abuse field, attention can be focused on key people who have contact with target populations. Subjective opinions can never replace objective data, but the sensitive accounts of key informants can help narrow the focus of the assessment by pointing in the direction of needed data sources and assisting in their analysis.

The use of data-gathering instruments, no matter how expertly done, cannot form the entire needs assessment process. An assessment tool can provide information, but people need to analyze and judge the information before priorities can be set. Possession of accurate data makes it possible for planners to analyze the current situation and set priorities based on reality. Needs assessment makes goal setting possible.

IDENTIFYING DESIRED OUTCOMES

Goal setting is the heart of the planning process. If needs assessment allows planners to identify community problems, goal selection lets them begin to find solutions.

All too often, substance abuse professionals focus on means rather than ends, insisting that certain services, and only those services, will bring about desired client outcomes. In fact, however, we cannot assume that a specific service will always bring about the desired outcome. Instead, we should begin with a set of goals for client outcomes and then select from among a number of alternate interventions. The key to effective planning, then, is to focus on desired outcomes before even beginning to consider the activities that might be expected to lead to these ends.

In general, goals are defined as broad statements regarding the outcomes sought by an agency or program. Objectives are more specific, limited, and measurable. Ideally, attainment of all of a program's objectives will imply that its general goals have been reached. It is less important to distinguish between goals and objectives, however, than to ensure that some statement of outcome is used to determine the selection of program activities. Outcomes should be stated so that they are clear, measurable, and realistic.

Once concrete and realistic outcome statements have been prepared, planners can begin to identify an array of activities that might lead to the desired accomplishments. When clear objectives form the basis of program planning, the resulting activities tend to be more innovative than they are in situations where planners assume that certain services are mandatory. Moreover, the existence of appropriate outcome statements at the planning stage simplifies evaluation by providing measurable standards and milestones.

DEVISING AND SELECTING ALTERNATIVES

When their objectives are clear, planners can identify alternative methods for accomplishing them, ideally considering a wide range of options before narrowing the program's focus. Brainstorming, for instance, can generate a large number of alternatives. Many of the activities listed might at first glance appear impractical, but untried approaches should receive as much consideration at this point as more customary methods. One problem in the substance abuse field is the assumption that a certain set of procedures must always be present in treatment. Reliance on a standard set of interventions may prevent us from being as creative as we should be in meeting the needs of an increasingly heterogeneous clientele. Good decision making requires that the planner generate as many alternatives as possible, consider the potential consequences of each, and search for any data that might possibly be relevant, always maintaining an openness to new information. In the substance abuse field there is a pressing need for more effective treatment alternatives. Planning has tended to be based on a few minimally acceptable methods. People involved in program planning need to examine as many alternatives as possible, weighing each, and stop the search only when the best possible options have been found. We need an approach that will open the field to innovation.

DEVELOPING IMPLEMENTATION AND EVALUATION PLANS

Once planners have completed the steps of assessing needs, setting goals, and deciding on preferred activities, they can develop the mechanisms for putting their plans into action. At this point, program developers should have in hand general statements of goals, lists of concrete objectives, and a set of specified methods or services selected to meet each objective. Every service listed should be clearly designed to meet a specified outcome objective; any activity that fails to connect with one of the objectives should be eliminated.

Each service that has withstood this final test should now be the subject of an implementation plan. The questions to be asked at this point include the following:

- What specific tasks need to be carried out?
- What personnel do we need to carry out these tasks?
- What are the reasonable target dates for completing each task?
- What resources do we need in order to meet our targets?

The answers to these questions form the framework for an implementation plan specifying who is to perform what activities, when, and with what resources.

The development of a plan for evaluation takes place concurrently with the initial program development process. While programming decisions are being made, planners also consider what methods they will be able to use for evaluating the success of the services to be delivered. The objectives that have been clearly specified in the interest of program efficiency also point the way toward effective evaluation. If evaluation criteria are identified at this point, planners can also create plans to carry out evaluation simply by deciding on the methods they will use for gathering data on a continual basis.

BUDGETING

The process of budgeting cannot be separated from the process of planning. A program is designed to meet the community's needs and the budget simply translates ideas into dollars.

> The budget itself is simply a projection of operational plans, usually for a one-year time span, with the plans being stated in terms of the allocation of dollars for varying functions or activities. Whether the budget helps or hinders the agency's efforts to set and meet its goals depends on the degree to which it is placed in perspective as a tool at the service of program planners.... The budget, then, should be the servant, rather than the master, of planning. (Lewis, Packard, & Lewis, 2007, p. 170)

Creating the annual budget depends on forecasting expected revenues and needs for the coming year. Analysis of budgetary needs involves scrutinizing the implementation plans that have been designed and making accurate estimates of the costs of the activities that have been selected. If this analysis forms the basis of the budgeting, the budget becomes what it should be: a decision-making tool transforming goals into realities.

EVALUATION

The purposes of evaluation are (1) to let us know whether services have taken place as expected and (2) to determine whether these services have succeeded in bringing about the client and community outcomes desired. Accomplishment of these distinct purposes requires two types of evaluation. Process evaluation assesses the agency's activities to determine whether programs are actually operating in accordance with plans and expectations. Outcome evaluation attempts to verify the impact of services by measuring the degree to which clients have changed as a result of the program's interventions. A useful evaluation plan must contain elements of each.

PROCESS EVALUATION

Process evaluation involves collecting and analyzing information that can verify whether planned services have been delivered consistently to the appropriate number and types of clients. As important as it is to find out whether programs have met their outcome goals, it is just as urgent to learn how these goals were met. If successful programs are to be duplicated or less successful programs changed, service providers need to know exactly what services were offered. Process evaluation lets program planners know whether clients have been reached in the numbers projected and whether the degree and quality of services meet expectations.

This information makes outcome evaluations more meaningful by specifying what number, type, and range of services have brought about the outcomes being assessed.

Process evaluation is possible only when planners have identified clear and measurable program objectives. With these objectives in place, programs can be monitored with a view toward learning whether progress toward meeting goals is proceeding appropriately. Successful monitoring, of course, depends on the existence of a good information system. How else can we find out what services were provided, by whom, for whom, in what time period, and at what cost? Comparing measurable accomplishments with objectives lights the way toward necessary program improvements. Only then does true accountability become part of the program's culture.

GOALS AND OBJECTIVES Because process evaluation depends on the evaluator's ability to identify gaps between planned activities and actual accomplishments, it can be performed only when program objectives are clear and measurable. Each program goal should specify some condition that program operations will bring about, and each goal must be capable of being divided into quantifiable objectives. Consider the following hypothetical example involving a community information and referral agency. This agency has conducted a needs assessment leading to the estimate that approximately 2,000 alcohol-dependent individuals below the poverty level live in the target community and are receiving no services. The program goal is that within 3 years, 2,000 alcohol-dependent individuals at or below the poverty level in the community will be referred to appropriate financial, rehabilitative, and family services.

Once all terms contained in such a program goal have been defined (What is meant by alcohol-dependent? What are the boundaries of the community? How is the poverty level defined?), planners can decide what activities must take place within what time span if the goal is to be reached. In this example, the objectives for the first 4 months of the program's 1st year might include the following:

- Identifying all appropriate services in the community within 3 months
- Establishing facilities and equipment to provide referral services within 2 months
- Employing and training a referral and administrative staff within 2 months
- Completing an operational program within 3 months
- Establishing liaison with all referral agencies within 4 months

Such objectives can be considered measurable only if they contain clear criteria and standards. The criterion is what is to be measured; the standard is the quantity or quality desired. For example, the first objective in the previous list is identifying all appropriate services in the community within 3 months. One criterion, "services," involves several standards: "all," "appropriate," and "in the community." The other criterion is time, and also involves a specified standard: "3 months." If all criteria and standards are clearly defined before the fact, the evaluator can readily determine whether the objective has been met.

These time-oriented objectives make continual process evaluation possible, as opposed to awaiting the development of an annual report. If, at the end of 4 months, liaisons with all referral agencies have not been completed, managers can analyze the difficulty and take action either to improve these relations or to adjust the plans for subsequent activities. In agencies without clear, time-oriented objectives, such problems go unrecognized, and failures to obtain overall goals are frequently unexplained.

MANAGEMENT INFORMATION SYSTEMS   The criteria and standards that form each objective also lead the way toward the kind of information that will be needed in order to measure the program's accomplishments. For example, the hypothetical information and referral agency discussed earlier has as one of its goals the referral of alcoholics at or below the poverty level. Information about income must therefore be obtained routinely from each client in order to determine whether the specified target population is being reached. Client information of this type is needed to determine whether the targeted group is being served, and service delivery information is needed to determine whether treatment is being delivered in accordance with plans.

Thus, the data needed for evaluation can be identified by examining each specified objective and clarifying the criteria and standards to be met. Once information requirements have been specified, planners can easily decide on the most appropriate source for the data. What is most important is that the collection of data needed for evaluation be built into the agency's routine operating procedures. As a part of program development, planners should decide who within an agency should record the necessary information, what methods or forms should be used, how the information should be reported and maintained, and who should be responsible for its analysis. Process evaluation becomes simplified when information about clients, communities, and services are maintained. Among the information needed are:

- information related to the community, such as demographic information, data on social and economic characteristics, identification of underserved populations, and listings of external services and resources
- information concerning individual clients, groups of clients, and the client population as a whole, including such data as presenting problem, history, type of service received, length of service, socioeconomic and family characteristics, employment, and even measurements of satisfaction and service outcome
- service information, including types of service provided by units within the agency, number of clients served, number of admissions and discharges in a given period, and specification of service-related activities
- staff information, including time spent in varying activities, number of clients served, volume of services, and differences among separate programs within the agency
- resource allocation information, including total costs, costs for specific types of services, and data needed for financial reporting.

These data do not require complex or expensive computer systems and can be obtained through normal agency routines. Planners and evaluators need to be concerned less about the amount of information available than about the appropriateness of the information.

The key to system effectiveness is the degree to which it meets the agency's unique planning, management, and evaluation needs. Agency personnel need to identify as specifically as possible the kinds of data needed, and the frequency with which they should be distributed. Beyond this, planning for effective gathering and disseminating of information involves working out the type of system that is most appropriate for the agency's functions, size, and degree of complexity. The same kinds of planning processes are needed for a small agency using one client data form as for the large institution with a full-fledged information department.

Of course, all of this information about the agency's activities is important only to the degree that it helps explain the client changes that have been achieved. Evaluation, if it is to be useful, must focus on outcome as well as process.

OUTCOME EVALUATION

Outcome evaluation in the substance abuse field has been plagued by a number of problems, including overly narrow and insensitive outcome measurements, difficulties in locating subjects for follow-up, and doubts about the accuracy of client self-reports concerning drinking or other drug use behavior. These problems, however insoluble they may seem on the surface, must be overcome in the interest of treatment effectiveness. Valid outcome research is needed both to enhance program planning and management and to improve the decisions made by each counselor concerning every client.

Information about the effectiveness of treatment interventions is needed for decision making, whether the decisions at hand concern the development of a program or the design of an individual treatment plan. This information can be trusted only if it is based on both appropriate outcome measurements and effective follow-up procedures.

OUTCOME MEASURES Traditionally, outcome evaluation in the drug and alcohol field has been based on simplistic, either/or measures but such measures fail to capture client change in all its permutations.

A multivariate conceptualization of drug and alcohol problems brings a change in focus concerning outcome evaluation. First, drinking and drug-taking behaviors are considered as continuous rather than nominal variables. Second, a number of additional outcome criteria are utilized in addition to measures of posttreatment substance use.

Considering drug or alcohol use as a continuous variable takes into account the complexity of this behavior and allows the evaluator to recognize the existence of varying degrees of involvement. The evaluator should use a more accurate gauge that follows individual clients over time and allows for some recognition of the direction of change. A practitioner following a multivariate approach might be as interested in how an individual client changes and adjusts in response to life events as in how a group's "success" can be measured at one point. Many psychosocial criteria in addition to drinking or drug-taking behaviors can also be considered more appropriately as continuous rather than nominal variables. For instance, it might be more useful to know the number of days the client worked during a given period instead of asking the dichotomous question of whether he or she is employed at any given moment. As researchers move away from a dichotomous view of treatment outcome, they also move toward a recognition that multiple outcome variables should be assessed.

Although drinking and drug-taking behaviors will always remain as major—even primary—criteria of treatment success, they are not the only variables that indicate the degree of a client's rehabilitation. Outcome evaluation should be applicable to the particular population being served, but as a general rule, client progress in the following areas should be tracked:

- physical health
- mental health
- career/employment success
- family stability
- social support
- solution or avoidance of criminal justice problems

It is important both to broaden outcome evaluation and to seek consistent and objective methods of measurement. Ideally, the use of these methods should not be reserved for researchers but should form part of the routine evaluations performed every day by treatment practitioners.

A joint effort of the ASAM and the American Managed Behavioral Health Care Association (now the Association for Behavioral Health and Wellness) led to a set of principles for outcome evaluation in the treatment of substance-related disorders (ASAM, 2001). The report generated by this collaboration identified a set of concepts and principles that capture the complexity of outcome evaluation. The principles include the following:

1. The multiple, often overlapping reasons for conducting outcome evaluation should be recognized, as should the often differing motivations of various parties who have interest in outcomes data....
2. Outcome evaluation should be meaningful....
3. Evaluation studies of the process of treatment or the outcomes of treatment should specify a number of different domains....
4. Parameters being evaluated should be measurable and comparable....
5. Addiction treatment outcome measures should be as consistent as possible with outcome measures utilized in generally accepted public health research and health care delivery research.
6. Abstinence should not be the only variable considered in evaluating the effectiveness of a treatment intervention for a substance-related disorder....
7. Treatment outcome studies should take into account that persons with addictive disorders are not a uniform population....
8. Outcome evaluations should creatively apply the available capabilities and recognize the limitations of currently existing data sets and methodologies....
9. Outcome studies in addiction treatment must comply with ethical standards for treatment services research....

ASSESSMENT INSTRUMENTS   Substance abuse practitioners often find it difficult to design valid instruments to be used in outcome evaluation. Rather than focusing too narrowly on dichotomous questions concerning drug or alcohol use, such practitioners can consider the use of instruments that have been designed and used by other evaluators. In addition to making evaluation more practical for small agencies, the use of standardized instruments can facilitate comparisons among programs. Many instruments are currently available, and some of the instruments described in earlier chapters for assessing individual progress are also appropriate for broader outcome studies. Among instruments with a long history of use for this purpose are the following:

- Behavior Rating Scale—Social, Employment, Economic, Legal, Drinking
- Alcohol Dependence Scale
- Addiction Severity Index
- Health and Daily Living Form
- Timeline Follow-back Assessment Method

FOLLOW-UP PROCEDURES   Effective outcome evaluation depends both on the selection and measurement of appropriate criteria and on the use of well-planned procedures. Even when evaluators utilize valid and reliable outcome measurements, they need to take further steps to ensure the accuracy of their data. Traditionally, research and evaluation in the substance abuse field has been troubled as much by procedural deficits as by poor criterion selection. If evaluation is to be useful at all, it must be based on methods that minimize losing track of patients after treatment and that encourage accuracy in the data collected from clients and collateral resources. Fortunately, we have known for some time that self-reports concerning drinking behaviors can be reasonably valid, especially if they are backed up by indicators from other sources Similarly, problems of attrition do appear to be surmountable if careful follow-up procedures are planned and prioritized. Completeness and accuracy in follow-up are possible if outcome evaluation, like process evaluation, becomes an integral part of the treatment program's ongoing work.

As far as individual clients are concerned, the focus on outcome follow-up should begin at the first intake interview. New clients should be briefed about the importance of follow-up, not only for evaluation purposes but also to ensure continuity in their care. Before the completion of treatment, the evaluator should again confirm the client's commitment to participate in the follow-up process.

This consistent attention to evaluation as part of an ongoing process from intake through treatment through follow-up helps to establish clients' understanding of its importance and to encourage their commitment to participation. This approach also improves the planning done by evaluators, because comparable measurements need to be taken both before and after treatment.

Clients leaving treatment with an understanding that follow-up contacts will ensue are likely to maintain their intent to cooperate if regular and positive contacts are made. Frequent contacts aid the evaluation process in several ways. The ongoing relationship between treatment providers and the former client enhances cooperation and commitment; the regularity of contact makes it far less likely than usual that the client will be lost track of; and the existence of the relationship may also serve as a form of treatment, preventing some problems from occurring at all and allowing for immediate intervention in others.

Routine and frequent contacts are likely to enhance the accuracy of client self-reports, but other sources of information must also be used before evaluators can have complete confidence in the information they have acquired. Multiple sources and measures should be used, not because clients are disbelieved but because no one measure can possibly be adequate to assess such complex behaviors as drinking, drug use, and life functioning. Treatment providers may feel overwhelmed by the prospect of maintaining frequent contacts with former clients and, at the same time, using multiple sources of information to measure treatment outcome. They might well consider the notion of performing outcome evaluation studies following up a limited number of randomly selected subjects. It is more useful to have a complete evaluation of all members of a random sample of clients than to have a partial and biased study of a larger number of individuals.

The effectiveness of this approach to outcome evaluation depends on the quality of the relationship formed between interviewer and interviewee, evaluator and client. A sophisticated and skilled interviewer who is able to establish a high level of rapport with a patient during the follow-up interview (and who can offer some continuity of care) will be far more successful in maintaining the sort of contact with a patient which facilitates the gathering of valid data than would be a less clinically skilled interviewer.

Each agency or program needs to develop mechanisms that are appropriate to its goals and staffing, sometimes having to balance a desire for interviewer objectivity, which would argue in favor of using outside evaluators, with an equally valid desire for making follow-up a more integral part of treatment. Whoever the follow-up interviewers may be, they must be trained to work with clients in an accepting and nonjudgmental manner, creating an atmosphere that encourages honest reporting. Evaluation, whether of process or of outcome, must be based on an openness to new information, whatever that information may be. Its purpose is not merely to justify support for current practices but rather to inform decision making concerning desirable changes. Objective evaluation takes planning to its logical conclusion by comparing the program's accomplishments with the goals that were selected at the outset of the planning process. Without this important step, the quality of substance abuse counseling could never be assured.

SUMMARY

Excellence in planning and evaluation can be as important to the success of a substance abuse program as the quality of the clinical treatment that is provided. In fact, good program management and good client services seem to go hand in hand. Substance abuse counselors, like other human service and health professionals, need to focus on meeting objectives that can be measured in client and community outcomes.

The current environment within which substance abuse treatment takes place focuses on accountability, cost-savings, and tailoring treatment to individual differences. Practitioners must be able to maneuver effectively within managed care systems and to use placement criteria appropriately.

Effectiveness in programming depends on the careful implementation of a planning process that includes the following steps: (1) assessing needs, (2) identifying desired outcomes, (3) generating alternative methods for reaching goals and judging and selecting among them, (4) developing implementation and evaluation plans, and (5) budgeting. Variations of the same steps are appropriate for such divergent activities as developing long-term agency strategies, making changes in specific programs, or even devising individual clients' treatment plans.

Program planning leads directly toward evaluation, which lets us know whether services have taken place as expected and whether desired client outcomes have been reached. Two types of evaluation are needed to provide this information. Process evaluation involves collecting and analyzing data to verify whether programs are operating in accordance with plans. Outcome evaluation attempts to measure the degree to which clients have changed as a result of the services provided.

In the substance abuse field, outcome evaluation has been plagued by problems such as insensitive outcome measurements and poorly planned follow-up procedures. Evaluation can be improved if drinking and drug-taking behaviors are considered continuous, rather than dichotomous, variables; if a number of outcome criteria are measured; and if carefully planned follow-up procedures are prioritized by treatment facilities. Attention to the results of truly objective evaluations can bring about what all substance abuse professionals desire: improvements in program effectiveness and enhancement of our ability to meet the unique needs of each client we serve.

Questions for Thought and Discussion

1. Suppose you and a group of your colleagues realized that your substance abuse treatment agency was not doing a good job meeting the needs of clients over the age of 65. You decide to design a program that will serve these clients more effectively. What might be some specific outcomes you would like the program to achieve?
2. Choose one of the outcomes you listed in your answer to question 1. What are some methods you might use to help your clients achieve this outcome?
3. Considering again the outcome statements you listed in your answer to question 1, how might you evaluate your agency's success in achieving the desired outcomes?

References

American Society of Addiction Medicine. (1996). *Patient placement criteria for the treatment of substance-related disorders* (2nd ed). Chevy Chase, MD: American Society of Addiction Medicine.

American Society of Addiction Medicine. (1999). *The impact of managed care on addiction treatment.* Chevy Chase, MD: American Society of Addiction Medicine.

American Society of Addiction Medicine (2001a). *ASAM Patient Placement Criteria for the Treatment of Substance-Related Disorders,* (Second Edition–Revised). Chevy-Chase, MD: American Society of Addiction Medicine.

American Society of Addiction Medicine, (2001b). *Principles for outcome evaluation in the treatment of substance-related disorders: A joint AMBHA-ASAM statement.* Chevy Chase, MD: ASAM.

Brown, B. S. (1997). *Drug abuse treatment needs assessment methodologies.* National Institute on Drug Abuse. Retrieved June 1, 2009, from http://www.drugabuse.gov/about/organization/despr/hsr/da-tre/BrownTreatmentNeeds.html

Center for Substance Abuse Treatment. (1995a). *Purchasing managed care services for alcohol and other drug treatment*. Technical Assistance Publication Series 16. DHHS Publication No. SMA 95-3040. Rockville, MD: Center for Substance Abuse Treatment.

Center for Substance Abuse Treatment. (1995b). *The role and current status of patient placement criteria in the treatment of substance use disorders*. Treatment Improvement Protocol Series 13. DHHS Publication No. SMA 95-3021. Rockville, MD: Center for Substance Abuse Treatment.

Lewis, J. A. (1997). Treating alcohol problems in a managed care environment. In S. R. Sauber (Ed.), *Managed mental health care: Major diagnostic and treatment approaches* (pp. 297–311). Bristol, PA: Brunner/Mazel.

Lewis, J. A., Packard, T. R., & Lewis, M. D. (2007). *Management of human service programs* (4th ed.). Belmont, CA: Thomson Brooks/Cole.

McGlynn, E. A., Asch, S. M., Adams, J., Keesey, B. A., Hicks, J., DeCristofaro, M. P. H., & Kerr, E. A. (2003, June 26). The quality of health care delivered to adults in the United States. *The New England Journal of Medicine, 348*(26), 2635–2645.

National Association of Addiction Treatment Providers. (2009a, February). Are you confused? Electronic health records are not the same as electronic medical records. *Visions, 1,* 4.

National Association of Addiction Treatment Providers. (2009b, March). It all begins with the NAATP benchmark survey. *Visions, 1,* 4.

Redhead, C. S. (2009). *The Health Information Technology for Economic and Clinical Health (HITECH) Act*. Congressional Research Service. Retrieved June 1, 2009, from http://ipmall.info/hosted_resources/crs/RL32858_050413.pdf

PREVENTING SUBSTANCE ABUSE

ALTHOUGH ALCOHOLISM EDUCATION was first mandated by Vermont in 1882, prevention has been, in many ways, "the lost child" of the substance abuse field. Traditionally, community responses to perceived substance abuse problems have focused on treatment or on legal approaches. Both of these alternatives have been of limited effectiveness in reducing what is perceived by many to be an epidemic of substance abuse problems. Thus, since the mid-1970s there has been a growing interest in the development of prevention strategies (DuPont, 1979). This chapter reviews some of the issues in substance abuse prevention in the expectation that identifying those problems will help prevention programs and substance abuse counselors become more effective.

THE CONCEPT OF PREVENTION

Prevention refers to activities that reduce or stabilize the incidence (occurrence of new cases) of substance abuse and thereby reduce or stabilize its prevalence (the total number of cases). As we will see, the development, implementation, and evaluation of substance abuse prevention programs has not been an easy process (Blane & Chafetz, 1979; Miller & Nirenberg, 1984; Bukoski, 1998).

PRACTICAL DIFFICULTIES

Preventing substance abuse involves two key difficulties. The first problem concerns the validity and reliability of data on the prevalence and incidence of substance abuse in society. Disagreements over how we should define and measure the existence of the problem coupled with methodological issues has made it difficult

213

to demonstrate that prevention programs were having their intended outcomes. Moreover, prevention professionals have been involved in social policy/ideological conflicts over the expected/intended outcomes of prevention (e.g., no use versus responsible use). Thus, there has been uncertainty over how widespread substance abuse is and the extent to which it can be reduced or prevented.

The second difficulty with prevention has been in identifying and carrying out programs and activities that work. This requires that we (1) understand the causal factors in the development of substance abuse, (2) design programs and activities that will modify these risk factors, (3) obtain the resources necessary to implement our programs, and (4) demonstrate the effectiveness of programs. Researchers have articulated an impressive array of possible risk factors for substance abuse (Jones & Battjes, 1985), and program designers have been energetic in developing activities to modify those risk factors (Glynn, Leukefeld, & Ludford, 1983). However, a risk factor is not necessarily a causal factor (Moskowitz, 1989; Jung, 2001) so that focusing on the risk factor may not change the substance-using behavior. Moreover, obtaining resources (including financial and social support) for substance abuse prevention has been difficult, and frequently those programs that have been implemented seemed unable to demonstrate desired effects, particularly long-term effects.

COMMUNITY RESPONSES TO SUBSTANCE ABUSE

Bourne (1974) argued that community responses to substance abuse could be viewed as evolving through the four stages depicted in Figure 10.1. The first stage is one of denial. Community leaders and members typically find it difficult to accept the idea that substance abuse is a problem in their community and may actively or passively resist the development of prevention and treatment programs on the basis that there is no need for them.

The second stage is typified by panic. This stage is generally initiated in response to a crisis of some sort (the drug-related death of a local athlete) but may be stimulated through a needs assessment survey or a similar demonstration of the extent of substance abuse. The panic stage is transitory and involves rather vociferous demands that "something must be done immediately."

Bourne's fragmentation stage involves the development of diverse proposals and counterproposals for how to respond to the crisis. Typically, one or more actions will be accepted and endorsed as "the solution." Such solutions often take the form of developing treatment alternatives for "those people" or increasing law enforcement to identify and remove drug users and dealers, reduce the availability of drugs, and deter the motivation to use drugs. The key characteristic of the fragmentation

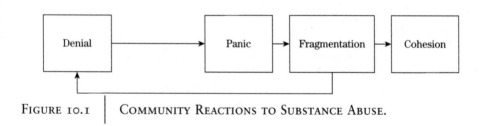

FIGURE 10.1 | COMMUNITY REACTIONS TO SUBSTANCE ABUSE.

stage is that the community response is based on considerations of cost, political clout, ease of implementation, and similar factors rather than being a comprehensive, integrated approach to the prevention of substance use, misuse, and abuse.

It should be noted that if the actions taken during the fragmentation stage are even partially "successful" (that is, the panic subsides and there is a general community consensus that the problem is being corrected), the community may regress to the denial stage or stagnate in the fragmentation stage. Successive "crises" or other information that substance abuse is continuing or increasing can result in increased commitment to the already existing programs and activities. After all, those existing programs and activities worked before, and therefore, if we renew our commitment and increase our resources, they will work again.

Bourne indicated that relatively few communities had progressed beyond the fragmentation stage. This assessment seems as valid today as it was in 1974. That is, when existing programs no longer seem to be working, the typical community response is to divert increased resources to the existing providers of substance abuse services and, perhaps, to add an additional program or two to satisfy perceived needs or funding initiatives.

Eventually, several factors can combine to move a community from a fragmentary to a cohesive response to substance abuse. These factors include the ever-increasing costs of supporting the existing and often competing programs, the persistence of substance abuse, and increasing community awareness of the inadequacies inherent in the ad hoc system that has been developed. The cohesive stage of a community's response to substance abuse is typified by a comprehensive planning process. This planning process is based on a thorough needs assessment to determine what services are needed and what are already available. The community can then begin to develop new or expanded programs to meet unmet needs as well as coordinate existing programs.

The importance of this discussion of community responses to substance abuse is that prevention programs have generally been one of the last components considered. Substance abuse prevention activities typically have not had the opportunity to develop the social support necessary for growth and to demonstrate their effectiveness.

GENERAL MODEL OF PREVENTION

Until recently, the National Institute on Drug Abuse (NIDA) and the National Institute on Alcohol Abuse and Alcoholism (NIAAA) used somewhat different conceptual schemes to organize prevention activities and programs. With the forming of the Office of Substance Abuse Prevention (OSAP) for overseeing federal prevention initiatives, a more unified approach has been promoted. OSAP generally subscribes to a public health model for prevention. The three interacting components to the model are agent, host, and environment. The model recognizes that (1) drugs (the agent) can affect users (hosts) differently; (2) hosts (users) may be differentially susceptible to drug use (agent) at various times in their lives; and (3) the drug–user relationship occurs within a context (environment) that influences such factors as drug availability and the acceptability of using a drug. Figure 10.2 portrays some of the factors that affect alcohol and drug use.

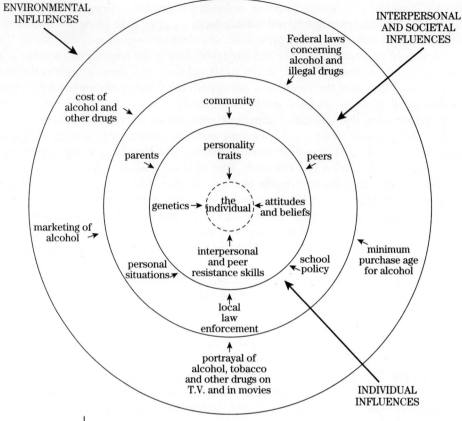

FIGURE 10.2 | FACTORS THAT INFLUENCE ALCOHOL AND OTHER DRUG USE.

Source: Office of Substance Abuse Prevention (OSAP). (1989). *Prevention Plus II—Tools for Creating and Sustaining Drug-Free Communities* (DHHS Publication No. (ADM) 89–1649).

In addition to the distinctions among agent, host, and environment, it is also useful to differentiate among levels or types of prevention (Davis, 1976). *Primary prevention* refers to activities that are designed to forestall the use of drugs. It is difficult to demonstrate the effectiveness of primary prevention because it requires demonstrating the nonoccurrence of an event that might have taken place. Secondary prevention targets experimenters and occasional users of drugs through early identification and intervention to prevent more serious drug use patterns or drug-related problems from developing. Tertiary prevention parallels treatment efforts by focusing on ameliorating existing drug-related problems and preventing relapse.

Two points should be noted from this discussion. First, treatment approaches constitute an incomplete response to substance-abuse-related problems because they tend to focus on problematic users/addicts and ignore (a) the agent and environment and (b) nonusers and nonproblematic users. The second point is that secondary and tertiary preventions have had higher social policy priority than primary prevention because of their focus on the more observable characteristics of substance abuse.

DETERMINING THE PURPOSE OF PREVENTION

One of the continuing problems in the area of substance abuse prevention is disagreement over the goals of prevention. There are two dominant perspectives on what should be the goals of prevention programs. The oldest and, perhaps, most widely endorsed perspective is that the purpose of prevention is to achieve or maintain abstinence. A newer perspective focuses on responsible use and harm reduction.

Abstinence, as used in the literature on substance abuse prevention, has at least two meanings. First, *abstinence* has been used to refer to a general prohibition against the use of any drug by any individual. A review of the history of substance use across time and cultures suggests that general prohibitions may be unattainable. A second meaning of abstinence targets either selected drugs or specific groups within society (e.g., minors). This second approach to abstinence has encountered difficulties in justifying differences among substances (e.g., alcohol versus marijuana) and among groups (e.g., drinking age). A variant of the specific abstinence approach is to focus on inappropriate or critical situations such as drinking and driving or substance use during pregnancy. Abstinence advocates have been bolstered during the last decade by research indicating that the age of first use of alcohol increased, illicit drug use decreased, and alcohol-related driving fatalities decreased (*Healthy People 2010*, 2000).

The successes of specific abstinence approaches coupled with the apparent failure of absolute abstinence have contributed to increased support for a harm reduction model. Harm reduction advocates emphasize identifying and reducing the harmful consequences of alcohol, tobacco, and other drug use rather than abstinence (Marlatt, 1998). Although abstinence may be the appropriate goal in some situations, other goals are also appropriate for prevention (e.g., changes in the pattern of use, choice of drug, or other behaviors). Although such an approach is conceptually consistent with the general model used by OSAP (as is abstinence) and is probably a more realistic goal than abstinence in a drug-using society, the harm reduction approach has been attacked as inconsistent with legal codes and popular conceptions regarding the dangers of drug use. Generally speaking, only with regard to the "social drugs"—that is, alcohol, caffeine, and nicotine—and prescription drugs has there been much support for controlled-use prevention programs.

MacCoun (1998) notes that in addition to the differences in goals between use reduction (abstinence) and harm reduction, each approach may have different unintended effects. For example, a use reduction drug education program may encourage some students to avoid using drugs while convincing others that their use of drugs is safe (Bensley & Wu, 1991). Conversely, a harm reduction program that promotes designated drivers to reduce alcohol-related crashes may encourage the "riders" to consume more alcohol than they otherwise would have.

Given that prevention programs can focus on either use reduction or harm reduction, we may ask why so many programs seem to be based on abstinence. There are several reasons. First, there is a historical tradition that emphasizes non-use of drugs. Second, there is a simplified logic that specifies that if people do not use drugs, they cannot abuse them. Third, a mystique and a mythology regarding the evils of drugs have developed. Finally, the emphasis on abstinence is easier to carry out than trying to define acceptable levels of controlled use.

There are, however, some very serious drawbacks to emphasizing abstinence as a prevention goal. First, many abused drugs also have legitimate and widely accepted therapeutic uses in medicine. Thus, there is a potential conflict and a difficult distinction to be made between the use of a substance under the direction of a physician and the use of the same substance without the approval of an authority. Second, abstinence denies the historical fact that virtually every known culture permits, if not actually encourages, the use of one or more psychoactive drugs for social and recreational purposes. By what criteria are we to distinguish between caffeine and other stimulants, tobacco and marijuana, or alcohol and other depressants? Third, and related to the second, the bulk of pharmacological, etiological, and epidemiological research provides little support for the so-called logic of abstinence or for much of the mystique and mythology that have been created around substance use and abuse. Fourth, abstinence as a prevention goal may be inconsistent with developmental processes emphasizing decision making, clarification of values, independence, and responsible behavior. Finally, the emphasis on abstinence is one reason so many prevention programs have been seemingly ineffective, because any use of a substance following completion of the program or activity would be construed as a negative outcome (Bacon, 1978). Thus, harm reduction programs focusing on controlled use or reducing the adverse consequences of substance abuse may show greater promise of being successful than the abstinence-oriented programs.

DEVELOPING A CAUSAL MODEL

Having determined the purpose, or goal, of a substance abuse prevention program, we need to determine how to achieve that goal. Achieving a change in the prevalence of substance abuse or the consequences of abusing drugs depends on the development of a causal model. Such a model specifies the presumed antecedents of substance abuse, so that we can identify those factors that are subject to change and thereby reduce the occurrence of abuse.

The causal model should account for biological, psychological, and sociocultural influences. Failure to fully articulate the presumed causal model can result in both overestimating the importance of the factors selected for inclusion and underestimating compensatory processes among correlated factors not included in the model. Both of these errors imply that even when we are successful in modifying our selected antecedents of substance abuse, the impact of the prevention program or activity can be insignificant or nonexistent.

For example, concern over drinking and driving generally focuses on either restricting drinking or identifying and punishing drivers who have been drinking. Restrictions on drinking are generally attempted by way of public education campaigns regarding the risks of drinking and driving. Identifying and punishing drunken drivers is a law enforcement concern. Although these approaches are needed, they are incomplete. Both approaches ignore the acute and chronic effects of alcohol on subjective perceptions and the lack of intent by many individuals to overuse alcohol and then drive. We need to develop activities that will deter driving by intoxicated individuals, such as devices to keep the people from entering or starting their automobile and the provision of alternative transportation. Only by focusing on both the factors that result in drinking and the factors that contribute to driving after drinking can we begin to develop successful programs to prevent driving while intoxicated.

Likewise, analyses of adolescent substance abuse suggest that a broad array of factors contribute to the initiation of illegal drug use. Preventing the initiation of adolescent substance abuse is a complex problem requiring a comprehensive approach. Such an approach would involve multiple strategies (information, life skills, alternatives, and social policy) targeted at multiple systems (youth, families, schools, and community).

As the preceding examples illustrate, developing substance abuse prevention programs requires a careful analysis of the factors that contribute to the use and abuse of drugs. Only through etiological research that identifies and explicates the relationships among causal factors can we hope to successfully reduce the incidence of substance-abuse-related problems.

PRODUCING CHANGE

Having identified a number of presumed causal factors that contribute to the occurrence of substance abuse problems, we will encounter several issues in actually changing the prevalence of those problems. These issues include (1) obtaining sufficient resources to initiate and maintain the change process, (2) anticipating counter prevention programs and activities, (3) allowing enough time for the prevention activities to work, (4) providing programs of sufficient intensity, (5) ensuring that the proposed changes do not create new problems, (6) targeting populations, and (7) demonstrating the effectiveness of prevention programs.

OBTAINING RESOURCES

Obtaining sufficient resources to begin and maintain prevention programs continues to be a major obstacle. Although it is difficult, if not impossible, to determine the total amount of private and public funds committed, prevention funding tends to account for a small percentage of the total funds for alcohol and drug abuse programs whereas the vast majority goes to law enforcement. As Nathan (1983) noted, federal and state commitment to substance abuse prevention is lacking.

The absence of federal and state resources can be largely attributed to both an inconsistent social policy on prevention and an entrenched treatment orientation to substance abuse. Substance abuse prevention often overlaps in several respects with an array of other social and personal problems, such as mental health, education, law enforcement, and health care. This overlap has resulted in competition among community agencies for funds, clients, and other resources. Although coordination and integration of these diverse agencies are desirable, it is clear that to fulfill this objective (e.g., reducing both teenage drinking and pregnancies) requires both social policy commitment and extensive staff training. At present, federal funding is far more committed to prevention through law enforcement than through other means.

A second obstacle to obtaining resources for prevention is the institutionalization and elaboration of a treatment system for substance abusers. Helping professionals are understandably more oriented toward services for afflicted individuals than toward preventive programs. It should be obvious that vested interests have developed around the concept of treatment. The treatment network has been elaborated in a number of directions, including earlier identification of, intervention with, and referral of suspected substance abusers; identification of special populations with special treatment needs (women, youth, older people); and increases in the number of agencies for indirectly afflicted individuals (spouses and children of substance abusers). The appropriateness of such elaboration is not at issue here. What is important is that prevention is often opposed, overtly or covertly, because it is perceived as diverting funds from needed treatment resources.

RESISTING COUNTERPREVENTION

Given the diversity of prevention models, purposes, and etiological factors, the absence of a clear social policy, and the vested interests of the treatment network, it should not be surprising that there is little consensus on how to prevent substance abuse. When prevention proposals, programs, and activities also infringe, or are perceived as infringing, on other established institutions such as the alcoholic beverage industry, pharmaceutical manufacturers, advertising, law enforcement, medicine, or education, there is controversy, debate, and resistance to the proposals. The ensuing disagreement over the means and ends of prevention can result in counterprevention (Low, 1979). For example, prevention and educational programs in the schools may encounter resistance from various community groups (including parents), who may oppose the programs on a wide variety of grounds. Thus, one of the problems a prevention initiative should anticipate is the development of counteractivities by those agencies or organizations that do not concur with the program's purpose or techniques.

ALLOWING ENOUGH TIME

A third issue to be considered in prevention activities is the amount of time required for the expected changes to accrue. Prevention programs or activities need to give careful attention to the period required to demonstrate expected changes. Unrealistic expectations by prevention planners in combination with demands from the community or funding sources can result in unrealistic promises of change within short time periods.

Within the general area of health promotion and risk reduction, there are numerous examples of this kind of delay. Antismoking programs (initiated about 1964) and seat belt usage campaigns (initiated around 1972) are two examples in considering the length of time necessary to substantially alter social behavior.

ENSURING INTENSITY

In addition to allowing enough time for prevention to work, we must recognize the importance of providing programs of sufficient intensity to make changes occur. The intensity of a program is particularly important when we examine school programs, but it should also be considered when designing other prevention activities.

Most educational institutions assume that knowledge and skill are acquired slowly, sequentially, and with practice. Thus, we teach spelling, writing, reading, mathematics, history, athletics, music, and the like, beginning in grammar school and extending into college. Even such activities as learning how to drive an automobile or handle a gun involve intensive learning processes. Substance abuse education, on the other hand, often seems to assume that a single film or guest speaker, or maybe a 4-week series of activities, is sufficient to prevent the use, misuse, or abuse of drugs.

Substance abuse in contemporary society is a multifaceted issue crosscut by moral, legal, medical, psychological, and sociological considerations. For prevention activities to have an impact, they must be intense enough and continue long enough to provide appropriate opportunities for acquisition, retention, and practice.

Maintaining Positive Balance

A program has a positive balance when its positive effects outweigh its negative effects (Low, 1979). In designing, implementing, and evaluating substance abuse prevention programs and activities, we must give careful attention to both their intended and their unintended effects at both the personal and social levels of analysis.

The importance of positive balance can be observed in several areas. First, as Low notes, the benefits of substance use are primarily personal and subjective, whereas the problems associated with such behavior are more likely to be interpersonal and objective. Thus, there is a distinct tendency to underestimate the benefits of substance use and to emphasize the problems associated with using drugs. Second, there is a clear tendency to overgeneralize research based on clinical populations and to assume that other users of drugs have (or will have) the same problems (health, occupational, legal, familial, or other) found among those already in treatment. Third, it seems that many, if not most, substance abuse professionals persistently view substance use as the cause of other problems when it is entirely possible that the substance use is the result of some other problem. Finally, it should be noted that agency definitions of behaviors as either desirable or undesirable are often constructed on the basis of implicit normative standards. These standards, in turn, are based on judgments of what should be, what is conventional, and what is politically acceptable rather than empirical assessments of the etiology and epidemiology of substance abuse.

An example of the importance of positive balance is found in the law enforcement approach to the control of substance abuse (Nadelmann, 1997). The underlying logic of this approach seems to be that (1) by reducing the availability or supply of drugs (through legal restrictions on the importation, manufacture, distribution, and sale of drugs) and (2) by reducing the demand for drugs (through imprisoning or deterring users and dealers), we can reduce the prevalence of substance use and abuse. Furthermore, it is often argued that reductions in the prevalence of substance use will result in a reduction in drug-related crime. Finally, a corollary of this approach contends that if legal restrictions are initially ineffective, we need to strengthen the penalties for noncompliance.

Advocates of the law enforcement approach use arrest, prosecution, and prison statistics and data from programs designed to divert substance abusers into treatment to support assertions that this approach can be effective in containing drug abuse. These possible benefits of drug laws and enforcement must be balanced against the costs of this approach, such as the following:

- financial costs, including billions of dollars spent by the federal, state, and local governments on law enforcement every year
- criminal justice problems, including the number of personnel diverted from other law enforcement areas; difficulty in enforcing a "victimless" crime; possible corruption of officers, prosecutors, and judges; and hostility and alienation of community members who oppose this approach or feel discriminated against stigmatization of individuals arrested under these laws
- increased health risks for users from the poor quality control of "street" drugs and from the spread of disease and septic problems in the use of drugs (e.g., AIDS)
- increased criminal activity in the form of both a black market to supply the drugs and the need to acquire the money to purchase drugs
- perpetuation of myths about drugs and drug use because of the difficulties in studying an illegal activity

Clearly, the concept of positive balance calls into question the efficacy of drug laws and their enforcement in preventing substance abuse.

TARGETING POPULATIONS

A sixth issue in prevention is the selection of target populations. Knowledge about a proposed target population's characteristics such as cognitive development, values, and cultural background is essential in developing activities that can be effective. Three general dimensions are relevant in deciding how to match a prevention program or activity to an audience: general versus specific, direct versus indirect, and distal versus proximal.

A general prevention program is one that is applicable to a wide array of individuals regardless of their degree of involvement in substance use and abuse. Specific prevention programs, on the other hand, focus on certain groups, with the specificity defined in terms of a presumed or empirically validated common characteristic. For example, drug information programs are usually general, because they try to enhance knowledge of how drugs affect behavior. However, specific information programs have been developed that target the drug use and abuse problems among, for example, Black Americans, Native Americans, older Americans, and Hispanic Americans.

The second variable in selecting a target population focuses on whether the prevention activities will be direct or indirect. Direct prevention activities are specific to substance abuse, whereas indirect activities focus on more general issues that are correlated in some way with substance abuse. Health promotion activities can be viewed as indirect substance abuse prevention, because they may not only affect the use and abuse of drugs but also have an impact on a variety of other behaviors (nutrition, exercise, and stress control). Substance abuse education, in contrast, will presumably focus on changing some combination of affective, behavioral, and cognitive factors related to the use and abuse of drugs and will involve nutrition, exercise, and stress control only to the extent that they are correlated with the use and abuse of drugs.

Finally, in targeting a prevention program, it is well to keep in mind the distinction between distal and proximal variables. For example, because both parent and peer behaviors have been found to correlate with adolescent substance abuse (Jung, 2001), prevention programs could focus on either or both variables. However, the development of functional families, appropriate parenting skills, and satisfactory parent–child relationships precedes and contributes to peer relationships. Thus, prevention programs targeting parents would have delayed effects, and peer-oriented programs would have more immediate effects on the use and abuse of substances.

Selection of a particular type of prevention program or a combination of types requires a determination of the characteristics of the population or group to be targeted by the prevention program. Thus, once a target population for substance abuse prevention has been provisionally selected, a needs assessment should be conducted.

Evaluating Programs

Well-designed studies to assess the effectiveness of substance abuse prevention programs are essential (Schaps, DiBartolo, Palley, & Churgin, 1978). There are extensive reviews of both general issues related to evaluation and specific concerns related to the evaluation of prevention programs and activities. We will not examine them here, but several issues do deserve special mention: (1) evaluation as a social judgment process; (2) the relationship between what is desired, what is intended, and what is accomplished; (3) the contrast between immediate and delayed effects; (4) the strength of the effects; and (5) the concept of declining marginal utility.

Evaluation research ultimately involves a social judgment regarding the utility or acceptability of a program or activity. Although the data used to support an evaluation are essentially neutral, decisions regarding what data to collect, how to collect them, and what their results mean involve a variety of implicit and explicit judgments. Thus, there may be considerable disagreement among the evaluation research team, the program developers and managers, and the community over the relative success or failure of a prevention program or activity.

For example, a drug education program may be designed to enhance students' knowledge of the benefits and risks of various substances in the expectation that such information will reduce the use and abuse of drugs. Evaluation research may show that although there appears to have been an increase in knowledge about drugs, the research design was inadequate to show that this change in knowledge was a direct result of the program. It may further indicate little or no impact on drug-using behavior. Thus, the results are inconclusive. The community, observing little change in adolescent behavior, may conclude that the program does not work.

One major source of disagreement regarding the effectiveness of programs to prevent substance abuse derives from the distinction among desired, intended, and achieved effects. The desired effects of a program represent what is hoped for by various community groups. Desired effects are often implicitly rather than explicitly stated and are often phrased in the language of morals (e.g., teenagers should not drink alcoholic beverages). The intended effects of a prevention activity represent the explicit purpose and objectives of the program, such as a reduction in the adolescent mortality rate related to drunken driving. The achieved effects of a prevention program represent both the intended and the unintended changes that are correlated with its implementation; for example, increased understanding of the risks associated with driving under the influence (DUI) results in increased utilization of designated drivers. Because the desired, intended, and achieved effects of a program or activity can be at variance, it may be unclear from the evaluation research whether the prevention program was successful. As indicated in the foregoing example, the prevention program may accomplish the intended objective in an unintended way without fulfilling community expectations.

The third evaluation issue concerns the distinction between immediate and delayed effects. For several reasons, the immediate effects of a program or activity may be both quantitatively and qualitatively different from the delayed effects (Bell & Battjes, 1985). For example, the effectiveness of an education program intended to reduce fetal and neonatal consequences of substance use and abuse among females but targeted at prepubescents can vary considerably over time. There may be immediate and significant cognitive, affective, and behavioral changes in the intended directions that gradually erode over time, so that statistical differences between the control and experimental groups are insignificant at pubescence. Likewise, the prepubescent changes in knowledge, values, and behaviors may not be transformed into expected behaviors during the childbearing years. Thus, the results of evaluation research may reveal different effects depending on how much time has elapsed between the program and the research.

A fourth issue related to the evaluation of prevention programs and activities concerns the relationship between statistical significance, the strength of an effect, and the size of the sample. Statistical significance is less likely to occur when either the effects of a prevention program are small or the number of units of analysis is small. Because the unit of analysis for many prevention programs is often small (that is, one class of 30 students), the magnitude of the effect must be large in order to achieve statistical significance. However, the same program could very well achieve statistical significance if more individuals, classes, schools, or communities were involved. Thus, in considering the apparent effectiveness of a program, we must consider both the strength of the effects and the size of the sample.

The fifth issue to be discussed in the context of evaluation concerns declining marginal utility. According to this concept, the less the discrepancy between an actual (empirically verified) event and the maximum (or minimum) occurrence of the event, the more difficult it will be to change the event. That is, if the prevalence of substance abuse in a community is much higher than the endemic rate (the minimally attainable rate), then it is relatively easy to reduce the prevalence. As the prevalence decreases, however, it becomes increasingly difficult to further reduce the prevalence rate, and further reductions will require increased resource allocations, more efficient programs, or more effective programs. Figure 10.3 depicts the concept of declining marginal utility as applied to prevention programs.

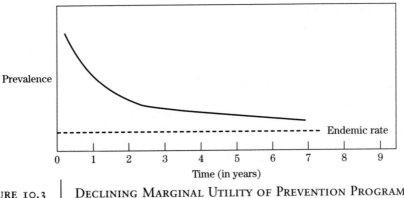

FIGURE 10.3 | DECLINING MARGINAL UTILITY OF PREVENTION PROGRAMS.

One year after a prevention program is begun, the prevalence rate may be 70% of what it was before the program. After 2 years, however, the prevalence is still 50% of its initial value. At the end of the 3rd year the prevalence is 40% of the baseline, and with each succeeding year the prevention program has less impact than it did the previous year.

Clearly, the context of a prevention program is important in determining the apparent effectiveness of the program. A program or activity implemented in a community with a very high prevalence rate can have considerable impact, and the same program in a community with a low prevalence rate may produce little or no discernible change (Bacon, 1978). Likewise, a program that is initially successful in reducing the prevalence of substance abuse in a community can, over time, seemingly become ineffective. Thus, if a program appears to be either effective or ineffective, we must be careful to specify the context in which it was implemented and recognize that it might have very different results in a different context.

A final caveat regarding the evaluation of substance abuse prevention activities and programs is in order. Prevention professionals have seemingly accepted and endorsed the concept of rigorous evaluation much more readily than their treatment-oriented brethren. Thus, as a rule, the literature on the evaluation of prevention programs more frequently addresses issues of research design than does the literature on treatment. Consider, for example, the basic importance of having both an experimental and a control group in assessing the effectiveness of a program. While control groups are seemingly routinely employed in prevention evaluation research, treatment programs only rarely utilize any form of control group. Hence, although both the effectiveness and scientific rigor of prevention programs have justifiably been questioned, those same criticisms and concerns are applicable to the vast body of "knowledge" regarding treatment.

EFFECTIVENESS OF PREVENTION PROGRAMS

This section reviews the evaluation research related to a broad variety of substance abuse prevention programs. As often occurs with applied research, these studies have frequently been criticized for their methodological weaknesses.

MASS MEDIA PROGRAMS

Mass media programs attempt to motivate avoidance of substance use (demand reduction) by influencing knowledge and attitudes. Wallack (1981) indicated that they are of limited effectiveness, and Bensley and Wu (1991) found a differential impact with high-threat messages increasing alcohol use, especially among heavy drinkers. Research based on alcohol advertising has found little relationship between substance use and either bans on such advertising or expenditures to promote sales (Smart, 1988). Although mass media campaigns and advertising can reach large audiences at low cost, they may be differentially attended to, interpreted, accepted, and acted on by recipients.

ECONOMIC CONTROLS

With respect to alcohol, there is evidence that when the price increases (through taxation), there is a decrease in consumption (Leung & Phelps, 1993). However, this effect was less pronounced for beer than for spirits and wine. Such research involving illicit drug use has been more difficult to conduct; however, heavy users can be expected to increase their criminal activity to compensate for price increases (Reuter & Caulkins, 1995). Similarly, heavy alcohol users may be less responsive to price increases than light and moderate drinkers.

EDUCATIONAL PROGRAMS

Perhaps the most common approach to substance abuse prevention has been through school-based drug education programs. Educational programs have incorporated a number of variations including knowledge/information, affective education, and behavioral skills training. Evaluations of school-based programs found little effect for knowledge-based (Schaps et al., 1978) or self-esteem–enhancing (Hopkins, Mauss, Kearney, & Wilsheit, 1988) programs. However, behavioral skills training (G. J. Botvin, Schinke, Epstein, Diaz, & E. M. Botvin, 1995) and normative education (Hansen, Graham, Wolkenstein, & Rohrbach, 1991; Pentz, 1995) have been shown to be effective.

Tobler (1997) conducted a meta-analysis of 120 programs that suggests that the method used in conducting prevention activities is more important than the content. Tobler placed programs into four categories and found that interactive programs were more effective than noninteractive programs. Interactive programs focus on intrapersonal and interpersonal development with the leader as a facilitator. Noninteractive programs focus on information dissemination with the leader as a teacher and students as passive participants.

DRUG ABUSE RESISTANCE EDUCATION

Project Drug Abuse Resistance Education (DARE) was initiated in 1983 as a cooperative project between the Los Angeles Police Department and public schools. The program consists of 17 components delivered by uniformed police officers. DARE spread rapidly so that by 1994 it was operating in every state; over 8,000 communities and more than half the nation's schools were using it. The federal government mandated financial support through the Drug-Free Schools and Communities Act. Though there are several positive elements to this approach, Ennett, Tobler, Ringwalt, and Flewelling (1994) found little effect on substance-using behavior and Tobler (1997) classified it as a noninteractive model. Thus, despite its popularity, DARE does not seem to have had its intended effect as a substance abuse prevention program.

MUTIPLE FACTORS APPROACHES

Three somewhat related approaches to prevention have evolved in the past 20 years: risk and protective factors theory (Hawkins, Catalano, & J. Y. Miller, 1992); resiliency model (Werner & Smith, 1992); and developmental assets approach (Leffert, Benson, & Roehlkepartain, 1997). These approaches are similar in recognizing that there are a large number of variables that can influence the onset of substance use.

Each of these approaches seeks to identify variables that reduce the likelihood of using drugs (protective factors, resiliency factors, or assets) and the types of events that increase the risk of using drugs. Unlike the DARE approach with its 17 components, these multiple factor approaches require a needs assessment to determine which factors are relevant and then the creation of activities to strengthen or ameliorate their influence. Because the selection of which factors to focus on and the choice of activities to engage in varies from one setting to another, it has been difficult to establish clear evaluative outcomes.

LEGAL RESTRICTIONS

In addition to taxation, a variety of federal and state laws have been passed that focus on the supply and demand for legal and illegal drugs. As such, these legal restrictions can be viewed as prevention measures. It is unclear how effective these measures have been. Proponents argue that the laws restrict supply and deter individuals from using the substances. Opponents point out that the effects of law enforcement on reducing the supply (availability) of drugs are questionable and may not affect demand (Institute of Medicine, 1996) but may increase prices and, consequently, criminal activity (MacCoun & Caulkins, 1996). Clearly, despite increased arrest rates, increased incarcerations, and the development of drug courts and diversion programs, illicit drug use remains high.

PARENTING PROGRAMS

Parenting programs utilizing some combination of information dissemination, skills training, support group access, and enhancement of family interaction patterns offer a forum for both primary and secondary prevention. A review of these interventions (Ashery, Robertson, & Kumpfer, 1998) indicates that they can be successful either on their own or when combined with other programs (e.g., school-based programs).

COMMUNITY PER-BASED PROGRAMS

A number of community programs designed to provide services to youth (e.g., Young Men's Christian Association (YMCA)/Young Women's Christian Association (YWCA), Big Brothers/Big Sisters, churches) have extended their activities to include substance abuse prevention. Typically, these programs incorporate educational content similar to that already discussed into their existing programs with similar results (Pentz, 1995).

DRUG-FREE WORKPLACES

During the 1980s, there was a rapid expansion of employee assistance programs designed to reduce corporate costs by identifying and intervening with troubled employees (e.g., poor work quality, excessive tardiness or time off from work, high accident rates). This movement was facilitated by federal mandates for drug-free workplaces. Though generally conceded to be cost-effective, the effects of such programs on alcohol and drug consumption are less clear (Jung, 2001).

CENTER FOR SUBSTANCE ABUSE PREVENTION STRATEGY

The Center for Substance Abuse Prevention (CSAP) developed and promoted a strategy for substance abuse prevention that utilizes six elements. These elements are: (1) information dissemination to increase awareness of the impacts of alcohol and drug use/abuse/dependence; (2) prevention education that uses interactive events to influence life skills; (3) alternative activities to foster involvement in substance-free activities; (4) community-based processes to enhance community substance abuse prevention, intervention, treatment, and relapse avoidance services; (5) environmental approaches that focus on community standards, attitudes, and regulations that can deter substance abuse; and (6) problem identification and referral for those individuals who have engaged in illegal drug use. CSAP funded research indicates that comprehensive approaches utilizing several strategies are more effective than models using one or two elements (Brounstein, Zweig, & Gardner, 1998).

It should be clear from the foregoing review of prevention approaches that prevention programmers have made considerable progress in designing, implementing, and demonstrating the effectiveness of their activities. Prevention can work. However, research remains to be done on the content, audience, presenter, methods of delivery, and their interactions. In other words, we need to determine what kinds of activities, implemented in what manner, by what kinds of facilitators, to what audience work best.

SUMMARY

Society's response to substance abuse problems has traditionally focused on treatment or legal approaches. However, the high cost and questionable effectiveness of these approaches have stimulated a growing interest in prevention, which is now viewed as an essential component of the substance abuse services network.

A review of contemporary prevention programs indicates that prevention initiatives have and are confronting the same types of issues that face treatment providers. These include the following:

- definition and measurement of substance abuse problems
- community and professional resistance
- controversy over the goals of prevention programs
- development of causal models
- utilization of research based interventions
- adequate resources
- sufficient time for expected changes to occur

- intensity to establish and strengthen behavioral changes
- defining the target population and matching the prevention program to population characteristics
- careful evaluation of effects

Several steps can be taken to develop more effective prevention programs. The first step is to utilize empirically validated planning processes that combine information from social, behavioral, educational, and health research. The second and third steps are to ensure that the prevention program is comprehensive and intensive, so it can both reach the intended target population and promote changes in behavior. Fourth, the internal and external consistency of the program must be monitored, in order to avoid mixed messages and to provide a message that can be assimilated by the target population. Fifth, prevention providers must be carefully selected and trained to achieve audience acceptance of them as credible sources of information. Sixth, prevention programs must be community owned; that is, they must become a part of the community. Finally, continual public evaluations of prevention programs are essential if we are to improve and adapt our programs to changing community needs.

Although efforts to prevent substance abuse have met with a number of problems, epidemiological studies indicate that most members of our society do not experience acute or chronic substance abuse problems. Prevention activities have been implemented to do that work. The challenge is to systematize these activities to increase their effectiveness and to develop new approaches that impact underserved populations. Prevention efforts have helped enhance our knowledge of substance-abuse-related problems and are contributing to the development of more successful substance abuse services networks.

QUESTIONS FOR THOUGHT AND DISCUSSION

1. You have been asked to design a substance abuse prevention program for a high school in your community. What do you think should be the primary components of such a program? Would it be possible to include aspects of both primary and secondary prevention aimed at both the students themselves and the school environment?
2. If you were to implement such a program, how would you go about making sure that you had broad agreement on the goals of the program? How would you get the support of the various groups affected by the program?
3. What challenges would you face in evaluating the effectiveness of the prevention program?

REFERENCES

Ashery, R., Robertson, E., & Kumpfer, K. (1998). *Drug abuse prevention through family interventions* (NIDA Research Monograph 177).

Bacon, S. D. (1978). On the prevention of alcohol problems and alcoholism. *Journal of Studies on Alcohol, 39*(7), 1125–1147.

Bell, C. S., & Battjes, R. (Eds.). (1985). *Prevention research: Deterring drug abuse among children and adolescents.* Rockville, MD: National Institute on Drug Abuse.

Bensley, L., & Wu, R. (1991). The role of psychological reactance on drinking following alcohol prevention messages. *Journal of Applied Psychology, 21,* 1111–1124.

Blane, H. T., & Chafetz, M. E. (Eds.). (1979). *Youth, alcohol, and social policy.* New York: Plenum.

Botvin, G. J., Schinke, S. P., Epstein, J. A., Diaz, T., & Botvin, E. M. (1995). Effectiveness of culturally focused and generic skills training approaches to alcohol and drug abuse prevention among minority youth: Two-year follow-up results. *Psychology of addictive behaviors, 9,* 183–194.

Bourne, P. G. (1974). Approaches to drug abuse prevention and treatment in rural areas. *Journal of Psychedelic Drugs, 6*(2), 285–289.

Brounstein, P., Zweig, J., & Gardner, S. (1998). Science-based practices in substance abuse prevention: A guide. Rockville, MD: Center for Substance Abuse Prevention.

Bukoski, W. (1998). Introduction. In W. Bukoski & R. Evans (Eds.), *Cost-benefit/cost-effectiveness research of drug abuse prevention: Implications for programming and policy* (NIDA Research Monograph 176).

Davis, R. E. (1976, Spring). The primary prevention of alcohol problems. *Alcohol Health and Research World,* 10–12.

DuPont, R. L. (1979). The future of drug abuse prevention. In R. L. DuPont, A. Goldstein, & J. O'Donnell (Eds.), *Handbook on drug abuse.* Rockville, MD: National Institute on Drug Abuse.

Ennett, S., Tobler, N., Ringwalt, C., & Flewelling, R. (1994). How effective is drug abuse resistance education? A meta-analysis of project DARE outcome evaluations. *American Journal of Public Health, 84,* 1394–1402.

Glynn, T. J., Leukefeld, C. G., & Ludford, J. P. (Eds.). (1983). *Preventing adolescent drug abuse-intervention strategies.* Rockville, MD: National Institute on Drug Abuse.

Hansen, W., Graham, J., Wolkenstein, B., & Rohrbach, L. (1991). Program integrity as a moderator of prevention programming effectiveness: Results for fifth-grade students in the adolescent alcohol prevention trial. *Journal of Studies on Alcohol, 52,* 568–579.

Hawkins, J. D., Catalano, R. F., & Miller, J. Y. (1992). Risk and protective factors for alcohol and other drug problems in adolescence and early adulthood: Implications for substance abuse prevention. *Psychological Bulletin, 112,* 64–105.

Healthy people 2010: Understanding and improving health (2nd ed.). (2000). Washington, DC: U.S. Department of Health and Human Services.

Hopkins, R. H., Mauss, A. L., Kearney, K. A., & Wilsheit, R. A. (1998). Comprehensive evaluation of a model alcohol education curriculum. *Journal of Studies on Alcohol, 49,* 38–50.

Institute of Medicine. (1996). *Pathways of addiction: Opportunities in drug abuse research.* Washington, DC: National Academy Press.

Jones, C. L., & Battjes, R. J. (Eds.). (1985). *Etiology of drug abuse: Implications for prevention.* Rockville, MD: National Institute on Drug Abuse.

Jung, J. (2001). Psychology of alcohol and other drugs—A research perspective. Thousand Oaks, CA: Sage.

Leffert, N., Benson, P., & Roehlkepartain, J. (1997). Starting out right: Developmental assets for children. Minneapolis, MN: Search Institute.

Leung, S. F., & Phelps, C. E. (1993). My kingdom for a drink ...? A review of estimates of the price sensitivity of demand for alcoholic beverages. In M. E. Hilton & G. Bloss

(Eds.), *Economics and the prevention of alcohol-related problems* (NIAAA Research Monograph No. 25).

Low, L. (1979). Prevention. In L. A. Phillips, S. R. Ramsey, L. Blumenthal, & P. Cranshaw (Eds.), *Core knowledge in the drug field*. Ottawa: Non-Medical Use of Drugs Directorate, National Health and Welfare.

MacCoun, R. (1998). Toward a psychology of harm reduction. *American Psychologist, 53*, 1199–1208.

MacCoun, R. J., & Caulkins, J. (1996). Examining the behavioral assumptions of the national drug control policy. In W. K. Bickel & R. J. DeGrandpre (Eds.), *Drug policy and human nature: Psychological perspective in the prevention, management, and treatment of illict drug use*. New York: Plenum.

Marlatt, G. (Ed.). (1998). *Harm-reduction: Pragmatic strategies for managing high-risk behaviors*. New York: Guilford Press.

Miller, P. M., & Nirenberg, T. D. (Eds.). (1984). *Prevention of alcohol abuse*. New York: Plenum.

Moskowitz, J. (1989). The primary prevention of alcohol problems: A critical review of the research literature. *Journal of Studies on Alcohol, 50*, 54–58.

Nadelmann, E. (1997). Drug prohibition in the United States: Costs, consequences, and alternatives. In C. Reinarman & H. Levine (Eds.), *Crack in America: Demon drugs and social justice*. Berkeley: University of California Press.

Nathan, P. E. (1983, April). Failures in prevention: Why we can't prevent the devastating effect of alcoholism and drug abuse. *American Psychologist, 459–467*.

Office of Substance Abuse Prevention (OSAP). (1989). *Prevention Plus II—Tools for Creating and Sustaining Drug-Free Communities* (DHHS Publication No. (ADM) 89-1649).

Pentz, M. (1995). Prevention research in multiethnic communities. In G. Botvin, S. Schinke, & M. Orlandi (Eds.), *Drug abuse prevention with multiethnic youth*. Thousand Oaks, CA: Sage.

Reuter, P. & Caulkins, J. P. (1995). Redefining the goals of national drug policy: Recommendations from a working group. *American Journal of Public Health, 85*, 1059–1063.

Schaps, E., DiBartolo, R., Palley, C. S., & Churgin, S. (1978). Primary prevention evaluation research: A review of 127 program evaluations. Prepared for the National Institute on Drug Abuse, Rockville, MD.

Smart, R. G. (1988). Does alcohol advertising affect overall consumption? A review of empirical studies. *Journal of Studies on Alcohol, 49*, 314–323.

Tobler, N. (1997). Meta-analysis of adolescent drug prevention programs: Results of 1993 meta-analysis. In W. Butoski (Ed.), *Meta-analysis of drug abuse prevention programs* (NIDA Research Monograph 170).

Wallack, L. (1981). Mass media campaigns: The odds against finding behavior change. *Health Education Quarterly, 8*, 209–260.

Werner, E. E. & Smith, R. S. (1992). Overcoming the odds: High-risk children from birth to adulthood. New York: Cornell University Press.

APPENDIXES

A PSYCHOSOCIAL AND SUBSTANCE USE HISTORY

Client's name _____ Date _____

Social Security no. _____ Nationality _____

Age _____ Birth date _____ Sex _____

Address _____ Telephone no. _____

In your own words, why did you come here?

_____

_____

_____

How do you feel about being here? _____

_____

_____

_____

A. Marital history (spouse refers to husband, wife, girlfriend, or boyfriend)

    1. Marital status (circle the word that best explains your status)

       single   engaged   married   separated   divorced

       widowed   divorced/remarried   common-law

    2. If you have been married, how many times? _____

    3. How old were you when you were first married? _____

Source: Adapted with permission from the South Suburban Council on Alcoholism, East Hazelcrest, IL, N. Haney, Executive Director.

4. How many years have you been married to your present spouse? _____
5. How old is your present spouse? _____

B. Educational history (please circle)

1. Grade school
2. High_school: 1 year   2 years   3 years   4 years   General Educational Development (GED)
3. College: 1 year   2 years   3 years   4 years   postgraduate
4. Have you ever been in special education classes? _____ yes _____ no
   If so, why were you in these classes?_____
   _____

5. Have you ever had tutoring? _____ yes _____ no
   If so, what for?_____
   _____

C. Drinking and drug history relative to school

1. Are you still in school? _____ yes _____ no
   Name of school _____
2. Has your drinking or drug use ever caused problems in school?
3. Have you ever been sent home from school because of drinking or drug use? _____ yes _____ no
4. Have you ever been suspended from school? _____ yes _____ no
5. Have you ever been expelled from school? _____ yes _____ no
   If so, why were you expelled? Please explain: _____
   _____
   _____

6. Are you in danger of being expelled now? _____ yes _____ no
   If so, please explain: _____
   _____
   _____

7. Have the school authorities suggested that you come here?
   _____ yes _____ no
   If they have, please explain: _____
   _____

8. Are you having any other school problems? _____ yes _____ no
   If so, please explain: _____
   _____
   _____

9. Do you have enough credits to graduate? _____ yes _____ no
   If not, please explain: _____
   _____
   _____

D. Military history

1. Have you ever been in the armed forces? _____ yes _____ no
   If yes, which branch? _____
2. What was your rating and rank? _____

3. How long were you in the service? _____

4. Date you enlisted _____
Date you entered service _____

5. Current status _____
Type of discharge _____

E. Employment history

1. Are you employed? _____ How long? _____

2. Name of employer _____

3. Job title _____ Gross annual income _____

4. What is your occupation? _____

5. How long have you been doing this type of work? _____

6. What type of work would you like to do, even though you may not have the necessary training or skills? _____

7. Employment history (list most recent jobs first)

Job Title	Date Started	Date Finished	Reason for Leaving
a.			
b.			
c.			

8. Describe any problems on the job (past or present) _____
_____
_____
_____

9. Do you have medical insurance? _____ yes _____ no

10. _____ Do you have public aid? _____ yes _____ no

F. Family history

1. Are your parents still living together? _____ yes _____ no

2. If your parents are separated or divorced, whom do you live with?
_____ mother _____ father

3. Describe your father: _____
_____

4. Describe your mother: _____
_____

5. List your brothers and sisters, and circle any stepbrothers or stepsisters.
a. _____
b. _____
c. _____
d. _____
e. _____
f. _____
g. _____
h. _____

6. Where are you in the order of birth (oldest to youngest)? _____

7. Which brother or sister are you closest to? _____
Please explain: _____
_____

8. Which brother or sister are you least close to? _____
   Please explain: _____
   _____

9. Which person in your family makes the decisions? _____
   Please explain: _____
   _____

10. If you needed to borrow money, which member of the family would you ask?
    Please explain: _____
    _____

11. Do you eat dinner with your family? _____ yes _____ no
    How many nights a week? _____
    Please explain: _____
    _____

12. What family activities does your family take part in? _____
    _____
    Please explain: _____
    _____

13. Do you believe in God? _____ yes _____ no
    What denomination? _____
14. Do you go to church regularly? _____ yes _____ no
15. Do you have a girlfriend/boyfriend? _____ yes _____ no
16. Do both of you spend a lot of time together? _____ yes _____ no
17. Would you say that your boyfriend/girlfriend has a drinking problem?
    _____ yes _____ no
    Please explain: _____
    _____

18. Would you say that your girlfriend/boyfriend has a drug problem?
    _____ yes _____ no
    Please explain: _____
    _____

19. Did anyone in your family suffer from the following (underline)?
    Nervous breakdown; fits or convulsions; nervousness; migraine headaches; visions; stuttering; times when they could not remember what they were doing; times when they acted strangely or peculiarly; alcohol problem; drug abuse.
    If you have underlined any of the choices in the previous list, state which family member and when and how you were affected.
20. Did you ever belong to a gang? _____ yes _____ no
21. What teams or clubs did you belong to as a child? _____
    _____
    List those in which you were an officer: _____
    _____

22. What do you do outside of work or school (hobbies, leisure)?
    _____
    _____

23. About how many close friends do you have? _____

Describe them by name, sex, and age: _____

_____

Has any of them ever had a drinking or drug problem? _____ yes _____ no
If so, please describe: _____

_____

_____

24. List your children, and circle those who are adopted or by a previous marriage.

    a. _____

    b. _____

    c. _____

    d. _____

    e. _____

G. Legal history

1. Do you have any arrest charges pending? _____ yes _____ no
If so, what are they? _____

Charge	Court Date	Location
a.		
b.		
c.		
d.		

2. Have you had previous arrests? _____ yes _____ no
If so, what were the charges and when were they filed?

Charge	Date
a.	
b.	
c.	
d.	

3. Are you on probation? _____ yes _____ no
On parole? _____ yes _____ no
Under court supervision? _____ yes _____ no

4. Have you attended or are you attending a class on alcohol or drug safety?
_____ yes _____ no
If so, where? _____

5. Were you referred to treatment by the class? _____ yes _____ no

6. Were you referred to treatment by the social services department of the circuit court? _____ yes _____ no

7. Were you ordered to treatment by the circuit court? _____ yes _____ no
If so, what county? _____
Who was the judge? _____

8. Do you have a lawyer or public defender? _____ yes _____ no
Which? _____

9. Were you referred to treatment by your lawyer? _____ yes _____ no
If so, what is your lawyer's name? _____
Phone no. _____

10. Would you consent to sign a release of information allowing us to communicate with any of the agencies mentioned earlier or authorities on specific treatment issues? _____ yes _____ no

11. What is your court date? _____

12. If not listed earlier, who referred you? _____

H. History of drinking, other drug use, and treatment (check all items that apply to you, or give the information requested; if not applicable, mark N/A)

1. Have you ever been treated for an alcohol problem before?
_____ yes _____ no
If yes, complete the following:

   a. Detoxification only _____ How many times? _____
   Places and dates: _____

   Did you finish treatment? _____ yes _____ no
   If no, please explain: _____

   b. Rehabilitation _____ How many times?_____
   Places and dates: _____

   Did you finish treatment? _____ yes _____ no
   If no, please explain: _____

   c. Outpatient therapy _____ How many times? _____

   Places and dates: _____

   Did you finish treatment? _____ yes _____ no
   If no, please explain: _____

   d. Would you consent to sign a release of confidential information allowing us to communicate with any of these programs on specific treatment issues? _____ yes _____ no

2. Have you been involved with Alcoholics Anonymous? _____ yes _____ no
If so, how often did/do you attend meetings? _____
Were they open or closed? _____
Did/do you have a sponsor? _____ yes _____ no

3. At what age did you first drink? _____ Describe the circumstances and consequences: _____

4. At what age did you first lose control of your drinking? _____
(I have never lost control of my drinking; I just drink daily.) _____

5. At what age did you have your first blackout? _____
   (I have never had blackouts.) _____

6. At what age did your blackouts begin to increase? _____

7. When and why did you first become concerned about your drinking?

   _____

   _____

   _____

8. What is the average amount of hard liquor you consume? (check one)

   _____ none   _____ about 1 pint a day
   _____ very little   _____ about 1 quart a day
   _____ occasional "benders"   _____ more than 1 quart a day
   _____ a couple of "shots" a day   _____ other

9. What is the average number of beers you consume? (check one)

   _____ none   _____ close to 20 a day
   _____ very few   _____ more than 20 a day
   _____ several a day   _____ occasional "benders"
   _____ about 5 to 10 a day

10. What is the average amount of wine you consume? (check one)

    _____ none   _____ more than 4 quarts a day
    _____ very little   _____ occasional "benders"
    _____ about 1 pint a day
    _____ about 1 quart a day
    _____ about 2 to 4 quarts a day

11. Do you ever go on "binges" (periods of uncontrolled drinking)?

    _____ yes _____ no
    _____ once a year   _____ every 1 to 3 months
    _____ every 6 to 8 months   _____ every weekend
    _____ every 3 to 6 months   other _____

12. Do you drink daily? _____ yes _____ no
    How long have you been drinking daily? (check one)

    _____ just this last month   _____ 1 year
    _____ 1 to 3 months   _____ 2 years
    _____ 3 to 6 months   _____ longer than 2 years
    _____ 6 to 9 months   _____ How long? _____

13. Do you notice that you have the "shakes" when you stop drinking?

    _____ yes _____ no
    If so, when did this first happen? _____

    _____

    Please describe: _____

    _____

    _____

    Have you ever seen or heard things that were not actually there?

    _____ yes _____ no
    If so, when? _____

    Have you ever had delirium tremens (DTs)? _____ yes _____ no

If so, when? _____

_____

Please describe: _____

_____

_____

Have you ever had a seizure? _____ yes _____ no
If so, when? _____

_____

Please describe: _____

_____

_____

14. Has a physician ever told you to stop drinking? _____ yes _____ no
    If so, why? _____

    _____

    _____

15. With whom do you usually drink? (check as many as apply)

    _____ spouse   _____ "buddies" on the street
    _____ other relatives   _____ strangers
    _____ neighbors   _____ by myself
    _____ people at work   _____ kids at school
    _____ friends at a bar

16. When drinking, how do you act?

    _____ seldom get angry or violent   _____ get into physical fights
    _____ get mean or surly   _____ get happy
    _____ get into angry arguments   _____ have fun
    _____ other

17. How do your parents, wife/girlfriend, or husband/boyfriend feel about
    your drinking?

    _____ don't seem to mind   _____ nag me about it
    _____ don't say much about it   _____ question doesn't apply
    _____ threatened to leave because of my drinking

18. Have your family activities changed because of your drinking?
    _____ yes _____ no

19. Has your sexual life changed because of your drinking?
    _____ yes _____ no

20. Have you ever quit drinking? _____ yes _____ no
    How long did you stay sober? _____
    When was the last time (date)? _____
    Did this dry period follow any form of treatment? _____ yes _____ no
    If so, what type and where? _____
    What things do you do to stay sober? _____
    Did you have any symptoms when you stopped drinking? _____

21. Have you ever used cough syrup or other medicines containing alcohol
    as substitutes for liquor or for the purpose of getting high?

    _____ yes _____ no
    _____ prescription   _____ nonprescription

Have you used any other alcohol substitutes? _____ yes _____ no
If so, please identify: _____
_____
_____
_____

22. What mood-altering drugs have you taken? (check as many as apply)

Prescribed by physician

_____ tranquilizers (Valium, Librium,   _____ yes _____ no
Miltown, etc.)
type _____

_____ psychotropics (Stelazine, Cogentin,   _____ yes _____ no
Thorazine, etc.)
type _____

_____ barbiturates (Quaaludes, phenobarbital,   _____ yes _____ no
Nembutal, Tuinal, Seconal)
type _____

_____ amphetamines (Dexedrine, Benzedrine,   _____ yes _____ no
Methedrine, etc.)
type _____

_____ sleeping pills   _____ yes _____ no
type _____

_____ opiates (heroin, morphine, opium, etc.)   _____ yes _____ no
type _____

_____ pain killers (Darvon, codeine, etc.)   _____ yes _____ no
type _____

_____ other type _____   _____ yes _____ no

_____ hallucinogens (LSD, STP, MDA, PCP,   _____ yes _____ no
mescaline, etc.)
type _____

_____ cocaine. If so, how often? _____

_____ marijuana. If so, how often? _____

_____ glue sniffing. If so, how often? _____

23. Have you ever received treatment for a drug problem?
_____ yes _____ no
If so, what type of treatment? _____
_____
_____
_____

Where? _____
When? _____

24. Have you ever been involved with Narcotics Anonymous?
_____ yes _____ no
If so, how often did/do you attend meetings? _____
Were they open or closed? _____
Did/do you have a sponsor? _____ yes _____ no

25. When do you usually drink or use drugs? (check as many as apply)

_____ weekends   _____ occasionally during the day

_____ after work or evenings   _____ frequent, short "benders"

_____ regularly during the day   _____ most of the time

_____ long, occasional "benders"

26. Which apply to you? (check as many as apply)

_____ I am losing control of my drinking/drug use.

_____ I'm an alcoholic/drug addict.

_____ I can't stop myself.

_____ I am deteriorating rapidly.

_____ I know why I drink/use drugs.

_____ I hate myself.

_____ I have a drinking problem.

_____ My tolerance is decreasing.

_____ I need a drink when I wake up.

_____ I'm not eating regularly.

_____ I'm strictly a social drinker.

_____ My tolerance is increasing.

_____ I can quit any time.

_____ I might be an alcoholic/drug addict.

_____ I have accidents or fall while drinking and sometimes injure myself.

_____ I'm a problem drinker/drug user but not an addict.

_____ I get arrested because of my drinking or drugging.

_____ I have been unable to complete a task (or begin a task) because I was drinking.

_____ I have a drug problem.

27. Which of these apply to you at this time?

_____ school problems   _____ financial problems

_____ marital problems   _____ threat to job

_____ physical problems   _____ loss of job

_____ family problems   _____ legal problems

_____ loneliness   _____ other

28. What do you expect from treatment? _____

_____

What might we expect from you? _____

29. In your own words, what is alcoholism/drug dependence? _____

_____

_____

30. Is alcoholism/drug dependence a disease, or is it a bad habit? _____

31. Have you ever been treated for emotional/psychiatric problems?
    _____ yes _____ no
    If so, complete the following.
    How many times?
    Where? _____ When? _____
    Where? _____ When? _____
    Where? _____ When? _____
    Have you ever attempted or considered attempting suicide?
    _____ yes _____ no
    How many times, and when? _____
    _____

32. Describe yourself: _____
    _____
    _____
    _____

33. What are your weaknesses? _____
    _____

    What are your strengths? _____
    _____

34. Are you interested in further treatment or help, and do you know what is
    available? _____

35. Please add any information that you feel could be important to your
    treatment: _____
    _____

36. Do you have any questions? _____
    _____

37. Next of kin _____
    Address _____

Client signature _____ Date _____
Staff signature _____ Date _____

INITIAL BEHAVIORAL ASSESSMENT AND FUNCTIONAL ANALYSIS

Date _____ Name of counselor _____

I. Background data

Name of client _____
Age _____ Marital status _____ Religion _____
Address _____
Previous substance abuse and psychiatric treatment (including hospitaliza-
tions)_____

II. Problems (frequency, intensity, inappropriate form, duration, inappropriate occasions)

A. Behavioral excesses _____
_____
_____

B. Behavioral deficits _____
_____
_____

III. Assets and strengths (indicate current and best past functioning)

A. Grooming _____
_____

Source: Compiled from various sources.

B. Self-help skills _____

_____

_____

C. Social skills (including conversation, recreation, and friendships)

_____

_____

_____

D. Education and vocational training _____

_____

_____

_____

IV. Functional analysis of problems

A. What are the consequences (both positive and negative) of the client's current problems? _____

_____

_____

_____

1. Who or what persuaded or coerced the client into treatment?

_____

2. Who reinforces the client's problems with sympathy, help, attention, or emotional reactions? _____

_____

3. What would happen if the problems were ignored? _____

_____

_____

Reduced in frequency? _____

_____

_____

4. What reinforcers would the client gain if the problems were removed? _____

_____

B. What stimulus determinants or conditions and settings serve as occasions for the occurrence of the problems? _____

_____

1. Where? _____
2. When? _____
3. With whom? _____

C. Congruence between client's self-description and that of other observers.

_____

_____

V. Reinforcement survey. Be sure to assess the correspondence between the client's verbal report and the observations made by you and significant others.

A. People. With whom does the client spend the most time (family, relatives, friends, coworkers)?

1. _____   4. _____
2. _____   5. _____
3. _____   6. _____

With whom would the client like to spend more time?

1. _____   3. _____
2. _____   4. _____

B. Places. Where does the client spend the most time (bedroom, kitchen, yard, car, work, store, church, etc.)?

1. _____   4. _____
2. _____   5. _____
3. _____   6. _____

Where would the client like to spend more time?

1. _____   3. _____
2. _____   4. _____

C. Things. What does the client spend most of his or her time with (books, hobbies, tobacco, foods, drinks, clothes, favorite possessions)?

1. _____   5. _____
2. _____   6. _____
3. _____   7. _____
4. _____   8. _____

What things and foods would the patient like to have greater access to?

1. _____   3. _____
2. _____   4. _____

D. Activities. What activities occur with the highest frequency or longest duration (work, smoking, sports, watching television, listening to music, dancing, napping, being alone, driving a car, reading, pacing)?

1. _____   5. _____
2. _____   6. _____
3. _____   7. _____
4. _____   8. _____

What activities would the client like to increase?

1. _____   3. _____
2. _____   4. _____

E. Negative reinforcers. What are relief stimuli and events for the client (people, substances, situations, activities, social isolation)?

1. _____   4. _____
2. _____   5. _____
3. _____   6. _____

F. Punishments. What are aversive stimuli and events for the patient (people, situations, activities, fears, social isolation, etc.)?

1. _____   4. _____
2. _____   5. _____
3. _____   6. _____

G. Natural reinforcers. Who, among those that the patient is in daily contact with, would make potential mediators in a counseling program?

1. _____   5. _____
2. _____   6. _____
3. _____   7. _____
4. _____   8. _____

VI. Biological analysis

A. Medical and surgical problems and limitations to activity

1. _____   3. _____
2. _____   4. _____

B. Date of last physical exam _____.
Name and address of the physician performing the exam: _____
_____
_____
_____

C. Current medical treatment and drugs _____
_____
_____

D. Psychotropic drugs

1. Current Drugs   Dose   Prescribed By   Date

   _____   _____   _____   _____
   _____   _____   _____   _____
   _____   _____   _____   _____

2. Past Drugs   Dose   Response

   _____   _____   _____
   _____   _____   _____
   _____   _____   _____

E. Family history. Which other members of the family have significant psychiatric or substance abuse behavioral disturbance? _____
_____
_____
_____

VII. Sociocultural analysis

A. Recent charges in milieu (migration, intergenerational conflicts in the family, work changes, etc.) _____
_____
_____

B. Recent changes in social relationships (separation, divorce, deaths, etc.)
_____
_____
_____

C. Language and values (conflicts between minority group and majority culture) _____

D. Other recent traumas or stresses _____

VIII. Formulation of behavioral goals (be specific)

A. Increase desirable behaviors (include strengthening assets)

   1. Short term (3 months)   2. Long term (9 months to 1 year)

B. Decrease or extinguish undesirable behaviors

   1. Short term (3 months)   2. Long term (9 months to 1 year)

C. Treatment techniques and interventions

   1. _____
   2. _____
   3. _____
   4. _____
   5. _____
   6. _____
   7. _____

D. Recording methods   Behaviors

   1. _____
   2. _____
   3. _____
   4. _____

Diagnosis: _____

Interview
Booklet

Comprehensive
Drinker Profile

G. Alan Marlatt, Ph.D.
and William R. Miller, Ph.D.

Date: _____   Interviewer: _____

Comprehensive Drinker Profile for:

Full name of client:

_____
(First)   (Middle)   (Last)

Prefers to be called: _____   Sex: (1) _____ F   (2) _____ M

A. Demographic Information

Age and Residence

A1. Date of birth: _____ _____ _____   Present age: _____
                         Month   Day   Year

A2. Present local address: Street address or box no. _____

City or town _____

State _____ Zip code _____

A3. Local telephone: Area code _____ Number _____

Best times to reach at this number: _____

A4. Name and address of a person through whom you can be located if we lose contact with you (must be different from A2.):

Name: _____ Relationship: _____

Street address or box no. _____

City or town _____ State _____ Zip code _____

Telephone: Area code _____ Number _____

A5. How did you first hear about this program? _____

If referred, by whom? _____
                              Name   Agency

Family Status

A6. Client's current living situation:

(1) ———— living alone

(2) ———— living with spouse or partner

(3) ———— living with roommate(s)

(4) ———— living with children only

(5) ———— living with parents

A7. Client's current marital status:

(1) ———— single, never been married

(2) ———— married, living with spouse

(3) ———— married, separated

(4) ———— widowed

(5) ———— divorced

A8. Number of times client has been married (including present): ————————————

OK to
call?

———— A9. Name of spouse, partner, or roommate: ————————————————————

OK to call?	A10. Children: Name	Age	Sex	Living with client?
——	———————————	——	——	—————
——	———————————	——	——	—————
——	———————————	——	——	—————
——	———————————	——	——	—————
——	———————————	——	——	—————

Number of children: ————————

A11. Other individuals living with client:

OK to call?	Name	Age	Sex	Relationship
——	———————————	——	——	—————
——	———————————	——	——	—————
——	———————————	——	——	—————
——	———————————	——	——	—————

Employment and Income Information

A12. Major occupation or skill (whether or not presently employed):

_____ Spouse's occupation: _____

A13. Currently employed or self-employed (not including school):

(1) _____ full time   (3) _____ retired   (5) _____ homemaker

(2) _____ part time   (4) _____ unemployed

A14. Title of present or most recent job (major job if more than one):

_____

If unemployed, how long? _____

OK to
call at
work?
_____
A15. Name of employer or firm: _____

Address: _____

_____

Telephone: Area code _____ Number _____

If OK, best time to reach client at work: _____

A16. Length of time in present or most recent job: _____ years

if less than 1 year, code as 1 year and indicate time: _____

A17. How many different jobs have you held in the past year? _____

in the past five years?

A18. How many years of active military duty have you served? _____

A19. Family income:

Source: _____ Annual $ _____

Source: _____ Annual $ _____

Source: _____ Annual $ _____

Total Annual Family Income in Dollars $ _____

A20. SES code: _____ (Socioeconomic status code)

Educational History

A21. Describe client's educational background: _____
_____ Degree? _____ Major? _____

A22. Code highest year of education completed: _____

A23. Are you currently pursuing education or training?

(1)_____ full time (2) _____ part time (3) _____ no classes now

B. Drinking History

Development of the Drinking Problem

B24. About how old were you when you first took one or more drinks? _____

B25. About how old were you when you first became intoxicated? _____

Do you remember what you were drinking? Beverage: _____

B26. How would you describe the drinking habits of:

_____ your mother?

_____ your father?

_____ spouse/partner?

0 = client does not know
1 = nondrinker (abstainer)
2 = occasional or light social drinker
3 = moderate or average social drinker
4 = frequent or heavy social drinker
5 = problem drinker (at any time in life)
6 = alcoholic (at any time in life)

B27. Do you have any <u>blood</u> relatives whom you regard as being or having been a problem drinker or an alcoholic?

	Number Males	Number Females
Parents?	_____ ×3= _____	_____ ×3= _____
Brothers or Sisters?	_____ ×3= _____	_____ ×3= _____
Grandparents?	_____ ×2= _____	_____ ×2= _____
Uncles or Aunts?	_____ ×2= _____	_____ ×2= _____
First Cousins?	_____ ×1= _____	_____ ×1= _____
TOTAL SCORES	Males: _____	Females: _____

Were you raised by your biological parents?_____ (1)YES _____ (2)NO

If not, who raised you?_____

B28. At what age (how long ago) did drinking begin to have an effect on your life which you did not approve of – when did drinking first begin to be a problem for you?

_____ Age at first problem   _____ Denies that drinking is a problem

_____ Years of problem duration (Age minus age at first problem)

At that particular time in your life when drinking first became a problem, were there any special circumstances or events that occurred which you feel were at least partly responsible for it becoming a problem?

_____

_____

_____

_____

_____

_____

B29. Did you arrive at your present level of drinking:

(1) _____ gradually over a long period of time? how long: _____

or (2) _____ by a more rapid increase (over several months or less)?

_____

_____

_____

Present Drinking Pattern

B30. Drinking Pattern (Check one)
Determine which of the following categories best describes the client's current drinking pattern:

____ (P) ──────┬─── PERIODIC DRINKER
           │   Drinks less often than once a week
           │   Is abstinent between drinking episodes
           └──── *Complete Episodic Pattern Chart*

____ (S) ──────┬─── STEADY DRINKER
           │   Drinks at least once per week
           │   Drinks about the same amount every week without periodic episodes of heavier drinking. (A
           │   heavy episode is defined as one or more days in which pattern fluctuates from the steady
           │   pattern by 5 or more SECs.)
           └──── *Complete Steady Pattern Chart*

____ (C) ──────┬─── COMBINATION PATTERN DRINKER
           │   Drinks at least once per week with a regular weekly pattern, but also has heavier episodes as
           │   defined above
           └──── *Complete both Steady and Episodic Charts.*

B31. Steady Pattern Chart

If the client drinks at least once per week complete the Steady Pattern Chart, then complete Q/F data summary. (If client does not drink at least once per week, proceed to B33.)

For each time period enter the type of beverage, % alcohol, amount consumed, and approximate time span during which it is consumed.

	Morning	Afternoon	Evening	Total for Day
Monday				Total SECs Monday
Tuesday				Total SECs Tuesday
Wednesday				Total SECs Wednesday
Thursday				Total SECs Thursday
Friday				Total SECs Friday
Saturday				Total SECs Saturday
Sunday				Total SECs Sunday

FORMULA FOR CALCULATING SECs: # oz. $\times$ % alcohol $\times$ 2 = SECs

A. TOTAL SECs per week . . . . _____
(transfer this total to item B32.)

B. TOTAL drinking (nonabstinent) days reported . . . . _____

C. AVERAGE SECs per drinking day (A $\div$ B) . . . . _____

D. ESTIMATED Peak BAC for week . . . . _____ mg%

B32. Quantity/Frequency Summary Data (Steady Drinking Pattern *Only*)

Total SECs per week from table: _____ SECs per week

Multiply by 13 weeks × 13 =

Total SECs in past 3 months: _____ SECs (From Steady Pattern *Only*)

B33. Episodic Pattern Chart (Periodic and Combination Patterns *Only*) (For Steady Drinkers, skip to B38.)

B34. Quantity/Frequency of Episodic Drinking

Multiply Quantity (SECs per episode by Frequency (episodes per 3 months) for each episode type:

Type and Amount of Beverages Consumed:		
	Number of episodes in past 3 months:	
Total SECs: _____ per episode	× _____ episodes per 3 mo.	= _____ SECs/3 months†
Hours: Peak BAC: _____ mg%		

Type and Amount of Beverages Consumed:		
	Number of episodes in past 3 months:	
Total SECs: _____ per episode	× _____ episodes per 3 mo.	= _____ SECs/3 months†
Hours: Peak BAC: _____ mg%		

Type and Amount of Beverages Consumed:		
	Number of episodes in past 3 months:	
Total SECs: _____ per episode	× _____ episodes per 3 mo.	= _____ SECs/3 months†
Hours: Peak BAC: _____ mg%		

_____ Total SECs/3 mo. from all episodic drinking

† For COMBINATION PATTERN DRINKERS, subtract from this total the number of SECs already accounted for in the Steady Pattern Chart (B31), and record here <u>only</u> SECs in excess of the steady drinking pattern. No drink should be counted both at B31 and B33. For PERIODIC DRINKERS, however, record all drinks here (since for these drinkers there is no Steady Pattern and B31 is left Blank).

B35. How would you describe the circumstances which mark the beginning of one of these heavy drinking episodes? That is, what factors determine when you <u>begin</u> heavy drinking?

_____

_____

B36. How would you describe the circumstances which mark the end of one of these heavy drinking episodes? That is, what factors determine when you finally <u>stop</u> drinking?

_____

_____

B37. Total Q/F. Add starred (*) lines from B32 and B34 above:

Calculate for <u>all</u> drinkers: _____ + _____ = _____ Q/F SECs past 3 mo.

Pattern History (All Drinkers)

B38. What is the largest amount of alcohol that you have ever drunk in one day?

Beverage   Amount

_____   _____

_____   _____ over _____ hours

TOTAL SECs:_____   Estimated Peak BAC: _____ mg%

B39. What is the longest period of continuous drinking that you have had? (Include hours of sleep if client began drinking again the next morning.)

Total hours: _____ hours

B40. Since drinking first became a problem for you, what is the longest period of time that you have gone without taking a drink?

_____ days   (convert to days)

B41. When was the last time that you went for 2 or 3 days without drinking any alcohol? (Ask whether client was taking tranquilizers or other withdrawal-inhibiting medication during this time.)

How long ago?_____ Medication? _____

B42. During this time, what was the main reason or reasons for stopping?

_____

_____

B43. After that period of no drinking, what were the circumstances when you started drinking again?

_____

_____

B44. Are there any particular days of the week on which you are more likely to drink (or to drink more) than on other days? If YES, list days and explain if there are any particular circumstances or factors which contribute to drinking (more) on these days.

_____

_____

Alcohol-Related Life Problems

B45. Now I'm going to ask you some more questions to help me understand your drinking pattern. Please answer them as honestly and as accurately as you can.

ITEM	RESPONSE	SCORE
1. Do you feel you are a normal drinker?	_____ (N)	_____ (2)
2. Have you ever awakened the morning after some drinking the night before and found that you could not remember a part of the evening before?	_____ (Y)	_____ (2) _____(1)
3. Does any member of your family (wife, husband, parents, etc.) ever worry or complain about your drinking?	_____ (Y)	_____ (1)
4. Can you stop drinking without a struggle after one or two drinks?	_____ (N)	_____ (2) _____(2)
5. Do you ever feel bad about your drinking?	_____ (Y)	_____ (1)
6. Do friends or relatives think you are a normal drinker?	_____ (N)	_____ (2)
7. Are you always able to stop drinking when you want to?	_____ (N)	_____ (2) _____(1)
8. Have you ever attended a meeting of Alcoholics Anonymous (AA)? (If YES, about how many? _____)	_____ (Y)	_____ (5)
9. Have you gotten into fights when drinking?	_____ (Y)	_____ (1)
10. Has drinking ever created problems with you and your spouse (husband/wife)?	_____ (Y)	_____ (2)
11. Has your spouse (or other family member) ever gone to anyone for help about your drinking?	_____ (Y)	_____ (2)
12. Have you ever lost friends or lovers because of your drinking?	_____ (Y)	_____ (2)
13. Have you ever gotten into trouble at work because of drinking?	_____ (Y)	_____ (2)
14. Have you ever lost a job because of drinking?	_____ (Y)	_____ (2)
15. Have you ever neglected your obligations, your family, or your work for two or more days in a row because you were drinking?	_____ (Y)	_____ (2)
16. Do you ever drink before noon?	_____ (Y)	_____ (1) _____(1)
17. Have you ever been told you have liver trouble?	_____ (Y)	_____ (2)
18. Have you ever had severe shaking after heavy drinking?	_____ (Y)	_____(3)
19. Have you ever heard voices or seen things that weren't there after heavy drinking?	_____ (Y)	$\overline{}$ (2) (18 or 19) _____(4)
20. Have you ever gone to anyone for help about your drinking?	_____ (Y)	_____ (5)
21. Have you ever been in a hospital because of drinking?	_____ (Y)	_____ (5)
TOTAL points, this page (total both columns)		_____ _____
		A-1 B-1

22. Have you ever been a patient in a psychiatric hospital or on a psychiatric ward of a general hospital?   _____

    If YES, was drinking part of the problem?   _____(Y)   _____(2)

    DESCRIBE: _____

    _____

23. Have you ever been seen at a psychiatric or mental health clinic, or gone to a doctor, social worker, or clergy for help with an emotional problem?   _____

    If YES, did drinking play a part in the problem?   _____(Y)   _____(2)

    DESCRIBE: _____

    _____

24. Have you ever been arrested, even for a few hours, because of drunk behavior? (other than driving)   _____(Y)   _____(2)

    DESCRIBE: _____

    _____

25. Have you ever been arrested for drunk driving or driving after drinking?   _____(Y)   _____(2)

    DESCRIBE: _____

    _____

26. Have you ever had a hangover?   _____(Y)   _____(1)

27. Have you ever had vague feelings of fear, anxiety, or nervousness after drinking?   _____(Y)   _____(1)

28. Have you ever felt a craving or strong need for a drink?   _____(Y)   _____(1)

29. Are you able to drink more now than you used to without feeling the same effect?   _____(Y)   _____(1)

30. Has drinking or stopping drinking ever resulted in your having a seizure or convulsion?   _____(Y)   _____(4)

31. Do you ever skip meals when you are drinking?   _____(Y)   _____(1)

    TOTAL points, this page (total both columns)   _____   _____
                                                                             A-2   B-2

TOTAL PROBLEM SCORES

Total Column A for both pages   _____ + _____ = _____ (MAST Score)[1]
                                   A-1   A-2

Total Column B for both pages   _____ + _____ = _____ (Ph Score)[2]
                                   B-1   B-2

[1]MAST Score is an indicator of severity and extent of life problems related to drinking. The Michigan Alcoholism Screening Test was originally designed by Selzer. (Selzer, M. L., The Michigan Alcoholism Screening Test: The quest for a new diagnostic instrument. *American Journal of Psychiatry*, 1971, *127:12*; 1653-1658. Copyright, 1971, the American Psychiatric Association. Reprinted by permission.)
[2]Ph Score is an index of severity of physical dependence on alcohol.

Drinking Settings

B46. Drinking Locations card sort
(Indicate rank ordering: 1 = most frequent setting; 9 = least)

_____ At Home (My own house, apartment or room)

_____ At Work

_____ In Other People's Homes

_____ Outdoors

_____ Private or Social Clubs

_____ Restaurants

_____ Social Events (such as Weddings, parties, Dances)

_____ Tavern or Bar

_____ While Driving

_____ Other places (if mentioned): _____

_____ TOTAL locations indicated as drinking locations

B47. Social Situations card sort
(Indicate rank ordering: 1 = most frequent; 9 = least frequent)

_____ I Drink Alone

_____ I Drink with my Spouse (Husband, Wife, Companion)

_____ I Drink with Relatives Other than my Spouse

_____ I Drink with a Male Friend or Friends (No Females Present)

_____ I Drink with a Female Friend or Friends (No Males Present)

_____ I Drink with Friends of Both Sexes

_____ I Drink with Strangers (or with People I Meet After I have Started Drinking)

_____ I Drink with Business Associates (for Business Purposes)

_____ Other companions (if mentioned): _____

_____ TOTAL situations indicated as drinking situations

Associated Behaviors (assure confidentiality)

B48. Do you smoke cigarettes? (Indicate number of cigarettes smoked per day. Enter 00 for nonsmoker.)

_____ cigarettes per day

If client used to smoke but does not smoke now, how long has it been since the last cigarette?

_____

Indicate any other use of tobacco (cigars, pipe, chewing):

_____

_____

B49. Are you satisfied with your present weight? (If YES, enter 00. If NO, indicate the number of pounds client regards self as overweight (+) or underweight (−) using proper arithmetic sign):

_____

B50. Describe <u>all</u> medications that you currently use, including vitamins, birth control, aspirin, etc. [Ask specifically about tranquilizers, sedatives, stimulants, diet pills, pain medications – by prescription or otherwise. Indicate name of each drug, dosage, frequency, purpose, and whether taken by prescription (Rx).]

Medication	Dosage	Frequency	Purpose	Rx?

B51. <u>Other Drugs card sort</u>

	Specify	Last Use?	Past 3 mo. Frequency	How?	Dose?
_____ Amphetamine					
_____ Barbiturates, etc.					
_____ Cannabis					
_____ Cocaine					
_____ Hallucinogens					
_____ Inhalants					
_____ Opiates					
_____ Phencyclidine					
_____ Other Drugs					

_____ Total Drug Classes Used   _____ Total Past 3 mo.

B52. What are your interests and hobbies (not associated with work), and how much time do you spend at each of them per month? (For each hobby or interest determine whether it is usually associated with or accompanied by drinking.)

Interest or Hobby	Hrs/mo	Assoc. with Drinking?

B53. Eating Behavior

In an average week (7 days), on how many days do you:

eat breakfast? _____ eat lunch? _____ eat evening meal? _____

Total regular meals/week _____ eat additional snacks besides regular meals? _____

If you overeat sometimes, what factors are most likely to lead to your overeating? (situations, kinds of food, feelings, etc.)

_____

_____

How many caffeine drinks do you have in an average day?   _____ cups coffee   _____ sodas

_____ cups tea   _____ other

_____ Total

B54. Driving Behavior

When you are driving or riding in a private automobile, on what percentage of occasions do you wear a seat belt or shoulder harness?
_____ %

When you are driving on open highway where the speed limit is 55 mph and there are no police around, what is the average speed at which you drive according to your speedometer?
_____ mph

During the past year, how often would you say that you drove shortly after having more than 3 drinks?
_____ approximate times in past year

B55. Exercise Behavior

What exercise do you get in the course of an average week?

Type of Exercise	Amount	Frequency

Beverage Preferences

B56. <u>Beverage Preferences card sort</u>
(Indicate rank order: 1 = most frequently consumed drink, etc.)

For preferences 1, 2, and 3, also note the preferred manner of drinking and preferred brand, if stated.

BEVERAGE LIST	PREFERRED MANNER OF DRINKING	BRAND
_____ Beer or Ale	_____	_____
_____ Brandy	_____	_____
_____ Gin	_____	_____
_____ Liqueurs (Cordials)	_____	_____
_____ Malt Liquor	_____	_____
_____ Pure Alc. or Nonbeverage Alc. (Specify)	_____	_____
_____ Rum	_____	_____
_____ Sparkling Wine	_____	_____
_____ Special Fortified Wine	_____	_____
_____ Tequila	_____	_____
_____ Vodka	_____	_____
_____ Whiskey (Scotch, Bourbon, etc.)	_____	_____
_____ Red, Dry Wine	_____	_____
_____ Red, Sweet Wine	_____	_____
_____ Rosé Wine	_____	_____
_____ White, Dry Wine	_____	_____
_____ White, Sweet Wine	_____	_____
_____ Other Alc. Beverage (Specify)	_____	_____
_____ TOTAL Number of Beverages Used		

B57. What are your three favorite nonalcohol beverages?

1. _____

2. _____

3. _____

Relevant Medical History

B58. Present weight: _____ Pounds   Present height: ___'___" = _____ inches

B59. Tell me any serious illness, hospitalization, or surgery you have had in the past 10 years. (Indicate illness, date, any continuing care.)

Illness	Required Hospitalization?	Required Surgery?	Date	Follow-Up Care?
_____	_____	_____	_____	_____
_____	_____	_____	_____	_____
_____	_____	_____	_____	_____
_____	_____	_____	_____	_____

B60. Have you ever had jaundice (yellowed skin, dark urine)? Swelling of the feet or ankles? Any diagnosed liver disease such as hepatitis? (If YES, Specify) (Indicate date, illness, continuing care if any.)

Illness	Date	Continuing Care?
_____	_____	_____
_____	_____	_____
_____	_____	_____

B61. Have you ever been told that you have high blood pressure? Have you ever had pain or tightness in your chest, especially with exercise? Unusual shortness of breath during exercise? A stroke or heart attack? Any other indication of heart problems? (If YES, Specify)

_____

_____

_____

B62. Have you ever had any of the following: Diabetes? Pancreatitis or inflammation of the stomach? Ulcer? Thyroid problem? Weakness or numbness in the legs? (If YES, Specify)

_____

_____

B63. Have you noticed, over a period of time, that you are more affected by alcohol than you used to be – that drinking less has more of an effect on you? (If YES, Specify)

_____

_____

_____

B64. Are you currently seeing a counselor; psychologist, or psychiatrist for counseling or therapy? (If YES, Specify)

_____

_____

B65. (Women) Are you pregnant, or planning to become pregnant? _____

C. Motivational Information

Reasons for Drinking

C66. What are the main reasons why you drink? In other words, when you are <u>actually drinking,</u> what for you is the most positive or desirable <u>effect</u> of alcohol? What do you like best about alcohol?

_____

_____

C67. Are you aware of any inner thoughts or emotional feelings, or things <u>within</u> you as a person, which "trigger off" your need or desire to take a drink at a particular moment in time?

_____

_____

C68. Are you aware of any particular situations or set of events, things which happen to you in the <u>outside world,</u> which would result in your feeling like having one or more drinks?

_____

_____

C69. In terms of your <u>life as a whole,</u> what are the most positive effects or consequences of drinking?

_____

_____

C70. When you are <u>actually drinking,</u> what for you is the most negative or undesirable <u>effect</u> of alcohol? In other words, what is the thing you like least about alcohol when you are drinking?

_____

_____

C71. In terms of your <u>life as a whole,</u> what do you see as the most negative effects or consequences of your drinking?

_____

_____

C72. Can you describe a situation or set of events which would be <u>least likely</u> to result in your feeling like drinking? In other words, when do you feel least inclined to drink?

_____

_____

Effects of Drinking

C73. Card sort: Check all effects that the client reports as having experienced <u>while drinking</u> during the past three months.

Group A	Group B	Group C	Group D	Group E
___ Calm	___ Angry	___ Afraid	___ Friendly	___ Inferior
___ Happy	___ Depressed	___ Excited	___ Outgoing	___ Insecure
___ Peaceful	___ Frustrated	___ Nervous	___ Secure	___ Unfriendly
___ Relaxed	___ Lonely	___ Restless	___ Strong	___ Weak
___ Unafraid	___ Sad	___ Tense	___ Superior	___ Withdrawn
TOTALS ___ A	___ B	___ C	___ D	___ E

Next spread out those cards identified as describing effects experienced by the client and ask client to rank order the five <u>most frequent</u> effects experienced <u>while drinking</u>. Specify below:

Rank	Effect	Comments, if any
1	_____	_____
2	_____	_____
3	_____	_____
4	_____	_____
5	_____	_____

Most representative emotion group (see decision rules): _____

C74. Suppose that we were to agree that you would not drink at all for the next two weeks. What problems do you think you might have if you did this? Would there be any special feelings or situations that might be more difficult for you to handle?

_____

_____

_____

_____

Other Life Problems

C75. Card sort. Have client sort into YES and No piles for current problems, then rank order. Indicate ranks for all YES cards: 1 = most important current problem.

Then for all YES cards inquire whether the problem is or is not at least partly related to drinking in the client's opinion. Check (✓) all problems indicated to be related to drinking.

Rank   ✓

_____ _____ Aggression (Fighting, Anger, Hostility)

_____ _____ Boredom

_____ _____ Conflicts with the Law (Being Arrested, Drunk Driving, Police Visits, Lawsuit, etc.)

_____ _____ Depression (or Negative Self-Concept)

_____ _____ Family Problems (Arguments with Spouse or Family Members etc.)

_____ _____ Fatigue, Tiredness

_____ _____ Financial Problems

_____ _____ Health Problems

_____ _____ Problems with not Being Assertive (Being Taken Advantage of, Always Giving in, Can't Express What I Feel, etc.)

_____ _____ Problems with Eating and Appetite (or Weight Problems)

_____ _____ Problems with Memory or Concentration

_____ _____ Problems with Sleeping (Insomnia, Early Waking, Nightmares)

_____ _____ Problems with Social Contact (Sociability and Meeting People, Losing Friends, Loneliness)

_____ _____ Sexual Problems

_____ _____ Suicidal Thoughts

_____ _____ Tension or Anxiety

_____ _____ Work Problems

_____ _____ Other Problems

TOTAL Number of Problems YES: _____

TOTAL Number of Problems Alcohol–Related: _____

Finally inquire further about the top three problems (Rank 1, 2, and 3) and describe below in greater detail.

Problem 1: _____

_____

_____

Problem 2:_____

_____

_____

Problem 3:_____

_____

_____

Motivation for Treatment

C76. On your own and without any outside help, what steps if any have you taken to try to stop or control your drinking? How well did these work?

_____

_____

_____

C77. What <u>outside</u> help, professional or otherwise, have you sought for your drinking problem (including A.A.)? What helped and what didn't?

_____

_____

_____

C78. Has anyone ever advised you to stop drinking completely? If so, who?

(1) _____ Yes   (2) _____ No   If YES: _____

C79. Has anyone ever advised you to cut down on your drinking? If so, who?

(1) _____ Yes   (2) _____ No   If YES: _____

C80. What are the main reasons for your seeking help for drinking <u>at this particular time?</u> Why now? In other words, what particular circumstances led you to come to this program now?

_____

_____

C81. What do you see as the most ideal outcome of treatment for you here? What would you like to happen?

_____

_____

C82. Which of these six statements best describes your own goal in this program? (Mark the one chosen. If more than one is chosen, prioritize.)

(1) _____ I think that total abstinence is the only answer for me, and I want to stop drinking completely.

(2) _____ I think that total abstinence may be necessary for me, but I am not sure. If I knew that controlled drinking were impossible for me, then I would want to stop drinking completely.

(3) _____ I think that total abstinence is not necessary for me, but I would like to reduce my drinking to a "light social" nonproblem level.

(4) _____ I think that total abstinence is not necessary for me, but I would like to reduce my drinking to a "moderate social" nonproblem level.

(5) _____ I think that total abstinence is not necessary for me, but I would like to reduce my drinking to a "heavy social" nonproblem level.

(6) _____ I think that total abstinence is not necessary for me, and I see no need to reduce my drinking.

C83. If you were to achieve your <u>ideal</u> goal in this program, what would your drinking be like? About how much would you be drinking in an average week? (Record specific beverage types and amounts; convert to SECs.)

Beverage   Amount

_____   _____

_____   _____

_____   _____   TOTAL SECs: _____

C84. In your honest and realistic opinion, what do you estimate your chances are – from 0 to 100% – of achieving this goal?

_____%

C85. How would it affect you if you did not achieve your ideal outcome of treatment here? In other words, what is most likely to happen if you do not meet your goals in this program?

_____

_____

_____

_____

C86. How would you define "alcoholism"?

_____

_____

_____

_____

C87. Some people say that alcoholism is a disease or sickness, while others say that it is not a disease, but rather is more like a bad habit that a person has learned. Do you see it more as a disease or as a bad habit? (If person says "both" have him or her indicate which they would agree with <u>more</u>.)

(1) _____ Disease   (2) _____ Bad Habit

Drinker Type Ratings

C88. Now I am going to give you a list of six different types of drinkers and I would like you to tell me which one, in your opinion, best describes you at the present time. (Obtain rating)

(If applicable): Now I'd like you to tell me the one that you think <u>your husband/wife</u> would choose as best describing you. (Obtain rating)

Which one do you think your <u>closest friend</u> would choose as best describing you? (Obtain rating)

Which one do you think <u>most people who know you</u> would choose as best describing you? (Obtain rating)

RATINGS: Self _____   Spouse _____   Friend _____   Most People _____

1 = Total Abstainer   4 = Heavy Social (Nonproblem) Drinker
2 = Light Social (Nonproblem) Drinker   5 = Problem Drinker
3 = Moderate Social (Nonproblem) Drinker   6 = Alcoholic

Compare self-rating with rating for "most people." Is self-rating:

(1) _____ higher than "most"   (2) _____ equal to "most"   (3) _____ lower than "most"

<u>END OF INTERVIEW</u>

Additional Comments:

FAMILY DRINKING SURVEY

	Yes	No
1. Does someone in your family undergo personality changes when he or she drinks in excess?	( )	( )
2. Do you feel that drinking is more important to this person than you are?	( )	( )
3. Do you feel sorry for yourself and frequently indulge in self-pity because of what you feel alcohol is doing to your family?	( )	( )
4. Has some family member's excessive drinking ruined special occasions?	( )	( )
5. Do you find yourself covering up for the consequences of someone else's drinking?	( )	( )
6. Have you ever felt guilty, apologetic, or responsible for the drinking of a member of your family?	( )	( )
7. Does one of your family members' use of alcohol cause fights and arguments?	( )	( )
8. Have you ever tried to fight the drinker by joining in the drinking?	( )	( )
9. Do the drinking habits of some family members make you feel depressed or angry?	( )	( )
10. Is your family having financial difficulties because of the drinking?	( )	( )

Source: These survey questions are modified or adapted from the Children of Alcoholics Screening Test (CAST), the Howard Family Questionnaire, and the Family Alcohol Quiz from Al-Anon.

	Yes	No
11. Did you ever feel like you had an unhappy home life because of the drinking of some members of your family?	( )	( )
12. Have you ever tried to control the drinker's behavior by hiding car keys, pouring liquor down the drain, and so on?	( )	( )
13. Do you find yourself distracted from your responsibilities because of a family member's drinking?	( )	( )
14. Do you often worry about a family member's drinking?	( )	( )
15. Are holidays more of a nightmare than a celebration because of a family member's drinking behavior?	( )	( )
16. Are most of your drinking family member's friends heavy drinkers?	( )	( )
17. Do you find it necessary to lie to employers, relatives, or friends in order to hide your spouse's drinking?	( )	( )
18. Do you find yourself responding differently to members of your family when they are using alcohol?	( )	( )
19. Have you ever been embarrassed or felt the need to apologize for the drinker's actions?	( )	( )
20. Does some family member's use of alcohol make you fear for your own safety or safety of your family?	( )	( )
21. Have you ever thought that one of your family members had a drinking problem?	( )	( )
22. Have you ever lost sleep because of a family member's drinking?	( )	( )
23. Have you ever encouraged one of your family members to stop or cut down on his or her drinking?	( )	( )
24. Have you ever threatened to leave home or to leave a family member because of his or her drinking?	( )	( )
25. Did a family member ever make promises that he or she did not keep because of drinking?	( )	( )
26. Did you ever wish that you could talk to someone who could understand and help the alcohol-related problems of a family member?	( )	( )
27. Have you ever felt sick, cried, or had a "knot" in your stomach after worrying about a family member's drinking?	( )	( )
28. Has a family member ever failed to remember what occurred during a drinking period?	( )	( )
29. Does your family member avoid social situations where alcoholic beverages will not be served?	( )	( )
30. Does your family member have periods of remorse after drinking occasions and apologize for his or her behavior?	( )	( )
31. Please write down any symptoms or medical or nervous problems that you have experienced since you have known your family member was a heavy drinker.	( )	( )

If you answer 'YES' to any two of the previous questions, there is a good possibility that someone in your family may have a drinking problem.

If you answer 'YES' to four or more of the previous questions, there is a definite indication that someone in your family has a drinking problem.

Useful Web Sites

Alcoholics Anonymous	www.aa.org
Alcohol MD	http://www.alcoholmd.com/
American Society of Addiction Medicine	http://www.asam.org/
Center for Substance Abuse Treatment and Prevention	http://www.samhsa.gov/index.aspx
Join Together	www.jointogether.org
Narcotics Anonymous	www.na.org
National Addiction Technology Transfer Center	http://www.attcnetwork.org/index.asp
National Association of Addiction Treatment Providers	http://www.naatp.org/
National Association of Alcohol and Drug Counselors	http://www.naadac.org/
National Center on Addiction and Substance Abuse	www.casacolumbia.org
National Council on Alcoholism and Drug Dependence, Inc.	http://www.ncadd.org/
National Institute on Alcoholism and Alcohol Abuse	http://www.niaaa.nih.gov/
National Institute on Drug Abuse	http://www.nida.nih.gov/NIDAHome.html

Office of National Drug Control Policy	http://www.whitehousedrugpolicy.gov/
Partnership for a Drug Free America	http://www.drugfree.org/
SAMHSA Office of Applied Studies	http://www.samhsa.gov/index.aspx
Substance Abuse and Mental Health Services Administration	http://www.samhsa.gov/index.html

VALUABLE TREATMENT MANUALS

APPENDIX

F

The United States Department of Health and Human Services developed a series of treatment manuals for use by treatment facilities and individual treatment providers as part of a huge treatment study called Project MATCH. This study was one of the largest initiatives ever undertaken by the National Institute on Alcoholism and Alcohol Abuse (NIAAA). The treatment manuals are free and they are presented to the alcoholism treatment community as standardized, well-documented intervention tools for alcoholism treatment. These manuals summarize reasonable intervention approaches based on present knowledge.

Volume 1: Twelve-Step Facilitation Therapy Manual. This volume describes, in full detail, 12-step facilitation therapy in which the overall goal is to facilitate a client's active participation in the fellowship of Alcoholics Anonymous. The therapy approach described here regards such active involvement as the primary factor responsible for sustained recovery and therefore is the desired outcome of participation in this treatment program. This therapy is grounded in the concept of alcoholism as a spiritual and medical disease.

Volume 2: Motivational Enhancement Therapy Manual. This volume fully describes Motivational Enhancement Therapy (MET), a systematic intervention approach for evoking change in problem drinkers. MET is based on the principles of motivational psychology and is designed to produce rapid internally motivated change. This treatment strategy does not attempt to guide and train the client, step by step, through recovery, but instead employs motivational strategies to mobilize the client's own change resources.

Volume 3: Cognitive-Behavioral Coping Skills Therapy Manual. This volume describes cognitive-behavioral coping skills therapy, which is based on the principles of social learning therapy and views drinking behavior as functionally related to major problems in a client's life. Emphasis is placed on overcoming skill deficits and increasing the client's ability to cope with high-risk situations that commonly precipitate relapse. The program consists of 12 sessions aimed at training the client to use active behavioral or cognitive coping methods to deal with problems rather than relying on alcohol as a maladaptive coping strategy.

Volume 1: Twelve-Step Facilitation Therapy Manual. A clinical research guide for therapists treating individuals with alcohol abuse and dependence. Joseph Nowinski, Stuart Baker, and Kathleen Carroll.

Volume 2: Motivational Enhancement Therapy Manual. A clinical research guide for therapists treating individuals with alcohol abuse and dependence. William R. Miller, Allen Zwegan, Carlo D. Clemente, and Richard Rychtarik.

Volume 3: Cognitive-Behavioral Coping Skills Therapy Manual. A clinical research guide for therapists treating individuals with alcohol abuse and dependence. Ronald Kadden, Kathleen Carroll, Dennis Donovan, Ned Cooney, Peter Monti, David Abrams, Mark Lih, and Reid Hester.

Ordering information for Volumes 1, 2 and 3: Cost: Free. NIAAA, P.O. Box 10686, Rockville, MD 10849-0686.

The National Institute on Drug Abuse (NIDA) also publishes excellent treatment manuals that are available at no cost to treatment providers. The NIDA manuals present clear, helpful information to aid drug treatment practitioners in providing the best possible care that science has to offer. They describe scientifically supported therapies for addiction and give guidance on session content and how to implement specific techniques.

Manual 1: Therapy Manuals for Drug Addiction. A Cognitive-Behavioral Approach: Treating Cocaine Addiction. This manual focuses on cognitive-behavioral coping skills treatment (CBT), which is a short-term, focused approach to helping cocaine-dependent individuals become abstinent from cocaine and other substances. The underlying assumption is that learning processes play an important role in the development and continuation of cocaine abuse and dependence. These same learning processes can be used to help individuals reduce their drug use. Very simply put, CBT attempts to help clients recognize, avoid, and cope. That is, recognize the situations in which they are most likely to use cocaine, avoid these situations when appropriate, and cope more effectively with a range of problems and problematic behaviors associated with substance abuse.

Manual 2: Therapy Manuals for Drug Addiction. A Community Reinforcement Plus Vouchers Approach: Treating Cocaine Addiction. This volume focuses on a treatment that integrates a community reinforcement approach (CRA), originally developed as an effective treatment for alcohol dependence, with an incentive program (vouchers) wherein clients can earn points exchangeable for retail items by remaining in treatment and abstinent from cocaine.

Manual 1: National Institute on Drug Abuse. Therapy Manuals for Drug Addiction. A Cognitive-Behavioral Approach: Treating Cocaine Addiction. Kathleen M. Carroll. NIH Publication #98-4308.

DETOXIFICATION AND SUBSTANCE ABUSE TREATMENT

The Treatment Improvement Protocol, Detoxification and Substance Abuse Treatment, provides information about the role of detoxification in the continuum of services for patients with substance use disorders, the physiology of withdrawal, patient placement procedures, and issues in the management of detoxification services within comprehensive systems of care. It also expands on the administrative, legal, and ethical issues commonly encountered in the delivery of detoxification services and suggests performance measures for detoxification programs. While not "treatment" by itself, it is included here because many clinicians believe detoxification to be "treatment" and, in fact a period of detoxification and stabilization needs to be considered for every client entering substance abuse treatment. For a complete discussion of detoxification procedures and issues please see http://www.ncbi.nlm.nih.gov/books/bv.fcgi?rid=hstat5.section.85295

Important principles regarding detoxification and its role in patient care include:

1. Detoxification, in and of itself, does not constitute complete substance abuse treatment.
2. The detoxification process consists of three essential components, which should be available to all people seeking treatment:
   - Evaluation
   - Stabilization
   - Fostering patient readiness for and entry into substance abuse treatment
3. Detoxification can take place in a wide variety of settings and at a number of levels of intensity within these settings. Placement should be appropriate to the patient's needs.
4. All persons requiring treatment for substance use disorders should receive treatment of the same quality and appropriate thoroughness and should be put into contact with substance abuse treatment providers after detoxification.
5. Ultimately, insurance coverage for the full range of detoxification services is cost-effective.
6. Patients seeking detoxification services have diverse cultural and ethnic backgrounds as well as unique health needs and life situations. Programs offering detoxification should be equipped to tailor treatment to their client populations.
7. A successful detoxification process can be measured, in part, by whether an individual who is substance-dependent enters and remains in some form of substance abuse treatment/rehabilitation after detoxification.

Name Index

Subject Index